PENGUI

ANCIEN

Dr Georges Roux was born at Salon-de-Provence in 1914. The son of an officer in the French Army, at the age of nine he accompanied his parents to the Middle East where he lived for twelve years in Syria and Lebanon before returning to France in 1935. He graduated in medicine at the University of Paris and practised in that city for several years; but he had by then become so interested in Ancient Near Eastern History that in his spare time he read assyriology at the École du Louvre and the École des Hautes Études, subsequently pursuing his oriental studies side by side with his medical career. In 1950 he joined the Iraq Petroleum Company as a medical officer and served for two years in Qatar and seven years in Iraq. His original research work in southern Mesopotamia and the articles he wrote for specialized periodicals such as *Sumer* and the *Revue d'Assyriologie* have won him admission to the restricted circle of professional archaeologists and assyriologists.

Dr Roux now lives in Burgundy.

ANCIENT IRAQ

GEORGES ROUX

THIRD EDITION

PENGUIN BOOKS

PENGUIN BOOKS

Published by the Penguin Group
Penguin Books Ltd, 27 Wrights Lane, London w8 5tz, England
Penguin Books USA Inc., 375 Hudson Street, New York, New York 10014, USA
Penguin Books Australia Ltd, Ringwood, Victoria, Australia
Penguin Books Canada Ltd, 10 Alcorn Avenue, Toronto, Ontario, Canada m4v 3b2
Penguin Books (NZ) Ltd, 182–190 Wairau Road, Auckland 10, New Zealand

Penguin Books Ltd, Registered Offices: Harmondsworth, Middlesex, England

First published by George Allen & Unwin Ltd 1964
Published in Pelican Books 1966
Second edition 1980
Third edition reprinted in Penguin Books 1992
5 7 9 10 8 6

Copyright © George Allen & Unwin Ltd, 1964, 1980, 1992
All rights reserved

The moral right of the author has been asserted

Printed in England by Clays Ltd, St Ives plc
Set in $10\frac{1}{2}/12\frac{1}{2}$ pt Monophoto Baskerville

CONTENTS

CONTENTS

CONTENTS

CONTENTS

PLATES

PLATES

Façade of the temple of the Kassite king Karaindash in Uruk. (*Courtesy Iraq Museum, Baghdad*)

Relief from Tell Halaf. (*Courtesy Prof. W. Caskel, Cologne*)

Assyrian statue at Nimrud. (*Photograph by the author*)

Specimen of Assyrian writing on stone, from Nimrud. (*Courtesy Iraq Petroleum Company*)

Stele of Esarhaddon, from Zenjirli. (*Courtesy Vorderasiatische Museum, Berlin*)

Assyrian scene of war. Relief from Nineveh. (*Courtesy Louvre Museum*)

ILLUSTRATIONS

CHRONOLOGICAL TABLES

MAPS

FOREWORD
TO THE THIRD EDITION

By the time this third edition of Ancient Iraq is published
twelve years will have elapsed since the second edition (1980).
During this relatively short period, Mesopotamian studies have
made tremendous strides. In archaeology, generally brief but
fruitful international 'rescue excavations' have been carried out
on some 140 *tells*, prompted by the building of three main dams
on the Euphrates, the Tigris and one of its tributaries, radically
altering our evaluation of prehistoric periods in particular,
whilst digging was started, resumed and/or extended on such
well-known sites as Mari, Isin, Larsa, Tell el-Oueili, Uruk, Tell
Brak, Abu Salabikh and Sippar, to mention only the main
ones. At the same time, Assyriologists were busy deciphering the
inscriptions discovered in these excavations as well as revising
and re-publishing hundreds of texts partially or inadequately
published long ago, thereby modifying and improving our
knowledge of the political, socio-economic and cultural history
of ancient Mesopotamia. This was not routine work but a
highly successful, unprecedented and, of course, computer-
assisted revolution.

In 1980 I retired from my employment with a leading British
pharmaceutical company. Having more time at my disposal and
access to the university libraries of Paris, I wrote in my native
language 'La Mésopotamie' (Le Seuil, 1985), largely based on
Ancient Iraq but more comprehensive and relatively up-to-
date. I realized then that some parts of my 'British baby' were
badly in need of correction and improvement, and I had no
difficulty in obtaining the agreement of Penguin Books (may
the god Nabû bless them!) for an even more thoroughly revised
and considerably enlarged third edition of Ancient Iraq, which

indeed is now one step ahead of the French book on several points.

To the persons listed in the Introduction who encouraged and helped me in various ways I wish to add, for the second edition, Professor W. G. Lambert in England, Professors S. N. Kramer and J. B. Pritchard in the USA, Professor J. Bottéro, Madame Florence Malbarn-Labat and M. J. P. Grégoire in France and, for this edition, Professors David and Joan Oates, J. V. Kinnier-Wilson and H. W. F. Saggs in England, M. Olivier Rouault, Madame Sylvie Lackenbacher and Professor Dominique Charpin in France, Madame Duchesne-Guillemin in Belgium and Professor A. K. Grayson in Canada. Last but not least, I wish to thank my wife Christiane for the innumerable tasks she performed to assist me.

Saint Julien du Sault, France, November 1991.

INTRODUCTION
TO THE FIRST EDITION

This is a revised version, substantially enlarged and entirely rewritten, of the series of articles which appeared between September 1956 and January 1960 in *Iraq Petroleum*, the now defunct magazine of the Iraq Petroleum Company, under the title *The Story of Ancient Iraq*. Written in Basrah with no other source of documentation than my own personal library, these articles suffered from many serious defects and were far from even approaching the standards required from a work of this nature. In my view, whatever merit they possessed resided more in the lavish manner in which they were printed and illustrated than in the quality of their content. Yet, much to my surprise, the 'Story' received a warm welcome from a large and distinguished public. From Japan to California, a number of persons who, directly or indirectly, had access to the magazine took the trouble to write to the editor or myself asking for back numbers, spare copies or reprints, and suggesting that these articles be put in book form. I have now at last complied with their wish and I must say that, had it not been for the encouragement I received from their indulgent appreciation, I would never have had the courage to embark upon such a task.

For the unexpected success of these articles I can find only one reason: imperfect as they were, they helped to fill a regrettable gap. The Tigris-Euphrates valley – the region once called Mesopotamia and now mostly in Iraqi territory – forms a large, coherent, well-defined geographical, historical and cultural unit. Throughout antiquity, its inhabitants – Sumerians, Akkadians, Babylonians and Assyrians – shared the same brilliant civilization and played the leading role in Near Eastern politics, art, science, philosophy, religion and literature. During the last hundred years an enormous amount of archaeological research has been carried out in Iraq proper and in the eastern provinces of Syria. Impressive monuments have been unearthed, and museums have been filled with works of art and inscribed tablets recovered from the buried cities of Mesopotamia. No less remarkable results have been achieved in the field of philology: little by little, the two main languages of ancient Iraq – Sumerian and Akkadian – have yielded their secrets, and tens of thousands of texts have been translated and published. In university libraries the number of books and articles devoted to one aspect or other of Mesopotamian archaeology, history and civilization is positively staggering. Yet while several excellent and detailed histories of ancient Egypt, Iran, Syria, Palestine and Anatolia are offered to scholars or laymen, until H. W. F. Saggs in 1962 published *The Greatness That Was Babylon* it was impossible to find one single recent general history of ancient Iraq in English or, to my knowledge, in any other language.

That professional people are reluctant to undertake such a task can easily be understood. To deal thoroughly and competently with *all* the aspects of a civilization which had its roots in prehistory and lasted for more than thirty centuries would keep several scholars fully occupied for years and would fill many large volumes. Moreover, as almost every new discovery alters our knowledge of the past, even such a work would be in danger of becoming obsolete within a decade. Assyriologists and archaeologists in general prefer to plough their own fields. Most of their works are accessible only to other scholars or to advanced students. Those among these specialists who aim at a wider audience write on the subjects they know best. 'Popular' books, such as Woolley's monographs on Ur, Parrot's publications on Mari or Kramer's editions of Sumerian epics and myths cannot be too highly praised, but they are spotlights illuminating small areas in a very large picture. The layman often fails fully to appreciate their value simply because he is unable to place the sites, monuments, events or ideas described in their proper chronological or cultural context. Historians, on the other hand, have adopted precisely the opposite attitude. The works of L. King (*A History of Sumer and Akkad*, London, 1910; *A History of Babylon*, London, 1915), Sidney Smith (*Early History of Assyria*, London, 1928), A. Olmstead (*History of Assyria*, New York, 1923), B. Meissner (*Babylonien und Assyrien*, Heidelberg, 1925) and L. Delaporte (*La Mésopotamie*, Paris, 1923), excellent in their time and still very useful, though on many points outdated, have never been replaced. Instead, the French and Germans and, to a lesser extent, the British have given us, in more recent years, vast syntheses embracing either the whole of Western Asia or the entire Near East (Egypt included), or even the totality of the ancient world. E. Meyer's *Geschichte des Altertums* (1913–37), H. Schmökel's *Geschichte des alten Vorderasien* (1957), or the chapters written by G. Contenau and E. Dhorme for *Peuples et Civilisations* (1950), by L. Delaporte for *Les Peuples de l'Orient Méditerranéen* (1948) and by G. Goossens for the *Encyclopédie de la Pléiade* (1956), or again, the monumental *Cambridge Ancient History* (1923–5), of which a revised edition is being prepared, are invaluable monuments of erudition and lack neither detail nor perspective. But it is the kind of perspective one can expect in an art gallery where even a masterpiece tends to lose its individual character among other paintings. No matter what place they give to Mesopotamia, these books fail to do full justice to the remarkable cohesion and continuity of her history and civilization.

In a modest way, the present work aims at bridging the gap between these two kinds of publications: monographs and encyclopedias. Devoted entirely to Iraq,* it is a concise and in many respects incomplete study of the political, economic and cultural

---

* The fact that all the ancient capital cities of Sumer, Babylonia and Assyria are in Iraqi territory and that Iraq covers about three-quarters of the Tigris-Euphrates valley justifies the title of this work. It must be clearly understood, however, that several important sites mentioned are, in fact, situated in Syria or Turkey. I apologize to the Syrians and Turks and hope that they will feel no more offended than would the Belgians if part of their country was included in a history of Gaul entitled 'Ancient France'.

history of Mesopotamia in antiquity, beginning with the first manifestations of human presence in north-eastern Iraq during palaeolithic times, and ending with the ultimate collapse of the Sumero-Akkadian civilization at the dawn of the Christian era. In addition, two introductory chapters purport to acquaint the reader with the geography and ecology of Mesopotamia and with the techniques and results of archaeological excavations in that country.

Ancient Iraq is intended not for scholars, but for laymen and students. Throughout the world there exists a growing number of persons from all walks of life who are deeply interested in history in general and in the ancient Orient in particular. Cultured and eager to learn, these persons have not yet found gathered in one volume of reasonable size all the information they desire on a country which, with very good reasons, fascinates them. It is for this enlightened public that this book has primarily been written. But among those kind enough to look with indulgence upon my articles in *Iraq Petroleum* were also several university professors. In private letters and conversation they expressed the opinion that a book written along the same lines as the articles would provide their students with a useful working instrument. In order to satisfy the requirements of this category of readers, I have enlarged on certain points, perhaps considered by many as of secondary importance, and provided each chapter with rather copious bibliographical and explanatory notes. The thought that this work could be of some help to young students of antiquity will, I hope, render the general public more tolerant to its occasional heaviness.

I have endeavoured to make this work as simple, clear and readable as humanly possible, but at the same time accurate and up to date. Needless to say that this was not an easy task. Writing for non-specialized readers on scientific matters is like walking on a tightrope: one is always afraid of falling into pedantry or triviality, and I am by no means sure that I have succeeded in keeping my balance all the way. In the enormous amount of material available, I had to make difficult, often

heart-breaking choices, but I have taken great care to avoid
over-simplification and dogmatism. History, especially where
antiquity is concerned, abounds in unsolved problems, and the
truth of today may be the proven error of tomorrow. I have
therefore taken the liberty of discussing at some length some of
the more debated problems – such as the origin of the Sumerians
– and I have underlined, on almost every page, the provisional
character of our knowledge. On frequent occasions I have
attempted to correlate historical events with previous events or
with geographical and economic conditions. In other words, I
have tried to 'explain' as much as to describe, for I feel that
without such 'explanations' – no matter how tentative they are
– history would be nothing but a meaningless and tedious
collection of dates and data. Finally, I have given archaeology,
art, literature and religion more importance than is usually
expected in a work of this kind, and I have quoted as many
texts as space would permit. The public nowadays wants to
know how ancient people lived and what they thought at least
as much as what they did, and the best way to make the past
alive is perhaps to let it speak by itself.

I wish to thank all those who have helped me in this work,
particularly my learned friends Monsieur René Labat, Professor
at the Collège de France, Paris, and Monsieur Georges Dossin,
Professor at the Universities of Brussels and Liège, who gave me
their encouragement; Mr T. E. Piggott, former editor of *Iraq
Petroleum*, who published my articles and obligingly put the
blocks at my disposal; Mr L. H. Bawden, who drew the maps
with consummate skill and art; Monsieur P. Amiet, of the
Louvre Museum, Dr R. D. Barnett and the Trustees of the
British Museum, Professor W. Caskel, of the University of
Cologne, Dr G. R. Meyer, of the Vorderasiatische Museum,
Berlin, and Dr Faisal al-Wailly, Director-General of Antiquities
to the Iraqi Government, who authorized the publication of
photographs of the monuments from their respective museums.
Above all, I owe a very special debt of gratitude to Dr D. J.

Wiseman, Professor of Assyriology at the University of London, who was kind enough to read the manuscript and to offer much invaluable advice, and to my wife, without whose self-sacrifice, moral support and linguistic assistance I would have been unable to write this book.

London, August 1963

CHAPTER I

THE GEOGRAPHICAL SETTING

Nowhere, perhaps, is the influence of geography upon history
as clearly demonstrated as in the group of countries which
extend from the Mediterranean Sea to the Iranian plateau and
form what we call the Near East. In the great deserts and
equatorial forests, or in the vicinity of the poles, man is overwhelmed by a hostile nature threatening his very existence. In
temperate areas, on the other hand, man is almost everywhere
at home in a favourable and challenging environment. But in
the arid, sub-tropical Near East the balance between man and
nature is more delicately poised. Man can live there and even
thrive, yet his various activities are largely conditioned by the
relief of the ground, the nature of the soil, the amount of
rainfall, the distribution of springs and wells, the course and
rate of flow of the rivers. These factors exert upon him a
profound influence: they mark the paths of his trade and of his
military ventures, incline him to settle as a farmer or condemn
him to the wandering life of a nomad, contribute to his physical
and moral qualities and, to some extent, command his thoughts
and religious beliefs. The history of any Near Eastern country
must therefore begin with a study of the map, and the antique
land of Iraq is no exception to the rule.

Since we possess no ancient treatise on geography, the following description will necessarily be based on present-day Iraq,
though there is no doubt that it applies to antiquity with but
minor amendments.[1] While in some parts of the country the
rivers do not follow exactly the same course as they did in the
past, and while regions which were once fertile are now sterile
and vice versa, the general pattern of mountains, plains and
valleys remains obviously unchanged, and a comparison between ancient and modern faunae and florae,[2] as well as the

I

evidence obtained from geological and meteorological studies,[3] indicate that climatic fluctuations over the last five thousand years have been so slight as to be practically negligible. Scientific proof of this kind, however, is almost superfluous, for any person with some knowledge of history who visits Iraq finds himself in familiar surroundings. Not only do bare mountains, stony deserts, fields of barley, palm-groves, reed-thickets and mud-flats form the landscape which ancient texts and monuments suggested, but living conditions outside the main cities are reminiscent of those of yore. On the hills shepherds straight from biblical ages graze sheep and goats; in the desert tribes of bedouins endlessly wander from well to well, as of old; in the plain peasants live in mud houses almost identical with those of the Babylonian farmers and often use similar tools, while fishermen in the marshes dwell in the reed-huts and punt the high-prowed boats of their Sumerian ancestors. If the moon, the sun, the winds, the rivers are no longer worshipped, their power is still feared or welcomed, and many ancient customs and beliefs can be explained by reference to present conditions. Indeed, there are few countries in the world where the past is more strangely alive, where the historian's dead texts are provided with a more appropriate illustration.

Our field of studies is a triangle covering an area of about 240,000 square kilometres, limited by arbitrary lines drawn between Aleppo, Lake Urmiah and the mouth of the Shatt-el-'Arab. The political frontiers of today divide this triangle between Syria and Iraq, the latter having the better share, while parts of Turkey and Iran protrude in the north and east. But these frontiers are recent, and the whole region constitutes in fact one large geographical unit having for its main axis the valleys of two great rivers, the Tigris and the Euphrates. We may therefore call it 'Mesopotamia', though the word, coined in antiquity by Greek historians, is somewhat too restricted, meaning '(the land) *between* the rivers'. Surprising as it may seem, the ancient inhabitants of 'Mesopotamia' had no name covering the totality of the country in which they lived, and the terms they used were either too vague ('the Land') or too precise ('Sumer', 'Akkad', 'Assur', 'Babylon'). So deeply embedded in their minds were the concepts of city-states and of narrow politico-religious divisions that they apparently failed to recognize the existence of a territorial unity which to us is obvious.

The geographical unity of Mesopotamia was matched in pre-Christian times by a striking cultural unity. Within our triangle flourished a civilization which in quality and importance was only equalled by the civilization of Egypt. According to the fashion of the day, we call it 'Chaldaean', 'Assyro-Babylonian', 'Sumero-Akkadian' or 'Mesopotamian' civilization, but these are one and the same thing. From roots set deeply in the darkness of prehistoric times, it slowly grew, blossomed in the dawning light of history and lasted for nearly three thousand years, remaining remarkably uniform throughout, though repeatedly shaken by political convulsions and repeatedly rejuvenated by foreign blood and influence. The centres which generated, kept alive and radiated this civilization over the entire Near East were towns such as Ur, Uruk, Nippur, Agade, Babylon, Assur and Nineveh, all situated on or near the Tigris or the Euphrates, within the boundaries of modern Iraq. At the beginning of the Christian era, however, the Mesopotamian civilization gradually declined and vanished for reasons which will be detailed in due course. Some of its cultural and scientific achievements were salvaged by the Greeks and later became part of our own heritage; the rest either perished or lay buried for centuries, awaiting the picks of archaeologists. A glorious past was forgotten. In man's short memory of these opulent cities, of these powerful gods, of these mighty monarchs, only a few, often distorted names survived. The dissolving rain, the sand-bearing winds, the earth-splitting sun conspired to obliterate all material remains, and the desolate mounds which since concealed the ruins of Babylon and Nineveh offer perhaps the best lesson in modesty that we shall ever receive from history.

The Twin Rivers

Herodotus's famous sentence 'Egypt is a gift of the Nile'[4] is often quoted. In many respects, it can also be said of Mesopotamia that she is a gift of the twin rivers. From time immemorial the Tigris and the Euphrates have deposited their alluvium on a bed of sedimentary rocks between the Arabian platform and the Iranian highland, creating amidst deserts a plain which in size and fertility has no equivalent in the 2,300 miles of barren land stretching from the Indus to the Nile. Was this plain also claimed from the sea? In other words, did the head of the Arabo-Persian Gulf reach the latitude of Baghdad in early prehistoric times, being gradually pushed southwards as millennia went by? Such is the classical theory long professed as a dogma and still to be found in most textbooks.[5] In 1952, however, a new theory was put forward, which claims that the Tigris and the Euphrates unload their sediment in a slowly subsiding basin and that in consequence the line of the seashore has probably varied very little in the course of time.[6]

However, further studies conducted in the 1970s, mainly on marine terraces and submarine sediments, have shown that this theory accounted for only part of a very complex process and that Pleistocene and Holocene changes in world climate were also major factors, being responsible for wide fluctuations in the level of the Gulf waters, which of course influenced the position of the shoreline and the gradient of river flow. Most scientists now agree that about 14000 B.C., at the peak of the last Ice Age, the Gulf was a deep and broad valley through which flowed the Tigris and the Euphrates united in a single river, and that this valley was gradually filled with sea water as the ice-cap melted. By 4000–3000 B.C. the level of the Gulf was approximately one or two metres above its present level, so that the shoreline lay in the vicinity of Ur and Eridu. Gradual regression combined with silting from the rivers brought it to where it is now.[7] There is some archaeological evidence that around 1500 B.C. the sea-shore was roughly half-way between

4

Ur and modern Basrah.[8] But many other factors must have intervened, and we shall probably never know the entire story.

Both the Tigris and the Euphrates have their sources in Armenia, the former to the south of Lake Van, the latter near Mount Ararat. The Euphrates, 2,780 kilometres long, first follows a zigzagging course across Turkey, while the Tigris, notably shorter (1,950 kilometres), almost immediately flows southwards. When they emerge from the Taurus mountains the two rivers are separated from each other by some 400 kilometres of open steppe. The Euphrates, which at Jerablus is only 150 kilometres from the Mediterranean, takes a south-easterly direction and leisurely makes its way towards the Tigris. Near Baghdad they nearly meet, being a mere thirty-two kilometres apart, but they soon diverge again and do not mingle their waters until they reach Qurnah, 100 kilometres north of Basrah, to form the Shatt-el-'Arab. In antiquity, however, this wide, majestic river did not exist, the Tigris and the Euphrates then running separately into the sea. This general pattern of river courses can be divided into two segments. To the north of a line Hît-Samarra the valleys of the Twin Rivers are distinct. The two streams cut their way across a plateau of hard limestone and shale and are bordered by cliffs, with the result that the river-beds have moved very little in the course of time, the ancient cities – such as Karkemish, Mari, Nineveh, Nimrud or Assur – still being on, or close by, the river banks, as they were thousands of years ago. But to the south of that line the two valleys merge and form a wide, flat alluvial plain – sometimes called the Mesopotamian delta – where the rivers flow with such a low gradient that they meander considerably and throw numerous side-branches. Like all meandering rivers they raise their own beds, so that they frequently flow above the level of the plain, their overflow tending to create permanent lakes and swamps, and they occasionally change their course. This explains why southern Mesopotamian cities, which were once on the Euphrates or on its branches, are now forlorn ruin-mounds in a desert of silt, several miles from modern waterways. Changes in river-beds are extremely difficult to study in retrospect and to date with accuracy, but they certainly occurred in antiquity. It is, however, remarkable that the ancient Mesopotamians managed to keep their rivers under control, since the two principal branches of the lower Euphrates followed approximately the same course for about three thousand years, passing through Sippar, Babylon, Nippur, Shuruppak, Uruk, Larsa and Ur, that is to say from 25 to 80 kilometres to the east of its present main channel. As for the Tigris, all that can be said about its ancient course in southern Mesopotamia is that it probably was the same as the course of the Shatt el-Gharraf, one of its present branches: straight from Kut el-Imara to the neighbourhood of Nasriyah. It seems to have played a relatively minor role in that region, either because its bed was dug too deep into the alluvium for simple canal irrigation or because it was surrounded – as indeed it is now – by extensive marshes.

The climate of central and southern Iraq is of the 'dry, subtropical' variety, with temperatures reaching 120° F. (50° C.) in summer and an average winter rainfall of less than ten inches. Agriculture therefore depends almost entirely upon irrigation, though the dimensions and profile of the plain, as well as the rate of flow of the rivers, preclude the cheap and easy 'basin type' of irrigation as practised, for instance, in Egypt, where the overflow of the Nile freely inundates the valley for a time and then withdraws. Since the combined flood periods of the Tigris and the Euphrates occur between April and June, too late for winter crops and too early for summer crops, the fields must be supplied with water at man's will, and this is achieved by a complex system of canals, reservoirs, dykes, regulator-sluices and the like ('perennial irrigation').[9] To create an efficient network of canals and to maintain them against rapid silting-up are clearly colossal and unending tasks which require large labour forces and the cooperation of many communities – factors which contain the germs of both local strife and political unity. But this is not all: year after year, two grave dangers threaten the Mesopotamian farmer. The more insidious of the two is the accumulation in flat, low-lying areas of the salt brought by irrigation and collected in the water-table which lies just beneath the surface. If no artificial drainage is installed – and it seems that such drainage was unknown in antiquity – fertile fields can become sterile in a comparatively short time, and in this way, throughout history pieces of land of ever-increasing size had to be abandoned and reverted to deserts.[10] The other danger lies in the capricious rate of flow of the twin rivers.[11] While the Nile, fed by the great lakes of East Africa acting as regulators, has an annual flood of almost constant volume, the volume of the combined floods of the Tigris and the Euphrates is unpredictable, for it depends upon the variable amount of rain or snow which falls on the mountains of Armenia and Kurdistan. If low waters over a few years mean drought and famine, one excessive flood often spells catastrophe. The rivers break through their embankments; the low land as far as the eye can see is submerged; the flimsy mud-houses and reed-huts are swept away; the crop is lost in a huge muddy lake, together with the cattle and the belongings of a large part of the population. It is a spectacle the horror of which will never be forgotten by those who witnessed the last great Iraqi inundation, in the spring of 1954. Thus Mesopotamia constantly hovers between desert and swamp. This double threat and the uncertainty it creates as regards the future are believed to be at the root of the 'fundamental pessimism' which, for some authors, characterizes the philosophy of the ancient Mesopotamians.

Despite these drawbacks, the plain watered by the Tigris and the Euphrates is a rich farming land and was even richer in antiquity before extensive salinization of the soil took place. The entire population of ancient Iraq could easily feed on the country and barter the surplus of cereals for metal, wood and stone, which had to be obtained from abroad. Though wheat, emmer, millet and sesame were grown, barley was – and still is – the main cereal, since it tolerates a slightly saline soil. Agricultural methods were, as might be expected, primitive, yet at the same time thorough. They are described in fairly great detail in an interesting text known as 'a Sumerian Farmer's Almanac', written about 1700 B.C.[12] According to this text – which purports to be a farmer's instructions to his son – the field was first watered with moderation, trampled over by shod oxen, then carefully dressed with axes to make its surface even. Ploughing and sowing were carried out simultaneously by means of a wooden seeding-plough that went 'two fingers' deep into the soil, the furrows being approximately two feet apart. Later, while barley was growing, the field was inundated again three or four times. The same document also describes the harvesting, the threshing by wagon and sled, and the winnowing. As in the Book of Ruth, the farmer is exhorted to 'make the earth supply the sustenance of the young and the gleaners' by leaving on the ground some of the fallen ears.

The initial watering and ploughing were performed in May–June, and the main harvest usually took place in April of the following year; but a catch-crop was often possible after the winter rains. The fields remained fallow every other year. There is no doubt that the alluvial soil of central and southern Mesopotamia was very fertile in antiquity, but the figure of two- or three-hundredfold given by Herodotus and Strabo for the yield of corn is grossly exaggerated,[13] and to state that the yield of wheat in the extreme south of Iraq in about 2400 B.C. could compare favourably with that of the most modern Canadian wheatfields seems to be over-enthusiastic. In fact, all figures put forward by modern authors must be taken with caution since they are based on very few cuneiform texts, some of which may be misleading; moreover, they only apply to a certain period and a certain region. However, the recently suggested overall estimate of forty- to fiftyfold (i.e. about twice the average figure in central Iraq in the fifties) appears to be acceptable.[14] The hot and humid climate of southern Mesopotamia and the availability of ample water supplies in that region also were conditions highly favourable to the cultivation of the date-palm which grows along rivers and canals, 'its feet in water and its head in the scorching sun', in the words of an

Arabian proverb. We learn from ancient texts that as early as the third millennium B.C. there were in the country of Sumer extensive palm-groves, and that artificial pollination was already practised.[15] Flour and dates – the latter of high calorific value – formed the staple food of ancient Iraq, but cattle, sheep and goats were bred and grazed in the uncultivated areas and in the fields left fallow, while rivers, canals, lakes and sea provided fish in abundance. A variety of fruit and vegetables, including pomegranates, grapes, figs, chickpeas, lentils, beans, turnips, leeks, cucumbers, watercress, lettuces, onions and garlic, was also grown in gardens sheltered by the palm-trees and watered by means of a very simple water-lifting instrument (*dâlu*) which is still used under its old name. There is no doubt that, apart from occasional famines due to war or natural disasters, the Mesopotamians generally enjoyed a rich and varied diet and were much better off in this respect than their neighbours of Syria, Iran or Asia Minor.[16]

Regional Variations

Up to now our attention has been focused on the main axis of the Mesopotamian triangle, the plain between the two rivers; but if we turn to the periphery we at once observe considerable differences in climate and landscape. Leaving aside minor local variations, four main regions can be described: the desert, the steppe, the foothills and the marshes.

Hilly in the north, dissected by deep *wadis* in the centre, flat and featureless in the south, the desert borders to the west the whole course of the Euphrates and extends for hundreds of kilometres into the heart of Arabia.[17] This great Syro-Arabian desert, however, was foreign to ancient Mesopotamia, and the sharp line which divides it from the Euphrates valley also marks the limit of pre-Islamic settlements. The Sumerians and Babylonians were essentially peasant-folk; unlike the Arabs, they turned their backs on the desert and remained firmly attached to the 'good land', the fertile alluvium. But they had to reckon with the uncouth nomads who attacked their caravans, raided their towns and villages and even invaded their country, as did the Amorites at the beginning of the second millennium and the Aramaeans eight hundred years later. As we shall see, long chapters in the history of ancient Iraq are filled with episodes of this age-old struggle between the sedentary society of the alluvial plains and the hostile tribes of the western desert. It must be added here that desert conditions can be found in various parts of Mesopotamia itself. Not only is the desert always potentially present between the twin rivers, ready to creep in and take the place of cornfields and palm-groves as soon as rivers change their course or canals become silted-up, but large areas on the left bank of the Tigris and of the Middle Euphrates have always been dreary wastes strewn with dry *wadis* and salt lakes, scarcely inhabited at the best of times and by-passed by the main trade routes.

In the north-western part of Mesopotamia, beyond the thin ridges formed by Jabal 'Abd-al-Aziz and Jabal Sinjar and up to the foot of the Taurus, the plain called by the Arabs al-Jazirah, 'the island', spans the 400 kilometres which separate the Tigris from the Euphrates. The many streams which converge and form the rivers Balikh and Khabur, affluents of the Euphrates, are spread like fans over this region, while the more than adequate winter rains are supplemented by a vast and super-ficial water-table fed by the snows of the nearby mountains. Cornfields and orchards stretch along the rivers or cluster around springs and wells, the meshes of this green network being filled by a steppe covered with grass in springtime and offering ideal conditions for the breeding of cattle, sheep and horses. This fertile plain forms a natural 'corridor', a transit area between the Upper Tigris valley and the plains of northern Syria, and the amazing constellation of 'tells' representing buried cities and villages testifies that it was heavily populated in antiquity.

Of particular interest for the historian is the north-eastern corner of Iraq, the foothill region between the Tigris and the mountains of Kurdistan.[18] There the annual rainfall varies between 30 and 60 centimetres. From a rolling plain alongside the river the ground rises through a series of parallel folds of gradually increasing height to the rugged, snow-covered peaks of the Zagros range (altitude 2,500 to 3,600 metres) which separates Iraq from Iran. Four tributaries of the Tigris, the Greater Zab, the Lesser Zab, the 'Adhem and the Diyala, flow diagonally across the region, sometimes cutting deep gorges through the limestone ridges, sometimes zigzagging around them. The climate is hot in summer but cool in winter. The hills are now rather denuded, but here and there on their slopes can be seen a meadow or a small forest of oaks or pine-trees, while wheat, barley, fruit-trees, vine and vegetables grow easily in the high-lying valleys. Successively the home of pre-historic cavemen, the cradle – or, rather, one of the cradles – of farming in the Neolithic Near East, and the fringe of the Assyrian kingdom, this attractive district played an important part in the history of Mesopotamia. Yet even in Assyrian times civilization remained confined to the cultivable land at the foot of the hills. The mountains themselves, difficult to penetrate and easy to defend, always formed a disputed borderland between the armies of Mesopotamian rulers and the 'barbarian' highlanders who, like the bedouins of the western desert, coveted and threatened the wealthy cities of the plain.

At the other end of Iraq, the extensive marshes which cover the southern part of the Tigris–Euphrates delta also form a special district, widely different from the rest of Mesopotamia. With their myriads of shallow lakes, their narrow waterways winding through dense thickets of reeds, their fauna of water-buffaloes, wild boars and wild birds, their mosquitoes and their stifling heat, they constitute one of the most strange, forbidding and fascinating regions of the world.[19] Although they may have varied in extent and configuration, ancient monuments and texts prove that they have always existed, and indeed, the Ma'dan, or marsh-Arabs, appear to have preserved to some extent the way of life of the early Sumerians established on the fringe of the swamps more than five thousand years ago. From an archaeological point of view, the Iraqi marshes are still largely *terra incognita*. Reports from travellers suggest that traces of ancient settlements are exceedingly rare, probably because they consisted of reed-hut villages similar to those of today, which have completely disappeared or lie buried beneath several feet of mud and water. It is hoped, however, that modern methods – such as the use of helicopters – will eventually open to exploration a region which is by no means lacking in historical interest.

Thus, under an apparent uniformity, Iraq is a land of contrasts. If the northern steppe and the southern marshes can be considered as local variants of the great Mesopotamian plain, there is a striking difference in topography, climate and vegetation between the plain and the foothill region, and this difference has its counterpart in history. Throughout antiquity, a definite opposition between the North and the South – or, in terms of political geography, between Sumer-and-Akkad (or Babylonia) and Assyria – can be detected, sometimes faintly perceptible and revealed only by cultural dissimilarities, sometimes open and manifested in violent conflicts.

Trade Routes

Long before they knew that a wealth of petroleum was lying beneath their feet, the inhabitants of Iraq exploited a parent-substance, bitumen, which they obtained from seepages in various parts of the country, in particular on the Middle Euphrates, between Hît and Ramâdi. They used bitumen in many ways, not only in architecture (as mortar for brickwork and waterproof lining for bathrooms and drains), but in sculpture and inlay-work, as a material for caulking boats, as fuel and even as a drug. There is some evidence that, at least during certain periods in their history, they exported it.[20]

But if Mesopotamia was rich in bitumen, clay and agricultural products, she lacked metal ores as she lacked hard stone and good timber. These materials were already being imported from abroad in proto-historical times, thus enabling a Chalcolithic culture to develop in a country conspicuous for the absence of metal. Copper was first discovered, it is generally believed, in north-western Iran or in the Caucasus, and was perhaps originally obtained from Azerbaijan or Armenia. Soon, however, were found alternative sources of supplies, such as Anatolia (which later produced iron), Cyprus and the country called in cuneiform texts *Magan*, which has tentatively been identified with the mountainous part of Oman. Tin seems to have been inported from Iran, the Caucasus, or perhaps even Afghanistan, before the Phoenicians in the first millennium B.C. brought it from Spain. Silver came mostly from the Taurus mountains, gold from various deposits scattered between Egypt and India.[21] Several districts of Iran could provide hard stones and semi-precious stones, and Magan was reputed for its beautiful black diorite used by the sculptors of the Third Dynasty of Ur. Ordinary timber could be found in the nearby Zagros mountains, but the valuable cedar was brought from Lebanon or the Amanus, while other varieties of wood came by sea from the mysterious country of *Meluhha* – possibly the ancient name for the Indus valley. At a very early date, therefore, an extensive network of trade routes was developed, which linked the various parts of Mesopotamia with each other and with the rest of the Near East.[22]

Within Mesopotamia transport from one locality to another was frequently effected by water. The Tigris and the Euphrates formed convenient thoroughfares from north to south, and the larger irrigation canals could also be used as waterways between villages and cities. The advantages offered by these means of communications can readily be appreciated if one remembers that the canals themselves are obstacles to land traffic, that most of the plain is covered with thick mud in winter and liable to local inundations during the spring, and that the only pack-animal available until the camel was introduced on a large scale in the first millennium B.C. was the ass.

Outside Mesopotamia two great roads led in a westerly direction towards Syria and the Mediterranean coast. These roads were, of course, simple desert tracks, for the paved highways which have been found outside the gates of several cities were unlikely to go very far inland. The first road started from Sippar (near Fallujah, at the latitude of Baghdad), followed the Euphrates as far as Mari or some other market-place in the Abu-Kemal–Deir-ez-Zor area, and, cutting straight through the desert via Tidmur (Palmyra), reached the region of Homs, where it divided into several branches to the Phoenician ports, Damascus or Palestine. The crossing of the desert – there no more than 500 kilometres wide – was inconvenient in summer and exposed at all times to attacks from the nomads; caravans and armies, therefore, usually preferred the second road, much longer but safer and well provided with water and fodder. It left the Tigris at Nineveh, opposite Mosul, ran through the steppe of Jazirah from the east to west via Shubat-Enlil (perhaps Tell Leilan), Guzana (Tell Halaf), Harranu (Harran), crossed the Euphrates at Karkemish (Jerablus) or at Emar (Meskene), passed through or near Aleppo and ended in the Orontes valley, with terminal branches to the Mediterranean coast and central Syria.[23] At various points on this road other tracks branched off in a north-westerly direction, ultimately ending in Cilicia and Anatolia. From Nineveh it was also possible to reach Armenia and eastern Anatolia by following the Tigris as far as Diarbakr and then crossing the Taurus through narrow passes.

Communications with the east were much more difficult. The tribes dwelling in the Zagros were generally hostile, and the mountain itself constituted a formidable barrier which could only be passed at three points: at Raiat, near Rowanduz, at Halabja, to the south-east of Suleimaniyah, and at Khanaqin, on the upper Diyala. The Raiat and Halabja passes gave access to Azerbaijan and the shores of Lake Urmiah, the Khanaqin pass to Kermanshah, Hamadan and, beyond Hamadan, the Iranian plateau. A fourth road, farther south, ran parallel to the Zagros from Dêr (near Badrah) to Susa (Shush, near Dizful), the capital city of Elam. It met with no physical obstacle, the lower valleys of the rivers Kerkha and Karun, which form the territory of Elam, being merely an eastward extension of the Mesopotamian plains, but the Elamites were the traditional enemies of the Mesopotamians, and this road was more often followed by invading armies than by peaceful caravans.

The last of the great trade routes between ancient Iraq and the rest of the world was through the Arabo-Persian Gulf, the 'Bitter River', the 'Lower Sea' or 'Sea of the Rising Sun', as it was then called. From early Islamic times onward the Gulf has been the 'lung' of Iraq, a window wide open on India and, later, the Far East and Western countries.[24] In antiquity, merchant ships sailed on it from Ur to Dilmun (Bahrain) and hence to Magan (Oman) and/or Meluhha (the Indus valley), probably putting into several as yet unidentified ports on their way. It has long been known from cuneiform texts and some objects, notably stamp-seals, that commercial relations between Mesopotamia and the Indus valley had been established as early as the third millennium, but until recent years the Arabian coast of the Gulf had been *terra incognita* on archaeological maps. In 1953, however, excavations started in Bahrain and subsequently extended to Saudi Arabia, Kuwait (Failakka Island), Qatar, the United Arab Emirates and Oman, with unexpected results. Not only have they brought to light material evidence of cultural and commercial intercourse between these countries and Mesopotamia (as well as south-eastern Iran and Pakistan) since the fifth millennium, but they have also revealed local cultures of considerable interest.[25] Later on, at certain periods the Gulf was sailed by ships transporting troops and possibly ambassadors, since we know that the kings of Akkad, c. 2200 B.C., and the kings of Assyria, in the first millennium, endeavoured to attract at least Dilmun and Magan within the sphere of their political and economic influence.

This brief and very incomplete description should have made

it clear that Mesopotamia, contrary to popular belief, did not offer ideal conditions for the development of an original civilization. Her two rivers form a fertile delta, but they can bring disaster as well as opulence. Through considerable and sustained effort agriculture is possible on a large scale, but metal, stone and timber are desperately lacking. Deserts and high mountains, both difficult to cross and inhabited by predatory people, surround the plain on all sides, leaving only one narrow access to the sea – a sea bordered for five hundred miles by the inhospitable shores of Arabia and Persia. All considered, the northern steppe and the foothills of Kurdistan would seem to offer a more favourable environment than the great alluvial plain, and it is not by chance that these regions were the seats of the Neolithic and Early Chalcolithic cultures of Mesopotamia. Yet it is in the extreme south of that country, on the fringe of the swamps, that the Mesopotamian civilization took shape. Whatever man achieved in ancient Iraq, he did it at the price of a constant struggle against nature and against other men, and this struggle forms the very thread of history in that part of the world. Before going farther, however, we must first examine the sources from which historians draw their raw material.

CHAPTER 2

IN SEARCH OF THE PAST

In order to reconstruct the past, historians make use of two kinds of documents: texts and objects, the word 'object' here meaning literally any artefact, from the most elaborate building to the humblest kitchen utensil. But while objects play a comparatively small part where recent periods are concerned, they grow in importance as one moves back along the scale of time, and as historians have no direct access to non-written documents, they usually must rely upon the publications of those men whose task it is to dig up ancient cities and necropoles: the field archaeologists.

Historians of the ancient Near East are even more dependent upon archaeologists than those of classical antiquity, for, in Mesopotamia, objects *and* texts lie, for reasons that we shall presently examine, deeply buried in the ground and can only be reached by means of excavation. Archaeological excavations began in Iraq in 1843 and have continued unceasingly ever since. At first the work of genial amateurs, they rose to scientific standards at the turn of this century when it was realized that filling museums with *objets d'art* was not an end in itself and that finding out how people lived was far more important. On the other hand, the very nature of their work, the fact that they were dealing with fragile material such as mud bricks and clay tablets, and the necessity, in order to reach deeper into the past, of destroying layer after layer of human occupation almost as soon as they uncovered them, obliged archaeologists to devise proper, elaborate techniques. Teams of experts trained in, and sponsored by, European or American museums and universities and backed by all the resources of modern science were brought in to direct and supervise the skilled workmen who handled the pick and the spade. During the last ninety years more than thirty sites – including practically all the main cities of ancient Iraq – have been extensively excavated and more than three hundred mounds 'sounded'. The results of this international effort are astounding. Our knowledge of ancient Mesopotamian history has been completely altered and broadened beyond all expectations. Historians, who 150 years ago had no other source of information than the scanty data supplied by the Bible and by a handful of classical authors, now confess that they can hardly handle the enormous amount of material put year after year at their disposal and gratefully acknowledge their debt to archaeologists.[1]

Courtesy alone would therefore justify this chapter, but other reasons have also prompted us to write it. Throughout this book we shall speak of the mounds or 'tells' which represent the buried cities of ancient Iraq; we shall refer to 'levels' and 'layers'; we shall, whenever possible, give 'absolute' and 'relative' dates. It seemed to us that the reader was entitled to know from the start what we were talking about, and that the best way of satisfying his curiosity would be to summarize the objects, methods and development of what is now commonly called 'Mesopotamian archaeology'.

The Buried Cities of Iraq

To most tourists, the first contact with the ancient sites of Iraq comes as a surprise. They are taken to a hillock rising above the plain and they are told that this was once an ancient city. As they go nearer they may find such splendid monuments as the stage-tower of Ur or the Ishtar Gate of Babylon, but in most cases they are confronted with unsightly bits of brickwork and heaps of earth littered with broken pottery. Quite naturally they are puzzled and wonder how this happened.

To answer this question it should be first explained that these ancient towns were built of nothing but mud. Stone is rare in Iraq, whereas clay is everywhere at hand. In very early times houses were made of piled-up mud (*pisé*) or of shapeless lumps of clay pressed together (*adobe*), but as early as in the ninth millennium B.C. it was soon found preferable to mix clay with straw, gravel or potsherds, mould it into bricks, let these bricks dry in the sun and bind them together with a gypsum mortar. In that way, thicker, stronger and more regular walls could be built. Of course, kiln-baked bricks were much more resistant and durable, especially when they were jointed with bitumen, but this was a costly material, as wood fuel was rare and bitumen had often to be shipped from comparatively distant regions. Burnt bricks therefore were in general reserved for the houses of gods and kings, though this was by no means the rule,[2] and the vast majority of ancient Mesopotamian buildings were of simple mud bricks. The roofs were made of earth spread over a structure of reed mats and tree-trunks, and the floors of beaten earth sometimes with a coating of gypsum. A coat of mud plaster was also usually applied to the walls.

These houses with their thick walls were relatively comfortable, being cool in summer and warm in winter, but they required constant attention. Every summer it was necessary to put a new layer of clay on the roof in anticipation of the winter rains, and every now and then the floors had to be raised. The reason for this was that rubbish in antiquity was not collected for disposal but simply thrown into the street, so that the street level gradually rose higher than the floor level of the houses that bordered it, allowing the rain and the filth to seep in. Earth was therefore brought into the rooms, rammed over the old floors and covered with another coat of plaster. It is not infrequent for archaeologists to find two, three or more superimposed floors in one house. Provided these things were done, mud-brick buildings could last for a great many years. But then one day something happened. Whether it was war, fire, epidemic, earthquake, flood or change in river course, the result was the same: the town was partly or totally deserted. The roofs left unattended collapsed and the walls, now exposed to weather on both faces, crumbled down, filling up the rooms and sealing off the objects left behind by the householders. In the case of war, the destruction was of course immediate, the victorious enemy usually setting fire to the city. These arsonists of yore unknowingly made modern 'cuneiformists' happy, since many sun-dried and therefore fragile tablets were baked by the fire and became almost indestructible.

After years or even centuries of abandonment, new settlers would perhaps reoccupy the site, attracted by such things as its strategically or commercially advantageous position, the abundance of its water supplies or, possibly, a lingering devotion to the god under whose aegis it had been built. Since they had no means of removing the enormous mass of debris, they levelled off the ruined walls and used them as foundations for their own building. This process was repeated several times in the course of years, and as 'occupation levels' succeeded one another the city gradually rose above the surrounding plain. Some sites, it is true, were abandoned early and for ever; others, like Erbil and Kirkuk, have been more or less continuously occupied from very ancient times until now; but the vast majority of them, after centuries or millennia of occupation, were deserted at some period or another of the long history of Iraq. It is not difficult to imagine what took place then: windborne sand and earth piled up against the remaining walls and filled in the streets and every hollow, while rainwater smoothed off the surface of the heaped-up ruins, spreading debris over a large area. Slowly but inexorably, the town took its present shape: that of a rounded, more or less regular ruin-mound or, as the Arabs say, using an old, pre-Islamic word, a 'tell'.[3]

The task of archaeologists is to dissect that closely woven fabric of standing or fallen walls and foundations, rubble, floors and earth-filling, to recover the plan of buildings, to collect and preserve the objects they may contain and to identify and date the successive 'levels' which constitute the tell. Depending upon the time and funds at their disposal, they use one of several methods.[4]

The quickest and cheapest way of knowing roughly what is in a tell is to carry out a 'sounding'. Several trenches are dug into the surface of the mound at various angles. As the trenches are deepened, objects such as pottery are collected for dating purposes and a record is made of the floors and segments of walls encountered. This method is obviously imperfect and should only be used for preliminary surveys or for comparatively unimportant sites. A variety of sounding often applied to high and narrow tells consists of cutting a long trench, not on the surface but on the side of the mound from summit to base, just as one cuts into a Christmas pudding. An impressive series of occupation levels can be detected in this way, though it is practically impossible to circumscribe any building.

Another method, in theory perfect, is to divide the surface of the site into squares, dig up each square in turn until a certain depth is reached and start all over again for the second horizontal 'slice'. The objects found in each square and in each layer are carefully numbered and plotted on maps. As the work goes on, monuments gradually take shape. This very slow and expensive method is rarely used. As a rule, archaeologists prefer what may be called 'extended sounding'. A certain area is carefully selected on the surface of the tell and a trench dug, but as soon as walls are encountered, they are followed and denuded on both faces until the whole building is unearthed. Several areas are treated in the same way and may or may not join together. Whenever desirable, digging is pushed in depth underneath the uppermost and consequently more recent buildings, which are destroyed in order to bring older buildings to light. In one or more points a shaft or 'test-pit' may be sunk down to the virgin soil, giving a cross-section of the mound, a summary as it were of its various occupation levels. Some parts of the site remain, of necessity, untouched, but this is of little importance if the main monuments such as temples and palaces and a selection of private houses have been unearthed. Nimrud, Babylon, Uruk, Ur, Nippur and all the main sites of Iraq were or still are excavated by this method with, in the main, highly satisfactory results.

Dating the Past

Dating the monuments and objects discovered can be very easy or very difficult. Obviously, a building whose bricks are stamped with the inscription 'Palace of Sargon, King of Assyria' is *ipso facto* dated, provided we know when King Sargon reigned. But this is the exception. By far the majority of objects found in archaeological excavations – and of course the totality where prehistory is concerned – bear no inscription. In such cases, dating can only be approximate and 'relative', and is based on such criteria as shape, dimensions and style. The cumulative experience derived from the excavation of many a tell has taught archaeologists that bricks of a certain size, vases of certain shapes and decoration, weapons of a certain type, sculptures of a certain style, etc., are exclusively or predominantly found at a certain level and, grouped together, form what is called a 'cultural horizon' or 'cultural stratum'. If only one of these objects is inscribed with a 'date', or if it is found in close and indisputable relation to a monument which is otherwise dated, then the whole cultural stratum easily falls in position within the scale of time. If not, attempts are made to correlate the period during which these objects were in use with more ancient and more recent periods. To take an example, in a number of southern Mesopotamian sites a certain category of painted vases (the so-called Jemdat Nasr pottery) appears immediately *below* a cultural stratum characterized, among other things, by 'plano-convex' bricks (i.e. bricks of which one side is flat and the other rounded) and immediately *above* a cultural stratum where plain, buff, dark or red ceramic predominates. Various inscriptions enable us to date the plano-convex bricks to the third millennium B.C. (Early Dynastic period: *c.* 2900–2334 B.C.). The plain pottery is undated but forms part of the cultural horizon called 'Uruk' after the site where it was first identified. The Jemdat Nasr stratum can therefore be given a 'relative' date. It is intermediate in time between the Uruk period and the Early Dynastic period and ends about 2900 B.C.

How long it lasted is another matter, but there are means of forming rough estimates.

When dealing with history it becomes necessary to express dates in figures, and it is not without interest to examine how these are obtained and to what extent we can trust them.

The ancient Greeks counted from the first Olympiad (776 B.C.), the Romans from the foundation of Rome (753 B.C.); the Moslems date from the *hijra* (A.D. 622) and we have our own Christian era. The ancient Mesopotamians, however, had no such fixed chronological system until late in their history, when they adopted the Seleucid era (311 B.C.). Before that time, they simply referred to the years of reign of their rulers. These could be expressed in three ways: (1) the years of the reign were given in plain figures, e.g. *12th year of Nabû-naʿid (Nabonidus), King of Babylon*; (2) or within each reign each year was defined by some important event such as victories, royal weddings, construction of temples, etc. that had taken place in the *previous* year, e.g. *Year (when) Uruk and Isin were conquered*; (3) or each year of a king's reign was named after some high official of the kingdom (eponyms or, in Assyrian, *limmu* system). In Early Dynastic Sumer all three systems seem to have been used. Then the second system (year-names) was adopted in Babylonia and used until the Kassite period when it was replaced by the first system. In Assyria, however, the *limmu* system was kept throughout history.[5]

These dating systems could only be of practical value for the Mesopotamians themselves if they possessed for each king a list of his year's names or a list of eponyms, for each dynasty a list of its kings with the duration of their reigns, and finally a list of the successive dynasties which ruled over the country. Such lists existed and several of them have fortunately survived. Here are some examples:

Date-list of King Hammurabi of Babylon[6]

(Year 1) Hammurabi became king.
(Year 2) He established justice in the country.

(Year 3) He constructed a throne for the main dais of the
   god Nanna in Babylon.
(Year 4) The wall of (the sacred precinct) Gagia was built.
(Year 5) He constructed the *en. ka.ash.bar.ra* (?).
(Year 6) He constructed the *shir* (?) of the goddess Laz.
(Year 7) Uruk and Isin were conquered.
(Year 8) The country Emutbal (was conquered).

   It will be seen from this list that the date quoted above is
the seventh year of King Hammurabi.

King list B, covering the First Dynasty of Babylon[7]

Sumuabi, king, (reigned) 15 (14) years.
Sumulail, 35 (36) years.
Sabu, his son, same (i.e. king), 14 years.
Apil-Sin, his son, same, 18 years.
Sin-muballit, his son, same, 30 (20) years.
Hammurabi, his son, same, 55 (33) years.
Samsuiluna, his son, same, 35 (38) years.
etc.
The list continues with four other kings and ends with the
statement 'eleven kings, dynasty of Babylon'. Thus we
learn that Hammurabi was the sixth king of Babylon and
that he reigned during 55 (43) years.*

Limmu-list (reign of Adad-nirâri III (810–783 B.C.)[8]

Adad-nirâri, king of Assyria (campaign) against Manna
Nergal-ilia, *turtânu* (field marshal), against Guzana
Bêl-daiân, *nâgir ekalli* (herald of the palace), against Manna
Ṣil-bêl, *rab shaqê* (chief cup-bearer), against Manna
Ashur-taklak, *abarakku* (superintendent), against Arpad
Ili-ittia, *shakin mâti* (governor of Assur), against the town of
   Hazâzu
Nergal-eresh, (governor) of Rasappa, against the town of Ba'li
etc.

---

* The figures in this list were compiled from damaged inscriptions and are
often erroneous. The correct figures are given in brackets.

The time-range of these lists varied. Some were restricted to one place and one dynasty. Others, like the king list B just quoted, included several dynasties which reigned – at least apparently – in succession. Others were even more ambitious and embraced very long periods and dynasties of several kingdoms. Such is the famous 'Sumerian King List' reconstructed by Th. Jacobsen, which ranges from the mythical rulers 'before the Flood' to Damiq-ilishu (1816–1794 B.C.), last king of the First Dynasty of Isin.[9]

To express such dates in terms of Christian chronology would have been impossible but for Claudius Ptolemeus (Ptolemy), a Greek from Alexandria who in the second century A.D. appended to one of his books a list of all the kings of Babylon and Persia from Nabonassar (747 B.C.) to Alexander the Great (336–323 B.C.). This list, known as 'Ptolemy's Canon', not only gives the length of each reign but the outstanding astronomical events that marked some of them. Now it so happens that by putting together data from several Assyrian tablets we can reconstruct a long, uninterrupted *limmu*-list covering the period between Adad-nirâri II (911–891 B.C.) and Ashurbanipal (668–627 B.C.), and this *limmu*-list also gives the main astronomical phenomena of these times. Between 747 and 631 B.C. the *limmu*-list and Ptolemy's Canon coincide, and so do the eclipses, the movements of stars, etc. they mention. Moreover, astronomers have found that an eclipse of the sun, which in the *limmu*-list is said to have occurred in the month of *Sivan* (May–June) of King Ashur-dân's tenth year, actually took place on 15 June 763 B.C., and this is precisely the date arrived at by proceeding backwards and adding together on the list the years of each reign. The absolute chronology of Mesopotamia is therefore firmly established from 911 B.C. onwards.[10] The chronology of early periods rests upon more fragile foundations. In theory, it should be possible to work it out from king lists and dynastic lists, but these have often proved to be misleading. Not only do they show significant differences, but they contain a number of gaps or scribal errors, or they give as successive dynasties which, in fact, partly overlapped or were contemporaneous.

IN SEARCH OF THE PAST

One should not therefore be surprised to find different figures in different textbooks and occasional changes of opinions. For instance, the accession date of King Hammurabi of Babylon was given as 2394 B.C. one hundred years ago (Oppert, 1888), 2003 after the First World War (Thureau-Dangin, 1927), and varies now between 1848 (Sidersky, 1940) and 1704 (Weidner, 1951), but most historians of the ancient Near East have pronounced in favour of the so-called 'middle' chronology according to which Hammurabi reigned from 1792 to 1750 B.C. and this is the chronology that will be found in this book.[11]

We cannot leave this subject without mentioning the attempts made to put chronology on a more scientific basis by means of physical methods and, in particular, the Carbon 14 or Radiocarbon method developed in 1946 by Professor W. F. Libby of Chicago.[12] Its principle is briefly as follows: all living organisms contain ordinary carbon of atomic weight 12 and a radioactive isotope of carbon of atomic weight 14 which is formed in the upper layers of the atmosphere through the action of cosmic rays on nitrogen, falls upon earth and is absorbed by vegetation and ultimately by animals. The ratio of carbon 14 to carbon 12 remains fixed throughout life: one-billionth of a gram for every gram of ordinary carbon. After death, when no more carbon 14 is absorbed, that part of it which is in the organism decreases slowly and regularly by reverting to nitrogen. As the curve of disintegration, or 'half-life' curve, of carbon 14 is known (this is 5,568 years), it is possible to find the date at which the organism died, and consequently its age. This method can be applied to organic matter, such as bone, wood, charcoal, shells, reeds, etc., found in archaeological excavations, but its usefulness is limited by a number of factors ('standard deviation' inherent in the radiation counting technique, contamination by older or more recent material, variations in atmospheric carbon 14 concentrations with time) and recent attempts to 'calibrate' radiocarbon estimations by dendrochronology (the study of tree-rings) have met with problems. This means that radiocarbon dates must be taken with caution; they are of considerable help when prehistory is concerned – since differences of a few hundred years matter little – but cannot be used for precise, historical chronology.

Archaeological Research in Iraq

The transformation of once flourishing cities into tells was more rapid than one might think.[13] Herodotus in the middle of the fourth century B.C. sees Babylon still alive, but neglects to visit Nineveh destroyed a century and a half before, and Xenophon leading ten thousand Greek mercenaries across Mesopotamia in 401 B.C. passed near the great Assyrian capital city without even noticing it.[14] Four centuries later, Strabo speaks of Babylon as of a town in ruins, 'almost completely deserted'.[15]

A thousand years went by. As the blanket of dust over the ancient cities grew thicker and thicker, their memory gradually faded away. Arab historians and geographers still knew something of Iraq's glorious past, but Europe had forgotten the East. The peregrinations of Benjamin of Tudela in the twelfth century and the travels of the German naturalist Rauwolff four hundred years later were isolated episodes. It was not before the seventeenth century that western interest in oriental antiquities was awakened, when an Italian nobleman, Pietro della Valle, gave an entertaining account of his journey across Mesopotamia and brought back to Europe, in 1625, bricks found at Ur and Babylon 'on which were writing in certain unknown characters'. Gradually, it dawned upon academics and royalty that here was a field worth investigating. For the first time, in 1761 a scientific mission was sent out east by the King of Denmark with orders to gather as much information as possible on various subjects, including archaeology. The numerous inscriptions copied at Persepolis by its leader Karsten Niebuhr – a mathematician by profession – were put at the disposal of philologists, who were soon at work deciphering the mysterious writing. From then on, nearly all those who visited, or lived in, the Orient made a point of exploring its ruins, collecting 'antikas' and copying inscriptions. Prominent among them are Joseph de Beauchamp, a distinguished French abbé and astronomer (1786), Claudius James Rich, a Resident of the East India Company and British Consul General in Baghdad (1807), Sir James Buckingham (1816), Robert Mignan (1827), James Baillie Fraser (1834) and that extraordinary army officer, sportsman, explorer and philologist, undoubtedly the greatest of all, Sir Henry Creswicke Rawlinson (1810–95). We should also mention here at least one important government-subsidized expedition of the early nineteenth century, the British 'Tigris – Euphrates Expedition' (1835–6) of F. R. Chesney, who studied the course of the two rivers and collected a wealth of information on the country around them.

With the exception of the two small pits dug by de Beauchamp and Mignan at Babylon, all these men confined their activities to the examination and measurement of the ruins as they saw them and were far from imagining what those 'desolate mounds' concealed. But in 1843 Paul Emile Botta, Italian-born French Consul in Mosul, started at Khorsabad the first archaeological excavations in Iraq, discovered the Assyrians and opened a new era. Almost at once (1845) an Englishman, Sir Henry Layard, followed his example at Nimrud and Nineveh, and soon a number of tells were excavated. In 1877 Ernest de Sarzec, French Consul in Basrah, having heard of some statues found by chance at Telloh, near Nasriyah, decided to dig there and discovered the Sumerians. Thus within thirty years a hitherto unknown civilization was revealed to a world astonished to learn that Mesopotamia could yield nearly as many treasures as Greece or Egypt. Botta, Layard, Sarzec, Loftus, Smith, the pioneers of that heroic period were all amateurs in every sense of the term. They had no experience and little method. Their main object was to discover and send to the museums of their respective countries statues, bas reliefs, inscriptions and *objets d'art* in general. They had no time for mud bricks and broken pots, destroyed much and preserved little, but they opened the road and, despite obstacles of all sorts, worked with an energy and enthusiasm which have never been surpassed.

Meanwhile, in the libraries of Europe no less enthusiastic but more patient pioneers were engaged in the fantastic task of deciphering the written documents which by then were pouring by the thousand into the museums. The story of this intellectual adventure, which lasted no less than a hundred years and taxed to the extreme the ingenuity of many scholars from several nations, cannot be told here even briefly.[16] We feel, however, that homage should be paid to such men as Grotefend, a teacher of Greek at Göttingen University, who made the first serious and partly successful attempt at reading the Old Persian inscriptions in cuneiform script copied by Niebuhr at Persepolis; Rawlinson, who between 1835 and 1844 not only copied at the peril of his life the long trilingual inscription which Darius had engraved high up on the rock of Behistun in Western Iran but also began to translate it – the inscription in Old Persian, Babylonian and Elamite has been called the 'Rosetta stone of Assyriology', with the difference that none of the three languages could initially be read – and to the Irishman Edward Hincks and his French colleague Jules Oppert, who, with Rawlinson, deserve to be called the 'holy triad' of cuneiform studies, since they overcame the greatest epigraphic and linguistic difficulties and, as one of their modern successors puts it, 'laid open the dusty pages of the clay "books" buried all over the ancient Near East'.[17] The decipherment of the Assyro-Babylonian language (now called Akkadian) was considered assured in 1848, and by 1900 the other language of ancient Mesopotamia, Sumerian, was broadly comprehended. The former now has virtually no secret; the latter still has its dark corners, but is read with increasing certainty. At a conservative estimate, half a million tablets are – or, since many of them have not yet been published, will eventually be – at the historian's disposal,[18] and countless more will be discovered as archaeological research progresses. It can be said without exaggeration that no other country in the world has yielded such a wealth of ancient texts in the very form in which they were written thousands of years ago.

The entry on to the stage by the Germans at the turn of the century heralded a new approach to excavation work. Robert Koldewey at Babylon (1899–1917) and Walter Andrae at Assur (1903–14) introduced strict, even meticulous techniques in a domain where luck and intuition had long reigned supreme. The German method was soon generally adopted, and the twenty years between the two world wars witnessed what should perhaps be considered as the most brilliant and fruitful period in the history of Mesopotamian archaeology. These were the days when Woolley was digging up the past at Ur and its celebrated Royal Cemetery (1922–34), when Heinrich and his team were working at Uruk, Parrot at Mari, the British at Ubaid, Nineveh, Arpachiyah and Chagar Bazar, the Americans at Tepe Gawra, Nuzi and in the Diyala valley, and both the British and the Americans at Kish and Jemdat Nasr. One by one, large and small tells were opened up and yielded their secrets. The main features of Mesopotamian history were defined piece by piece, and beyond history older, fascinating cultures appeared which threw new light on the origins of civilization in that part of the world.

During this time Iraq had emerged as a nation. Baghdad now had its own museum. Young Iraqi archaeologists had been trained, and excavations, far from coming to a complete standstill during the Second World War, continued with the most interesting results at 'Uqair (1940–1), Hassuna (1943–4) and 'Aqar Quf (1943–5). The war over, work was resumed by the Germans (Lenzen) at the huge site of Uruk, by the Americans (Haines and McCown) at Sumer's religious capital, Nippur, and by the French (Parrot) at Mari, the metropolis of the Middle Euphrates. Mallowan, on behalf of the British Museum, reopened Nimrud, the Assyrian military capital city which had not been touched for over seventy years. Seton Lloyd, Taha Baqir, Fuad Safar dug up for the Iraq Museum three virgin sites: Eridu, one of the most ancient sacred cities of Iraq,

Harmal, a modest mound unexpectedly rich in texts, and Hatra, the strange capital of a pre-Islamic Arab kingdom. After 1958, the young Republic of Iraq opened its doors even wider to foreign archaeologists. Whilst the Germans and Americans continued working on the inexhaustible sites of Uruk and Nippur, whilst the Iraqis themselves discovered at Tell es-Sawwan a new prehistoric culture and sounded numerous smaller mounds, fresh excavations were undertaken by the British at Tell al-Rimah, Umm Dabaghiyah, Choga Mami and Abu Salabikh, by the French at Larsa and the Belgians at Tell ed-Der, by the Germans at Isin, by the Italians at Seleucia, by the Russians at Yarim Tepe and the Poles at Nimrud, and even by the Japanese at Telul ath-Thalathat, to mention only the main sites. At the time of writing, several of these excavations are still in progress and others are being planned. All the large cities of ancient Mesopotamia and many less renowned towns have been, or are being, unearthed and a considerable amount of restoration work has been done, or is going on, notably at Nineveh, Nimrud, Babylon, Ur and Hatra.

In the late 1970s a new and rewarding type of archaeological activity developed: the so-called 'salvage excavations' made necessary by the building, for agricultural purposes, of several dams on the Euphrates, the Tigris and some of their tributaries in both Syria and Iraq. The lakes created by these dams were bound to submerge a great number of tells, and it was imperative to explore as many of them as possible before this happened. These huge tasks were performed by Syrian and Iraqi archaeologists working in cooperation with colleagues from Europe, America, Australia and Japan. The first of these large-scale rescue operations was prompted by the construction of the Assad dam on the great bend of the Syrian Euphrates; then came, in Iraq, the 'Hamrin basin project' in the valley of a tributary of the Diyala river, the Haditha (or Qadissiyah) salvage excavations on the middle Euphrates, and the Eski Mosul project in the Tigris valley upstream of Mosul. Altogether, almost two hundred sites, ranging from prehistoric to late Islamic times, were explored, some of them partially and briefly, others extensively and for several months or years. The results of this international effort were very interesting: they brought to light not only a few large cities, like Emar (Meskene), but also some relatively minor towns, such as Haradum on the Iraqi Euphrates, which probably would have never been excavated; they provided a great deal of information on settlement patterns at different periods and filled many gaps in our knowledge of proto-historic cultures hitherto poorly documented.[19]

The 'Gulf War' has put an end to all archaeological research in Iraq, but there is no doubt that sooner or later such peaceful activities will be resumed there. Some six thousand tells in Iraq alone are awaiting the diggers – enough to keep busy several generations of archaeologists and epigraphists. And as though in our search for the past we were proceeding backwards, after the Assyrians, after the Babylonians, after the Sumerians, after the nameless peoples of the fourth and fifth millennia B.C, the Stone Age of Iraq has been brought under the searchlight. Despite inevitable gaps in our knowledge, it has at last become possible to write a complete history of ancient Mesopotamia, starting from those very remote days when men chose the hills and caves of Kurdistan for their dwellings and left behind them the humble tools of chipped flint which betray their presence.

CHAPTER 3

FROM CAVE TO FARM

Until 1949 textbooks and scientific journals alike were silent on the prehistory of Iraq. Archaeological work had concentrated on the Mesopotamian plain, where prehistoric remains, if they ever existed, would by now be buried under a very thick layer of alluvium. The lowest levels of several tells had supplied enough material for historians to build up a sequence of five proto-historic cultures which announced and explained the dawn of the Sumero-Akkadian civilization in about 3000 B.C., but all these cultures belonged to the late Neolithic and to the Chalcolithic ages and covered, at the most, a couple of thousand years. Prehistory proper, the Stone Age of Iraq, was practically unknown. True, a few worked flints had been found on the surface in various parts of the Syro-Mesopotamian desert,[1] and as early as 1928 Professor D. A. E. Garrod, the lady archaeologist well known for her studies on prehistoric Palestine, had visited Kurdistan and found palaeolithic artefacts in two caves near Suleimaniyah; but these discoveries attracted little attention outside a small circle of specialists. Twenty years were to elapse before Professor R. J. Braidwood publicized the Neolithic site of Jarmo and aroused enough interest to promote further research in this long-neglected field.[2] Since then, the American excavations at Barda-Balka, Palegawra and Karim-Shehir (1951), the survey of the Zab basin by the Oriental Institute of the University of Chicago (1954–5) and the startling discoveries made by Dr R. Solecki in Shanidar cave[3] since 1951 have contributed considerably to our knowledge of Iraq's most ancient past and filled a very regrettable gap in Near Eastern prehistory.

Palaeolithic

Among the three classical subdivisions of the Stone Age –
Palaeolithic, Mesolithic and Neolithic – the first named is by
far the longest. It entirely fills the geological period called
Pleistocene because it is 'the most recent' (*pleistos kainos*) chapter
in the very long history of the earth. The Pleistocene began
approximately two million years ago and ended in about 10000
B.C., to be replaced by the Holocene ('latest') period in which
we are still living. Pleistocene and Holocene together constitute
the Quaternary era.

· The beginning of the Pleistocene was marked by the ultimate
and weaker convulsions of the previous period, the Pliocene,
which in the Near East led to the formation of the Taurus and
Zagros ranges, which are part of the Alpine-Himalayan system,
to the deep fault of the Rift Valley linking the Dead Sea and
the Red Sea to the great East African lakes, and to the creation
of the Mesopotamian plain and the Arabo-Persian Gulf due to
sliding of the rigid Arabian platform underneath the not less
rigid Iranian plateau. These tectonic movements were accompanied by a considerable plutonic activity, as witnessed by the
numerous volcanoes, most of them nowadays extinct, that are
scattered all over Turkey, the Caucasus range and Iran, as well
as by the extensive lava fields to be found, for example, in
Syria, south of Damascus.

About one million years ago, the surface of the earth, which by
then had almost reached its present configuration, entered a
period of relative rest, the main activity being erosion of the
relief. This was largely facilitated by the expansion and retraction
of four successive ice-caps lying over the northern parts of Europe
and America: the four glaciations called, at least in Europe:
Günz, Mindel, Riss and Würm, and their consequences. It must
be noted that in tropical, subtropical and equatorial regions long
periods of heavy rains (pluvials) alternating with periods of
relative drought (interpluvials) corresponded approximately to
the glacials and interglacials of Europe and North America.

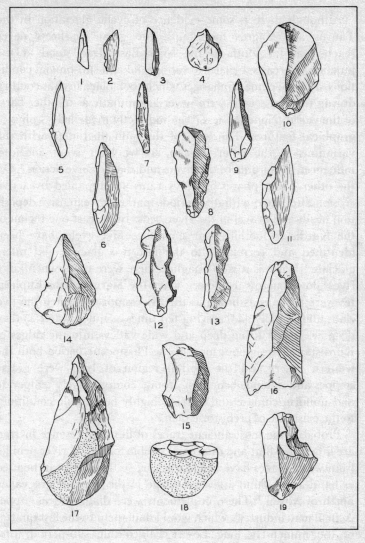

Stone industries in Iraqi Kurdistan: 1–4, microlithic (Shanidar B); 5–13,
Aurignatian (Baradostian, Shanidar C); 14–16, Mousterian (Shanidar D);
17–19, Levalloisian-Acheulaean (Barda Balka).
After R. Solecki and H. Wright Jnr, Sumer, VII, 1951 and VIII, 1952.

Although there is some evidence of cyclic glaciation in the Taurus and Zagros mountains, the great ice-sheets never reached as far south as the Near East. Iraq stood at the junction of areas subjected to sub-glacial and sub-pluvial conditions, and the climatic changes which took place in that country during the Pleistocene were never as dramatic as in other parts of the world. None the less, they indirectly modelled its physiographical features. The level of the Gulf fluctuated with the variations in the polar ice-cap, as we have seen, and this influenced the profile of the rivers and their erosive action.[4] On the other hand, phases of heavy rains accompanied by active erosion alternated with dry periods marked by extensive deposition of silt and gravel in the river beds. In at least one region of the Kurdistan foothills four such successive cycles have been identified and correlated to the last two glacials and interglacials.[5] Hard as it is to imagine, there were times when large rivers flowed across the desert, when the Tigris and the Euphrates were perhaps as broad as the Mississippi and when the two Zabs and the Diyala, carrying ten times as much water as they do now, were cutting deep and wide valleys into the ridges of Kurdistan. Throughout most of the Pleistocene period both the western desert and the foothill region of Iraq were grassy steppes and uplands benefiting from a comparatively temperate and uniform climate and offering highly favourable conditions to the existence of prehistoric men.[6]

Probably the most ancient traces of human presence in Iraq are limestone, flint and quartzite 'pebble tools' (i.e. river pebbles from which flakes have been struck off so that they can be used as hand-axes) found a few years ago in the upper Tigris valley north of Mosul.[7] These implements were diagnosed as 'upper Acheulaean industry', which would date them to the last quarter of the immensely long Lower Palaeolithic sub-period, *circa* 500,000–110,000 B.P. Then comes, on the scale of time, the interesting site of Barda-Balka near Chemchemal, between Kirkuk and Suleimaniyah, discovered in 1949 by Iraqi archaeologists. There, around a megalith of Neolithic age, were palaeolithic flint tools lying on the ground. A sounding made in 1951 by two American archaeologists traced their origin to a once open 'workshop' or 'camp site' now buried under three to five feet of silt and gravel.[8] The flint implements consisted of heart-shaped or almond-shaped hand-axes and of side-scrapers made out of flakes. There were also limestone 'pebble-tools'. This industry has strong affinities with the Acheulaean, Tayacian (a derivative of Clactonian) and Mousterian cultures and has been attributed to the end of the Riss-Würm interglacial, about 80,000 years ago.

A further step into the Middle Palaeolithic is represented by the mixed Levalloiso-Mousterian industry discovered in 1928 by Miss Dorothy Garrod in the lowest level of the 'Dark Cave' of Hazar Merd, about nineteen kilometres south of Suleimani-yah.[9] But nowhere is the true Mousterian better illustrated than at Shanidar cave, excavated between 1951 and 1960 by Dr R. Solecki of the University of Michigan.[10]

Shanidar cave is a very large rock shelter (the size of four tennis courts) in the southern flank of the Baradost mountains overlooking the valley of the Upper Zab, not far from the small town of Rowanduz. It is still used in winter by Kurdish shepherds. Digging through its floor, Dr Solecki was able to reach a depth of fourteen metres and to identify four occupation levels. In level D, the lowest and thickest (8.50 metres), successive layers of hearths and ash deposits mixed with bones and flint implements proved that the cave had been inhabited at various periods in Middle Palaeolithic times. The stone artefacts consisted of points, scrapers and borers typical of the Mousterian culture in its last phase. Animal bones were those of oxen, sheep and goats, suggesting a moderately cold climate, and there were numerous tortoise shells. Of special interest are the nine human skeletons in level D: those of two small children and of seven adults. The bones generally were in poor condition, but the skull of skeleton I – a man about thirty-five years old, 1·50 metres tall – could be restored with a fair degree of accuracy.[11] It exhibited all the features of the Neanderthal man: the thick bones, the massive chinless jaw, the sloping forehead, the prominent brow-ridges; and there is every reason to believe that the other individuals belonged to the same race. Dr D. T. Stewart, who examined these remains, could also diagnose that the arm of one of the Shanidar men, already crippled from birth, had later been amputated with a crude flint knife. Some of these people had been killed by huge blocks falling from the roof of the cave, though by no means at the same time. The body of a cave-dweller rested on a bed of branches and flowers and these flowers, when examined, enabled the date of death to be estimated as 'between late May and early July'. The ages of three skeletons were determined by radiocarbon: two were dated 46,000 and 50,000 B.P. respectively and the third one, stratigraphically lower, was as old as 60,000 years.[12]

Level C of Shanidar cave takes us well into the Upper Palaeolithic period. By means of carbon 14 tests carried out on the charcoal of its hearths, it has been possible to fix its lower and upper limits at 'more than 34,000 years' and 'about 25,500 B.C.' respectively. The stone material was of the blade-tool type characteristic of the Aurignacian cultures. As it contained some well-made gravers of unusual form, Dr Solecki has proposed for this industry the name of 'Baradost' or 'Baradostian' from the mountains in which the cave opens. The upper part of level C and the greater part of level B immediately above yielded samples of the same industry, but with a tendency for the artefacts to be undersized (microliths). This late Aurignacian or 'extended Gravettian' culture is represented in several palaeolithic sites of Northern Iraq. Small round scrapers and 'pen knife' blades, and bladelets with deeply notched edges, in particular, were found in abundance in the cave of Zarzi, near Suleimaniyah, by Miss Garrod[9] and in the cave of Palegawra, 32 kilometres to the east of Chemchemal, by B. Howe.[13] They also occur in various caves explored by Professor Braidwood and his co-workers in 1954–5, especially Kaiwanian and Barak, west and south of Rowanduz. It appears that some at least of these small objects could be hafted and used as weapons to kill wild horses, deer, goats, gazelles, sheep and swine, which then lived in a still cool but already drier country.

The Palaeolithic men of Iraq were not isolated. Through the Syrian desert – where Stone Age artefacts have been found in various places – they were in contact with the Palaeolithic men of Syria–Palestine, and it is not by chance that the flint industries of the two countries have some features in common. They also had commercial intercourse with the Anatolian plateau and the Iranian highlands. The material of Shanidar D and Hazar Merd, for instance, is almost identical with that of Bisitun cave in Western Iran and in many details similar to that of Korain cave in Turkey. In Upper Palaeolithic times the men of Shanidar made some of their tools of obsidian (volcanic glass), the nearest source of which was in the Lake Van district of Armenia. Indeed, from camp to camp stone-working techniques were taken as far away as Europe, if we are to believe with some authorities that the Aurignacian culture originated in the Near East. Yet Iraqi Kurdistan, because of its semi-secluded position in a corner of the 'Fertile Crescent', retained its own characteristics. According to Solecki, the 'Baradost' industry is unique in the Near East, and the Neanderthal men of Shanidar, though somewhat more recent than those of Mount Carmel, do not seem to have mixed with or evolved towards *Homo sapiens* like the latter, and remained 'conservative' in their physical features. Finally, the Solutrean and Magdalenian cultures which, in Western Europe, succeeded the Aurignacian and flourished in late Palaeolithic times never reached Iraq – nor, for that matter, any other part of Western Asia. In those countries the passage from Aurignacian to microlithic (Mesolithic) was direct, and the Mesolithic period was but a short step from the Neolithic revolution.

Mesolithic

Mesolithic (or Epipalaeolithic) is the name given to a transitional period between the Palaeolithic and the Neolithic or, in terms of economy, between hunting and food-gathering and food-producing. It is characterized by lithic industries consisting of very small and extremely varied flint or obsidian tools (microliths) and by a tendency to full or partial sedentism with all its social and economic consequences, notably the need for storing food and controlling its sources. In Iraq, the Mesolithic period lasted from about 9000 B.C. (the upper limit of Shanidar B1 level as determined by radiocarbon analysis) and 7000 B.C. (the approximate date of pre-pottery neolithic Jarmo).[14]

The first stage of Mesolithic in Iraqi Kurdistan is represented by the B1 level of Shanidar cave and by the open-air site of Zawi Chemi Shanidar, on the left bank of the Upper Zab.[15] The only trace of settlement at this site is a low and curving wall made of field stones and river pebbles, which might have surrounded a hut or a tent. In the cave as in the camp the stone tools were microlithic flint flakes or 'impoverished Zarzian' type and bigger implements, such as grinders, querns, mortars and pestles, which did not exist in Lower Palaeolithic times and were most probably used to pound wild grains and pigments. Other novelties were awls made of bone and sometimes decorated with geometric designs, and such body ornaments as bone beads and pendants, animal teeth and coloured stones. The people who presumably lived there part of the year and spent the winter in the nearby Shanidar cave ate wild goat, wild sheep, wild pig and red deer, as well as fish, fresh-water mussels and turtles. Most of the twenty-six human skeletons found in Shanidar cave level B1 were gathered in a 'cemetery', lying on stone platforms, and each of the eight adults buried at Zawi Chemi was accompanied by a child, which suggests some awful ritual. All the skulls studied were of the Protomediterranean type, and many showed signs of trepanation and disease, notably tooth decay. Radiocarbon tests yielded a date of 8920 ± 400 years B.C. for the open-air site.

A gap of perhaps a thousand years separates Zawi Chemi Shanidar from two other sites which are roughly of the same date: Karim-Shehir and Mlefaat.

Karim-Shehir, ten kilometres east of Chemchemal,[16] covers two acres and consists of one occupation level only, just below the surface. The flint artefacts, microlithic in character, are associated with objects which can be regarded as agricultural tools: flint sickle blades, chipped-and-ground stone hoes, and milling stones. In addition, a very irregular pebble pavement spread over the whole area suggests hut floors, though no plans of habitations are recognizable. If Karim-Shehir was, as it is thought, a camp site of semi-nomads, it represents a very early stage in the development towards sedentary life.

A more permanent type of agricultural community probably occupied the third site, Mlefaat.[17] In that small mound near the Kirkuk-Erbil road were found pit-houses, some of them surrounded by walls of piled-up stones and paved with pebbles. The tools consisted mostly of stone celts and mortars.

Outside Iraq, but still in Mesopotamia, or very close to it, one can find mesolithic sites of great interest as they provide good sequences and examples of regional variations. These are Tell Mureybet in Syria and Tepe Ali Kosh in south-west Iran.

At Tell Mureybet,[18] located on the great bend of the Euphrates, American, then French archaeologists have revealed evidence of continuous occupation for more than 1,300 years (from before 8600 to 7300 B.C.) and divided it into three phases. The phase I settlement was a camp of hunters and fishers using the 'Natufian' type of stone tools that was then common in the whole of Syria and Palestine. In phase II, this camp had become a village of round houses built of pressed mud (*tauf* in Arabic), and in phase III these round houses had partly been replaced by wider, multi-roomed rectangular houses built of limestone blocks. There, the goats and sheep of Kurdistan did not figure on the menu, and all meat (and hides) came from the wild and fast animals of the neighbouring steppe (wild asses, gazelles, aurochs, fallow deer, wild boars, hares) shot down by arrows. The wild plants consumed were einkorn and two-row barley, lentils, vetches and pistachios. It must be noted that wild wheat and barley do not grow at all in that region, and it has been hypothesized that they were imported from the nearest source: the region of Gaziantep, in Turkey, ninety-three miles away, and replanted locally. Another remarkable feature of Mureybet is that some buildings contained horns, skulls and bones of wild oxen buried under a clay podium or hung on the walls, thus resembling the remarkable but more recent Neolithic shrines of Çatal-Hüyük in central Anatolia.

Tepe Ali Kosh,[19] one of several mounds excavated by American archaeologists in the Deh Luran valley (Luristan), was stratified into three different cultures. The lowest, neolithic level of occupation (c. 8000–7000 B.C.) yielded very small houses of mud-bricks with thin walls. The people who lived there, possibly in the winter only, hunted the same animals of the steppe as the inhabitants of Mureybet, but they also herded goats and sheep, as did their contemporaries in Kurdistan. They collected the seeds of a very wide variety of legumes and wild grasses, but it seems that they imported emmer wheat and barley *already domesticated* from the region of Kermanshah. The presence on the site of obsidian tools in fair amounts and of cowrie shells as ornaments indicate relations with faraway Armenia and with the much nearer Gulf.

Neolithic

From these examples and from the results of excavations on other Near-Eastern sites, it appears clearly that the Mesolithic period was a time of settlement and of slow but tremendous advances in several fields. During these crucial millennia, not only were the chipped stone techniques perfected to produce very fine tools for all kinds of household purposes, but the house-building technology was acquired and, above all, innumerable experiments were performed to ensure a permanent supply of vegetable and animal foods, available in all seasons in the vicinity of the settlement. These experiments eventually resulted, in various places and at different times, in the development of a primitive but fairly efficient 'food technology' which made it possible to cultivate and store selected strains of wheat and barley and to herd and breed goats and sheep first, and later cattle and pigs.[20] Mesolithic men and women of course continued to hunt and fish and to collect wild edible plants and fruit, but this gradually became a relatively small part of their activities. When a given community began to live principally on agriculture and animal husbandry, it had played its role in the so-called 'Neolithic revolution'.

It has often been said that this revolution took place on the hilly flank of the 'Fertile Crescent' (as defined by the line of 25 centimetres of rain) because this was – and still is – the only part of the world where emmer wheat (*Triticum dicoccum*), einkorn (*T. boetium*) and two-row hulled barley (*Hordeum distichum*) grow naturally. However, in 1966, two American botanists, J. R. Harlan and D. Zohary, who worked in Eastern Turkey, noticed that these wild cereals still covered thousands of hectares. Harlan went out with a flint-toothed sickle and within one hour collected enough wheat to produce one kilo of pure grain with a protein content that was twice as high as that of domesticated wheat. He calculated that after three weeks of moderate work, a family could have harvested more grain than they could eat in a year. The botanists exclaimed: 'If wild cereal grasses can be harvested in illimited quantities, why should anyone bother to till the soil and plant the seed?'[21]

A number of theories have been put forward to answer this question. The most plausible one, based on Bingford's 'equilibrium model', was developed by Flannery.[22] According to this author, all groups of Palaeolithic hunters-gatherers lived in limited 'ecological niches' and tried to keep their number below maximum capacity of their environment. However, when some of these 'central' areas became relatively over-populated a number of their inhabitants had to move into 'marginal' areas with poorer natural resources, and this stimulated a search for new sources of food, notably cereals. Mureybet and Ali Kosh might have been settlements of this kind. This theory is concordant with the 'broad spectrum revolution' observed on some sites of the Late Upper Palaeolithic period, where the presence around hearths of the remains of small animals (notably snails) in huge amounts seems to indicate a need for the exploitation of all potential nutriments, probably because of over-population.

In Iraq the most important Neolithic site is Jarmo, not far from Chemchemal, excavated by Professor R. J. Braidwood of the University of Chicago in 1948, 1950–51 and again in 1955.[23] The 7-metre-high artificial mound rests on top of a very steep hill and is formed of sixteen layers of superimposed habitations. Eleven of these layers are characterized by the absence of pottery and belong to the same 'pre-ceramic Neolithic' cultural stratum. The inhabitants of Jarmo lived in square, multi-roomed houses built of pressed mud (*pisé*), with mud-ovens and baked-in clay basins sunk in the ground. They ate with bone spoons, sewed with bone needles, and their stone spindle-whorls show that they could weave or plait flax and perhaps wool. They used microlithic and normal-sized flint and obsidian blade tools, in particular sickles made of flint fixed with bitumen to a wooden backing, but most of the heavy objects lying about in the rooms, such as axes, celts, saddle-querns, hand-rubbers, mortars, pestles and vases, were of limestone, often beautifully ground. These objects, together with carbonized grains of wheat and barley, leave no doubt concerning the agricultural activities practised at Jarmo, while ninety-five per cent of the animal bones found were those of domesticated animals: sheep, cattle, pigs and dogs. Lentils, peas, vetches and acorns completed the menu. They were probably eaten as thick soups brought to ebullition by throwing red-hot stones in large round or oval clay-lined pits sunk into the ground. Other foods were roasted in clay ovens provided with a chimney. These people adorned themselves with simple clay or stone necklaces, grooved bracelets of marble and shell pendants, buried their dead under the floor of their houses, and modelled clay figures of animals and of a steatopygous, pregnant woman who presumably embodied for them the mysterious forces of fecundity. Pre-ceramic Jarmo was first dated by radiocarbon tests on snail shells at about 4750 B.C., but further tests on charcoal gave higher figures, and *c.* 6750 B.C. is a more likely date.

Several other Neolithic sites have been discovered in northern Iraq, but among these two are of special interest. The first site is represented by the lower levels of the otherwise mainly historic Tell Shimshara, situated in the upper valley of the Lower Zab, not far from the town of Rania, and excavated by Danish archaeologists from 1957 to 1959.[24] The only difference between Shimshara and Jarmo lies in its stone industry, and notably in the predominance of obsidian (85%) from Armenia or Anatolia, but it has also the merit of filling, at least partly, the chronological gap between Jarmo and Hassuna (*c.* 5800 B.C.), the first of a long series of proto-historic settlements. The second site is Maghzaliyeh, an important tell on the plain west of the Tigris, excavated by Soviet archaeologists between 1977 and 1980.[25] The most important feature of this Neolithic village is a curving wall with semi-circular projections suggesting towers. If this is the case, then we are confronted with the most ancient fortified settlement ever discovered in Mesopotamia.

Thus, around 7000 B.C. in northern Iraq and in other parts of the Near East man ceases to be a wandering hunter depending for his living upon his luck and skill and becomes a farmer attached to the small piece of land from which he obtains a regular food supply. Out of clay he builds himself a house. He uses new tools to perform new tasks. He secures in sheep and cattle a permanent and easily available source of milk, meat, wool and hide. At the same time his social tendencies develop, for the care and defence of the land call for close cooperation. Each family probably erects its own farm, cultivates its own field, grazes its own flock and makes its own tools; but several families are grouped together and form a hamlet, the embryo of a social organization. Later other revolutions will occur: metal will replace stone, villages will grow into cities, cities will be united into kingdoms and kingdoms into empires. Yet the essentials of life, the labour of man bent over mother earth and enslaved to the cycle of seasons, has not changed since those remote days.

The absence of pottery in eleven out of sixteen occupation levels makes Jarmo one of the earliest agricultural communities in Western Asia, together with Ali Kosh and Tepe Guran in Iran, Hacilar in Anatolia and Jericho in Palestine, to mention only the main 'aceramic' sites. With the exception of Jericho which, with its well-built houses and strong city-wall of undressed stones, must have looked like a small medieval town, all these were modest villages covering only a few acres and apparently unfortified. The people who lived in those villages used stone bowls, baskets made waterproof with bitumen and probably skins and gourds as containers, but they already handled clay with some skill to build the walls of their houses, to line pits or basins dug into the ground and to model figurines of animals and women.[26] From this to baked clay, and therefore pottery, there were but a few steps which seem to have been made much earlier than formerly believed, since coarse, lightly fired clay vessels have been found at Mureybet, in northern Syria, in a level dated *c.* 8000 B.C. by a radiocarbon sample, and at Ganj Dareh, an eighth millennium site in western Iran. Similar vessels also occur at Jarmo, *c.* 6300 B.C., but they already coexist with a decorated pottery characterized by lines of oblique tadpole-shaped blobs painted in red on a pinkish-buff surface, also found at the contemporary site of Tepe Guran.

Ceramic by itself is perhaps not as momentous an invention as agriculture, but for the archaeologist it heralds a new era where bowls, cups, plates and vases will henceforth play for him the same role as fossils for the geologist. From about 6000 B.C. to the beginning of history more than three millennia will elapse, and these long years will of course be filled with cultural developments, commercial ventures, ethnic movements and no doubt wars and conquests, but because written documents are lacking, the actors will always remain nameless and silent. All we have to try and reconstruct the events of that distant past are material remains among which pottery is of special interest, as it is found in abundance on all sites and lends itself to comparative studies. Interpreted with caution – for changes in pottery styles may be due to many reasons and do not necessarily betray the replacement of one population by another[27] – the distinctive wares found at different levels in archaeological excavations represent both the hall-marks of successive cultures in late prehistoric Mesopotamia and fairly reliable indicators of the relationship between these cultures and those of surrounding countries.

CHAPTER 4

FROM VILLAGE TO CITY

The story of the passage from Neolithic to History, from the humble villages of the Zagros foothills to the relatively large and highly civilized Sumerian cities of the lower Tigris–Euphrates valley cannot be told in full detail because our information, though rapidly progressing, remains imprecise and patchy. Yet each new prehistoric *tell* excavated, each buried city dug down to the virgin soil, confirms what forty years of archaeological research in Iraq already suggested: the Sumerian civilization was never imported ready-made into Mesopotamia from some unknown country at some ill-defined date. Like all civilizations – including ours – it was a mixed product shaped by the mould into which its components were poured over many years. Each of these components can now be traced back to one stage or another of Iraqi prehistory, and while some were undoubtedly brought in by foreign invasion or influence, others had roots so deep in the past that we may call them indigenous. In addition, excavations conducted at an ever increasing pace in Iran, Syria, Palestine and Turkey at the same time as in Iraq have thrown considerable light on the interplay of Neolithic and Chalcolithic cultures in the Near East and have supplied enough comparative material and radiocarbon dates to draw up a rough, tentative chronological scale along the six divisions of Mesopotamian proto-history:

The Hassuna period	*c.* 5800–5500 B.C.
The Samarra period	*c.* 5600–5000 B.C.
The Halaf period	*c.* 5500–4500 B.C.
The Ubaid period	*c.* 5000–3750 B.C.
(Ubaid 1 and 2 included)	
The Uruk period	*c.* 3750–3150 B.C.
The Jemdat Nasr period	*c.* 3150–2900 B.C.

Each of these periods is characterized by a distinct cultural assemblage and has been named after the site, not necessarily the largest nor even the most representative, where this assemblage was first identified.

As will be seen, the areas covered by these cultures vary from one period to the other; moreover, cultures long thought to be successive are in fact contemporaneous or at least overlapping, and within each period there is room for a variety of regional and interesting subcultures. The above divisions therefore, are somewhat artificial, but they provide a convenient framework into which can be fitted the changes that occurred during those three millennia when Mesopotamia was pregnant, so to speak, with Sumer.[1]

The Hassuna Period

The site type for this period is Tell Hassuna, a low mound thirty-five kilometres south of Mosul, excavated in 1943-4 by the Iraqi Directorate of Antiquities under the direction of Seton Lloyd and Fuad Safar.[2] There, resting on the virgin soil, were coarse pottery and stone implements suggestive of a Neolithic farming community living in huts or tents, for no trace of building was found. Overlying this primitive settlement, however, were six layers of houses, progressively larger and better built. In size, plan and building material these houses were very similar to those of present-day northern Iraqi villages. Six or seven rooms were arranged in two blocks around a courtyard, one block serving as living quarters, the other as kitchen and stores. The walls were made of pressed mud, the floors paved with a mixture of clay and straw. Grain was kept in huge bins of unbaked clay sunk into the ground up to their mouths, and bread was baked in domed ovens resembling the modern *tanur*. Mortars, flint sickle-blades, stone hoes, clay spindle-whorls and crude clay figurines of naked and apparently seated women were present. Large jars found inside the houses contained the bones of deceased children accompanied by tiny cups and pots for after-life refreshment while, strangely enough, much liberty seems to have been taken with the disposal of adult skeletons piled up in the corner of a room, thrown into clay bins 'without ceremony' or buried in cist graves without the usual funerary gifts. The few skulls that have been studied belong, like those from Byblos and Jericho, to a 'large-toothed variety of the long-headed Mediterranean race', which suggests a unity of population throughout the Fertile Crescent in late Neolithic times.[3]

The pottery discovered at Hassuna has been divided into two categories called 'archaic' and 'standard'. The *archaic ware* ranges from level Ia, at the bottom of the tell, to level III and is represented by: (1) tall, round or pear-shaped jars of undecorated coarse clay; (2) bowls of finer fabric varying in colour from buff to black according to the method of firing and 'burnished' with a stone or bone, and (3) bowls and globular jars with a short, straight neck, sparingly decorated with simple designs (lines, triangles, cross-hatchings) in fragile red paint and also burnished. The Hassuna *standard ware*, predominant in levels IV to VI, is made up of the same painted bowls and jars and the designs are very similar, but the paint is matt brown and thicker, the decoration more extensive and executed with greater skill. A number of vessels are almost entirely covered by shallow incisions, and some are both painted and incised.

While the archaic pottery has several traits in common with that found in the deepest layers of Turkish (Sakçe Gözü, Mersin), Syrian (Kerkemish, 'Amuq plain) and Palestinian (Megiddo, Jericho) sites, the standard pottery seems to have developed locally[4] and is distributed over a relatively small area of northern Iraq. Sherds of Hassuna ware can be picked up on the surface of many unexcavated mounds east and west of the Tigris down to Jabal Hamrin, and complete specimens have been found in the lowest levels of Nineveh, opposite Mosul, at Matarrah,[5] south of Kirkuk and at Shimshara[6] in the Lower Zab valley. They were also present throughout the thirteen levels of mound 1 at Yarim Tepe,[7] near Tell 'Afar, associated with the remains of square or round houses, with tools and weapons of flint and obsidian, with pieces of copper ore and a few copper and lead ornaments, with small seated clay figurines and with minute stone or clay discs with a loop at the back, engraved with straight lines or criss-cross patterns. These objects, probably worn on a string around the neck, may have been impressed as a mark of ownership on lumps of clay fastened to baskets or to jar stoppers, in which case they would represent the earliest examples of the stamp-seal, and the stamp-seal is the forerunner of the cylinder-seal, a significant element of the Mesopotamian civilization. Some authors, however, regard them, at least in this period, as mere amulets or ornaments.

Forty-eight kilometres due south of Yarim Tepe, at the limit of the rain-fed plain and the desert of Jazirah, lies Umm Dabaghiya, excavated by Diana Kirkbride between 1971 and 1973.[8] Umm Dabaghiya was a small settlement, a simple trading post where nomads from the desert brought the onagers and gazelles they had hunted to be skinned, the raw hides being later sent elsewhere to be tanned. Related by its coarse and painted pottery to the archaic levels of Hassuna but most probably older, the site has many distinctive and strangely sophisticated features. For instance, the floors of the houses are often made of large clay slabs which announce the moulded bricks of later periods; floors and walls are carefully plastered with gypsum and frequently painted red, and in one building were found fragments of frescoes representing an onager hunt, a spider with its eggs and perhaps flying vultures. Several houses contained alabaster bowls beautifully carved and polished. Predominant among the clay vessels are bowls and jars with 'applied decoration', i.e. small figurines of animals and human beings stuck on the vessels before firing. Other sites representative of this Hassunan subculture are Tell Sotto and Kül Tepe,[9] near Yarim Tepe, and mound 2 at Tulul ath-Thalathat,[10] in the same Tell 'Afar area. Not unexpectedly for places lying on the trade routes to the west and north-west, some

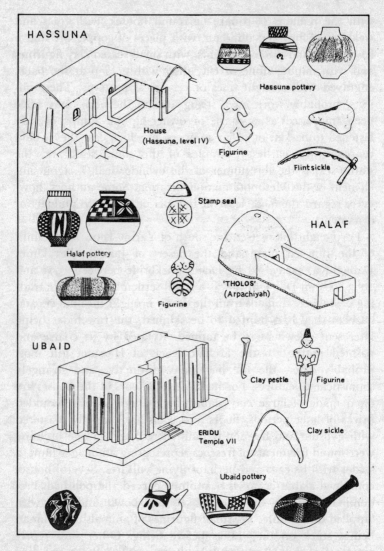

Buildings, potteries, figurines, seals and tools characteristic
of the Hassuna, Halaf and Ubaid periods.

elements of the 'Umm Dab culture', such as plastered floors and arrow-heads, point to Syria (Buqras on the Euphrates and even Ras Shamra and Byblos), whilst the red and frescoed walls are reminiscent of contemporary Çatal Hüyük in remote Anatolia.

The Samarra Period

In the upper levels of Hassuna, Matarrah, Shimshara and Yarim Tepe the Hassuna ware is mixed with, and gradually replaced by, a much more attractive pottery known as *Samarra ware* because it was first discovered, in 1912–14, in a prehistoric cemetery underneath the houses of the medieval city of that name, famous for its spiralled minaret.[11] On the pale, slightly rough surface of large plates, around the rim of carinate bowls, on the neck and shoulder of round-bellied pots, painted in red, dark-brown or purple, are geometric designs arranged in neat, horizontal bands or representations of human beings, birds, fish, antelopes, scorpions and other animals. The motifs are conventionalized, but their distribution is perfectly well balanced and they are treated in such a way as to give an extraordinary impression of movement. The people who modelled and painted such vessels were undoubtedly great artists, and it was long thought that they had come from Iran, but we now know that the Samarra ware was indigenous to Mesopotamia and belonged to a hitherto unsuspected culture which flourished in the middle Tigris valley during the second half of the sixth millennium B.C.

This culture was revealed in the 1960s by the Iraqi excavations at Tell es-Sawwan, a low but large mound on the left bank of the Tigris, only eleven kilometres to the south of Samarra.[12] The inhabitants of Tell es-Sawwan were peasants like their Hassunan ancestors and used similar stone and flint tools, but in an area where rain is scarce they were the first to practise a primitive form of irrigation agriculture, using the Tigris floods to water their fields and grow wheat, barley and

linseed.[13] The yield must have been substantial if the large and
empty buildings found at various levels were really 'granaries'
as has been suggested. The central part of the village was
protected from invaders by a 3-metre-deep ditch doubled by a
thick, buttressed mud wall. The houses were large, very regular
in plan, with multiple rooms and courtyards, and it must be
noted that they were no longer built of pressed mud, but of
large, cigar-shaped mud bricks plastered over with clay or
gypsum. A thin coat of plaster covered the floors and walls.
Apart from numerous pots and plates of coarse or fine Samarra
ware, these houses contained exquisite, translucent marble vessels. The bodies of adults, in a contracted position and wrapped
in matting coated with bitumen, and of children, placed in
large jars or deep bowls, were buried under the floors, and it is
from these graves that have come the most exciting finds in the
form of alabaster or terracotta statuettes of women (or occasionally men) squatting or standing. Some of the clay statuettes
have 'coffee-bean' eyes and pointed heads that are very similar
to those of the Ubaid period figurines, whilst other clay or stone
statuettes have large, wide-open eyes inlaid with shell and
bitumen and surmounted by black eyebrows, that are 'astonishingly reminiscent of much later Sumerian technique'.[14] Could
the Samarran folk be the ancestors of the 'Ubaidians' and even
perhaps of the Sumerians?

So far, no other settlement comparable to Tell es-Sawwan
has been excavated,[15] but apart from copies or imports in
Baghuz, on the middle Euphrates, and Chagar Bazar, in central
Jazirah, the Samarra pottery has been found in a limited but
fairly wide area along the Tigris valley, from Nineveh to Choga
Mami near Mandali, on the Iraqi–Iranian border.[16] In the
latter site, where canal-irrigation was practised, not only do we
find statuettes resembling the 'coffee-bean'-eyed statuettes of
Sawwan, but the Samarra ware seems to have developed locally
into new ceramic types (called 'Choga Mami Transitional')
similar to the Eridu and Hajji Muhammad wares of southern
Iraq, themselves considered as early forms of the Ubaid pot-

tery.[17] This unexpected discovery might provide the beginning of an answer to our question.

The Halaf Period

The third period of proto-historic Mesopotamia takes its name from Tell Halaf, a large mound overlooking the Khabur river near the village of Ras el-'Ain, on the Turkish–Syrian border. There, just before the First World War, a German archaeologist, Max Freiherr von Oppenheim, came upon a thick layer of beautifully painted pottery immediately beneath the palace of an Aramaean ruler of the tenth century B.C. The discovery was not published until 1931.[17] At that time little was known of Near Eastern prehistory and the date of von Oppenheim's 'Buntkeramik' was the subject of much controversy. But in the following years British excavations a Nineveh,[18] Tell Arpachiyah near Mosul[19] and Tell Chagar Bazar,[20] as well as American excavations at Tepe Gawra, put the Halaf period into its proper chronological place and supplied a complete assortment of its cultural assemblage. The Russian excavations of mound 2 at Yarim Tepe and, more recently, the stratigraphic exploration of Arpachiyah by the Iraqi Ismail Hijara,[21] as well as soundings and partial excavations of several sites in the Hamrin basin and the upper Tigris valley, have considerably added to our knowledge.[22]

Compared with the previous cultures, the Halaf culture offers a number of new and highly distinctive features. The settlements are still of village type and size, but cobbled streets, at least at Arpachiyah, indicate some municipal caretaking. Pressed mud or mud bricks remain the standard building materials, but rectangular houses tend to be smaller than before while round houses called *tholoi* (plural of *tholos*) by analogy with the Mycenaean tombs of much later date become predominant. The *tholoi* of Yarim Tepe are usually small; some are divided into two rooms, others are surrounded by rectangular rooms or concentric walls of pressed mud. Those of Arpachiyah, however, are much larger structures, up to 10 metres in diameter; they rest on stone foundations and to some of them is appended a long antechamber which further increases the resemblance with the Mycenaean tombs. Since they had been built and rebuilt with great care and since they were found empty, it was long thought that they were shrines or temples, but the finds at Yarim Tepe clearly show that most *tholoi* were simple, beehive-shaped houses such as can still be seen around Aleppo, in northern Syria. In fact, the only building of that period that might be considered a sanctuary is a small, square structure with mud pedestals and an ox skull on the threshold of a doorway, excavated by Mallowan at Tell Aswad, on the Balikh river. At Arpachiyah the dead were buried in pits beneath the floors or around *tholoi*, but there are examples of collective burials of dismembered bodies there as at Tepe Gawra and of cremation, perhaps for ritual purposes, at Yarim Tepe.

No less interesting than the *tholoi* are some of the small objects found at Arpachiyah and elsewhere. We allude, in particular, to amulets in the form of a house with gabled roof, a bull's head or a double-axe, and to terracotta figurines of doves and women. The latter are not new in Mesopotamia, but they now differ from previous models. The woman is usually squatting or sitting on a round stool, her arms supporting her heavy breasts. The head is reduced to a shapeless lump, but the body is realistic and covered with painted strips and dots which may stand for tattoo marks, jewels or clothes. It is probable that these figurines were talismans against sterility or the hazards of childbirth rather than 'Mother Goddesses', as too often assumed.

Last but not least comes a very remarkable painted pottery, the most beautiful ever used in Mesopotamia.[23] The Halaf ware is made by hand in a fine, ferruginous clay slightly glazed in the process of firing. The walls of the vessels are often very thin, the shapes varied and daring: round pots with large, flaring necks, squat jars with rolled-out rims, footed chalices, large and deep 'cream bowls' with an angular profile. The decoration perhaps

Examples of decorated pottery in proto-historic Mesopotamia:
1. Neolithic (Jarmo); 2–3, Hassuna culture (3 is an incised jar); 4–6,
Samarra culture; 7, Eridu (Ubaid 1) culture; 8, Hajji Muhammad (Ubaid
2) culture; 9–10, Halaf culture; 11–13, Ubaid 3 and 4 cultures; 14–15,
Nineveh V culture; 16 Jemdat Nasr culture.
All drawings are not on the same scale.

lacks the bold movement of the Samarra ware, but it is perfectly adapted to the shapes, minutely executed and pleasant to the eye in the manner of Persian rugs. On a cream or peach 'slip' is laid, originally in black and red, later in black, red and white, a closely woven pattern covering most of the vessel. Triangles, squares, checks, crosses, scallops and small circles are among the favourite designs, though flowers, sitting birds, crouching gazelles and even a leaping cheetah are also encountered. Most characteristic of all and perhaps loaded with religious symbolism are the double-axe, the 'Maltese square' (a square with a triangle on each corner) and the *bucranum*, or stylized bull's head.

It has recently been proven by neutron activation analysis[24] that this attractive pottery was manufactured in large quantities in certain specialized centres, such as Arpachiyah, Tell Brak, Chagar Bazar and Tell Halaf, and exported to specific settlements from which it gradually reached more distant places. The people who transported this ware (perhaps on the back of cattle or on ox-drawn sledges) presumably returned loaded with such 'luxury' goods as marine shells, gem stones and particularly obsidian, which is predominant in most Halafian sites. It has also been suggested that the Halafian formed a 'ranked society' (i.e. with social, but not economic, classes) and that the pottery-producing centres were the residences of local chieftains. The inhabitants of these relatively small villages were farmers and pastoralists. They grew emmer, wheat, einkorn, barley, lentils, flax and other vegetables and bred sheep, goats, pigs, cattle and domestic dogs.

Judging from the distribution of true Halaf pottery, at the peak of its expansion the core of the Halaf culture occupied a wide, crescent-shaped area entirely located in the dry-farming zone. It extended from the region of Aleppo to the Diyala valley, covering the whole of Jazirah and of future Assyria, and it was surrounded by a halo of peripheral areas where this pottery was copied or merely imported; these included the heart of eastern Anatolia, Cilicia and northern Syria up to the

Mediterranean coast, the Harim basin and parts of western Iran and Transcaucasia.

While the Samarra culture may be regarded as a derivative of the Hassuna culture, the Halaf culture has no ancestor in prehistoric Mesopotamia. It is strikingly intrusive and clearly has some connections with Anatolia (virtually all the symbolic designs painted on the Halaf ware and many of the artefacts already described are reminiscent of those found in Anatolian Neolithic sites), but it is not possible to be more precise at present.[25] Whatever the origin of the 'Halafians', there is no evidence of brutal invasion; in fact all we know of them points to a slow infiltration of peaceful people who came to settle in regions that might have then been sparsely populated.

The Ubaid Period

Between 4500 and 4300 B.C. several Halafian settlements in northern Mesopotamia were abandoned, while in many others the *tholoi* and the painted pottery typical of the Halaf culture were gradually replaced by square houses and by another type of pottery which bears the name of Ubaid because it was first found in the 1920s during excavations of a small mound called al-'Ubaid, in the vicinity of the celebrated Sumerian city of Ur.[26] This name is significant as it implies that for the first time in proto-history one single culture extended from the Jazirah (and even beyond) to the Tigris–Euphrates delta. The lack of rupture between the Halaf and Ubaid cultures excludes a conquest of northern and central Iraq by 'Ubaidians' coming from the south, and the most plausible hypotheses are a peaceful infiltration or the adoption by the 'Halafians' of the culture of another population after a long period of contact.

That southern Iraq had been inhabited long before the middle of the fifth millennium was demonstrated in 1946–9 by the excavations conducted at Eridu (Abu Shahrain, nineteen kilometres to the south-west of Ur).[27] The ruins of Eridu are now marked by low mounds and sand dunes surrounding a much dilapidated 'ziqqurat', or stage-tower, erected by Amar-Sin, king of the Third Dynasty of Ur (2046–2038 B.C.), but under one corner of the ziqqurat Seton Lloyd and Fuad Safar unearthed an impressive series of seventeen temples[28] built one above the other in proto-historic times. The lowest and earliest of these temples (levels XVII–XV) were small, one-roomed buildings which contained altars, offering tables and a fine quality pottery (*Eridu ware*) decorated with elaborate, often elegant geometric designs in dark-brown colour and presenting affinities with the Choga Mami transitional ware. The poorly preserved remains of temples XIV–XII yielded a slightly different ceramic characterized by its crowded designs and 'reserve slip' decoration, which was identical with the pottery found in 1937–9 by German archaeologists at Qal'at Hajji Muhammad, near Uruk.[29] This *Hajji Muhammad ware*, as it is called, is also present on other sites of southern Iraq, notably Ras el 'Amiya, eight kilometres north of Kish,[30] where, it must be noted, fragments of walls, clay vessels and other objects lay buried (as indeed at Qal'at Hajji Muhammad itself) under a few metres of alluvium and were discovered by chance. Finally, temples XI to VI, generally well preserved, contained numerous specimens of standard *Ubaid ware*, whilst temples VI–I could be dated to the early stages of the Uruk period. Since the Eridu, and Hajji Muhammad wares are closely related to the early and late Ubaid ware, these four types of pottery are now commonly called Ubaid 1, 2, 3 and 4 respectively.

More recently, a startling discovery was made at a site called Tell el-'Oueili by the French archaeologists who were digging at the nearby city of Larsa. Oueili is a relatively small mound partly above and partly below the present level of the surrounding plain, and it has the advantage of being entirely Ubaidian. Two deep soundings conducted in 1981 and 1983 respectively enabled the explorers to divide it into twenty levels of occupation.[31] The uppermost levels (1 to 8) contained Ubaid 4, 3 and 2 pottery, and samples of Ubaid 1 (Eridu) ware were recovered from levels 8 to 11. But this was not the end, as would have been expected, for below these were no less than eight additional levels (12 to 19) which yielded a pottery (tentatively classified as Pre-Ubaid or Ubaid Zero) that was hitherto unknown but had affinities with the Samarra ware, while the cigar-shaped mud-bricks of a wall in level 12 were reminiscent of the bricks found at Tell es-Sawwan. Furthermore, below level 20 (in the water table and therefore unexplorable) other layers of occupation could vaguely be seen, and no one knows how far back into the sixth millennium the roots of this modest South Mesopotamian village go.

Clearly, then, large parts of southern Mesopotamia had been occupied long before the Ubaid period proper perhaps by people related to those Samarra folk who, it will be remembered, invented irrigation agriculture on the middle Tigris and in the Mandali area. Moreover, while a progressive architectural development can be followed throughout the superimposed temples of Eridu, there is no break in ceramic styles or techniques. The Ubaid ware – so the experts tell us – derives from the Hajji Muhammad ware, which derives from the Eridu ware, which in turn appears to derive from, or at least to share common ancestors with, the Samarra ware. Another, inescapable, conclusion to be drawn from the Eridu temples is that the same religious traditions were handed down from century to century on the same spot from about the middle of the sixth millennium B.C. until historical times, and from the relatively recent finding of two Ubaid shrines near to Anu's 'White Temple' at Uruk (see Chapter 5). Thus the more we dig, the more we find that the Sumerian civilization was very deeply rooted in the past.

Even easier to identify than the Halaf ware is the Ubaid ware, the hall-mark of that period, which is less sophisticated and much less attractive. The clay, frequently overfired, varies in colour from buff to green. The paint is matt, dark brown or bluish-black and the decoration restricted as a rule to only parts of the vessels. Although occasional plants, animals and broad sweeping curves are not without charm, the monotony of the common motifs (triangles, striped or cross-hatched bands, broken or wavy lines) betrays a lack of imagination. Yet the fabric is often fine, some specimens seem to have been made on a slow wheel or 'tournette', and spouts and loop-handles appear for the first time. Among the most characteristic forms are a bell-shaped bowl, a jar with basket-handle, a cream bowl with pouring lip and a lenticular vessel with a flat base and a long, tubular spout, called 'tortoiseshell'. With a few exceptions (Kish, for example), this pottery was found on all sites of southern Iraq and on many sites of northern Mesopotamia, but there are marked differences between the north and the south in the other elements of the Ubaid cultural assemblage.

The words 'clay and water' would aptly qualify the Ubaid culture in southern Iraq. As stone is rare in that part of the country, its use was limited to heavy tools and a few ornaments. All other objects, including bent 'nails' (in fact, probably mullers), sickles, spindle-whorls, loom-weights, net-sinkers, sling pellets and even models of axes, adzes and knives, were made of terracotta. The erroneously called 'Mother Goddess' type of clay figurines – a slim, standing woman with a lizard-like head crowned by a coil of hair made of bitumen and whose 'coffeebean' eyes recall those of Tell es-Sawwan and Choga Mami – was very popular, and there were figurines of men as well. A number of houses were frail structures of reed matting supported by wooden poles and sometimes plastered with clay, such as can be seen around Basrah today, but pressed mud or mud bricks were widely used for more comfortable buildings. The Ubaid period temples of Eridu were made of large mud bricks set in clay mortar and consisted of a long, oblong nave, or *cella* surrounded by small rooms projecting forward at the corners. At one end of the *cella*, against the wall, was a low podium which had once supported the statue of the god, while at the other end stood a brick altar. The walls were adorned externally with shallow buttresses and niches that caught the light and broke the monotony of the plastered brickwork. Let us also note that these temples were raised on mud-brick platforms which tended to be increasingly larger and higher, foreshadowing the ziqqurats of later times.

Virtually unknown for many years, the secular architecture of the Ubaid period is now well illustrated in Lower Mesopotamia and in the Hamrin basin. In the upper, late Ubaid levels of Tell el'Oueili, for example, the French archaeologists have unearthed the remnants of several large and carefully constructed mud-brick houses separated from each other by open spaces. One of these houses was remarkable in that within and around it were dozens of small, square and shallow cavities between thin walls of *tauf*, which is rather puzzling but can probably be interpreted as infrastructures of granaries. The village was in a very flat region criss-crossed by streams and partly marshy. Its inhabitants grew barley, date-palms and other edible plants; they bred almost exclusively zebus and pigs which fed on aquatic plants, and they cut reeds for wickerwork with their baked clay sickles. The presence of obsidian and bitumen testifies to a certain amount of long-distance trade.[32]

Half-way between the extreme south and the extreme north of Iraq lies the Hamrin basin where about twelve Ubaid settlements have been explored. Among them, Tell Madhhur, excavated by a British expedition in 1977–80, is of particular interest as it contained 'one of the best preserved prehistoric buildings ever to have been found in Mesopotamia'.[33] This was a relatively small house built on the 'tripartite plan' characteristic of all the main buildings of the Ubaid period (temples included), with a central cruciform hall and smaller rooms on two sides. The walls were still more than six feet high, and the doors and windows remained perfectly visible. A ramp in one of the rooms suggested an upper floor, but this could not be proven. The house had been destroyed by fire, which preserved most of its contents, including pottery *in situ* and basically the same agricultural tools and household implements as elsewhere in those days, with thousands of clay sling-bullets, but no baked clay sickle.

If we now turn to the north, we are confronted by a somewhat different picture. Reed habitations are unknown and all buildings are made of bricks. Stone is commonly used and stone stamp-seals, very rare in the south, are here quite numerous; they bear linear designs, but also representations of animals and human beings arranged in what may perhaps be considered as mythical scenes or ritual dances. At Tepe Gawra,[34] the most important site of that period in northern Iraq, the three large temples with painted walls that form a grandiose 'acropolis' in level XIII closely match the Eridu temples, but two *tholoi* betray the persistence of regional traditions, as do the Halaf-style sitting and painted female figurines. More important, perhaps, the burial customs are very different from those of the south. At Eridu, in a large cemetery outside the settlement, adults and children alike are lying supine on a bed of potsherds in cist-graves lined and covered with mud bricks. At Gawra there is only one burial of that type; the other graves are simple pits grouped around the houses, and the bodies lie, flexed, on one side; children are buried in urns. This would suggest that the bearers of the Ubaid culture were in the minority in the north. Outnumbered but not eliminated, the descendants of the 'Halafians' still probably formed a large part of the population, whereas the south was entirely 'Ubaidian'. In the next chapter we shall see how the gap between the north and the south gradually widened and how the south took the lead in the march towards civilization.

These differences, however striking, do not fundamentally alter the unity of the Ubaid culture. Whether imported from south-western Iran or, as is increasingly probable, developed locally, this culture – which lasted at least a thousand years – spread all over the cultivable areas of the Mesopotamian plain with the notable exception of the middle Euphrates and lower Tigris valleys. The highest chains of the Taurus and the Zagros mark its limits, but neither these mountains, nor the rivers, nor even the sea offered an insuperable barrier to commercial intercourse. The reality and extent of this trade is attested by the presence of obsidian on many sites of southern Iraq and of gold and amazonite (a semi-precious stone obtainable only from India) at Ur, as well as by the presence of unmistakable

Ubaid pottery at Ras Shamra, on the Syrian coast, and on the Arabian shores of the Gulf.[34] In southern Mesopotamia the Ubaid settlements were situated along the Euphrates and its branches and communicated with each other by water, as illustrated by the clay models of boats found at Eridu and Ur. Most of them were villages, but there were larger centres from which were to spring later on all the main cities of ancient Sumer. Another fact has yet wider implications: of all the buildings of the Ubaid period, the temple was always the largest and best constructed. It therefore looks as though the future Sumerian cities grew not around a palace or a castle, but around a shrine, and it is perhaps not unreasonable to think that the temple was already the hub around which most social and economic activities revolved. It would be bold at this early stage to speak of 'Sumerians', but there is strong reason to believe that the Ubaid period represents the first stage in the development of the Sumerian civilization.

CHAPTER 5

BIRTH OF A CIVILIZATION

During the fourth millennium B.C. the cultural development already perceptible during the Ubaid period proceeded at a quicker pace and the Sumerian civilization finally blossomed. This, however, took place only in the southern half of Iraq, the northern half following a somewhat different course and lagging behind in many respects. Much attention has been paid in recent years to the reasons that concurred to endow the south with such a privilege,[1] and an oversimplified, though plausible, sequence of events is described below. The reader must be warned, however, that all such 'explanations' are largely conjectural and that we shall probably never know what really happened.

In the middle of the fourth millennium B.C. the climate of the Near East, which for some two thousand years had been warm and humid, slowly began to change and became increasingly cooler and drier. Irrigation agriculture had by then proved so successful in southern Iraq that immigrants from the dry-farming plains and hills of northern Mesopotamia moved into the lower Euphrates valley, where archaeological surface surveys have detected a sharp increase in the number of village-size settlements for that period.[2] The new villages, like the old ones, were situated on river banks, but they tended to cluster around those Ubaid period settlements which were both the abodes of the great gods upon whom all prosperity depended and the centres of sizeable agricultural communities. The need to feed a much increased and fast-growing population challenged man's natural ingenuity: the plough was invented, and also the sled for dragging grain, the chariot for carrying goods and the sail for travelling faster on waterways. These technical improvements generated a large surplus of food that could be stored, redistributed or exchanged for imported raw materials and luxuries, while other inventions – such as the potter's wheel and the casting of copper alloys – opened the era of industrial production.

This went on for three or four centuries, but towards the end of the millennium the effects of desiccation started to be felt in southern Mesopotamia. As the Euphrates carried less and less water, many of its tributaries dried up. The hitherto familiar landscape of anastomotic watercourses and extensive marshes was gradually replaced by a new landscape not very different from the present one: bands of palm-groves, fields and orchards along the few remaining streams and, in between, patches of steppe or even desert. Many villages disappeared, their inhabitants regrouping themselves within and around the larger centres, which rapidly grew to the size of towns. To extend the areas of cultivable land artificial irrigation was developed, but the enormous common effort required to dig and maintain big canals and the need for an equitable distribution of water considerably reinforced the authority of the traditional town chiefs, the high priests. This, together with the scarcity of fertile land, led to the concentration of power and wealth in a few hands and in a few places, to further technical progress, to remarkable architectural and artistic achievements, to the invention of writing as a means of recording transactions, but also to armed conflicts. Thus, it would seem, were born the city-states of ancient Sumer, with their fortified cities and well-defined territories, with their population of priests, scribes, architects, artists, overseers, merchants, factory workers, soldiers and peasants and their religious rulers or war leaders.

The five hundred years which saw these developments have been divided, somewhat artificially, by archaeologists into a 'Uruk period' (c. 3750–3150 B.C.) and a 'Jemdat Nasr period' (c. 3150–2900 B.C.) but there is little doubt that the people responsible for the urbanization of southern Mesopotamia were closely related to, or had been absorbed by, the Ubaidians, for there is no clear-cut break between the Ubaid culture and the

Uruk culture and no sign of armed invasion and destruction. On all the sites excavated, such as Eridu, Uruk and Ur, the new temples are built over old ones, on the same plans and with the same materials, and the distinctive *Uruk ware* – a wheelmade, mass-produced, unpainted but sometimes highly polished buff, grey or red pottery, which in some of its forms seems to copy the metal vessels now used by the wealthy – very slowly replaces the Ubaid ware. As for the other elements of the Uruk and Jemdat Nasr cultures (cylinder-seals, cone-mosaic wall decoration, reliefs and sculptures in the round, temples on high terraces), they either derive from older Mesopotamian models or can be credited to the inventiveness of local artists and architects. We are therefore confronted here not with a civilization imported ready-made, but with the final stages of an evolution that had begun with the foundation of Eridu and possibly even earlier in northern Iraq.

The Uruk Period

The site which gave its name to that period is Uruk (biblical Erech, modern Warka), whose large and impressive ruins lie in a non-desert area about half-way between Baghdad and Basrah, not far from the small town of Samawa. It is one of the most important sites of the Near East, not only by its huge size (four hundred hectares), but also by its virtually uninterrupted occupation from Ubaidian to Parthian times and by the rich archaeological and epigraphic material it has yielded.[3]

The city of Uruk was born of the coalescence of two towns 800 metres apart: Kullaba, devoted to the sky-god An (or Anu), the supreme god of the Mesopotamians, and E-Anna ('House of Heaven'), the main abode of the love goddess Inanna (called Ishtar by the Semites). In the centre of E-Anna can still be seen the remains of a mud-brick stage tower (*ziqqurat*) built by the Sumerian king Ur-Nammu (*c.* 2112–2095 B.C.) over a large temple raised on a platform and dating to the Jemdat Nasr period. It is in this area that the German archaeologists, who since 1912 have been digging on and off at Warka for about fifty years, have unearthed at least seven adjacent or superimposed temples and various other cultic installations dating to the second half of the Uruk period. It is also there that they sunk a twenty metre deep well reaching the virgin soil and obtained a stratigraphic section of the site, apparently founded during the Ubaid period.

The archaic temples of Uruk were very similar in plan to those of the Ubaid period at Eridu already described: the buttressed façade, the long *cella* surrounded by small rooms, the doors on the long side testify to the persistence of architectural traditions as well, probably, as of belief and cult. In E-Anna, they were arranged in pairs, a fact that led Professor H. Lenzen to suggest that they were dedicated not only to Inanna but also to her lover the fertility-god Dumuzi.[4] Particularly remarkable were the lowermost levels with their enormous temples – one of them, built on limestone foundations, measured 87 by 33 metres – and their extraordinary 'mosaic building'. The latter consisted of a large courtyard extending between two sanctuaries, with a raised portico of eight massive mud-brick columns, three metres in diameter, arranged in two rows. The side walls of the courtyard, the columns themselves and the platform on which they rested were entirely clad in a coloured pattern of geometrical design formed by the flat end of terracotta cones, seven to ten centimetres long, which had been painted in black, red or white and then stuck into the mud plaster. This original and very effective type of decoration was widely used during the Uruk and Jemdat Nasr periods, and loose clay cones can still be picked up by the thousand in the ruins of Warka. The colour, when preserved, has lost its brightness, but little effort is required to imagine what a fresh cone-mosaic façade must have looked like in the glaring oriental sunlight. This taste for colour is also manifest in the use of wall painting. One of the archaic temples of E-Anna, the so-called 'Red Temple', owes its name to the pink wash which covered its walls, and at Tell 'Uqair, eighty kilometres south of Baghdad, the Iraqis excavated in 1940–1 a temple of the Uruk period decorated with frescoes which, when discovered, were 'as bright as the day they were applied':[5] human figures, unfortunately damaged, formed a procession, and two crouching leopards guarded the throne of an unknown god. All these temples, it must be noted, rested on low brick platforms, as did the temples of the Ubaid period at Eridu; but with time the platform became higher, tending to be more important in size than the building itself. Here in all probability is the origin of the *ziqqurat*, the stage-tower topped by a shrine so typical of the Mesopotamian civilization in historical times. This evolution is illustrated by the Anu temple of Uruk, where six temples built in succession were finally included in a truly monumental platform rising some fifteen metres above the plain. At the top of this platform are the amazingly well-preserved remains of a sanctuary dating to the late Uruk period, the so-called 'White Temple', and to stand between these walls, at the very place where officiated, five thousand years ago, the priests of the sky-god, is an experience which no visitor will easily forget.

Domestic architecture is poorly represented in southern Iraq, but we may catch a glimpse of it on other, distant sites – for the Uruk culture progressively spread throughout Mesopotamia and covered roughly the same area as the Ubaid culture. Near Erbil, for instance, at Tell Qalinj Agha,[6] two large residential quarters were separated by a main street, 2 to 3 metres wide, intersected by smaller streets at a right angle, and the same regular plan can be seen at Habuba Kabira, on the great bend of the Euphrates, a city which covered not less than 22 hectares and was surrounded by a wall with square towers.[7] In both places the houses, carefully built of oblong bricks, consisted of three buildings of two to four spacious rooms each, around a large hall or courtyard.

The magnificence of the Uruk temples and the near-luxurious aspect of private houses tend to dwarf the other forms of art. Yet the seal impressions of the Uruk period are little masterpieces. At that time the stamp-seal of earlier periods was almost entirely superseded by the cylinder-seal. This was a small

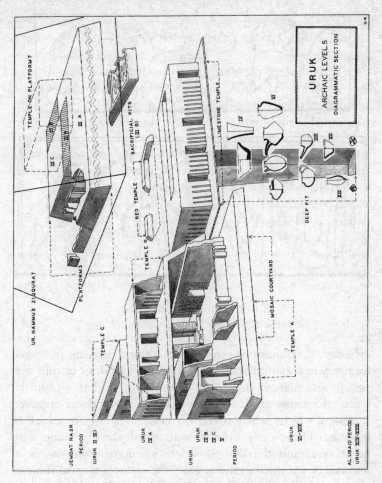

URUK
ARCHAIC LEVELS
DIAGRAMMATIC SECTION

Diagrammatic section through the archaic layers of Uruk (E-Anna). Successive temples on 3 levels. Note the temple on platform (Jemdat Nasr period) under the ziqqurat built by Ur-Nammu (Ur III period) and the test pit with models of pottery, going down to the Ubaid period. *Reconstruction by the author based on H. Lenzen's plans in Zeitschrift für Assyriologie, XLIX, 1949.*

Cylinder-seals of the Uruk period.
A. Parrot, Archéologie Mésopotamienne, *II, 1953*.

cylinder of ordinary or semi-precious stone, varying in length from 2.5 to 8 centimetres, as thick as the thumb or as thin as a pencil, and pierced lengthwise throughout, so that it could be worn on a string around the neck. On its surface was engraved a design which, when rolled on clay, could be repeated *ad infinitum*. These early cylinder-seals were already made with great skill, and the designs – which ranged from friezes of animals or plants to scenes of daily life or mythological subjects – were composed and arranged with considerable ingenuity. Their interest, however, goes far beyond their artistic value, for they are the only objects of the Uruk period that are alive with people and give us an inkling of their occupations. For instance, a cylinder-seal representing a massacre of prisoners bespeaks war, while the frequent occurrence of cattle walking in herds, gathered around their pens or attacked by lions evokes the farmers' main preoccupation. Mysterious ceremonies performed by naked priests are also frequently represented. We have here for the first time, besides an art in miniature, a source of information which at all periods will prove useful to the historian of ancient Mesopotamia.[8]

But the Uruk period witnessed another novelty immensely more important than the wheel, the cylinder-seal or the cone mosaic decoration, an epoch-making invention comparable only to the invention of agriculture in Neolithic times. It is towards the end of the period, c. 3300 B.C. in the archaic temples of E-Anna in Uruk, that writing appears for the first time in the form of pictographic tablets.[9]

The writing used in Mesopotamia throughout history and known as 'cuneiform' was originally – as all primitive writings, past or present – a collection of small, simplified drawings, or pictograms. The earliest texts from Uruk and elsewhere are already too complex to represent the first attempt made by men to preserve their thoughts, and in all probability the first pictograms were engraved on wood or painted on skins or leaves, but such media must have disintegrated long ago in the humid subsoil of Iraq, and the only documents that have survived are written on clay. The process of writing was in itself very simple: the scribe took a lump of fine, well-washed clay and shaped it as a small, smooth cushion, a few centimetres square. Then, with the end of a reed stalk cut obliquely he drew lines dividing each face of the cushion into squares and filled each square with incised drawings. The 'tablet' was then either baked or left unbaked. Baked tablets are nearly as hard as stone; old, unbaked tablets crumble into dust between the fingers, but if they are collected with care, allowed to dry slowly in the shade and hardened in an oven they become almost indestructible. It must be added, however, that a number of archaic inscriptions were engraved in stone, at first with a bronze point, then with a cold chisel.

In the course of time the Mesopotamian script gradually lost its pictographic character. The signs were laid down in horizontal lines rather than in squares or in vertical bands. They

	Head	Hand	Foot	Fish	Bird	Reed
Archaic c. 3500						
UR III c. 2500						
Old Babylonian c. 1800						
Middle Assyrian c. 1100						
Neo-Assyrian c. 750						
Neo-Babylonian c. 600						
Sumerian	SAG	SHU	DU, GIN GUB. TUM	HA	NAM	GI
Akkadian	sak, sag shak, rish, ris	shu qad, qat	du, tu kub, gub qub	ha	nam sim	gi, ge ki, ke qi, qe

Examples of changes in cuneiform signs throughout centuries.
Beside their phonetic value in the Akkadian language, most signs have one
of several logographic values. Thus, SHU (in Sumerian the hand) can be
read in Akkadian *qâtu*, hand; *emûqu*, strength; *gamâlu*, protection, etc.

became smaller, more compact, more rigid, more 'abstract',
finally bearing no resemblance to the objects they represented.
The awkward curves disappeared and were replaced by straight
lines, at first, of equal width, then – as the prismatic stylus was
forced into the clay prior to being drawn on its surface –
vaguely triangular or wedge-shaped. Towards the middle of the
third millennium B.C. this evolution was completed and the

true 'cuneiform' writing (from Latin *cuneus*: wedge, nail) was born, though minor changes never ceased to occur thereafter, enabling the specialists to date a text as surely as archaeologists date a piece of pottery.[10]

The earliest texts in our possession were probably written in Sumerian. This language being largely monosyllabic, writing was based, as in Chinese, on the principle: one object or idea equals one sound equals one sign. The first pictograms were therefore extremely numerous (more than two thousand). Some of them represent objects that are easy to identify, such as agricultural tools, vases, boats, heads of animals or parts of the human body, while others appear to be purely conventional. But because it is very difficult to represent abstract ideas graphically, one pictogram was often used to express several words and could be read in several ways. For instance, a foot would not only mean 'foot' (pronounced *du* in Sumerian) but also ideas related to the foot such as 'to stand' (*gub*), 'to go' (*gin*), 'to come' or 'to bring' (*tum*). Reciprocally, some concepts totally unrelated but pronounced with the same sound were grouped under the same sign. Thus the sign of the bow was used for 'arrow' (*ti*), but also for 'to live' (*ti* or *til*). In classical Sumerian, the correct reading of a sign is normally indicated either by the context or by other signs called 'phonetic complements', 'determinatives' or 'grammatical particles'; but the archaic texts had nothing of this kind. Moreover, the signs were laid down in apparent disorder, and some of them, used only in the earliest periods, were later abandoned so that their phonetic value (or values) is unknown. For these reasons we cannot *read* the pictographic tablets. All we can say is that they have all the characteristics of economic documents (lists of workmen, lists of goods, receipts, etc.). This is not surprising since writing was invented purely for accounting purposes. As early as the seventh millennium, there appeared on several sites in Iraq and Iran small balls, cubes and cones of baked clay which were first thought to be toys but were later recognized as token or 'calculi' the size and shape of which indicated units and subunits or undetermined goods that were exchanged. In about 3500 B.C. these calculi were found in envelopes of clay bearing drawings of their contents.[11] Simple tablets with nothing but numerals (circles and short lines) were also found in illiterate places such as Khafaje, in the Diyala valley, Tell Brak and Habuba Kabira.[12] It is remarkable that from such humble beginnings writing developed in southern Mesopotamia within a relatively short time into an extremely sophisticated system which was used to express all mental activities, including a vast and admirable literature.

The Jemdat Nasr Period

In 1925 a distinctive pottery consisting, in the main, of large thick jars decorated with geometrical or naturalistic designs in black and/or red paint applied directly on the buff clay was discovered at Jemdat Nasr, between Baghdad and Babylon.[13] Later, the 'Jemdat Nasr ware' was found, usually in small quantities, on other Mesopotamian sites and was taken as the hallmark of a cultural period immediately preceding history, the so-called 'Jemdat Nasr period'. It must be borne in mind, however, that between the cultural elements of that period and those of the Uruk period there is no fundamental difference, but simple variations in style and quality. Architectural remains are rare but sufficient to prove the absence of drastic changes in the plan and decoration of temples, though emphasis is now laid on their platforms, and the cone-mosaic decoration is generally applied in panels instead of covering every inch of the walls. Cylinder-seals carry the same religious and secular scenes, though these tend to become stereotyped and conventional. Writing is more and more in use, but the pictograms are less numerous, less 'realistic' and often used for their phonetic value alone. The bulk of the ceramic is identical with the plain Uruk pottery and the rare 'Jemdat Nasr ware', perhaps of Iranian inspiration, may represent nothing more than a transient local fashion. All things considered, sculpture is perhaps the only original contribution of the new period to the progress of the arts.

Almost forgotten since the Samarra period, sculpture suddenly reappears, soon reaches a high degree of perfection and is applied with passion to a large variety of objects. Lions attacking bulls, heroes mastering lions, sullen boars, peaceful ewes and rams are carved in relief or in the round on stone vases and bowls, on troughs, on mural plaques and on the back of the rare stamp-seals that have survived. Also from that time date numerous statuettes of worshippers offered as *ex-votos*, and a rather crude basalt stele found at Warka, which represents two bearded men killing lions with spear and arrows, is the oldest known ancestor of the famous Assyrian hunting scenes. If all this is not always of excellent quality, two objects – both found at Uruk – are as yet without rival in the whole world for that period.[14] One is a one-metre-high alabaster vase carved in low relief with perfect skill, where the goddess Inanna is shown receiving gifts from a man of high rank, perhaps a priest, a chief or even a god. This vase was already regarded as a valuable *objet d'art* in antiquity, for it had been repaired with metal clips. The other masterpiece is an almost life-size mask of a woman made of marble. The eyes are unfortunately missing, but the face is modelled with a mixture of realism and sensitivity rarely found before the classical period of Greek sculpture.

Progress in techniques, achievements in art, writing, all these are the symptoms of a fully mature civilization which should be called without hesitation 'Sumerian' since it is practically certain that the tablets from Jemdat Nasr and the contemporary levels of Ur and Tell 'Uqair are written in that language. Born and bred in southern Iraq, this civilization radiated over the entire Near East and exerted a deep influence on the other oriental cultures. We may well imagine that the as yet undeciphered 'Proto-Elamite' script on clay, which appears about that time in near-by Elam (south-west Persia), was inspired by the archaic Sumerian writing or invented by a people related to the Sumerians, but it is more difficult to understand through which channel and in what circumstances Egypt borrowed from Mesopotamia.[15] Yet the late prehistoric graves of Naqadah have yielded typical Jemdat Nasr cylinder-seals, and the object itself was adopted by the Egyptians, who engraved it with their own traditional designs and, having no clay tablets on which to roll it, used it for centuries as an amulet. Similarly, favourite Mesopotamian motifs, such as hunting scenes, lions devouring cattle or beasts with long, intertwined necks were copied by Egyptian sculptors just as the Egyptian architects of the First Dynasty built their royal tombs with the recessed façades of the Mesopotamian temples. Indeed, some authorities believe that the Sumerian pictograms antedate the earliest hieroglyphs and may well have inspired their inventors. This one-way influence is the more remarkable, since contacts between the two great focuses of civilization in the Near East have always been surprisingly rare and superficial throughout ancient history.

Less unexpected, though no less striking, was the Sumerian influence over northern Syria. Little is known so far of the first settlement at Ebla, but when that great city flourished, in the third millennium, much of its architecture and art had a strong Sumerian flavour, and the library of its royal palace contained both Sumerian and Semitic texts in standard cuneiform writing, which suggests close previous contacts with southern Iraq. The same can be said of Mari, on the middle Euphrates, where art and script in the Early Dynastic period are purely Sumerian, though here again the people are Semites. Furthermore, the finding of Mesopotamian cylinder-seals in Iran (Susa, Tepe Sialk, Tepe Hissar), as well as in Turkey (Alişar, Troy), Lebanon and Palestine, and the discovery of typical Jemdat Nasr pottery in Oman bear witness to extensive commercial relations between lower Mesopotamia and its neighbours.

Strangely enough, in Mesopotamia proper the archaic Sumerian civilization remained confined for a long time to the southern half of the country. Whilst traces of the Uruk culture are almost omnipresent in the north, traces of the Jemdat Nasr culture are limited to a few sites, thought to be Sumerian colonies, such as Tell Brak, in the Khabur basin, and Grai Resh,[16] in the Sinjar area, where temples on platform with clay-cone mosaic and small southern-type idols – some with staring eyes, others spectacle-shaped – were found in the late thirties, or again Tell Asmar and Khafaje, in the Diyala valley, where soundings brought to light Jemdat Nasr pottery, sculptures, cylinder-seals and tablets.[17] It therefore looks as though, for some obscure reason, most of Jazirah and the entire upper Tigris valley had been impervious to the cultural developments that had taken place some 300 kilometres to the south. The only important site in future Assyria at that time is Tepe Gawra; yet throughout the Uruk and Jemdat Nasr periods the inhabitants of Tepe Gawra fought with maces and slings, continued to use stamp-seals, made their pottery by hand and ignored writing, though they drove in four-wheeled chariots and buried their chiefs with a wealth of grave furniture unequalled in the south at that time. The 'Gawra culture' was eventually replaced by the 'Nineveh 5 culture' (level 5 of the deep sounding at Nineveh) characterized by a wheel-made, rather attractive, painted or incised pottery and by Sumerian weapons and seals. But by that time Sumer had already entered history, and the whole of the Early Dynastic period (c. 2900–2334 B.C.) was to elapse before the first written documents appeared in the north in the wake of the Akkadian conquerors.

The gap opened at the end of the fourth millennium between the north and the south was never entirely filled in ancient history. After the Akkadians, successively the Sumerian kings of the Third Dynasty of Ur and Hammurabi of Babylon held under their sway the Upper Tigris and the foothills of Kurdistan. Yet from their inscriptions one forms the impression that these districts were considered somewhat foreign and culturally inferior. The Hittite raid on Babylon (1595 B.C.) and the long period of semi-anarchy that followed the Kassite domination put an end to the political supremacy of the south. The north then took its revenge and the kings of Assur and Nineveh ruled over the whole of Mesopotamia. But the Babylonians never willingly accepted government by these 'barbarians' and repeatedly tried to shake off the yoke, while the mighty monarchs of Assyria themselves, who piously collected the old Sumerian texts and regularly took part in the New Year Festival of Babylon, implicitly acknowledged their debt to a very ancient and venerable civilization.

The Sumerian Problem

Who are these Sumerians, whose name can now be pronounced for the first time and who are going to occupy the stage of history for the next thousand years? Do they represent a very ancient layer of population in prehistoric Mesopotamia, or did they come from some other country, and if so, when did they come and whence? This important problem has been debated again and again ever since the first relics of the Sumerian civilization were brought to light more than a century ago, and is still with us. The most recent discoveries, far from offering a solution, have made it even more difficult to answer, but at least they have supplied fresh and solid arguments to an old debate and it is in this new light that the 'Sumerian problem' should be examined.[18]

The word 'Sumerian' comes from the ancient name of the southern part of Iraq: *Sumer* or, more exactly, *Shumer*, usually written in cuneiform texts with the signs KI.EN.GI.[19] At the beginning of historical times three ethnic groups lived in close contact within that region: the Sumerians, predominant in the extreme south from approximately Nippur (near Diwaniyah) to the Gulf, the Semites, predominant in central Mesopotamia (the region called *Akkad* after 2400 B.C.), and a small, diffuse minority of uncertain origin to which no definite label can be attached. From the point of view of the modern historian, the line of demarcation between these three components of the first historical population of Mesopotamia is neither political nor cultural but linguistic. All of them had the same institutions; all of them shared the way of life, the techniques, the artistic traditions, the religious beliefs, in a word the civilization which had originated in the extreme south and is rightly attributed to the Sumerians. The only reliable criterion by which we can separate and identify these three peoples is therefore their language. *Stricto sensu*, the appellation 'Sumerians' should be taken as meaning 'Sumerian-speaking people' and nothing else; similarly, the 'Semites' were those who spoke a Semitic dialect; and indeed we would be unaware of the existence of the third ethnic element were it not for a few strange, non-Sumerian and non-Semitic personal and geographical names which occur here and there in ancient texts. This, incidentally, explains why all efforts to define and to assess the relations between Sumerians and Semites in other fields than philology are doomed to failure.[20] Another point should be made quite clear: there is no such thing as a Sumerian 'race' neither in the scientific nor in the ordinary sense of the term. The skulls from Sumerian graves that have been examined are either dolicho- or brachycephalic and indicate a mixture of the so-called Armenoid and Mediterranean races, the latter being somewhat predominant.[21] As for the physical features depicted on monuments, they are largely conventional and have therefore no real value. The big, fleshy nose, the enormous eyes, the thick neck and flat occiput long considered to be typical of the Sumerians also belong to the statues of individuals bearing genuine Semitic names found in the almost exclusively Semitic district of Mari, while more realistic portraits, such as those of Gudea, the Sumerian governor of Sumerian Lagash, show a short, straight nose and a long head.

Philology alone is often a good index of ethnic relationship. Thus the Greeks, the Hittites and the Indo-Aryans, though dispersed over a wide area, were related to each other through the Indo-European languages they spoke and probably came from a common homeland in south-eastern Europe. But in the case of the Sumerians philology is of no help. The Sumerian language is 'agglutinative', which means that it is formed of verbal radicals modified or inter-connected by the apposition of grammatical particles. As such, it belongs to the same category as numerous dialects spoken from Hungary to Polynesia, though it bears no close resemblance to any known language, dead or living. The Sumerian literature presents us with the picture of a highly intelligent, industrious, argumentative and deeply religious people, but offers no clue as to its origins. Sumerian myths and legends are almost invariably drawn against a background of rivers and marshes, of reeds, tamarisks and palm-trees – a typical southern Iraqi background – as though the Sumerians had always lived in that country, and there is nothing in them to indicate clearly an ancestral homeland different from Mesopotamia.

We are therefore obliged to fall back on archaeology, that is to say on the material elements of the Sumerian civilization. The question here is: which of the various ethnic groups responsible for the successive proto-historic cultures of Mesopotamia can be identified with the Sumerian-speaking people of history? Put in this way the problem is of course insoluble, since we do not know what languages were spoken in Mesopotamia before the Uruk period. Whatever answer is given can only rest on broad generalization, intuitive thinking or mere guesswork. On this question scholars in general are divided into two groups: for some the Sumerians came to Mesopotamia during the Uruk period; for others they were already there in Ubaid times at the latest. We cannot enter here into a detailed discussion, but we are personally rather inclined to agree with the tenets of the second theory. True, the Sumerian *writing* appears for the first time at the end of the Uruk period, but this does not imply that the Sumerian language was not spoken before. Again, there are in ancient Mesopotamian literature place names that are neither Sumerian nor Semitic, but do they necessarily represent the traces of an older and *exclusive* population? As for the change in pottery style which marks the beginning of the Uruk period, we have seen that it was probably due to mass production rather than to foreign invasion or influence. In fact, in all respects the Uruk culture appears as the development of conditions that existed during the Ubaid period. In any case, if we assume that the Sumerians were invaders where did they come from? Some authors have sought their origin in the mountainous countries to the east of Mesopotamia where they arrived by land or by sea, while others believe that they came from Anatolia following the Euphrates down to its mouth; but the arguments afforded in favour of these theories are not very convincing. Furthermore, since the Second World War numerous archaeological excavations have been conducted in Turkey, Iran, Baluchistan, Afghanistan and Central Asia, and none of them has revealed anything resembling, even vaguely, the Uruk and Jemdat Nasr cultures; nor have they produced any inscription written in Sumerian which of course would be the only decisive evidence. In these circumstances, why not turn to Mesopotamia itself?

It has been shown in Chapter 4 that many material elements of the Sumerian civilization – mud-brick buildings, coloured walls and frescoes, stone vases and statuettes, clay figurines, seals, metal work and even irrigation agriculture – originated in northern Iraq during the sixth and fifth millennia B.C., and the excavations at Choga Mami have established a definite link between the Samarra culture and the partly contemporary Eridu and Hajji Muhammad cultures, now recognized as the early stages of the Ubaid culture. To equate the Samarrans with the Sumerians, or even the Ubaidians, on the sole basis of their pottery and extraordinary statuettes would be unacceptably rash, but there is little doubt that the first settlers in southern Mesopotamia were in some way related to, or at least influenced by, their northern neighbours. And the Samarrans, in turn, might have descended from the Neolithic farmers of Hassuna or Umm Dabaghiya. Thus the more we try to push back the limits of our problem, the more it thins out and vanishes in the mist of prehistory. One is even tempted to wonder whether there is any problem at all. The Sumerians were, as we all are, a mixture of races and probably of peoples; their civilization, like ours, was a blend of foreign and indigenous elements; their language belongs to a linguistic group

large enough to have covered the whole of Western Asia and
much more. They may therefore represent a branch of the
population which occupied the greater part of the Near East in
early Neolithic and Chalcolithic times. In other words, they
may have 'always' been in Iraq, and this is all we can say. As
one of the most brilliant orientalists put it: 'The much discussed
problem of the origin of the Sumerians may well turn out to be
the chase of a chimera.'[22]

CHAPTER 6

THE GODS OF SUMER

Whatever the real origin of the Sumerians, there is no doubt that their civilization sprang from the prehistory of Iraq itself. It reflected the mood and fulfilled the aspirations of the stable, conservative peasant society which has always formed the back-bone of that country; it was 'Mesopotamian' in origin and in essence. For this reason, it survived the disappearance of the Sumerians as a nation in about 2000 B.C. and was adopted and carried over with but little modification by the Amorites, Kassites, Assyrians and Chaldaeans who, after them, ruled in succession over Mesopotamia. The Assyro-Babylonian civilization of the second and first millennia is therefore not fundamentally different from that of the Sumerians, and from whatever angle we approach it we are almost invariably brought back to a Sumerian model.

This is particularly true of religion. For more than three thousand years the gods of Sumer were worshipped by Sumerians and Semites alike; and for more than three thousand years the religious ideas promoted by the Sumerians played an extra-ordinary part in the public and private life of the Mesopotamians, modelling their institutions, colouring their works of art and literature, pervading every form of activity from the highest functions of the kings to the day-to-day occupations of their subjects. In no other antique society did religion occupy such a prominent position, because in no other antique society did man feel himself so utterly dependent upon the will of the gods. The fact that the Sumerian society crystallized around temples had deep and lasting consequences. In theory, for instance, the land never ceased to belong to the gods, and the mighty Assyrian monarchs whose empire extended from the Nile to the Caspian Sea were the humble servants of their god Assur, just as the governors of Lagash, who ruled over a few square miles of Sumer, were those of their god Ningirsu. This of course does not mean that economics and human passions did not play a part in the history of ancient Iraq, as they did in the history of other countries; but the religious motives should never be forgotten nor minimized. As an introduction to the historical periods which we are about to enter, a brief description of the Sumerian pantheon and religious ideas will surely not be out of place.[1]

The Sumerian Pantheon

Our knowledge of Mesopotamian religious and moral ideas derives from a variety of texts – epic tales and myths, rituals, hymns, prayers, incantations, lists of gods, collections of precepts, proverbs, etc. – which come, in the main, from three great sources: the sacerdotal library of Nippur (the religious centre of Sumer), and the palace and temple libraries of Assur and Nineveh. Some of these texts are written in Sumerian,[2] others are usually Assyrian or Babylonian copies or adaptations of Sumerian originals, even though, in a few cases, they have no counterpart in the Sumerian religious literature discovered so far. The dates when they were actually composed vary from about 1900 B.C. to the last centuries before Christ, but we may reasonably assume that they embody verbal traditions going back to the Early Dynastic period and possibly even earlier, since a number of Sumerian deities and mythological scenes can be recognized on the cylinder-seals and sculptured objects from the Uruk and Jemdat Nasr periods. Before these, positive evidence is lacking, but the unbroken continuity of architectural traditions, the rebuilding of temple upon temple in the same sacred area suggest that some at least of the Sumerian gods were already worshipped in southern Iraq during the Ubaid period.

The formulation of religious ideas and their expression as divine families and in myths were certainly slow processes, carried out by several 'schools' of priests simultaneously; but somehow, in the end a general agreement on principles was reached, and while each city retained its own patron-god and its own set of legends, the whole country worshipped a common pantheon.[3] The divine society was conceived as a replica of the human society of Sumer and organized accordingly. The heavens, the earth and the netherworld were populated with gods – at first in hundreds but later less numerous owing to an internal syncretism that never reached monotheism. These gods, like the Greek gods, had the appearances, qualities, defects and passions of human beings, but they were endowed with fabulous strength, supernatural powers and immortality. Moreover, they manifested themselves in a halo of dazzling light, a 'splendour' which filled man with fear and respect and gave him the indescribable feeling of contact with the divine, which is the essence of all religions.[4]

The gods of Mesopotamia were not all of equal status, but to classify them is not an easy talk. At the bottom of the scale we would perhaps put the benevolent spirits and the evil demons who belonged more to magics than to religion proper, and the 'personal god', a kind of guardian angel attached to every person and acting as an intermediary between this person and the higher gods.[5] Then would come the humble deities who were responsible for such tools as the plough, the brick-mould or the pickaxe, and for such professions as potters, blacksmiths, goldsmiths and the like, as well as the gods of Nature in the broad sense of the term (gods of rivers, mountains, minerals, plants, wild and domesticated animals, gods of fertility, birth and medicine, gods of winds and thunderstorms), originally perhaps the most numerous and important as they personified 'élan vital, the spiritual cores in phenomena, indwelling wills and powers',[6] all concepts that are characteristic of the so-called primitive mentality. One step higher would be found the gods of the Netherworld, Nergal and Ereshkigal, side by side with warrior gods such as Ninurta. Above them the astral deities, notably the moon-god Nanna (called Sin by the Semites), who controlled time (the lunar months) and 'knew the destinies of all' but remained in many ways mysterious, and the sun-god Utu (Shamash), the god of justice who 'laid bare the righteous and the wicked' as he flooded the world with blinding light. Finally, atop of the scale would naturally stand as dominant figures in the vast Mesopotamian pantheon the three great male gods An, Enlil and Enki.

An (Anu or Anum in Akkadian) embodied 'the overpowering personality of the sky' of which he bore the name, and occupied first place in the Sumerian pantheon. This god, whose main temple was in Uruk, was originally the highest power in the universe, the begetter and sovereign of all gods. Like a father he arbitrated their disputes and his decisions, like those of a king, brooked no appeal. Yet An – at least in the classical Sumerian mythology – did not play an important part in earthly affairs and remained aloof in the heavens as a majestic though somewhat pale figure. At some unknown period[7] and for some obscure reason the patron-god of Nippur, Enlil, was raised to what was in fact the supreme rank and became in a certain sense the national god of Sumer. Much later he himself was in turn wrested of his authority by the hitherto obscure god of Babylon, Marduk; but Enlil was certainly less of an usurper than Marduk. His name means 'Lord Air', which, among other things, evokes immensity, movement and life (breath), and Enlil could rightly claim to be 'the force in heaven' which had separated the earth from the sky and had thereby created the world. The theologians of Nippur, however, also made him the master of humanity, the king of kings. If An still retained the insignia of kingship it was Enlil who chose the rulers of Sumer and Akkad and 'put on their heads the holy crown'. And as a good monarch by his command keeps his kingdom in order, so did the air-god uphold the world by a mere word of his mouth:

> Without Enlil, the Great Mountain,
> No city would be built, no settlement founded,
> No stalls would be built, no sheepfolds established,
> No king would be raised, no high priest born ...

The rivers – their floodwaters would not bring over flow,
The fish in the sea would not lay eggs in the canebrake,
The birds of heaven would not build nests on the wild earth,
In heaven the drifting clouds would not yield their moisture,
Plants and herbs, the glory of the plain, would fail to grow,
In fields and meadows the rich grain would fail to flower,
The trees planted in the mountain-forest would not yield their
fruit . . .[8]

The personality of the god Enki is better known but much more complex. Despite the appearances, it is not certain that his Sumerian name means 'lord earth' (en.ki), and linguists are still arguing about the exact meaning of his Semitic name Ea. However, there is no doubt that Enki/Ea was the god of the fresh waters that flow in rivers and lakes, rise in springs and wells and bring life to Mesopotamia. His main quality was his intelligence, his 'broad ears' as the Sumerians said, and this is why he was revered as the inventor of all techniques, sciences and arts and as patron of the magicians. Moreover, Enki was the god who held the me's, a word used, it seems, to designate the key-words of the Sumerian civilization, and which also played a part in the 'attribution of destinies'.[9] After the world was created, Enki applied his unrivalled intelligence to the laws devised by Enlil. A long, almost surrealist poem[10] shows him putting the world in order; extending his blessings not only to Sumer, its cattle sheds, fields and cities, but also to Dilmun and Meluhha and to the nomads of the Syro-Mesopotamian desert; transformed into a bull and filling the Tigris with the 'sparkling water' of his semen; entrusting a score of minor deities with specific tasks and finally handing over the entire universe to the sun-god Utu. This master architect and engineer who said that he was 'the ear and the mind of all the land' was also the god who was closest and most favourable to man. It was he who had the brilliant idea to create mankind to carry out the gods' work, but also, as we shall see, who saved mankind from the Flood.

Side by side with the male pantheon there was a female

Mural painting from the second millennium palace at Mari.
Above, the goddess Ishtar appoints Zimri-Lim king of Mari by giving him
the sceptre and the ring of kingship. Below, two unnamed goddesses holding
vases spurting out water, as a symbol of fertility.
After A. Parrot, Mission Archéologique de Mari, *II, 2, 1958.*

pantheon composed of goddesses of all ranks. Many of them were merely gods' wives whilst others fulfilled specific functions. Prominent among the latter stood the mother-goddess Ninhursag (also known as Ninmah or Nintu), and Inanna (Ishtar for the Semites) who played a major role in Mesopotamian mythology.

Inanna was the goddess of carnal love and as such had neither husband nor children, but she entertained many lovers whom she regularly discarded. Beautiful and voluptuous as she undoubtedly was imagined and portrayed, she often acted perfidiously and had violent outbursts of anger which made this incarnation of pleasure a formidable goddess of war. In the course of time, this second aspect of her personality raised her to the rank of the male gods who led the armies into battle.[11] Dumuzi, the only god she seems to have loved tenderly, probably resulted from the fusion of two prehistoric deities, for he was both the protector of herds and flocks and the god of the vegetation that dies in the summer and revives in the spring. The Sumerians believed that the reproduction of cattle and the renewal of edible plants and fruit could be secured only by a ceremony, on New Year's Day, in which the king, playing the role of Dumuzi, consummated a marital union with Inanna, represented by one of her priestesses. Love poems where overt erotism mixes with tender affection celebrate this 'Sacred Marriage',[12] while the ritual itself is described in some royal hymns, the most explicit of which is a hymn to Iddin-Dagan (1974–1954 B.C.), the third king of the dynasty of Isin.[13] A scented bed of rushes is set up in a special room of the palace and on it is spread a comfortable cover. The goddess has bathed and has sprinkled sweet-smelling cedar oil on the ground. Then comes the King:

> The King approaches her pure lap proudly,
> He approaches the lap of Inanna proudly,
> Ama'ushumgalanna * lies down beside her,
> He caresses her pure lap.

* One of Dumuzi's names.

When the Lady has stretched out on the bed, in his pure lap,
When the pure Inanna has stretched out on the bed, in his pure lap,
She makes love with him on her bed,
(She says) to Iddin-Dagan 'You are surely my beloved'.

Thereafter the people, carrying presents, are invited to enter, together with musicians, and a special meal is served:

> The palace is festive, the King is joyous,
> The people spend the day in plenty.

However, the rapports between Inanna and Dumuzi were not always harmonious, as shown by a famous text called 'Inanna's descent to the Netherworld' of which two versions have been preserved, one Sumerian, the other Assyrian.[14] In the Sumerian text Inanna goes down to the 'land of no return', casting off a piece of clothing or a jewel at each stage, in order to snatch this lugubrious domain from the hands of her sister Ereshkigal, the Sumerian equivalent of Persephone. Unfortunately, Inanna fails; she is put to death, then resurrected by Enki, but she is not allowed to return to earth unless she finds a replacement. After a long voyage in search of a potential victim, she chooses none other than her favourite lover. Dumuzi is promptly seized by demons and taken to the Netherworld, to the sorrow of his sister Geshtin-anna, the goddess of vines. Finally, Inanna is moved by Dumuzi's lamentations: she decides that he will spend one half of the year underground, and Geshtin-anna the other half.

The Sacred Marriage rite probably originated in Uruk, but it was performed in other cities, at least until the end of the dynasty of Isin (1794). After that date, Dumuzi fell to the rank of a relatively minor deity, although a month bore his name in its Semitic form Tammuz, and still bears it in the Arab world. In the last centuries of the first millennium B.C., however, the cult of Tammuz was revived in the Levant. A god of vegetation more or less akin to Osiris, he became *adon* ('the Lord'), i.e.

Adonis who died each year and was mourned in Jerusalem, Byblos, Cyprus and later even in Rome. In a Greek legend, Persephone and Aphrodite were quarrelling for the favours of the handsome young god when Zeus intervened and ruled that Adonis would share the year between the two goddesses.[15] Thus, the old Sumerian myth of Inanna's descent to the Netherworld had not been entirely forgotten: slightly distorted but recognizable, it had reached the Aegean Sea by some unknown channel, as did a number of Mesopotamian myths and legends.

Tales of Creation

The Mesopotamians imagined the earth as a flat disc surrounded with a rim of mountains and floating on an ocean of sweet waters, the *abzu* or *apsû*. Resting on these mountains and separated from the earth by the atmosphere (*lil*) was the sky vault along which revolved the astral bodies. A similar hemisphere underneath the earth formed the Netherworld where lived the spirits of the dead. Finally, the whole universe (*anki*:[9] sky-earth) was immersed like a gigantic bubble in a boundless, uncreated, primeval ocean of salt water. The earth itself consisted of nothing more than Mesopotamia and the immediate centre stood for the Babylonians or, probably, Nippur for the Sumerians.

How and by whom had the world been created? The answers to the question varied, no doubt because they were founded on different traditions.[16] One legend stated that Anu had created the heavens and Enki the *apsû*, his abode. Another attributed the creation of the universe to the general assembly of all the gods and yet another to only four great gods acting collectively. The beginning of an incantation against the 'worm' responsible for toothaches says that Anu created the sky, which created the earth, which in turn created the rivers, the rivers the canals, the canals the marshes and the marshes the worm. But this sounds rather like the nursery rhyme 'The house that Jack built' and

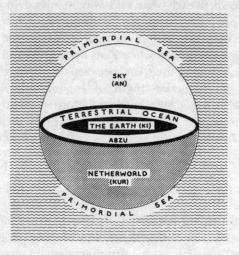

How the Sumerians conceived the world. The earth is a flat disc
surrounded by an ocean; above and below the hemispheres of sky (heavens
residences of the gods) and netherworld (hell) with special gods.
The whole world floats in a primordial ocean.
From S. N. Kramer, L'Histoire commence à Sumer, *1975.*

should perhaps not be taken too seriously. More interesting is a
version from the town of Sippar, according to which the great
Babylonian god Marduk had 'built a reed platform (or raft) on
the surface of the waters, then created dust and poured it
around the platform', because this is actually how the marsh-
Arabs of southern Iraq make the artificial islands upon which
they erect their reed-huts.[17] In general the Sumerians believed
that the primeval ocean, personified by the goddess Nammu,
had begotten alone a male sky and a female earth intimately
joined together. The fruit of their union, the air-god Enlil, had
separated the sky from the earth and, with the latter, had
engendered all living creatures. The theory that the ocean was
the primordial element from which the universe was born, that

the shape of the universe had resulted from the forceful separation of heaven from earth by a third party was generally
adopted in Sumer, Babylonia and Assyria, and forms the basis
of the most complete and detailed story of creation that we
possess: the great Babylonian epic called, from its opening
sentence, *Enuma elish*, 'When on high . . .' But the Babylonian
genesis has still wider philosophical implications; it describes
the creation not as a beginning but as an end, not as the
gratuitous and inexplicable act of one god but as the result of
a cosmic battle, the fundamental and eternal struggle between
those two aspects of nature: Good and Evil, Order and
Chaos.

Enuma elish is a long poem in seven tablets originally composed
during the Old Babylonian period (beginning of the second
millennium), though all the copies found so far were written
during the first millennium B.C. In most copies the main part
is played by Marduk, the patron-god of Babylon, but an
Assyrian version substitutes the name of Ashur, the national
god of Assyria, for that of Marduk. On the other hand, Marduk
is once called in the poem 'the Enlil of the gods', and as we
know that Marduk had usurped the rank and prerogatives of
the Sumerian god Enlil, we may confidently surmise that the
hero of the epic was originally Enlil, as in the Sumerian cosmogony already mentioned.[18]

The Mesopotamian mythographers took their inspiration
from their own country. If we stand on a misty morning near
the present Iraqi sea-shore, at the mouth of the Shatt-el-'Arab,
what do we see? Low banks of clouds hang over the horizon;
large pools of sweet water seeping from underground or left
over from the river floods mingle freely with the salty waters of
the Persian Gulf; of the low mud-flats which normally form the
landscape no more than a few feet are visible; all around us sea,
sky and earth are mixed in a nebulous, watery chaos. This is
how the authors of the poem, who must have often witnessed
such a spectacle, imagined the beginning of the world. When
nothing yet had a name, that is to say when nothing had yet

been created, they wrote, Apsu (the fresh waters), Tiamat (the salt waters) and Mummu (the clouds[19]) formed together one single confused body:

> *Enuma elish la nabú shamamu . . .*
> When on high the heaven had not been named,
> Firm ground below had not been called by name,
> Naught but primordial Apsu, their begetter.
>   (And) Mummu (and ?) Tiamat, she who bore them all,
> Their waters commingling as a single body;
> No reed-hut had been matted, no marsh land had appeared;
> When no gods whatever had been brought into being,
> Uncalled by name, their destinies undetermined –
> Then it was that the gods were formed within them.

In the landscape described above larger patches of land emerge from the mist as the sun rises, and soon a clear-cut line separates the sky from the waters and the waters from the earth. So in the myth the first gods to emerge from the chaos were Lahmu and Lahamu, representing the silt; then came Anshar and Kishar, the twin horizons of sky and earth. Anshar and Kishar begot Anu, and Anu in turn begot Ea (Enki). At the same time, or shortly afterwards, a number of lesser deities were born from Apsu and Tiamat, but of these gods the poem says nothing except that they were turbulent and noisy. They 'troubled Tiamat's belly' and disturbed their parents so much that they decided to destroy them. When they heard of this plan the great gods Lahmu and Lahamu, Anshar and Kishar, Anu and Ea were shocked and amazed: 'they remained speechless', no doubt thinking that the exuberance of Life was preferable to the peace of a sterile Confusion. However, 'Ea the all-wise' soon found a means of wrecking the evil scheme. He 'devised and set up a master design': he cast a magic spell upon Mummu and paralysed him; in the same way Apsu was put to sleep and slain. After this double victory Ea retired to his temple, now founded on the abyss of sweet waters (*apsû*) and with his wife

Damkina engendered a son, Marduk, who possessed outstanding qualities:

> Perfect were his members beyond comprehension . . .
> Unsuited for understanding, difficult to perceive.
> Four were his eyes, four were his ears;
> When he moved his lips, fire blazed forth.
> Large were all four hearing organs,
> And the eyes, in like number, scanned all things.
> He was the loftiest of the gods, surpassing was his stature;
> His members were enormous, he was exceedingly tall.

Meanwhile, Tiamat was still alive and free. Delirious with rage, she declared war on the gods. She created a number of fierce dragons and monstrous serpents 'sharp of tooth, unsparing of fangs, with venom for blood', and placed one of her sons, Kingu, at the head of the gruesome army. The gods were terrified. Anshar 'smote his loins and bit his lips' in distress, and declared that Kingu should be put to death. But who was to do this? One after another, the gods declined to fight. Finally, Marduk accepted under one condition: that he be made their king. 'Set up the assembly,' said he, 'proclaim supreme my destiny, let my word, instead of yours, determine the fates.' The gods had no alternative but to agree. They met at a banquet and, slightly inebriated, they endowed Marduk with the royal powers and insignia. Marduk chose his weapons: the bow, the lightning, the flood-storm, the four winds, the net. He clad himself with 'an armour of terror, a turban of fearsome halo', and mounted on his storm-chariot went forth alone to fight the forces of Chaos. At the sight of him, the army of monsters disbanded; Kingu, their chief, was captured. As for Tiamat, she was caught in Marduk's net and, as she opened her mouth, he at once blew the four winds into her stomach. He then pierced her heart with an arrow, smashed her skull with his mace, and finally split her body open 'like a shell-fish'. Half of her 'he set up and ceiled it as sky', the other half he placed beneath the earth.

After his victory Marduk put the universe in order. Having in the new sky fixed the course of the sun, the moon and the stars, he decided to create mankind:

> I will establish a savage (*lullu*), 'man' shall be his name.
> Verily, savage-man I will create.
> He shall be charged with the service of the gods
>   That they might be at ease!

On Ea's advice Kingu was put to death, and from his blood Marduk and his father fashioned the first human being. Thereafter Marduk divided the gods into two groups: three hundred of them to dwell in heaven, three hundred to live on earth side by side with humanity. As a reward for his victory the gods built Marduk's great temple in Babylon, Esagila, and, assembled at another great banquet, they 'proclaimed his fifty names'.

Childish as this story may sound, it was loaded with grave significance for the Babylonians. To their deeply religious minds it offered a non-rational but nevertheless acceptable 'explanation' of the universe. Among other things, it described how the world had assumed its alleged shape; it made good the fact that men must be the servants of the gods; it accounted for the natural wickedness of humanity, created from the blood of evil Kingu; it also justified the exorbitant powers of Marduk (originally Enlil) by his election and his heroic exploit. But, above all, it had, like the Sacred Marriage, a powerful magical virtue. If every year for nearly two millennia *Enuma elish* was recited by the priests of Babylon on the fourth day of the New Year Festival it was because the Babylonians felt that the great cosmic struggle had never really ended and that the forces of Chaos were always ready to challenge the established Order of the gods.

Life, Death and Destiny

The commerce of men with the gods, like the commerce of men between themselves, had its degrees. If the King of Babylon was

directly under Marduk's orders the Babylonian peasant was in
closer contact with Ashnan, the barley-god, or Shumuqan, the
cattle-god, than with Anu or Enlil. Besides, there were enough
deities to cater for the important events of life; whenever required, an invocation and an offering of dates would propitiate
Gula, the goddess of childbirth, or Pasag, the protector of
travellers. In case of dire emergency, the greater deities could
be approached through the clergy or, more directly, through
the offices of his 'personal god'.

Sumerians, Babylonians and Assyrians looked up to their
gods as servants look to their good masters: with submission and
fear, but also with admiration and love. For kings and common-
ers alike, obedience to divine orders was the greatest of qualities,
as the service of the gods was the most imperative of duties.
While the celebration of the various festivals and the performance of the complicated rituals of the cult were the task of
priests, it was the duty of every citizen to send offerings to the
temples, to attend the main religious ceremonies, to care for the
dead, to pray and make penance, and to observe the innumerable rules and taboos that marked nearly every moment of his
life. A sensible man 'feared the gods' and scrupulously followed
their prescriptions. To do otherwise was not only foolish but
sinful, and sin – as everyone knew – brought on man's head the
most terrible punishments. Yet it would be wrong to think of
the Mesopotamian religion as a purely formal affair, when
hymns and prayers disclose the most delicate feelings and burst
with genuine emotion.[20] The Mesopotamians put their confidence in their gods; they relied upon them as children rely
upon their parents, they talked to them as to their 'real fathers
and mothers', who could be offended and punish, but who
could also be placated and forgive.

Offerings, sacrifices and the observance of religious prescriptions were not all that the Mesopotamian gods required from
their worshippers. To 'make their hearts glow with libation', to
make them 'exultant with succulent meals' was certainly deserving, but it was not enough. The favours of the gods went to

those who led 'a good life', who were good parents, good sons, good neighbours, good citizens, and who practised virtues as highly esteemed then as they are now: kindness and compassion, righteousness and sincerity, justice, respect of the law and of the established order. Every day worship your god, says a Babylonian 'Counsel of Wisdom', but also:

> To the feeble show kindness,
> Do not insult the downtrodden,
> Do charitable deeds, render service all your days . . .
> Do not utter libel, speak what is of good report,
> Do not say evil things, speak well of people . . .[21]

As a reward for piousness and good conduct the gods gave man help and protection in danger, comfort in distress and bereavement, good health, honourable social position, wealth, numerous children, long life, happiness. This was perhaps not a very noble ideal by Christian standards, but the Sumerians and Babylonians were contented with it, for they were practical, down-to-earth people who loved and enjoyed life above everything. To live for ever was the dearest of their dreams, and a number of their myths – in particular Adapa and the Gilgamesh cycle (see next chapter) – aimed at explaining why man had been denied the privilege of immortality.

But only the gods were immortal. For men death was ineluctable and had to be accepted:

> Only the gods live for ever under the sun,
> As for mankind, numbered are their days,
>   Whatever they achieve is but wind.[22]

What happened after death? Thousands of graves with their funerary equipment testify to a general belief in an after-life where the dead carried with them their most precious belongings and received food and drink from the living. But such details of the Mesopotamian eschatology as we can extract from the myth 'Inanna's descent to the Netherworld' or the Sumerian cycle of Gilgamesh are scanty and often contradictory. The 'land of no return' was a vast space somewhere underground, with a huge palace where reigned Ereshkigal and her husband Nergal, the god of war and pestilence, surrounded by a number of deities and guards. To reach this palace the spirits of the dead had to cross a river by ferry, as in the Greek Hades, and take off their clothes. Thereafter, they lived a wretched and dreary life in a place:

> Where dust is their food, clay their sustenance;
> Where they see no light and dwell in darkness,
> Where they are clad like birds with garments of wings,
> Where over door and bolt dust has spread.[23]

Yet we learn from other sources that the sun lit the Netherworld on its way round the earth, and that the sun-god Utu pronounced judgement on the dead, so that they were probably not all treated with the same severity. It would seem that the Sumerian idea of hell was as vague as ours, and that a great deal of this literature is just poetical embroidery on a loose theme.

Death, however, was not the Mesopotamians' sole preoccupation. They had, like us, their share of disease, poverty, frustration and sorrow, and like us they wondered: how could all this happen when the gods ruled the world? How could Evil prevail over Good? To be sure, it was often possible to put the blame on man himself. So tight was the network of rules and prohibitions that surrounded him that to sin and offend the gods was the easiest thing to do. Yet there were occasions when the irreproachable had nevertheless been punished, when the gods seemed to behave in the most incomprehensible way. A Babylonian poem called *Ludlul bêl nemeqi*, 'I will praise the Lord of Wisdom', pictures the feelings of a man, once noble, rich and healthy, now ruined, hated by all and afflicted with the most terrible diseases. As it turns out, in the end the god Marduk takes pity on him and saves him; but our Babylonian Job had had time to doubt the wisdom of Heaven. Bitterly he exclaimed:

Who knows the will of the gods in heaven?
Who understands the plan of the underworld gods?
Where have mortals learnt the way of a god?
He who was alive yesterday is dead today.
For a minute he was dejected, suddenly he is exuberant.
One moment people are singing in exaltation,
Another they groan like professional mourners . . .
I am appalled at these things; I do not understand their
    significance.[24]

But the so-called Babylonian 'pessimism' was much more than a temporary outburst of despair. It was metaphysical in essence, not ethical, and had its roots in the natural conditions which prevailed in Mesopotamia itself. The Tigris–Euphrates valley is a country of violent and unexpected changes. The same rivers that bring life can also bring disaster. The winters may be too cold or rainless, the summer winds too dry for the ripening of the dates. A cloudburst can in a moment turn a parched and dusty plain into a sea of mud, and on any fine day a sandstorm can suddenly darken the sky and blow devastation. Confronted with these manifestations of supernatural forces, the Mesopotamian felt bewildered and helpless. He was seized with frightful anxiety. Nothing, he believed, was ever sure. His own life, the life of his family, the produce of his fields and of his cattle, the rhythm and measure of the river floods, the cycle of seasons and indeed the very existence of the universe were constantly at stake. If the cosmos did not revert to confusion, if the world order was none the less maintained, if the human race survived, if life came again to the fields after the scorching heat of the summer, if the moon and the sun and the stars kept revolving in the sky, it was by an act of will of the gods. But the divine decision had not been pronounced once and for all at the origin of all things; it had to be repeated again and again, particularly at the turn of the year, just before that terrible oriental summer when nature seems to die and the future appears loaded with uncertainty. The only thing man could do in these critical circumstances was to provoke the decision of the gods and

secure their goodwill by performing the age-old rites that ensured the maintenance of order, the revival of nature and the
permanence of life. Each spring, therefore, a great and poignant
ceremony took place in many cities and especially in Babylon:
the *akitu* or New Year Festival, which combined the great
drama of Creation and the annual reinstatement of the king,
and culminated in the gathering of all the gods who solemnly
'decreed the Destinies' (see Chapter 24) Only then could the
king go back to his throne, the shepherd to his flock,
the peasant to his field. The Mesopotamian was reassured:
the world would exist for another year.

CHAPTER 7

AN AGE OF HEROES

If the Sumerians were not short of theories as to the origin of the universe, they were regrettably more discreet about their own origins, thereby standing in sharp contrast with, for instance, the Israelites who never forgot that Abraham, their ancestor, had come from Ur and who located the earthly paradise in the garden of Eden (a word derived from the Sumerian *edin* meaning 'plain' or 'open country'), between the Tigris and the Euphrates. The Sumerians have left two texts which allude to a golden age but unfortunately do not provide information on their ancestral cradle. The first one is a passage of the epic tale *Enmerkar and the Lord of Aratta*[1] which speaks of very remote times when there were no dangerous animals and when 'all peoples together paid homage to Enlil in one single language'. This blissful unity ended when rivalries between Enki and Enlil led to a 'confusion of tongues', a theme which recurs in the biblical story of the Tower of Babel.

The second text is a strange and complicated myth called *Enki and Ninhursag*[2] (in which the action takes place in Dilmun the island of Bahrain and neighbouring regions). To put it briefly, in this myth the god Enki makes Dilmun a fertile country by creating freshwater springs, while the goddess Ninhursag creates a number of healing gods, one of these being Enshag who appears as Inzak in stone inscriptions found in Bahrain and in the island of Failaka, near Kuwait. The first lines of the myth describe Dilmun as a clean, pure and bright country where old age, disease and death are unknown, and where:

> The raven utters no cries,
> The *ittidu*-bird utters not the cry of the *ittidu*-bird

The lion kills not,
The wolf snatches not the lamb,
Unknown is the kid-devouring wild dog . . .

Does this mean that the Sumerians originated from, or at least had once lived in this blessed island? There is nothing in the myth that suggests it, and we are inclined to see in these lines an indirect reference to the East, traditionally 'the land of the living' and the West, 'the land of the dead', perhaps combined with an attempt by the Sumerians to include in their pantheon Inzak and all other gods of Dilmun – a country with which they had very close commercial relations in the third millennium B.C. In reality, the Sumerians, like most ancient peoples, saw their country as the hub of the universe and themselves as the direct descendants of the first human beings. They used the same ideogram for *kalam*, 'The Country' (i.e. Summer) and for *ukú*, 'people in general' and 'the people of Sumer' in particular. Significantly, the other ideogram for 'country', *kur*, pictures a mountain and was originally used in connection with foreign countries only. Clearly the Sumerians identified themselves with the earliest inhabitants of Mesopotamia and indeed with the initial population of the earth. How, then, did they imagine their own 'prehistory'?

From 'Adam' to the Deluge

In the preceding chapter we have seen how, in the great Babylonian Epic of Creation, the first and nameless 'savage-man' had been created from the blood of the evil god Kingu. Other myths such as '*Atrahasis*' (see below) refer to the making by the gods of one or two human beings either from clay or from the blood of minor deities, or both. But nowhere are we told what happened to these Adams or Eves. Up to now the Sumerian literature has offered no close parallel to the biblical story of the Lost Paradise, and to find a Mesopotamian account of the Fall of Man we must turn to the legend of Adapa,[3] written in the middle of the second millennium B.C.

Created by the god Ea (Enki) as 'the model of men', Adapa was a priest of Eridu who fulfilled various tasks in Ea's temple, the most important being to supply his master with food. One day, as he was fishing on the 'great sea', the South Wind suddenly blew with such violence that his boat capsized and he himself was nearly drowned. In his anger Adapa uttered a curse whereby the wings of the South Wind – that big demon-bird – were broken, and for a long time 'the South Wind blew not upon the land'. It so happens that the south(-easterly) wind is of capital importance to agriculture in southern Iraq, for it brings what little rain there is in winter, and in summer causes the ripening of the dates.[4] When the great god Anu heard what Adapa had done he was naturally much angered and sent for the culprit. But Ea came to Adapa's aid. He told him that upon his arrival at Anu's gate in heaven he would meet the two vegetation gods, Dumuzi and Ningishzida (whom Adapa, it seems, had indirectly 'killed' by suppressing the South Wind), but if he clad himself in mourning and showed signs of grief and contrition the two gods would be appeased; they would 'smile' and even speak to Anu in Adapa's favour. Anu would then no longer treat Adapa as a criminal but as a guest; he would, after oriental fashion, offer him food and water, clothes to put on and oil with which to anoint himself. The last two Adapa could accept but, warned Ea:

> When they offer thee bread of death,
> Thou shalt not eat it. When they offer thee water of death,
> Thou shalt not drink it . . .
> This advice that I have given thee, neglect not; the words
> That I have spoken to thee, hold fast!

Everything happened as Ea had said even beyond expectation, for Anu, touched no doubt by Adapa's repentance and sincere confession, offered him instead of the food and drink of death the 'bread of life' and the 'water of life'. But Adapa, following strictly his master's advice, refused the gifts that would have rendered him immortal. Whereupon, Anu dismissed him with these simple words:

Take him away and return him to earth.

Whether Ea's proverbial foresight had failed him, or whether he had deliberately lied to Adapa is difficult to determine. But the result was that Adapa lost his right to immortality. He lost it through blind obedience as Adam lost it through arrogant disobedience. In both cases man had condemned himself to death.

The biblical parallel, however, goes no farther for the time being, for even if we see in Adapa a Mesopotamian Adam, we are lacking that long line of posterity which in the Bible links the first man with the Hebrews' true ancestor, Abraham. The Sumerians were not possessed of the passion for genealogy that was characteristic of the nomadic Semites. They viewed their own history from a different angle. The gods, they reasoned, had created mankind for a definite purpose: to feed and serve them. They had themselves fixed the details of this service, they had 'perfected the rites and exalted the divine ordinances'. Humanity, however, was but a great, rather stupid flock. It needed shepherds, rulers, priestly kings chosen and appointed by the gods to enforce the divine law. At some remote date, therefore, almost immediately after the creation of mankind, 'the exalted tiara and the throne of kingship' were 'lowered from heaven', and from then on a succession of monarchs led the destinies of Sumer and Akkad on behalf of and for the benefit of the gods. Thus was justified by reference to the most distant past the theory of divinely inspired kingship, current in Mesopotamia from the third millennium onwards. Yet some modern scholars hold different views. They believe that the original political system of Sumer was what they call a 'primitive democracy'. Monarchy, they say, developed comparatively late in proto-history, when the warrior chief (*lugal*), formerly elected by an assembly of citizens for short periods of crisis, took over for good the control of the city-state.[5] This theory, first put forward by Th. Jacobsen in a penetrating study cannot be lightly dismissed. Thus the passage in the Epic of Creation describing the election of Enlil (or Marduk) to the rank of 'champion of the gods' for the specific purpose of waging war against Tiamat may reflect what happened on earth in similar circumstances. There is also no doubt that there were in Early Dynastic Sumer local assemblies, especially of older men, which played a part in the government of each city. But as pointed out by other Sumerologists, these assemblies (*ukin*) appear to have been purely consultative bodies summoned by the rulers on rare occasions, so that the word 'democracy' in this context is perhaps a misnomer. Judging from the texts at our disposal, there is no clear-cut evidence in the Sumerian tradition of a period when the city-states were ruled by collective institutions, and as far as we can go back into the past we see nothing but rulers or monarchs second only to the gods.

We possess by chance a document that gives us an uninter-rupted list of kings from the very beginnings of monarchy down to the eighteenth century B.C. This is the famous 'Sumerian King List' compiled from about fifteen different texts and pub-lished by Th. Jacobsen in 1939.[6] Despite its imperfections, this document is invaluable: not only does it embody and summarize very old Sumerian traditions but it provides an excellent chrono-logical framework in which can be placed most of the great legends of the Sumerian heroic age. For the Sumerians, like the ancient Greeks, Hindus and Germans, had their heroic age, their age of demigods and superhuman kings who stood on equal term with the gods and performed fantastic feats of valour. Only now do we begin to realize that some at least of these heroes are only half-mythical and belong, in fact, to history.

According to the Sumerian King List, kingship was first 'lowered from heaven' in the city of Eridu, a remarkable statement if we remember that Eridu is one of the most ancient Sumerian settlements in southern Iraq (see Chapter 4). Then, after no less than 64,800 years during which only two kings reigned in Eridu, for some untold reason kingship was 'carried' to Bad-tibira (three kings, one of them the god Dumuzi himself, 108,000 years). From Bad-tibira it passed on successively to

Larak (one king, 28,800 years), to Sippar (one king, 21,000 years) and to Shuruppak (one king, 18,600 years).[7] These incredible figures, strangely reminiscent of Adam's posterity in the Bible, have no hidden significance; they simply express a widespread belief in a golden age when men lived much longer than usual and were endowed with truly supernatural qualities. But an even closer comparison with the Old Testament is called for by the brief sentence which follows the mention of Ubar-Tutu, King of Shuruppak, and closes the first paragraph, as it were, of the Sumerian King List:

> The Flood swept thereover.

Here we feel irresistibly compelled to interrupt our narrative and examine one of the most controversial and fascinating problems of Mesopotamian archaeology and mythology: the problem of the Great Flood.

The Great Flood

In 1872 George Smith, then a young British assyriologist, announced to an astonished world that he had discovered, among the many tablets from Ashurbanipal's library in the British Museum, an account of the Deluge strikingly similar to that given in the Bible (*Genesis* vi. 11–viii. 22). The story he had in hand was but an episode from a long poem in twelve tablets known as the Gilgamesh Epic of which we shall speak later. The hero of the epic, Gilgamesh, King of Uruk, is in search of the secret of immortality and eventually meets Ut-napishtim, the only man to have been granted eternal life and the son, incidentally, of Ubar-Tutu, King of Shuruppak. This, briefly, is what Ut-napishtim tells Gilgamesh:[8]

At some indefinite date, 'when Shuruppak was already an old city', the gods decided to send a deluge in order to destroy the sinful human race. But Ea took pity on Ut-napishtim and, secretly speaking to him through the thin wall of his reed-hut, advised him to tear down his house, abandon his possessions, build a ship of a certain size, take with him 'the seed of all living creatures' and prepare himself for the worst. The next day work was started on the ark and soon a huge, seven-decked vessel was ready, caulked with bitumen and loaded with gold, silver, game, beasts and Ut-napishtim's family, relations and workmen. When the weather became 'frightful to behold' our Babylonian Noah knew that the time for the deluge had come. He entered the ship and closed the door. Then, 'as soon as the first shimmer of morning beamed forth, a black cloud came up from out of the horizon', announcing the most terrible tempest of wind, rain, lightning and thunder that man had ever witnessed. The dykes gave way, the earth was shrouded in darkness; even the gods were panic-stricken and regretted what they had undertaken:

> The gods cowered like dogs and crouched in distress.
> Ishtar cried out like a woman in travail . . .
> 'How could I command war to destroy my people,
> For it is I who bring forth my people' . . .
> The Anunnaki gods wept with her;
> The gods sat bowed and weeping . . .
> Six days and six nights
> The wind blew, the downpour, the tempest and the flood
> overwhelmed the land . . .

On the seventh day, however, the tempest subsided. Says Ut-napishtim:

> I opened a window and light fell upon my face.
> I looked upon the 'sea', all was silence,
> And all mankind had turned to clay.

The ark landed on mount Nisir,[9] but no land was visible besides the rock that held fast the ship. After a week had elapsed Ut-napishtim sent forth a dove, but it came back; he sent forth a swallow, but it also came back; he sent forth a raven, and this time the raven found land and did not return. Ut-napishtim then poured a libation on top of the mountain and offered a sacrifice of sweet cane, cedar and myrtle:

> The gods smelled the savour,
> The gods smelled the sweet savour,
> The gods gathered like flies over the sacrificer.

If Ishtar, in particular, was delighted, Enlil, who had ordered the deluge and whose plans were frustrated, was filled with anger and put the blame on Ea. But so well did Ea plead his own cause and the cause of mankind that Enlil's heart was touched. He entered the ship and blessed Ut-napishtim and his wife, saying:

> Hitherto Ut-napishtim has been but a man,
> But now Ut-napishtim and his wife shall be like unto us gods.
> In the distance, at the mouth of the rivers, Ut-napishtim shall
> dwell.

Needless to say, George Smith's publication of this story made headlines in the newspapers of the time. As new cuneiform texts became available, however, other versions of the Flood legend, less complete but older than the Gilgamesh version (written at Nineveh in the seventh century B.C.), were discovered. The name of the hero varied. In a Sumerian text from Nippur dated about 1700 B.C. he was called Ziusudra, while in a Babylonian epic of slightly later date he was called Atrahasis, 'Exceedingly Wise', probably a nickname for Ut-napishtim himself.[10] But, allowance being made for other minor variations, the theme was always the same: a gigantic Flood had swept over the earth and all but one (or two) human beings had perished; in the long history of mankind the deluge marks a definite break and the replacement of one race of men by another. The resemblance with the biblical story is, of course, striking; furthermore, it seems probable that the Hebrews had borrowed from a long and well-established Mesopotamian tradition. Quite naturally, the question arose: are there traces of such a cataclysm in Mesopotamia?

Hitherto, sizeable deposits of water-borne clay and sand due to a major and prolonged inundation have been found on only three Mesopotamian sites: Ur, Kish and Shuruppak. At Ur, seven out of the fourteen test pits dug by the late Sir Leonard Woolley between 1929 and 1934 have revealed such deposits at different levels. The deepest and thickest of these was sandwiched between two occupational layers of the Ubaid period, and Woolley always maintained, without convincing reasons, that this was the biblical Flood.[11] The other, and thinner, Ur deposits were dated to about 2800–2600 B.C., and so were the several deposits discovered at Kish. As for the single 'sterile layer' found at Shuruppak, its probable date is 2900 B.C. The presence on these sites of such alluvial deposits raises difficult geophysical problems,[12] but it does not provide evidence of a widespread inundation covering hundreds of square kilometres, let alone the entire Near East. The only events it reflects are *limited* inundations probably due to overflows and changes in river courses. It must be noted, for instance, that Eridu, which lies in a shallow depression some 20 kilometres from Ur and has been excavated down to the virgin soil, has yielded no trace of a flood.

But if there never was in Mesopotamia (and elsewhere) a cataclysmic Flood of biblical dimensions, what then was at the root of the Mesopotamian legend? Several theories have been put forward, ranging from an alleged universal desire to cancel a slice of the past to a vague remembrance, handed down through generations, of the torrential Pleistocene rains. However, none of these theories is satisfactory or even relevant, for it appears clearly from the cuneiform texts that the Flood was not a natural accident but a deliberate attempt by the gods at getting rid of mankind. Why should the gods want to do this? The Gilgamesh epic and the Sumerian flood story are silent on this point, but a recently published fragment of *Atrahasis* may give us a clue.[13] This remarkable epic begins with the creation of male and female human beings who would relieve the lesser gods, the *Anunnaki*, from their exhausting work on earth. All goes well at first, but:

> Twelve hundred years had not yet passed
> When the land extended and the people multiplied.

> The earth was bellowing like a bull,
> The gods got distressed with their uproar.

In order to reduce this noisy crowd to silence, the gods unleash an epidemic followed by a terrible drought, but these are of no avail: men and women continue to multiply, even though starvation forces them to eat their own children. Finally, the gods release the Flood, not knowing that Ea will warn and save Atrahasis, the 'Exceedingly Wise'. The Flood itself is described in about the same words as in *Gilgamesh*, but it is the end of our epic which deserves our attention, for Ea now appears as a precursor of Malthus, advocating infertility, infantile mortality and celibacy as remedies against over-population. Turning to Mami/Nintu, the mother-goddess, Ea says:

> O Lady of Birth, creatress of the Fates . . .
> Let there be among the people bearing women and barren women,
> Let there be among the people a *Pashittu*-demon,
> Let it seize the baby from the mother's lap,
> Establish *Ugbabtu*-priestesses, *Entu* priestesses and *Igisitu*-priestesses.
> They shall indeed be tabooed, and thus cut off child-bearing.*

This presumably means that in the future the population increase must be controlled to prevent the gods from sending another Flood, this being the ultimate solution obviously inspired by the damage caused by major local inundations.

As for the Flood mentioned in the Sumerian King List as a specific event, a switch of power from one city to another that occurred at a certain date, it is perhaps not unreasonable to suggest that it might have been introduced in the list by the scribes of Shuruppak who had witnessed two or three simultaneous disasters in that city around 2900 B.C.: a military defeat, a severe inundation and possibly a (relative) 'demographic explosion'. If this were the case, then the Flood-event would merge with the Flood-myth, but of these two tales it is the myth that

---

* All these priestesses were forbidden to bear children.

has survived and will never cease to fascinate us and arouse our curiosity.

Dynasties of Supermen

After the Flood, says the Sumerian King List, kingship was again 'lowered from heaven', this time in Kish, a city now represented by an important group of tells, about sixteen kilometres due east of Babylon.[14] The first 'dynasty' * of Kish comprises twenty-three reigns with an average duration of one thousand years per reign. If we omit one king whose name could not be read by the scribe who compiled the list from old tablets, we observe that out of twenty-two monarchs twelve bear Semitic names or nicknames, such as *Kalbum*, 'dog', *Qalumu*, 'lamb', or *Zuqaqip*, 'scorpion'; six have Sumerian names and four have names of unknown origin. This is important because it shows the mixture of ethnic elements in southern Iraq at an early date, the predominance of Semites in the region of Kish and the apparent absence of rivalry between Sumerians and Semites within the same city-state. As we shall see in the next chapter, we have good reason to believe that this dynasty was at least partly historical and should be placed shortly after 2800 B.C. Yet one of its kings is expressly designated as a mythical figure: 'Etana, a shepherd, the one who ascended to heaven', and as it happens that we possess Babylonian and Assyrian tablets which give us more details about Etana, we can enlarge on this point.[15]

The Etana legend begins like a fable. The serpent and the eagle lived on the same tree and helped each other as good neighbours should. But the eagle one day devoured the young of the serpent. The serpent went weeping to the sun-god Sha-

---

* The word 'dynasty' in Mesopotamian history should not be taken as meaning a royal *family*, but a succession of kings ruling over the same city-state for a period of time. The Sumerian King List mentions only the dynasties which ruled, over the *whole* country of Sumer.

mash, who prompted the following stratagem: the serpent hid in the belly of a dead ox, and when the eagle came to devour the carcass, the reptile took his revenge; he caught the big bird, broke his 'heel'; plucked him and threw him into a pit. Now a certain Etana, who had no children and was desperately in need of the 'plant of birth' which grows only in heaven, also cried to Shamash, and Shamash advised him to rescue the eagle, win his friendship and use him as a vehicle to fly to heaven. This Etana did. 'Upon the eagle's breast he placed his breast, upon the feathers of his wings he placed his hands, upon his sides he placed his arms' and, in this uncomfortable position, he took off for a series of breathtaking flights that took him to the gates of Anu, Enlil, Ea, Sin, Shamash, Adad and Ishtar. Then, moved, perhaps, by a spirit of adventure, he went even higher. Gradually he saw the earth shrink to the size of a furrow and the sea to the size of a bread basket. But when land and sea were no longer visible Etana panicked: 'My friend, I will not ascend to heaven!' he shouted and, loosening his grip, he plunged head down towards the earth, followed by the eagle. The end of the tale is unclear, due to lacunae in the tablets, but we may assume that Etana reached his goal, for not only did he live a respectable 1,560 years but, according to the King List, he had a son and heir called Balikh.

The Sumerian King List gives the impression that the last king of the First Dynasty of Kish, Agga, was defeated in battle by the first king of the first dynasty of Uruk; but we know that the two dynasties overlapped and that Agga, in fact, was contemporary with the *fifth* King of Uruk, Gilgamesh. We owe this information to a short Sumerian poem[16] which describes how Agga sent Gilgamesh an ultimatum demanding that Uruk submit to Kish, how the ultimatum was rejected and Uruk besieged and how, at the sight of mighty Gilgamesh peering over the wall, the enemy was overwhelmed with fear and 'cast itself down'. In the end it was Agga who became the vassal of Gilgamesh, and Kish which submitted to Uruk, as indicated in the King List. Yet if the predecessors of Gilgamesh did not rule over the whole country of Sumer but only over Uruk they were prominent figures all the same, since we have in order of succession: Meskiaggasher, son of the sun-god Utu, who 'went into the sea and came out (from it) to the mountains'; Enmerkar, 'the one who built Uruk'; divine Lugalbanda, a 'shepherd', and finally, Dumuzi, the vegetation-god called here 'a fisherman'. The deeds of at least two of these heroes and demigods are now familiar to us, owing to the publication of four Sumerian epic tales which once formed parts of a 'cycle of Enmerkar' and of a 'cycle of Lugalbanda'.[17] All these legends revolve around the usually strained relations between Uruk and Aratta, a far-away country separated from Sumer by 'seven mountains' and probably to be located in Iran.[18] In one of these tales we are told at length of the considerable difficulties encountered by Enmerkar in obtaining gold, silver, lapis-lazuli and precious stones from the Lord of Aratta, either by threats or in return for grain – a situation which must have repeated itself again and again in the long history of Mesopotamia and which perhaps underlies the endless wars between that country and mountainous Elam. In another tale we see Uruk besieged by the MAR.TU folk, i.e. the nomadic Amorites of the Syrian desert who, as will be told later, settled in Iraq and took over from the Sumerians at the beginning of the second millennium B.C. If we could be sure that these legends reflected the political situation as it was at the dawn of history and not at the date when they were actually written down (about 1800 B.C.) we would find in them matter of considerable interest to the historian.

Finally, we come to Gilgamesh, the fifth king of the first dynasty of Uruk and the son, we are told, of the goddess Ninsun and of a high priest of Kullab, a district of Uruk. Gilgamesh, whose exploits are reminiscent of those of both Ulysses and Hercules, was the most popular of all Mesopotamian heroes and appears in the form of a brawny, bearded man fighting bulls and lions on a very large number of monuments, from the cylinder-seals of the Jemdat Nasr period to the sculptured reliefs of the Assyrian palaces. Like Enmerkar and Lugal-banda, he had his own cycle of Sumerian legends, apparently unconnected episodes of his life, of which five are known to us.[19] But this is not all. Early in the second millennium a long poem was composed, which amalgamated some of the older Sumerian legends with new material. The resulting 'Gilgamesh Epic' has by chance survived practically complete, and as it is without any doubt the masterpiece of Assyro-Babylonian literature and, indeed, one of the most beautiful epic tales of the ancient world, we must at least try to give a brief summary of its content, referring the reader to the several excellent translations that have been published.[20]

The Story of Gilgamesh

'He who saw everything to the ends of the world', as the title of the poem has it, Gilgamesh was two-thirds god and one-third man. He was supremely strong, brave and handsome, and cared much for Uruk, his city. The Babylonians admired in particular the strong wall which he had built around it – perhaps the 9.7 kilometre long wall of Early Dynastic times that still encircles the ruins of Warka. Yet his arrogance, ruthlessness and depravity were a subject of grave concern for the citizens of Uruk. They complained to the great god Anu, and Anu instructed the goddess Aruru to create another 'wild ox', a 'double' of Gilgamesh, who could challenge him and distract his mind from 'the warrior's daughter and the nobleman's spouse' whom, it appears, he would not leave in peace. So, out of clay Aruru modelled Enkidu, a huge, brutish, hairy creature who lived in the steppe among the wild beasts:

> With the gazelles he feeds on grass,
> With the wild beasts he jostles at the watering places,
> With the teeming creatures, his heart delights in water.

Now, one day a hunter saw Enkidu at a distance and understood why the traps he was setting were always out of action, and why the game kept slipping out of his hands. He reported the matter to Gilgamesh, who set a trap of another kind against the wild man. A woman, a prostitute, was sent forth to the steppe with orders to seduce Enkidu and convert him to civilized life. The harlot had no difficulty in fulfilling the first part of her mission. She then took Enkidu by the hand 'like a mother' and led him to Uruk, where he soon learnt to bathe, anoint himself with perfumed oil, eat bread and indulge in strong drinks. But while in Uruk, Enkidu heard that Gilgamesh was once more going to exercise his *ius primae noctis* in the communal house and bravely barred his way. A terrible fight ensued which ended in mutual affection and peace, Gilgamesh having found a companion of his own stature and Enkidu a master: 'They kissed each other and made a friendship.'

The exuberant Gilgamesh, however, was anxious to make himself a name and persuaded Enkidu to accompany him to the vast and remote Cedar Forest, abode of Huwawa (or Humbaba), a frightening giant 'whose mouth was fire, whose breath was death'. Having prepared their weapons and prayed to the gods, the two friends left Uruk and, covering in three days the distance it normally took six weeks to travel, they reached the Cedar Forest:

> They stood still and gazed at the forest,
> They looked at the height of the cedars . . .
> From the face of the mountains
> The cedars raise aloft their luxuriance,
> Good is their shadow, full of delight . . .

Having caught the guardian unaware, they entered the forbidden land, and already Gilgamesh was felling tree after tree when Huwawa rose in anger and would have massacred the two adventurers if Shamash had not come to their rescue; he sent all the eight winds against Huwawa, who, paralysed, acknowledged himself beaten and begged for his life. But Gilgamesh and Enkidu cut off his head and triumphantly returned to Uruk.

Following this exploit, the goddess Ishtar herself fell in love with Gilgamesh and offered to marry him; but Gilgamesh would have none of it. Reminding the unfaithful goddess how she had treated her numerous lovers, from Tammuz, for whom she had 'ordained wailing year after year', to the shepherd and the gardener, whom she had turned into wolf and spider, he abused her in the most outrageous terms:

> Thou art but a brazier which goes out in the cold,
> A backdoor which does not keep out blast and windstorms,
> A waterskin which soaks through its bearer,
> A shoe which pinches the foot of its owner!

Bitterly offended, Ishtar asked Anu to send the Bull of Heaven to ravage Uruk. But after the Bull had knocked down man after man, Enkidu seized it by the horns while Gilgamesh thrust a sword into its neck, and as Ishtar was cursing the ruler of Uruk, he tore off the beast's right thigh and tossed it in her face.

Such impudence was more than the gods could stand. They decided that one of the pair should die. Enkidu, therefore, was seized with a long and painful disease and, having reviewed his past life, cursed the harlot and dreamed of the sombre Netherworld, he passed away, mourned by his companion for seven days and nights 'until a worm fell out of his nose'.

The death of Enkidu affected Gilgamesh deeply. For the first time the fiery and fearless King of Uruk realized the full horror of death. Could he also disappear like this? Could he not escape the dreadful fate of the human race?

> Fearing death I roam over the steppe;
> The matter of my friend rests heavy upon me.
> How can I be silent? How can I be still?
> My friend, whom I loved, has turned to clay,
> Must I, too, like him, lay me down
> Not to rise again for ever and ever?

Gilgamesh decided to meet Ut-napishtim, the man who survived the Deluge, and obtain from him the secret of immortality.

First he had to cross the mountain of Mashu, the vast and dark mountain of the setting sun whose entrance was guarded by scorpion-men; but they took pity on him and let him pass. On the other side of the mountain he met Siduri 'the barmaid who dwells on the edge of the sea', and Siduri's advice was to stop worrying and wandering and enjoy life. Yet, touched by his sorrow, she told him where Ut-napishtim could be found: on the other side of an immense and dangerous sea barred by 'the waters of death'. Our hero did not hesitate. He enlisted the help of Urshanabi the boatman, crossed the sea and finally met Ut-napishtim, who told him his own story, the story of the Flood. Could Ut-napishtim do something for Gilgamesh? Yes, he should get hold of a certain thorny plant, the plant of life which grew in the depths of the ocean. Gilgamesh, like a pearlfisher of the Persian Gulf, tied heavy stones to his feet, dived and picked the plant. Alas, on his way home, while he lay asleep near a spring, a snake came out from the water and carried away the precious harvest. There would be no eternal life for Gilgamesh. The conclusion implicit in the story is as pessimistic as Ut-napishtim's address to our hero:

> Do we build houses for ever?
> Does the river for ever raise up and bring on floods?
> The dragon-fly leaves its shell
> That its face might but glance at the face of the sun.
> Since the days of yore there has been no permanence;
> The resting and the dead, how alike they are!

Such is – briefly outlined and unfortunately robbed of its poetical fragrance – the story of Gilgamesh, unquestionably the most famous epic tale in the ancient Near East, judging from the numerous Assyro-Babylonian 'editions' and from the Hittite and Hurrian translations that have come to us.[21] Gilgamesh-the-hero is, of course, a myth. But what of Gilgamesh-the-king? A few years ago one would have strongly doubted his existence; today there are good reasons to believe that a king of that name actually ruled over Uruk, though definite proof is still lacking.

For some time we have had the impression of standing at the moving, ethereal border which separates fiction from reality; we now have the certitude that the time of Gilgamesh corresponds to the earliest period of Mesopotamian history.

CHAPTER 8

THE EARLY DYNASTIC PERIOD

The history of ancient Iraq is divided, like its prehistory, into periods characterized by major political changes often accompanied by changes in the social, economic and cultural fields. The first of these periods begins around 2900 B.C. and ends with the conquest of Sumer by the Semitic king of Akkad, Sargon, in 2334 B.C. or thereabouts. For this reason, it is sometimes called 'Presargonic', though the term 'Early Dynastic' (abbreviated ED) is usually preferred by English-speaking scholars. The Early Dynastic period, in turn, has been broken down into three parts: ED I (c. 2900–2750 B.C.), ED II (c. 2750–2600 B.C.) and ED III (c. 2600–2334 B.C.), but it must be made quite clear from the start that if by 'history' is meant records of political events, or at least genuine incriptions from local rulers, then only part of ED II and the whole of ED III are historical; ED I and the first decades of ED II belong to prehistory in the narrow sense of the term until the chance discovery of an inscription, from one of the earliest kings of Uruk or Kish mentioned in the Sumerian King List, pushes back overnight into the past the beginnings of history, as has already happened twice.

Until the First World War, our knowledge of the Early Dynastic period was almost entirely derived from the excavations carried out by the French at Lagash – or rather Girsu[1] – nowadays Tell Luh or Telloh, a large mound near the Shatt al-Gharraf, forty-eight kilometres due north of Nasriya.[2] Besides remarkable works of art, these excavations have yielded numerous inscriptions which have made it possible to reconstitute in fairly great detail the history of Lagash and to draw up a list of its rulers from about 2500 to 2000 B.C. Unfortunately, the information thus obtained was practically restricted to one city, and its rulers did not figure on the King List, probably because they were not considered to have held sway over the whole of Sumer.

Then, in the winter of 1922–3, Sir Leonard Woolley found atl-'Ubaid, among the debris of magnificent bronze sculptures and reliefs which had once decorated a small Early Dynastic temple, a marble tablet with an inscription reading:

(To) Ninhursag: A-annepadda, King of Ur, son of Mesannepadda, King of Ur, for Ninhursag has built (this temple)

Both A-annepadda and his father figured on the Sumerian King List, the latter being the founder of the First Dynasty of Ur which succeeded the First Dynasty of Uruk. Thus for the first time one of those early Sumerian princes long held as mythical was proven to have actually existed. There is reason to believe that Mesannepadda reigned in about 2560 B.C.

Finally, in 1959 a German scholar, D. O. Edzard, found in the Iraq Museum a fragment of a large alabaster vase, engraved with three words in a very archaic script:

Me-bárag-si, King of Kish

This monarch, as Edzard showed,[3] was none other than Enmebaragesi of the King List, twenty-second king of the 'legendary' First Dynasty of Kish and the father of Agga who, as we have seen, fought against Gilgamesh. Since another inscription of that king was found at Khafaje in an archaeological context suggesting the end of ED II, and since Gilgamesh, king of Uruk, had seven successors whose reasonably long reigns totalled 140 years before his dynasty was overthrown by Mesannepadda, we may safely assume that Mebaragesi reigned around 2700 B.C. and take that date as a provisional starting-point for the history of ancient Iraq.

The twenty-one kings of Kish preceding Mebaragesi and the four contemporary kings of Uruk preceding Gilgamesh would nicely fill the gap between 2900 and 2700 B.C., provided we ignore the incredibly long reign assigned to each of them by the

Sumerian King List. There is no reason to doubt that these monarchs existed, despite the fact that they were later turned into heroes and semigods, but we have no genuine royal inscription from these three centuries, and our knowledge of ED I and ED II is entirely based on archaeological data, the archaic texts from Ur (ED I or ED II) being extremely difficult to understand and of limited historical interest.

From about 2500 B.C. onwards, however, we have just enough royal inscriptions, as well as economic, legal, administrative and even literary texts – notably from Fara, Abu Salabikh and, later, Girsu[4] – to sketch a rough outline of the political and social history of Sumer. But apart from a few very short inscriptions (mostly kings' names) found at Mari, on the middle Euphrates, and from fragments of inscribed vases and statuettes discovered at Khafaje, in the Diyala valley, all these texts come from southern Mesopotamia, the northern part of this country remaining regrettably illiterate. However, one must not lose all hope, and the thousands of clay tablets recently found at Ebla show us that archaeology may still hold many surprises.

The impact of this discovery cannot be fully appreciated unless one remembers that until 1974 virtually nothing was known about Northern Syria in the third millennium B.C. By a stroke of good luck, in that and the following two years the Italian archaeologists who during a decade had been excavating at Tell Mardik – a large mound lying sixty kilometres southwest of Aleppo – brought to light, in the ruins of a palace dated 2400–2250 B.C., some fifteen thousand clay tablets bearing cuneiform signs of the type used in the Sumerian city of Kish.[5] Many words and sentences were written in Sumerian 'logograms' but others, written in syllables, left no doubt that Tell Mardik was the ancient city of Ebla – a name that had previously appeared in a handful of Mesopotamian texts – and that the language spoken at Ebla was a hitherto unknown Semitic language, promptly baptized 'Eblaite', which to some extent differed from Akkadian and from the West-Semitic languages (Amorrite, Cananaean) of the second millennium B.C.

As these tablets were slowly being deciphered, their importance became increasingly obvious. Not only did they reveal that Ebla was the capital city of a relatively large and powerful North Syrian kingdom, but they provided a wealth of information on the organization, social structure, economic system, diplomatic and commercial relations, areas of influence and cultural affinities of this long forgotten kingdom. No Sumerian city-state of the Early Dynastic period has left us such vast and detailed archives, but with a few exceptions (see page 142) the contribution of the Ebla texts to the history of ancient Mesopotamia, although non-negligible, has up to now remained limited, and as more of these texts are being published, it does not seem that this situation will be greatly modified.

The Archaeological Context

Surface exploration and excavations have shown that at the beginning of the third millennium B.C. the urbanization process, which had commenced during the Uruk period, reached its acme, involving the whole of Mesopotamia. In southern Iraq many villages disappeared to the benefit of already large or growing cities, the best example being Uruk which became a huge metropolis covering more than 400 hectares and giving shelter to 40 or 50,000 inhabitants. At the same time, urban centres appeared or developed from proto-historic settlements in the northern part of Iraq. The best known of these towns are Mari (Tell Hariri),[6] half-way between northern Syria and Sumer, Assur (Qala'at Sherqat),[7] ninety kilometres south of Nineveh (opposite modern Mosul), and others of unknown ancient name but which must have been important: Tell Taya, for instance, at the foot of Jabal Sinjar,[8] and Tell Khueira on the Turkey–Syria border, between the rivers Balikh and Khabur.[9] Urban growth, exceptionally coupled with rural proliferation, also occurred in the Diayala basin, north-east of Baghdad, where surveys have revealed the traces of ten major cities, nineteen small towns and sixty-seven villages in a area of about 900 square kilometres. Incidentally, it is to the American archaeologists who, in the 1930s, excavated three sites in this region, Tell Asmar (Eshnunna), Khafaje (Tutub) and Tell 'Aqrab, that we owe the classical and sometimes criticized tripartite division of the Early Dynastic period.[10]

As a rule, the Mesopotamian towns of the early third millennium B.C. were surrounded by a wall, sometimes double and often reinforced by towers. These fortifications bespeak of frequent wars, and this is supported in Sumer by ED III texts mentioning struggles between city-states and against foreign invaders. We shall never know, however, who were the enemies so much feared by the inhabitants of Tell Taya that they built a citadel and raised their city wall on a three-metre high stone base.

With few exceptions, all the northern towns were subjected to varying degrees of Sumerian influence in matters of art, religious architecture and sometimes pottery and glyptics. How this came about remains uncertain. Some authors have postulated the existence of 'Sumerian colonies' in the midst of predominantly Semitic populations, but there is no textual or archaeological evidence to support this theory, at least in the Early Dynastic period, and the most plausible carriers of Sumerian culture would be itinerant artisans and merchants.

Most archaeologists agree that the Early Dynastic period culture is issued from the Uruk-Jemdat Nasr culture, and this is true in many respects, but some discontinuities are striking and raise difficult questions. Thus, there seemed in the ED II period to disappear, for an unknown reason, before the end of ED III, a very peculiar and diagnostic building material which has never been used in Mesopotamia before and after: the so-called 'plano-convex' bricks, shaped like flat-based bread loaves, laid on their edges and arranged in a herring-bone pattern. A more important problem is the quasi-total abandonment of the classical 'tripartite' Mesopotamian sanctuaries and their replacement by temples and shrines of various plans and sizes,[11] some of them often indistinguishable from the surrounding houses until one went inside, others standing alone, like the large and splendid 'oval temple' of Khafaje, with its two eccentric enclosures and its *cella* raised on a platform; this type of temple goes back to the Uruk period (oval temple of Tell 'Uqair). Some Early Dynastic sanctuaries clearly reflect non-Mesopotamian influences, possibly for geographical reasons. At Mari, for instance, the temple of the local goddess Nini-zaza contained a conical monolith, a *baetyl*, which would have been at home in an open-air West-Semitic temple of Syria or Palestine. Further north, the multiple temples of Tell Khueira, so near to the present Turkish border, rest on stone bases and have open porticoes that are reminiscent of Anatolian dwelling-houses.

Apart from a few interesting wall-plaques, some of them inscribed, and pieces such as the celebrated 'Stele of the Vultures' from Girsu, the sculpture of that period is represented mainly by statues of worshippers which once stood on the brick benches that ran around the *cella* of most temples. Usually upright but sometimes seated, their hands folded in front of their chest, these long-haired or bald, shaven or bearded men wearing the traditional Sumerian woollen skirt, and these women wrapped in a kind of saree were staring at some divine statue with their shell-and-lapis eyes set in bitumen – the eyes we have already encountered at Tell es-Sawman two and a half millennia ago. But these statuettes are not all of the same quality.[12] Those found at Tell Khueira are rather crude and clumsy, those discovered in the archaic Ishtar temple at Assur are mediocre, and those, widely publicized, which come from the 'square temple' of Tell Asmar are stiff, angular and, with their huge, haunting eyes and their corrugated beards, more impressive than beautiful. In contrast, many of the statues unearthed at Mari are marvellous portraits extremely well-carved, but Mari is very far from Sumer and these remarkable sculptures cannot be regarded as being representative of Sumerian art: in all probability, they were the work of local artists drawing their inspiration from Sumer, the ancestors of the great sculptors of the Akkad period. What is strange is that

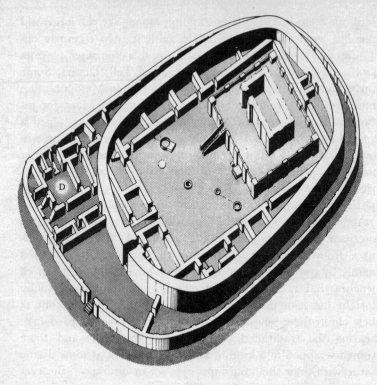

The oval temple at Khafaje, Early Dynastic III period. The two areas enclosed by walls measure 103 × 74 and 74 × 59 metres respectively. We do not know to which god or goddess this temple was dedicated.
From P. Amiet, L'Art Antique du Proche-Orient, *1977; after P. Delougaz*, The Oval Temple at Khafaje, *1940.*

the statues of worshippers discovered at Nippur and Girsu, in the Sumerian heartland, give the impression of being mass-produced and cut a sorry figure when compared with the masterpieces of the Uruk period. Were they made in work-shops for 'impoverished pilgrims',[13] or do they reflect the inevi-table decline that seems to follow all exceptional periods in the history of art?

To be fair, it must be said that in other fields the art of the Early Dynastic period was far from being decadent. Thus, in a limited area of central Mesopotamia there flourished, in ED I, an attractive polychrome pottery called *scarlet ware* clearly derived from the Jemdat Nasr ware. On the other hand, many sites of the upper Tigris valley and the Khabur basin have yielded samples of the very elegant 'Ninevite 5' ceramic, at first painted, then heavily incised, and remarkable for its shapes: tall fruit stands with pedestal bases, high-necked vases with angular shoulders, carinated bowls.[14] The scarlet ware was short-lived, the Ninevite 5 ware vanished towards the middle of ED III after a very long existence, and both were replaced, throughout Mesopotamia, by an unpainted pottery with very few artistic qualities.

The art of the stone-cutter followed a contrary course towards improvement.[15] The short and narrow cylinder-seals of the ED I period bearing monotonous friezes of schematized animals or geometric designs (the so-called 'brocade' style) were replaced, in ED II and III, by longer and wider seals with totally different compositions depicting either 'banquet scenes' or 'animal-contest scenes'. The former showed men and women drinking from cups or from tall jars through a tube. The latter consisted of cattle attacked by lions and defended by naked heroes and bull-men. There were also some religious motifs, such as the sun-god on a boat. As time went by, the compositions remained basically the same, but they were executed with greater skill. Some seals, notably those of kings, were made of lapis-lazuli or other semi-precious stones, or even of gold, and they were sometimes capped with silver at both ends. An important novelty was the appearance, at Ur, Jemdat Nasr and Uruk, of the first short cuneiform inscriptions on cylinder-seals.

However, it is in metal work that the Sumerians made the most striking advances due to a great extent to the introduction of two new techniques: *cire perdue* (lost wax) for bronze and *repoussé* for precious metals. As we shall see in going through the marvellous pieces found in the Royal Cemetery of Ur, the Early

Dynastic period was the time when the art of the goldsmith reached a degree of proficiency unequalled in any other contemporary civilization. But the raw material had to be imported and paid for with what southern Mesopotamia could offer: cereals, hides, wool, textiles, manufactured objects and bitumen. How, then, were the Sumerians organized to run their economy? What was their social structure? Who were their rulers and what can we know of their political history? To try to answer these questions (and some others) we must leave archaeology and turn to the few texts that are available.

The Sumerian City-states

Because our attention is now focused on Sumer we are tempted to forget what a small country it really was: thirty thousand square kilometres, a little less than the area of Belgium, about the size of four or five English counties. As life remained concentrated along the Euphrates, its branches and irrigation canals, the 'cradle of civilization' was in fact a fairly narrow strip of land extending from the latitude of Baghdad to the swamps that bordered the shores of the Arabo-Persian Gulf. In addition, a linguistic barrier, somewhere between Kish and Nippur, separated the Semitic-speaking people of the north (the future Akkad) from the Sumerian-speaking people of the south, making Sumer proper even smaller.

In the third millennium B.C. both Sumer and Akkad were divided into political units which we call 'city-states'. Each city-state consisted of a city, its suburbs and satellite towns and villages, and of a well-defined territory comprising gardens, palm-groves and fields of barley and wheat. The open steppe between irrigated areas served as pasture land. The average surface of a city-state is unknown, but one of the largest, Lagash, is said to have measured some 2,880 square kilometres and to have numbered 30,000–35,000 people.

For the Early Dynastic period our sources do not list more than eighteen major cities in the whole of Sumer and Akkad.

These were, from north to south: Sippar, Kish, Akshak, Larak, Isin, Nippur, Adab, Zabalam, Shuruppak, Umma, Girsu, Lagash, Nina, Badtibira, Uruk, Larsa, Ur and Eridu. But many other towns and villages, as yet unlocated, are also mentioned, whilst archaeologists have unearthed settlements – such as al-'Ubaid and Abu Salabikh – whose ancient names remain unknown.

Each Sumerian city was formed of several districts, and each district had its own god with his temple. The city as a whole and its territory were under the protection of a 'national' god who ideally *owned* the city-state. Lagash, for example, 'belonged' to Ningirsu as its rival Umma belonged to Shara and Ur to the moon-god Nanna. This fictitious concept and the fact that the first administrative records available in large numbers came from a temple – that of the goddess Baba in Girsu – have led to the hasty conclusion that all the land of the city-state was the property of the temples and that all its inhabitants were temple servants or clients. This might have been true for the Uruk period, but the picture that emerges from other Presargonic tablets now in our possession and from a careful reappraisal of old and new data by modern scholars is very different from the picture presented some years ago.[16]

It is now estimated that about one-third of the arable land surrounding the city was owned by the temples. This temple-land could neither be sold nor exchanged and was divided into three parts: the 'land of the Lord' (*gàna-nì-enna*), which fed the priests and the numerous persons employed by the temple; the 'food land' (*gàna-shukura*), which was allotted in small parcels to the farmers who worked the 'land of the Lord' and to some temple officials for their subsistence, but which did not fully belong to them and could be taken away at any time; and the 'plough land' (*gàna-uru-lá*), which was let out to tenants against one-seventh or one-eighth of the harvest. The temples also exploited or hired out orchards, pastures, fisheries, as well as cattle and flocks of sheep and goats. Taken collectively, the revenues of the temples in cereals, fruit, livestock and by-products were therefore considerable. They were partly used for the maintenance of the priests, scribes and other temple officials, partly stored as provision against drought and partly exchanged for imported goods. Probably the largest part, however, was redistributed as wages or gratuities to the thousands of people – mostly women, but also men and slaves of both sexes – who permanently laboured in temple workshops and premises, milling grain, spinning and weaving wool or hair, brewing beer or acting as cooks, gardeners and servants. Also paid in kind (usually barley) were the temple farmers, who could be mobilized by the ruler in case of war or for such large-scale public works as the building of sanctuaries and fortifications and the digging of canals. The scale of wages seems to have varied considerably from place to place and also with time.

All this required continuous planning, control and book-keeping, but the Sumerians had meticulous minds and were extremely well organized. Not only did their 'bureaucrats' leave us thousands of payrolls, vouchers, lists of workers and other similar documents, but we learn from tablets found at Girsu and Shuruppak that members of the same profession were divided into highly specialized groups. For instance, there were separate shepherds for male and female asses and separate fishermen according to whether they fished in fresh, brackish or sea water; even the snake-charmers formed a 'corporation', which had its own chief. Artisans and merchants, similarly organized, worked partly for private citizens and partly for the state (temple or palace), though trade with foreign countries as far away as Afghanistan and the Indus valley was largely in the hands of the latter. An army of scribes, controllers, overseers and other officials, directed by chief inspectors (*nu-bànda*) and by superintendents (*agrig*) under the leadership of the high priest (*sanga*) of each temple kept this intricate machinery running.

The other single major economic unit was the palace, although much less is known about its role and administration. Tablets from Shuruppak, *c.* 2600 B.C., indicate that the ruler maintained six or seven hundred soldiers with their equipment – no doubt his own bodyguards and the regular army of the city-state – and employed people of various professions on his estates. We also learn from a handful of contracts that he occasionally purchased land from wealthy individuals or high officials. We have no means of assessing the total size of the royal domain, but if we include the possessions of the princes and their families, it might have been as large as the temple-land.

Finally, other contracts – more numerous, it is true, in Semitic Akkad than in Sumer proper – tell us that private persons of all ranks could freely sell, exchange, donate or let out houses, fields, gardens, fishery ponds, livestock and slaves belonging to them – or rather, perhaps, to family communities.[17] Naturally, the area of the plots of land in private possession varied according to the social status of the owner: it could reach more than 240 hectares for a high official and be as small as 6 hectares or even one hectare for a simple civil-servant, a currier or a stone-cutter, all people attested as vendors in these contracts.

As for the social structure of the city-state, our texts mention only freemen and slaves, but it is clear from the tripartite economic system described that in Early Dynastic times the Sumerian society was divided into three main layers: at the bottom the slaves, usually recruited among prisoners of war or kidnapped in foreign countries but never very numerous; then those peasants and workers who served the temple or the palace, were maintained by them and possessed no land; and then the group of landowners or 'freemen', which covers the whole range from artisans to members of the royal family. And above all these, of course, the ruler of the city-state about whom more will now be said.

Early Sumerian Rulers

For the Sumerians, the ruler was the 'shepherd' chosen by the gods and responsible to them for the safety and prosperity of the city-state. On the archaic tablets from Uruk the ruler is called *en*, a title translated by 'lord' but implying both secular and religious functions. The *en* probably resided in the temple precinct, and it is reasonable to assume that he was also the high priest of the 'national' god, the head of the temple around which the Sumerian city had grown. This title persisted until the middle of the nineteenth century B.C., but in other Early Dynastic states the ruler was known as either *ensi*, 'governor', or *lugal*, 'king'. *Ensi* is written PA.TE.SI, a compound logogram of uncertain meaning; *lugal* simply means 'great man'. Why some rulers called themselves *ensi* and others *lugal*, or sometimes took both titles according to circumstances, is by no means clear.[18] In some cases at least it seems that the *lugal* reigned over several city-states and that the *ensi* was the vassal of a *lugal*. The ruler's wife, known in any case as *nin*, 'lady', 'queen', played an important part in public life. In Girsu, for example, she managed the affairs of the temple of the goddess Baba.

The ruler and his family lived in a palace (*é-gal*, 'big house') distinct from the temple. Three such palaces have been excavated in Mesopotamia: one at Eridu, another at Kish and yet another – or rather two superimposed palaces built in succession – at Mari.[19] They differed in a number of details but were strikingly similar in plan. All had a square central courtyard surrounded by chambers on three sides and communicating, on the fourth side, with a long, rectangular room which probably served as an audience hall. Two parallel thick walls separated by a narrow corridor surrounded the building. In Mari, the palace contained numerous ritual installations suggesting royal chapels. In Kish, a second building alongside the palace included a spacious hall with four central mud-brick columns and a pillared loggia.

The ruler governed the city-state on behalf of the gods. As most ancient and modern kings, he led his troops against the enemy, signed peace treaties and saw to it that fair judgements were rendered. One of his most sacred duties was the building, maintenance and restoration of the temples, in keeping with the

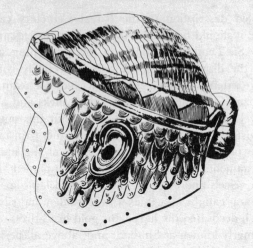

Meskalamdug's helmet (or, more exactly, wig) in massive gold,
from the Royal Cemetery of Ur.
After Sir Leonard Woolley, Ur Excavations, *II, 1934.*

belief that humanity had been created for the service of the gods
and that he was only the first of their servants. Numerous
inscriptions refer to such building activities, and from Ur-Nanshe
to Ashurbanipal several Mesopotamian monarchs have been
portrayed in stone or bronze with baskets on their heads, carrying
bricks for the new sanctuaries. *Lugals* and *ensis* also played a
leading role in feasts, processions and other religious ceremonies.
In Uruk, but also possibly elsewhere, the Early Dynastic ruler
acted as the male god in the Sacred Marriage rite and, indeed,
there is reason to believe that early in the third millennium B.C., in
the days of Lugalbanda, Dumuzi and Gilgamesh – all qualified as
'divine' in the Sumerian King List – some royal couples were
considered as 'living gods' or, more correctly, as human replicas
of the divine couple to whom the city-state belonged. This,
might be one of the answers to the many questions raised by the
most startling discovery ever made in the course of Mesopotamian
excavations: the Royal Cemetery of Ur.

A detailed description of the Royal Cemetery cannot be given here; it should be read in the excellent articles and books written by Sir Leonard Woolley on this fascinating subject.[20] None but the discoverer himself could effectively convey the feeling of excitement that seized him and his team as gold literally oozed from the earth under their picks and as marvel after marvel was brought to light. None but this outstanding archaeologist could describe the delicate and painstaking removal, the patient and skilled restoration of the magnificent objects, ornaments and weapons that accompanied the dead: the golden vessels and daggers, the gold and lapis-lazuli statuettes of a ram 'caught in a thicket', the golden and silver bulls' heads which decorated the harps, the gold head-dress of 'Queen Puabi' formerly known as Shubad, and, above all perhaps, the splendid golden helmet of Meskalamdug – to quote only the main pieces. Woolley's dramatic evocation of these strange funerals where musicians with their harps, soldiers with their weapons and court ladies in gorgeous attire willingly followed their masters into the awesome pits where they were drugged to a painless death never fails to leave the reader with a poignant, unforgettable feeling of horror, mingled with wonder and admiration.

But the Royal Cemetery of Ur presents the historian with very difficult problems. There is no doubt that it belongs to the dawn of history, to the period immediately preceding the First Dynasty of Ur (c. 2600 B.C.). It would seem at first sight that the people so lavishly buried could be no other than kings, queens and princes, but in the seventeen royal tombs where several inscriptions were found, most of them on cylinder-seals, two names only, Meskalamdug ('The hero of the good land') and Akalamdug ('The son of the good land'), are followed by the title *lugal*, 'king', and two other names, those of Ninbanda, wife of Meskalamdug, and of Puabi, spouse of an unknown monarch, are qualified by the title *nin*, 'queen'; and while the fact that all but two tombs had been plundered in antiquity might account for the absence of other royal inscriptions, this absence is nevertheless disconcerting. Even more puzzling is the practice of collective burials involving from three to seventy-four attendants, mostly female here – practically a whole royal household. It is attested on a smaller scale and mostly with male servants in other countries and in other times – in Egypt during the First Dynasty, among the Scythians and the Mongols, in Assam, and even among the Comans of southern Russia as late as the thirteenth century A.D.[21] – but nowhere in Mesopotamia outside Ur and possibly Kish. Again, it can be argued that practically all the royal tombs in ancient Iraq were found plundered and that we have no written description of a royal funeral. Yet this silence about a ceremony which must have been of paramount importance is surprising and can only be explained by assuming that royal burials with human sacrifices fell into disuse at a very early date, probably during the Early Dynastic period. But why this sacrifice? The only text in our possession alluding to a king going to the grave with his retinue is, significantly, a Sumerian epic tale known as 'the death of Gilgamesh'.[22] Now, we know that Gilgamesh and Meskalamdug were but a few generations apart, and we also know from other sources that Gilgamesh was considered to be a god of the Netherworld. This would tend to confirm the theory first propounded by Woolley that Meskalamdug, Akalamdug, Puabi and the other anonymous kings and queens of the Royal Cemetery were more than monarchs: they were gods, or at least they represented the gods on earth and, as such, were entitled to take their court with them into another life, a life no doubt incomparably more enjoyable than that of the human being. However, this theory, as all others, is open to criticism, and the drama of the Cemetery of Ur remains a mystery.[23]

If the kings of Mesopotamia ceased early to be 'substitute gods' they always retained some of their priestly functions. Yet the general trend throughout history was towards a gradual separation of the Palace from the Temple, and this development began in Early Dynastic times. Already in about 2400 B.C. Entemena, *ensi* of Lagash, was no longer high priest of that city, for on a beautiful silver vase which he dedicated to Ningirsu an inscription expressly mentions: 'In those days Dudu was priest (*sanga*) of Ningirsu.' There were even times when the ruler and the priests were, it seems, in open conflict. About a century after Entemena, Uruinimgina (formerly called Urukagina), the last prince of Lagash, tells us in a famous inscription[24] how he, as champion of the gods, put an end to the abuses that existed before his reign: inspectors of the ruler interfered in all affairs, fantastic taxes were levied on burials and, apparently, on weddings, houses were bought below their price by rich officials, corruption was rife and the poor suffered much; but, more important, the *ensi* was building up vast estates, his 'onion and cucumber gardens' encroached on the best fields of the gods and were tilled by oxen and asses belonging to the temples. Uruinimgina revoked many officials, reduced taxation and 'reinstated Ningirsu' in the buildings and fields of the ruler:

He freed the citizens of Lagash from usury, monopoly, hunger, theft and assault; he established their freedom.

But these reforms, if they were applied at all, had no lasting effect, for it was under Uruinimgina's reign that Lagash and the rest of Sumer fell into non-Sumerian hands.

Outline of History

To reconstruct the sequence of events during the Early Dynastic period is not an easy task. Not only are historical texts proper extremely rare and usually concise, but the co-existence of several local 'dynasties' and the part played by some rulers not mentioned in the King List add considerably to the difficulty. We shall therefore aim at nothing more than a brief outline of Early Dynastic history, warning the reader that many points in our reconstruction are highly controversial.

This history is essentially one of wars between city-states and against foreigners. Many of these wars undoubtedly had economic causes that are seldom mentioned, such as the appropriation of land or the control of trade routes and irrigation canals, but some had geopolitical or religious motives. Thus Kish lay in the heart of a Semitic area – even though most of its rulers bore good Sumerian names* – and to conquer it meant to unite the two main ethno-linguistic groups of Sumer under the same rule. The title 'King of Kish' therefore seems to have been more coveted than any other, being almost synonymous with 'King of Sumer and Akkad' or 'King of the (whole) Country' which occur later in royal inscriptions. Another goal worthy of any prince, whether Sumerian or Semite, was to possess Nippur, or at least to be recognized by its *ensi* and clergy. Contrary to Kish, Uruk and Ur, Nippur never gained nor claimed ascendancy over other city-states and does not even figure among the 'dynasties' of the Sumerian King List, but it was the seat of Sumer's supreme god, Enlil, and the religious capital, the Rome or Mecca of the Sumerians. In consequence, *lugals* and *ensis* competed in sending to Enlil's shrine the most valuable gifts; those who could include Nippur in their kingdom restored or rebuilt its temples, and at the end of the third millennium the words 'chosen by Enlil in Nippur' became part of the standard royal titles. Did this attitude towards Nippur merely reflect religious fervour, or was it – as the supporters of the 'primitive democracy' believe – a survival of the times when, faced with the threat of foreign invasion, delegates from all city-states met in Nippur to elect a common war leader? Or again, did the priests and theologians of Nippur exert upon the kings some strong, if untold, political influence, as did the priests of Heliopolis in Egypt? As with so many questions in ancient history, these have no definite answer.

Mebaragesi (*c.* 2700 B.C.) is the first Early Dynastic king authenticated by two inscriptions, but these give us only his name and title, whereas the Sumerian King List yields the interesting information that 'he carried away as spoil the

---

* *Me-barage-si*, for instance, means: 'the *me* (powers inherent in nature and human institutions) fill the throne'.

weapons of Elam'. This is the first mention, though probably not the first episode, of a very long conflict between Mesopotamia and Elam which had its roots in prehistoric times and was to last for almost three thousand years. When Mebaragesi's son, Agga, surrendered to Gilgamesh, the age-old First Dynasty of Kish came to an end, and for a century (c. 2660–2560 B.C.) Gilgamesh's seven successors – unfortunately mere names on the King List – reigned over both Uruk and Kish. Soon after that period, however, we have three short inscriptions from a prince of unknown origin named Mesalim, who calls himself 'King of Kish' but seems to have had close links with Lagash, where he erected a temple to Ningirsu and arbitrated a border dispute between that city and Umma (Tell Jokha, twenty-nine kilometres to the west of Girsu), setting up his stele as a boundary stone.

During that time, maritime trade with the East had immensely enriched the city and rulers of Ur (which was then a port near the mouth of the Euphrates),[25] as shown by the treasures buried with Meskalamdug and Akalamdug in the famous 'Royal' Cemetery (c. 2600 B.C.). Who the ancestors and descendants of those two kings were we do not know, but c. 2560 B.C., Mesannepadda ('hero chosen by An') – whom we have already met – founded the First Dynasty of Ur. He was soon powerful enough to overthrow the last king of Uruk as well as his contemporary, Mesalim of Kish. Nippur appears to have been in his possession, since he and his second successor, Meskiagnunna, rebuilt there a temple called Tummal which had been originally erected by Mebaragesi but which had 'fallen into ruin for the first time'. Lagash was then at peace with Umma, and its prince Ur-Nanshe was busy building temples, digging canals, importing wood from Dilmun and having himself portrayed on a well-known wall-plaque with his wife, his seven sons and three of his officials. Even relations with distant Mari were friendly, if we judge from the finding in Mari of a hoard of precious objects apparently offered by Mesannepadda to one of its kings.[26] This *pax sumerica* under the aegis of Ur lasted about one hundred years, but ended in disaster.

Kish, probably lost early to the local rulers of its Second Dynasty, was briefly occupied by people from Hamazi, a town or a country probably located beyond the Tigris, between the Diyala and the Lesser Zab, whilst hordes of Elamites came from the district of Awan (probably around modern Shushtar) and imposed their law over part of Sumer. And as though this was not enough, Lagash became very troublesome under one of its rulers – a ruler who has left us some of the most extensive and detailed historical records of the entire Early Dynastic period.

Like his grandfather Ur-Nanshe, Eannatum,*ensi of Lagash (c. 2455–2425 B.C.), was a great builder of temples and digger of canals; circumstances also made of him a great warrior. He purged Sumer from the Elamite bands and protected its eastern flank by conquering if not, as he claims, 'Elam the great mountain that strikes terror, in its entirety', at least several towns on the border of Elam. He overthrew Ur and Uruk and 'added to the princeship (nam-ensi) of Lagash and the kingship of Kish'. But the war about which we are best informed is a localized conflict, the war against Umma.[27] The bone of contention was a certain field called Gu-edin which lay at the border between the two states and was claimed by both; but now:

The ensi of Umma, at the command of his god, raided and devoured the Gu-edin, the irrigated land, the field beloved of Ningirsu ... He ripped out the steel (set up by Mesalim) and entered the plain of Lagash.

The infantry of Lagash, armed with long spears and protected by heavy shields, met in battle the soldiers of Umma. Eannatum won:

By the word of Enlil, he hurled the great net upon them and heaped up piles of their bodies in the plain ... The survivors turned to Eannatum, they prostrated themselves for life, they wept ...

The fight ended in a peace treaty. The ensi of Lagash 'marked off the boundary with Enakalli, the ensi of Umma; he restored

* E-anna-tum: 'worthy of the E-anna' (temple of Inanna in Lagash).

Mesalim's stele to its former place' and levied on Umma a heavy tax in barley. Eannatum's victory – or rather the victory of Ningirsu, the god of Lagash, over Shara, the god of Umma, as the texts present it – was commemorated by a masterpiece of early Sumerian sculpture, unfortunately found in fragments: the stele 'of the Vultures', so called because of the birds of prey that tear up the corpses of the vanquished. Towards the end of his reign, Eannatum had to fight a coalition of the men of Kish and Mari led by Zuzu (or Unzi), King of Akshak.[28] Although he claimed victory, there is little doubt that this war marked the end of the small empire he had built.

Only a few years ago, very little was known about the history of the kingdom of Mari during the Early Dynastic period. Mari figures on the Sumerian King List with six kings totalling 136 years of reign, but only one or two names are legible. Two inscriptions from Ur mention an otherwise unknown Ilshu, king of Mari, and four of the statues of worshippers found at Mari itself bear inscriptions giving their name (Ikun-Shamash, Lamgi-Mari, Iblul-Il, Ishkun Shamagan), but there is no means of knowing in which order they reigned. But now, some light has been shed on the subject by the Ebla archives, and notably by a letter from a certain Enna-Dagan, *en* of Mari, to an unnamed *en* of Ebla, reminding him of a series of successful military campaigns led in northern Syria by three of his predecessors and in particular Iblul-Il who seems to have devastated or occupied a large number of towns belonging to the Ebla kingdom.[29] The purpose of this letter is not stated, but there can be little doubt that Enna-Dagan was trying to put some pressure on his rival and keep some kind of control over Ebla. This seems to be supported by administrative documents from Ebla which suggest that the rulers of this kingdom regularly sent large 'gifts' (read: tribute) of gold and silver to the court of Mari, at least until the reign of Ebrium, the most powerful king of Ebla.[30] Other documents of this type also show that Mari and Ebla were not always on bad terms: many artisans and artists from Mari actually worked in Ebla, and these two cities exchanged a variety of goods, either for their own use or acting as 'trading ports' between the Mediterranean coast and Anatolia at one end and lower Mesopotamia and beyond at the other.[31]

When exactly the Mari-Ebla wars took place is impossible to say for lack of synchronisms between the rulers of these kingdoms and those of the Sumerian city-states, and also because of the uncertainties attached to the order and duration of their reign, the meaning of their title and indeed the existence of some of them. However, for reasons which cannot be developed here, it seems that Iblul-Il of Mari, Arennum of Ebla and Eannatum of Lagash were more or less contemporary (c. 2460–2400 B.C.).

The century following Eannatum's death (c. 2425) is rather confused. It appears that En-shakush-anna, King of Uruk, and Lugal-anne-mundu, King of Adab (nowadays Bismaya, twenty-six kilometres north of Tell Fara[32]), successively occupied Kish and Nippur and were recognized as suzerains of Sumer. In Lagash, under Eannatum's nephew Entemena * war broke out again with Umma. In a long inscription on two clay cylinders Entemena recalls what happened in the past, tells us how he 'slew the Ummaite forces up into Umma itself', then stood firm against the pretensions of the new ensi of Umma, 'that plunderer of fields and farms, that speaker of evil', and dug a boundary ditch as a permanent frontier between the two rival cities. We also know from other sources that Entemena concluded a 'brotherhood pact' with his powerful neighbour Lugal-kinishe-dudu of Uruk, who had united Uruk and Ur into a single kingdom, and that his reign ended in peace and prosperity. But a few years later the situation deteriorated again in Lagash. The priests of Ningirsu seized the throne and occupied it for about two decades, enlarging, as we have seen, their personal properties at the expense of the gods. They were overthrown by Uru-inimagina, famous for his social reforms, but the victor reigned

---

* *En-temena*: 'lord of the (temple) platform'.

only for eight years. An energetic and ambitious *ensi* of Umma, Lugalzagesi*, marched against Girsu, took it and destroyed it, thus avenging two centuries of defeat. On the smouldering ruins of the city, an unknown scribe sat later to write a lamentation which has come down to us:[33]

The men of Umma have set fire to the (temple) Antasurra, they have carried away the silver and the precious stones ... They have shed blood in the temple E-engur of the goddess Nanshe; they have carried away the silver and the precious stones ... The men of Umma, by the despoiling of Lagash, have committed a sin against the god Ningirsu ... As for Lugal-zagge-si, ensi of Umma, may his goddess Nidaba make him bear his mortal sin upon his head!

But the curse had no immediate effect. After Lagash, Lugalzagesi took Uruk and established himself as king of that city. He then proceeded to conquer the rest of Sumer and apparently succeeded. Indeed, on a vase dedicated to Enlil in Nippur he claims conquests embracing the whole of Mesopotamia as well as Syria:

When Enlil, king of sovereign countries, had given him the kingship over the nation (Sumer), had directed upon him the eyes of the nation, made all sovereign countries wait upon him, and made (everyone) from where the sun rises to where the sun sets submit to him; then he drew toward himself the feet of (everybody) from the Lower Sea (Arabo-Persian Gulf) (along) the Tigris and the Euphrates to the Upper Sea (Mediterranean). From where the sun rises to where the sun sets, Enlil lets him have no opponent. All sovereign countries lay (as cows) in pasture under him; the nation was watering (its fields) in joy under him; all the dependent rules of Sumer and the ensis of all independent countries bowed to him before his arbitral office in Uruk.[34]

It is difficult to believe that Lugalzagesi possessed in fact such an empire. Perhaps this is no more than a piece of grandiloquence; perhaps the King of Uruk had managed to obtain the submission or the alliance of the Semites of Mari, who, in turn,

---

* *Lugal-zage-si*: 'king who fills the sanctuary'.

might have held the Semites of Syria under their political influence. In any case, the 'Sumerian Empire' of Lugalzagesi lasted no longer than his reign: twenty-four years (c. 2340–2316). A newcomer, a Semitic prince, Sargon of Akkad, gave it the fatal blow.

CHAPTER 9

THE AKKADIANS

We have previously seen that in the Early Dynastic period
Sumer exerted a considerable cultural influence outside its
natural boundaries, particularly along the Euphrates from Kish
to Mari and from Mari to Ebla, whereas the Tigris valley, for
some unknown reason, seems to have been relatively neglected.
However, there is nothing to suggest that the dissemination of
Sumerian arts, writing and literature was achieved by armed
forces. If the Sumerian rulers fought during four centuries, it
was more to repel invaders from the East and to establish their
supremacy over other city-states than to conquer foreign lands.
However, towards the end of the twenty-fourth century B.C.
the fulgurant campaign of Lugalzagesi heralded a policy of
territorial expansion and domination which was almost immediately taken up by Semitic princes from central Iraq. Not only
did Sargon and his successors subdue all the Sumerian city-
states, but they conquered the entire Tigris–Euphrates basin as
well as parts of the adjacent countries, embarked upon expeditions in the Persian Gulf and built the first great Mesopotamian
kingdom. For the first time since the prehistoric Ubaid period
the two halves of Mesopotamia, till then connected only by
loose cultural ties, were bound together as one large domain
extending from the Taurus to the 'Lower Sea', from the Zagros
to the Mediterranean. To the people of those days this territory
appeared immense; it encompassed 'the Four Regions of the
World', it was 'the Universe'. The Sargonic empire was to last
for about two hundred years and to collapse under the combined
pressure of the Zagros tribes and internal rebellion, but it had
set an example never to be forgotten. To reconstruct the unity
of Mesopotamia, to reach what we would call its natural limits
became the dream of all subsequent monarchs, and from the

middle of the third millennium until the fall of Babylon in 539 B.C. the history of ancient Iraq consists of their attempts, their successes and their failures to achieve this aim.

Who then were these Semites who made such a brilliant entry into history?

The Semites

The adjective 'Semitic' was coined in 1781 by a German scholar, Schlözer, to qualify a group of closely related languages, and subsequently the people who spoke these languages were called 'Semites'. Both words come from Shem, son of Noah, father of Ashur, Aram and Heber (*Genesis* x. 21–31) and alleged ancestor of the Assyrians, Aramaeans and Hebrews. Among the Semitic languages Arabic is today the most widely spoken; then come Ethiopic and Hebrew, the latter recently revived in script. Others, like Akkadian (Babylonian and Assyrian) or the Canaanite dialects are dead, while Aramaic survives, much altered, in the liturgic tongue of some Oriental Churches (Syriac) and in the dialects spoken by small, isolated communities in the Lebanon and northern Iraq. All these languages have many points in common and form a large and coherent family. One of their main characteristics is that almost all the verbs, nouns and adjectives derive from roots usually composed of three consonants. The insertion of long or short vowels between these consonants gives precision and actuality to the concept expressed by the root in a general way. Thus in Arabic the radical *ktb* conveys the vague idea of 'writing', but 'he wrote' is *kataba*, 'he writes' *yiktib*, 'writer' *kâtib*, etc. Languages of this type are called inflected and contrast with languages, such as Sumerian, which are of the agglutinative type.

As long as they are used for linguistic purposes, the words 'Semitic' and 'Semite' are convenient and acceptable to everyone. But because the Semitic languages, before the great Islamic expansion, were spoken in a limited area, a number of authors have considered the Semites as a particular race, or rather –

since the concept of a Semitic race is rejected by modern anthropologists – as an homogeneous community of persons sharing not only the same language but also the same psychology, laws and customs and the same religious beliefs. In other words, the Semites are taken to be one great single 'people'. Is this view justified? The problem, of course, is of importance and must be examined.[1]

The area inhabited by the Semitic-speaking peoples in early historical times consists of the Arabian peninsula and its northern appendages: the Syrian desert, Syria-Palestine and part of Mesopotamia. It is a well-defined, compact region, limited on all sides by seas and high mountains. According to the classical theory, all Semites were originally nomadic tribes living in the central part of this area. At various intervals large groups of them left the Syro-Arabian desert to settle, peacefully or by force, in the peripheral districts, mostly Mesopotamia and Syria-Palestine. They were:

the Akkadians in Mesopotamia during the fourth millennium B.C.;
the Western Semites (Cananeo-Phoenicians, Eblaites and Amorites) in Mesopotamia and Syria-Palestine during the third and second millennia;
the Aramaeans all around the Fertile Crescent in the twelfth century B.C.;
the Nabateans and other Pre-Islamic Arabs from the second century B.C. to the sixth century A.D.;
and finally, the Moslem Arabs from the seventh century A.D.

This theory holds good – especially for the last ethno linguistic group – inasmuch as it describes in broad outline a certain sequence of events. In detail, however, it cannot be accepted without serious amendments.[2] To consider the Syro-Arabian desert as the centre of diffusion of the Semites is out of the question. Only the Yemen, parts of Hadramaut and Oman, and a few oases in Arabia proper offer favourable living conditions, and it is extremely doubtful whether the great desert of central Arabia was inhabited at all between the Palaeolithic period – when it was not a desert but a savanna – and the first millennium B.C. Life in extensive desert areas presupposes long-range seasonal migrations in search of pastures, but only short-range migrations were possible before the widespread use of domestic camels in the Near East from the twelfth century B.C. onwards. Before that time the nomads, who rode on asses and practised sheep-rearing, were much more restricted in their movements than the bedouins of today and could not wander far beyond the limits of the grassy steppe which extends between the Tigris and the Euphrates and at the foot of the Zagros, the Taurus and the Lebanon. There they were in close and constant touch with the agricultural populations which bought their sheep and supplied them with grain, dates, tools, weapons and other utilitarian objects and amenities. The relationship between nomads and peasants could take various forms.[3] In general the two groups met regularly in villages or on marketplaces outside the gates of the cities, and exchanged goods, together, no doubt, with a number of ideas. Then the nomads returned to the steppe, perhaps only a few kilometres away. Occasionally, individuals left the tribe to find work in towns as mercenaries, craftsmen or merchants. Sometimes a family, a clan, or a whole tribe would acquire (or be granted) land and devote itself partly to agriculture, partly to sheep-breeding. Not infrequently the local governments exercised some control over the nomads, using them in particular as auxiliary troops whenever required. But in times of political unrest the situation could be reversed: tribes or confederations of tribes waged war against the sedentary society, ransacked the towns and occupied a territory, large or small, where they eventually settled. The sedentarization of the nomads was therefore a slow, almost continuous process with occasional episodes of armed intrusion. It took the form not of an outward movement from the central desert to the fertile periphery, but of a series of short- or medium-range movements within the periphery itself, from the steppe to the irrigated land. Thus the Fertile Crescent and possibly parts of the outskirts of the Arabian peninsula appear as the true homeland of the Semitic-speaking peoples. They were there, as far as we can judge, from prehistoric times, but they *reveal* themselves to us at different periods, either because they adopt some sort of writing or because, at a given moment, they become militarily active or politically influential and are mentioned in the written records of the civilized sedentary society.

Because most nomadic tribes in the ancient Near East spoke Semitic languages, it does not necessarily follow that all Semitic-speaking people were nomads. The failure to recognize this point has resulted in a great deal of confusion. The features attributed, rightly or wrongly, to the Semites in general – their 'spirited, impatient, mercurial, and emotional type of mentality',[4] their 'monotheistic anti-mythological and antiritualistic religious ideas',[5] their socio-political concepts revolving around the tribe – all this applies in fact only to the *nomadic* Semites and results, to a great extent, from their particular way of life. But if some of the Arabs, Aramaeans and Western Semites fall within this category, we have no proof whatsoever that the Akkadians in Mesopotamia – nor, for that matter, the Eblaites and Cananaeans in Syria-Palestine – were originally nomads. As to Mesopotamia, we do not know when the Semites first entered the country, if indeed they *entered* at all. Attempts have been made to correlate one or the other of the great ethnic migrations of proto-historic times with a Semitic invasion, but the wide divergence of opinions among scholars on this subject is tantamount to a confession of ignorance. Semitic personal names and a few texts written in Semitic language appear during the Early Dynastic period,[6] their geographical distribution suggesting that the Semites were in a minority among the Sumerians of the south, but were powerful and active, if not predominant, in the region of Kish. Judging from the Mari inscriptions and from later documents, it seems certain that they already formed the greater part of the population of northern Iraq. From the Sargonic period onwards the central part of Mesopotamia from Nippur up to perhaps Hît and Samarra, including the lower Diyala valley, was called 'the country of *Akkad*', this name being usually written with the Sumerian ideogram URI. We may therefore call the earliest Semites of Mesopotamia *Akkadians*. Their language, also called Akkadian, constitutes a particular branch of the Semitic family, and they wrote it with the cuneiform script invented by the Sumerians to express their own language – a delicate and awkward adaption, since the two languages are as unrelated to each other as, say, Chinese and Latin. While a number of Sumerian words passed into Akkadian, the Sumerians borrowed a fairly large amount of Akkadian words such as *hazi*, 'axe', *shám*, 'price', or *súm*, 'garlic'. This is about all the sources available at present enable us to say. But it must be pointed out that not one single Sumerian text refers to the Akkadians as enemies, invaders or nomads.[7] And although it is possible, albeit far from proven, that the social organization and political system of the Akkadians differed from those upon which the Sumerian city-state was founded, it appears clearly that the Akkadians practised agriculture, lived in villages and towns and shared the way of life, the religion and the culture of their Sumerian neighbours. So far as we know at the present time, the only obvious difference between the Akkadians and the Sumerians is a linguistic one; in all other respects these two ethnic groups are indistinguishable. The Akkadian domination in Sargonic times changed the course of history; it did not fundamentally alter the predominantly Sumerian character of the Mesopotamian civilization.

Sargon of Akkad

The reign of Sargon, the first Akkadian King, made such an impression on the Sumero-Akkadians that his personality was surrounded with a lasting halo of legend. A text written in Neo-Assyrian times (seventh century B.C.) describes his birth and early childhood in terms reminiscent of Moses, Krishna and other great men:

My mother was a changeling (?), my father I knew not.
The brothers of my father loved the hills.
My city is Azupiranu, which is situated on the banks of the
    Euphrates.
My changeling mother conceived me, in secret she bore me.
She set me in a basket of rushes, with bitumen she sealed my lid.
She cast me into the river which rose not over me.
The river bore me up and carried me to Akki, the drawer of water.
Akki, the drawer of water, took me as his son and reared me.
Akki, the drawer of water, appointed me as his gardener.
While I was a gardener, Ishtar granted me her love,
And for four and . . . years I exercised kingship.[8]

This is, at best, strongly fictionalized history, though we learn from more reliable sources[9] that the man who was to call himself *Sharru-kîn*, 'the righteous (or legitimate) king', was of humble origin. The cup-bearer of Ur-Zababa, King of Kish, he managed – we do not know how – to overthrow his master and marched against Uruk, where reigned Lugalzagesi, then overlord of Sumer. This king who had fifty *ensis* under his command, was defeated, captured, put 'in a carcan' and exposed at Enlil's gate in Nippur. Thereafter the usurper attacked Ur, Lagash and Umma; everywhere he was victorious and of every town he 'tore down the walls'. To show that he had conquered Sumer in its totality and that he now held the key to the Gulf, at Eninkimar, the port of Lagash he made a symbolic gesture, a gesture which will later be repeated by other monarchs on other shores: he washed his weapon in the Lower Sea.

Sargon could have contented himself with the prestigious title 'King of Kish', but he had other ambitions. Somewhere on the Euphrates he founded a new capital, Agade – the only royal city of ancient Iraq whose location remains unknown[10] – wherein he built a palace as well as temples for his tutelary goddess, Ishtar, and for Zababa, the warrior-god of Kish. The major innovation of the reign, however, was the ascendancy given to the Semites over the Sumerians. Akkadian governors were appointed in all the main city-states, and Akkadian became, as much as Sumerian, the language of official inscriptions. Yet it seems that the vanquished *lugal* and *ensi* remained in function and that only newly created offices and provinces were given to Akkadians. Moreover, the religious institutions of Sumer were respected. Sargon's daughter Enheduanna – a poetess who wrote a beautiful hymn to Inanna[11] – was made a priestess of Nanna, the moon-god of Ur, and by calling himself 'anointed priest of Anu' and 'great *ensi* of Enlil' the King of Agade proved that he did not wish to break with ancient and respectable traditions.

Having consolidated his political and moral authority over Sumer and considerably enlarged his army, Sargon launched several military campaigns in at least two directions: across the Tigris towards Iran, and along the Euphrates towards Syria. To the east, he met with strong resistance: the troops of four rulers of south-western Persia led by the King of Awan. The enemies were eventually defeated, several cities were sacked, and the various governors, viceroys and kings of Elam, Warahshe and neighbouring districts became the vassals of Sargon. It was at that time that Susa was raised by Sargon's viceroy from the rank of a modest market-place to that of a capital city and that Akkadian was imposed as the official language of Elam. Whether he sponsored or merely accepted this transfer of power from the mountains of Awan to the Elamite plain, the King of Akkad could hardly have foreseen that a governor of Elam would contribute to the fall of his own dynasty, or that the name of Susa would, for centuries to come, be symbolic of Mesopotamian defeat and humiliation. The campaign to the north-west appears, perhaps wrongly, almost as an armed promenade: Sargon says that in Tutul (Hit) he 'prostrated himself in prayer before Dagan' (the grain-god worshipped all along the Middle Euphrates) and that 'Dagan gave him the Upper Region: Mari, Iarmuti[12] and Ebla as far as the Cedar Forest and the Silver Mountain', the former standing for the Lebanon or the Amanus and the latter for the Taurus range. As these mountain names indicate, Sargon had secured a supply of wood and precious metal which could now be floated safely and freely down the Euphrates to Agade, but the victory over Mari and Ebla – both Semitic kingdoms like his own – had rid the King of Akkad of two dangerous rivals.

This is as far as the authentic sources – Sargon's own inscriptions – take us. None of them, however, alludes to northerly campaigns in the upper Tigris region, and it is probably to Sargon's grandon, Narâm-Sin, that must be attributed the magnificent bronze head found at Nineveh and likely to portray an Akkadian sovereign, as well as the introduction in future Assyria of the first tablets and inscriptions.[13] But what are we to think of the several chronicles, omens and literary compositions of later date which give us a detailed and often poetic description of Sargon's campaigns and conquests? Where, for instance, does history end and legend begin in the text known as the 'Epic of the King of the Battle' which shows the King of Akkad advancing deep into the heart of Asia Minor to protect merchants from the exactions of the King of Burushanda?[14] We can accept successful campaigns in Kurdistan and perhaps expeditions on the Gulf as far as Oman, but can we really believe that Sargon 'crossed the Sea of the West' and set foot in Cyprus and Crete, as an omen and a rather obscure geographical list would suggest? The figure of the first great Mesopotamian conqueror enflamed the ancient writers' imagination. For them, the king who had said:

> Now, any king who wants to call himself my equal,
> Wherever I went, let him go![15]

was perfectly capable of having conquered 'the world'. Yet extreme scepticism is as undesirable as extreme credulity, for some of these stories, and notably the Anatolian expedition, must contain at least a grain of truth.

The glorious reign of Sargon lasted for no less than fifty-five years (c. 2334–2279 B.C.). 'In his old age,' says a late Babylonian chronicle,[16] 'all the lands revolted against him, and they besieged him in Agade.' But the old lion still had teeth and claws: 'he went forth to battle and defeated them; he knocked them over and destroyed their vast army'. Later on, we are told, 'Subartu – i.e. (the nomadic tribes of) Upper Jazirah – in their might attacked, but they submitted to his arms, and Sargon settled their habitations, and he smote them grievously.'

The Akkadian Empire

The events which darkened the last years of Sargon announced the general revolt which broke out in Sumer and in Iran after his death. His son and successor, Rimush, repressed it with extreme vigour, but his authority was challenged even in his own palace: after only nine years of reign (2278–2270), during which he led a successful campaign in Elam, 'his servants', says a Babylonian omen,[17] 'killed him with their *kunukku*', a word which usually designates both the cylinder-seal and the sealed tablet but which, in this context, probably has a different meaning. Rimush was replaced by Manishtusu, perhaps his twin brother as his name 'Who is with him?' might suggest.

One of the main events in Manishtusu's reign (2269–2255) was an expedition across the Persian Gulf. It is described as follows:

Manishtusu, King of Kish, when he had subjugated Anshan and Shirikum (in S.W. Iran), he crossed the Lower Sea in ships. The kings of the cities on the other side of the sea, 32 of them assembled for battle. He defeated them and subjugated their cities; he overthrew their lords and seized the whole country as far as the silver mines. The mountains beyond the Lower Sea – their stones he took away, and he made his statue, and he presented it to Enlil.[18]

These 'mountains beyond the sea' were most probably those of Oman, rich in copper and hard stone. The goal of the expedition is clearly stated, and if we look at the situation in Mesopotamia at that time we understand the reasons behind it. The northern regions had probably been crossed by the armies of Sargon but not effectively occupied. The populations of Jazirah and northern Syria were free again, or rather, had returned under Eblaite rule. Farther north, a people which will later play an important part in the history of ancient Iraq, the Hurrians, occupied part of the great half-circle of the Taurus mountains from Urkish, near Nisibin, to Nawar, probably somewhere in Kurdistan, and perhaps as far south as the Upper Zab. Their eastern neighbours, the Lullubi, were entrenched in the Shehrizor plain, near Suleimaniyah. Below the Lullubi, around Hamadan in the central Zagros, were the savage Guti and farther south, the turbulent tribes around Elam. All these peoples were on anything but friendly terms with the Akkadians, and as they held all the passes leading from Anatolia, Armenia and Azerbaijan to Mesopotamia, the latter was cut off from her traditional supplies of copper, tin and silver. The 'bronze routes' were closed, and the Akkadians had only two alternatives: either to secure other sources of metal, such as Oman or south-eastern Persia, or to fight in the north.

Narâm-Sin ('Beloved of Sin'), the son of Manishtusu, chose war and, at least for a while, was rewarded with success. To the title of 'King of Agade', he could proudly add those of 'King of the Four Regions (of the World)' (*shar kibrat 'arbaim*) and 'King of the Universe' (*shar kishshati*). Furthermore, his name was preceded by the star, the ideogram for 'god', read in Sumerian *dingir*, in Akkadian *ilu*. Thus the king had become a god, like Lugalbanda and Gilgamesh. Megalomania? Perhaps, although the mighty Assyrian kings of the first millennium B.C. were never deified. But we must confess that the deification of a limited number of monarchs in ancient Mesopotamia is a strange practice not yet fully understood. It has been assumed that the divine title was taken only by those sovereigns who played the part of the male god in the Sacred Marriage ceremony. Others believe that posing as a god was the only way in which these early Mesopotamian empire-builders could secure absolute obedience from the various *ensis* of their kingdom. Both explanations, however, are highly conjectural.

Narâm-Sin was of the same stamp as his grandfather Sargon and like him became a hero of legend. His long reign (2254–2218) was almost entirely filled with military operations, and they all took place at the periphery of Mesopotamia. In the west he 'slew Arman (Aleppo?) and Ebla with the weapon of the god Dagan', partly destroying the palace of Mari on his way. And 'he overpowered the Amanus, the Cedar Mountain'.[19] In the north a campaign against the Hurrians is attested by a royal relief carved in the rock at Pir Hussain, near Diarbakr, and a royal city was built at Tell Brak, a key position in the heart of the Khabur basin, which controlled all the roads of Jazirah.[20] In the extreme south Magan (Oman) probably revolted, for Narâm-Sin 'marched against Magan and personally caught Mandannu, its king'. But the main campaign was directed against the powerful Lullubi. The Akkadian victory over them is commemorated by another rock sculpture at Darband-i-Gawr, near Sar-i-Pul (Iran) and by a masterpiece of Mesopotamian sculpture: the famous stele found at Susa and now the pride of the Louvre museum.[21] There Narâm-Sin, armed with the bow and the horned tiara of the gods on his head, is shown climbing a steep mountain and treading upon the corpses of his enemies; his infantry, pictured on a smaller scale, follows him. The gods, who dwarfed the humans in Early Dynastic Sumerian sculpture, are now, significantly, reduced to discreet symbols: two stars in the sky.

Did the reign end in semi-disaster? A document known as 'the Cuthean Legend of Narâm-Sin' shows the King of Akkad 'bewildered, confused, sunk in gloom, sorrowful, exhausted' from an overwhelming invasion;[22] but, here again, the mixture of facts and fancy calls for extreme caution. There is no doubt, however, that Narâm-Sin was the last great monarch of the Akkadian dynasty. No sooner was he dead than the pressure at the frontiers of the empire became formidable. Throughout his reign Elam and Mesopotamia had lived on friendly terms: the king had bestowed his favours upon Susa, and the energetic governor of Elam, Puzur-Inshushinak, had subdued on his behalf the tribes of the southern Zagros. But under Narâm-Sin's successor, Shar-kali-sharri, Puzur-Inshushinak declared himself independent, abandoned the Akkadian language for his own tongue, Elamite, and dared take the supreme title 'King of the Universe'. The King of Agade, whose name, ironically, meant 'King of all Kings', was powerless to intervene, so busy was he with the repression of revolts in Sumer and with wars against the Lullubi, the Guti and the nomads of Syria, the Amorites whom we shall soon meet again.

Shar-kali-sharri, like Rimush and Manishtusu, disappeared in a palace revolution (2193 B.C.), and the Akkadian empire collapsed as rapidly as it had been built up. The state of anarchy in the capital was such that the Sumerian King List simply says:

> Who was king? Who was not king?
> Was Igigi king?
> Was Nanum king?
> Was Imi king?
> Was Elulu king?
> Their tetrad was king, and reigned 3 years!

Several Sumerian cities became independent, following the example set by Uruk where a local dynasty (Uruk IV, five kings, thirty years) reigned from the last days of Narâm-Sin. From Elam Puzur-Inshushinak conducted a raid into Mesopotamia and reached the neighbourhood of Agade. In Kurdistan Annubanini, King of the Lullubi, carved his image on the rock with an inscription in Akkadian boasting of widespread conquests.[23] Yet it was neither the Elamites nor the Lullubi, but the Guti who won the decisive battle, although we do not know how, where and when. Under the last puppet kings of Akkad they were already installed in Mesopotamia, and for about a century the Sumerians and Akkadians were to obey sovereigns who responded to such strange names as Inimagabesh or Jarlagab, but they did not feel responsible for the disaster. A long and moving Sumerian poem called 'The Curse of Agade' places the burden on Narâm-Sin who is accused of having destroyed Enlil's temple in Nippur – a sacrilege which could not pass unpunished.[24]

The rise and fall of the Akkadian empire offers a perfect preview of the rise and fall of all subsequent Mesopotamian empires: rapid expansion followed by ceaseless rebellions, palace revolutions, constant wars on the frontiers, and in the end, the *coup de grâce* given by the highlanders: Guti now, Elamites, Kassites, Medes or Persians tomorrow. A civilization based on agriculture and metal work in a country like Iraq required, to be viable, two conditions: perfect cooperation between the various ethnic and socio-political units within the country itself, and a friendly or at least a neutral attitude from its neighbours. Unfortunately, neither one nor the other ever lasted for any length of time. The narrow nationalism of the Sumerians, inherited from a distant past and founded on their attachment to the local gods, could not accommodate itself to obedience to a common ruler, always necessarily 'foreign'. On the other hand, the treasures accumulated in the prosperous cities of the plain attracted the poor shepherds of the hills no less than those of the steppe, and they were bent upon pillage. It was not enough for the Mesopotamians to keep them at a respectful distance: they had to conquer them, to subdue them if they wished to keep open the vital arteries of their trade. In this endless guerrilla war on two fronts the kings of Akkad, as later the kings of Ur, Babylon and Assyria, used up their strength and, sooner or later, their empires collapsed.

The death of Shar-kali-sharri practically marks the end of the 'Akkadian period' as it is often called; but short as it was, this period exerted a deep and lasting influence on Mesopotamian history. The geographical horizon of Sumer was considerably enlarged. The Semitic language of the Akkadians found a wider audience, and the first two historical populations of Iraq were intimately blended for future destinies. The Sumero-Akkadian culture and its support, the cuneiform writing, were adopted not only by the people of northern Mesopotamia, but by the Hurrians, the Lullubi and the Elamites. Conversely, Mesopotamia was immensely enriched by the introduction of bronze, silver, wood and stone in large quantities, while numerous prisoners of war working as slaves provided cheap and abundant labour. Elam, Bahrain (Dilmun), Oman (?Magan) and the whole Gulf came under Mesopotamian influence, while Proto-Indian seals, vases and ornaments found in Iraq testify to commercial relations with the Indus valley (perhaps the Meluhha of our texts), where flourished the brilliant civilization of Harappa and Mohenjo-Daro.[25] In art the new tendencies were towards realism, and true portraits replaced the more or less conventional figures of Early Dynastic times. Politically, the period rings the knell of the small city-states and heralds the advent of large, centralized kingdoms. In the social and economic fields the Akkadian preference for private property and the constitution of large royal estates[26] eroded the domain and power of the temples, at least in Sumer. Even the Sumerian reaction which succeeded the Akkadian interlude could not entirely revert to old-fashioned ideas and customs, and in many respects the kings of Ur followed the pattern laid down by Sargon and his dynasty.

CHAPTER 10

THE GREAT KINGDOM OF UR

About the Guti who overthrew the Akkadian empire and ruled over Mesopotamia for almost a hundred years we know next to nothing.[1] The Sumerian King List gives 'the hordes of Gutium' twenty-one kings, but very few of them have left us inscriptions, and this, coupled with silence from other sources, points to a period of political unrest. The invaders were certainly not very numerous; they ravaged the country, probably plundered Agade and occupied Nippur and a few strategic points. Yet we know from a recently published inscription that at least one of their kings, Erridu-Pizir, fought against the Lullubi and the Hurrians of Kurdistan in defence of Akkad,[2] and many cities must have enjoyed almost complete freedom, keeping alive a spirit of national resistance which, eventually, culminated in the liberation of Sumer and Akkad. When, in about 2120 B.C., Utuhegal, *ensi* of Uruk, mustered an army and rose against 'the stinging serpent of the hills' several princes in southern Iraq followed him. The hated foreigners were defeated; Tiriqan, their king, tried to escape, was captured and handed over to the Sumerian leader:

Utu-hegal sat down; Tiriqan lay at his feet. Upon his neck he set his foot, and the sovereignty of Sumer he restored into his (own) hands.[3]

Nippur was no doubt recovered, and Uruk, the city which since the days of Gilgamesh had given Sumer no less than four dynasties, could stand once again at the head of the city-states. But its fifth dynasty was short-lived: after seven years of reign Utu-hegal was evicted by one of his own officials, Ur-Nammu,* governor of Ur, who took the titles 'King of Ur, King of Sumer

---

* 'Warrior of the goddess Nammu'.

and Akkad'. Thus was founded the Third Dynasty of Ur (*c.* 2112–2004 B.C.), which represents one of the most brilliant periods in the history of ancient Iraq, for not only did Ur-Nammu and his successors restore the Akkadian empire throughout its length and breadth but they gave Mesopotamia a century of relative peace and prosperity and sponsored an extraordinary renaissance in all the branches of Sumerian art and literature.

Ur-Nammu and Gudea

Compared with the Sargonic period, the time of the Third Dynasty of Ur – the 'Ur III' or 'Neo-Sumerian' period, as it is sometimes called – is conspicuously poor in historical inscriptions and, much as we should like to, we cannot follow Ur-Nammu in the battles which served to enlarge his kingdom. The collapse of the Guti followed by the accidental death of Utu-hegal ('his body was carried off by the river') must have resulted in complete political vacuum, and we may assume that the whole of Mesopotamia fell into the hands of the King of Ur in a comparatively short time. The rest of the reign (2112–2095) was devoted to the fulfilment of more domestic but none the less urgent and important tasks: the restoration of order and prosperity and the care of the gods. Ur-Nammu 'freed the land from thieves, robbers and rebels' and has long been thought to have dictated what is considered to be the most ancient collection of laws in the world, although it appears from a newly found tablet that the true author was his son Shulgi.[4] In its present state, this 'code' is incomplete, but what remains of the laws is of considerable interest, for it appears that at least some crimes (such as physical injury) were not punished by death or mutilation, as later in the Code of Hammurabi or the Hebraic law, but the offender was obliged to pay compensation in silver, the weight of which varied according to the gravity of the crime. This, of course, is the sign of a society far more polished and civilized than is usually imagined.[5] Ur-Nammu

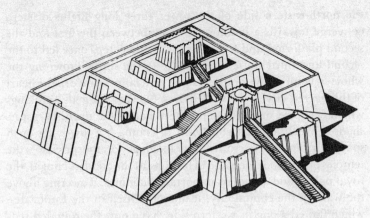

Reconstruction of the ziqqurat of Ur, as it probably looked at the
time it was built by Ur-Nammu or Shulgi.
After Sir Leonard Woolley, Ur Excavations, V, 1939.

also revived agriculture and improved communications by digging a number of canals; towns were fortified against future
wars, and an enormous amount of rebuilding was carried out.
But in the minds of archaeologists the name of Ur-Nammu will
for ever be associated with the *ziqqurats*, or stage-towers, which
he erected in Ur, Uruk, Eridu, Nippur and various other cities
and which are still the most impressive monuments of these
sites.[6]

The best preserved of these stage-towers, the ziqqurat of Ur,
may be taken as an example.[7] Built of mud bricks, but covered
with a thick 'skin' of baked bricks set in bitumen, the stage-
tower of Ur measured at its base 60.50 by 43 metres. It had at
least three tiers, and though only the first and part of the
second tiers have survived, its present height is about twenty
metres. Yet this enormous mass gives an astonishing impression
of lightness due partly to its perfect proportions and partly to
the fact that all its lines are slightly curved, a device long
thought to have been invented by the Greek architects who
built the Parthenon, nearly two thousand years later. Against

the north-eastern side of the tower three long flights of steps converge towards a landing half-way between the first and the second platforms, and from this point other steps once led to the second and third stories and finally to the shrine crowning the whole structure. The ziqqurat stood on a large terrace in the heart of the 'sacred city' – the walled area reserved for gods and kings which occupied most of the northern half of the town. It cast its shadow over the great courtyard of Nanna – a low-lying open space surrounded by stores and lodgings for the priests – the temples of the moon-god and of his consort the goddess Ningal, the royal palace and other less important buildings. Towering above the walls of the capital city, it mirrored itself in the Euphrates, which flowed along its western side. Even now the rounded red-brown pyramid topping the enormous greyish mound of the ruins forms a landmark visible from many miles away. The ziqqurats of other cities are not so well preserved and differ from that of Ur in several details, but their shape, their orientation and their position in relation to the main temples remain essentially the same. What then, it may be asked, was the purpose of these monuments?

The pioneers of Mesopotamian archaeology naïvely thought that the ziqqurats were observatories for 'Chaldaean' astronomers, or even towers 'where the priests of Bel could spend the night away from the heat and mosquitoes', but this obviously does not make sense. Comparison with Egypt comes immediately to mind, and indeed, Sumerian architects may well have inspired their Egyptian counterparts; but it must be emphasized that the ziqqurats, contrary to the pyramids, do not contain tombs or chambers; they were built as a rule upon older, more modest structures erected during the Early Dynastic period, and these low, one-tiered, archaic ziqqurats derived, it is now generally believed, from the platforms that supported the temples of the Ubaid, Uruk and Jemdat Nasr periods. But why these platforms, why these towers? Philology throws no light on the problem, since the word *ziqqurat* (sometimes transcribed ziggurat or zikkurat) comes from a verb *zaqaru*, which simply means 'to build high', and we have the choice of several theories.

Some authors believe that the Sumerians were originally highlanders who worshipped their gods upon the mountain-tops, and so built these towers to serve as artificial mountains in the flat Mesopotamian plain. Others, rejecting this over-simplified and questionable explanation, think that the purpose of the temple platform (and therefore of the ziqqurat) was to raise the main god of the city above the other gods and to protect him from the promiscuity of laymen. Yet another group of scholars sees in the monument a colossal staircase, a bridge between the lower temples, where the routine ceremonies of the cult were performed, and the upper sanctuary, half-way between heaven and earth, where men and gods could meet on certain occasions; and this, we believe, is nearer the truth. All considered, perhaps the best definition of the ziqqurat is given by the Bible (*Genesis* xi. 4), where it is said that the 'Tower of Babel' (i.e. the ziqqurat of Babylon) was meant 'to reach unto heaven'. In the deeply religious mind of the Sumerians these enormous, yet curiously light constructions were 'prayers of bricks' as our Gothic cathedrals are 'prayers of stone'. They extended to the gods a permanent invitation to descend on earth at the same time as they expressed one of man's most remarkable efforts to rise above his miserable condition and to establish closer contacts with the divinity.

Judging from the dispersion throughout southern Iraq of bricks stamped with Ur-Nammu's name, it would appear that the building of temples was the king's privilege, and indeed it was, when the Ur III empire was firmly established, but before that we know of a city not far from the capital where a grandiose building programme was carried out by the local ruler with truly royal magnificence: this was Lagash under its famous *ensi* Gudea (*c.* 2141–2122 B.C.).

We have seen (Chapter 8) that Lugalzagesi of Umma had put an end to the protracted conflict between his city and Lagash by setting fire to the monuments of Girsu and turning it into a mass of ruins. But in the ancient Orient towns were rarely as completely destroyed as the texts would have us believe, and somehow Girsu survived. Towards the end of the

Gutian period it was in the hands of energetic princes who apparently managed to remain independent and set themselves the task of reinvigorating the faded glory of their city. One of them was Gudea,* a contemporary of the last Gutian kings, whose numerous statues and inscriptions provide the most admirable examples of Sumerian achievement in art and literature.

Gudea built – or rather rebuilt – at least fifteen temples in the city-state of Lagash, but on none of them was he so lavish as on the E-ninnu, the temple of Ningirsu, the city-god of Girsu. On two large clay cylinders and on some of his statue inscriptions[8] he explains at length why and how he built it, giving us, incidentally, invaluable details on the complicated rites essential to the foundation of sanctuaries in ancient Mesopotamia. It is typical of Sumerian thinking that the decision to erect a temple is given not as an act of will of the ruler, but as the fulfilment of a wish of the god expressed in the form of a mysterious dream:

In the heart of a dream, here was a man: his height equalled the sky, his weight equalled the earth . . . To his right and to his left lions were crouching . . . He told me to build him a temple, but I did not understand his heart (= his desire) . . .

Here was a woman. Who was she not, who was she? . . . She was holding in her hand a stylus of flaming metal; she was holding the tablet of good writing of heaven; she was immersed in her thoughts . . .

Troubled and perplexed, Gudea first sought comfort from his 'mother', the goddess Gatamdug, and then proceeded by boat to the temple of the goddess Nanshe 'interpreter of dreams'. Nanshe explained that the man was Ningirsu and the woman Nisaba, the goddess of science; she advised Gudea to offer Ningirsu a chariot 'adorned with shining metal and lapis-lazuli':

Then, inscrutable as the sky, the wisdom of the Lord, or Ningirsu, the son of Enlil, will soothe thee. He will reveal to thee the plan of His temple, and the Warrior whose decrees are great will build it for thee.

* 'the one called (to power)'.

Gudea obeyed. Having united the citizens of Girsu 'as the sons of the same mother' and made peace reign in every house, he desecrated the old temple and purified the city:

He purified the holy city and encircled it with fires . . . He collected clay in a very pure place; in a pure place he made silt into the bricks and put the bricks into the mould. He followed the rites in all their splendour: he purified the foundations of the temple, surrounded it with fires, anointed the platform with an aromatic balm . . .

When this was done, craftsmen were brought from afar:

From Elam came the Elamites, from Susa the Susians. Magan and Meluhha collected timber from their mountains . . . and Gudea brought them together in his town Girsu.

Gudea, the great *en*-priest of Ningirsu, made a path into the Cedar mountains which nobody had entered before; he cut its cedars with great axes . . . Like giant snakes, cedars were floating down the water (of the river) . . .

In the quarries which nobody had entered before, Gudea, the great *en*-priest of Ningirsu, made a path and then the stones were delivered in large blocks . . . Many other precious metals were carried to the ensi. From the Copper mountain of Kimash . . . its mountains as dust . . . For Gudea, they mined silver from its mountains, delivered red stone from Meluhha in great amount . . .

Finally the construction work proper began, and within one year the sanctuary was completed, beautifully appointed and ready for the god's ceremonial entry:

Respect for the temple – says Gudea proudly – pervades the country; the fear of it fills the strangers; the brilliance of the Eninnu enfolds the universe like a mantle!

Alas, of this magnificent temple practically nothing remains, and we would be tempted to tax Gudea with gross exaggeration were it not for the seventeen odd statues of the *ensi* that have come to us, mostly as the result of illicit digging.[9] Carved out of hard, polished black diorite from Magan, they are executed with a simplicity of line, an economy of detail, a sensitivity of expression which give them a prominent place in the gallery of world sculpture. If such masterpieces were displayed in the sanctuaries of Girsu we can well believe that the rest of the decoration and the buildings themselves were of no inferior quality.

This young man sitting calmly, a faint smile upon his lips, his hands clasped in front of his chest, the plan of a temple or a foot rule across his knees, is the finest example of a figure unfortunately soon to disappear: the perfect Sumerian ruler, pious, just, cultured, faithful to the old traditions, devoted to his people, filled with love and pride for his city and, at least in this particular case, pacific – in all the inscriptions of Gudea, only one military campaign in Anshan (East of Elam) is mentioned; there is therefore no doubt that the timber, metal and stone used in his buildings were acquired by trade and not by territorial conquests. What was given in exchange is not disclosed, but the widespread commercial undertakings of the *ensi* of Lagash testify to the almost unbelievable prosperity of a Sumerian city-state after one hundred years of Akkadian government and almost fifty years of foreign occupation.

Shulgi, Amar-Sin and the Sumerian Empire

'Abandoned on the battlefield like a crushed vessel',[10] Ur-Nammu died in an untold war and was succeeded by his son Shulgi,* who reigned forty-seven years (2094–2047 B.C.). The first half of this long reign was spent in peaceful activities: the temples and ziqqurats founded by Ur-Nammu were completed and new buildings erected; the gods were reinstated in their shrines under the care of high-priests appointed by the king; the calendar was reformed and a new measure of grain, the royal *gur* (about six bushels) superseded the local measures formerly in use; in all probability, a thorough political, economic and

---

* This name, which probably means 'noble young man', was formerly read *Dungi*.

administrative reorganization of the kingdom took place during this period. Furthermore, this king who claimed to have mastered the science of the scribe founded the two great schools of Ur and Nippur to which we owe so many masterpieces of Sumerian literature. On his twenty-fourth year of reign, however, Shulgi embarked upon a long series of annual military campaigns in the plains and hills of Kurdistan. The theatre of these operations was a triangular region delimited by the towns of Shashrum, Urbilum and Harshi and having for its centre Simurrum, an apparently mighty stronghold which had to be captured and 'devastated' nine times before it succumbed.[11] This region was inhabited by Hurrians who, with their Lullubi allies, were probably threatening two major trade routes: one along the Diyala river to central Iran, the other along the Tigris to Armenia and Anatolia. The threat must have been strong, for between two of the three 'Hurrian wars' the Sumerians built a fortified wall somewhere between the Tigris and the Zagros range. In the end, Shulgi was victorious and turned this part of Kurdistan into a Sumerian province (2051). In South-West Iran, the Sumerian king pursued a more diplomatic and easier policy. The Guti had put an end to Puzur-Inshushinak's reign and plunged Elam into a state of anarchy worse than that of Mesopotamia. Shulgi took advantage of the situation to assert his authority over the former Akkadian protectorate. He married his own daughters to the rulers of Warahshe and Awan, took possession of Susa where he installed a Sumerian governor but built a temple to Inshushinak, Elam's supreme god, crushed a revolt in Anshan and finally enlisted Elamite soldiers into a kind of 'foreign legion' entrusted with the defence of Sumer's south-eastern border. Following the example set by Narâm-Sin, Shulgi called himself 'King of the Four Quarters (of the World)' and was worshipped as a god during and after his lifetime. Twice monthly offerings were made to his statues throughout the empire, hymns were written praising him,[12] and the name of 'divine Shulgi' was given to a month of the Sumerian calendar.

Amar-Sin,* son of Shulgi, reigned only nine years (2046–2038). Like his father, he divided his time between the building of temples and the conduct of wars in the same north-easterly districts, was deified and, with complete lack of modesty, referred to himself as 'the god who gives life to the country' or 'the god sun (i.e. judge) of the Land'. According to a late omen-text, Amar-Sin died of an infection caused by a shoe-bite. He was buried, side by side with Shulgi, in a vast and remarkable underground mausoleum found intact though plundered in the sacred city of Ur, near the famous 'Royal Cemetery'.[13]

During the reigns of Shulgi and Amar-Sin the Sumerian 'empire't reached its zenith. Within borders that are hazy for us, three different zones can be identified. At the periphery were independent states, such as Elam or Mari, which had been drawn into the sphere of influence of Ur by a policy of matrimonial alliances introduced by Ur-Nammu at Mari[14] and pursued by Shulgi elsewhere. Then came conquered countries transformed into provinces and put under a civilian governor (*ensi*) or a military governor (*sagin* in Sumerian, *shakkanakkum* in Akkadian), often of local origin; this was the case with Susa, Assur and probably a great portion of Northern Mesopotamia, as suggested by the fact that Ur-Nammu repaired and renovated the palace of Narâm-Sin at Tell Brak, where it had been destroyed, presumably by the Guti. Finally, in the heart of the kingdom (Sumer and Akkad), the former city-states were now treated as provinces. The only *lugal* was the King of Ur, and the once proud *ensi* had become mere administrators appointed by him to maintain order, dispense justice, implement royal instructions concerning public works and collect duties and taxes. The different parts of this vast territory were interconnected by a network of roads with fixed halting-places, a day's

---

* The name, formerly read *Bur-Sin*, is sometimes transcribed *Amar-Su'en*. It means 'bull calf of (the god) Sin'.

† It must be noted that neither the word nor even the concept of 'empire' has ever existed in the ancient Near East.

walk apart, where the official travellers, escorted by soldiers and gendarmes, received a ration that varied in importance according to their rank.[15] These were royal couriers (*lu-kasa*) but also *sukkal*, that is to say royal inspectors periodically sent by the king to ensure that the local and regional administrations worked smoothly. Their chief, the *sukkalmah* ('great sukkal'), held the highest post in the central government: he was the 'grand chancellor' responsible only to the sovereign.

One of the most specific institutions of the kingdom of Ur was the *bala* (literally 'rotation'), a taxation system whereby each *ensi* of Sumer and Akkad in turn paid the State a monthly tax, usually in cattle or sheep.[16] These taxes converged towards a large collecting centre called Sellush-Dagan, nowadays Drehem, a few kilometres south of Nippur. There, they were sorted, some of them going to Nippur – more than ever the religious capital of Sumer – and the rest to Ur. To these taxes must be added the tribute (*gun*) in silver, cattle, hides and various objects paid by far-away provinces and by some countries under Sumerian tutelage, as well as the 'gifts' sent by foreign rulers.[17] All in-going and out-going goods were carefully recorded by the scribes of Sellush-Dagan.

These Drehem archives, together with those found at Ur, Nippur, Girsu and Umma, constitute a huge mass of administrative documents of which about forty thousand have already been published[18] and as many, if not more, are still lying in the drawers of museums, universities and private collections. In spite of this apparent wealth of information, our knowledge of the social and economic systems in Sumer under the Third Dynasty of Ur will never be complete for the simple reason that, apart from a few contracts, letters and judgements, all these texts are only accounts of State institutions, the private sector, if any, being completely occluded. Moreover, the sheer number of tablets to be studied, the uncertain meaning of some Sumerian titles and functions and the methodological problems raised by an undertaking of that size mean that it will be a long time before the coherent synthesis expected by all historians becomes available.

In our present state of knowledge, the general impression created by these documents is that the type of central government which had developed around the Temple and the Palace in the Early Dynastic period (pp. 131–4) persisted but with the emphasis now on the Palace. On all his lands and subjects the king of Ur exerted absolute power based on his personal qualities and on a mandate he claimed to have received from Enlil with as sole condition the respect of traditions – a respect which went so far that 'dynasties' of *ensi* and *shagin* were tolerated, and even a provincial judge could oppose a royal verdict.[19] In theory the owner, on behalf of Enlil, of all goods and estates, the king seems to have possessed only the 'food land' in the small territory of the city of Ur. On the other hand, the Palace received from everywhere an unceasing flow of taxes, duties, tributes and gifts which provided the monarch, his family and his court with a very substantial income. It is only fair to add that large chunks of this income were spent on financing the building of temples, the digging and maintenance of canals and the undertaking of other public works throughout the Sumerian 'empire'.

As in the remote past, the wheat and barley fields were cultivated and managed by the numerous persons who worked for the temples under command of a 'prefect' (*shabra*) assisted by an army of supervisors, controllers and scribes. The cultivable lands were still divided into lord's land (i.e. god's land), food land and plough land, and the yield was considerable: in the second year of Amar-Sin, for example, almost 255,000 hectolitres of wheat were harvested around Girsu. We are not so well informed on the pastoral sector of the economy, although we occasionally read about large herds and flocks bred and fed by the State (i.e. the Temple and the Palace); but we return to firmer ground with the Sumerian 'industry', that is to say the transformation of agricultural and pastoral products – but not metal work which remained in the hands of artisans.[20] Throughout southern (and probably also central) Mesopotamia were big, self-sufficient factories producing such commodities as leather, textiles or flour and employing thousands of workers, most of them female. Thus, in the region of Girsu fifteen thousand women were employed in the local textile industry,[21] and in the same area a cereal transformation unit was producing not only flour (1,100 tons per year) and bread, but also beer, linseed oil, grindstones, mortars, clay pots, woven reeds and leather. This particular factory employed 134 specialists and 858 skilled workers, including 669 women, 86 men and 103 teenagers. While there is some evidence of private merchants and 'businessmen',[22] the international trade seems to have been exclusively in the hands of the State which supplied the necessary capital. The majority of the so-called merchants (*damgar*) were in fact civil servants acting as intermediaries. Silver was still rare and mainly used as standard for exchanges, but sometimes also as 'money'. It was hoarded by high officials and did not circulate unless authorized by the Palace.

In the Ur III period, the Sumerian society – as seen through the administrative texts that are available and discounting a possible private sector of unknown size – seems to have been divided into two categories of persons. On one side, the relatively few officials of the central and provincial governments, from *sukkalmah* to *hazzanum* (village mayor), whose revenues and social status varied according to their rank. On the other side, the bulk of the population, employed by the great production units. These units were run by a large number of managers specialized in different activities, while the manpower was provided by teams of male (*gurush*) and female (*geme*) workers, skilled or unskilled. This labour force was also used either permanently or for long periods to carry out such seasonal work as harvesting cereals or gathering dates and reeds, or for occasional corvées, such as digging and maintaining irrigation canals, hauling river-boats or building fortifications. For some very extensive public works, soldiers (*eren*) were enlisted, and the whole population could be mobilized if needed. Slaves (*arad*) were in small numbers and exclusively recruited among those prisoners of war who had not been put to death after battle.[23] They were incorporated with units of *eren* or teams of *gurush*, while their wives and children were 'vowed' to temples or allocated to the great factories as employees or servants. All slaves enjoyed the same rights as the other labourers, and they could be set free by the institutions for which they worked.

As in the Early Dynastic period, salaries were paid in yearly, monthly or daily rations the nature and amounts of which varied according to age, sex and rank.[24] The minimum ration of an unskilled factory worker consisted of twenty litres of barley per month, plus three and a half litres of oil and two kilos of wool per annum. This sounds, and indeed was, very little, but it was to some extent supplemented by the smaller rations allotted to wives and children and by seasonal or occasional distributions of dates, beans, spices, fish, meat and clothes. On the other hand, an *engar*, who was a chief ploughman but also a kind of agricultural expert, received twice the above rations. In addition, he would be given a piece of food land and perhaps a small kitchen garden under palm-trees where he would grow fruit and vegetables, breed geese and goats. This would leave him with a surplus that would enable him to buy one or two servants and perhaps a house for his children. On the whole, it would appear that a large proportion of the Sumero-Akkadian population lived rather miserably and that some of them merely subsisted. These people often had to borrow goods or even silver from public or private lenders at a very high interest rate (thirty-three per cent for barley); some of the poorest were forced to hire out as servants their children and sometimes their wife until they were free of debt.

We shall never know what the 'man in the street' thought of the society in which he lived. He may have been the victim of abuse and injustice from the wealthy and the powerful, but he probably put up with a system in which he was only a cog; after all, he had never known anything else and he had to comply with the order established by the gods. In the days of Shulgi and Amar-Sin, the huge economic machine which ensured everybody's life and the prosperity of Sumer seemed to be working smoothly. To the contemporaries of these kings the empire must have looked like a large, well-kept, almost inde-structible edifice. But the soldiers keeping watch along the dusty roads of the desert knew that the nomads were already on the move. Across the Euphrates and the Khabur, they now trickled towards the green valley in harmless little streams; in a not too distant future, however, their bellicose tribes would form a rushing torrent which no power could stem.

The Fall of Ur

The first indication that things were not as quiet as they had been on the western frontier occurs during the reign of Shu-Sin* (2037–2029 B.C.), the brother and successor of Amar-Sin. Like the previous kings of Ur, 'divine' Shu-Sin restored a number of temples and campaigned in the Zagros mountains, where he defeated a coalition of several Iranian rulers.[25] He also helped his son-in-law, the king of Simanum (a town north of Mardin, in southern Turkey) to quell a rebellion, brought the rebels to Sumer and built a camp for them near Nippur: the first P.O.W. camp in Mesopotamia!). But the formula for his fourth year strikes an unfamiliar note, for in that year, we are told, the king 'built the fortress of MAR.TU (called) which keeps away *Tidnum*'.[26] We know from other sources that MAR.TU in Sumerian and Tidnum (or, more usually, Amurrum) in Akkadian were different names for the country west of the Euphrates and its inhabitants. This vast region corresponds to present-day Syria, including the desert around Palmyra, the Orontes valley and the mountains which border the Mediterranean Sea. Part of its population lived in towns and villages, but when the Sumerians or Akkadians spoke of the MAR.TU or *Amurrû* – the 'Amorites' as we call them – they had in mind those people with whom they were in particularly close contact: the nomadic tribes who roamed the Syrian desert and often crossed the

---

* Or *Shu-Su'en*, 'The one of (the god) Sin'.

rivers to graze their flocks in the steppes of Mesopotamia.[27] Since Early Dynastic times these wandering Amorites were well known to the Sumerians, either as individuals who had abandoned their tribe to live and work in the cities or as bedouins whose uncouth way of life was considered with disgust and contempt:

The MAR.TU who know no grain . . . The MAR.TU who know no house nor town, the boors of the mountains . . . The MAR.TU who digs up truffles . . . who does not bend his knees (to cultivate the land), who eats raw meat, who has no house during his lifetime, who is not buried after his death . . .[28]

Or again:

They have prepared wheat and *gú-nunuz* (grain) as a confection, but an Amorite will eat it without even recognizing what it contains![29]

Against these savages who raided villages and attacked the caravans frequent police operations were directed, and on occasion a full-scale campaign was launched. Thus one of the years of Shar-kali-sharri, the last great king of Agade, was named, after his victory over the MAR.TU 'in mount Basar', i.e. Jabal Bishri, between Palmyra and Deir-ez-Zor, and there are references to Amorite prisoners of war in texts of Shulgi and Amar-Sin. But the situation was now reversed: the Sumerians were on the defensive; somewhere between Mari and Ur they had to build a fortress in order to keep the nomads at bay.

For a time this measure must have proved effective, since we do not hear about the Amorites during the next ten years. Meanwhile, Shu-Sin died and was succeeded in 2028 by his son, Ibbi-Sin.* What happened during the change of reign we shall probably never know, but no sooner was the new king enthroned than the empire literally disintegrated.[30] One by one, the eastern provinces – beginning with Eshnunna in the second year of Ibbi-Sin and Susa in his third year – declared

* 'Sin has called'.

themselves independent and broke away from Ur. At the same time the Amorites were exerting an ever-increasing pressure on the borders of the kingdom. In the fifth year they broke through the defences and penetrated deep into the heart of Sumer. How critical the situation had become is shown by two letters exchanged between the king and one of his generals, Ishbi-Irra, a native from Mari, who had been ordered to buy a large quantity of grain in Nippur and nearby Isin and to convey it to Ur. Ishbi-Irra declares himself unable to carry out his mission because the MAR.TU have ravaged the country and cut off all roads leading to the capital city, and are ready to attack Isin and Nippur; he asks to be formally entrusted with the defence of the two cities. In his reply the king agrees, advises his officer to seek the help of other *ensis* and offers to buy the grain at double its normal price. Soon afterwards Ibbi-Sin succeeded in defeating the MAR.TU, but his subjects were starving and his authority was challenged by his own officials. In the eleventh year (2017) Ishbi-Irra proclaimed himself king in Isin – the very city he had pledged to protect on behalf of his lord – and a few years before, an Amorite sheikh called Nablânum had been crowned in Larsa, only twenty-five miles from Ur. To make matters worse, the Elamites took advantage of the situation to invade Sumer, as they had done so often in the past. Abandoned by the gods, beset with famine, attacked on two fronts, practically reduced to the capital city and its immediate neighbourhood, the great Sumerian empire was by now only the shadow of a kingdom. Ibbi-Sin fought to the last and apparently attempted to secure the alliance of the Amorites against the Elamites and the troops of his rival Ishbi-Irra. But this plan also failed. In 2004 B.C. the Elamites were at the walls of Ur – those walls which Ur-Nammu had built 'as high as a shining mountain'. They attacked the great city, took it, sacked it, burned it down and withdrew, leaving behind a small garrison. The unfortunate Ibbi-Sin was taken prisoner to Iran, 'to the end of Anshan whose cities he himself, like a bird, had devastated', and died there. Years later, when Ur was again a flourishing city, its destruction was still remembered and lamented by the Sumerians as a national catastrophe:

O Father Nanna, that city into ruins was made . . .
Its people, not potsherds, filled its sides;
Its walls were breached; the people groan.
In its lofty gates, where they were wont to promenade, dead bodies
    were lying about;
In its boulevards, where the feasts were celebrated, scattered they lay.
In all its streets, where they were wont to promenade, dead bodies
    were lying about;
In its places, where the festivities of the land took place, the people
    lay in heaps . . .
Ur – its weak and its strong perished through hunger;
Mothers and fathers who did not leave their houses were overcome by
    fire;
The young lying on their mothers' laps, like fish were carried off by
    the waters;
In the city, the wife was abandoned, the son was abandoned, the
    possessions were scattered about.
O Nanna, Ur has been destroyed, its people have been dispersed![31]

CHAPTER 11

THE AMORITES

The fall of Ur at the close of the third millennium B.C. is one of
the major turning-points in the history of ancient Iraq: it does
not only ring the knell of a dynasty and of an empire, it marks
the end of the Sumerian nation and type of society. Intervening
at the last moment, the Elamites had taken the capital-city, but
the secession of entire provinces, the revolt of Ibbi-Sin's officials
and the Amorite invasion were the real causes of the Sumerian
defeat. The Elamites were soon expelled from Iraq; the Semites
remained. From then on they were to hold the reins of government for nearly fifteen hundred years.

Even before Ur was captured, the Sumerian empire had
collapsed, and Mesopotamia had been shattered into a mosaic
of large or small kingdoms, the most important being those of
Isin and Larsa in the south, Assur and Eshnunna in the north.
For about two centuries (c. 2000–1800 B.C.) these kingdoms
coexisted, though by no means peacefully, those of the south
fighting each other for the possession of Ur and the sovereignty
over Sumer and Akkad; those of the north, for the control of
the great trade routes which crossed Upper Mesopotamia.
Meanwhile, waves of nomadic Semites continued to enter Iraq
from the west, pitching their tents up to the foot of the Zagros
or founding new kingdoms around the towns they occupied.
The rulers of one of these towns, Babylon, soon became powerful
enough to compete with their neighbours, and during the first
half of the eighteenth century B.C. Hammurabi succeeded in
eliminating his rivals and subdued the whole of Mesopotamia.
The empire he built alone – the 'Old Babylonian Empire' as it
may be called – was short-lived, but even after its fall Babylon
remained, together with its rival Assur, one of the two poles of
Mesopotamian history and civilization.

The rulers who replaced the Sumerians on the political stage were either Akkadians from Iraq or Western Semites – 'Amorites' in the broad sense of the term – from Syria and the western desert. The former were highly civilized; the latter, allegedly uncouth bedouins, assimilated the Sumero-Akkadian culture with remarkable ease and rapidity, partly because they came from regions long under its influence, and partly because the language presented them with no major difficulty. As they spoke Semitic dialects they adopted in writing the Akkadian language, and slowly in the south, rapidly in the north, the latter prevailed over Sumerian in private and official inscriptions. But this linguistic revolution hardly affected the religious, ethical and artistic concepts current in Mesopotamia since proto-historic times. The newcomers worshipped the Sumerian gods and the old Sumerian myths and epic tales were piously copied, translated or adapted with in general only minor alterations. As for the scarce artistic production of the period, there is practically nothing to distinguish it from that of the preceding Ur III period. Generally speaking, the civilization created by the Sumerians outlived them and survived these years of turmoil as it had survived the Akkadian domination and the Gutian conquest.

The advent of the Western Semites, however, had deep and lasting repercussions on the political, social and economic structure of ancient Mesopotamia.[1] The division of the country into kingdoms erased all traces of city-states, and with the city-states disappeared most of the principles upon which they were founded. Men, land and cattle ceased to belong physically to the gods, as in proto-historic times, or to the temples and the king, as under the Third Dynasty of Ur. The new monarchs seized or purchased large pieces of land, parts of which were worked by peasants for the Palace while others were distributed to their families and courtiers who in turn let them out to tenant farmers against payments in kind. Thus emerged a mixed society of big or medium-sized landowners and tenants who made up the bulk of the population. The 'industrial' production units inherited from the Third Dynasty of Ur were now much smaller, but craft workshops multiplied. Trade with foreign countries was in the hands of merchants[2] who remained State employees but also worked for themselves: organized into associations (*karum*), they embarked upon fruitful commercial ventures, sharing capital, risks and profits; they also benefited from government loans, bought the left-overs from the Palace and sold them at a much higher price, and acted as lenders to chronically endebted people. Deprived of their privileges, the temples became 'land-owners among other land-owners, tax-payers among other tax-payers'.[3] The priests assumed the service of the gods and cared for the spiritual needs of the people, while the king governed and cared for the welfare of his subjects, but the economic life of the country was no longer exclusively – or almost exclusively – in their hands. If, as in the past, each kingdom identified itself with its chief-god, if each sovereign claimed to owe his sceptre to divine favour, the traditional view according to which no prince could rule over Sumer and Akkad unless he had been elected by Enlil in Nippur became obsolete. The Sumerian *lugals* had invoked Enlil's blessings to justify their conquests; to the ruthless sheikhs who had seized the power by the sword and knew no other law than that of razzia, the investiture of the local god appeared sufficient. Thus Nippur lost its importance and Enlil his royal prerogative.

The period which opens with the fall of Ur and ends with the reign of Hammurabi – the so-called 'Isin-Larsa period' – is extremely rich in events. For greater clarity we must treat separately northern and southern Mesopotamia, beginning with the latter.

Isin, Larsa and Babylon

The kingdoms of Isin and Larsa[4] were founded within eight years of each other, but for almost a century Isin overshadowed Larsa. While the Amorite prince of Larsa, Naplânum, had to content himself with hardly more than the town he had conquered, Ishbi-Irra of Isin possessed the three important centres of Nippur, Uruk and Eridu. Towards the end of his reign he captured the Elamite garrison of Ur and recovered the ruined, but still prestigious city. His son, Shu-ilishu (1984–1975 B.C.) managed to bring back from Elam the statue of Nanna, the moon-god of Ur. The occupation of Sippar by Iddin-Dagan (1974–1954 B.C.), brought the frontiers of the kingdom from the Persian Gulf to the latitude of Baghdad; it now extended along the whole course of the Lower Euphrates, the vital artery of Sumer. As for Ishme-Dagan (1953–1935 B.C.) he attacked without success the famed city of Kish, then the capital of a small independent kingdom.

Ishbi-Irra was, it will be recalled, an Akkadian from Mari, and in the names of two of his descendants appears the great god of that city, the wheat-god Dagan. Yet these Semites considered themselves as the true successors of the Sumerian kings of Ur. Most of them were deified, like Shulgi and Amar-Sin, and hymns were composed in their honour.[5] They took the titles 'King of Ur, King of Sumer and Akkad', restored and embellished the former capital-city, renewed active commercial relations with Dilmun,[6] and ironically were obliged to defend their kingdom against those to whom they owed it, fighting the Elamites, building fortresses against the MAR.TU and imposing tribute upon their nomadic tribes. In official inscriptions from Isin the Sumerian language is used exclusively, and it must be emphasized that practically all the great pieces of Sumerian literature found in the famous 'library' of Nippur were com-posed or copied during that period at the request of monarchs craving for Sumerian culture. Sumer in those days was like the declining Roman empire where everything was Latin, save the emperors.

The supremacy of Isin went on unhindered until the reign of Lipit-Ishtar (1934–1924 B.C.), the author of a 'Code' of Law of which some forty-three articles and parts of the prologue and epilogue have survived.[7] As it happens, these laws deal mostly with succession, real estates, hire contracts and the condition of privately owned slaves, and therefore give us a limited but interesting insight into the society which was then taking shape. Unfortunately, this peaceful legislator entered into conflict with a formidable warrior whose name sounds like the beat of a battle-drum, Gungunum, King of Larsa. Gungunum had already campaigned in the Zagros when, in his eighth year (1924 B.C.), he attacked the kingdom of Isin and occupied Ur, claiming sovereignty over Sumer and Akkad. A few years later Lagash, Susa and perhaps Uruk fell into his hands. Larsa now possessed one-half of southern Iraq and a door on the 'Lower Sea'.

The loss of its main town and seaport was for Isin a severe setback further aggravated by the extinction of the ruling family. Lipit-Ishtar – who died the year he lost Ur – was replaced by an usurper, Ur-Ninurta, who in turn was defeated and killed by Abi-sare of Larsa. About twenty years later another usurper called Irra-imitti lost Nippur to his rival Sumu-El, and soon the kingdom was reduced to Isin and its immediate neighbourhood. The story of Irra-imitti's death and succession deserves to be told, since it illustrates a rare and strange Mesopotamian institution: on occasions, when omens were exceptionally sombre and the king feared the wrath of the gods, a commoner was placed upon the throne as 'substitute king', reigned for a certain time and was then put to death. This is how a Babylonian chronicle describes what happened in Isin:[8]

That the dynasty might not end, King Irra-imitti made the gardener Enlil-bâni take his place upon his throne and put the royal crown upon his head. Irra-imitti died in his palace because he had swallowed boiling broth. Enlil-bâni who was upon the throne did not relinquish it and was installed as king.[9]

We must add that the lucky gardener was deified and managed for twenty-four years (1860–1837) to govern what little remained of the kingdom of Isin, while Nûr-Adad and Sin-idinnam of Larsa, pushing their troops northwards, conquered city after city. By now, however, the two rivals had in that region a common enemy, Babylon.

The first kings of Isin had kept the Amorites at bay, but after their decline the latter once again crossed the Euphrates in large numbers and poured into Iraq. In Kish, Uruk, Sippar, Marad[10] and other towns their chiefs proclaimed themselves kings, adding to the political confusion. In the first year of Sumu-El of Larsa (1894 B.C.) one of these sheikhs, Sumuabum, chose for his capital a city a few miles to the west of Kish, on the left bank of the Euphrates, in that 'waist' of Mesopotamia the historical importance of which has already been stressed. This city had been governed by an *ensi* at least under the Third Dynasty of Ur, but had never played a part in Sumerian politics. Its name in Sumerian was KÁ.DINGIR.RA, in Akkadian *Bâb-ilâni*, both meaning 'The Gate of the Gods'; we call it, after the Greeks, Babylon. It was clear from the start that the energetic and clever rulers of Babylon were strongly determined to make it not only a great and rich city but the capital of the whole country. The war waging between Isin and Larsa and the multiplicity of small Amorite kingdoms gave them all the pretexts they needed. It took them nearly sixty years, but with infinite patience, using sometimes diplomacy and sometimes brute force, the first five kings of the First Dynasty of Babylon piece by piece, conquered the whole country of Akkad. They were approaching Nippur, key of Sumer, when they met with the strongest resistance from the foreign princes who now held the sceptre in Larsa.

The Elamites, as we well know, never missed an opportunity of interfering in Mesopotamian affairs. In 1834 B.C. the throne of Larsa was vacant, Silli-Adad having been killed in the war with Babylon after a brief reign. Kudur-Mabuk, an Elamite official who controlled the Amorite tribes established between the Tigris and the Zagros, occupied Larsa and appointed one of his sons king in that city, contenting himself with the title 'Father (i.e. protector) of Amurru'. It is remarkable that the two sons of Kudur-Mabuk, Warad-Sin ('slave of Sin') and

Rîm-Sin ('bull of Sin'), who reigned successively in Larsa, bear Semitic and not Elamite names. Even more remarkable is the fact that these freshly imported foreigners behaved in every respect like genuine Mesopotamian monarchs, building no less than nine temples and a dozen important monuments in the city of Ur alone. In other times they would have been great pacific rulers like Ur-Nammu, but as long as Isin was still alive and Babylon active there could be no peace in Sumer. Rîm-Sin defeated a dangerous coalition led by his Babylonian rival and in 1794 B.C. succeeded in taking Isin, overthrowing at last Larsa's oldest enemy. Two years later, Hammurabi ascended the throne of Babylon.

At this point we must leave the south for a while and turn our attention towards the northern half of Iraq. There again we meet with 'warring kingdoms' in fierce competition, but the cultural setting and the political and economic motives of the conflict are markedly different.

Eshnunna and Assur

Situated between the Tigris and the Zagros mountains, sixteen kilometres to the east of the Diyala River, Eshnunna (Tell Asmar) was a relay on the road from Upper Mesopotamia to Elam, and as such was subject to a triple current of influences: it lay within the sphere of the Sumero-Akkadian civilization, had close contact with the northern countries – its main god Tishpak was probably identical with the Hurrian god Teshup – and was linked to Elam by strong economic, political and cultural ties.[11] It was therefore perhaps not mere coincidence if Eshnunna was, with Susa, the first city-state to break away from Ur in the second year of Ibbi-Sin (2027 B.C.). As far as we know, the passage to freedom was swift and smooth: the rulers of Eshnunna called themselves 'servant of the god Tishpak' instead of 'servant of the King of Ur' and replaced by local names the names of months and years in use throughout the Sumerian empire; in the capital-city the temple once built for the deified King of Ur Shu-Sin was secularized, and a large palace was erected beside it; in official inscriptions Akkadian replaced the Sumerian language. These early rulers, who responded to Semitic or Elamite names, immediately enlarged their kingdom far beyond its original boundaries: with the help of Amorite bands they occupied the entire valley of the lower Diyala, including the important centre of Tutub (Khafaje), and went as far north as the region of Kirkuk. One of them, Bilalama – a contemporary of the second king of Isin – is credited by some scholars with a 'Code' of Law, written in Akkadian, which antedates by about one century the Code of Hammurabi and has with it many points in common.[12] The 'Laws of Eshnunna', incidentally, were not found at Tell Asmar but at Tell Harmal, a small mound at the outskirts of Baghdad, excavated by the Iraqis between 1945 and 1949.[13] Tell Harmal (ancient *Shaduppum*) was the administrative centre of an agricultural district of the kingdom of Eshnunna, and a copy of the royal laws was kept in the 'town-hall' for easy reference. The same site has also yielded a number of interesting tablets, in particular date-lists and mathematical problems.

The reign of Bilalama was followed by a period of repeated setbacks during which Eshnunna was sacked by the King of Dêr (modern Badrah, about one hundred kilometres east of Tell Asmar), defeated in war by the ruler of Kish and deprived of most of its possessions. But the fortune of the kingdom was eventually restored, and in about 1850 B.C., with 'the enlarger of Eshnunna', as Ipiq-Adad II called himself, began a new period of expansion marked by the occupation of Rapiqum on the Euphrates (somewhere near Ramâdi). The situation of this town clearly indicates that the king of Eshnunna aimed at establishing a bridgehead on that river in order to control one of the main 'tin roads' which from the north and west converged towards his capital city in the general direction of Susa. The strenuous efforts made by his successors were at first successful, but they finally met with failure since three other major powers, Babylon, Larsa and the great 'Upper Mesopotamian Kingdom', were soon to encircle Eshnunna and oppose a strong barrier to the ambitions of its rulers.

The birth and development of the Assyrian kingdom which, from the thirteenth century onwards was to play an ever increasing role in the history of Mesopotamia and the whole Near East, are worth retracing here. The city which gave its name to this kingdom, Assur[14] (or, more exactly, *Ash-shur*) * lay in a strong strategic position: built on a hill overlooking the Tigris just upstream of the point where it enters the Fat-ha gorge through Jabal Hamrîn, protected on one side by the great river, on the other by a canal, and strongly fortified, it commanded the road which, from Sumer or Akkad, went up the Tigris valley either to Kurdistan or to Upper Jaziah. Successively Sargon, Narâm-Sin and the kings of Ur had occupied this key place, the origins of which went back to the Early Dynastic period and probably earlier, and there is no evidence that Assur was independent before the second millennium B.C. Yet the northern equivalent of the Sumerian King List, the great Assyrian King List found at Khorsabad and published by A. Poebel in 1942,[15] gives a series of seventeen kings of Assur who, if we were to take the list at its face value, would have lived in Early Dynastic times. But here, as in the Sumerian list, dynasties recorded as successive may have been in fact parallel; in addition, our document states that these kings 'lived in tents', which may mean that they did not actually govern the city of Assur but some important tribe in the neighbourhood; and finally, it must be noted that the names of several early Assyrian monarchs – such as Tudia, Ushpia, Sulili or Kikkia – are neither Semitic nor Sumerian, but belong to some other ethnic stratum, possibly Hurrian.[16]

After the fall of the Sumerian Empire Assur, like many other

---

* In ancient texts the city, the kingdom and their god are all called *Ashshur*. To avoid any ambiguity we have used throughout this work the spellings Assur for the city and Ashur for the god, keeping the traditional Latin name Assyria for the kingdom.

cities, became independent. Puzur-Ashur I, who must have reigned about 2000 B.C., opens a new line of kings bearing such genuine Akkadian names as Sargon or Narâm-Sin. Two of them, Ilushuma and Erishum I, have left inscriptions mentioning the building of temples for Ashur, Adad and Ishtar in the city.[17] Moreover, Ilushuma is known to have raided deep into southern Iraq during the reign of Ishme-Dagan of Isin (1953–1935 B.C.). But the true founders of the *future* Assyrian might were the Western Semites, who during the first centuries of the second millennium flooded northern Iraq as they flooded the southern regions. Halê, the chief of an Amorite tribe, pitched his tent somewhere between the Khabur and the Tigris, and his alleged descendants made of northern Mesopotamia (Assyria included) a large, prosperous and powerful kingdom in which the true Assyrians played a very small role.

Mari and the Kingdom of Upper Mesopotamia

The reader may remember that we left Mari at the time when Narâm-Sin of Akkad seized this town on his way to northern Syria. Thereafter, for about three centuries Mari was governed by rulers who called themselves *shakkanakku* (literally 'military governor', a title they had initially received from their Akkadian overlords and continued to use, although they behaved as kings). Little is known about the history of Mari during this long period, but recent excavations on the site have brought to light the palace of the *shakkanakku* – a vast building with impressive underground tombs – and inscriptions from which could be drawn a list of these rulers in chronological order, from 2266 to 1920 B.C., when we lose their trail.[18]

When light shines again on Mari, we find it, and the greatest part of northern Mesopotamia, occupied by a large group of Amorites called the Hanaeans (*Hana*) divided into two main tribes: the *Beni-Iamina* or Iaminites (literally 'sons of the right', i.e. the South) and the *Beni-Sima'al* or Simalites ('sons of the left, i.e. the North).[19] The majority of Iaminites were semi-nomads in the desert west of Mari, but several of their clans lived in villages and towns on the Euphrates and the lower Khabur river. In contrast, most of the Simalites were settled in clusters of small or medium-sized 'kingdoms' in the region called Idamaras, the very fertile triangle formed by the many tributaries of the Khabur. The eastern part of Jazirah and the Tigris valley were also populated by Amorite tribes.

In about 1830 B.C., a 'Simalite' chief named Iaggid-Lim established friendly relations with another Amorite, Ilâ-kab-kâbu, who reigned over the small kingdom of Ekallâtum, an as yet unidentified town on the banks of the middle Tigris. The two chiefs exchanged 'solemn oaths', but for some untold reason the friendship was broken. Ilâ-kabkâbu attacked Iaggid-Lim, destroyed his fortress and seized his son Iahdun-Lim. A few years later the king of Ekallâtum died, leaving the throne to one of his two sons, Samsi-Addu (the Amorite form of Akkadian Shamshi-Adad).* We do not know when Iaggid-Lim passed away, nor when his son was set free, but in *c.* 1820 Iahdun-Lim took possession of Mari and proclaimed himself 'king of Mari and of the country of the Hanaeans', that is to say the Khabur basin. The renown of the old city, its wealth as the major trading station between Syria and Babylonia and, probably, the 'charisma' of the new king enabled him to exert a kind of benevolent protection over a large number of small independent states in Jazirah. Iahdun-Lim rebuilt the city wall of Mari and its neighbour Terqa, opened canals, founded a town bearing his name and erected a temple to the sun-god Shamash. He also embarked on an adventurous military and economic expedition in northern Syria, up to the Mediterranean Sea. In a long inscription repeated on nine large bricks used as foundation deposits for the temple of Shamash, he says that he offered sacrifices to the 'Ocean', had his soldiers bathe in it and removed quantities of trees from the high mountains, then

* 'The god Adad (the rain-god) is my sun'.

imposed a perpetual tribute on countries bordering the sea.[20] This must have frightened the chiefs of other Amorite tribes, for three of them attacked him in the same year and, not surprisingly, Sumu-Ebuh, King of Iamhad (the region of Aleppo) and master of northern Syria, whose territory had been invaded and plundered, lent them his support. In the same inscription Iahdun-Lim claims to have defeated them all.

Meanwhile, on the eastern side of Jazirah a series of momentous events had taken place. Soon after Samsi-Addu ascended the throne of Ekallâtum, Narâm-Sin, the king of Eshnunna who had succeeded Ibiq-Adad, took his army across the Diyala River into the Tigris valley, seized Ekallâtum and other towns further north, and occupied the Euphrates valley up to the vicinity of Mari. Samsi-Addu fled and took refuge in Babylon whence he returned after a while to reconquer his capital-city (c. 1815 B.C.).[21] Five years later, he liberated Assur. In 1800 B.C. or thereabouts Iahdun-Lim, who had defeated Samsi-Addu at Nagar, was assassinated by his own son (?) and successor Sumu-Iaman, who reigned for barely two years before being murdered by his servants. This gave Samsi-Addu an opportunity to seize Mari without shooting an arrow and to put his younger son Iasmah-Addu in charge of the town and its territory (c. 1796). Five years earlier, he had appointed another of his sons, Ishme-Dagan, viceroy of Ekallâtum. As for him, he seems to have moved from place to place; towards the end of his reign, he took up residence in the third-millennium town of Shehna which he renamed Subat-Enlil, now definitively identified as Tell Leilan, a large mound between two eastern tributaries of the Khabur.[22] The son of Ilâ-kabkâbu had solidly established his power on two pillars: the Tigris and the Euphrates.

The first task of Samsi-Addu was to obtain, by diplomacy or by force, the submission of the numerous princes of the Hanaeans and to consolidate his authority over the inhabitants of Northern, or Upper, Mesopotamia. It was most probably at that time that Nineveh, hitherto an independent city-state, was made subservient to Assur. As far as they can be reconstructed, the frontiers of the new kingdom at its greatest extent roughly followed the present Syro-Turko-Iraqi border from the great bend of the Euphrates to the extreme north of modern Iraq, ran along this river down to the vicinity of Ramadi and, in the east, skirted the foothills of the Zagros range to reach the Diyala River. In modern terms, they embraced the northern half of Iraq and the whole of Transeuphrataean Syria. This vast territory has been, and is still frequently referred to as 'Assyria' or 'The First Assyrian Empire', but it should be called the 'Kingdom of Upper Mesopotamia' because, as a Danish Assyriologist put it briefly: 'Shamshi-Adad's empire did not originate in, and was not built upon the men and the power of the city-state Assur'.[23] Besides, although Samsi-Addu figures (as Shamshi-Adad) on the Assyrian King List, he was in fact a usurper, later rejected by the Assyrian tradition.

In the whole history of ancient Iraq few periods are as well documented as the reign of Samsi-Addu and his sons. Moreover, our information is derived not from the usual official inscriptions, but from the most accurate and reliable documents that an historian can expect: the letters exchanged between the three princes and between Iasmah-Adad and other rulers, and the reports from various officials to their masters; in all, more than five thousand tablets forming part of the royal archives found in the palace of Mari.[24] While these letters are generally undated and therefore difficult to arrange in chronological order, they throw an invaluable light on the daily routine of the court and on the relationship between the governments of Assur, Mari and Ekallâtum and the various peoples, kingdoms and tribes surrounding them. Besides – and this is not the least of their interest – they offer a first-hand moral portrait of the three rulers. For the first time we are in the presence not of mere names but of living persons with their qualities and defects: Ishme-Dagan, a born warrior like his father, always ready to go to battle and proud to announce his victories to his brother – 'At Shimanahe we fought and I have taken the entire country. Be glad!'[25] – but on occasion taking him under his wing:

Do not write to the king. The country where I stay is nearer the capital city. The things you want to write to the king, write them to me, so that I can advise you . . .

Iasmah-Adad of Mari, on the contrary, docile, obedient, but lazy, negligent, cowardly:

You remain a child, writes his father, there is no beard on your chin, and even now, in the ripeness of age, you have not built up a 'house' . . .

Or again:

While your brother here is inflicting defeats, you, over there, you lie about amidst women. So now, when you go to Qatanum with the army, be a man! As your brother is making a great name for himself, you too, in your country, make a great name for yourself!

And finally, Samsi-Addu the father, wise, cunning, meticulous, sometimes humorous, who advises, reprimands or congratulates his sons and keeps Mari under very close control.

The kingdom of Samsi-Addu was more rigidly organized than that, more modest, of his predecessor. It was divided into provinces with, in the main cities, governors assisted by professional civil servants and controlled by the king, his sons and royal inspectors. Iasmah-Adad lived in the palace of Iahdun-Lim which he had received intact (an inventory had even been made on that occasion). The scribes of the kingdom wrote the purest Old Babylonian language introduced by Iahdun-Lim to replace the archaic Mari dialect loosely related to the language of Ebla.

The main internal problems faced by the governors, the viceroys and, when needed, the great king himself were of two kinds: on the one hand, the rivalries, disputes and even wars between the petty rulers of Upper Mesopotamia (notably in Idamaras and the Jabal Sinjar region), which could be solved by arbitration, and occasional rebellions which had to be crushed; on the other hand, the unruly behaviour of certain semi-nomadic clans in the vicinity of Mari,[26] and in particular the Iaminites, always ready for a razzia, who tried to escape control, dodged the royal census and recruitment, and sometimes even lent assistance to foreign invaders, not to mention the Sutû, inveterate bandits who attacked caravans and ravaged entire districts. In Ekallâtum, Ishme-Dagan had to fight on frequent occasions against the Turukkû of what is now Kurdistan, people more feared than had ever been their predecessors, the Lullubi and Guti, and who raided all the way to the rich Idamaras.

Relations between the Upper Mespotamian kingdom and its neighbours varied with time and circumstances. Iamhad (Aleppo), the greatest kingdom in the west was hostile, mainly because Samsi-Addu supported Qatna and even sent troops there in a protracted conflict between this smaller state and Aleppo.[27] The marriage of Iasmah-Adad to the daughter of the King of Qatna could only increase the hostility of the Aleppine monarch, but there is so far no evidence that war broke out between the two main major powers. Conversely, Iasmah-Adad entertained excellent relations with, for example, Karkemish whose king Aplahanda sent 'very good wine', food, ornaments and fine clothing to his 'brother', granted him the monopoly over certain copper mines in his territory and offered to give him 'whatever he desired'.[28]

The situation was very different in the East, where the kings of Eshnunna were as keen as ever to enlarge their domain, both to the north in the 'corridor' between the Tigris and the Zagros range in the direction of Assur and Ekallâtum, and to the west along the Euphrates towards Mari. The chronology here remains uncertain. Assuming that Narâm-Sin withdrew his troops from the middle Euphrates when Samsi-Addu conquered Upper Mesopotamia, hostilities in that region were probably resumed either by him or by his successor Dadusha, causing panic in Mari, since Iasmah-Adad wrote to his brother 'promptly send me numerous troops, the distance is long'.[29] Then we have an inscription of Samsi-Addu, who seems to have tried, without much success, to dislodge the Eshnunaeans from the key-town of Qabra which commanded the passage of the Lower Zab, coming from the south. In this inscription, the king says that he 'crossed the Zab, made a razzia in the land of Qabra, destroyed the harvest in that land, captured the fortified cities in the land of Urbêl (Erbil) and established garrisons everywhere'.[30] At an as yet undetermined date, an attack of Eshnunna was stopped, and a peace treaty was signed by the two belligerents. A recently found but not yet fully published stele of Dadusha tends to support the hypothesis of an alliance between the man of Eshnunna and the powerful north Mesopotamian monarch. This inscription, thought to have been written one year before Dadusha's death, describes a war against one Bunnu-Eshtar, King of Urbêl, and curiously states that Dadusha abandoned the territory conquered to Samsi-Addu, 'King of Ekallâtum'.[31]

Finally, we come to Babylon, the third powerful neighbour of Assyria. With Babylon relations were cold but polite, since neither Sin-muballit (1812–1793 B.C.) nor Hammurabi (1792–1750 B.C.) – both contemporaries of Samsi-Addu – had yet turned their ambition towards the north. Thus Shamshi-Adad dispatched to Hammurabi tablets copied at his request, and Iasmah-Adad returned to Babylon a caravan which had been delayed in Mari and a Turrukû captive who had escaped and sought refuge in that city.[32] In only one letter do we feel a shadow of anxiety: apparently, Iasmah-Adad had been informed of certain unfriendly projects of 'the man of Babylon', but after inquiry one of his officials reassures him:

Now, may my lord's heart be at ease, for the man of Babylon will never do harm to my lord.[33]

Some thirty years later, however, Hammurabi was to take and destroy Mari.

CHAPTER 12

HAMMURABI

The victory over four powerful princes and the unification of Mesopotamia are in themselves remarkable achievements sufficient to single out Hammurabi * as one of the greatest Mesopotamian monarchs. But the King of Babylon was not merely a successful war leader: his handling of his opponents reveals the qualities of a skilful diplomat; his Code of Law displays a passion for justice which, to a great extent, balances the repulsive cruelty of punishments; his inscriptions show a genuine concern for the welfare of his subjects and a deep respect for the traditions of a country which was, after all, foreign to his race; his letters prove that the descendant of an Amorite sheikh could administer a vast kingdom with the same care and attention to detail as the ruler of a Sumerian city-state. Hammurabi raised Babylon to the rank of a major capital-city and made its god Marduk one of the greatest deities.

Moreover, his forty-three years' long reign (1792–1750 B.C.) marked the peak of a series of cultural changes which had started in the previous century and were to last until the abrupt fall of the First Dynasty of Babylon, 155 years after his death. These changes deeply affected the art, language, literature and philosophy of the Mesopotamians. The official sculpture, directly derived from that of the Akkad and Ur III period, remained frozen in a sober and powerful beauty,[1] but a 'popular' art had emerged which was characterized by its realism and its love of movement. It was expressed in some bronze statuettes (such as an unnamed, four-headed god from Ischali who was astonishingly shown walking), in certain steles and

---

* The name – which should be written *Hammurapi* – probably means 'the god *Hammu* (a western Semitic god) is a healer'.

sculptures in the round (a roaring lion's head, a goddess smelling a flower), in parts of the beautiful frescoes in the royal palace of Mari (a date-gatherer climbing a palm-tree, a bird about to fly away) and above all, in a large number of terracotta plaques depicting scenes of daily life, such as a carpenter at work, a peasant on his zebu, a bitch feeding her puppies and even couples making love).[2] In no other period has the art of Mesopotamia been so lively and free.

Hammurabi's reign was also the time when the Akkadian language reached perfection, not only in its grammar – the Code of Hammurabi is the classic model for students of Assyriology – but also in its clear and elegant cuneiform signs. From then on used alone in royal inscriptions, letters and all administrative and legal documents, 'Old Babylonian', as it is called, became a literary language, a language whose 'vigour and freshness was never matched later'.[3] The scribes continued to copy the major Sumerian texts, but they adapted them freely, giving them a Semitic flavour, and also wrote original works. This resulted in admirable pieces of literature, such as the legends of Etana and Anzu – the storm-god who robbed Enlil's tablets of destiny – the Atrahasis myth and the Gilgamesh epic.

Finally, this was the time when personal religion flourished, as witnessed by innumerable clay figurines or votive plaques representing gods and demons and by moving prayers, 'letters to the gods' and street corner chapels. But although they were told that 'God cares about Man personally and deeply',[4] the Mesopotamians began to wonder, to doubt and to ponder on the great mysteries of Life and Death or Good versus Evil. Prompted by an extraordinary curiosity for the world around them, they refined and classified the knowledge acquired by their predecessors and by themselves, exercised their intelligence and tried to predict their own personal future. Hence the first rough drafts of a sapiential literature[5] which reached its full development during the Kassite period, and the multiplication of scientific texts of all kinds, including divination and magic.

All these changes contribute to make the first half of the eighteenth century B.C. a decisive period in the history of ancient Iraq, and without any doubt the figure of Hammurabi, the statesman and the lawgiver deserves special attention.[6]

The Statesman

When Hammurabi ascended the throne he inherited from his father Sin-muballit a comparatively small kingdom, some one hundred and fifty kilometres long and sixty kilometres wide, extending from Sippar to Marad or, in terms of modern topography, from Fallujah to Diwaniyah. All around were larger states and more powerful kings: the south was entirely dominated by Rîm-Sin of Larsa who two years before had taken Isin and put an end to the rival dynasty (1794 B.C.); to the north the horizon was barred by the great Kingdom of Upper Mesopotamia; and to the east, just across the Tigris, Dadusha, allied to the Elamites, still reigned in Eshnunna. The new King of Babylon was no less determined than his ancestors to enlarge his domain, but he patiently waited for five years before making the first move. Then, when he felt secure enough on the throne, he attacked in three directions: he snatched Isin from the King of Larsa and advanced along the Euphrates as far south as Uruk (sixth year), campaigned in Emutbal, between the Tigris and the Zagros range and occupied the key to that district, Malgum (tenth year), and finally took Rapiqum, upstream of Sippar (eleventh year). Thereafter, it would seem from his date-formulae that for twenty successive years he devoted his time solely to the embellishment of temples and the fortification of towns.[7]

This short series of military operations infringed on the territories of Larsa and Eshnunna and no doubt aroused considerable hostility from Rîm-Sin and from Ibal-pî-El II, who in 1779 B.C. had succeeded Dadusha, but we have no means of knowing if and how they retaliated. As for the Assyrians, they would have rejoiced at the humiliation of 'the man of Eshnunna' had they not been occupied with more serious problems.

It has very recently been established that both Samsi-Addu and Iasmah-Adad died, probably in a battle, in 1776 B.C. (about five years later than in previous estimates),[8] leaving Mari wide open to Zimri-Lim *, a son (or perhaps only a close relative) of Iahdun-Lim.[9] Ishme-Dagan, however, remained in possession of Ekallâtum and Assyria. The most urgent task of Zimri-Lim was to assert his authority over a kingdom smaller than before and that was beginning to disintegrate, and for this he used either force or astute diplomacy: he crushed a rebellion of Iaminites in the lower Khabur valley and summoned the princes of Idamaras and the Sinjar region to a meeting where he convinced them to recognize him as their 'lord and father'. Moreover, he gave several of his numerous daughters in marriage to some of his vassals.[10] Zimri-Lim's foreign policy was aimed at securing peace wherever possible, while discouraging all aggressions. Early in his reign, he made an alliance with the King of Iamhad and later on married his daughter Shibtu. He also dedicated a statue to Adad, the patron-god of Aleppo, and travelled as far as Ugarit, on the Syrian coast, for some unknown but pacific purposes. Against Eshnunna, the traditional enemy in the east, he tried to use the Elamites as a shield. Helped by troops from Mari and Babylon, the Elamites succeeded in capturing the strongly fortified city of Eshnunna. Unfortunately, this success whetted the appetite of the ruler (*sukkal*) of Elam who, in the following year, sent two armies into Mesopotamia: one marching on Babylon, the other on Ekallâtum. Hammurabi defeated the first army at Hiritum (an as yet unidentified site), but Ekallâtum, Shubat-Enlil and other towns of north-eastern Jazirah were occupied, which stirred up disturbances and unrest among these small kingdoms. In 1771 B.C., Ibal-pî-El of Eshnunna, the energetic successor of Dadusha, retaliated with the same two-pronged strategy: one army in the Tigris valley, another along the Euphrates. Ekallâtum was occupied once more, but Mari was spared. Following an inconclusive battle in

* *Zimri-Lim*: '(the god) Lim is my protection'.

the Sinjar region, Ibâl-pî-El preferred to negotiate and in the
end forced Zimri-Lim to sign a treaty recognizing his supremacy. However, no sooner had the Eshnunaeans gone than
the vassals of the King of Mari renewed their submission to him.

The movements of the rulers of Eshnunna and Elam were
watched with equal anxiety by Zimri-Lim's best friend, Hammurabi. Since Babylon and Mari commanded the entire course of
the Euphrates, the two rulers had everything to gain in joining
hands together. Zimri-Lim's ambassador at the court of Babylon
kept him fully posted on 'all the important affairs' of that
kingdom, and reciprocally Babylonian messengers reported to
Hammurabi all the news they heard in Mari, this bilateral
'intelligence service' functioning, it seems, with the full knowledge and approbation of the two sovereigns. The two kings lent
each other troops – Zimri-Lim's soldiers helped Hammurabi
when he destroyed the rival kingdom of Larsa – and rendered
each other the minor or major services expected of good neighbours. But in the light of later events the attitude of Hammurabi
was perhaps less disinterested than it appears, and he may have
used his ally merely to consolidate his power. Piece by piece
emerges from these archives the figure of a patient and cunning
politician who observes more than he acts and waits for the
right time to strike with the certainty of winning.

At long last, in the twenty-ninth year of his reign this time
arrived – sooner perhaps than Hammurabi had expected, since,
according to his own version of the events, Babylon was attacked
by a coalition of Elamites, Guti, 'Subarians' (Assyrians) and
people from Eshnunna:

The leader beloved of Marduk, after having defeated the army which
Elam ... Subartu, Gutium, Eshnunna and Malgum had raised in
masses, through the mighty power of the great gods consolidated the
foundations of Sumer and Akkad. (Year-formula 30.)

The following year (1763 B.C.) Hammurabi took the offensive
and, 'encouraged by an oracle', attacked Larsa. Rîm-Sin –
whom he contemptuously calls 'the King of Emutbal', Emutbal

being the homeland of Rîm-Sin's family – was overthrown after a reign of sixty years, the longest in Mesopotamian annals.

In the thirty-first year a new coalition comprising the same enemies as before was formed. The 'hero' not only 'overthrew their army' but advanced 'along the bank of the Tigris' as far as 'the frontier of Subartu'. Implicitly, this was the end of Eshnunna.

Now the master of southern and central Mesopotamia, Hammurabi was not a man to stop there. The great empires of Akkad and Ur must have been in his mind when he decided to attack his old friend Zimri-Lim; accused of not having taken Hammurabi's side in his war against Eshnunna.

Mari and Malgum he overthrew in battle and made Mari and ... also several other cities of Subartu by a friendly agreement (listen) to his orders. (Year-formula 32.)

These last words seem to indicate that Zimri-Lim did not lose his throne but was made a vassal of Hammurabi. Two years later, however, the Babylonian troops were again sent to Mari, perhaps to quell a rebellion. This time the city wall was dismantled, the beautiful palace of Zimri-Lim was sacked and burnt down, and the great metropolis of the Middle Euphrates was turned into ruins (1761 B.C.).

Finally, in the thirty-sixth and thirty-eighth years of his reign Hammurabi 'overthrew the army of the country Subartu (Assyria)' and 'defeated all his enemies as far as the country of Subartu'. What treatment was reserved for Assur we do not know. Somehow the Assyrian dynasty managed to survive, but the Assyrian domination in northern Iraq had come to an end.

Thus in ten years all but one of the five Mesopotamian kingdoms had successively disappeared, and Mesopotamia now formed one single nation under Babylonian rule. How far Hammurabi's power extended is difficult to say. A stele with his inscription is said to have been found near Diarbakr, in southeastern Turkey,[11] but Elam and Syria remained independent. In those days they were stronger countries and to subdue them would have required more time and forces than were at Hammurabi's disposal. The Babylonian monarch called himself 'mighty King, King of Babylon, King of the whole country of Amurru, King of Sumer and Akkad, King of the Four Quarters of the World' but, wisely no doubt, he did not attempt to gain effective control over 'the Universe'.

The Lawgiver

While achieving by arms the unity of Mesopotamia, Hammurabi carried out a series of administrative, social and religious measures which aimed at concentrating in his hands and in those of his successors the government of a nation made up of several ethnic groups and conspicuous for the multiplicity of its laws and customs, the complexity of its pantheon and the persistence of local traditions and particularism. Domestic affairs were handled by the king with the same mixture of ruthless energy and astute moderation as he so successfully used in his foreign policy. A corpus of letters exchanged between Hammurabi and two high officials residing in Larsa shows that they were subjected to a very strict royal control.[12] On the other hand, the Babylonians may have had an illusion of self-government since in each city the administration that judged petty court cases, collected taxes and handled purely local affairs was composed of the mayor (rabiânum), the Elders, the assembly of wealthy and influential citizens and the 'chamber of commerce' (kârum). But the more important tasks (managing the royal estates, seeing to it that that the regional resources were exploited properly) were performed by officials appointed by the monarch and occasionally inspected by royal inspectors. Soldiers were garrisoned in the main towns where they acted as police force, army reserve and guards of labourers engaged in public works; these troops were placed under a high-ranking officer called 'inspector of the Amorites' (wâkil amurri). An 'inspector of the merchants' (wâkil tamkari) represented the king at the meetings of the kârum. Towards the middle of his reign, the monarch went a step further in his dictatorship: he extended his control over the judges of the temples who from then on called themselves on their seal 'servant of Hammurabi' instead of the traditional 'servant or such or such god'.[13] In order to legalize his dynasty and to curtail any future claim to the kingship over Sumer and Akkad, Hammurabi gave the god of Babylon, Marduk – hitherto a third-rank deity – a high rank in the pantheon; but he tactfully proclaimed that this rank had been conferred to Marduk by Anu and Enlil and that he, Hammurabi, had been 'called' by the same great gods 'to promote the welfare of the people'.[14] Docile to royal instructions, the priests rearranged divine genealogies, endowed Marduk with the qualities of other gods. Yet the old Sumero-Akkadian beliefs were not fundamentally altered. Everywhere, including Nippur, the temples were rebuilt, repaired or embellished in the true Mesopotamian royal tradition, and any steps that might have hurt the religious feelings of the population were carefully avoided.

The famous Code of Law issued by Hammurabi[15]

> To cause justice to prevail in the country
> To destroy the wicked and the evil,
> That the strong may not oppress the weak,

can no longer be considered as 'the most ancient in the world' – we now possess similar documents from the reigns of Ur-Nammu, Lipit-Ishtar and Bilalama, not counting the 'reforms' of Urukagina – but it is still the most complete and as such deserves more than a few words. It should be stressed, however, that the word 'Code' is somewhat misleading, since we are not confronted here with a thorough legislative reform, nor with an exhaustive corpus of logically arranged legal dispositions, such as Justinian's *Institutes* or Napoleon's *Code Civil*. Indeed, the Mesopotamians were never ruled by any other system than a 'common law', handed down from reign to reign and occasionally modified to fit the social and economic conditions prevalent at a given period. One of the first acts of every ruler, at least since Urukagina, was to 'ordain *mêsharum*', a word which can be translated by 'justice', but which in this context covered a number of other things, such as remitting certain debts and obligations and fixing the prices of certain commodities – an efficient way of regulating the economy of the country. This is what is meant, for instance, by the formula of the second year of Hammurabi: 'he established justice in the country', and a good example of a *mêsharum*-act has survived in the 'edict' of King Ammiṣaduqa, one of Hammurabi's successors, published in the late fifties (see Chapter 15). In all other matters the new king simply applied the laws of his predecessors, thereby ensuring a continuity in tradition which, in this domain as in others, was one of the main features of the Mesopotamian civilization.[16] In the course of the reign, however, social and economic changes occurred which required the laws to be adjusted, and the king pronounced sentences on a number of isolated cases for which no precedent could be found. These royal decisions (*dînat sharrim*), duly recorded and eventually collected together to be used for reference by the judges of future generations, formed the so-called 'Codes of Law', and we possess several such copies of the Code of Hammurabi on clay tablets, ranging from the Old Babylonian period to the time of the Chaldean dynasty (sixth century B.C.).

Towards the end of his reign Hammurabi ordered his royal decisions to be carved on steles which were placed in temples, bearing witness that the king had performed his important function of 'king of justice' satisfactorily and had acted according to the gods' hearts. One of these steles, found in an excellent state of preservation, is in itself a remarkable work of art. Erected originally in the temple of Shamash at Sippar, it was taken to Susa as war booty by the Elamites in the twelfth century B.C., discovered there by the French in 1901 and transported to the Louvre Museum. It is an eight-foot-high stele of polished basalt, roughly conical in shape. On its upper part is carved a scene representing Hammurabi in the attitude of prayer facing a god – either Marduk or Shamash, the sun-god and god of justice – seated on his throne. The rest of the stele, front and back, is covered with vertical columns of text beautifully engraved and written in the purest Babylonian language. After a long prologue enumerating the religious deeds of the king, come at least 282 laws[17] dealing with various offences, with trade and commerce, marriage, family and property, the fees and responsibilities of professional men, legal problems connected with agriculture, wages and rates of hire, and the sale and purchase of slaves. Finally, a long epilogue calls for divine punishments against whoever would deface the monument or alter 'the just laws which Hammurabi, the efficient king, set up'.

It appears from the Code and various other documents that the Babylonian society was divided into three classes: free men (*awêlu*), *mushkênu* and slaves (*wardu*). The term *mushkênum*, here left untranslated, has been rendered by 'plebeian', 'commoner', 'villein' or 'poor' (cf. Arabic *meskîn*), but it seems to indicate, in fact, some kind of military or civilian 'state dependant' who submitted to certain obligations and restrictions in return for certain privileges.[18] The slaves were recruited partly among prisoners of war and their descendants, partly among impoverished free men who sold themselves or their children to their creditors. Shaven and branded with a distinctive mark, they were considered as belonging to their masters, and severe penalties were pronounced against those who assisted or harboured fugitive slaves. Yet their condition was not as hopeless as one would imagine: they could be set free or adopted by their masters, and, as under the Third Dynasty of Ur, at least some of them could acquire property or even marry the daughters of free men (§§ 175–6). Fees and punishments varied according to the social condition. For instance, the cost of a life-saving operation was fixed at ten shekels of silver for an *awêlum*, five shekels for a *mushkênum* and two shekels for a slave (§§ 215–17). Similarly, 'if a man has pierced the eye of an *awêlum*, they shall pierce his eye', but 'if he has pierced the eye or broken the bone of a *mushkênum*, he shall pay one mina of silver', and in the case of a slave, one half of his value (§§ 196, 198, 199). Compensation in kind or money, which formed the basis of the Sumerian penal system, was now partly replaced by death, mutilation or corporal punishment, and when the victim or plaintiff was a free man the terrible Law of Retaliation was usually applied, even if the offence was unintentional. Thus:

If a surgeon performed a major operation on an *awêlum* with a bronze lancet and has caused the death of this man ... they shall cut off his hand (§ 218).

If an architect built a house for an *awêlum* but did not make his work strong, and if the house that he built collapsed and has caused the death of its owner, that architect shall be put to death (§ 229).

If it has caused the death of a slave of the owner, he shall give slave for slave to the owner of the house (§ 231).

Cruel as it sometimes appears to civilized minds, the Code of Hammurabi, in many of its laws is surprisingly close to our modern ideas of justice. The laws concerned with family and property, in particular, represent a remarkable effort to protect women and children from arbitrary treatment, poverty and neglect, and if penalties, in this section also, are exceedingly severe, their application is mitigated by the admission of forgiveness and extenuating circumstances. The wife's adultery is punished by death, but the husband may pardon his spouse and the king her lover, thus saving them from being 'bound together and thrown into the river' (§ 129). The prisoner's wife who, in her husband's absence, has 'entered the house of another man' incurs no punishment if she has done so because 'there was nothing to eat in her house' (§ 134). A man may divorce his wife without giving her anything if she misbehaved (§ 141), but if he divorces her because she has not borne him sons, 'he shall give her money to the value of her bridal gift and shall make good to her the dowry which she has brought from her father's house'[19] (§ 138). The husband of a diseased woman may marry another woman, but he must keep his wife in his house and maintain her 'so long as she lives' (§ 148). When a man dies his property is divided between his sons, but his widow has the usufruct of this property (§ 171) and may dispose freely of any 'field, plantation, house or chattel' he may have given her (§ 150). When a woman dies her dowry does not return to her father, but goes to her sons (§ 162). Similar dispositions protect the sons of the 'first wife' against those of the 'slave-girl' or concubine and guarantee the children's rights against undeserved disherison (§ 168).

Another point of general interest in the Code is the frequent reference to the institution called *ilkum* (§§ 26–41). Apparently, persons of certain professions, such as the *rêdum* (gendarme), the *ba'irum* (sailor) or the *nash biltim* (literally 'tribute-bearer') received from the king corn, land, sheep and cattle in return for certain duties, the most explicit of which is military service. The fief (*ilkum*) thus acquired remained the personal property of the fief-holder throughout his life and was divided between his heirs after his death. It could not be sold nor assigned by the holder to his wife or daughters, though it could be used to pay his ransom if he was captured in the service of the king, or forfeited to a substitute if he refused to fulfil his military duties or deserted. Clearly then, the granting of an *ilkum* was not a simple reward for services rendered to the crown, but a measure probably introduced by Hammurabi himself[20] to tie firmly to the land a number of his subjects and to create between them and the king a bond comparable to the feudal bond which, in medieval Europe, attached lord and liegeman.

Such are, very briefly, some of the main features of this famous Code. Less original perhaps than it was thought, it remains unique by its length, by the elegance and precision of its style and by the light it throws on the rough, yet highly civilized society of the period. Written in the last years of Hammurabi, it crowns his long and successful reign. Looking at this achievement, the King of Babylon could proudly proclaim:

> I rooted out the enemy above and below;
> I made an end of war;
> I promoted the welfare of the land;

I made the people rest in friendly habitations;
I did not let them have anyone to terrorize them.
The great gods called me,
So I became the beneficent shepherd whose sceptre is righteous;
My benign shadow is spread over my city.
In my bosom I carried the people of the land of Sumer and Akkad;
They prospered under my protection;
I have governed them in peace;
I have sheltered them in my strength.[21]

CHAPTER 13

IN THE DAYS OF HAMMURABI

No matter how fascinating the ever-changing spectacle of political and economic situations, there are times which call for a pause; there are periods so richly documented that the historian feels compelled to leave aside monarchs and dynasties, kingdoms and empires, wars and diplomacy, and to study the society in a static condition as it were. How did people live? What did they do in everyday life? These are questions which come naturally to mind and deserve an answer.[1]

In Mesopotamia the days of Hammurabi – or, more exactly, the century which begins sixty years before his reign (1850–1750 B.C. in round figures) – is one of these periods. Here our sources, both archaeological and literary, are particularly copious. It is true that we know very little about the capital cities of southern Iraq: Isin and Larsa have just begun to yield their secrets, and eighteen years of excavations at Babylon have barely scratched the surface of the huge site, the height of the water-table having prevented the German archaeologists from digging much below the Neo-Babylonian level (609–539 B.C.). In the small area where deep soundings were possible only a few tablets and fragments of walls pertaining to the First Dynasty were found, some twelve metres below the surface. But on other sites other archaeologists have been more fortunate. The monuments they have unearthed – the royal palace of Mari, the palace of the rulers at Tell Asmar, the temples and private houses of Ur, to mention only the most important – are perhaps not very numerous, but they are of outstanding quality. As regards written documents we are even better provided, for not only do we have the Code of Hammurabi, but his correspondence, the royal archives of Mari, Tell Shimshara and Tell al-Rimah,[2] and many legal, economic, administrative, religious and scientific texts from Mari, Larsa, Sippar, Nippur, Ur, Tell Harmal and various other sites; in all, perhaps thirty or forty thousand tablets. Indeed, it can be said without exaggeration that Mesopotamia 1,800 years before Christ is much better known to us than any European country a thousand years ago, and it would be in theory possible for historians to draw a fairly complete and detailed picture of the Mesopotamian society in the eighteenth and nineteenth centuries B.C. As this would go far beyond the boundaries of the present work, we shall limit ourselves to the sketching of the three main aspects of this society: the god in his temple, the king in his palace, the citizen in his house.

The God in his Temple

The temples – the 'houses' (*bitu*) of the gods as they were called – varied in size and layout. Some were small wayside chapels which were part of a block of houses and consisted of hardly more than an open courtyard with an altar and a pedestal for the divine statue,[3] others were larger detached or semi-detached buildings, comprising several courtyards and rooms,[4] and finally, there were the enormous temple-complexes of the greater gods, which often included several shrines for the minor deities of their household and retinue.[5] These temples no longer retained the admirable simplicity of the early Sumerian sanctuaries (see Chapter 4). Throughout the ages they had increased in complexity to incorporate the numerous services of a strongly organized religious community. Moreover, their plan reflects a high degree of specialization in the performance of the cult, and it appears that a distinction was made between the parts of the temple open to the public and those reserved for the priests, or perhaps for certain categories of priests only. Whether the concept that the great gods could only be approached by degrees was developed by the Sumerians or introduced by the Semites is a much debated problem which cannot be discussed here.

All the main Mesopotamian temples had in common certain features.[6] They all comprised a large courtyard (*kisalmahhu*) surrounded by small rooms which served as lodgings, libraries and schools for the priests, offices, workshops, stores, cellars and stables. During the great feasts the statues of the gods brought from other temples were solemnly gathered in this courtyard, but on ordinary days it was open to all, and we must imagine it not as an empty and silent space, but as a compromise between a cloister and a market-place, full of noise and movement, crowded with people and animals, unceasingly crossed by the personnel of the temple, the merchants who did business with it and the men and women who brought offerings and asked for help and advice. Beyond the *kisalmahhu* was another courtyard, usually smaller, with an altar in its middle, and finally, the temple proper (*ashirtu*), the building to which none but the priests called *erib bîti* ('those who enter the temple') had access. The temple was divided by partitions into three rooms, one behind the other: vestibule, ante-*cella* and *cella* (holy of holies). The *cella* contained the statue of the god or goddess to whom the temple was dedicated. Usually made of wood covered with gold leaves, it stood on a pedestal in a niche cut in the back-wall of the *cella*. When all doors were open the statue could be seen shining faintly in the semi-darkness of the shrine from the small courtyard but not from the large one, as it was at a right angle with the temple doorway, or hidden behind a curtain, depending on the layout of the temple. Flower pots and incense burners were arranged at the god's feet, and low brick benches around the *cella* and ante-*cella* supported the statues of worshippers, together with royal steles and various *ex-votos*. A two-step altar, a table for the sacred meals, basins of lustral water, stands for insignia and dedicated weapons made up the rest of the temple furniture. Rare and expensive materials were used in the construction of the building: cedar beams supported its roof, and its doors were made of precious wood, often lined with copper or bronze sheets. Lions, bulls, griffins or genii made of stone, clay or wood guarded the entrances. At the corners of the

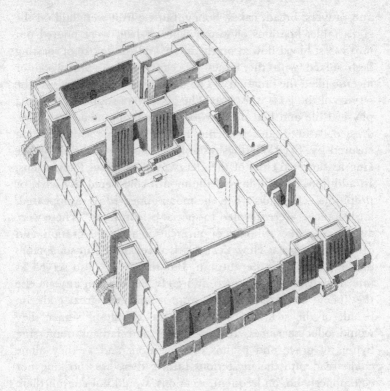

The temple of Ishtar-kititum at Ischâli (Diyala valley). First half of
the second millennium B.C.
Reconstruction by H. D. Hill. From H. Frankfort, The Art and Architecture
of the Ancient Orient, *1954.*

temple precinct and buried under the pavement were brick
boxes containing bronze or clay 'nails', royal inscriptions and
the statuettes of the kings who had founded or restored the
sanctuary. These 'foundation deposits' (*temenu*) authenticated
the sacred ground, marked its limits and kept the netherworld
demons at bay.[7]

Every day throughout the year religious ceremonies were
performed in the temple: the air vibrated with music,[8] hymns

and prayers; bread, cakes, honey, butter, fruit were laid on the god's table; libations of water, wine or beer were poured out into vases; blood flowed on the altar, and the smoke of roasting flesh mixed with the fumes of cedar-wood, cyprus-wood or incense filled the sanctuary. The main object of the cult was the service of the gods, the *dullu*. The gods were supposed to live a physical life and had daily to be washed, anointed, perfumed, dressed, attired and fed, the regular supply of food being ensured by 'fixed offerings' established once and for all by the king as supreme chief of the clergy, and by pious foundations. In addition, certain days of the month considered as sacred or propitious – the days when the moon appeared or disappeared, for instance – were devoted to special celebrations.[9] There were also occasional ceremonies of purification and consecration, and of course the great New Year Festival celebrated in some cities in the spring and the autumn. But the priests also served as intermediaries between men and gods. Better than anyone else they knew the proper way of approaching the great gods; on behalf of the sick, the sorrowful, the repentant sinner they would offer sacrifices, recite prayers and lamentations, sing hymns of grace and psalms of contrition; and as they alone could read into the mysterious future, there was no king nor commoner who, on frequent occasions, would not consult them and ask for an omen. For each of these acts of cult a strict and complicated ritual was laid down. Originally prayers and incantations were in Sumerian, but under the First Dynasty of Babylon the Akkadian language was allowed into the Temple, and we possess, for instance, a 'Ritual for the Covering of the Temple Kettle-drum', where it is said that a certain prayer should be whispered 'through a reed tube' in Sumerian into the right ear of a bull and in Akkadian into its left ear.[10]

The chief administrator of the temple was the *shanga*, a high dignitary who, in the reign of Hammurabi, was appointed by the king himself. He was assisted by inspectors and scribes who registered all that entered or went out of the temple stores and commanded low-grade employees, such as guards, cleaners and even barbers. The wheat and barley fields of the temple were run by *ishakku*'s (Akkadian for *ensi*, which shows how low this once prestigious title had fallen), and were worked by farm hands and sometimes corvées which involved the entire population of the town or district.

A large number of priests were attached to the main temples.[11] Sons and grandsons of priests, they were brought up in the sanctuary and received a thorough education in the temple school, or *bît mummi* (literally 'House of Knowledge'). At their head was the high-priest, or *enum* (Akkadian form of the Sumerian word *en*, 'lord') and the *urigallum* originally the guardian of the gates but now the main officiant. Among the specialized members of the clergy, the *mashmashshum* who recited incantations, the *pashîshum* who anointed the gods and laid their table, the *ramkum* who washed the statues of the gods, the *nishakum* who poured out libations and the *kâlum* who chanted incantations but also fulfilled some mysterious functions, were the most important. These priests were assisted by the sacrificer (*nash patri*, 'sword bearer'), as well as by singers and musicians. Although he took part in religious ceremonies, the *ashipum* (exorcist) cannot be considered a priest in the narrow sense of the term, since he served the public and notably the sick. The same remark applies to the *sha'ilum*, who interpreted dreams, and even more the *barûm* or diviner, a very busy and rich man in a society where divination was part of everyday life. Unfortunately, we know almost nothing about the temples of female deities. There is no doubt, however, that the temples of Ishtar, the goddess of carnal love, were the sites of a licentious cult with songs, dances and pantomimes performed by women and transvestites, as well as sexual orgies. In these rites, which may be found shocking but were sacred for the Babylonians, men called *assinu*, *kulu'u* or *kurgarru* – all passive homosexuals and some of them perhaps castrates – participated together with women who are too often referred to as 'prostitutes'. In fact, the true prostitutes (*harmâtu, kezrêtu, shamhâtu*), such as the one who seduced Enkidu (page 118), were only haunting the temple surrounds and the taverns. Only those women who were called 'votaress of Ishtar' (*ishtarêtu*) or 'devoted' (*qashshâtu*) were probably part of the female clergy.[12]

In sharp contrast with all this were the *nadîtu*, who usually came from the best families and could marry but were not allowed to bear children so long as they remained in the temple 'cloister' (*gagû*) where they lived in communities. Loosely attached to the temple, the *nadîtu* were, in fact, remarkable business women who made fortunes from buying and letting out houses and land. On their death their wealth was left to their parents or relatives, thereby preventing the estates from being fragmented through the marriage of daughters.[13]

All these people formed a closed society which had its own rules, traditions and rights, lived partly from the revenues of the temple land, partly from banking and commerce and partly 'from the altar',[14] and played an important part in the affairs of the state and in the private life of every Mesopotamian. Yet the days when the temple controlled the entire social and economic life of the country were over, for the vital centre, the heart and brain of the state, was now the royal palace.

The King in his Palace

The importance given to the royal palace (Sum. *é-gal*, Akkad. *ekallum*, 'great house') is a striking feature of the Old Babylonian period. The concentration of authority in the hands of the monarch, the requirements of a centralized administration, the costly exigency of prestige had concurred to transform the king's residence – hitherto a relatively modest building – into a vast compound of apartments, reception rooms, offices, workshops and stores surrounded for safety reasons by strong defensive walls. Mansion, castle and serai, the palace had become a city within the city.

Of such royal abodes there is no finer example than the palace of Mari.[15] Found in an excellent state of preservation, it is remarkable not only for its size – it measures some 200 by 150

metres and covers an area of about two and a half hectares –
but for its intelligent and harmonious layout, the beauty of its
decoration and the quality of its construction. Archaeologists
have called it 'the jewel of archaic Oriental architecture',[16] and
such was its fame in antiquity that the King of Ugarit, on the
Syrian coast, did not hesitate to send his son 600 kilometres
inland for the sole purpose of visiting 'the house of Zimri-
Lim'.[17]

The enormous outer wall of the palace (fifteen metres thick
in places), laid on stone foundations and reinforced by towers,
was pierced with only one gate on its northern side. Passing
through a guarded vestibule, a small courtyard and a dark
corridor, one would enter the great courtyard of the palace, a
truly majestic open space (1617 square metres) flooded with
sunlight and paved with gypsum slabs. On the side opposite the
entrance three elegantly curved steps led to a high, oblong
room which is now taken as being the chapel of the goddess
Ishtar of the Palace. Through a door in the western wall of the
'courtyard of honour' and an L-shaped passage, royalties, ambassadors, high officials of the kingdom and other visitors of importance were introduced into another courtyard, smaller but
particularly neat and attractive with its floor of hard, white
plaster and its walls covered with frescoes, some of them sheltered from rain and excessive heat by a light canopy resting on
wooden poles. The brightly coloured paintings, which have in
part survived and are now the pride of the Louvre and Aleppo
museums, represent religious state ceremonies: a bull brought to
sacrifice, the King of Mari 'touching the hand' of Ishtar (a
ritual of investiture performed during the New Year Festival),
offerings and libations to a goddess and other fragmentary
scenes.[18] Beyond this courtyard were two long rooms, one
behind the other. The first room contained a plastered and
painted *podium* which once supported a statue – perhaps the
'goddess with the flowing vase' found nearby, beheaded and
thrown down on the ground. The other room was the throne-
room. At one end, against the wall, was a low stone pedestal

which must have supported a wooden throne, while at the other end a long, magnificent flight of steps led to a raised platform where probably stood the statues of the king's ancestors. From another room started a staircase leading to the king's apartment overlying a large group of stores.

Audience-room and throne-room with their annexes formed the heart of the palace. Around them were various quarters. On either side of the gate were lodgings for guests and for the palace garrison. Near the north-western corner of the building was a group of nicely decorated rooms and bathrooms – one with two terracotta baths still in place – which, together with a long room containing rows of clay benches and long mistaken for a school, formed part of what is now regarded as the apartment of the queen and her court. Further south were the royal administration quarters. From the courtyard of honour a long series of corridors gave access to a double chapel – presumably dedicated to the goddesses Anunit and Ishtar – for the king's private devotions. The remainder of the three hundred odd rooms and courtyards of the palace was occupied by kitchens, stores, servants' quarters, smithies and potters' kilns.

No less remarkable than its plan was the construction of the building. The walls, extremely thick as a rule and rising in places to a height of sixteen feet, were made of large mud bricks covered with several layers of clay and plaster. In many rooms – especially the bathrooms and lavatories – a coating of bitumen protected the floor and the lower part of the walls. No window was found, and it is likely that the rooms received light either through their wide and high doors opening on to courtyards or through round apertures in the ceiling, which could be blocked with mushroom-shaped clay 'plugs'. The existence of a second floor, at least in certain parts of the palace, is suggested by the remains of staircases. As for the drainage, it was effected by means of brick gutters laid under the pavement and of bitumen-lined clay pipes going down ten metres underground. The whole system had been so skilfully planned and installed that the waters of a violent rainstorm which burst one day

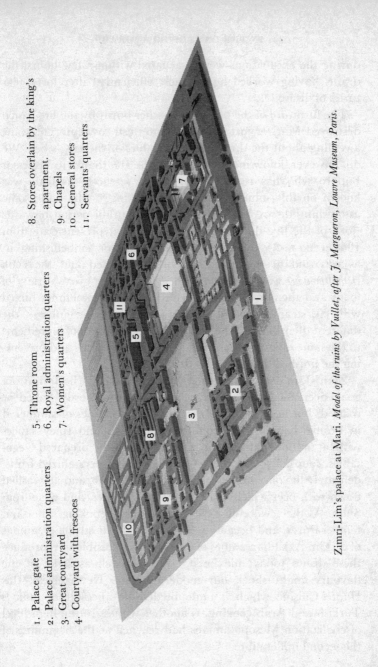

1. Palace gate
2. Palace administration quarters
3. Great courtyard
4. Courtyard with frescoes
5. Throne room
6. Royal administration quarters
7. Women's quarters
8. Stores overlain by the king's apartment.
9. Chapels
10. General stores
11. Servants' quarters

Zimri-Lim's palace at Mari. *Model of the ruins by Vuillet, after J. Margueron, Louvre Museum, Paris.*

during the excavations were evacuated within a few hours, the drains having worked again, most efficiently, after forty centuries of disuse![19]

The furniture of the palace was either burnt by the fire which destroyed Mari or just crumbled into dust, so we do not know anything about the thrones, chairs, tables or the king's bed. We do, however, know more or less what he ate, thanks to Professor Bottéro who has recently done some research, as little was known on this subject: Babylonian cooking.[20] He made some astonishing discoveries. From the Hammurabi period onwards (four of the five documents known to us at present date from 1800–1700 B.C.), the art of preparing food, or 'embellishing' it, as was said at the time, had been perfected and the cook (*nuhatimmum*) was an accomplished artist. The great variety of foods and their preparation (boiled in water sometimes mixed with fat, steamed, baked, cooked under ashes or embers), the different utensils used, the way of adding a variety of ingredients to the same mixture, thus producing subtle flavours and presenting the finished dishes in appetizing ways.

Zimri-Lim's servants dished up various meats (beef, mutton, goat, deer and gazelles), fish, birds, poultry, mostly grilled or roasted, but also stewed in earthenware casseroles or simmered in bronze cauldrons, accompanied by rich and spicy sauces with a predominant garlic flavour, carefully prepared vegetables, soups, assorted cheeses, fresh, dried or crystallized fruits, delicately flavoured cakes of all shapes and sizes, and all washed down with beer which came in several qualities, and wine from Syria. As there were no exact indications of cooking times and temperatures, and because we do not understand the meanings of certain Akkadian names of foods, it is impossible to reproduce these dishes today; maybe it is just as well as some of the flavours might shock our modern palate. Nevertheless, this Haute Cuisine which is undoubtedly the ancestor of today's Turkish and Arab cooking, is another witness to the high level of civilization Mesopotamians had reached at the beginning of the second millennium.

As the palace of Mari illustrates the surroundings in which the Mesopotamian kings lived, so do the tablets discovered in various rooms of the palace – together with Hammurabi's letters discovered in other Mesopotamian cities – give us a clear picture of their routine occupations. Perhaps the most striking fact emerging from these documents is the interest taken by the king himself in the affairs of the kingdom. Provincial governors, army chiefs, ambassadors to foreign courts, officials of all ranks and even simple individuals constantly wrote to their sovereign, keeping him informed of what was happening in their particular field of activities and asking for advice. In return the king gave orders, encouraged, blamed, punished or asked for more information. A steady flow of letters carried by escorted messengers came in and out of the palace. Military and diplomatic matters, justice and public works naturally formed the bulk of the state correspondence and we see, for instance, Hammurabi intervening in Larsa, now the capital-city of his southern provinces, to pronounce legal decisions, appoint officials, summon civil servants to his court and order the digging or clearing-out of canals. Similarly, Iasmah-Adad and Zimri-Lim give instructions for the census of nomads and the mobilization of troops and exchange presents and ideas with their royal 'brothers'. But more trivial subjects were also touched upon, as will be shown from a few examples taken at random. The daughters of Iahdun-Lim, held captive in Mari by the Assyrian usurper Iasmah-Adad, are now grown up; Shamshi-Addu writes to his son suggesting that they be sent to his palace at Shubat-Enlil, where they will be taught music. The chariots made in Mari are of much better quality than those made in Ekallâtum; Ishme-Dagan asks his brother to send him a few, together with good carpenters.[21] In Terqa[22] locusts have appeared, and the governor of that city sends basket-loads of the insects to his master Zimri-Lim, who, like the modern Arabs, appreciates this delicacy.[23] In Terqa again a man has had a strange, ominous dream which is the talk of the town; the king will be interested to hear it.[24] A certain Iaqqim-Addu, governor of Sagaratim,[25] has captured a lion; he has put it in a wooden cage and is shipping it to Zimri-Lim. Near Mari the mutilated body of a child has been found; Bahdi-Lim, the palace superintendent, assures the king that an inquest will be made at once. A female servant of the royal palace has escaped and fled from Assur to Mari; Shamshi-Addu requests his son to return her under escort. A woman exiled to Nahur, near Harran, is unhappy and begs Zimri-Lim: 'Could my Lord write so that they take me back and that I see again the face of my Lord, whom I miss?'[26] And so it goes, tablet after tablet, in a simple, matter-of-fact style contrasting sharply with the pompous tone of the official inscriptions: 'To My Lord, say this: thus speaks X, your servant'.[27] This is the rare occasion when we really live with these people, when we understand their problems and share their worries. At the same time we realize how widespread was already the art of writing, how numerous the scribes, how efficient the royal chancellery, how busy and conscientious the kings and their officials. Nothing conveys a stronger impression of travelling back into time than a visit to the royal palace of Mari and a glimpse at the contents of its archives.

The Citizen in his House

It now remains for us to examine how the ordinary citizens of Mesopotamian towns, the *awêlum*, lived almost four thousand years ago. For this we must travel some nine hundred kilometres down the Euphrates, from Mari to the great city of Ur. There again architectural remains combined with texts give us nearly all the information wanted. So well preserved were the 8,000 square metres of streets and private houses excavated in 1930–1 by Sir Leonard Woolley that even today, after years of exposure to wind and rain, they conjure up the past with a vividness such as can be found only in the ruins of Pompeii and Herculaneum.[28]

Muddy in winter, dusty in summer, soiled by the rubbish thrown out of the houses and never collected, the streets are all but attractive. They wind without much planning between compact blocks of houses: blank, windowless façades pierced by occasional small doors. Here and there, however, little shops grouped in bazaars or set among the houses throw a note of gaiety in the austere scenery. Like the shops of a modern Oriental *suq*, they consist of a showroom opening widely on to the street, and of one or several back-rooms for the storage of goods. What was sold there we do not know: pottery, perhaps, tools, clothes, food? Or were they shops of barbers, shoe-makers, tailors and cleaners such as the one whose quarrel with a customer is narrated in a British Museum tablet found at Ur.[29] At intervals the red glow of a furnace in the smithy's dark workshop, the brick counter of a 'restaurant' where one can purchase and eat from clay bowls onions, cucumbers, fried fish or tasty slices of grilled meat, or a small chapel advertised by terracotta figurines hung on either side of the doorway. To enter the courtyard, drop a handful of dates or flour on the altar and address a short prayer to the god smiling in his niche takes only a few minutes and confers long-lasting blessings.

Very little traffic in the streets: they are too narrow for carts and even a donkey carrying a bulky load would obstruct most of them. Servants who go shopping, water-carriers, pedlars avoid the sun and hug the shadows of the walls, but in the early morning or late afternoon a public writer or a story-teller reciting 'Gilgamesh' would gather small crowds around him at the cross-roads, while two or three times a day flocks of noisy children invade the streets on their way to or from one of the schools.

If we push one of the doors and enter a house a pleasant surprise awaits us, for it is cool, comfortable and much larger than it appears from outside. Having washed our feet in a small lobby, we pass into the central courtyard and notice that it is paved and that a vertical drain opens in its centre, so that it can be rinsed clean and will not be flooded during the rainy season. All around us is the building. The walls are uniformly plastered and white-washed, but we know that their upper part

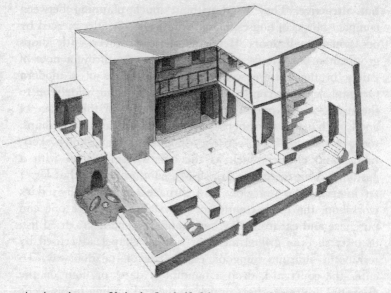

A private house at Ur in the first half of the second millennium B.C. Note the
family's chapel above the family's grave on the left of the drawing.
Reconstruction by the author from the plan of Sir Leonard Woolley in Ur Excavations,
VII, 1976.

is made of mud bricks and their lower part of burnt bricks
carefully laid and jointed with clay mortar. A metre wide
gallery supported by wooden poles runs around the courtyard,
dividing the building into two storeys: on the first floor live the
owner of the house and his family, while the ground floor is
reserved for servants and visitors. We recognize the kitchen, the
workshop and store-room, the ablution room and lavatories,
and that constant feature of all Oriental residences: the long,
oblong chamber where the guests are entertained and eventually
spend the night, the 'diwan'. The house furniture, now of
course vanished, would consist of a few tables, chairs, chests and
beds and of quantities of rugs and cushions.[30]

The above description, valid for most houses of the Isin-Larsa
and Old Babylonian periods at Ur, will sound familiar to those

who have visited the Near East. It would apply word for word to any Arab house of the old style, such as can still be seen today in some parts of Aleppo, Damascus or Baghdad. Kingdoms and empires have vanished, languages and religions have changed, many customs have fallen into disuse, yet this type of house has remained the same for thousands of years merely because it is best suited to the climate of that part of the world and to the living habits of its population. But our Babylonian houses had something which no longer exists: behind the building was a long narrow courtyard, partly open to the sky and partly covered with a penthouse roof. The roof protected a brick altar and a grooved pillar upon which stood the statuettes of the household gods, the 'personal gods' so dear to the Babylonians' hearts. In the open part of the courtyard, under the brick pavement, was a vaulted tomb where all the members of the family were buried in turn, except for the small children, who were buried in vases in or around the domestic chapel. Thus the cult of the tutelary gods and the cult of the ancestors were closely associated within the house precincts. The deceased were no longer interred in cemeteries distant from the town as in earlier days, but continued to take part in the life of the family.

The objects and tablets found in the houses throw precious light on the occupations of their owners. We know, for instance, that the headmaster of a private school was called Igmil-Sin and that he taught writing, religion, history and mathematics. Other texts found elsewhere provide a great deal of interesting and sometimes amusing information on the time-table, actual work, competitive spirit, achievements, truancy and corporal punishment of the future scribes, and some of them even disclose the fact that certain fathers eager to see their son with better marks do not hesitate to bribe the teacher.[31] Although we can hardly believe that the Sumero-Akkadian grammar found in the factory of Gimil-Ningishzida, the bronzesmith, was for his own use, we perfectly understand how Ea-nâṣir the copper merchant and unlucky speculator of 'No. 1, Old Street', came to sell part of his house to a neighbour.[32] All these people were modest, middle-class citizens, and it would appear from the size, construction and comfort of their houses that their standard of living was fairly high. Yet if some of them were prosperous, others were half-ruined. The transfer of power and wealth from the southern to the central part of Iraq under Hammurabi, combined with the restriction of maritime trade on the Gulf, must have seriously affected the rich merchants of Ur.[33] Their city, however, was no longer passing from hand to hand as it had done so often during the struggle between Isin and Larsa. Mesopotamia was now united under a powerful and respected monarch, and for many of Hammurabi's subjects the future may have appeared full of promise. But this period of peace and stability was short: ten, twenty years at most. The next generation would have to face new wars and witness the beginning of formidable changes affecting not only Mesopotamia but the entire Near East.

CHAPTER 14

NEW PEOPLES

Between 2300 and 2000 B.C. – the period of the Akkadian, Gutian and Ur III dynasties in Mesopotamia – important events took place beyond the Taurus and the Zagros mountains. Peoples coming from far away regions entered Asia Minor and founded in the heart of Anatolia what would be known later as the Hittite Kingdom. About the same time, in Armenia and in Iran other foreigners settled among the Hurrian and Kassite tribes as a ruling aristocracy. Four hundred years later the Hittites raided Babylon, the Kassites overthrew the great kingdom painstakingly built by Hammurabi, and the Hurrians, under their 'Mitannian' leaders, firmly occupied the northern half of Mesopotamia.

Hittites, Mitannians and the ruling class of the Kassites belonged to a very large ethno-linguistic group called 'Indo-European', and their migrations were but part of wider ethnic movements which affected Europe and India as well as Western Asia. In all these regions, the arrival of these peoples had multiple, deep and lasting consequences, the most important of which, in the field of this study, were the emergence in Mesopotamia and on its northern and western flanks, of young and energetic nations and the involvement of Egypt in Near Eastern politics. From 1600 B.C. onwards political issues in the Orient are raised to truly international scale, and it is no longer possible to treat Iraq as though it were isolated – or almost isolated – from the rest of the world. Mesopotamian history will have to be drawn against an increasingly wider background, including now Egypt and Anatolia, tomorrow Iran with the Medes and Persians, and finally Europe with the Greco-Macedonian conquerors. If we want to understand the next sequence of events we must at this stage broaden our horizon considerably.

The present chapter will attempt to give a bird's-eye view of
Indo-European migrations, followed by an outline of Hittite,
Hurrian, Syrian and Egyptian history from the twentieth to the
sixteenth century B.C. in round figures.

The Indo-Europeans

The adjective Indo-European applies to a vast linguistic family
comprising languages now spoken in countries as far apart as
America and India, Scandinavia and Spain. All modern European languages (with the exception of Basque, Finnish and
Hungarian), as well as Armenian, Persian and several Hindu
dialects, belong to this group as belonged to it in antiquity
Hittite, Sanskrit, Greek, Latin and several other tongues. In
spite of obvious differences, it is easy to demonstrate that these
languages are closely interrelated, and it is generally believed
that they all derive from a 'Common Indo-European Language'
which has left no written trace.[1] Moreover, a comparative study
of vocabularies had led certain scholars to the conclusion that
all Indo-European-speaking peoples had originally similar ways
of life and institutions: essentially herdsmen and skilled in
horse-breeding, they practised intermittent agriculture, knew
the wheel, the boat and metal techniques, were organized in
families and tribes, worshipped anthropomorphic gods and
obeyed chiefs issued from a martial aristocracy. Finally, it has
been inferred from the distribution of linguistic provinces in
early historical times that the homeland of the Indo-Europeans,
before they divided into several branches, lay somewhere between the Baltic and the Black Sea, probably in the plains of
southern Russia. But difficulties arise when one tries to correlate
the various Chalcolithic cultures which have left traces in
Eastern Europe with the Indo-European-speaking peoples, since
writing does not appear in those regions until a very late date
and precise identifications are impossible. All these 'Pontic'
cultures, however, have a common feature: the presence of
stone or copper battle-axes in tumulus-graves, and most histori-

ans agree that the 'Battle-Axe Warriors' have more claim than anyone else to represent the 'original' Indo-Europeans. These considerations should make it clear that the following reconstruction of Indo-European movements lies, to a great extent, in the realm of speculation, and should be taken with due caution.

The first Indo-European migrations took various forms, reached different countries at different times and were certainly very slow, covering decades and even centuries. As far as can be ascertained, they started about the end of the third millennium B.C. and spread in all directions from the south Russian 'homeland'. In Europe[2] the Battle-Axe folk moved northwards along the Volga and westwards across the open plains of Poland and Germany. By 1600 B.C. they had reached Denmark and the Rhine valley, where they mingled with another ethnic group, the 'Beaker Folk' (so called because of their large, bell-shaped drinking vessels), who probably originated in Spain, and the resulting culture is taken by some scholars as being the prototype of the great Celtic (and therefore linguistically Indo-European) civilization which flourished in Central Europe towards the end of the second millennium B.C. But the Battle-Axe warriors cannot be credited with the introduction of metal into Europe, although they certainly hastened its diffusion. Before their arrival copper had already been brought from the Caucasus and from Anatolia by peaceful tradesmen and artisans who followed the Danube valley or crossed the Mediterranean Sea, so that there were, in the middle of a still Neolithic continent, old islands of metal cultures, notably in the Balkans,[3] Hungary, Spain, Greece and Crete. The last two countries are of special interest to us, owing to the close relationship which has always existed between the Aegean countries, Egypt and Western Asia.

The first Bronze Age culture of Greece,[4] the Early Helladic culture, seems to have been founded at the beginning of the third millennium by immigrants from Anatolia and benefited from intensive commercial intercourse with Asia Minor, the Cyclades and Crete. In about 1900 B.C., however, the Greek peninsula was the setting for a large-scale invasion followed by radical changes in architecture, burial customs and ceramics. Sizeable towns were built on the ruins of humble villages; a grey, wheel-made pottery replaced the dark, hand-made ware of the preceding period, and as the new settlers were buried with numerous bronze weapons, including occasional battle-axes, it has been suggested that the Middle Helladic culture was introduced by the Indo-Europeans. The following Late Helladic or Mycenaean culture in many respects appears to result from the internal development of Middle Helladic, and as the Mycenaeans spoke an Indo-European (Greek) dialect and were, in fact, Greeks – as proved by Ventris' genial decipherment of their 'Linear B' writing[5] – one may reasonably conclude that Indo-European migrations reached continental Greece at the beginning of the eighteenth century B.C., i.e. about the time Hammurabi reigned in Babylon.

While Greece was thus conquered and organized, the brilliant Minoan civilization flourished in the island of Crete.[6] Crete was the meeting-point of Egyptian and Asiatic influences, and indeed, the development of its civilization had been triggered off by early contacts with Egypt, while the local bronze industry was certainly of Anatolian origin, and the *tholoi* tombs and double-axe amulets of the Early Minoan culture (? 2500–1850 B.C.) recall similar though much older monuments and objects found in proto-historic Mesopotamia. Yet the final product of this mixture was extremely original and surprisingly 'Western European' in character. If the palaces erected at Cnossos, Mallia and Phaistos resemble in their layout the contemporary palace of Mari, their architecture and decoration owed no more to foreign arts than did the egg-shell 'Kamares' pottery; nor were the Minoan hieroglyphic and 'Linear A' writings on clay tablets – both as yet undeciphered – of foreign origin. During this Middle Minoan period (1850–1550 B.C.), which corresponds to the Middle Egyptian Kingdom and to the First Dynasty of Babylon, Crete gave more than she received: she exported her products throughout the Aegean and eastern Mediterranean countries and aided the young Mycenaean civilization of continental Greece to mature. In 1450 B.C., however, the Minoan civilization was brutally destroyed – by social and/ or political upheavals the nature of which has not yet been fully elucidated. The Mycenaeans landed in the island, in turn impressed their mark on its culture and built an insular empire which spanned the Aegean: the Indo-Europeans had conquered the sea.

Turning now from Europe to Asia, we find another group of Indo-European-speaking peoples – the Aryans or Indo-Aryans – moving southwards from Russia at the end of the third millennium. In the course of a long periple, two branches detached themselves from a common stem: through Iran or the Caucasus the first branch penetrated into the massif of Armenia and hence to the Taurus foothill region, where it mingled with a very old 'Asianic' people, the Hurrians; the second branch seized control over other Asianic tribes, the Kassites, established farther south in the folds of the Zagros and on the Iranian plateau. The bulk of the Aryans continued their course in a south-easterly direction and eventually reached the former Indian provinces of Sind and Punjab, now in Pakistan. Fourteen years of excavations at two sites of the Indus valley, Mohenjo-Daro and Harappa, have shown that during the third millennium B.C. this region was the centre of a flourishing civilization known as the Indus Civilization or Harappa culture.[7] With its well-planned towns and comfortable brick houses, its attractive painted pottery and its delicately carved and inscribed seals, the Harappa culture is strangely reminiscent of, and can favourably compare with the Sumerian civilization, and indeed there is some evidence of commercial intercourse between the 'Proto-Indians' and the inhabitants of Mesopotamia during the Akkadian period. According to the classical theory, the Harappa culture was destroyed c. 1550 B.C. by the Aryans, but other hypotheses have recently been put forward to explain the disaster which brutally plunged the Indus valley in the dark for many centuries. Some authors blame a gigantic flood, while others believe that the destruction occurred at an earlier date

(1750 B.C.) and was the work of Chalcolithic tribes of central and southern India.[8]

Such is the general background against which we must now examine more closely two peoples which, by virtue of their geographical position, had intimate contacts with Mesopotamia and exerted a considerable influence on its history: the Hittites and the Hurrians.

Asia Minor and the Hittites

The earliest settlements discovered so far date back to Neolithic times, (c. 7000–5400 B.C.), and are situated on the South Anatolian plateau (Hacilar, Çatal Hüyük, Kizilkaya) and in the plain of Cilicia (Mersin, Tarsus). Roughly contemporaneous with Jericho, Jarmo and Hassuna, they resemble these sites in many respects, such as tool equipment, figurines, architecture, etc., though the findings at Çatal Hüyük have revealed a much more elaborate and original pre-ceramic Neolithic phase.[9] Even in Cilicia and in the neighbouring 'Amuq plain, near Antioch,[10] these Neolithic cultures with their buff, brown or black burnished pottery owe nothing to either Syria-Palestine or Mesopotamia, but in the following Early and Middle Chalcolithic periods (c. 5400–3500 B.C.) numerous sherds of Halaf and, later, Ubaid ware appear in these areas, whilst an indigenous painted pottery is produced in Çatal Hüyük, Hacilar and, further west, Beycesultan.

During the Early Bronze Age (c. 3500–2300 B.C.) other parts of Asia Minor became densely populated and a rather brilliant civilization blossomed in the western half of Anatolia (Troy, Alişar, Alaca, Polatli and many other sites), whence it spread over Macedonia, Thessaly and the Aegean Isles. By comparison, the eastern half of the country as well as Armenia seem to have lagged behind, though this may be a false impression due to the rarity of archaeological excavations in that part of Turkey. The Bronze Age cultures vary in detail from region to region, but a number of features give the whole of prehistoric Asia Minor a certain unity: the pottery is predominantly monochrome, 'burnished', dark in colour and attractive; the houses are built of stone and mud bricks, their walls being strenghened by wooden beams, and metal work reaches a high degree of perfection, as illustrated by the so-called 'Priam treasure' of Troy II (c. 2600 B.C.) and by the lavish furniture of the 'Royal Cemetery' at Alaca (c. 2400 B.C.).[11]

In about 2200 B.C., a violent and widespread destruction caused by invaders – most probably the Luwians (see page 271) – marks the end of this unnamed civilization. The western part of Asia Minor was plunged into semi-darkness for several centuries, but central Anatolia soon recovered, and the Middle Bronze Age in that region is characterized by important architectural remains of fortified cities and by the increasing use of indigenous painted wares, including the attractive 'Cappadocian pottery'. It is also in this period that history begins in Anatolia, though the first written documents are in fact of foreign origin.

Asia Minor was one of the main metallurgic centres of the ancient Near East, and a very old and active trade between Mesopotamia and her northern neighbour had eventually resulted in the foundation of Assyrian trading colonies beyond the Taurus range during the reign of Sargon I of Assyria (c. 1900 B.C.), if not earlier.[12] One of these colonies was situated at Boghazköy, the future capital-city of the Hittites; another – the most important of all – was discovered at Kültepe (ancient *Kanesh*), near the town of Kayseri in Cappadocia. There German and Turkish excavations carried out over a number of years have unearthed the traders' houses together with hundreds of their 'business letters'. These, of course, are clay tablets, often contained in a sealed clay envelope, written in a dialectal variety of Akkadian known as 'Old Assyrian'. Since they cover at least six generations, they tell us a great deal about the merchants and their trade. We learn, for instance, that they exported to Assyria silver, gold and large amounts of copper, and imported tin (*annakum*) and woven material. Tin, probably obtained by the Assyrians from Azerbaijan, Elam, or perhaps Afghanistan appears to have been used by the Anatolians for making bronze with the copper produced locally. Payments were generally made in silver. The goods were transported by caravans of donkeys, and we can trace the 1,500 kilometre long track they followed from Assur to Kültepe, and vice versa, through Jazirah and the Taurus passes. The activities of the Assyrian communities were financed by rich families of Assur and controlled by an organization called *karum*, which functioned as Chamber of Commerce, tribunal and consulate under an annually appointed chairman or *limmu*. But perhaps the main interest of this correspondence is that it is our only source of information on the ethnic and political structure of Anatolia at the dawn of her history. Although they practically held in their hands the whole economy of the country, the Assyrian merchants were generally on good terms with the natives and their chieftains who enriched themselves with taxes levied at almost every stage of the commercial transactions. The country was divided into about ten small kingdoms which seemed to obey one ruler called 'prince of princes'. Several local names belong to the old 'Asianic' layer of population (*Hattians*), but the presence of Indo-European names in large numbers indicates that the 'Hittites' had already crossed the Bosphorus and crept into Asia Minor.

Taken in its broader sense, the word 'Hittite' covers the totality of the intruders – three peoples speaking different, though closely related Indo-European languages: Luwian, Palaic and Nesite. The Luwians arrived first and are probably responsible for the destructions which mark the end of the Early Bronze Age; the others came later. Soon they were scattered all over the peninsula. The Luwians, whose language was later written in hieroglyphs, settled to the west of Cilicia, along the coast, the Palaites probably in the hilly region of Sivas, and the so-called Nesites in Cappadocia – indeed, the city of Nesa or Nesha has been tentatively identified with Kanesh-Kültepe. Centuries later those Nesite-speaking invaders conquered the centre of the Anatolian plateau, east of Ankara, the country called *Hatti* by its indigenous population, and took their name from it. They became the *Hittites* proper who played such an important part in Near Eastern history during the second millennium B.C.[13]

From the nearest civilized country, Syria, the Hittites borrowed the cuneiform script invented in Mesopotamia and adapted it to their own Indo-European language. Most of the Hittite texts in our possession are not older than the fourteenth or thirteenth centuries B.C., but they sometimes refer to events which took place in what was already the remote past. One text, for instance, speaks of Pitkhanas, King of Kussara, and his son Anittas, who subdued five neighbouring kingdoms (including Hatti) and transferred his residence to Nesa. As the names of these rulers also appear in the tablets from Kültepe, and as Anittas' campaigns seem to have put an end to the Assyrian colonies in Cappadocia, it is possible to date these events to *c.* 1750 B.C. A palace revolution thereafter took place, and another King of Kussara, Labarnas I (*c.* 1680–1650 B.C.) is said to have 'made the sea his frontiers' and divided the territories conquered between his sons. The origins of Labarnas are obscure, but he was considered by the Hittite monarchs as their true ancestor, and must be credited with having laid the foundations of what is known as the Old Hittite Kingdom, a period of brief but considerable glory for the Hittites, as will be seen in the next chapter.

Leaving, for the time being, the Hittites, we must now turn to one of their most interesting neighbours: the Hurrians.

Hurrians and Mitannians

Known ninety years ago from one single cuneiform text (a letter found at el-Amarna in Egypt) and from a reference in the Bible (the '*Horites*' of *Genesis* xxxvi. 20–30), the Hurrians have become a subject of considerable interest to historians and archaeologists. Unlike the Hittites, they played little part in Near

Eastern politics until the fifteenth century B.C., and then only for a short period, although there is now ample evidence that they formed an important and active element in the population of Mesopotamia and Syria during the second millennium B.C. Yet they still remain in many respects an elusive people, and what we know of them can be told in a few words.[14]

Their language, written in cuneiform script, is neither Semitic nor Indo-European, but belongs to the vague so-called 'Asianic' group, its nearest relative being Urartian, the language spoken in the country of Urartu (Armenia) in the first millennium B.C. Their national gods were Teshup, a storm-god of the mountains, and his consort Hepa, a form of mother-goddess. Whether the Hurrians had an art of their own is open to discussion, but the ceramics associated with their presence in certain sites are most characteristic. These elegant goblets decorated with flowers, birds and geometrical designs painted in buff colour on a dark-grey background contrast with the plain Mesopotamian pottery of the time and date a level as surely as did the Halaf or Ubaid painted wares in proto-historic ages.

Language and religion point to the mountainous north, more precisely to Armenia, as the original homeland of the Hurrians, but they were never strictly confined to that region. We have already seen (p. 156) Hurrian kingdoms established on the upper Tigris and on the Upper Euphrates during the Akkadian period. Under the Third Dynasty of Ur isolated personal names in the economic records from Drehem, near Nippur, suggest that the Hurrians formed in Sumer small groups of immigrants comparable to Armenians in modern Iraq. During the first quarter of the second millennium Hurrian infiltrations in the 'Fertile Crescent' amounted, at least in some regions, to a peaceful invasion. In the Syrian town of Alalah, between Aleppo and Antioch, the Hurrians formed the majority of the population as early as 1800 B.C.[15] At the same time Hurrian personal names and religious texts in Hurrian are found in the archives of Mari and Chagar Bazar. A century or so later the Hurrians practically possess northern Iraq. They occupy the city of Gasur, near Kirkuk, change its name into Nuzi, adopt the language and customs of its former Semitic inhabitants, and build up a very prosperous Hurrian community.[16] Tepe Gawra and Tell Billa,[17] near Mosul, equally fall under their influence. After 1600 B.C. the Hurrian pottery replaces the crudely painted pottery peculiar to the Khabur valley, and the Hurrian element dominates in northern Syria, northern Iraq and Jazirah. We should therefore not be surprised to find in those regions, at the beginning of the fifteenth century B.C., a Hurrian kingdom powerful enough to hold in check the Assyrians in the east, the Hittites and Egyptians in the west. The heart of this kingdom lay in the Balikh-Khabur district, in the region called *Hanigalbat* by the Assyrians and *Naharim* ('the Rivers') by the Western Semites, and it is probable that the name of our 'Hurrians' (*Hurri*) survived in Orrhoe, the Greek name for modern Urfa.

In a number of texts the Hurrian kingdom of Jazirah is called *Mitanni*, and from this word derives the appellation 'Mitannian' applied to the Indo-European element discernible in the Hurrian society at a certain period. We do not know when and how the Indo-Aryans came to be mixed with the Hurrians and took control over them, but there is little doubt that, at least during the fifteenth and fourteenth centuries B.C., they were settled among them as a leading aristocracy. The names of several Mitannian kings, such as Mattiwaza and Tushratta, and the term *mariannu*, which is applied to a category of warriors, are most probably of Indo-European origin. Moreover, in a treaty between Mitannians and Hittites, the gods Mitrasil, Arunasil, Indar and Nasattyana – which are, of course, the well-known Aryan gods Mithra, Varuna, Indra and the Nasatyas – are invoked side by side with Teshup and Hepa. Undoubtedly it was those ancient nomads of the Russian plains who taught the Hurrians the art of horse-training – a Hurrian living in Boghazköy wrote a complete treatise on this subject, using Indo-European technical terms – and in this way introduced or rather popularized the horse in the Near East.[18]

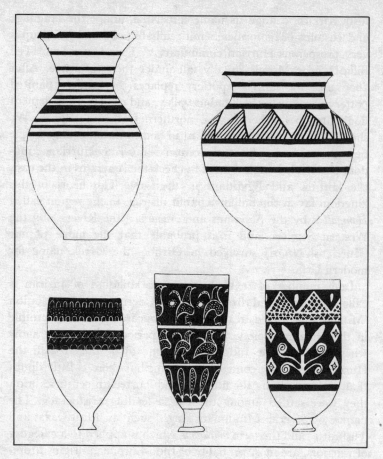

Above: samples of the so-called 'Khabur pottery' (16th century
B.C.), from Chagar Bazar. Below, samples of the so-called 'Nuzi pottery'
(15th century B.C.), from Alalah and Nuzi.
After M.E.L. Mallowan, Iraq, *III (1936) and Sir Leonard Woolley,*
A Forgotten Kingdom, *1953.*

If the contribution of the Hurrians to the civilization of
Mesopotamia was negligible, their impact on the less advanced
cultures of Syria must have been considerable, though difficult

to define. In any case, their large-scale intrusion in the latter country seems to have started a series of political disturbances and ethnic movements, the effects of which were felt as far away as Egypt.

Syria and Egypt

A line corresponding roughly to the present western and southern borders of the Syrian Republic divides ancient Syria* into two parts – the rolling plains of the north and the mountains, hills and deserts of the south – which in prehistory followed a different development. Space does not allow us to describe it, however briefly,[19] but what we think is of interest to our subject is the fact that from very early days the north was wide open to Mesopotamian influences, as it was the link between the Tigris–Euphrates valley, the Mediterranean and, to some extent, Anatolia. If the north, with its hundreds of tells, had been as thoroughly explored as Lebanon or Palestine, the discovery at Ebla of a large and powerful kingdom, dating to the middle of the third millennium B.C., and which owed much to the Sumero-Akkadian civilization (see above, page 142) would not have come as a complete surprise. What could not have been expected, however, is that the people of Elba spoke a hitherto unknown Semitic dialect, akin to Akkadian though definitely West-Semitic.

During that time, the south – certainly inhabited by other Semites – looked towards Egypt.[20] Relations between that country and Lebanon or Palestine, already attested in the Pre-Dynastic period, are well documented under the Old Egyptian Kingdom (c. 2800–2400 B.C.). This was the time of the great pyramids, and Egypt looked like its monuments: lofty, massive, apparently indestructible. Docile to the orders of Pharaoh – the incarnate god who sat in Memphis – and of his innumerable

---

* The term *Syria* is taken here in its broadest sense and includes Syria proper, Lebanon, Palestine and Transjordan.

officials, toiled a hard-working people and an army of foreign slaves. But if the Nile valley was rich, it lacked an essential material: wood. The mountains of Lebanon, within easy reach, were thick with pine, cypress and cedar forests. Thus a very active trade was established between the two countries to their mutual profit. Byblos (Semitic *Gubla*, Egyptian *Kepen*), the great emporium of timber, became strongly 'Egyptianized', and from Byblos Egyptian cultural influence spread along the coast. The relations between the Egyptians and the populations of the Palestinian hinterland, however, were far less friendly. The nomads who haunted the Negeb, in particular, repeatedly attacked the Egyptian copper mines in the Sinai peninsula and on occasion raided the Nile delta, obliging the Pharaohs to retaliate and even to fortify their eastern border. The downfall of the Old Kingdom left Egypt unprotected, and we know of the large part played by the 'desert folk', the 'Asiatics', in the three hundred years of semi-anarchy which followed.

The first centuries of the second millennium witnessed the expansion of the Western Semites in Syria as well as in Mesopotamia, as proved by a break between the Early Bronze and Middle Bronze cultures, and by the predominance of West-Semitic names among the population of Syria-Palestine. While Amorite dynasties rose to power in many Mesopotamian towns, northern Syria was divided into several Amorite kingdoms, the most important being those of Iamhad (Aleppo), Karkemish and Qatna. Around the palaces of local rulers large fortified cities were built, and the objects and sculptures discovered in the palace of Iarim-Lim, King of Alalah, for instance, are by no means inferior in quality to those found in the contemporary palace of Zimri-Lim, King of Mari. We have already seen that the archives of Mari offer ample proof of intimate and sometimes friendly contacts between Mesopotamia and Syria, and indeed, one cannot escape the impression of a vast community of Amorite states stretching from the Mediterranean to the Persian Gulf. At the same time commercial relations between Syria and Crete were intensified. A colony of Minoan traders established

itself in the port of Ugarit (Ras Shamra),[21] and the exquisite
Kamares crockery found its way to the tables of Syrian monarchs. Egypt, then in the full revival of its Middle Kingdom
(2160–1660 B.C.), renewed and consolidated the ties which
attached it to the Lebanese coast and endeavoured to counter
the growing Hurrian influence in northern Syria by lavishing
presents on the Amorite courts. This, at any rate, is a possible
explanation for the vases, jewels and royal statues sent to
Byblos, Beirut, Ugarit, Qatna and Neirab (near Aleppo) by the
Pharaohs of the Twelfth Dynasty.[22]

The region to the south of the Lebanon presents us with a
very different picture. Much poorer than northern Syria and
less open to foreign influences, Palestine in the Middle Bronze
Age (2000–1600 B.C.) was a politically divided and unstable
country 'in the throes of tribal upheaval'[23] where the Egyptians
themselves had no authority and apparently little desire to
extend their political and economic ascendancy. The arrival
among those restless tribes of Abraham and his family – an
event whose after-effects are still acutely felt in the Near East –
must have passed almost unnoticed. Small clans or large tribes
constantly travelled in antiquity from one side to the other of
the Syrian desert, and there is no reason to doubt the reality of
Abraham's migration from Ur to Hebron *via* Harran as described in *Genesis* xi. 31. A comparison between the biblical
account and the archaeological and textual material in our
possession suggests that this move must have taken place 'about
1850 B.C., or a little later',[24] perhaps as the result of the difficult
conditions which prevailed then in southern Iraq, torn apart
between Isin and Larsa. The historical character of the Patri-
archal period was further reinforced – so it was thought some
years ago – by the mention in cuneiform and hieroglyphic texts
dating mostly from the fifteenth and fourteenth centuries B.C. of a
category of people, generally grouped in bellicose bands, called
habirû (or *'apiru* in Egyptian), a name which sounded remarkably like biblical *'Ibri*, the Hebrews. There was at last the long-
awaited appearance in non-hebraical sources of Abraham's kin!

Unfortunately, recent and thorough reappraisals of these sources have shown beyond any doubt that the Habiru have nothing in common with the Hebrews but a similitude of name. They were neither a people nor a tribe, but a class of society made up of refugees, of 'displaced persons' as we would now say, who frequently turned into outlaws.[25]

In about 1720 B.C. the Palestinian chieftains, whose turbulence and hostile attitude had already worried the last Pharaohs of the Twelfth Dynasty, succeeded in invading Egypt, which they governed for nearly one hundred and fifty years. They are known as Hyksôs, the Greek form of the Egyptian name *hiqkhase*, 'chieftain of a foreign hill-country'. Although they never occupied more than the Nile delta, their influence on the warfare, the arts and even the language of that country was considerable. In the end, however, the kings of the Eighteenth Dynasty overthrew the Hyksôs, chasing them up to the gates of Gaza, and with this exploit opens what we call the New Empire (1580–1100 B.C.), undoubtedly the most glorious period in the history of ancient Egypt. By contrast, Mesopotamia fell, at about the same time (1595 B.C.) into the hands of other foreigners, the Kassites, and entered into a long period of political lethargy.

CHAPTER 15

THE KASSITES

After this broad, if sketchy, survey of the Near East, we must now return to Mesopotamia, which we left, it will be remembered, at the end of Hammurabi's reign, in the middle of the eighteenth century B.C.

The ethnic movements just described were then about to bear fruit: the Hittites were enforcing their rule upon the indigenous populations of Anatolia; the Hurrians were peacefully invading northern Syria and northern Iraq; and behind the Zagros range an Aryan aristocracy was organizing the Kassites into a nation of warriors. If the Babylonian court was aware of these changes, it probably saw in them little cause for alarm, since none of these peoples yet appeared to constitute an immediate danger to Iraq, and indeed, the first cracks in the edifice erected by Hammurabi resulted not from foreign aggression, but from its own intrinsic weakness. The empire of Babylon was the work of one man and rested almost entirely upon his powerful personality. Built up in a few years through the aggregation of five sovereign states, each of them with a long tradition of independence, it had been forcefully and prematurely centralized. The efforts made by the king to concentrate in Babylon the political, economic and spiritual life of the country might in the long run have benefited Mesopotamia as a whole, but their immediate effect was to ruin the provinces and to create a considerable amount of discontentment particularly in the once prosperous cities of Sumer and in Assyria, where the memory of Shamshi-Adad's great deeds was still alive. Small wonder, therefore, that the death of Hammurabi (1750 B.C.) was followed by an outburst of revolts leading to the rapid disintegration of his kingdom. These revolts were relatively easy, three of the four states annexed by Hammurabi being vassal kingdoms, and they were also popular since the king of Babylon had purchased or simply taken vast estates, the market was in the hands of rapacious businessmen, and the provinces, notably in southern Mesopotamia, were getting increasingly poorer to the benefit of the capital-city and its immediate surroundings.

The kings who succeeded Hammurabi tried in vain to quell the general rebellion, then resigned themselves to the breaking down of the Babylonian empire, but they proved unable to cope with the new situation by applying the right policies.[1] To compensate for their loss of revenues from tenant farmers' rents and taxation, they tried to increase agricultural production in the smaller territory that remained in their possession. To replace the dwindling profits of a declining trade with the Gulf countries, many merchants acted as bankers: in collusion with the Palace, they offered the small farmers and shopkeepers loans for equipment.[2] Thousands of families were endebted for ever, while many private lenders were enriched to the point of threatening the power of the State. Moreover, it seems that in order to produce more and more cereals, landowners violated the rule of fallow, thereby reducing the fertility of the soil and accelerating its salinization.[3] Thus, within a century (1700–1600 B.C. in round figures) Babylonia went from political disintegration to economic disorders and ecological disaster. The kingdom became decrepit and a small blow, a short-lived raid of the Hittites, brought about its collapse and that of its First Dynasty.

Ironically, it was the princes of the Kassites, a people regarded as inferior and semi-barbaric, who ascended the throne left vacant, apparently took the necessary measures and gradually transformed Babylonia into a prosperous kingdom honoured and respected by its powerful neighbours. The Kassites reigned for more than four centuries, and we can only regret that the paucity of our sources makes this long and interesting period one of the least-known in the history of ancient Iraq.

Hammurabi's Successors

Hammurabi's son and heir, Samsu-iluna (1749–1712 B.C.), was apparently endowed with some of his father's qualities, for he fought with remarkable endurance against the various enemies of Babylon.[4] But it was like mending a ragged cloak: for every rent patched a new one appeared, and the final result was an enormous loss of territory. Thus in the ninth year of the reign an adventurer calling himself Rîm-Sin, like the last King of Larsa, led a revolt in the districts bordering Elam and kept afield for at least five years before he was caught and slain.

The King of Eshnunna, who had sided with him, was captured and strangled in Babylon. During the long and bloody war which followed, Samsu-iluna pulled down the walls of Ur, plundered and set on fire all its temples and partly destroyed that city.[5] Uruk shared about the same fate, which gave the Elamites a pretext to intervene: Kuturnahhunte I entered that city and took away, among other treasures, a statue of the goddess Inanna which Ashurbanipal recovered a thousand years later. After a few years of respite, a certain Iluma-ilu – pretendedly a descendant of Damiq-ilishu, the last king of Isin – raised the flag of independence in Sumer, became the master of the entire country south of Nippur and founded the so-called 'Second Dynasty of Babylon' or Dynasty of the Sea-Land which lasted until 1460 B.C.[6] At about the same time the north-eastern districts, under Babylonian obedience as a result of Hammurabi's last campaign, also recovered their freedom – probably through the rebellion of one of Shamsi-Addu's obscure successors, Adasi, who remained famous in Assyrian annals for having 'ended the servitude of Assur'.[7] In addition to facing this series of domestic disasters, Samsu-iluna had to protect his kingdom against the threat of foreign invasion: we learn from year-names that he defeated a Kassite army in his ninth year and an Amorite army in his thirty-fifth year – not to mention the frequent incursions of Sutaean raiders who captured men and women and sold them as slaves to the Mesopotamians themselves. At the end of this disastrous reign Babylon was safe, but the kingdom, amputated of its northern and southern provinces, had shrunk back to its original boundaries: those of the country of Akkad.

Samsu-iluna's four successors, however, managed to preserve their reduced heritage for about a century. Abi-eshuh (1711–1684 B.C.) repelled a second Kassite attack, tolerated or perhaps encouraged the settling of Kassite individuals in Babylonia as agricultural workers, but was unable to prevent the Kassite chief Kashtiliash I from becoming King of Hana in about 1700 B.C.[8] In a grandiose effort to dislodge Iluma-ilu from the swamps where he had taken refuge he dammed the Tigris, but failed to catch his rival, who continued to reign unchallenged over Sumer. There is some evidence that Ammi-ditana (1683–1647 B.C.) reconquered, at least temporarily, some of the territories lost by his predecessors. Ammi-ṣaduqa (1646–1626 B.C.) is famous not for his military achievements, if any, but for his 'edict of justice' (meshârum). This document is of considerable interest for the light it indirectly throws on the economic situation of the time and the efforts made by the king to alleviate the burden of his subjects. It proclaims, for the whole population, the remitting of all debts and an amnesty for arrears, rents due and loans 'for necessities', and for some categories of people the suppression or reduction of licences and certain taxes, as well as the abolition of imprisonment for debt, going as far as threatening with death penalty the bailiffs who would dare take debtors to court.[9] All that the last king of the dynasty, Samsu-ditana (1625–1595 B.C.), has left us is a list of the year-names of his reign. As did all good Mesopotamian kings, all the successors of Hammurabi restored temples, dug canals and built fortified towns in many parts of their reduced and impoverished kingdom. It is doubtful whether these keen, capable and pious monarchs, who year after year offered to the gods their own statues, ever suspected that the storm which was to sweep away their throne was gathering in the distant north-west, far beyond the snow-capped Taurus mountains.

We have said earlier that a Hittite prince of whom very little is known, Labarnas I, had founded in Anatolia and immediately enlarged a kingdom which he ruled from the unidentified city of Kussara. Labarnas II, his son (*c.* 1650–1620 B.C.), added to the royal domain the principality of Hatti, in the great bend of the Kizil-Irmak River, took for residence the then deserted city of Hattusas (modern Boghazköy) and from then on called himself Hattusilis, 'the man from Hattusas'. This warlike monarch soon found the frontiers of his kingdom too narrow and looked for other lands to conquer, but the fierce Gasgas tribes who dwelt in the Pontic range to the north, the Luwians to the west and the Hurrians to the east opposed to his ambitions a triple barrier. Only to the south was the road relatively free – it had been opened, it seems, by Labarnas I as far as Cilicia – and it led beyond the Taurus to Syria, and beyond Syria to either Egypt or Mesopotamia, fertile lands where a thousand years of civilization had accumulated an enormous amount of alluring wealth. The Hittites, therefore, marched southwards. The fragmentary annals of Hattusilis,[10] mention at least two campaigns in that direction, in the course of which Alalah was destroyed, Urshu (a town on the Euphrates, to the north of Karkemish) besieged and taken, and the troops of Aleppo defeated in Commagene. Aleppo itself (*Halpa*), then the capital-city of the powerful Amorite kingdom of Iamhad, could not be conquered, and Hattusilis appears to have lost his life in the war. But his adopted son and successor, Mursilis I (*c.* 1620–1590 B.C.), succeeded where his father had failed:

'He destroyed the city of Halpa,' says a Hittite text, 'and took to Hattusas prisoners from Halpa and its treasures.'[11]

After Aleppo, Karkemish succumbed. From Karkemish the Hittite army followed the Euphrates downstream and suddenly appeared at the gates of Babylon. Just what happened then we do not know. Babylonian writers are naturally reticent about this painful affair, and only in a chronicle of much later date do we find the laconic entry:

Against Samsu-ditana the men of Hatti marched, against the land of Akkad.

But the Hittite text already quoted is more explicit:

Thereafter he (Mursilis) went to Babylon and occupied Babylon; he also attacked the Hurrians and kept the prisoners and possessions from Babylon at Hattusas.

Thus Babylon was taken and plundered. We know from other sources that the statues of Marduk and his consort, the goddess Sarpanitum, were taken away as booty and, for some obscure reason, left behind at Hana when the Hittites retreated. As for Samsu-ditana, he lost his crown as well, probably, as his life. Thus disappeared in one day and presumably without much resistance the dynasty which an obscure Amorite sheikh had founded and which Hammurabi had made famous. It had lasted three hundred years (1894–1595 B.C.).

Iraq under Kassite Rule

The Hittite campaign, if it had been followed by the permanent occupation of Babylon, might have changed the course of Oriental history. It proved, however, to be no more than a daring razzia. Soon after his victory Mursilis returned to Hattusas, where dangerous palace intrigues required his presence, and never came back. After the withdrawal of the Hittite army the fate of Babylon is not known with certainty. It would appear that the Kassite ruler of those days – most probably the eighth king of the dynasty, Agum II (Kakrime) – sat on the throne left vacant by the death of Samsu-ditana, and from then on a long line of Kassite monarchs was to govern Mesopotamia or, as they called it, *Kar-Duniash* for no less than four hundred and thirty-eight years (1595–1157 B.C.).[12]

Established in Iran from time immemorial, the Kassites (Akkadian *kashshû*) originally occupied the central part of the Zagros range known today as Luristan, immediately to the south of

Hamadan. Unlike their northern neighbours, the Guti and the Lullubi, they played no part in Near Eastern politics during the third millennium. Their sudden aggressiveness, in the middle of the eighteenth century, seems to have been stimulated by the Indo-European warriors who had come from the east a century or two before, taught them the art of horse-rearing and taken control of their tribes. Since we possess no text entirely written in Kassite, but only Akkadian texts containing Kassite words and expressions, a short bilingual list of gods and a list of personal names, all we can say about the Kassite language is that it was agglutinative and perhaps distantly related to Elamite.[13] The Indo-European element is attested by the presence in the Kassite pantheon of Aryan gods such as Shuriash (Ind. Surya), Maruttash (Ind. Marut) and Buriash (perhaps identical with Boreas, the Greek god of the north wind), side by side with Sumero-Akkadian deities and with Kassite gods proper (Kashshu, Shipak, Harbe, Shumalia, Shuqamuna). On such scanty evidence rests our knowledge of the ethnic and cultural background of these highlanders.

Unfortunately, we are not much better off as regards the period of Kassite domination in Iraq. As archaeological excavations progress no doubt more documents will come to light, but all we have at present is about two hundred royal inscriptions – most of them short and of little historical value – sixty *kudurru* (see below) and approximately 12,000 tablets (letters and economic texts), less than 10 per cent of which has been published. This is very little indeed for four hundred years – the length of time separating us from Elizabeth I. The bulk of our information derives, in fact, from sources foreign to the kingdom of Babylon, such as the el-Amarna correspondence found in Egypt (see Chapter 16) or the 'Synchronous History', a chronicle written by an Assyrian scribe in the seventh century B.C.[14] This silence makes the Kassite period one of the most obscure in Mesopotamian history, and the words 'dark age' and 'decadence' come easily to mind. Nevertheless, if we make full use of our sources and if we take into account the monuments erected by the

Kassite kings, these long years of political stagnation appear, compared with the last years of the First Dynasty of Babylon, as an epoch of revival and even of progress, at least in some fields. There is no doubt, for instance, that the Kassites restored order, peace and unity in a country devastated by half a millennium of war, kept up with Mesopotamian traditions and behaved in every way like good, sensible Mesopotamian monarchs. Thus one of the first acts of Agum Kakrime (c. 1570 B.C.) after he became King of Babylon was to bring back from Hana the statues of Marduk and Sarpanitum and to reinstate them in their temples lavishly furnished for the occasion.[15] This gesture was calculated to win him the heart of his subjects, but it had a deeper significance: it meant that the foreigner recognized Marduk as the master of his new kingdom and intended to pose as the legitimate successor of the extinct dynasty. Some eighty years later Ulamburiash defeated Ea-gâmil, King of the Sea-Land, thereby recovering for Babylon the entire country of Sumer (after 1500 B.C.). Whether there were other, unrecorded and less successful wars between Babylonia and Assyria, or whether the Kassites gave up all hopes of imposing their authority over the former northern provinces of Hammurabi's empire, we do not know; but one of Agum's successors, Burn-aburiash I, signed an agreement with the Assyrian prince Puzur-Ashur III concerning the frontier which, somewhere around Samarra, separated the two kingdoms. A century or so later, a similar treaty was signed between Kara-Indash and Ashur-bêl-nisheshu (1419–1411 B.C.).[16] Thus was consecrated the division of Mesopotamia into two parts: Assyria and Babylonia, a dichotomy whose effects were to be felt for nearly a thousand years. In their own domain the Kassite kings undertook to rebuild and embellish the old and famous sanctuaries of Nippur, Larsa, Ur and Uruk. One of them, Kara-Indash, has left in the E-Anna precinct of Uruk a very interesting piece of work: a temple, the façade of which was made of bricks moulded in such a way that, when put together, they made up life-size figures of divine beings in low relief.[17] This ingenious technique

– perhaps a substitute for rock carving – was then new in Mesopotamia; it was used later by the Chaldean dynasty in Babylon and by the Achaemenians in Susa and Persepolis. The most enthusiastic of Kassite builders, however, was Kurigalzu I (c. 1400 B.C.), who not only restored the sacred city of Ur destroyed under Samsu-iluna but founded a new and important town, now represented by the ruins of 'Aqar Quf.

The 57 metre high tower of 'Aqar Quf, casting its shadow over the plain and standing a conspicuous landmark thirty-three kilometres due west of Baghdad, is the core of a huge ziqqurat which once rose in the middle of Dûr-Kurigalzu, the fortified city (dûru) and royal residence of King Kurigalzu. Excavations carried out at 'Aqar Quf have unearthed the base of the ziqqurat with its monumental staircase, three temples and part of a palace.[18] The palace was decorated with frescoes and comprised an ambulatory with square pillars, another architectural novelty. The temples were dedicated to the divine family Enlil, Ninlil and their son Ninurta. The presence of these Sumerian gods in a city founded by a Kassite king shows to what degree the foreigners had been assimilated. Various objects of interest were found in the temples and the palace, including a more than life-size statue of Kurigalzu engraved with a long Sumerian inscription, painted terracotta figurines modelled with considerable skill, and splendid gold jewels.

The Kassites are sometimes credited with the introduction of the horse into Mesopotamia. This is not strictly correct. The 'ass from foreign countries' (anshe-kur-ra), as the Sumerians called it, appears sporadically in texts of the Ur III period, and horses are mentioned under their Akkadian name sîsû in the royal correspondence from Mari.[19] But the use of the horse as a draught animal was certainly made more common during the Kassite period by the Hurrians and by the Kassites themselves. The appearance on Near Eastern battlefields of fast horse-driven chariots created, as expected, a revolution in warfare, while the replacement of load-carrying donkeys by horse-driven wagons made commercial transport easier and faster. Several other

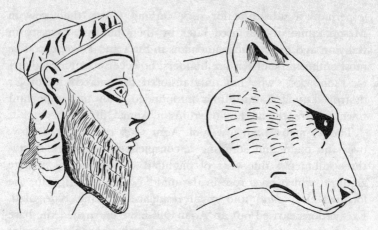

Terracotta heads of a man and a lioness from Dûr-Kurigalzu ('Aqar Quf),
Kassite period.
After Taha Baqir, Iraq, *VIII, 1946.*

major or minor changes were wrought by the Kassites or, at
least, took place during their reign. They range from the way of
measuring fields to the fashion of dressing and cannot be described here in detail. Two of them, however, are of particular
interest to the historian. One is the substitution for the old
dating system of year-names of a simpler system, whereby the
years of each reign, counting from the first New Year following
coronation, were expressed in figures, e.g. 'first, second, etc.,
year of King N'. The other novelty is the *kudurru*. The Akkadian
word *kudurru* means 'frontier, boundary', and these little steles
are often called 'boundary stones', although they were in reality
donation charts, records of royal grants of land, written on
stone and kept in temples, while copies on clay were given to
the landowners.[20] A *kudurru* was usually divided into two parts:
on the *recto* or on the upper part of the stele were sculptured in
low relief the images of the gods – often replaced by their
symbols: a sun-disc for Shamash, a moon-crescent for Sin, a hoe

for Marduk, etc. – under whose guarantee was placed the donation made by the king,[21] on the *verso* or under the sculptures was engraved a long inscription giving the name of the person who benefited from the grant, the exact location and measurements of the estate, the various exemptions and privileges attached to it, a list of witnesses and finally, multiple and colourful maledictions against 'whosoever in the future should deface, alter or destroy' the *kudurru*.

These small monuments are, with cylinder-seals and terracotta statues and figurines, about the only works of art of the Kassite period that have survived. While the sculpture on *kudurru* is predominantly symbolic and static, the designs on the seals comprise novel geometric figures (lozenges, crosses, crescents) and a variety of animals previously not represented, such as the fly, the bee, the grasshopper, the dog or the monkey, usually 'in motion'. Many seals bear a relatively long inscription giving the name, father's name and profession of the owner sometimes followed by a prayer or an incantation.[22] In literature the Kassite period was marked by considerable efforts to salvage the cultural heritage handed down from more creative ages and by a new, typically priestly approach to ethical problems. Scientific works, such as medical and astronomical observations compiled during the Isin-Larsa and Old Babylonian periods were copied and grouped into collections; dictionaries and lists of cuneiform signs were composed. Under the First Dynasty of Babylon, most of the great Sumero-Akkadian myths and legends had been rethought, recast into a simple, clear, elegant language and rejuvenated; under the Kassite rule they were edited by generations of temple scribes and couched in a rather sophisticated dialect, 'Standard Babylonian', markedly different from the vernacular 'Middle Babylonian'. The religious and philosophical concepts traditional in Mesopotamia were preserved, but in the relationship between men and gods the stress was put on resignation rather than on confidence, on superstition rather than on faith. Pieces of wisdom literature, such as *Ludlul bêl nêmeqi* (see p. 101), are highly representative of the new spirit,[23] while the current bigotry is reflected in 'hemerologies' (i.e. calendars of propitious and ill-fated days) and in collections of incantations against demons. All this was perhaps not very original, but at least the erudite priests of Babylon saved the Mesopotamian culture from oblivion, just as the European monks in the Middle Ages saved the Graeco-Roman culture. Such was the prestige of Mesopotamian literature in the ancient Near East that it was adopted in many countries from Anatolia to Egypt: the Epic of Gilgamesh, for instance, was translated into Hittite and Hurrian, and copies of Babylonian legends were found on the banks of the Nile. Moreover, the Babylonian language was *lingua franca* in all Oriental courts and diplomatic circles throughout the second half of the second millennium, at a time when Babylonia was, politically speaking, almost inactive. Thus if in the new international concert Mesopotamia played only third or fourth fiddle, she still ranked very high in the field of civilization.

CHAPTER 16

KASSITES, ASSYRIANS
AND THE ORIENTAL POWERS

Three out of the four centuries covered by the Kassite period were occupied by violent conflicts between the great nations of the Near East. The main reasons for these conflicts were the conquest of Syria by the Egyptians, the renewed claims of the Hittites over that country and the formation of a large Hurri-Mitannian Kingdom extending from the Mediterranean to the Zagros and acting as an obstacle to Egyptian, Hittite and, later, Assyrian ambitions. But while the territories disputed – Syria and Jazirah – lay within a short distance of Babylon, the Kassite monarchs were either too weak or too wise to allow themselves to become involved in the conflagration, and it was not until the middle of the fourteenth century that Assyrian pressure forced them into war. From 1600 to 1350 B.C. in round figures the Babylonians enjoyed almost complete peace, with the exception of their victorious war against the Sea-Land and of skirmishes along their northern frontier; and when the whole Orient after 1480 B.C. went up in flames they alone sat back, watching what has been aptly described as 'a scrum of empires'. Because of the comparatively minor role played by Babylonia and, for a long time, by Assyria in the great political turmoil of the second millennium, we need not give here more than a summary of these intricate events, the details of which can be found in any history dealing with the wider aspects of the ancient Near East. Some emphasis, however, will be placed on those events which took place in Mesopotamia proper or influenced the destinies of that country.[1]

253

Egypt versus Mitanni

The effects of the new political situation arising from the invasion of Egypt by the Hyksôs (*c.* 1700 B.C.) and from the fall of the First Dynasty of Babylon (1595 B.C.) were not felt immediately. In the light of the few available data, the sixteenth century appears as a relatively stable period during which the nations whose armies were later to stand face to face on the battlefields of Syria were dressing their wounds or furbishing their weapons. In the reign of Amosis I (1576–1546 B.C.) the Hyksôs were driven out of the Nile delta, but the first Pharaohs of the Eighteenth Dynasty were too busy enforcing their authority within their own country to engage in foreign adventures, and even the famous campaign of Tuthmosis I across Syria up to the Euphrates (*c.* 1520 B.C.) was a raid without lasting consequences. In Anatolia the Old Hittite Kingdom was slowly crumbling, undermined by palace revolutions no less than by foreign attacks. The king who had taken Aleppo and Babylon, Mursilis I, was assassinated in 1590 B.C., and his successors surrendered all claims over the territories south of the Taurus mountains. In Assur reigned the descendants of Adasi, the prince who had shaken off the Babylonian yoke; but for a few building inscriptions and for a reference to Puzur-Ashur III in the Synchronistic History² these princes would remain for us mere names on a list. As for Babylonia, she was being reunited and reorganized by the Kassites, obviously unwilling or unable to indulge in dreams of expansion. Perhaps the most active of all Oriental peoples during that period were the Hurrians and their Mitannian war-lords. While the complete absence of textual evidence precludes any positive statement, we may at least surmise, on the basis of subsequent events, that the Hurri-Mitannians were taking advantage of the vacuum created in northern Syria and northern Iraq by the collapse of the Hammurabian empire and the withdrawal of the Hittites to build themselves a great kingdom in those regions.

Then, suddenly, at the dawn of the fifteenth century, trouble broke out in the Near East, coming from an unexpected direction. Sheltered by the deserts which border the Nile valley, Egypt had lived for two thousand years isolated politically, though not commercially, from the rest of the Orient. Its north-eastern frontier, it is true, was vulnerable, and on several occasions the 'vile 'Amu', the 'Sand-farers', the hated Asiatics had crossed the isthmus of Suez, made armed incursions into the delta and given cause for serious concern; they had, however, never succeeded in gaining full control of the country. But the long and humiliating Hyksôs episode had taught the Egyptians a lesson: in order to avoid a similar invasion, they must fight the Asiatics in their country of origin and reduce them to servitude. It was with this idea in mind that Tuthmosis III in 1480 B.C. undertook the conquest of Syria, opening new fields to Egyptian ambitions and setting a pattern of Egyptian politics which can be followed throughout history down to the present day. The fact that it took him seventeen years to become the master of Palestine and of the coastal strip of Lebanon and Syria proves that he was up against forces far superior to those of the Syro-Palestinian princelings, or that his opponents received all the support in men, horses and weapons that only a powerful state could afford. The true enemies of Egypt in Syria were neither the Canaanites nor the Amorites, but the Hurri-Mitannians, long entrenched in those regions and now strongly organized. The kingdom of Mitanni occupied the region called *Hanigalbat* by the Assyrians, that is the steppe between the Euphrates and the Tigris, to the south of the Taurus range, and somewhere in this area – possibly near the head of the Khabur river – lay its capital Washukkanni, the exact location of which has not yet been determined.[3] Its northern and southern frontiers were probably as ill-defined for the Hurri-Mitannians as they are for us, though we know from Hittite sources that the Hurrians were established in Armenia, threatening the Hittite kingdom. During the fifteenth century northern Syria to the west and Assyria to the east were under Mitannian allegiance. The first king of Mitanni whose name has survived, Paratarna (*c.* 1480 B.C.), is mentioned in the statue inscription of Idrimi, King of Alalah, who refers to him as his overlord, as well as in a tablet found at Nuzi, near Kirkuk.[4] Also found in this city was the seal of Paratarna's successor, Shaushatar.[5] In addition, there is ample evidence of a Hurri-Mitannian political influence in Ugarit, in Qatna and, indirectly, in Palestine. An even greater influence can be detected in northern Iraq, and there is every reason to believe that all the Kings of Assur who reigned between 1500 and 1360 B.C. were the vassals of the King of Mitanni: when one of them dared to revolt, Shaushatar, we are told, plundered Assur and took to Washukkanni 'a door of silver and gold'.[6]

The victories of Tuthmosis III put only part of this vast kingdom under Egyptian domination. In Syria the Mitannians kept Alalah and Karkemish, whence they were able to foster in the districts they had lost rebellions serious enough to justify three Egyptian campaigns under Amenophis II. Under Tuthmosis IV (1425–1417 B.C.), this state of permanent though indirect hostility came to an end, and the most friendly relations were established between the courts of Thebes and Washukkanni: 'seven times' the pharaoh asked Artatama I of Mitanni for the hand of his daughter,[7] and Amenophis III (1417–1379 B.C.) married Shutarna's daughter Kilu-Hepa.[8] The fear of the Hittites is often given as the reason for this sudden and complete change in politics, but this is by no means certain. In about 1450 B.C. Tudkhaliyas II in Anatolia had founded a new dynasty and immediately reasserted Hittite rights upon the districts south of the Taurus by taking Aleppo – possibly acting in collusion with Tuthmosis III.[9] His immediate successors, however, entangled as they were in Anatolian wars, could hardly be considered so dangerous for both Egypt and Mitanni as to provoke a *rapprochement* between the two countries. The truth, in all probability, is that the Egyptians realized their inability to occupy the whole of Syria, and the Mitannians their inability to regain ground in Palestine and on the Syrian coast; both accepted the *status quo* and turned an old enmity into a friendly alliance.

The Time of Suppiluliumas

After the time of Shamshi-Adad and Hammurabi the fourteenth century B.C. is the most copiously documented period in the second millennium. Hittite annals and treaties, Assyrian inscriptions, Assyrian and Babylonian chronicles and, above all, the four-hundred-odd letters written by the kings of Western Asia, great or small, to Amenophis III and IV and found at el-Amarna in Egypt[10] throw on these years of armed conflicts and subtle diplomatic moves the most welcome light. Moreover, these documents bring out with particular clarity some of the most powerful or fascinating personalities of the ancient Orient: Amenophis IV (Akhenaten), the mystic pharaoh more interested in religion than in politics; Kurigalzu II, the only Kassite king who could pose as a conqueror; Ashur-uballit, the shrewd prince who liberated Assyria and turned it again into a great nation; and surpassing them all in merit, the energetic Hittite monarch who imposed his mark upon the whole period: Suppiluliumas.[11]

During the first quarter of the century the diplomatic and matrimonial ties already existing between Egypt and Mitanni were reinforced and extended to other nations, giving the entire Near East the appearance of a happy family in which Egypt played the part of the wealthy relative. Tushratta, having succeeded his father Shutarna on the Mitannian throne (c. 1385 B.C.), gave his daughter Tadu-Hepa to Amenophis III as spouse, and when the old Pharaoh fell ill he sent him the image of Ishtar of Nineveh, who was reputed to cure the most intractable diseases. Similarly, the Kassite Kadashman-Enlil I added his sister and his daughter to Amenophis's opulent harem and received from him large quantities of gold. Even the Assyrians, no doubt with the consent of their Mitannian overlord, sent ambassadors to the court of Thebes. But in 1380 B.C. Suppiluliumas became king in Boghazköy and a few years later led the Hittite army into Syria. A direct attack against Aleppo – now once more in Mitannian hands – having failed, in a second campaign he crossed the Euphrates near Malatiya, entered the land of Mitanni from the north, plundering Washukkanni on his way, turned westward, again crossed the Euphrates near Karkemish, subdued the region called Nuhashshe to the south of that city, ravaged Qatna and captured the stronghold of Qadesh (Tell Nebi Mend, south of Homs), which marked the northern limit of Egyptian dominion in Syria. At the same time he skilfully played on the rivalry between Syrian princelings and managed to put under Hittite suzerainty the kingdoms which did not lie directly across his path, including Ugarit and Alalah. Finally, leaving behind him a number of ardent support-ers, he returned to the Anatolian homeland, where important and difficult tasks were to absorb his activities for about twenty years.

This brilliant military and diplomatic exploit was a severe blow to the Egyptians and a near disaster for the Mitannians, who found themselves deprived of all their possessions west of the Euphrates. In Syria some of the most enterprising local rulers backed by the Hittites fell upon their neighbours, who cried to Egypt for help, and their clamour – mingled with the clamour of Palestinian chieftains continuously attacked by bands of *habirû* – fill the el-Amarna archives. But most of these letters remained unanswered. Amenophis III, too old and too ill to intervene, died soon after the Hittite campaign, leaving the throne to the weak, effeminate and theologically minded Amenophis IV (1379–1362 B.C.), himself for a long time under the influence of the queen-mother Teye. For various reasons Amenophis IV refused to be involved in the Syrian imbroglio, but otherwise pursued the foreign policy of his predecessor, marrying the youngest of his father's Mitannian wives, Tadu-Hepa – perhaps the same person as the charming 'Nefertiti' – and remaining on the best possible terms with his contemporary, the Kassite Burnaburiash II (1375–1347 B.C.). Details of the good relations between the pharaoh and the king of 'Kar-Duni-ash' can be read in the el-Amarna correspondence. The two monarchs, the two 'brothers' as they call each other, exchange presents, the Kassite offering horses, lapis-lazuli and other precious stones, the Egyptian, ivory, ebony and above all gold. Occasionally the quantity of gold received did not quite tally with the quantity announced, and the King of Babylon complained bitterly:

'The former gold which my brother sent – because my brother did not look to it himself, but an officer of my brother sealed and sent it – the forty minas of gold which they brought, when I put them in the furnace did not come out full weight.'[12]

But these were only passing clouds. In spite of the distance – 'the road is very long, the water supply cut off and the weather hot'[13] – messengers went to and fro between the two countries at the risk of being attacked by Canaanite bandits or by bedouins. We also learn that Amenophis IV married one of Burnaburiash's daughters and that on this occasion the pharaoh sent to Babylon an enormous number of bridal gifts, the list of which makes up more than 307 lines of text in four columns![14]

If the Egyptians closed their ears to the appeals of their Syrian vassals, why, it may be asked, did the Mitannians remain passive in front of the Hittite aggression and did not even attempt to recover their former dominion? The answer is that they were themselves in the throes of civil war. Tushratta owed his crown to the murder of his elder brother, and his authority was challenged by several members of the royal family. As he ascended the throne of Mitanni, another of his brothers, Artatama, declared himself 'King of Hurri' and founded a separate dynasty, though it is by no means certain that the kingdom was divided between the two rivals as some historians believe. The Kings of Hurri – Artatama and his son Shutarna II – sought assistance outside their own country and engaged in friendly relations with the Assyrian princes still under Mitannian obedience. Soon there was a strong pro-Hurrian and pro-Assyrian party in Washukkanni itself. Palace intrigues, no doubt fomented by the two allies, culminated, in about 1350 B.C., in the death of Tushratta, murdered by one of his sons. Unable to preserve his throne, the legitimate heir, Mattiwaza, fled to Babylon, where Burnaburiash, faithful to his neutral policy, refused to grant him asylum, and finally took refuge at the Hittite court, while Assyria and another small state of the Upper Tigris valley, Alshe, 'divided the land of Mitanni between themselves'.[15] Thus without shooting an arrow Ashur-uballiṭ I of Assyria (1365–1330 B.C.) not only freed his country from Mitannian domination but brought about the downfall of the kingdom to which his fathers had paid tribute. Encouraged by this success, he took the titles 'Great King' and 'King of the Universe', corresponded directly with his 'brother' Amenophis IV,[16] and gave his daughter in marriage to Burnaburiash in the hope that his grandson would one day reign over Babylonia.

All this happened shortly after Suppiluliumas departed from Syria. When he returned, twenty years later, the political situation in the Near East had changed to his advantage. In Egypt Amenophis IV had died in 1362 B.C. and his successors – including the famous Tut-ankh-Amôn – were too busy repairing the disastrous results of his religious policy to pay much attention to Syrian affairs. In northern Mesopotamia the Mitannian kingdom had disintegrated, and Ashur-uballiṭ was building up his Assyrian forces. In Babylonia, after a short civil war provoked by the murder of Ashur-uballiṭ's grandson,[17] Kurigalzu II had ascended the throne in 1345 B.C.; but the eyes of this great builder and warrior were turned not towards the west but towards the east: he attacked and defeated Hurpatila, King of Elam, and governed that country for at least part of his reign.[18] The main objective of Suppiluliumas was therefore to liquidate any remaining pocket of resistance and to organize the territories conquered. He signed treaties with obedient Syrian princes, gave Aleppo to one of his sons and Karkemish to another, with the mission of helping Mattiwaza to recover his throne.[19] In the ensuing war Mattiwaza was successful for a while but finally defeated, and the Assyrians advanced as far as the Euphrates, erasing all traces of the Mitannian kingdom. When Suppiluliumas died (1336 B.C.) the whole of Syria up to the region of Damascus was firmly in Hittite hands, but Assyria was the second great power in the Near East.

Assur and Susa versus Babylon

For the Hittites, to whom the Achaeans and other warlike people established along the coasts of Asia Minor denied access to the Mediterranean, the possession of active and prosperous ports, such as Ugarit and Sumur,[20] was undoubtedly an asset. Moreover, Syria itself was fertile and could also be used as a starting point for future military operations in Mesopotamia or in Egypt. But these advantages were to a great extent upset by the duplicity and unruly behaviour of the local chieftains: rebellions soon followed Suppiluliumas's death, obliging his son and successor, Mursilis II (1335–1310 B.C.), to intervene in person, and it might have been of some comfort for him to know that at the same time the King of Egypt, Seti I, had to bear a similar burden in his Palestinian dominion. Probably fomented by the Hittites in Palestine and by the Egyptians in Syria, these revolts were but the symptoms of a deeper conflict between the two great nations, a conflict which reached its acme when the young and ambitious Ramesses II (1304–1237 B.C.) decided to repeat Tuthmosis's exploits and to bring the frontier of his kingdom up to the Euphrates. The war he waged against the Hittite Muwatallis ended in one of the most famous battles of antiquity, Qadesh (1300 B.C.), but no decisive result was obtained.[21] Both enemies claimed victory and retained their respective positions. Sixteen years later, however, Ramesses signed with Hattusilis III of Hatti a peace treaty of which we possess by chance the Egyptian as well as the Hittite version[22] – the latter, incidentally, in Akkadian language – and even married a Hittite princess. Were the two champions tired of fighting, or did the growing strength of Assyria reconcile them as the Hittite menace had once reconciled Egyptians and Mitannians? The importance given in the treaty to clauses of mutual assistance in case of war, together with the overtures made at the same time by Hattusilis to the Kassites, seem to give weight to the second theory.

Ever since Assyria had become a nation her fortune had been written on the map. To the north and east the narrow strip of Tigris valley belonging to the god Ashur was surrounded by high, almost inaccessible mountains haunted by predatory peoples, such as the Guti and Lullubi, which could only be kept at bay by frequent and difficult police operations. To the west the steppe of Jazirah stretched for hundreds of miles, wide open to hostile armies or to nomadic raiders; the possession of that steppe spelled safety for the Assyrians, but it also meant the control of important trade-routes and, eventually, of northern Syria, with a window on the Mediterranean. Finally, to the south and within a short distance lay the rich plain and opulent cities of the Mesopotamian delta, a constant source of temptation but also of worry, since Akkadians, Sumerians and Babylonians had always claimed lordship over the northern half of Mesopotamia. During the second millennium the frontier in this area was heavily fortified, and when Babylon was strong all the Assyrians could expect to gain was a few villages; when it was weak, however, all hopes were permissible, including that of access to the Gulf. These geographical considerations account for the triple series of wars which fill Assyrian annals from the thirteenth century onwards: guerrilla wars in the mountains, wars of movement in Jazirah and wars of position on the middle Tigris. These were the price Assyria had to pay not only for her expansion but also for her freedom.

As soon as Ashur-uballiṭ had delivered his country from Mitannian domination hostilities opened on these three fronts. His son, Enlil-nirâri, was attacked by Kurigalzu but they soon made peace and, we are told, 'they divided the fields, they divided the district, they fixed (anew) the boundaries'.[23] The fragmentary annals of Arik-dên-ilu speak of campaigns in the Zagros, while we learn from those of his successor, Adad-narâri I, that he threw his armies across Jazirah and conquered – at least momentarily – that region 'as far as Karkemish which is on the bank of the Euphrates';[24] another text shows him forcing the Kassites into a new frontier agreement.[25] But the greatest warrior of the dynasty was undoubtedly Shalmaneser I (1274–1245 B.C.), who, having subdued 'the mighty mountain fastnesses' of Uruadri (Urarṭu, Armenia) and 'the land of the Guti who know how to plunder', turned against Assyria's former allies, the Hurrians, attacked Shattuara, 'King of Hanigalbat' and his Hittite and Ahlamû mercenaries and defeated them:

'I fought a battle and accomplished their defeat. I killed countless numbers of his defeated and widespreading hosts ... Nine of his strongholds and his capital city I captured. One hundred and eighty of his cities I turned into tells and ruins ... Their lands I brought under my sway, and the rest of their cities I burned with fire.'[26]

It was perhaps this exploit, performed a few years after the battle of Qadesh, that brought together Egyptians and Hittites, for the Hurrians had now lost their last stronghold, and the Assyrians in Karkemish were at the gates of Syria.

In the middle of the thirteenth century the critical situation of Babylon, already threatened by its powerful neighbour, was aggravated by the sudden reappearance of Elam on the political stage after an absence of about four hundred years. The new dynasty which occupied the throne in Susa was made of energetic princes determined, among other things, to assure their authority over the Kassites of Iraq as well as over those who had remained in Iran. Shortly after 1250 B.C. the unfortunate Kashtiliash IV found himself caught between two enemies: Untash-napirisha – the Elamite ruler who built the magnificent ziqqurat and temples of Chogha-Zambil, near Susa – and the Assyrian Tukulti-Ninurta I (1244–1208 B.C.).[27] The Elamite won a battle, but Tukulti-Ninurta occupied the capital-city. This exploit filled the Assyrians with considerable pride and forms the subject of the only Assyrian epic tale that has come to us: a poetic and, naturally, strongly biased, narrative known as the 'Tukulti-Ninurta Epic'.[28] In this the blame is put entirely on Kashtiliash, who is accused of having broken his oath and plotted against Assyria, thus deserving to be abandoned by the gods of his country and defeated. Yet the shorter account of the war in a building inscription found in Assur gives the impression that Tukulti-Ninurta acted without being provoked:

'I forced Kashtiliash, King of Kar-Duniash, to give battle; I brought about the defeat of his armies, his warriors I overthrew. In the midst of that battle my hand captured Kashtiliash, the Kassite king. His royal neck I trod on with my feet, like a *galtappu* (stool). Stripped and bound, before Ashur my lord I brought him. Sumer and Akkad to its farthest border I brought under my sway. On the lower sea of the rising sun I established the frontier of my land.'[29]

Three princes, puppets of the Assyrian, sat in quick succession on the throne of Babylon and were in turn attacked by the Elamites, who advanced as far as Nippur. But after seven years of servitude the Babylonians themselves restored their national dynasty. Says a Babylonian chronicle:

The nobles of Akkad and Kar-Duniash revolted, and they sat Adad-shum-uṣur on the throne of his father.[30]

As for the Assyrian monarch who had been the first to reach the Persian Gulf, he died ignominiously several years later, no doubt in punishment for his crimes:

As for Tukulti-Ninurta who had brought evil upon Babylon, Ashur-nadin-apli, his son, and the nobles of Assyria revolted, and they cast him from his throne. In Kâr-Ninurta they besieged him in his palace and slew him with the sword.[31]

Weakened by family dissensions and internecine warfare, his successors launched only small-scale offensives against Babylonia, and it was the Elamites and not the Assyrians who, in 1160 B.C., delivered the mighty blow which brought the Kassite dynasty to its knees. That year Shutruk-nahhunte left Susa at the head of a vast army, invaded southern Iraq and plundered it as it had never before been plundered. Famous monuments, masterpieces of Mesopotamian sculpture such as the stele of Narâm-Sin, the Code of Hammurabi and the Obelisk of Manish-tusu were carried away to Susa for ever. Shutruk-nahhunte's elder son, Kutir-nahhunte, was appointed governor of Babylonia. A Kassite prince with the good Babylonian name of Enlil-nadin-ahhê ('Enlil gives brothers') managed to stay on the throne for three years but was finally defeated and captured by Kutir-nahhunte after a fierce struggle (1157 B.C.). Babylon was occupied. Supreme humiliation: the god Marduk was taken in captivity by the Elamites as he had been taken by the Hittites 438 years before. Thus ended the longest dynasty in the history of Babylon.[32]

The fall of the Kassite dynasty may be used as a convenient landmark in the history of ancient Iraq, but it was almost insignificant compared with the events which took place in the Near East during the twelfth century B.C. When the Elamites invaded Babylonia the Hittite kingdom of Boghazköy had already disappeared; Egypt, which had just escaped another invasion from the east, was greatly weakened by internal divisions; the Philistines were established in Canaan, Moses was leading his people into the Promised Land, the nomadic Aramaeans were threatening both the Syrian princes and the Assyrian monarchs, and far away in the west the Dorian Greeks were invading the Hellenic peninsula. Once again the Indo-Europeans had moved into Western Asia, spreading the use of iron as their forebears had spread the use of the horse, and opening a new age in the history of humanity, but also starting a chain reaction of ethnic movements accompanied by political convulsions which rapidly changed the face of the Orient.

CHAPTER 17

THE TIME OF CONFUSION

The mass-movements of Indo-European population which took place in south-eastern Europe during the thirteenth century B.C. escapes analysis and can only be deduced from the profound repercussions they had upon Greece and Western Asia. It was probably the arrival in the Balkans of prolific and pugnacious tribes, the Illyrians, which thrust out the Thraco-Phrygians into Anatolia, where they overthrew the Hittite kingdom shortly after 1200 B.C., and drove the Dorians, Aeolians and Ionians into the Hellenic peninsula, the Aegean islands and the western districts of Asia Minor, where they destroyed the Mycenaean (or Achaean) empire (Trojan war, c. 1200 B.C.). Dislodged by this double current of invaders, the inhabitants of the Aegean shores and isles, the 'Peoples of the Sea' as the Egyptians called them,[1] fled southward along the coasts of Asia Minor and Syria and arrived, threatening, at the gate of Egypt. Ramesses III defeated them both at sea and on land (1174 B.C.), but some of the warriors went into the Pharaoh's service, while others settled on the maritime fringe of Canaan. Among the latter were the *Peleset*, or Philistines, who eventually gave to the whole country its name, Palestine. At about the same time another less known but equally important ethnic movement started somewhere around the Caspian Sea. The Indo-European-speaking peoples which we call 'Iranians' entered Iran from the north, following approximately the same route as the earlier Indo-Aryan emigrants. The *Parthava* (Parthians) and the *Haraiva* remained on the borders of Turkestan and Afghanistan, while the *Madai* (Medes), *Parsua* (Persians) and *Zikirtu* marched farther west and occupied the plateau from Lake Urmiah to Isfahan, rapidly gaining control over the poorly equipped indigenous population.[2]

Above: Alabaster head of a woman (or a goddess) found at Uruk. Proto-historic Uruk period (*c.* 3500 B.C.)

Below: Archaic inscription on a clay tablet from proto-historic Uruk (*c.* 3300 B.C.)

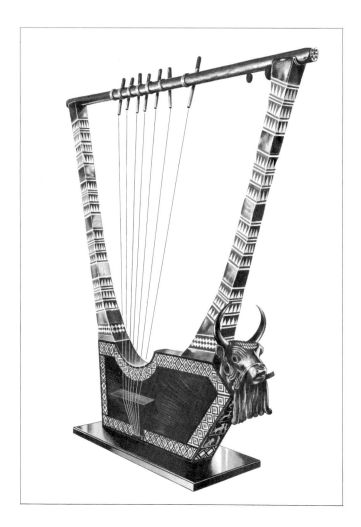

From the Royal Cemetery of Ur. A harp found in the 'Great Death Pit' and partly restored. Beneath the bearded bull's head, made of solid gold, is a set of shell plaques engraved with scenes of animal life

Above: Head-dress and necklaces of a woman found in a collective tomb of the Royal Cemetery at Ur (*c.* 2600 B.C.). The ornaments are made of gold, lapis-lazuli and cornelian

Below: From an anonymous grave of the Royal Cemetery of Ur. A gold dagger with a hilt of lapis-lazuli, in its gold sheath

Left: Fragment of the Stele of the Vultures, representing the army of Eannatum, *ensi* of Lagash (Telloh)

Right: This beautifully worked bronze head, three-quarters life-size, was found at Nineveh and is presumed to be a portrait of King Sargon of Akkad (*c.* 2334–2279 B.C.) or, more probably, his grandson Marâm-Sìn (*c.* 2254–2218)

One of the many statues of Gudea, *ensi* of Lagash, who lived *c.* 2141–2122 B.C., just before the first kings of the Third Dynasty of Ur. Only sixteen inches high and made of diorite

Stele of pink sandstone commemorating the victory of the
Akkadian king Narâm-Sîn over the Lullubi (a people of
the Zagros mountains) (c. 2230 B.C.)

The central stairs of the ziqqurat of Ur: looking as they probably did when the priests were treading the steps on the way up to the upper temple

The statue of Ebih-Il, an official from Mari, is one of
the finest pieces of Early Dynastic sculpture. The name
is Semitic, but the attitude and costume, as well as the
sculptor's technique, are typically Sumerian

A votive dog dedicated to the goddess Nin-Sin by a high official of Lagash, 'for the life of Sumu-El', King of Larsa (1894–1866 B.C.)

Believed to be the work of a Hurrian artist: the head of an unknown god found at Jabbul, near Aleppo

Above: Upper part of the stele bearing the text of Hammurabi's 'Law Code'. Hammurabi, king of Babylon (1792–1750 B.C.) stands in front of the Sun-god Shamash, supreme chief justice, with his hand over his mouth as a sign of prayer

Below: Façade of the temple of the Kassite king Karaindash (*c.* 1420 B.C.) in Uruk, showing the new technique of bricks with moulded motifs

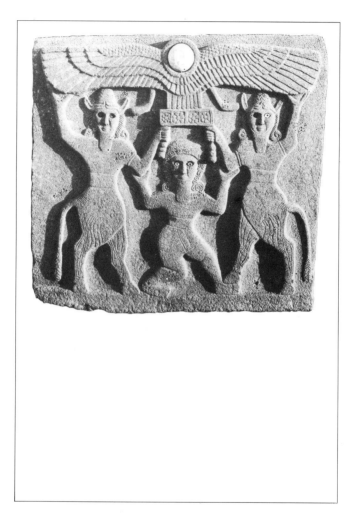

One of the reliefs decorating the walls of the palace of Kapara, the
Aramaean ruler of Guzana-Tell Halaf

A colossal Assyrian statue emerges from the earth at Nimrud

Specimen of Assyrian writing on stone (Nimrud)

Stele of Esarhaddon, King of Assyria (680–699
B.C.), found at Zenjirli, in the Amanus mountains.
Taharqa, King of Egypt (kneeling) and Abdi-
Milkuti, King of Sidon (standing) supplicate Esar-
haddon, who is holding them captive

The Assyrian army at war. In a mountainous and wooded country, foot-soldiers and cavalrymen fighting with bows, lances and slings, are progressing. A mounted officer shouts orders. Relief from Nineveh. Reign of Ashurbanipal (668–627 B.C.)

This cascade of migrations, involving as they did the Mediterranean and the central parts of Anatolia and Iran, left Iraq unaffected. But it coincided with a period of increased activity among the nomadic Semites who roamed the Syrian desert: Sutû, Ahlamû and, above all, the vast confederation of Aramaean tribes. The vacuum created in Syria by the collapse of the Hittite empire and the relative weakness of Assyria and Babylonia encouraged the Aramaeans to invade the Syrian hinterland, to cross the Euphrates and to penetrate deeper and deeper into Mesopotamia, settling as they advanced and forming, throughout the Fertile Crescent, a network of kingdoms, large or small, which enclosed Assur and Babylon in an ever-narrowing circle and nearly submerged them. Simultaneously, other Semites, the Israelites, coming from the Sinai desert and taking advantage of the confusion which reigned in Canaan after Egypt had withdrawn from Asia, conquered a large band of territory on either side of the Jordan and made it their homeland. Up to a point the progress of the Aramaeans in Iraq can be followed through the Assyrian royal inscriptions, and the conquest of Canaan by the Israelites, through the biblical narrative; but the rest of the Near East is plunged in profound darkness between 1200 and 1000 B.C. The Hittite archives from Boghazköy come abruptly to an end in about 1190 B.C., and there is just enough information from Egypt for us to perceive the decadence of that great country under the last Ramessides and its separation into two rival kingdoms at the dawn of the eleventh century. When the light again comes in about 900 B.C., the political geography of Western Asia has profoundly changed: Aramaean principalities flourish from the Lebanon to the Zagros; the remnants of the 'Peoples of the Sea', Philistines and Zakkalas, share Canaan with the Israelites; along the Lebanese coast the 'Phoenicians' enter a period of great prosperity, while the extreme north of Syria and the Taurus massif are the seats of several 'Neo-Hittite' kingdoms; Egypt is divided and weak; the kings who ascend the throne of Babylon in quick succession have little real power but in Assyria a line of energetic princes is busy loosening the Aramaean grip and rebuilding an Empire; and behind the Zagros the Medes and Persians are firmly established though not yet ready to play their historical role. These are the peoples which the Assyrians are going to meet, fight and conquer in their great movement of expansion during the first millennium B.C., and with which the reader should now become acquainted.

Israelites and Phoenicians

So familiar are we with the Bible that for most of us no more than a brief outline of early Hebraic history is needed here. We have already seen (p. 239) that Abraham and his family came from Ur in Sumer to Hebron in Canaan, probably about 1850 B.C., and there are good reasons for placing Joseph's migration to Egypt during the Hyksôs period (1700–1580 B.C.). For at least four centuries those who now called themselves 'Israelites' lived, multiplied and prospered in the Nile delta, until they were driven out by a Pharaoh 'whose heart the Lord had hardened' – more probably Ramesses II (1304–1237 B.C.) than his successor Mernephtah.[3] A man of supreme intelligence and powerful personality, the first great religious reformer in the history of humanity, Moses united the Israelites around the cult of a unique and universal God, led their long march across the Sinai peninsula and died when they reached the threshold of the 'Promised Land'. Joshua was their next leader, but the conquest of Canaan was in fact achieved by each of the twelve tribes fighting for its own territory under elected chiefs or 'Judges' and must have taken at least a hundred years. The formation of an Israelite kingdom under Saul and the victories won by David (1010–970 B.C.) over the Philistines, the Canaanites and the states lying east of the Jordan (Amon, Edom and Moab) consecrated the supremacy in Palestine of Abraham's progeny. Allowances being made for Oriental emphasis, the reign of Solomon was a period of considerable glory for the young nation.[4] For the first time in history Palestine obeyed one ruler whose authority extended 'from Dan (at the foot of mount Hermon) to Beersheba (on the border of Negeb)'. Jerusalem, formerly a small, unimportant town, took the rank of capital-city, and nearly 200,000 workmen – so we are told – took part in the building of its temple. The Israelite army was armed with weapons of iron and well provided with horses and chari-ots. From Ezion-Geber, near Akaba, Solomon's ships sailed down the Red Sea and returned from Arabia and Ethiopia loaded with gold. The King himself, though credited with proverbial wisdom, lived in a sumptuous palace among 'seven hundred wives and three hundred concubines'. Such extrava-gance was more than this small and austere nation could stand financially and morally. The glorious reign ended in revolts, and after Solomon's death (931 B.C.) the kingdom was divided by plebiscite into two parts: Israel in the north, with Samaria for capital city, Judah in the south, still commanded from Jerusalem. The period of united monarchy had lasted a bare century.

To the north-west of Israel the Canaanites of Lebanon and of the Syrian coast – the 'Phoenicians' as the Greeks were later to call them – were among the first victims of the great turmoil of the twelfth century. The richest of their cities, Ugarit, was for ever destroyed by the Peoples of the Sea,[5] while the great emporium of timber, Byblos, already ravaged by local wars during the el-Amarna period, was ruined by the decadence of its traditional client Egypt under the successors of Ramesses III. But by 1000 B.C. the situation in that area had taken a turn for the better. Because of their position at the points where the roads crossing the Lebanon mountains reach the sea, Arvad (Ruâd island), Sidunu (Sidon, modern Saida) and Sûri (Tyre, modern Sûr) had become the ports of the powerful Aramaean kingdoms of central Syria, and the southernmost of these towns, Tyre, benefited from the proximity of the Israelites, whom it supplied with timber, expert craftsmen and sailors.[6] The three cities soon grew rich on this trade and formed the new political and economic centres of Phoenicia.

The Syro-Lebanese coast has always been the meeting-point of Europe and Asia. At the dawn of the first millennium B.C. two thousand years of intimate contact with the Cretans, Mycenaeans and Cypriots, on the one hand, and with all the nations of the Near East, on the other, had resulted in the development of a composite but brilliant Phoenician civilization.[7] The main contribution of the Phoenicians to the cultural treasure of humanity was undoubtedly the invention of the alphabet, which was taken, in modified forms, by the Greeks throughout Europe and the Aramaeans throughout Western Asia, where it eventually superseded all previous syllabic and ideographic writing systems. The exact date and place of invention are thorny problems which need not be touched upon here, however briefly,[8] but we should at least mention that of the three alphabets simultaneously in use on the Mediterranean coast during the last quarter of the second millennium – the 'classical' and the 'pseudo-hieroglyphic' alphabets of Byblos and the 'cuneiform' alphabet of Ras-Shamra (Ugarit) – the last named served as a support for a copious and extremely interesting literature, the discovery of which has considerably enlarged and modified our ideas on ancient Canaanite religion and mythology.[9] In the domain of the arts the Phoenicians were perhaps not so creatively minded, but proved excellent pupils. Inspired by Aegean and Egyptian artists, their craftsmen were unrivalled in the Near East, at least during the first millennium B.C. They wove beautiful clothes, which they embroidered or dyed with the famous Sidonian purple, made vials of translucent glass, chiselled delicate jewels, carved exquisite ivories and were masters in wood- and metal-work. Their own country produced, besides timber, well-reputed wine and oil. All this formed a light, yet valuable cargo which the Phoenicians, sailors at heart, could now carry around the world themselves, the Dorian invasion of Greece having liberated the sea from its former masters, the Mycenaeans. Soon Tyrians, Sidonians and Arvadites became the leaders of an astonishing movement of maritime and colonial expansion which reached its peak between

the ninth and the sixth centuries B.C. with the foundation of
Carthage (814 B.C.), the creation of numerous warehouses in
Malta, Sicily and Spain, and the exploration of the Atlantic
coasts of Europe and Africa.

The Neo-Hittites

Proceeding northward along the Mediterranean shore we reach
in the extreme north of Syria the realm of the people called
'Hieroglyphic Hittites' or, more simply, 'Neo-Hittites'.[10] These
terms require some explanation. We know that the Hittites who
had Hattusas (Boghazköy) for capital-city used a cuneiform
script borrowed from Mesopotamia to write on clay tablets
their Indo-European language. But at the same time another
kind of script was used in Asia Minor to write on rock or stone
official or religious inscriptions. This script consisted of drawings
or hieroglyphs bearing no relation to the archaic Sumerian
pictograms nor to the Egyptian or Cretan hieroglyphs. Many
such inscriptions also appear in various sites of the Taurus
mountains and of northern Syria in association with monuments which can be dated from the first centuries of the first
millennium B.C., i.e. after the fall of the Hittite empire. The
decipherment of hieroglyphic Hittite by various scholars – confirmed and completed by the discovery in 1947 of bilingual
Phoenician-Hittite inscriptions at Kara Tepe, in Cilicia[11] – has
shown that the language of these inscriptions was a dialectal
variety of Luwian, the Luwians being one of the more or less
closely related Indo-European-speaking peoples which entered
Asia Minor at the beginning of the second millennium. It looks,
therefore, as though in the great reshuffling of population which
took place in the twelfth century the Luwians, who originally
occupied the south-western part of Asia Minor, had moved, or
been pushed, southward and eastward and had established
themselves in the southern provinces of the former Hittite
empire, provinces which had been spared by the Phrygians and
by-passed

highly conjectural. Moreover, it should be emphasized that there was no break in the transmission of Hittite culture in those regions, and that the term 'Neo-Hittite' is no more than a convenient appellation. The Hittite influence brought into Syria by Suppiluliumas and his predecessors outlived them by nearly five hundred years.

From the tenth century onwards a compact mosaic of Neo-Hittite kingdoms covered the territory comprised between the Taurus range and the Orontes river, forming what the Assyrians called *Hatti* or *Great Hatti* – (the province of Antioch is still called 'Hatay' by the Turks). Starting from the north, we find in the heart of the Taurus mountains about twelve city-states forming the confederation of Tabal (the *Tubal* of the Bible) and along the Upper Euphrates, the kingdom of Kummanu with Milid (modern Malatiya) for capital-city. Then come Kummuhu, the classical Commagene, and Gurgum around the town of Marqasi (Marash). Farther west the rich plain of Cilicia is occupied by the Danuna-folk, who obey the King of Ataniya (Adana) and hold sway over the surrounding highlanders. To the north of Aleppo lie Ya'diya (capital Sam'al, modern Zencirli) in the Amanus moutains, and Karkemish and Til-Barsip (Tell Ahmar), which command the passage of the Euphrates. Aleppo itself, so often taken and lost by the Mitannians and the Hittites, had lost much of its importance to Arpad, while Alalah, in the 'Amuq plain (*Hattina*), was governed first from 'Azaz, then from the as yet unidentified city of Kunalua. Finally, hieroglyphic inscriptions found at Hama testify to periodical occupation of the city by the Neo-Hittites.

Excavations at Zencirli, Sakçe-Gözü, Karkemish, Tell Tayanat and, more recently, Kara Tepe (ancient Azitawandas) have shed considerable light on the art and architecture of the Neo-Hittites and enable us to understand the resistance encountered by the Assyrians when they tried to overthrow these small but very strong kingdoms. The towns, roughly circular in plan, were protected by a double, massive wall: an outer wall around the lower town and an inner wall around the acropolis. The royal palace, in the centre of the city, often had its entrance preceded by a portico of wooden columns resting on stone bases sculptured with crouching lions and sphinxes. Its plan was usually of the type called by the Assyrians *bît hilâni*: a series of oblong rooms, one behind the other, the long sides of which ran parallel with the front of the building. The avenue leading to the acropolis as well as the façade of the palace were decorated with sculptured slabs of basalt or limestone lining the lower part of the walls. The subjects most commonly represented on these 'orthostats' are hunting scenes, royal banquets and marching soldiers, frequently intermingled with hieroglyphic inscriptions. The sculptures are too often crude and unskilled, though not devoid of movement and life, and some indeed attain a high standard of barbaric beauty. Most archaeologists agree that we meet here with a provincial version of Hittite art tempered with Assyrian, Egyptian and even Aegean influences.

The Neo-Hittite kingdoms flourished from the tenth to the eighth centuries B.C., and their full history will be revealed when all the hieroglyphic Hittite inscriptions are accurately translated and published. Between 745 and 708 B.C. they fell one by one into Assyrian hands[12] and disappeared as independent states, but long before that date some of them had already yielded to their immediate neighbours, the Aramaeans.

The Aramaeans

As usual in such matters, the problem of Aramaean origin is a very difficult one.[13] The Aramaean language, or Aramaic, belongs, like Canaanite and Hebrew, to the north-western group of Semitic dialects, but on many points shows strong affinities with Arabic, which might perhaps suggest that the Aramaeans originated or had lived in Arabia. On the other hand, there are several reasons to believe that their homeland was the Syrian desert and the Fertile Crescent, and it must be recalled that the memory of a close, though unspecified, ethnic relationship between Aramaeans and Hebrews has been preserved in the

Bible, where Jacob (Israel) himself is once qualified as a 'wandering Aramaean'.[14] At what period the Aramaeans made their first appearance in cuneiform inscriptions is another debatable point. In texts of the Akkadian, Ur III and Old Babylonian periods occasional mention is made of a city *Arami* and of individuals by the name of *Aramu*, but since this may be no more than a phonetic resemblance, two dates only must be considered: the fourteenth or the twelfth century, depending upon the acceptance of some kind of relationship between the Aramaeans and the Ahlamû. The Ahlamû are first mentioned in a mutilated letter from el-Amarna alluding to the King of Babylon; during the same period their presence is attested in Assyria, at Nippur and even at Dilmun (Bahrain), and we have seen (p. 263) that Shalmaneser I defeated the Hurrians and their Hittite and Ahlamû allies in Jazirah. In the following century they cut the road from Babylon to Hattusas, and Tukulti-Ninurta I (1244–1208 B.C.) claims that he conquered Mari, Hana and Rapiqum on the Euphrates and 'the mountains of the Ahlamû'.[15] We are thus confronted with a confederation of troublesome tribes active in the Syrian desert, along the Euphrates and about the Persian Gulf, at least from the fourteenth century B.C. But an inscription of Tiglathpileser I (1115–1077 B.C.) refers for the first time to the 'Ahlamû-Aramaeans' (*Ahlamê Armaia*),[16] and from then on the Ahlamû rapidly disappear from Assyrian annals to be replaced by the Aramaeans (*Aramû, Arimi*). In the text just quoted the word *Armaia* is 'gentilic' (adjective), and the expression could be translated '(Those of) the Ahlamû (who are) Aramaean', in which case we might be entitled to consider the Aramaeans as an important and in time dominant faction of the Ahlamû tribes. It is possible, however, that the two peoples had nothing in common, but operated in the same area and were regarded by the sedentary Mesopotamians as one and the same detestable desert folk.

In any case, there can be no doubt that the Aramaeans were established in Syria as early as the eleventh century B.C. We read in the Bible that Saul, David and Solomon fought against

the Aramaean kingdoms which lay across the northern frontier
of Israel: Aram-Sôbah in the Beq'a, Aram-Bêt-Rehob and
Aram-Ma'akah around Mount Hermon, Geshur in the Hauran,
and the state which was soon to govern them all: Damascus
(*Dimashqa, Dammesheq*). Farther north the Aramaeans were in
possession of Hama on the Orontes and were soon to become
strong enough to dissociate the Neo-Hittite block. During the
tenth or the ninth century they conquered Sam'al (Zencirli),
the region of Aleppo which they renamed Bît-Agushi, and Til-
Barsip, which became the chief town of Bît-Adini. Only the
plain of Antioch (Pattina) and Karkemish remained Hittite in
Syrian land. At the same time the Aramaeans invaded the
steppe to the east of the Euphrates, where they settled in such
numbers that the whole region became known as *Aram Naharaim*,
'Aram of the Rivers'. One of their earliest kingdoms in Mesopotamia was Bît-Bahiâni, which had for capital-city the very
ancient site of Tell Halaf abandoned since proto-historic times
(see above, p. 55) and now called Guzana. The Aramaean
progression in Mesopotamia will be described later. For the
present we would simply like to draw attention to the names of
the Aramaean kingdoms, usually formed with the word *bît*(*u*),
'house', followed by the name of an ancestor. Despite the
apparent similarity with our 'House of Hanover', 'House of
Windsor' and so forth, we have here a typically tribal way of
expressing land ownership: the state, the 'kingdom' is both the
territory around the tent (or house) of the chief and all the
chief's relatives forming the clan.

Whether merchants, peasants, shepherds, soldiers or bandits,
the Aramaeans were originally uncouth bedouins and contributed nothing to the civilizations of the Near East. Whatever
their ancestral religion, it appears from their inscriptions as well
as from their own names that they worshipped Sumero-
Akkadian and Canaanite gods, such as Hadad (Adad), the
storm-god, El, the supreme deity of Canaan, Sin, Ishtar (whom
they called 'Attar), the Phoenician goddess 'Anat ('Atta) and
others. Nor was there originality in the field of the arts, the

Aramaeans following the traditions of the countries where they settled. The King of Damascus, for instance, employed Phoenician sculptors and ivory-carvers, and Sam'al under its new masters retained all the features of a Neo-Hittite city. Archaeological excavations at Tell Halaf-Guzana have brought to light the palace of Kapara, an Aramaean ruler who probably lived at the beginning of the ninth century B.C.[17] It was a building of the *bît hilani* type, decorated with orthostats perhaps cruder than the contemporary sculptures of northern Syria, and with strange-looking, almost morbid statues which, on analysis, display a mixture of Mesopotamian, Hittite and Hurrian influences, as would be expected in a region – the Khabur valley – where the three cultures converged.

Yet to these barbaric Aramaeans befell the privilege of imposing their language upon the entire Near East. They owed it partly to the sheer weight of their number and partly to the fact that they adopted, instead of the cumbersome cuneiform writing, the Phoenician alphabet slightly modified, and carried everywhere with them the simple, practical script of the future. As early as the eighth century B.C. Aramaic language and writing competed with the Akkadian language and script in Assyria, and thereafter gradually spread throughout the Orient.[18] About 500 B.C., when the Achaemenian monarchs looked for a tongue which could be understood by all their subjects, they chose Aramaic, which became the *lingua franca* of their vast empire. At the close of the pre-Christian era Sumerian and even Hebrew were already dead languages, Akkadian was dying and Greek, introduced by the Macedonian conquerors, was mostly used for official purposes, but Aramaic – the language spoken by Jesus – reigned unchallenged as the common dialect of all the peoples of the Near East and was to remain so until the Arab invasion (seventh century A.D.). The Arabic script itself derives from a cursive form of Aramaic, as do all present and past alphabets used in Asia. Moreover, during the sixth century A.D. the Aramaic language gave birth in northern Mesopotamia to the extremely rich Syriac literature which the

Nestorian missionaries carried as far as Mongolia, and Syriac has survived as the liturgic tongue of several Oriental Churches. Indeed, Aramaic dialects are still spoken in some parts of the Near East, in particular among the Christian communities of northern Iraq. Few languages in the world can claim such a long and continuous tradition.

But it is time for us to return to our subject, Iraq, which we have left at the end of the Kassite dynasty, nearly twelve hundred years before Christ.

The Dark Age of Mesopotamia

After their victory over the Kassites the Elamites did not occupy Babylonia for long, either because the conquest of vast territories in western Iran absorbed all their energy or because they already felt the presence of the newly arrived Medes and Persians as a dagger in their back. However this may be, the Elamite garrisons withdrew or were expelled, and princes native of Isin founded the Fourth Dynasty of Babylon, also called 'Second Dynasty of Isin'.[19] Soon the new kings were powerful enough to interfere in Assyrian domestic affairs, and when Elam sank into anarchy after the brilliant reign of Shilak-Inshushinak, the Babylonian Nebuchadrezzar I * (c. 1124–1103 B.C.) attacked that country. A first campaign met with failure – 'the Elamite followed and I fled before him; I sat down on the bed of weeping and sighing'[20] – but the defection of one of the Elamite lords, Shitti-Marduk, who fought on the Babylonian side, made the second campaign a glowing success. The account of the war, written on a *kudurru* granting privileges to Shitti-Marduk as a reward for his assistance, is one of the most poetic military records of antiquity.[21]

From Dêr, the holy city of Anu, he (the King of Babylon) made a leap of thirty double-leagues. In the month of Tammuz (July–August) he

---

* *Nabû-kudurri-uṣur*: 'O Nabû, protect my offspring'.

took the road. The blades of the picks burn like fire; the stones of the track blaze like furnaces; there is no water (in the wadis) and the wells are dry; stop the strongest of the horses and stagger the young heroes. Yet he goes, the elected king supported by the gods; he marches on, Nebuchadrezzar who has no rival . . .

The battle was fought on the banks of the River Ulaia (Karun):

At the command of Ishtar and Adad, the gods of the battle, Hulteludish, King of Elam, fled and disappeared for ever, and King Nebuchadrezzar stood up in victory: he took Elam and plundered its treasures.

Among the booty was the statue of Marduk, taken to Elam at the end of the Kassite dynasty. This gave Nebuchadrezzar an aura of glory, and perhaps enabled Marduk to reach the top of the Mesopotamian pantheon,[22] but his victory had no lasting political results. Elam was not truly conquered, and Nebuchadrezzar's successors had to fight not for the possession of foreign lands but for the protection of their own kingdom against the eternal rival: Assyria.

Despite a serious crisis of succession and the temporary loss of their eastern provinces to Shilak-Inshushinak, the eleventh century as a whole was for the Assyrians an epoch of prosperity. Ashur-dân I, 'who attained to grey hair and a ripe old age',[23] and Ashur-rêsh-ishi, both contemporaries of the first kings of the Fourth Dynasty of Babylon, received tribute from the Sutû, kept the Ahlamû at bay, won a few battles over the Babylonians and did a considerable amount of repair work on the palace and temples of their capital-city. But at the end of the century storms gathered at the four points of the compass, which could have destroyed Assyria had it not been for the restless energy of one of the two or three great Assyrian monarchs since the days of Shamshi-Adad: Tiglathpileser I (1115–1077 B.C.).* To the north the Mushki – perhaps related

* Tiglathpileser is the Hebraic form of *Tukulti-apil-Esharra*: 'My trust is in the son of Esharra (i.e. the god Ashur)'.

to the Phrygians – had crossed the Taurus with twenty-thousand men and were marching down the Tigris valley in the direction of Nineveh; to the east the Zagros tribes were hostile; to the west the Aramaeans – now mentioned for the first time – were established in force along the Euphrates and had started crossing the river; and to the south Marduk-nadin-ahhê, King of Babylon, had captured Ekallâtum, bringing his frontier up to the Lower Zab, thirty kilometres only from the city of Assur. Tiglathpileser first marched against the Mushki and massacred them and their allies. Then, anxious to secure his northern frontier, he went up 'to the heights of the lofty hills and to the top of the steep mountains' of the land of Nairi, penetrated into Armenia and set up his 'image' at Malazgird, far beyond Lake Van, while one of his armies chastised, the lands of Musri and Qummani at the foot of the Taurus range. The Aramaeans were forced beyond the Euphrates and pursued to their stronghold Jabal Bishri, west of Deir-ez-Zor, but the Syrian desert was swarming with this new, tough enemy:

'Twenty-eight times,' says the king, 'I fought the Ahlamû-Aramaeans; (once) I even crossed the Euphrates twice in a year. I defeated them from Tadmar (Tidmur, Palmyra), which lies in the country Amurru, Anat, which lies in the country Suhu, as far as Rapiqu, which lies in Kar-Duniash (Babylonia). I brought their possessions as spoils to my town Assur.'[24]

It was probably in the course of these campaigns that Tiglathpileser 'conquered' Syria and reached the Phoenician coast, where he received tribute from Arvad, Byblos and Sidon. Finally, came the victorious war against Babylon:

'I marched against Kar-Duniash . . . I captured the palaces of Babylon belonging to Marduk-nadin-ahhê, King of Kar-Duniash. I burned them with fire. The possessions of his palace I carried off. The second time, I drew up a line of battle chariots against Marduk-nadin-ahhê, King of Kar-Duniash, and I smote him.'[25]

To these military exploits, the King of Assyria added hunting activities, and he was out for big game: four wild bulls 'which were mighty and of monstrous size' killed in the country of Mitanni, ten 'mighty bull elephants in the country of Harran and in district of the River Khabur', 120 lions slain on foot, 800 lions laid low from the royal chariot and even a narwhal 'which they call sea-horse' killed in Mediterranean waters near Arvad.

The murder of Tiglathpileser, however, put an end to this glorious period. The mounting tide of Aramaean invasion, the desperate efforts made by the Assyrians to dam it up, the irremediable decadence of Babylon, Sumer and Akkad wide open to the Sutû and the Aramaeans, foreign wars, civil wars, floods, famine, such is the pitiful picture offered by Iraq during the tenth and ninth centuries B.C. If ever there was a time of 'troubles and disorders',[26] of confusion and hardship, a dark age rendered even darker by the paucity of our sources, it was the 166 years which elapsed between the death of Tiglathpileser I (1077 B.C.) and the advent of Adad-nirâri II (911 B.C.).

Through the fragmentary annals of the Assyrian kings we can follow in broad outline the Aramaean progression in northern Mesopotamia. Under Ashur-bêl-kala (1074–1057 B.C.) they were still on the right bank of the Euphrates, but fifty years later they had crossed the river and advanced as far as the Khabur. A few decades later, during the reign of Tiglathpileser II (967–935 B.C.), we find them around Nisibin, half-way between the Khabur and the Tigris. Ashur-dân II (934–912 B.C.) tried to push them back and claimed great success, but it appears clearly from the annals of Adad-nirâri II and of his successors (see next chapter) that at the dawn of the ninth century the Aramaeans had settled en masse all over the steppe of Jazirah: there were Aramaean kingdoms on the Euphrates (Bît-Adini) and on the Khabur (Bît-Bahiâni, Bît-Hadipê), and powerful Aramaean tribes occupied the mountain Tûr 'Abdîn, north of Nisibin, and the banks of the Tigris. Caught between the nomads and the highlanders, Assyria was threatened with asphyxia.

In Babylonia the situation was even worse, as shown by the ancient chronicles.[27] Under the reign of Nebuchadrezzar's fourth successor, Adad-apal-iddina (1067–1046 B.C.), the Sûtu plundered and ruined one of the greatest sanctuaries of Akkad: the temple of Shamash in Sippar – an event which probably gave rise to the great Babylonian poem of war and destruction known as the Erra epic.[28] Between 1024 and 978 B.C. Babylon had seven kings divided between three dynasties. The first of these dynasties (Babylon V) was founded by a Kassite born in the Sea-Land; the second (Bît-Bazi), probably by an Aramaean; the third, by a soldier, also born in the Sea-Land but bearing an Elamite name. Under Nabû-mukin-apli (977–942 B.C.), the first King of Babylon VIII, all kinds of bad omens were observed and 'the Aramaeans became hostile'. They cut off the capital-city from its suburbs, with the result that for several years in succession the New Year Festival (which required the free movement of divine statues to and from Babylon) could not be celebrated: 'Bêl (Marduk) went not forth and Nabû went not (from Barsippa to Babylon)'.[29] The following monarchs are hardly more to us than mere names on a list, but in all probability it was during this obscure period that a number of Aramaean tribes known from later Assyrian inscriptions – the Litaû, Puqudû, Gambulû – settled between the lower Tigris and the frontier of Elam, and that the Kaldû (Chaldeans) invaded the land of Sumer.[30] No one could have then imagined that three hundred years later the Kaldû would give Babylon one of its greatest monarchs, the second Nebuchadrezzar. But in that short interval the Assyrian empire had grown, reached its peak and collapsed.

CHAPTER 18

THE RISE OF ASSYRIA

Towards the end of the tenth century B.C. Assyria was at her lowest ebb. The lack of unity among her enemies had saved her from rapid destruction, but economic collapse was impending. She had lost all her possessions west of the Tigris, and her vital arteries, the great trade routes that ran across Jazirah and through the mountain passes, were in foreign hands. Hostile highlanders occupied not only the heights of the Zagros but the foothills down to the edge of the Tigris valley, while Aramaean tribes pitched their tents almost at the gates of Assur. Her territory consisted of no more than a narrow strip of land, hardly 1,600 kilometres long and 800 kilometres wide alongside the river, mostly on its left bank. Yet reduced, cornered and exposed as she was, Assyria was still a compact, solid and tough nation. Her main cities were free; she had chariots, horses and weapons; her men, trained by years of almost constant fighting, were the best warriors in the world; above all, her dynastic line remained unbroken, the crown having passed from head to head in the same family for more than two centuries.[1] In the fragmented and chaotic Near East of the time no other kingdom could claim such privileges: Babylonia was partly occupied and regularly plundered by the Aramaeans; since the victory of Nebuchadrezzar I over 'Hulteludish' (Hutelutush-Inshushi-nak), Elam had disappeared from the political stage; Egypt, ruled by Libyan princes in the Nile delta and by priests of Amon in Thebes, was almost powerless; the latest invaders – the Phrygians in Anatolia, the Medes and Persians in Iran – were still remote and relatively harmless competitors, and in Armenia, the great rival kingdom of tomorrow, Urartu, was not yet fully grown. Of all these nations Assyria, despite appearances was undoubtedly the strongest, and many must have thought that if only she could awake and fight back, she would be second to none.[2]

Genesis of an Empire

Assyria awoke in 911 B.C. The prince who ascended the throne that year, Adad-nirâri II (911–891 B.C.), does not rank among the illustrious, and his name did not go down to posterity, as did those of Sargon and Ashurbanipal. But it is he who loosened the grip of Assyria's enemies and unknowingly opened the last and most brilliant chapter in the history of the northern kingdom. The war he waged and won was, in his own view, a war of national liberation.[3] The Aramaeans were driven out of the Tigris valley and dislodged from the Kashiari mountains (Tûr 'Abdin, a rugged volcanic massif lying to the east of Mardin) from which they threatened Nineveh. Several cities in eastern Jazirah, which had been 'torn away from Assur', were recovered and their walls either dismantled or fortified against possible counter-attacks. Other campaigns saw the Assyrian army in Kurdistan, whose inhabitants were 'cut down in heaps' and pushed back to the mountains. Finally, the King of Babylon – who was then Shamash-mudammiq, of the eighth dynasty – was twice attacked, twice defeated and lost not only a large piece of land to the north of the Diyala river, but also Hît and Zanqu, border-towns on the Middle Euphrates.[4] Another campaign against his successor, Nabû-shuma-ukîn, was apparently less successful but ended in a treaty which ensured peace between the two kingdoms for about eighty years.[5] Tukulti-Ninurta II (890–884 B.C.), apparently as energetic as his father, did not live long enough to substantially enlarge the royal domain, but he rebuilt the wall of Assur 'from its foundation to its top', and a circular expedition in the south-western districts reconquered by Adad-nirâri won him the respect of the Aramaeans settled therein.[6] When he died the frontier of Assyria encompassed the whole of northern Iraq from the Khabur to the Zagros and from Nisibin to Anat and Samarra. His son, the young Ashurnaṣirpal II, inherited this already large and powerful kingdom and took the first steps towards transforming it into what we call an empire.

It would be a mistake, however, to think of the Assyrian empire as a planned enterprise, an organized body formed by the deliberate addition of land after land, province after province to the original nucleus. The wars which the Assyrian monarchs waged year after year and which eventually resulted in the conquest of the greater part of the Near East, these wars which fill their annals and make us almost forget their other achievements, had different, though closely interwoven motives.[7] There can be no doubt that some of them were defensive or preventive measures aimed at protecting from avowed or potential enemies the relatively narrow plain on either side of the Tigris which formed the core of Assyria and to keep open the vital trade roads that traversed the Jazirah towards Syria, crossed the Taurus and the Zagros towards Anatolia and Iran, and ran southward along the Tigris. At the end of the tenth century B.C., some of these roads were blocked by tribes from the steppe or the mountains and others by the Babylonians, the rulers and soldiers of a large country which the Assyrians coveted for its riches, revered as the holder of the great Sumero-Akkadian traditions but also feared, for since the days of Narâm-Sin of Akkad the kings of the South had never ceased claiming possession of the North, as witnessed by the multiple 'border wars' they had deliberately started. To fight on all these fronts was the price the Assyrians had to pay for their political and economic freedom, but if they won, then there would be no limit to their ambitions, including to obtain access to the Mediterranean Sea or the Gulf. It must be borne in mind that Assyria was the only country of the Near East that had no 'window' on a sea.

But it was not enough for the Assyrians to survive: they had to become wealthy in order to finance major architectural or agricultural projects, to provide their kings and their gods with the luxury to which they were entitled. During most of the second millennium B.C., Assyria had obtained the surplus she needed first from the fruitful operations of her merchants in Cappadocia, then from the 'royal trade' which flourished in the 15th and the 14th centuries, until the economic equilibrium of the entire Orient was toppled by the great invasions that took place around 1200 B.C. But since that time, the campaigns of Tukulti-Ninurta I and Tiglathpileser I had shown how much bold armed expeditions could pay and how useful it was to possess a vast hunting ground, 'a geographical area through which one could raid without encountering effective opposition',[8] bringing back a heavy booty. As long as foreign countries could be plundered and/or persuaded to pay the ransom of their independence, there was no need to annex and govern them directly.

To these economic motives must be added, of course, the greed and ambition of the Assyrian kings, their typically oriental desire to cover themselves with glory, to pose as invincible demigods in front of their subjects.

Moreover, as vicars and representatives on earth of their national god regarded as standing well above all other gods, they felt it their duty to impose the cult of Ashur in what was for them the whole world.[9] This in general could only be achieved by force, but it did not matter since the king's enemies were *ipso facto* the god's enemies and therefore wicked devils who deserved to be punished whatever they had done.[10] Thus, brigandry and occasional massacres were justified by the politico-religious ideology of the Assyrians; each of their campaigns was a measure of self-defence, an act of gangsterism but also a crusade.

Almost every year, usually in the spring, the King of Assyria mustered his troops 'at the command of Ashur' and led them on the dusty tracks of the Mesopotamian plain or on the perilous paths of the Taurus and of the Zagros. In the early days his opponents in those regions were merely chiefs of tribes or local princelings. Some fought bravely, though rarely with success; others fled to the desert or hid on inaccessible mountain peaks;

others 'embraced the feet' of the Assyrian war-lord, brought presents, promised to pay regular tribute and were spared. But woe to those who failed to keep their promise! In the course of another campaign a punitive expedition was directed against them and a storm swept over their country: the rebels were tortured, the population massacred or enslaved, the towns and villages set on fire, the crops burned, the trees uprooted. Terror-stricken, the neighbouring chieftains hastened to offer gifts and to swear allegiance. Then, its duty accomplished, loaded with spoil, trailing behind it human captives, flocks and herds, the army returned home and disbanded. As an example of what Assyria gained from these wars, here is a list of the *tamartu* (the 'spectacular gift for display') taken by Ashurnaṣirpal in one single, small district of Bît-Zamâni, the region of modern Diarbakr.

> 40 chariots 'equipped with the trappings of men and horses'
> 460 horses 'broken to the yoke'
> 2 talents of silver, 2 talents of gold
> 100 talents of lead, 100 talents of copper
> 300 talents of iron
> 1,000 vessels of copper
> 2,000 pans of copper
> bowls and cauldrons of copper
> 1,000 brightly coloured garments of wool and linen
>   tables of *sha*-wood and 'couches made of ivory and
>   overlaid with gold' from the ruler's palace
> 2,000 heads of cattle
> 5,000 sheep,

not counting the ruler's sister, the 'daughters of his nobles with their rich dowries' and his 15,000 Ahlamû-Aramaean subjects 'snatched away and brought to Assyria'. The local prince was put to death, and an annual tribute was imposed on his successor, consisting of 1,000 sheep, 2,000 *gur* of grain, 2 minas of gold and 13 minas of silver.[11] In the same campaign Ashurnaṣirpal gathered presents and spoil from no less than five countries and nine major cities.

As years went by, the boundaries of the Assyrian hunting ground were pushed farther and farther afield. Behind the petty states of their immediate neighbourhood, the kings of Assur found larger and more powerful kingdoms: Urarṭu in Armenia, the Medes in Iran, Elam and Egypt. The raids of rapine became wars of conquest. Assyria had grown stronger, but her opponents were bigger and tougher. The increased distances rendered more difficult the collection of tribute and the suppression of revolts. In most places it became necessary to replace the native rulers and their courts by Assyrian governors and civil servants and to extend to these far-away regions the division into provinces which had prevailed in Assyria proper since very early days. In this way an empire took shape with its huge, complex and perfectly organized administrative machinery. But the original objectives were never forgotten, and the extortion of taxes remained the foundation of Assyrian government. It is certain that the Aramaean merchants and the Phoenician sailors and craftsmen benefited to a certain extent from the facility and security of communications throughout this vast territory and from the ever-increasing demands of the Assyrian palaces for luxury goods. It is probable that some of the more backward districts received a thin varnish of civilization.[12] But outside Assyria proper – which now included the entire steppe between the Euphrates and the Tigris – there is no evidence that the conquerors made much effort to diffuse their highly advanced culture, to care for the economic development of the distant provinces and satellite states, to improve, even indirectly, the welfare of their populations. The silence on this subject of the royal correspondence found at Nineveh and at Nimrud, the almost complete absence of Assyrian texts in Syria, Palestine, Armenia and Iran, the generally poor character of the Assyrian level in excavated sites of these countries, the frequent references to spoil, massacres and destruction in the royal annals (however exaggerated they may be), everything points to impoverishment or, at best, stagnation. The men, horses, cattle and sheep brought into Assyria by the thousand, the enormous yearly income in silver, gold, copper, iron, grain and other commodities so accurately registered by the palace scribes, all this was generally not purchased but taken by force. Wealth was constantly being transferred from the periphery to the centre, from the dependencies and 'protectorates' to the Mesopotamian homeland.[13] The Assyrians took much and gave very little, with the result that if the state was rich its distant subjects were destitute and in almost constant rebellion. The system upon which the empire was founded had in itself the germs of its own destruction.

Ashurnaṣirpal

With Tukulti-Ninurta's son we meet the first great Assyrian monarch of the new period. Ambition, energy, courage, vanity, cruelty, magnificence, Ashurnaṣirpal II* (883–859 B.C.) possessed to the extreme all the qualities and defects of his successors, the ruthless, indefatigable empire-builders. There is no smile, no piety, almost no humanity in the statue of him found at Nimrud and now in the British Museum, but the rigid attitude of a conceited despot, the aquiline nose of a bird of prey, the straight-looking eyes of a chief who demands absolute obedience, and in his hands the mace and the curved spear.[14]

No sooner was he upon the throne than, without the shadow of a pretext, he went forth to ransack the hilly countries to the north of Mesopotamia.[15] This took him as far as the land of Kutmuhu in the Upper Tigris valley, where he received tribute from several local princes and presents from the Mushki, or Phrygians, who held outposts on the southern slopes of the Taurus mountains. While he was there he received news that a vassal Aramaean city on the lower Khabur had revolted, and he immediately proceeded to punish the rebels – a march of at least three hundred kilometres, in the middle of the summer:

* The exact spelling of the name is *Ashshur-nâṣir-apli*, meaning 'the god Ashur is guardian of the heir'.

'To the city of Sûru of Bît Halupê I drew near, and the terror of the splendour of Ashur, my lord, overwhelmed them. The chief and the elders of the city, to save their lives came forth into my presence and embraced my feet, saying: "If it is thy pleasure, slay! If it is thy pleasure, let live! That which thy heart desireth, do!" ... In the valour of my heart and with the fury of my weapons I stormed the city. All the rebels they seized and delivered them up.'[16]

Further campaigns in the course of the reign were directed against other rebels in the Kashiari mountains, in the land of Zamua (the region around modern Suleimaniyah) and on the Middle Euphrates. Then, when the kingdom was pacified, the first stride was made towards reaching Syria and the Mediterranean, a goal which Shamshi-Adad I once had set and which no Assyrian monarch of value could overlook. Beyond the Khabur and the Balikh, within the great bend of the Euphrates, lay the important Aramaean kingdom of Bit-Adini. Ashurnaṣirpal invaded it and 'with mines, battering rams and siege engines' took Kaprabi (possibly Urfa), a city which 'was exceedingly strong and hung like a cloud from heaven'. The ruler of Bît-Adini, Ahuni, brought tribute and left hostages in Assyrian hands: the way was clear for the great Syrian expedition of the following year (877 B.C.). The annals go into considerable detail over this campaign, and we can follow the king and his army step by step, by daily marches of about thirty kilometres from Karkemish to the plain of Antioch, across the Orontes and finally, 'along the side of mount Lebanon and to the Great Sea of the land of Amurru'. There Ashurnaṣirpal repeated the gesture of his predecessors:

'I cleaned my weapons in the deep sea and performed sheep-offerings to the gods. The tribute of the sea-coast – from the inhabitants of Tyre, Sidon, Byblos, Mahallata, Maiza, Kaiza, Amurru, and (of) Arvad which is (an island) in the sea: gold, silver, tin, copper, copper containers, linen garments with multi-coloured trimmings, large and small monkeys, ebony, boxwood, ivory from walrus tusk – (thus ivory) a product of the sea – (this) their tribute I received and they embraced my feet.'[17]

The Assyrians returned home *via* the Amanus mountains, where trees were cut down and sent to Assur, and a royal stele set up. Taken by surprise, the Neo-Hittite and Aramaean princes of northern Syria had offered no resistance. Contrary to the claims made by the king, however, this triumphal campaign was not a conquest but another razzia, the first long-range Assyrian razzia since the days of Tiglathpileser I, two hundred years before. Even in Mesopotamia the territory gained by Ashurnaṣirpal was comparatively small, and the main result of the reign was to pave the way for the following kings. Fortresses such as Tushhan on the Upper Tigris, Kar-Ashurnaṣirpal and Nibarti-Ashur on the Middle Euphrates were founded and staffed with garrisons.[18] The position of Assyria in northern Iraq was consolidated, its nearest neighbours in the mountainous half-circle counted as vassals. The entire Near East learnt that the Assyrians were once again on the move and trembled with fear.

They had every reason to tremble, for Ashurnaṣirpal was preceded by a well-deserved reputation for cruelty. Humanitarian concepts in warfare were unknown in those days, and a few spectacular examples duly recorded and displayed in writing and pictures in various places were no doubt necessary to inspire respect and enforce obedience. All conquerors in antiquity (and some in modern times) practised a policy of terror, and the Assyrians were no exception. But Ashurnaṣirpal surpassed them all. Not only were the rebellious or recalcitrant rulers put to death, flayed and their skin 'spread over the walls of their city', but in a few, exceptional cases unarmed prisoners and innocent civilians, were tortured with sadistic refinements:

'I built a pillar over against his city gate and I flayed all the chiefs who had revolted, and I covered the pillar with their skin. Some I walled up within the pillar, some I impaled upon the pillar on stakes, and others I bound to stakes round about the pillar . . . And I cut the limbs of the officers, of the royal officers who had rebelled . . .

'Many captives from among them I burned with fire, and many I took as living captives. From some I cut off their noses, their ears and their fingers, of many I put out the eyes. I made one pillar of the living and another of heads, and I bound their heads to tree trunks round about the city. Their young men and maidens I burned in the fire.

'Twenty men I captured alive and I immured them in the wall of his palace . . .

'The rest of their warriors I consumed with thirst in the desert of the Euphrates . . .'[19]

It must be noted, however, that these atrocities were usually reserved for those local princes and their nobles who had revolted and that in contrast with the Israelites, for instance, who exterminated the Amalekites for purely ethno-cultural reasons, the Assyrians never indulged in systematic genocides.[20]

It is only fair to add that the memory of Ashurnaṣirpal must be credited with other, more commendable achievements. Part of his thirst for blood was quenched by the hunting prowesses which his sculptors have immortalized. He had a taste for zoology and botany and brought back 'from the lands in which he had travelled and the mountains he had passed' all kinds of beasts, trees and seeds to be acclimatized in Assyria. Above all, he was possessed with that passion for building which is the mark of all great Mesopotamian monarchs. Without neglecting the traditional restoration of temples in Assur and Nineveh, he decided early in his reign to build himself a new 'royal residence' away from the old capital-city. Had the Aramaean invasion shown that Assur, on the right bank of the Tigris, was dangerously exposed to attacks coming from the west, or was the move prompted by pride alone? We do not know, but if safety was sought, the site selected by Ashurnaṣirpal, Kalhu (biblical Calah, modern Nimrud, thirty-five kilometres south of Mosul) was strategically excellent, protected as it was by the Tigris to the west and by the Upper Zab flowing at some distance to the south. Shalmaneser I in the thirteenth century B.C. had founded a town there, but it had long fallen into ruins. Thousands of men were put to work: the ruin-mound,

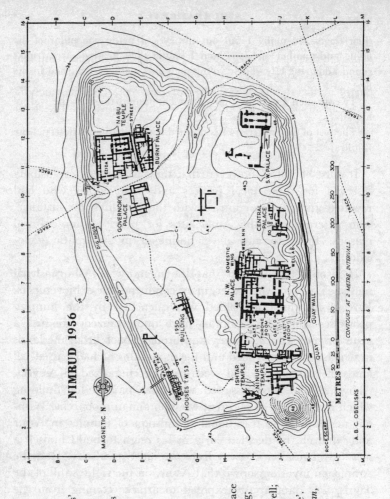

NIMRUD 1956

MAGNETIC N

A B C OBELISKS

METRES 50 25 0 50 100 150 200 250 300

CONTOURS AT 2 METRE INTERVALS

Plan of Nimrud.
1, The archaeologists'
    house;
2, temple of Nabū;
3, palace of the city's
    governor;
4, 'burnt palace';
5, street;
6, private houses;
7, building;
8, Ishtar's temple;
9, Ninurta's temple;
10, ziqqurat;
11, Ashurnaṣirpal's palace
    with A; domestic wing;
B, throne room;
C, archives room; D, well;
12, 'central palace';
13, 'south-west palace'.
*From M. E. L. Mallowan,
Iraq, XIX, 1957.*

the 'tell', was levelled, and the building site extended; a massive wall reinforced with towers was erected, enclosing a rectangle about eight kilometres in perimeter, and a partly natural, partly artificial hill in a corner of this rectangle became the acropolis supporting the ziqqurat, several temples and the royal palace:

'A palace of cedar, cypress, juniper, boxwood, mulberry, pistachio-wood and tamarisk, for my royal dwelling and for my lordly pleasure for all time I founded therein. Beasts of the mountains and of the seas of white limestone and alabaster I fashioned and set them up in its gates ... Door-leaves of cedar, cypress, juniper and mulberry I hung in the gates thereof; and silver, gold, lead, copper and iron, the spoil of my hand from the lands which I had brought under my sway, in great quantities I took and placed therein.'[21]

At the same time a canal called *Patti-hegalli* ('stream of abundance') was dug from the Zab with the double purpose of sheltering the town further and of watering the surrounding plain. Prisoners from the subdued lands were settled in the new capital-city, whose tutelary god, significantly, was the war-god Ninurta.

Ashurnaṣirpal's palace at Nimrud was one of the first monuments ever excavated in Mesopotamia. Between 1845 and 1851 Layard worked on its central part and – much to the awe and wonder of his labourers – dug up a number of colossal winged bull-men, lions, genii and slabs covered with reliefs and inscriptions.[22] Some of these treasures were sent to England and are now the pride of the British Museum; others, too heavy to be removed, were reinterred, to be unearthed again just over a century later by other British archaeologists.[23] We now possess the complete plan of the palace, which covered an area of more than three hectares and was divided into three parts: the administrative quarters (a series of rooms around a large court-yard), the ceremonial block with its spacious reception-hall and throne-room and, finally, the domestic wing, including royal apartments, harem, stores and ablution-rooms. In the ceremonial block the main gates were flanked by huge *lamussû*, or protective genii, the mud-brick walls decorated with frescoes and with carved and inscribed orthostats, the floors paved with burnt bricks stamped with the name of the king. An interesting feature of the domestic wing was the presence of an 'air conditioning' system in the form of broad air-vents cut in the thickness of the walls to admit fresh air from above. The door leaves of precious wood have perished in the fire which destroyed Nimrud, like other Assyrian cities, in 612 B.C., but a number of objects have survived, in particular beautifully incised or carved panels of ivory, often covered with gold, which once decorated the royal furniture. There were also weapons and tools of bronze or iron, clay jars and a number of tablets. As it now stands, Ashurnaṣirpal's palace is the best preserved of Assyrian royal dwellings, and the visitor who wanders through this maze of rooms and courtyards, who walks along these narrow corridors lined with huge slabs to be suddenly confronted, in the dim light of a doorway, with some terrifying monster of stone, can well imagine the emotion which must have seized those who entered the building to approach 'the wonderful shepherd who fears not the battle'.

Among the finds made in the palace was a very large stele bearing the figure of the king and a long inscription from which we learn of the festivities that accompanied the opening ceremony in 879 B.C.[24] An enormous banquet – the menu of which is given in detail – was offered by Ashurnaṣirpal to the entire population of the town as well as to foreign ambassadors, in all no less than 69,574 guests for ten days. And the final sentence makes us for a moment forget the other, unsavoury aspects of this great monarch:

'The happy people of all the lands together with the people of Kalhu for ten days I feasted, wined, bathed, anointed and honoured and sent them back to their lands in peace and joy.'

Shalmaneser III

Constantly on the battlefield, starting his campaigns from Nineveh or from one of his provincial palaces, Ashurnaṣirpal's son, Shalmaneser III* (858–824 B.C.), appears to have spent only the last years of his life in Kalhu. Yet it is from that city and its neighbourhood that come his most famous monuments. One of them is the 'Black Obelisk' found by Layard in the temple of Ninurta over a century ago and now in the British Museum.²⁵ It is a two-metre-high block of black alabaster ending in steps, like a miniature ziqqurat. A long inscription giving the summary of the king's wars runs around the monolith, while five sculptured panels on each side depict the payment of tribute by various foreign countries, including Israel, whose king Jehu is shown prostrate at the feet of the Assyrian monarch. More recent excavations at Nimrud have brought to light a statue of the king in the attitude of prayer, and a huge building situated in a corner of the town wall, which was founded by him and used by his successors down to the fall of the empire. This building, nicknamed by the archaeologists 'Fort Shalmaneser', was in fact his palace as well as the *ekal masharti* of the inscriptions, the 'great store-house' erected 'for the ordinance of the camp, the maintenance of stallions, chariots, weapons, equipment of war, and the spoil of the foe of every kind'.²⁶ In three vast courtyards the troops were assembled, equipped and inspected before the annual campaigns, while the surrounding rooms served as armouries, stores, stables and lodgings for the officers. Finally, we have the remarkable objects known as 'the bronze gates of Balawat'. They were discovered in 1878 by Layard's assistant Rassam, not at Nimrud, but at Balawat (ancient Imgur-Enlil), a small tell a few kilometres to the north-east of the great city. There Ashurnaṣirpal had built a country palace later occupied by Shalmaneser, and the main gates of this palace were covered with long strips of bronze,

* *Shulanu-asharedu*, 'the god Shulmanu is pre-eminent'.

about twenty-five centimetres wide, worked in 'repoussé' technique, representing some of Shalmaneser's armed expeditions; a
brief legend accompanies the pictures.[27] Besides their considerable artistic or architectural interest, all these monuments are
priceless for the information they provide concerning Assyrian
warfare during the ninth century B.C.

In the number and scope of his military campaigns Shalmaneser surpasses his father.[28] Out of his thirty-five years of reign
thirty-one were devoted to war. The Assyrian soldiers were
taken farther abroad than ever before: they set foot in Armenia,
in Cilicia in Palestine, in the heart of the Taurus and of the
Zagros, on the shores of the Gulf. They ravaged new lands,
besieged new cities, measured themselves against new enemies.
But because these enemies were much stronger than the Aramaeans of Jazirah or the small tribes of Iraqi Kurdistan, the
victories of Shalmaneser were mitigated with failures, and the
whole reign gives the impression of a task left unfinished, of a
gigantic effort for a very small result. In the north, for instance,
Shalmaneser went beyond 'the sea of Nairi' (Lake Van) and
entered the territory of Urarṭu, a kingdom which had recently
been formed amidst the high mountains of Armenia. The Assyrian claims, as always, complete success and describes the sack
of several towns belonging to the King of Urarṭu, Arame. Yet he
confesses that Arame escaped, and we know that during the
next century Urarṭu grew to be Assyria's main rival. Similarly,
a series of campaigns in the east, towards the end of the reign,
brought Shalmaneser or his commander-in-chief, the *turtanu*
Daiân-Ashur, in contact with the Medes and Persians, who
then dwelt around Lake Urmiah. There again the clash was
brief and the 'victory' without lasting results: Medes and Persians were in fact left free to consolidate their position in Iran.

The repeated efforts made by Shalmaneser to conquer Syria
met with the same failure. The Neo-Hittite and Aramaean
princes whom Ashurnaṣirpal had caught by surprise had had
time to strengthen themselves, and the main effect of the renewed Assyrian attacks was to unite them against Assyria.

Three campaigns were necessary to wipe out the state of Bît-Adini and to establish a bridgehead on the Euphrates. In 856 B.C. Til-Barsip (modern Tell Ahmar), the capital-city of Bît-Adini, was taken, populated with Assyrians and renamed Kâr-Shulmanashared, 'the Quay of Shalmaneser'. On top of the mound overlooking the Euphrates a palace was built, which served as a base for operations on the western front.[29] But whether the Assyrians marched towards Cilicia through the Amanus or towards Damascus via Aleppo, they invariably found themselves face to face with coalitions of local rulers. Thus when Shalmaneser in 853 B.C. entered the plains of central Syria, his opponents, Irhuleni of Hama and Adad-idri of Damascus (Ben-Hadad II of the Bible), met him with contingents supplied by 'twelve kings of the sea-coast'. To the invaders they could oppose 62,900 infantry-men, 1,900 horsemen, 3,900 chariots and 1,000 camels sent by 'Gindibu, from Arabia'. The battle took place at Karkara (Qarqar) on the Orontes, not far from Hama. Says Shalmaneser:

'I slew 14,000 of their warriors with the sword. Like Adad, I rained destruction upon them . . . . The plain was too small to let their bodies fall, the wide countryside was used up in burying them. With their corpses, I spanned the Orontes as with a bridge.'[30]

Yet neither Hama nor Damascus were taken, and the campaign ended prosaically with a little cruise on the Mediterranean. Four, five and eight years later other expeditions were directed against Hama with the same partial success. Numerous towns and villages were captured, looted and burned down, but not the main cities. In 841 B.C. Damascus was again attacked. The occasion was propitious, Adad-idri having been murdered and replaced by Hazael, 'the son of a nobody'.[31] Hazael was defeated in battle on mount Sanir (Hermon), but locked himself in his capital-city. All that Shalmaneser could do was to ravage the orchards and gardens which surrounded Damascus as they surround it today and to plunder the rich plain of Hauran. He then took the road to the coast, and on Mount Carmel received the tribute of Tyre, Sidon and *Iaua mâr Humri* (Jehu, son of Omri), King of Israel, the first biblical figure to appear in cuneiform inscriptions. After a last attempt to conquer Damascus in 838 B.C. the Assyrian confessed his failure by leaving Syria alone for the rest of his reign.

In Babylonia Shalmaneser was luckier, though here again he failed to exploit his success and missed the chance which was offered to him. Too weak to attack the Assyrians and too strong to be attacked by them, the kings of the Eighth Dynasty of Babylon had hitherto managed to remain free. Even Ashurnaṣirpal had spared the southern kingdom, giving his contemporary Nabû-apal-iddina (887–855 B.C.) time to repair some of the damage caused by the Aramaeans and the Sutû during 'the time of confusion'.[32] But in 850 B.C. hostilities broke out between King Marduk-zakir-shumi and his own brother backed by the Aramaeans. The Assyrians were called to the rescue. Shalmaneser defeated the rebels, entered Babylon, 'the bond of heaven and earth, the abode of life', offered sacrifices in Marduk's temple, Esagila, as well as in the sanctuaries of Kutha and Barsippa, and treated the inhabitants of that holy land with extreme kindness:

For the people of Babylon and Barsippa, the protégés, the freemen of the great gods, he prepared a feast, he gave them food and wine, he clothed them in brightly coloured garments and presented them with gifts.[33]

Then, advancing farther south into the ancient country of Sumer now occupied by the Chaldaeans (Kaldû), he stormed it and chased the enemies of Babylon 'unto the shores of the sea they call Bitter River (*nâr marratu*)', i.e. the Gulf. The whole affair, however, was but a police operation. Marduk-zakir-shumi swore allegiance to his protector but remained on his throne.[34] The unity of Mesopotamia under Assyrian rule could perhaps have been achieved without much difficulty. For some untold reason – probably because he was too deeply engaged in the north and in the west – Shalmaneser did not claim more than nominal suzerainty, and all that Assyria gained was some territory and a couple of towns on its southern border. The Diyala to the south, the Euphrates to the west, the mountain ranges to the north and east now marked its limits. It was still a purely northern Mesopotamian kingdom, and the empire had yet to be conquered.

The end of Shalmaneser's long reign was darkened by extremely serious internal disorders. One of his sons, Ashurdanin-aplu, revolted and with him twenty-seven cities, including Assur, Nineveh, Arba'il (Erbil) and Arrapha (Kirkuk). The old king, who by then hardly left his palace in Nimrud, entrusted another of his sons, Shamshi-Adad, with the task of repressing the revolt, and for four years Assyria was in the throes of civil war. The war was still raging when Shalmaneser died and Shamshi-Adad V ascended the throne (824 B.C.). With the new king began a period of Assyrian stagnation which lasted for nearly a century.

CHAPTER 19

THE ASSYRIAN EMPIRE

The great revolt of 827 B.C. was not a dynastic crisis in the usual sense of the term; it was an uprising of the rural nobility and of the free citizens of Assyria against the great barons of the kingdom: the rich and insolent provincial governors to whom Ashurnaṣirpal and his successor had entrusted the lands they had conquered, and the high officials of the court, such as the *turtanu* Daiân-Ashur, who, in the last years of Shalmaneser, had assumed powers out of proportion to the real nature of their duties. What the insurgents wanted was a king who really governed and a more even distribution of authority among his subordinates. They were fighting for a good cause, with the crown prince himself at their head, but a thorough administrative reform at this stage would have shaken the foundations of the still fragile kingdom. Shalmaneser judged that the revolt had to be crushed and no one was better qualified to crush it than his energetic younger son. It took Shamshi-Adad V five years to subdue the twenty-seven cities wherein his brother had 'brought about sedition, rebellion and wicked plotting', and the remainder of his reign (823–811 B.C.) to assert his authority over the Babylonians and the vassal rulers of the mountainous north and east, who had taken advantage of the civil war to shake off the Assyrian 'protection' and to withhold their tribute.[1] In the end, peace and order were restored, but no drastic changes were made in the central and provincial governments, and the malaise persisted giving rise, in the course of the following years, to other major or minor outbreaks of violence. This permanent instability affecting the infrastructure of the State, combined with other factors such as the lack of youth and slackness of some of Shamshi-Adad's successors and the ever-growing part taken by the rival kingdom of Urarṭu in

Near Eastern politics, accounts for the temporary weakness of Assyria during the first half of the eighth century B.C.

Assyrian Eclipse

Shamshi-Adad's son, Adad-nirâri III (810–783 B.C.), was very young when his father died, and for four years the government of Assyria was in the hands of his mother Sammuramat – the legendary Semiramis. How this queen, whose reign has left hardly a trace in Assyrian records,[2] acquired the reputation of being 'the most beautiful, most cruel, most powerful and most lustful of Oriental queens'[3] is a most baffling problem. The legend of Semiramis, as told in the first century B.C. by Diodorus Siculus[4] – who drew his material from the now lost *Persica* of Ctesias, a Greek author and physician at the court of Artaxerxes II (404–359 B.C.) – is that of a manly woman born of a Syrian goddess, who became queen of Assyria by marrying Ninus, the mythical founder of Nineveh, founded Babylon, built astonishing monuments in Persia, conquered Media, Egypt, Libya and Bactria, conducted an unsuccessful military expedition in India and turned into a dove on her death. This legend contains many ingredients, including a possible confusion with Naqi'a/Zakûtu (the wife of Sennacherib, who supervised the reconstruction of Babylon destroyed by her husband), as well as reminiscences of the conquests of Darius I, of the Indian war of Alexander the Great, and even of the Achaemenian court with the terrible queen-mother Parysatis. Semiramis also shares some traits with Ishtar as a war goddess who, like her, destroyed her lovers. At first sight, all this has nothing to do with what we know of Adad-nirari's mother. Yet both Herodotus and Berossus,[5] who said very little about Semiramis, have indirectly made it clear that she and Sammuramat were one and the same person. Where, then, is the link between the two women? The whole story has a strong Iranian flavour. Perhaps Sammuramat did something which greatly surprised and impressed the Medes (she might have led a battle against them), and her prowess was transmitted through generations, distorted and embroidered, by Iranian story-tellers, until they reached the ears of Ctesias. But this, like other hypotheses, cannot be substantiated. Presented in many forms, Diodorus's account of the Semiramis legend has met with an enormous success, notably in Western Europe, until the beginning of this century. And thus, by an ironical trick of fate the memory of the virile Assyrian kings has passed to posterity under the guise of a woman.

As soon as he was of age to perform his royal duties, Adad-nirâri displayed the qualities of a capable and enterprising monarch.[6] In his first year of effective reign (806 B.C.) he invaded Syria and imposed tax and tribute upon the Neo-Hittites, Phoenicians, Philistines, Israelites and Edomites. Succeeding where his grandfather had failed, he entered Damascus and received from Ben-Hadad III 'his property and his goods in immeasurable quantity'.[7] Similarly, the Medes and Persians in Iran were, in the emphatic style of his royal inscriptions, 'brought in submission to his feet', while 'the kings of the Kaldû, all of them' were counted as vassals. But these were mere raids and not conquests. The spasmodic efforts of this true offspring of Shalmaneser III bore no fruit, and his premature death marks the beginning of a long period of Assyrian decline.

Adad-nirâri had four sons who reigned in succession. Of the first, Shalmaneser IV (782–773 B.C.), very little is known, but his authority seems to have been singularly limited, for his commander-in-chief, Shamshi-ilu, in an inscription found at Til-Barsip (Tell Ahmar) boasts of his victories over the Urartians without even mentioning the name of his master, the king – a fact unprecedented in Assyrian records.[8] The reign of the second son, Ashur-dân III (772–755 B.C.), was marked by unsuccessful campaigns in central Syria and Babylonia, an epidemic of plague and revolts in Assur, Arrapha (Kirkuk) and Guzana (Tell Halaf) – not to mention an ominous eclipse of the sun. It is this eclipse, duly recorded in the *limmu* list and which can be dated June 15, 763 B.C., which served as a basis of Mesopotamian chronology in the first millennium (see page 25).

As for the third son, Ashur-nirâri (754-745 B.C.), he hardly dared leave his palace and was probably killed in a revolution which broke out in Kalhu and put upon the throne Tiglathpileser III,[9] a man whose membership of Adad-nirâri's family remains controverted and who might have been a usurper.

Thus for thirty-six years (781-745 B.C.) Assyria was practically paralysed, and during that time the political geography of the Near East underwent several major or minor changes. Babylonia, twice defeated on the battlefield by Shamshi-Adad V but still independent, fell into a state of quasi-anarchy recalling the worst decades of the tenth century. In about 790 B.C. for several years 'there was no king in the country', confessed a chronicle, while Eriba-Marduk (c. 769 B.C.) claimed as a great success a simple police operation against the Aramaeans who had taken some 'fields and gardens' belonging to the inhabitants of Babylon and Barsippa.[10] In Syria the Aramaean princes were too absorbed in their traditional quarrels to achieve anything like unity. Attacked on two fronts, humiliated by the Assyrians of Adad-nirâri and defeated by the Israelites of Ahab, the kings of Damascus lost their political ascendancy to the benefit first of Hama, then of Arpad (Tell Rifa'at, near Aleppo), the capital-city of Bît-Agushi.[11] In Iran the Persians began migrating from the north to the south towards the Bakhtiari mountains,[12] and the Medes were left free to extend their control over the whole plateau. Around Lake Urmiah the Mannaeans (*Mannai*), a non-Indo-European people which excavations have shown to be far more civilized than one would have thought,[13] organized themselves into a small but solid nation. But the main development took place in Armenia, where in the course of the ninth and eighth centuries Urartu grew from a small principality on the shores of Lake Van to a kingdom as large and powerful as Assyria itself. Under Argistis I (c. 787-766 B.C.) it extended approximately from Lake Sevan, in Russian Armenia, to the present northern frontier of Iraq and from Lake Urmiah to the upper course of the Euphrates in Turkey. Outside the national boundaries were vassal states or tribes which paid tribute to Urarṭu, acknowledged its suzerainty or were tied to it by military agreements. Such were the Cimmerians in the Caucasus, all the Neo-Hittite kingdoms of the Taurus (Tabal, Milid, Gurgum, Kummuhu) and the Mannai in Iran. Argistis's successor, Sardur II (c. 765–733 B.C.), also succeeded in detaching Mati'-ilu, King of Arpad, from the alliance he had just signed with Ashur-nirâri V and through Arpad the political influence of Urarṭu was rapidly spreading among the Aramaean kingdoms of northern Syria.

Old and recent excavations in Turkish and Russian Armenia – in particular at Toprak Kale (ancient Rusahina), near Van, and at Karmir Blur (ancient Teisbaini), near Erivan – have supplied us with copious information on the history and archaeology of the kingdom of Urarṭu.[14] Its main cities were built of stone or of mud bricks resting on stone foundations; they were enclosed in massive walls and dominated by enormous citadels where food, oil, wine and weapons were stored in anticipation of war. Urartian artisans were experts in metallurgy, and they have left us some very fine works of art displaying a strong Assyrian influence. All over Armenia numerous steles and rock inscriptions in cuneiform script and in 'Vannic' language – an offspring of Hurrian – bear witness to the heroism and piety of Urartian kings, while hundreds of tablets give us an insight into the social and economic organization of the kingdom, essentially based on vast royal estates worked by warriors, prisoners of war or slaves. The pastures of the Ararat massif and the fertile valley of the Arax river made Urarṭu a fairly rich cattle-breeding and agricultural country, but most of its wealth came from the copper and iron mines of Armenia, Georgia, Commagene and Azerbaijan, which it possessed or controlled.

The emergence of such a large, prosperous and powerful nation had a decisive influence on the history of Assyria. The ever-growing part assumed by Urarṭu in Near Eastern economics and politics, no less than its presence at the gates of Iraq, was for the Assyrians a source of constant worry but also a challenge. A series of unfortunate experiences under

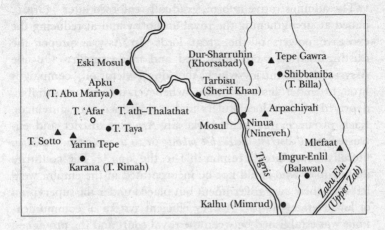

Principal sites in the vicinity of Mosul.

Shalmaneser IV had taught them that any attempt at striking a direct blow at Urarṭu in the present state of affairs would meet with failure. Before they could stand face to face with their mighty rivals they had to strengthen their own position in Mesopotamia and to conquer, occupy and firmly hold Syria and western Iran, those two pillars to Urartian dominion outside Armenia. The time of quick, easy, fruitful razzias was over. Assyria had no choice but to become an empire or perish.

Tiglathpileser III

Fortunately, Assyria found in Tiglathpileser III (744–727 B.C.) an intelligent and vigorous sovereign who took a clear view of the situation and applied the necessary remedies. Not only did he 'smash like pots' – to use his own expression – the Syrian allies of Urarṭu and the Medes but he turned the subdued lands into Assyrian possessions, reorganized the Army and carried out the long-awaited administrative reform which gave Assyria the internal peace it needed. From every point of view Tiglathpileser must be considered the founder of the Assyrian empire.

The administrative reform, gradually enforced after 738 B.C. aimed at strengthening the royal authority and at reducing the excessive powers of the great lords. In Assyria proper the existing districts were multiplied and made smaller. Outside Assyria the countries which the king's victorious campaigns brought under his sway were, whenever possible or suitable, deprived of their local rulers and transformed into provinces. Each province was treated like an Assyrian district and entrusted to a 'district lord' (*bel pihâti*) or to a 'governor' (*shaknu*, literally: 'appointed') responsible to the king.[15] The countries and peoples who could not be incorporated in the empire were left with their own government but placed under the supervision of an 'overseer' (*qêpu*). A very efficient system of communications was established between the royal court and the provinces. Ordinary messengers or special runners constantly carried reports and letters sent by the governors and district-chiefs or their subordinates to the king and the court officials, and the orders (*amât sharri*, 'king's word') issued by the monarch. In some cases the king sent his personal representative, the *qurbutu*-official, who reported on confidential affairs and often acted on his own initiative. District-chiefs and province governors had large military, judicial, administrative and financial powers, though their authority was limited by the small size of their charge and by the constant interference of the central government in almost every matter. Their main task was to ensure the regular payment of the tribute (*madattu*) and of the various taxes and duties to which Assyrians and foreigners alike were subjected, but they were also responsible for the enforcement of law and order, the execution of public works and the raising of troops in their own distruct. The last-mentioned function was of considerable importance to the motherland. Formerly, the Assyrian Army was made up of crown-dependents doing their military services as *ilku* (see page 206) and of peasants and slaves supplied by the landlords of Assyria and put at the king's disposal for the duration of the annual campaign. To this army of conscription, Tiglathpileser III added a permanent army (*kisir sharruti*, 'bond of kingship') mainly formed of contingents levied in the peripheral provinces. Some Aramaean tribes, such as the *Itu'* provided excellent mercenaries. Another novelty was the development of cavalry as opposed to war-chariots. This change was probably due to the frequency of battles in mountainous countries against people like the Medes who utilized mostly horsemen.[16]

Another of Tiglathpileser's initiatives was the practice of mass-deportation. Whole towns and districts were emptied of their inhabitants, who were resettled in distant regions and replaced by people brought by force from other countries. In 742 and 741 B.C., for instance, 30,000 Syrians from the region of Hama were sent to the Zagros mountains, while 18,000 Aramaeans from the left bank of the Tigris were transferred to northern Syria. In Iran in 744 B.C. 65,000 persons were displaced in one single campaign, and another year the exodus affected no less than 154,000 people in southern Mesopotamia.[17] Such pitiful scenes are occasionally depicted on Assyrian bas-reliefs: carrying little bags on their shoulders and holding their emaciated children by the hand, long files of men walk with the troops, while their wives follow in carts or riding on donkeys or horses. A pitiful and no doubt partially real spectacle, but deliberately intensified for propaganda purposes, for while one of the aims of deportation was to punish rebels or prevent rebellions, it also had other objectives: to uproot what would now be called 'national feelings' – i.e. fidelity to local gods, ruling families and traditions; to fill new towns on the borders, in conquered countries and in Assyria proper; to repopulate abandoned regions and develop their agriculture; to provide the Assyrians not only with soldiers and troops of labourers who would build cities, temples and palaces, but also with craftsmen, artists and even scribes and scholars.[18] We know from the royal correspondence that provincial governors were told to ensure that the deportees and their military escort would be well treated, supplied with food (and in at least one case, with shoes!) and protected against any harm. We also know that many of these displaced persons soon became used to new horizons and remained faithful to their new masters, and that some of them were given important posts in the imperial administration. The deportees were not slaves: distributed through the empire as needs arose, they had no special status and were simply 'counted among the people of Assyria', which means that they had the same duties and rights as original Assyrians. This policy of deportation – mainly from Aramaic-speaking areas – was pursued by Tiglathpileser's successors, and the number of persons forcibly removed from their home during three centuries has been estimated at four and a half million. It has largely contributed to the 'Aramaization' of Assyria, a slow but almost continuous process which, together with the internationalization of the army, probably played a role in the collapse of the empire.

The campaigns of Tiglathpileser III bear the imprint of his methodical mind.[19] First, an expedition in southern Iraq 'as far as the Uknû river (Kerkha)' relieved Babylon from the Aramaeans, pressure and reminded Nabû-nâṣir that the King of Assyria was still his protector. As usual, 'pure sacrifices' were offered to the gods in the sacred cities of Sumer and Akkad, from Sippar to Uruk. Then Tiglathpileser attacked Syria or, more precisely, the league of Neo-Hittite and Aramaean princes led by Mati'-ilu of Arpad, who obeyed Sardur III, the powerful King of Urarṭu. Sardur rushed to help his allies, but he was defeated near Samsat, on the Euphrates, and fleeing ignominiously on a mare, 'escaped at night and was seen no more'. Arpad, besieged, resisted for three years, finally succumbed and became the chief town of an Assyrian province (741 B.C.). In the meantime a victorious campaign against Azriyau, King of Ya'diya (Sam'al), and his allies of the Syrian coast resulted in the annexation of north-western Syria, and probably Phoenicia (742 B.C.). Numerous princes of the neighbourhood took fright and brought presents and tribute. Among them were Rasunu (Rezin), King of Damascus, Menahem, King of Israel,[20] and a certain Zabibê, 'Queen of the Arabs'. In all probability, the starting-point of the Syrian campaigns was Hadâtu (modern Arslan Tash), between Karkemish and Harran, where archaeological excavations have unearthed one of Tiglathpileser's provincial palaces, an elaborate building strikingly similar in layout to Ashurnaṣirpal's palace in Nimrud, though smaller. Near the palace a temple dedicated to Ishtar has yielded interesting pieces of sculpture, and in another building were found sculptured panels of ivory which once decorated the royal furniture of Hazael, King of Damascus, taken as booty by Adad-nirâri III.[21]

Having thus disposed of the Syrian vassals of Urarṭu, Tiglathpileser turned his weapons towards the east (campaigns of 737 and 736 B.C.). Most of the central Zagros was 'brought within the borders of Assyria', and an expedition was launched across the Iranian plateau, in the heart of the land occupied by 'the powerful Medes', as far as mount Biknî (Demavend) and the 'salt desert', to the south-west of Teheran. Never before had an Assyrian army been taken so far away in that direction. The scanty remains of another of Tiglathpileser's provincial palaces found at Tepe Giyan, near Nihavend and a stele recently discovered in Iran, testify to the reality of the campaigns and to the interest taken by the king in Iranian countries.[22] Later (probably in 735 B.C.) an attack was organized directly against Urarṭu, and Sardur's capital Tushpa (Van) was besieged, though without success.

In 734 B.C. Tiglathpileser returned to the Mediterranean coast where the situation was anything but peaceful. Tyre and Sidon were restless because of the restrictions imposed by the Assyrians on the export of timber to Philistia and Egypt; the troops had to intervene and made 'the people crawl with fear'.[23] Still worse, an anti-Assyrian coalition comprising all the kingdoms of Palestine and Trans-Jordania had been organized by the Philistine rulers of Ascalon and Gaza. Tiglathpileser himself crushed the rebels. The Prince of Ascalon was killed in action; the 'man of Gaza' fled like a bird to Egypt; Amon, Edom, Moab and Judah, as well as another queen of the Arabs called Shamshi paid tribute. Two years later Ahaz, King of

Judah, pressed by Damascus and Israel, called the Assyrians to the rescue. Tiglathpileser took Damascus, annexed half of Israel and established Hoshea as king in Samaria.[24]

Meanwhile, a series of *coups d'etat* had taken place in southern Iraq, following the death of Nabû-nâṣir, in 734 B.C. When the Aramaean chieftain Ukîn-zêr claimed the Babylonian throne (731 B.C.) the Assyrians tried to persuade the citizens of Babylon to rise against him and promised tax-exemption to any Aramaean who would desert from his chief. But after diplomacy had proved useless Tiglathpileser sent his troops against the usurper who was killed, together with his son, and decided to govern Babylonia himself. In 728 B.C. he 'took the hand of Bêl (Marduk)' during the New Year Festival and was proclaimed King of Babylon under the name of Pulû. The following year he died or, to use the Babylonian expression, 'he went to his destiny'.

Sargon II

The short reign of Tiglathpileser's son, Shalmaneser V (726–722 B.C.), is obscure. All we know for certain is that Hoshea, the puppet King of Israel, revolted and that Shalmaneser besieged Samaria for three years; but whether it was he or the next King of Assyria who captured the city is still a debated question.[25] Equally obscure are the circumstances which brought his successor to the throne, and no one can say whether he was a usurper or another of Tiglathpileser's sons. In any case, the name he took was in itself a promise of glory, for he called himself *Sharru-kîn* (Sargon), like one of the earliest kings of Assur and like the illustrious founder of the Dynasty of Akkad.[26]

Shortly before Sargon was enthroned two events of capital importance, which were to influence Assyrian strategy and diplomacy for a hundred years, took place in the Near East: the interference of Egypt in Palestine and of Elam in Babylonia. Both were the consequences of Tiglathpileser's victory, since his advance on the Iranian plateau had cut across the only trade routes left open to Elam, while his conquest of Phoenicia had wrested from Egypt one of her main clients. Elamites and Egyptians therefore joined the Urartians as Assyria's avowed enemies, but since neither of them were yet capable of attacking a nation at the peak of its power, they had recourse to slower but safer methods: they fostered revolts among the vassals of Assyria, and whenever the Aramaean sheikhs of southern Iraq or the princelings of Palestine threatened by the invincible Assyrian army begged for help, they lent them all the support they could in men and weapons. The political history of Sargon's reign is in fact nothing but the beginning of a long struggle against such rebellions.

Trouble, however, began at home, and for a year Sargon had his hands tied by domestic disorders which ended after he had freed the citizens of Assur from 'the call to arms of the land and the summons of the tax-collector' imposed upon them by Shalmaneser V. Only then could he deal with the critical situation which had arisen in Babylonia and Syria during the change of reign. In Babylonia – now the second jewel of the Assyrian crown – a Chaldean ruler from Bît-Iakin, on the shores of the Persian Gulf, Marduk-apal-iddina * (Merodach-Baladan of the Old Testament), had ascended the throne in the same year as Sargon and was actively supported by Humbanigash, King of Elam. In 720 B.C. Sargon marched against him and met his enemies at Dêr (Badrah), between the Tigris and the Zagros. His inscriptions claim complete victory, but the more impartial 'Babylonian Chronicle' clearly states that the Assyrians were defeated by the Elamites alone, while Merodach-Baladan in another text proudly declares that 'he smote to overthrow the widespread hosts of Subartu (Assyria) and smashed their weapons'.[27] Amusing detail: Merodach-Baladan's inscription was found at Nimrud, where Sargon had taken it from Uruk after 710 B.C., replacing it in that city with a clay cylinder bearing

* 'The god Marduk has given me an heir'.

311

his own radically different version of the event. This shows that political propaganda and 'disinformation' are not the privilege of our epoch. There can be no doubt, however, that the Assyrians met with a check, for we know that Marduk-apal-iddina reigned over Babylonia for eleven years (721–710 B.C.), behaving not as a barbarian chieftain but as a great Mesopotamian monarch and leaving traces of his building activities in various cities.

Not less dangerous for Assyria was the coalition of revolted Syrian provinces headed by Ilu-bi'di, King of Hama, and the rebellion of Hanuna, King of Gaza, assisted by an Egyptian army. But here Sargon had better luck. Ilu-bi'di who, with his allies, was defeated at Qarqar, was captured and flayed, whilst Hanuna was spared. As for the Egyptian general Sib'e, he 'fled alone and disappeared like a shepherd whose flock has been stolen' (720 B.C.).[28] Eight years later the Egyptians fomented another revolt in Palestine. This time the leader was Iamani, King of Ashdod, followed by Judah, Edom and Moab and supported by 'Pi'ru of Musru', i.e. Pharaoh of Egypt (probably Bocchoris). Again Sargon was victorious: Iamani fled to Egypt, but he was soon extradited by the Nubian king Sabakho who then held sway over the Nile valley:

He threw him in fetters, shackles and iron bands, and they brought him to Assyria, a long journey.[29]

The friendly attitude of the new ruler of Egypt towards Assyria accounts for the calm which reigned in Palestine during the rest of Sargon's reign.

We do not know for sure whether the Elamites had a hand in the dissensions which broke out among the ruling families of the central Zagros and gave Sargon in 713 B.C. the opportunity of conquering various principalities and towns in the regions of Kermanshah and Hamadan and to receive tribute from the Medes, but there can be no doubt as to who fomented trouble among the Mannaeans, the Zikirtu and other tribes of Azerbai-

jan, for Urarṭu remained in the north the main enemy of
Assyria. A glance at Sargon's correspondence shows at once the
care with which the Assyrian officials posted in those mountainous districts 'kept the watch of the king' and informed him of
every move made by the Urartian monarch or his generals, of
every change in the political loyalties of the surrounding peoples.[30] Yet, despite repeated interventions by Sargon, Rusas I of
Urarṭu managed, between 719 B.C. and 715 B.C., to replace the
Mannaean rulers friendly to Assyria by his own creatures. In
714 B.C. the Assyrians launched a large-scale counter-offensive.
The great campaign of Sargon's eighth year is recorded in
his Annals, but a more detailed account of it has reached us in
the form of a letter curiously addressed by the king to 'Ashur,
father of the gods, the gods and goddesses of Destiny, the city
and its inhabitants and the palace in its midst' – most certainly
a document written to be read in public at the end of the
annual campaign, with the view of creating a strong impression.[31] The march through the mountains of Kurdistan was
exceptionally difficult, owing to the geography of the region no
less than the resistance of the enemy, and our text abounds in
poetic passages like this:

'Mount Simirria, a great peak which stands like the blade of a lance,
lifting its head above the mountains, abode of Bêlit-ilâni; whose
summit on high upholds the heavens and whose roots below reach the
centre of the netherworld; which, like the spine of a fish, has no
passage from side to side and whose ascent from back to front is
difficult; on whose flanks gorges and precipices yawn, whose sight
inspires fear ... with the wide understanding and the inner spirit
endowed to me by Ea and Bêlit-ilâni, who opened my legs to overthrow
the enemy countries, with picks of bronze I armed my pioneers. The
crags of high mountains they caused to fly in splinters; they improved
the passage. I took the head of my troops. The chariots, the cavalry,
the fighters who went beside me, I made fly over this mountain like
valiant eagles ...'[32]

Sargon crossed rivers and mountains, fought his way around
Lake Urmiah and perhaps Lake Van and finally conquered

Urarṭu's most sacred city Muṣaṣir (south of Lake Van), taking away the national god Haldia. Urarṭu was not destroyed, but it had suffered a crushing defeat. At the news of the fall of Muṣaṣir, Ursâ (Rusas) was overwhelmed with shame: 'With his own dagger he stabbed himself through the heart like a pig and ended his life.'

But the Urartians had already had time to rouse anti-Assyrian feelings in other countries. In 717 B.C. the still independent ruler of Karkemish plotted against Sargon and saw his kingdom invaded and turned into an Assyrian province. During the next five years the same fate befell Quê (Cilicia), Gurgum, Milid, Kummuhu and part of Tabal, in other words all the Neo-Hittite kingdoms of the Taurus. Behind these plots and 'revolts' were not only 'the man of Urarṭu', but also Mitâ of Mushki (that is, Midas, King of Phrygia), whom Rusas had managed to attract into his sphere of influence.

At the beginning of 710 B.C. Sargon was everywhere victorious. The whole of Syria-Palestine (with the notable exception of Judah) and most of the Zagros range were firmly in Assyrian hands; the Medes were regarded as vassals; Urarṭu was dressing its wounds; the Egyptians were friendly, the Elamites and Phrygians hostile but peaceful. Yet Babylon under Merodach-Baladan remained as a thorn in the side of Assyria, and in that same year Sargon attacked it for the second time in his reign. The Chaldaean had enlisted the help of all the tribes dwelling in the ancient country of Sumer, and for two years he offered strong resistance to the Assyrian Army. Finally, encircled in Dûr-Iakîn (Tell Lahm) and wounded in the hand, he 'slipped in through the gate of his city like mice through holes' and took refuge in Elam. Sargon entered Babylon and, like Tiglathpileser III, 'took the hand of Bêl'. The repercussions of his victory were enormous: Midas the Phrygian offered him his friendship; Upêri, King of Dilmun (Bahrain), 'heard of the might of Assur and sent him gifts'. Seven kings of Iatnana (Cyprus), 'whose distant abodes are situated a seven days' journey in the sea of the setting sun', sent presents and swore allegiance to the

mighty monarch whose stele has actually been found at Lar-
naka. The repeated efforts made by its enemies to undermine
the Assyrian empire had been of no avail; at the end of the
reign it was larger and apparently stronger than ever.

As a war-chief Sargon liked to live in Kalhu (Nimrud), the
military capital of the empire, where he occupied, restored and
modified Ashurnaṣirpal's palace. But moved by incommensura-
ble pride, he soon decided to have his own palace in his own
city. In 717 B.C. were laid the foundations of 'Sargon's fortress',
Dûr-Sharrukîn, a hitherto virgin site twenty-four kilometres to
the north-east of Nineveh, near the modern village of Khorsabad.[33] The town was square in plan, each side measuring more
than one and a half kilometres, and its wall was pierced by
seven fortified gates. In its northern part an inner wall enclosed
the citadel, which contained the royal palace, a temple dedicated to Nabû and the sumptuous houses of high-ranking
officials, such as Sin-ah-uṣur, the vizier and king's brother.
The palace itself stood on a sixteen-metre-high platform over-
riding the city wall and comprised more than two hundred
rooms and thirty courtyards. Part of it, erroneously called
'harem' by the early excavators, was later found to be made of six
sanctuaries, and near by rose a ziqqurat of which the seven storeys
were painted with different colours and connected by a spiral
ramp. A beautiful viaduct of stone linked the palace with the
temple of Nabû, for in Assyria the religious and public functions of the king were closely interwoven. As expected, the
royal abode was lavishly decorated. Its gates and main doors –
as, indeed, the gates of the town and of the citadel – were
guarded by colossal bull-men; blue glazed bricks showing
divine symbols were used in the sanctuaries, and in most rooms
the walls were adorned with frescoes and lined with sculptured
and inscribed orthostats, a mile and a half long. Thousands of
prisoners of war and hundreds of artists and craftsmen must
have worked at Dûr-Sharrukîn, since the whole city was built
in ten years. In one of his so-called 'Display Inscriptions'
Sargon says:

The citadel of
Dūr-Sharrukin
(Khorsabad).
A, ziqqurat;
B, Sargon's palace;
C, C-E, residences
of high officials;
F, Nabû's temple;
G, outer wall of
the town;
H, lower town.
*From G. Loud and
Ch. B. Altman,
Khorsabad, II,
1938.*

'For me, Sargon, who dwells in this palace, may he (Ashur) decree as my destiny long life, health of body, joy of heart, brightness of soul.'[34]

But the god hearkened not to his prayer. One year after Dûr-Sharrukîn was officially inaugurated Sargon 'went against Tabal and was killed in the war' (705 B.C.). His successors preferred Nineveh to the Mesopotamian Brazilia, but Khorsabad remained inhabited by governors and their retinue: until the final collapse of Assyria.[35]

CHAPTER 20

THE HOUSE OF SARGON

Sargon's descendants – the Sargonids, as they are sometimes called – governed Assyria in unbroken succession for almost a century (704–609 B.C.), bringing the Assyrian empire to its farthest limits and the Assyrian civilization to its zenith. Yet the wars of Sennacherib, Esarhaddon and Ashurbanipal, which through the inflated language of the royal inscriptions look like glorious wars of conquest, were, at their best, nothing but successful counter-attacks. At the end of Sargon's reign the Assyrians ruled, directly or indirectly, over the entire Fertile Crescent and over parts of Iran and Asia Minor. They had a window on the Mediterranean and a window on the Gulf; they controlled the entire course of the Tigris and the Euphrates as well as the great trade routes crossing the Syrian desert, the Taurus and the Zagros. Supplied with all kinds of goods and commodities by their subjects, vassals and allies, they lived in prosperity and could have lived in peace, had it not been for the increasingly frequent revolts provoked by their oppressive policy and encouraged – at least in Palestine and Babylonia – by Egypt and Elam. The conquest of Egypt by Esarhaddon and the destruction of Elam at the hands of Ashurbanipal were therefore neither long-range razzias in the traditional style nor the fruits of a planned strategy: they were defensive measures taken by these monarchs to put an end to an unbearable situation; they represent the final outcome of long and bitter conflicts more imposed upon Assyria by her enemies than desired by her. In this endless struggle the Assyrians used up their strength, ruined their own possessions and failed to pay sufficient attention to the capital event which was taking place during that time behind the screen of the Zagros: the forma-tion of a powerful Median kingdom, the future instrument of their downfall. About 640 B.C. when total victory seemed at last achieved, when Ashurbanipal rose in triumph over all the foes of Assyria, it suddenly became apparent that the colossus had feet of clay.

Sennacherib

As implied by his name, Sennacherib – *Sin-ahhê-eriba*, 'the god Sin has compensated (the death of) the brothers' – was not Sargon's first-born son, but for some untold reason he was chosen as his legitimate heir, brought up in the 'House of Succession' and entrusted early with high administrative and military functions, especially on the northern frontier. He was thus well prepared for his royal duties when in 704 B.C. he ascended the throne of Assyria.[1]

Throughout his reign the northern and eastern frontiers, once the theatre of so many of his father's wars, were comparatively calm. Sargon's victories in Kurdistan, in Armenia and in the Taurus had struck such damaging blows at Urarṭu and Phrygia that they were no longer to be feared as potential aggressors. Moreover, these two nations were under attack by a new enemy: the Cimmerians (Assyr. *Gimirrai*), a warlike people from southern Russia, which at the end of the eighth century had crossed the Caucasus and entered Western Asia.[2] Already during the last years of Sargon's reign the Cimmerians, established in what is at present the Republic of Georgia, had risen in revolt against their Urartian suzerain and inflicted upon him a crushing defeat.[3] Now they were pushing forward along the southern shore of the Black Sea, in the folds of the Pontic range, harassing both Phrygia and her western neighbour, the young and fabulously rich kingdom of Lydia. At the same time other Cimmerians were penetrating the north-western corner of Iran, making alliance with the Mannai and the Medes. Sennacherib was no doubt informed of these events, but he was unable to intervene in these far-away regions. The four campaigns he launched to the north and the west were of medium scale and medium range; they were directed not against the Cimmerians or the Medes, but against restive vassals: princes of the central Zagros, city-chiefs of Kurdistan, rulers of Cilicia – probably supported by Ionian troops[4] – and one of the kings of Tabal.

In reality, the attention of Sennacherib was almost entirely absorbed by the extremely serious rebellions which had broken out in the Mediterranean districts and in Babylonia as soon as the news of Sargon's death was made public. In Phoenicia and Palestine Egyptian propaganda had persuaded Lulê, King of Sidon, Sidka, King of Ascalon, Ezekiah, King of Judah, and the inhabitants of Ekron to sever their links with Nineveh. In his fourth year of reign (701 B.C.) Sennacherib went forth to chastise the rebels. Lulê fled to Cyprus, Sidka was carried away to Assyria, an Egyptian army sent to the rescue of Ekron was defeated, and in all these cities more friendly rulers were put upon the throne. Then Sennacherib attacked Judah, besieged and captured the strongly fortified town of Lachish[5] and sent an army against Jerusalem. Here must be placed the dramatic scene described in the Second Book of Kings.[6] Over the wall of the sacred city three of Ezekiah's officials parley 'in the Jews' language' with three dignitaries of the Assyrian court – the turtânu, the rab-shaqê and the rab-sharish. The Assyrians mock the Jews, who trust 'upon the staff of this bruised reed, Egypt', promise 'two thousand horses' if they capitulate and finally resort to threats. But Ezekiah, encouraged by Isaiah the prophet, stubbornly refuses to open the gates of Jerusalem. A compromise is reached; the Assyrians withdraw and the city is spared, but at what price! Ezekiah has to give 30 talents of gold, 800 talents of silver, 'all kind of valuable treasures as well as his daughters, his harem, his male and female musicians', not counting several cities cut off from his land and given to the Philistines. It has long been thought that later in his reign Sennacherib had launched a second campaign in Palestine and, from there, planned to invade Egypt. He had already reached Pelusium (Tell el Farama, thirty miles east of the Suez canal) when his camp was ravaged 'by the angel of the Lord, who went out at night and smote one hundred fourscore and five thousand', says the Bible, 'by a legion of rats gnawing everything in the weapons that was made of rope or leather', says Herodotus, or, as Berossus tells us, 'by a pestilential sickness' killing '185,000 men with their commanders and officers'.[7] However, this episode is very controversial and rejected by most scholars.

In Babylonia the situation was far worse than in Palestine, and the war against the Aramaeans and their Elamite allies went on during most of Sennacherib's reign.[8] In 703 B.C. a year after he ascended the throne, Sargon's old rival, Marduk-apal-iddina (Merodach-Baladan), left Elam, where, it will be remembered, he had taken refuge, and assisted by Elamite officers and troops raised the entire Aramaean population of southern Iraq against the Assyrians, entered the capital-city and proclaimed himself King of Babylon. A few weeks later the King of Assyria led his armies against him. Defeated under the walls of Kish, the Chaldaean escaped and hid 'in the midst of the swamps and marshes' where he could not be found. Sennacherib plundered his palace, captured innumerable prisoners, deported 208,000 persons to Assyria and gave Babylon a king of his choice, Bêl-ibni, 'the son of a master-builder' who had grown up in Nineveh 'like a young puppy'. But three years later Merodach-Baladan reappeared in Bît-Iakin, his native country, and stirred up enough trouble to provoke a second Assyrian intervention. Bêl-ibni, more than suspect of collusion with the rebels, was taken away and replaced by Sennacherib's own son, Ashur-nadin-shumi. As for Merodach-Baladan, he refused to offer battle:

He gathered together the gods of his whole land in their shrines, and loaded them into ships and fled like a bird to the (Elamite) swampland of Nagite, which is in the midst of the sea.[9]

Six relatively peaceful years elapsed. Then in 694 B.C., under pretext of capturing the Elamite cities 'on the other side of the Bitter River, whither the people of Bît-Iakin had scattered before the mighty weapons of Ashur', Sennacherib organized a formidable combined land and sea operation aimed at securing for the Assyrians an access to the Gulf through the hostile Sea-Land.[10] A fleet of ships, built at Nineveh by Syrian craftsmen and manned by Phoenician and Cypriot sailors, was sent down the Tigris as far as Upâ (Opis).[11] There it was necessary to change rivers, probably because the Tigris in those days emptied its waters into extensive swamps and its lower course was not navigable. The ships were therefore carried overland to the Arahtu canal and continued their course on the Euphrates, while the army advanced on dry land. The meeting-point was at Bab-Salimeti, near the mouth of the river. The Assyrian troops embarked, crossed the head of the Gulf, landed in Elamite territory, conquered a few cities and returned loaded with spoil. Of Marduk-apal-iddina there is no longer question and we know that he died in exile. But the Elamites immediately retaliated. Hallushu (Halutush-Inshushinak), their king, invaded Mesopotamia, took Sippar. The Babylonians then seized Ashur-nadin-shumi and handed him over to the Elamites, who sent him to Iran where he disappeared, probably murdered.[12] Hallushu put on the throne of Babylon one of his favourites, soon expelled by the Assyrians and replaced by Mushezib-Marduk, a Chaldaean prince chosen by the local population. Again, there was a general upheaval of the inhabitants of Babylonia against the Assyrians. In 689 B.C. they used the treasures of Marduk's temple to buy the help of the then new King of Elam, Umman-menanu (Humban-nimena). A great battle took place at Hallulê, on the Tigris. Described as a victory in the Assyrian records, it was in fact a near-defeat.[13] Blind with rage, Sennacherib avenged himself on Babylon and dared to accomplish the unthinkable: he destroyed the illustrious and sacred city, the second metropolis of the empire, the 'bond of heaven and earth' which his forebears had always treated with infinite patience and respect:

'As a hurricane proceeds, I attacked it and, like a storm, I overthrew it . . . Its inhabitants, young and old, I did not spare and with their corpses I filled the streets of the city . . . The town itself and its houses, from their foundations to their roofs I devastated, I destroyed, by fire I overthrew . . . In order that in future even the soil of its temples be forgotten, by water I ravaged it, I turned it into pastures.

'To quiet the heart of Ashur, my lord, that peoples should bow in submission before his exalted might, I removed the dust of Babylon for presents to the (most) distant peoples, and in that Temple of the New Year Festival (in Assur) I stored up (some) in a covered jar.'[14]

The great gods of Sumer and Akkad could not leave such a crime unpunished. Eight years later in Nineveh, on the twentieth day of Tebet (January 681 B.C.), Sennacherib, while praying in a temple, met with the end he deserved: he was stabbed to death by one of his sons or, according to another version, crushed by the winged bulls that protected the sanctuary.[15]

Brutal and cowardly – most of his wars were fought by his generals – Sennacherib has been severely judged. Yet let us give him his due: the king who destroyed Babylon did an enormous amount of constructive work in Assyria. Not only were temples and public buildings erected or restored in several towns and colossal hydraulic works undertaken throughout the country, giving a fresh impulsion to agriculture, but the very old city of Nineveh (*Ninua*), hitherto a simple 'royal residence', was enlarged, fortified, embellished and turned into a capital-city worthy of the vast empire it commanded. Within a few years its circumference passed from three to twelve kilometres, embracing two separate boroughs now represented by the mounds of Kuyunjik and Nebi Yunus, opposite Mosul, on the left bank of the Tigris.[16] The outer wall, made of great limestone blocks, was 'raised mountain high', while the inner wall was pierced by fifteen gates leading in all directions. The squares of the town were widened; its avenues and streets were paved and 'caused to shine like the day'. In the northern part of the city (Kuyunjik) stood the old palace, but it had been neglected, and an affluent of the Tigris, the Tebiltu river, had ruined its foundations. The monument was torn down, and on a large terrace thrown over the Tebiltu was built Sennacherib's magnificent abode, the 'Palace without a Rival':

'Beams of cedar, the product of mount Amanus, which they dragged with difficulty out of (these) distant mountains, I stretched across their roofs. Great door-leaves of cypress, whose odour is pleasant as they are opened and closed, I bound with a band of shining copper and set them up in their doors. A portico patterned after a Hittite palace, which they call in the Amorite tongue *bit hilâni*, I constructed inside for my lordly pleasure.'[17]

Enormous copper pillars resting on lions of bronze were cast in moulds 'like half-shekel coins' – a technique which Sennacherib boasts of having invented – and adorned the palace gates. Protective genii of silver, copper and stone were set 'towards the four winds'. Huge slabs of limestone sculptured with war scenes were dragged through the doors and made to line the walls. Finally, at the side of the palace was opened 'a great park like unto mount Amanus, wherein were planted all kinds of herbs and fruit-trees'. To increase the vegetation in and around the town, water was brought from far-away districts by means of a canal cut 'through mountain and lowland', and the remains of a remarkable aqueduct visible near the village of Jerwan testify to the veracity of the royal annals as well as to the ability of the king's engineer.[18] Proud of himself and of his work, Sennacherib liked to be portrayed on the hills of his own country, of this 'land of Assur' to which he was fanatically devoted. At Bavian, near Jerwan, at Maltai, near Dohuk, and on the Judi Dagh, on the Turkish-Iraqi frontier,[19] can still be seen, carved in the rock, the gigantic image of the 'mighty king, ruler of widespread peoples', standing in front of the gods whom he had so gravely offended.

Esarhaddon

The murder of Sennacherib plunged Assyria into a violent, though fortunately short dynastic crisis, and Esarhaddon* had

---

* *Ashur-aha-iddin*, 'The god Ashur has given a brother'.

to conquer by the sword the throne he had legally inherited.[20] He was Sennacherib's youngest son, borne of his second wife, the very influential Naqi'a/Zakûtu and the fact that he had been chosen as the crown prince aroused the jealousy of his brothers. In the opening chapter of his annals Esarhaddon tells how their slanderous accusations turned his father's heart against him to the point where he was obliged to leave his own country and seek refuge 'in a hiding place' – possibly Cilicia or Tabal. The parricide is not mentioned, but it is clear that Sennacherib was dead when his sons 'butted each other like kids to take over kingship', thereby losing popular support among the Assyrians themselves. Encouraged by the gods, the exile hastened towards Nineveh, determined to claim his rights to the throne. The usurpers had deployed their army in the steppe to the west of the Tigris, blocking the road to the capital-city; but no sooner did Esarhaddon attack than their soldiers deserted to him, while the people of Assyria came to meet him and kissed his feet. Making his own army 'jump over the Tigris as if it be a small ditch', he entered Nineveh, and in March 681 B.C. 'sat down happily on the throne of his father'. The wicked brothers had fled 'to an unknown country', but the officers who had assisted them were put to death, together with their progeny.[21]

The first act of the new monarch was to atone for Sennacherib's sin by rebuilding Babylon. The gods in their anger had decreed that the town should lie in ruins for seventy years, but the priests found an easy way of overcoming this difficulty: 'The merciful Marduk turned the Book of Fate upside down and ordered the restoration of the city in the eleventh year', for in the cuneiform script the figure 70 becomes 11 when reversed, just as our figure 9 becomes 6. All the people of Kar-Duniash could then be summoned to 'carry the basket', and in due course Babylon was not only rebuilt but 'enlarged, raised aloft and made magnificent'.[22] Although the great city was probably not as thoroughly destroyed as Sennacherib would have us believe, the work of restoration occupied the whole reign, and it was not until the accession year of Ashurbanipal (669 B.C.) that Marduk and the other gods of Akkad could return from Assur, where they were held captive, to be reinstated in their temples. This act of justice won Esarhaddon the friendship of many of his Babylonian subjects: with the exception of an abortive attempt made in 680 B.C. by Merodach-Baladan's son to capture Ur, there was no serious trouble in southern Iraq during the rest of the reign, and indeed the Babylonians themselves repulsed the Elamite Humba-haldash when in 675 B.C. he invaded their country[23] In that other troublesome area of the empire, Phoenicia, Esarhaddon proved that if he could forgive he could also punish. Abdi-Milkuti, King of Sidon, who revolted in 677 B.C., was caught and beheaded; Sidon was 'torn up and cast into the midst of the sea', its inhabitants deported to Assyria and its territory given to the rival city of Tyre.[24] These drastic measures ensured – at least for a while – peace on the Mediterranean coast and left Esarhaddon free to deal with the serious problems that had arisen along the northern and eastern borders.

At the beginning of his reign another nomadic people from southern Russia, the Scythians (Assyr. *Ishkuzai*), had crossed the Caucasus and joined the Cimmerians already established in Asia Minor, Armenia and Iran.[25] The arrival of these warlike tribes, with which they were closely related, gave a new impetus to the predatory activities of the Cimmerians. In 679 B.C. they suddenly broke through the Taurus mountains, threatening the Assyrian garrisons in Tabal and causing some unrest among the vassal rulers of Cilicia. Esarhaddon swiftly counter-attacked, 'tramped upon the neck' of the Cilician rebels and 'cut with the sword' Teushpa and his hordes, forcing them to retreat beyond the Kizil-Irmak river. Cimmerians and Scythians then fell upon the kingdom of Phrygia, which they overthrew three years later with the help of the Urartians. Happy to see this human flood diverted from his own kingdom, Esarhaddon made peace with the Cimmerians, gave an Assyrian princess in marriage to the Scythian chief Bartatua (the 'Protothyes' of Herodotus) and repelled a weak attack from Rusas II of Urarṭu. On the eastern side of the Armenian massif, however, the repeated efforts made by the Assyrians to obtain tribute from the Mannai – now under strong Cimmerian and Scythian influence – met with failure, despite claims to the contrary in the royal inscriptions. To the south-east of Lake Urmiah the vast Iranian plateau was occupied by the Medes, in theory under Assyrian control but in fact independent, and this was the time (c. 680 B.C.) when Khshathrita ('Phraortes'), son of Daiakku ('Deioces'), was uniting their numerous tribes under his authority. Esarhaddon did all he could to prevent the development of a situation whose immediate effect was to cut down the supply of Median horses to the Assyrian Army and whose remote consequences were perhaps dimly foreseen. Several raids of cavalry were launched across the plateau as far as the desert to the east of Teheran, and three important princes of the Medes, who had begged Esarhaddon's help against their own vassals, were placed under Assyrian protection and imposed regular tribute. Farther south a series of successful operations in the central Zagros and an alliance sealed with the Gambulû – an Aramaean tribe settled on the left bank of the lower Tigris – aimed at forming a barrier of buffer states between Elam and Mesopotamia; but Esarhaddon struck an even greater victory when, after the death of Humba-haldash, he succeeded in putting on the Elamite throne a prince friendly to Assyria: Urtaki (675 B.C.).

While obtaining by a remarkable combination of force and diplomacy a precarious peace in Babylonia, in Phoenicia and along the 2,000 kilometres of his northern and eastern frontiers, Esarhaddon was preparing for his great project: the conquest of Egypt.[26] Already in 679 B.C. he had captured the city of Arzani 'on the border of the Brook of Egypt' (Wadi al 'Arish, in the Negeb). Then he had endeavoured to win the friendship of the Arabs, by now settled in large numbers in the Syrian desert, since without their cooperation no large-scale military campaign in the south-western regions of the empire could be undertaken. For example, he had given back to its former ruler, Hazail, the stronghold of Adumatu (al Jauf) which Sennacherib had conquered, together with his gods, and when a certain Uabu (Wahab) revolted against Hazail's son the latter received full military support from the Assyrians.[27] Finally, in the spring of 671 B.C., when he felt all the frontiers secure and the Arabs friendly or neutral, Esarhaddon led his army into Syria, the first step on the road to Egypt. An attempt was made to besiege Tyre, whose king had revolted, but the city resisted, and no time was wasted in trying to capture it. Marching southwards, the Assyrians reached Rapihu (Tell Rifah, south of Gaza) and crossed the Sinai desert, where they saw, among other dreadful things, 'two-headed serpents whose attack spelled death' and 'green animals whose wings were batting'. After fifteen days of considerable hardship they entered the green land of Egypt.

Despite the strong resistance offered by the pharaoh Taharqa and his army, the conquest of this vast country took surprisingly little time:

'From the town of Ishhupri as far as Memphis (*Mempi*), his royal residence, a distance of fifteen days (march), I fought daily, without interruption, very bloody battles against Tahasqa (*Tarqû*), King of Egypt and Ethiopia, the one accursed by all the great gods. Five times I hit him with the point of (my) arrows (inflicting) wounds (from which he should) not recover, and then I laid siege to Memphis, his royal residence, and conquered it in half a day by means of mines, breaches and assault ladders. His queen, the women of his palace, Ushanahuru, his "heir apparent", his other children, his possessions, horses, large and small cattle beyond counting I carried away as booty to Assyria. All Ethiopians I deported from Egypt – leaving not even one to do homage (to me). Everywhere in Egypt, I appointed new (local) kings, governors, officers, harbour overseers, officials and administrative personnel. I installed regular sacrificial dues for Ashur and the (other) great gods, my lords, for all times. I imposed upon them tribute due to me (as their) over-lord, (to be paid annually) without ceasing.'[28]

But Egypt was not to be an easy prey. Two years later, Taharqa came back from the south, where he had fled, recovered

Memphis and fomented a rebellion against the Assyrians in the Nile Delta. Esarhaddon was, once again, on his way to Egypt when he fell sick in Harran and died (669 B.C.).

Three years before, in May 672, in the presence of the Army and nobles of Assyria, foreign ambassadors and representatives from subject countries, he had solemnly proclaimed his son Ashurbanipal the legitimate heir to the throne and appointed another of his sons, Shamash-shum-ukîn, viceroy in Babylonia. That same day the vassal princes had signed a long and detailed treaty of loyalty to the crown prince, copies of which have been found at Nimrud.[29] Even Esarhaddon's mother, the Aramaean-born Naqi'a-Zakutu, had thrown the weight of her influence into the balance and obtained from the Babylonians and their future viceroy an oath of allegiance to the future ruler of Assyria.[30] Esarhaddon, the brave and wise king who left nothing to chance, had ensured that no dynastic crisis would follow his death.

Ashurbanipal

The change of reign took place smoothly, and the two princes sat upon their respective thrones: Ashurbanipal in Nineveh one month after his father's death, Shamash-shum-ukîn in Babylon one year later. The empire, however, was not divided. In all probability, the purpose of the arrangements made by Esarhaddon was to satisfy his Babylonian subjects by granting them sovereignty, though it had been made clear to all concerned that Ashurbanipal took precedence over his brother. The latter had full authority within his own kingdom; the former held sway over Assyria proper, the distant provinces and the vassal rulers, and was responsible for the conduct of war and the foreign policy of the empire as a whole. It was perhaps an awkward solution, but it worked perfectly well for sixteen years.

With the crown of Assyria Ashurbanipal* (668–627 B.C.)[31]

* *Ashur-ban-apli*, 'The god Ashur is the creator of the son'.

inherited the task, interrupted by his father's death, of repressing the Egyptian revolt.[32] The commander-in-chief (*turtânu*) was at once dispatched to that remote country with a small army corps which met Taharqa and his troops in the plain south of Memphis. The Assyrians won the battle and recovered the city, but Taharqa escaped them as he had escaped Esarhaddon's army. Ashurbanipal then ordered the formation of a larger armed force composed of Assyrians, Phoenicians, Syrians and Cypriots, but also of Egyptian soldiers recruited in the Nile delta. This army left Memphis and began marching towards Thebes (Assyr. *Ni'*), but it stopped on its way when the news broke that the princes of Lower Egypt were about to revolt:

All the kings . . . talked about rebellion and came, among themselves, to the unholy decision: 'Taharqa has been driven out of Egypt, how can we, ourselves, stay?' And they sent their mounted messengers to Taharqa, King of Nubia, to establish a sworn agreement: 'Let there be peace between us and let us come to mutual understanding; we will divide the country between us, no foreigner shall be ruler among us!'[33]

Betrayed by one of them, the conspirators were captured. Some were executed and others – notably Necho, King of Sais – were sent to Nineveh. The Assyrians knew that they could not proceed with their long march leaving behind them an ebullient Delta. Moreover, they were now some two thousand kilometres away from their homeland, in the heart of an unknown and hostile country with utterly foreign languages, customs and religion and which, in any case, they could not rule directly for a lack of administrators and troops in sufficient numbers. The only solution was to forgive and indeed cajole the kings of the Delta and win them over to their side, hoping that their hatred for Taharqa the Kushite (i.e. the Sudanese) would do the rest. Ashurbanipal, therefore, released the prisoners and put his stake on Necho, whose ancestors had reigned over the whole of Egypt. He sent him back to Sais, 'clad in a brilliant garment' and loaded with rich presents.

Two years elapsed, during which Taharqa died in exile. In 664 B.C., his son Tanutamûn (whom the Assyrians called *Tandamane*) entered Thebes amidst rejoicing, then sailed down the Nile to Memphis, in the vicinity of which he hit a thin screen of enemy troops, mostly Egyptians, and easily beat them. Necho was killed in the skirmish; the other kings of the Delta took refuge in the marshes whence they could not be dislodged. It was then that the large Assyrian army, stationed somewhere south of Memphis, began to move and march on Thebes. Entering that great and beautiful city at long last, they ransacked and destroyed it 'as if by a floodstorm' and carried away 'booty heavy and beyond counting', including two tall electrum-coated obelisks, each weighing almost thirty-eight tons. The metropolis of Southern Egypt never recovered from the devastation.

Although the inscriptions of Ashurbanipal are written in the first person, it is very unlikely that he visited Egypt. On the other hand, it seems certain that on two occasions he intervened personally in Phoenicia: in 667 B.C. to 'put under his yoke' Iakinlu, King of Arvad, who forced foreign vessels to unload their cargo in his own port instead of the Assyrian port, then in 662 B.C. against Ba'alu of Tyre who refused to continue paying tribute. Tyre which, like Arad, was built on an island but much closer to the Lebanese coast was reputed impregnable: it was besieged, reduced to famine and obliged to surrender. Similar tactics were probably used against Arvad, bringing the same results. Yet the rulers of these two cities were treated with astonishing leniency, no doubt because Ashurbanipal, whose army was fully engaged in the Egyptian venture, could neither afford to lose his Phoenician vassals nor spare troops for other fronts. He merely received the homage of the rebels as well as their presents and their daughters for his harem. For the same reason, he remained deaf to the calls of Gyges (*Gugu*), King of Lydia in western Anatolia – 'a distant country whose name the kings, my fathers, had never heard' – harassed by the Cimmerians. Gyges defended his kingdom alone and proved his success by sending two prisoners of war to Nineveh.[34]

The victory over Tanuatamûn and the Phoenicians gave Ashurbanipal a few years of respite during which he was able to devote his attention to the northern and eastern frontiers. The chronology of the reign is extremely uncertain, but it is probably between 665 and 655 B.C. that must be placed the campaign against the Mannai and the Medes described in the royal records, perhaps the alliance with Madyes, chief of the Scythians, which was to prove so useful a few years later, and the war against Urtaki, King of Elam, 'who gave no thought to the good done to him' by Esarhaddon and 'overran Akkad like a dense swarm of grasshoppers'[35] and was repelled. It seems that the alliance of the Cimmerians with the king of Tabal, their victory over Lydia and the death of Gyges killed in the battle, as well as their foray towards Mesopotamia, checked by the Assyrians, took place between 650 and 640 B.C.

Shortly before the middle of the seventh century the gods, who had always stood at Ashurbanipal's side, suddenly seemed to abandon him. About 655 B.C. Psamtik (*Psammetichus I*) – possibly a son of Necho – raised the flag of independence in the Nile Delta and, with the help of Ionian and Carian mercenaries, expelled the Assyrians from Egypt, pursuing them as far as Ashdod in Palestine. We owe this information to Herodotus,[36] for there is naturally no mention of this disaster in the cuneiform records, except for a passage in the 'Rassam cylinder' where Ashurbanipal states that Gyges 'sent his force to the aid of Tushamilki, King of Egypt, who had thrown off the yoke of his (Ashurbanipal's) sovereignty'. In other times an army would have been sent against Psammetichus, and Egypt would not have slipped so easily out of Assyrian hands. But it so happened that the bulk of the Assyrian army was engaged in a fierce struggle with the Elamites, and Ashurbanipal had to give up Egypt in order to save Mesopotamia. The King of Elam was then Tept-Humban (the *Teumman* of Assyrian inscriptions), a usurper who, six or seven years before, had seized the throne, obliging the sons of Urtaki to take refuge in Nineveh. War broke out when Teumman demanded their extradition, which

Ashurbanipal refused. The Elamites attacked, aided by the unfaithful Gambulû. Driven back into their own country, they were defeated at Tulliz on the Kerkha river. Teumman was killed in the battle; his head was cut off and triumphantly taken to Nineveh, where – as shown in a famous bas-relief – it was hung on a tree in the garden of the royal palace.[37] The Gambulû were punished, and Elam was divided between two members of the Urtaki family: Humbanigash and Tammaritu. There, as in Egypt, the Assyrians would not or could not put the vanquished country directly under their rule, and the half-measures they adopted left ultimately no choice but withdrawal or utter destruction.

This episode of the Elamite war was hardly concluded when Babylonia revolted. For sixteen years Shamash-shum-ukîn had behaved as a faithful brother, but gradually the virus of Babylonian nationalism overtook him and he came to think that, after all, Babylon was as much entitled to world domination as Nineveh. In 652 B.C. he closed the gates of Sippar, Babylon and Barsippa to the Assyrians and contrived a huge coalition comprising Phoenicia, the Philistines, Judah, the Arabs of the Syrian desert, the Chaldaeans of southern Iraq, the Elamites and even Lydia and Egypt. Had all these peoples attacked simultaneously, Assyria would have been overwhelmed. Fortunately, the plot was discovered in time. In a strongly worded proclamation Ashurbanipal warned the people of Babylon:

'Regarding the empty words which this false brother told you, I have heard all that he has said. They are nothing but wind. Do not believe him ... Do not, for a moment, listen to his lies. Do not contaminate your own good name, which is unsullied before me and before the whole world, nor make yourselves sinners against the divinity.'[38]

But the Babylonians refused to listen, and the King of Assyria marched against his brother. For three years, says a Babylonian chronicle, 'the war went on and there were perpetual battles'.[39] In the end Shamash-shum-ukîn lost hope; the legend has it that he set fire to his own palace and perished in the flames (648

B.C.).[40] Sumer and Akkad were pacified and Ashurbanipal put on the throne of Babylon a shadowy figure called Kandalanu, of obscure origin.[41] Soon afterwards, he proceeded to punish the other rebels and became at once entangled in a war against the Arabs,[42] who had not only lent their support to Shamash-shum-ukîn but were continuously raiding the western vassal-states. It was a difficult war, waged against elusive enemies fighting bravely and vanishing in a dreadful desert 'where parching thirst is at home, where there are not even birds in the sky'. Yet, here again, the Assyrian Army accomplished marvels: Uate' and his allies, the Nabataeans – who already dwelt around the Dead Sea – were defeated; Abiate' and his Qedar tribe were surrounded, cut off from water wells and forced 'to cut open their camels and drink blood and filthy water against their thirst'. Another Uate', son of Hazail, was caught and, a ring in his jaw and a collar around his neck, was 'made to guard the bar at the east gate at Nineveh'. The booty taken in this campaign was such, says Ashurbanipal, that:

Camels were bought within my country for less than one shekel of silver on the market place. The *sutammu*-workers received camels and (even) slaves as a present, the brewer as baksheesh, the gardener as an additional payment![43]

The Arabs subdued, Ashurbanipal sent his troops against his former protégé the King of Elam, who had accepted bribes from the rebellious King of Babylon and given him assistance. The vicissitudes of this long Elamite war, and the plots and revolutions which brought three princes in succession to the throne in Susa, are wearisome details that have no place here.[44] Suffice it to say that in 639 B.C. the Assyrians won the last battle. The entire land of Elam was devastated and its capital-city thoroughly plundered. This, incidentally, was mere retaliation, for among the spoil were found 'the silver, gold, property and goods of Sumer and Akkad and of the whole of Babylonia, which the former Kings of Elam had carried off in some seven raids'. The ziqqurat of Susa was destroyed, its sanctuaries

violated, its gods taken captive or 'thrown to the winds'. The
vanquished Elamites were even chased beyond the grave, and
their country symbolically erased from the map:

'The sepulchre of their earlier and later kings who did not fear Assur
and Ishtar, my lords, and who had plagued the kings, my fathers, I
destroyed, I devastated, I exposed to the sun. Their bones, I carried
off to Assyria. I laid restlessness upon their shades. I deprived them of
food-offerings and libations of water.

'For a distance of a month and twenty-five days' journey I devasted
the provinces of Elam. Salt and *sihlu* (a prickly plant) I scattered over
them . . . The dust of Susa, Madaktu, Haltemash and the rest of their
cities I gathered together and took to Assyria . . . The noise of people,
the tread of cattle and sheep, the glad shouts of rejoicing, I banished
from its fields. Wild asses, gazelles and all kinds of beasts of the plain I
caused to lie down among them, as if at home.'⁴⁵

Thus were avenged countless insults and settled a three-
thousand-year-old quarrel between Elamites and Mesopotamians.

Shortly after the sack of Susa Ashurbanipal celebrated his
triumph. From his sumptuous palace at Nineveh this learned,
magnificent and ruthless monarch could contemplate 'the whole
world' prostrate at his feet. Three Elamite princes and a 'King
of Arabia' were, literally, harnessed to his chariot. His treacher-
ous brother had met with a death appropriate to his crimes,
and he himself governed the Babylonians. The proud merchants
of Tyre and Arvad, the stiff-necked Jews,⁴⁶ the restive Aramaeans, had been subjugated. The Mannai had been 'smashed'
and the Cimmerians kept at bay. The rulers of Tabal and
Cilicia, at first hostile, had brought their daughters to the royal
couch. For having aided Psammetichus, Gyges of Lydia had
seen his country set afire by the wild warriors of the north and
lost his life, but now Ardys, his son, was asking as a favour to
bear the Assyrian yoke. Nineveh was overflowing with the
booty taken in Memphis, Thebes, Susa and countless other
cities, and the 'great name of Ashur' was respected and feared
from the green shores of the Aegean to the burning sands of

Arabia. Never had the Assyrian empire looked so strong, the Assyrian might so invincible. And yet how many shadows were there to this dazzling picture! The rich land of Egypt lost for ever; Elam conquered but turned into ruins; Babylonia devastated and, with the exception of a pro-Assyrian party of unknown size, inflamed with hatred for the Assyrians; the Phoenicians enslaved and losing their maritime and colonial empire to their Greek rivals; the vassal princes unreliable; the Assyrian army tired and depleted by a century of hard and bloody wars; the frontiers brought back from the Nile to the Dead Sea, from Mount Ararat to the first folds of the Taurus, from the Caspian Sea to the Zagros range; and beyond the Zagros, doubtful allies – the Scythians – and redoubtable foes – the Medes. The Assyrian empire, despite appearances, was weaker than it had ever been, and many must have thought secretly what the Israelite prophets dared to proclaim:

> And it shall come to pass
> that all they that look upon thee
>   shall flee from thee,
> and say: Nineveh is laid waste:
>   who will bemoan her? . . .
> There shall the fire devour thee;
> the sword shall cut thee off,
> it shall eat thee up like a cankerworm . . .
> There is no healing of thy bruise;
> thy wound is grievous:
> all that hear the bruit of thee
>   shall clap the hands over thee:
> for upon whom hath not thy wickedness
>   passed continually?[47]

CHAPTER 21

THE GLORY OF ASSYRIA

The reign of Ashurbanipal, like the reign of Hammurabi, is a momentous period in the history of ancient Iraq and calls for a pause. Having described at length how the Assyrian empire was formed, to be logical we should now examine what went on behind the façade of wars and diplomatic moves. What was, for instance, the social and economic structure of this vast political unit embracing the entire Fertile Crescent and stretching – at least for a while – from the Caspian Sea to the Nile valley? What were the materials, the routes and the volume of its internal and external trades? What ties linked in time of peace Nineveh with the vassal-states? What influence did the Assyrian domination have on the material and spiritual life of the Babylonians, Syrians, Iranians and other subject peoples and on the life of the Assyrians themselves? In short, what *was* the Assyrian empire?

This extremely difficult question could only be answered if the Assyrian empire were apprehended *in its entirety* and in great detail, but this would require much more material than is at present available. The peripheral areas, in particular, are poorly documented, since very few Assyrian administrative centres in Syria, Phoenicia, Anatolia, Armenia and Iran have been excavated, or even located on the map. For the moment, the bulk of our information comes from the state archives of Assur, Nineveh and Kalhu and from various official or private documents found in a few other cities of Assyria proper and Babylonia. Numerous and interesting as these texts are, they only provide occasional glimpses at the distant provinces, and, even with regard to the heart of the empire, the knowledge that can be derived from them on such topics as social and economic

337

conditions, land tenure and internal trade, for example, remains very limited and full of gaps or uncertainties.[1] All things considered, the subjects on which we are best informed are the king and his court, the central and regional administration, the army and, of course, the arts, and as these subjects constitute, after all, the main components of Assyria's vanished might and everlasting glory, it is on them that we shall concentrate. In a second chapter we shall take advantage of Ashurbanipal's famous library to describe the stage reached by the various Mesopotamian sciences in the seventh century B.C. By so doing we hope to dispel an impression which is all too readily gained from the reading of endless war-records: it would be utterly wrong to regard as a pack of wolves[2] an intelligent and often highly civilized people less thirsty of blood than of knowledge and culture.

The Assyrian State

'Great king, mighty king, king of the Universe, king of the country of Assur', the man who sat on the throne in Nineveh embodied all the overwhelming power of a preying nation and assumed the highest religious and governmental responsibilities. The officials who assisted him, the provincial governors who obeyed his orders, the ambassadors who conveyed his messages were not his ministers but merely his 'servants'. In many ways the king was the state. Yet the difference between an Ashurbanipal, absolute master of millions of people, and the *ensi* of an early Sumerian city-state, who ruled over a few acres of land, lay in the extent of their authority, not in its nature, and ideally the King of Assyria was only a human being selected among others to act on behalf of the gods for the benefit of the community.[3] He was the earthly representative and instrument of Ashur, just as Gudea of Lagash was the representative and instrument of Ningirsu. Indeed, before Shamshi-Adad I in the eighteenth century B.C. took the title of 'king' (*sharrum*) all the early rulers of Assyria called themselves *ishakkum* (= *ensi*) of the god Ashur, and this appellation remained for a long time in the long list of Assyrian royal titles.

The principle of divine election was much too old and theoretical ever to be questioned, but a principle of co-optation, which probably went back to the times when the Assyrian king 'lived in a tent' and was just a sheikh among others, explains both the *limmu* system – whereby high officials gave their name to reignal years – and the relative instability of the monarchy. The sovereign chose his successor from among his sons, yet his choice – although allegedly inspired by Ashur and confirmed by Sin and Shamash through oracles – had to be endorsed by other members of the royal family and by the nobility of the empire, and the domestic peace of the kingdom depended on whether they accepted it or not. The palace revolutions which, as we have seen, followed upon the reigns of Ashur-nirâri V and Sennacherib were essentially due to jealousy between brothers and to some high officials supporting other princes than the king designate. On the whole, however, the hereditary system was respected, and in their inscriptions several Assyrian monarchs take great pride in their long line of royal ancestors going back, in some cases, to the mythical hero Adapa.

Once chosen, the crown prince left his father's palace and entered the *bît redûti*, or 'House of Succession', situated in Tarbiṣu (modern Sherif Khan) on the Tigris, a few miles upstream of Nineveh.[4] There he was prepared for his royal functions and gradually entrusted with important military and administrative duties, which included replacing the king as head of the state in time of war. Some princes received a very thorough education. Ashurbanipal, for instance, describes his scholarly and military training as follows:

'The art of the Master Adapa I acquired: the hidden treasure of all scribal knowledge, the signs of heaven and earth ... and I have studied the heavens with the learned masters of oil divination; I have solved the laborious problems of division and multiplication, which were not clear; I have read the artistic script of Sumer and the obscure

Akkadian, which is hard to master, taking pleasure in the reading of the stones from before the flood ... This is what was done of all my days: I mounted my steed, I rode joyfully, I went up to the hunting lodge (?). I held the bow, I let fly the arrow, the sign of my valour. I hurled heavy lances like a javelin. Holding the reins like a driver, I made the wheels go round. I learned to handle the *aritu* and the *kababu* shields like a heavy-armed bowman ... At the same time I was learning royal decorum, walking in the kingly ways. I stood before the king, my begetter, giving commands to the nobles. Without my consent, no governor was appointed; no prefect was installed in my absence.'[5]

When the king died, mourned by all Assyrians, he was buried not in Nineveh or Kalhu, but in the oldest capital-city of the kingdom, Assur, where five heavy sarcophagi of stone, which once contained the bodies of Ashur-bêl-kala, Ashurnaṣirpal, Shamshi-Adad V, and perhaps of Sennacherib and Esarhaddon's wife, Esharhamat, but which had been plundered in antiquity, were found in vaulted chambers underneath the Old Palace. A recently published tablet indicates that the bodies of deceased kings most probably floated in oil in their sarcophagus.[6] An idea of the treasures contained in Assyrian royal tombs is provided by the startling discovery made at Nimrud in 1989 by a team of Iraqi archaeologists. There, under the floor of the domestic wing of Ashurnaṣirpal's palace were three tombs which had not been plundered. One of them yielded the skeleton of a man accompanied by no less than 200 pieces of gold jewellery. In another tomb were two female bodies, tentatively identified as those of Taliya, the wife of Sargon II, and Yaba, probably the spouse of Shalmaneser V. According to one of the most reliable reports,[7] this tomb contained some 200 gold jewels, such as necklaces, earrings, rings, bracelets, anklets and garment fasteners, as well as hundreds of small gold dress decorations and three solid gold bowls. To this must be added an ivory box, a bronze and ivory mirror and two alabaster jars with remnants of food for the after-life. The third tomb was that of Ashurnaṣirpal's wife Mulisu, but the great stone sarcopha-

gus in the middle was empty, suggesting that the queen's body
had been transferred elsewhere. Yet, 440 items of gold jewellery,
including a royal crown, were found in three bronze coffins
surrounded by remains of several skeletons. The total weight of
gold found in these three tombs has been estimated at fifty-
seven kilos, but the real value of these objects lies in their
beauty, the attractive marriage of gold with ivory, alabaster,
glass and semi-precious coloured stones and the skill with which
they were fashioned: in some pieces of filigree work some
threads were so thin that they could be seen only with a
magnifying lens. Further excavations in search of other tombs
were being planned when the Gulf War broke out.

The coronation followed the royal funeral after a short interval and took place in Assur. It was a simple ceremony. Carried
on a portable throne and preceded by a priest who called out
'Ashur is king! Ashur is king!', the crown prince went to Ekur,
the temple of the national god. He entered the sanctuary,
offered a golden bowl full of oil, a *mana* of silver and a richly
embroidered garment. Prostrate before the deity, he was
anointed by the high-priest and given the insignia of kingship:
'the crown of Ashur and the sceptre of Ninlil', * while these
words were prononounced:

'The diadem on thy head – may Ashur and Ninlil, the lords of the
diadem, put it upon thee for a hundred years.
Thy foot in Ekur and thy hands stretched towards Ashur, thy god –
may they be favoured.
Before Ashur, thy god, may thy priesthood and the priesthood of thy
sons find favour.
With thy straight sceptre make thy land wide.
May Ashur grant thee quick satisfaction, justice and peace.'[8]

The new king then proceeded to the palace, where the nobles
and officials did homage to him and relinquished their badges

* The goddess Ninlil, originally the female counterpart of Enlil, was the
spouse of the god Ashur.

of office. In most cases this gesture was purely symbolic, but it was meant to remind all those present that they were the king's servants and could be dismissed at any time. We may safely assume that the ceremony was followed by public rejoicing.

The King of Assyria governed in much the same way as all Mesopotamian monarchs, although the state letters suggest that more initiative was left to local authorities than, for instance, in the days of Hammurabi. Day by day he was kept informed of all matters of importance arising within the empire and in foreign countries; he gave orders and advice, appointed administrators, dealt with complaints, received and entertained high officials and foreign ambassadors, and carried on a voluminous correspondence with the aid of an army of scribes. As the supreme chief of the army, he drew up plans for military campaigns, inspected the troops and often personally conducted the operations. Off the battlefield he displayed his courage and skill by shooting wild game with the bow from his chariot, or by fighting lions with the spear in the palace grounds. Office work, receptions, hunting, these activities would be comparable to those of a modern head of state but for the fact that the King of Assyria was also a priest and as such was the slave of a complicated system of magico-religious practices which took much of his time and added to the heavy burden of his daily tasks. As the first servant of the gods and head of the clergy, he saw that temples were built or maintained, appointed some of the priests and took an active part in the main religious ceremonies of Assyria and Babylonia, such as the feast of the New Moon or the New Year Festival, as well as in certain rituals which seem to have been designed especially for him, in particular the *tâkultu* ('eating') ritual – a banquet offered to all the gods in exchange for their protection – and the *bît rimki* ('bathhouse') ritual – a royal bath during which prayers were addressed to various deities.[9] As the representative of his people, the king was 'manipulated like a talisman – or he became the scapegoat charged before the gods with all the sins of the community'.[10] He had to submit to occasional fasting, ritual

342

shaving and other humiliations, and when the omens were desperately bad for Assyria he escaped death only through the subterfuge of a 'substitute king'. We have already seen (p. 183) an example of this strange Mesopotamian institution in the Isin-Larsa period. A letter written during the reign of Ashurbanipal alludes to a similar situation:[11] it appears that to save the life of Shamash-shum-ukîn a certain Damqi, the son of the superintendent of Akkad, had been chosen by a prophetess in a trance, given a lady of the court in marriage and put to death with his wife after a short 'reign'. This was but an extreme and exceedingly rare application of a widespread belief. The Mesopotamians believed that the gods expressed their will in many ways and were constantly on the watch for signs and portents. Whether it was based on the movements of stars and planets, the interpretation of dreams and of natural phenomena, the configuration of the liver of sacrificed sheep, the flight of birds, the birth of monsters, the behaviour of drops of oil thrown on water, or the aspect of flames, divination was in Assyria a highly developed and offical 'science'.[12] The king was duly warned, verbally or by letter, of favourable and unfavourable omens, and no decision of importance was taken without first consulting the *barû*-priests (or diviners) or the royal astrologers. Here are two examples taken from the royal correspondence. Bêl-ushezib writes to Esarhaddon:

When a star shines forth like a torch from the sunrise and in the sunset fades away, the army of the enemy will attack in force.

When the south wind rises suddenly and having risen continues, and as it continues becomes a gale, and from a gale increases to a tempest – a day of destruction – the prince, on whatever expedition he goes, will obtain wealth.[13]

From Zakir to Ashurbanipal:

On the 15th day of the month of Tebet, in the middle watch, there was an eclipse of the moon. It began on the east (side) and turned to the west. The evil disturbance which is in the land of Amurru and its

343

territory is its own harm. The disturbance is the fault of the King of Amurru and his land for allowing the enemy of the king, my lord, to be in the land of Amurru. Let the king, my lord, do as he wishes. The hand of the king, my lord, shall capture him. The king shall accomplish his defeat . . .[14]

It would be a mistake, however, to think that the home and foreign policy of Assyria was ruled by superstition, when all we know of her history bears the print of realism. Astrologers and diviners gave the king a general set of circumstances within which he felt free to 'do as he wished', and there were even cases when he asked for several omens in succession until he obtained one that fitted his plans.

To run his vast empire the King of Assyria relied upon an administration which has been compared with that of the Ottoman empire (eunuchs included),[15] but was probably much more efficient. Around him were high dignitaries, such as the *turtânu* (commander-in-chief), the *rab shaqê* (chief cup-bearer), the *nâgir ekalli* (palace herald), the *abarakku* (superintendent) and the *sukallu dannu* (great chancellor), not to mention lesser officials who looked after the palace, its stables and its stores. Those who bore these time-honoured titles were not ministers in the modern sense of the term. With the exception of the *turtânu*, they seem to have acted mainly as advisers and to have performed various duties as the occasion arose, including provincial government. The latter, however, was generally entrusted to other high officials whom we have already met under Tiglath-pileser III, and we find here well-defined functions (see above, page 306) and a more firmly structured organization, for under the province governors (*bêl pihâti* or *shaknu*) came the district chiefs (*rab alâni*, literally 'chief of towns') and under these the 'mayors' (*hazannu*) and the Councils of Elders of small towns and villages. The higher officials resided in comfortable houses in capital cities[16] or in provincial palaces. They had their own courts and their own lands, employed hundreds of workers and slaves and could raise substantial armies if they so wished. Powerful and rich, they might have threatened the throne – as indeed they had done in the past – if the king had not kept them under control by a mixture of fear and rewards: fear of breaking the oath of obedience (*adû*) they had sworn and of being dismissed or even put to death (though there is no evidence that capital punishment was ever applied to them), and rewards in the form of grants of royal estates,[17] carefully spread over several provinces, distributions of war booty and shares in the multiple taxes exacted in Assyria and vassal countries. For greater safety some posts were divided and there was, for instance, under Sennacherib a *turtânu* 'of the right' and a *turtânu* 'of the left'.

A similar control was exerted by the king over the great cities of the empire and their population of priests, diviners, scribes, physicians, artisans and artists which, like all intelligentsia, occasionally tended to be troublesome. They too had sworn the *adû* and could be severely punished if they revolted, but they were the object of royal attention and favours. It is to this urban 'bourgeoisie' that Sargon addressed his account of the great campaign in Kurdistan, and some cities, like Assur, enjoyed almost complete freedom whilst others, even in Babylonia, were exempted from taxes, tolls and corvées.

Owing to the imprecision of terms and relative scarcity of documents, the economic conditions in the Assyrian empire remain imperfectly understood. The basis of the economy was, as always, agriculture, industry being reduced to artisan workshops around the cities. In theory, all the land belonged to the king, and indeed much of it did and was worked by peasants at his service or by people performing their *ilku*, but we learn from a census discovered at Harran and from land sale contracts[18] that there were small private landowners and fairly large estates belonging to the royal family or the temples, or purchased by high officials. Of internal trade we know almost nothing, probably because from the eighth century onwards most business transactions were couched in Aramaic on parchment or papyrus and have therefore perished.

Encouraged by the kings,[19] foreign trade was flourishing,

involving Egypt, the Gulf countries *via* Dilmun and the Aegean region visited by Phoenician ships. The goods most frequently exchanged were metals and rare items such as cotton, lint, dyes, precious stones and ivory.[20] It must be noted that their territorial conquests had given the Assyrians free access to the iron mines of Lebanon and the silver mines of Anatolia. Silver was used for payment in all transactions. Taxes were levied on merchandise that transited through the empire.

The population of Assyria was divided into three categories: free men (whatever their social status and including nomads), people who depended on the State or on rich landowners (the word *mushkênu* is used in some texts) and 'slaves' recruited among endebted families and prisoners of war; but slaves benefited from legal rights and could rise to important posts in the administration. To designate the inhabitants of their country the Assyrian officials only used vague terms such as *nishê* ('the people'), *napshâti* ('human beings') and *ardâni* ('servants') without distinction of rank, function or profession.[21] This suggests that in the eyes of bureaucrats the whole population of the empire was regarded as a human mass entirely at the king's service (*dullu sharri*), a service which included not only corvées for public works but also participation in what has been called 'the national industry of Assyria': war.

The Assyrian Army

Called up almost every year during three centuries, driven from the snow-capped mountains of Armenia and Iran to the swamps of the Sea-Land and the burning sands of Egypt, indefatigable and nearly always victorious, the army was the unrivalled instrument of Assyrian might.[22] Like the Macedonian phalanx and the Roman legion, the secret of its success lay in the quality of its troops, the superiority of its weapons and, as we may well imagine, the rigidity of its discipline.

Originally, the Assyrian Army was recruited among the peasants of northern Iraq, a mixed race of born warriors who combined the boldness of the bedouin with the tenacity of the farmer and the toughness of the highlander.

Since the reign of Tiglathpileser III, however, there were three categories of soldiers who may be called professional soldiers, conscripts and reserves.[23] Professional soldiers, selected, recruited and stationed in the main cities of Assyria and in all provinces of the empire, formed the bulk of the standing army (*kisir sharruti*). Some of them were Assyrian by birth but the majority came from formerly independent countries such as Babylonia or the Syrian kingdoms. Aramaeans were predominant, and among them the Itusi' and Guraya tribes provided numerous and much appreciated shock-troops. There were also auxiliary troops from among the Medes, Cimmerians, Arabs and even Elamites. Some units of the standing army formed the royal guard. The conscripts in turn may be divided into two groups: the king's soldiers and the reserves. The king's soldiers (*sabê sharri*) were generally young men who were temporarily mobilized in fulfilment of their *ilku* duty. They too were recruited throughout the empire and from all classes of society; they received a daily ration and waited, at home or in camps, to be called up, if needed, for the duration of a campaign. The reserves (*sha kutalli*, literally 'those behind') were men destined to be mobilized whenever necessary, to replace losses, for instance. Finally, all males of a population could be levied, together with the above listed categories of troops, in case of exceptionally long or dangerous conflict. In some wars, as in the Egyptian expedition, the King of Assyria asked his vassals to put their armed forces at his disposal.

This complex recruitment system had enormous advantages. For one thing, there were troops in every part of the empire, ready to quell a local rebellion or to repel a sudden attack on the Assyrian border. Secondly, the existence of a standing army made it possible to rapidly organize the forces that were required for a major military operation and to fight prolonged wars, whereas with the old system some campaigns had to be cut short so that the men could resume their agricultural activities.[24] We must add that the Assyrian army had other major assets, notably a well-organized system of communications by fast couriers or sometimes fire signals, and a state security and espionage system that would compare favourably with that of modern nations.[25]

Despite the wealth of war-records that have survived, we know surprisingly little about the size, organization and tactical methods of the Army. The number of soldiers engaged in action is very rarely given – Ashurnaṣirpal once speaks of 50,000 men; at the battle of Qarqar, Shalmaneser III fielded 120,000 men to the enemy's 70,000 troops – and if the enemy losses are grossly inflated, the casualties suffered by the Assyrians are practically never mentioned. If an overall figure were requested, we would venture to guess that in the seventh century B.C. the King of Assyria was in a position to mobilize an army of 400,000 to 500,000 men, reserves excluded. There are several gaps in our knowledge of the military hierarchy: from the *turtânu* and the *rab shaqê* (who often acted as his lieutenant) we pass almost immediately to the 'captains of seventy' and the 'captains of fifty'. We learn, however, that there were various grades among the cavalry officers, for instance, and that the king's bodyguard, the 'dagger-men', and other units had their own 'colonels'. The battles are invariably described in vague, though colourful terms, so that we are left in the dark as to the tactics applied, and only on rare occasions do we find references to ambushes and surprise attacks. All considered, our main source of information remains the innumerable scenes of war sculptured on slabs in the palaces of Nimrud, Khorsabad and Nineveh or carved in 'repoussé' on the bronze gates of Balawat.[26] The infantrymen depicted fall into two categories: light infantry (bowmen and slingers) and heavy infantry (lancers). The light infantrymen were clad in a short tunic and had no defensive weapon, whereas the lancers were protected by a coat-of-mail and by a round or oblong shield, sometimes taller than themselves. Slingers were, as a rule, bare-headed, but archers and lancers wore a tall conical helmet or, more rarely, a crested helmet resembling the Greek one. Besides their distinctive weapons,[27] most infantrymen carried a short sword, a dagger or a mace. All of them, at least since Tiglathpileser III, had half-boots laced in front. Cavalrymen wore a similar 'uniform' and were armed with a small bow or a long spear. They rode without a saddle or stirrups, but in late Sargonid times horses were protected by armour, so that both riders and mounts strangely resemble our medieval knights. A third category of soldiers fought on light, two-wheeled chariots drawn by two or three horses, each chariot carrying three to four men: a driver, one or two bowmen and two shield-bearers. Male and female servants, as well as wagons loaded with supplies and baggage followed the Army in campaign. Rivers were crossed either in ordinary boats or in reed-boats sealed with bitumen (the *qûfa* of the Arabs, still in use on the Upper Tigris), or on inflated goatskins.

One of the major assets of the Assyrian Army was its equipment in efficient siege-weapons. Many towns, particularly in Armenia and Syria, were strongly fortified, and to capture them was no mean task. But the Army included an important corps of engineers who filled in the moats, threw earthworks against the ramparts and dug tunnels, while the assailants shot arrows from fixed or mobile towers, battered weak points, doors or walls with enormous rams and progressed under cover of large shields. The besieged enemy tried to resist by hurling oil fire and torches on the war engines or by entwining the rams with chains. The final assault was made through breaches or from ladders. Once the town had been taken and looted and its inhabitants massacred or captured, it was either set on fire, dismantled and razed, or fortified anew, depending on its strategic interest.

War being an object of immense pride to the Assyrian monarchs, the official sculptors have depicted it in all its multiple aspects and with a profusion of detail. Scores of reliefs, obviously intended to illustrate the written descriptions that ran endlessly on orthostats, on steles, on monoliths, on mountain rocks and around statues, represent soldiers parading, fighting, killing, plundering, pulling down city-walls and escorting prisoners. In this series of pictorial war-records without equivalent in any country, among this almost monotonous display of horrors must be set apart some reliefs which have no parallel in the inscriptions and show soldiers at rest in their camps and under their tents, grooming horses, slaughtering cattle, cooking food, eating, drinking, playing games and dancing. These little scenes teeming with life give the tragedy of war a refreshing human touch. Through the ruthless killer of yore emerges a familiar and congenial figure: the humble, simple, light-hearted, 'rank-and-file' of all armies, past, present and future.

Assyrian Arts

The Assyrian Army has vanished long ago, routed and destroyed in the great disaster of the years 614–609 B.C., but the monuments of Assyrian art have mercifully survived, no less impressive by their quality than by their number.

Ever since the colossi of stone 'whose icy eyes had contemplated Nineveh' reached Europe for the first time, over a hundred years ago, the words 'Assyrian arts' have been suggestive of sculpture and particularly of reliefs. Sculpture in the round is poorly represented on the banks of the Tigris during the first millennium B.C. For some unknown reason, the capital cities of Assyria have yielded very few statues, and the best ones – such as the statue of Ashurnaṣirpal in the British Museum – are conventional, lifeless and inferior in many respects to the works of the great Neo-Sumerian masters. Reliefs, on the contrary, are always interesting, often attain to real beauty and undoubtedly represent 'the greatest and most original achievement of the Assyrians'.[28]

The technique of relief is almost as old as Mesopotamia itself, but it was for a long time confined to steles set up in temples. It found its first expression in the 'hunting stele' of Warka (Uruk or Jemdat Nasr period) and was carried on through such masterpieces as the 'Stele of the Vultures' of Eannatum and the

'Stele of Victory' of Narâm-Sin down to the Kassite and Middle Babylonian *kudurrus*. The Assyrians followed the tradition with a few religious subjects (e.g., the god Ashur as vegetation-god in the Berlin Museum),[29] but soon broke away from it to concentrate on representations of the king. The imperial steles, usually erected in conquered countries to commemorate Assyrian victories, are at best honest works of art, more remarkable perhaps for their historical value than for the quality of their execution. Reliefs carved on slabs, on the other hand, are probably of foreign origin. The idea of applying sculpture to the decoration of architectural elements seems to have originated in Anatolia among the Hittites, who, as early as the second millennium B.C., adorned the walls of their palaces with 'orthostats'. In the hills of their own country the Assyrians found in abundance a calcareous rock, rather porous and brittle but sufficient for most purposes, or they imported better materials from abroad. They had unlimited labour to quarry and transport the blocks, excellent artists to draw the subjects, skilful artisans to handle the chisel. They adopted the Hittite invention and raised it to an extraordinary degree of perfection. The colossal, yet lively winged bull-men and lion-men who guarded the gates of their palaces and seemed to emerge from them are treated with a harmonious sobriety in their masses and a wealth of precision in their detail which are probably unique. The slabs carved in low relief, which lined rooms and corridors and were made to be looked at more closely, are striking for the perfect balance of their composition, the sharpness of observation they reveal – especially where animals are concerned – and the sense of movement which pervades them. This is really 'grand art', superior to all that the world had already produced in this domain and second only to the sculpture of classical Greece.

While it is impossible for us to give here even a brief analysis of Assyrian reliefs, we would like to underline a peculiarity of this form of art which sets it apart from similar productions of the ancient Near East. All the monuments of Mesopotamia had hitherto possessed a religious significance and revolved, in one way or other, around the gods. In Assyrian sculpture, however, the central subject is usually the king – not a king supernatural in heroism and in size as the god-king of Egyptian reliefs, but a human, albeit dominating and exceedingly valorous, monarch. Moreover, while the king is portrayed parading, hunting, resting, receiving homage or tribute, or leading his armies in war, he is practically never shown performing his priestly functions. Genii, demi-gods, heroes are also represented, but the gods are conspicuously absent – except on rock sculptures – or reduced to their symbols: a spear stuck in an altar or a winged disc in the sky. Since kingship in Assyria was just as immersed in religion as in Sumer and Babylonia, there is only one possible explanation: the sculptured slabs which adorned the royal palaces were a form of political propaganda; narrative as much as decorative, they were intended not to please or placate the gods, but to inspire respect, admiration and fear in the human race. From a general point of view, the work of the Assyrian sculptors appears as one of the first attempts ever made to 'humanize' the arts and to deprive them of magical or religious meaning inherited from prehistoric ages.

It had been known for a long time that some statues and reliefs were painted. On the other hand, brightly coloured glazed bricks bearing ornamental or pictorial motifs were used in temples and palaces forming, as it were, a transition between reliefs and frescoes.[30] On the basis of recent excavations we may now assume that mural paintings adorned the walls of most, if not all, official buildings and of many private residences. Because the paint was laid on fragile plaster, it has generally disappeared, but at Khorsabad, Nimrud and Tell Ahmar (Til-Barsip) large fragments have been copied *in situ* or removed to museums. Mural paintings, like reliefs, had deep roots in the country and, at least in Assyria, favoured profane subjects. These varied according to the size and function of the room. They ranged from simple friezes of geometrical designs to elaborate panels covering the greater part of the walls and combining floral motifs, animals, scenes of war and hunting scenes and royal effigies, arranged in horizontal bands. From the examples recovered Assyrian painting appears as being by no means inferior to Assyrian sculpture, and the frescoes of Tell Ahmar,[31] display a great freedom of expression as well as high qualities of craftsmanship.

The Assyrians were expert – or perhaps we should say employed experts – in metal work, and they have left us some very fine pieces of bronze, gold and silver plates, vessels and ornaments of various kinds. Their female slaves, working in royal factories, wove carpets of elaborate design and embroidered with fairy hands, as can be seen from the robes worn by the kings and their courtiers and reproduced in stone in the most minute detail.[32] Their stone-cutters, contrary to their sculptors, preferred the traditional religious and mythological motifs to profane subjects, and the Neo-Assyrian cylinder-seals, engraved with extreme skill and care, exhibit a cold though often fascinating beauty. But among the so-called 'minor arts', a place of honour must be given to the ivories found in Assyria.

Known in Mesopotamia in Early Dynastic times, ivory-work fell into disuse, to reappear in the middle of the second millennium in countries under Egyptian influence: Palestine (Lachish, Megiddo) and the Mediterranean coast (Ugarit). The prosperity of the Phoenician cities, of the Israelite kingdom and of the Armaean states of Syria, and their intensive commercial relations with Egypt (which supplied the raw material) account for the extraordinary development of this form of art not only in Syria-Palestine (Samaria, Hama) but also in Assyria, Iran (Ziwiyeh) and Armenia (Toprak Kale) at the beginning of the first millennium B.C. There is no doubt that the majority of the ivories discovered at Assur, Khorsabad, Arslan Tash (Hadâtu) and particularly at Nimrud – the richest site of all[33] – had been received as tribute or taken as booty from the western districts of the empire. But a number of pieces, which are purely Assyrian in style and inspiration, must have been made in Assyrian workshops, though it is difficult to decide whether they were executed by foreign Syro-Phoenician artists or by the Mesopotamians themselves. Applied to the decoration of chairs, thrones, beds, screens and doors, or shaped into boxes, bowls, vases, spoons, pins, combs and handles, ivory was worked in many different ways: engraved, sculptured in relief, in the round or in open-work, inlaid with semi-precious stones, plain, painted or gold-plated. Not less remarkable was the variety of the subjects treated. Beside the purely Egyptian motifs, such as the birth of Horus or the goddess Hathor, there are 'women at the window', cows, deer and griffins which are more specifically Phoenician in style, and animals fighting together, heroes struggling with wild beasts, nude women or goddesses, hunting scenes and processions which are regarded by the experts as partly Syrian and partly Mesopotamian. These subjects, it is worth noticing, are emphatically peaceful. A few pieces portray the stiff figure of 'the mighty King of Assur' alone or accompanied by his soldiers, but those smiling women – the admirable 'Mona Lisa' from Nimrud, for instance – those gay musicians and dancers, those calm, enigmatic sphinxes, those cows suckling their calves, and in a graceful, loving movement turning their heads to lick them, are pleasantly relaxing. Whether they were made in Assyria or not, the ivories throw a new light on the mentality of their owners. They bear witness that the Assyrians were sensitive to charm and delicacy, just as their libraries testify to their taste for erudition.

CHAPTER 22

THE SCRIBES OF NINEVEH

In 1849 Sir Henry Layard, the pioneer of British archaeology in Iraq, was excavating Sennacherib's palace in Nineveh when he opened 'two large chambers of which the whole area was piled a foot or more deep in tablets'.[1] Three years later Layard's assistant, Hormuz Rassam, made a similar discovery on the same mound of Kuyunjik, in the palace of Sennacherib's grandson, Ashurbanipal. In all more than 25,000 tablets and fragments were gathered and sent to the British Museum, where they form the richest collection of their kind in the world.[2] On examination, it was found that 'Ashurbanipal's library' * could be divided into two parts: on the one hand, a relatively small number of 'archive documents', such as royal inscriptions, letters and administrative texts; on the other hand, 'library documents' consisting of literary texts proper (e.g. myths and legends) and a mass of 'scientific' texts among which those on divination, omina and exorcism were largely predominant. Many of these tablets were copies of ancient Sumerian and Babylonian texts made in Nineveh at the king's request, whereas others had been obtained from Babylon. Several letters preserved in the royal correspondence afford evidence that the kings of Assyria were craving for culture and had organized a widespread search for old inscriptions, particularly in the highly civilized countries of Sumer and Akkad.

When you receive this letter [writes Ashurbanipal to a certain Shaduna] take with you these three men [their names follow] and the learned men of the city of Barsippa, and seek out all the tablets, all those that are in their houses and all those that are deposited in the temple Ezida. . . .

---

* Most tablets found in Sennacherib's palace, belonged in fact, to Ashurbanipal, this monarch having used his grandfather's residence in his earlier years.

Hunt for the valuable tablets which are in your archives and which do not exist in Assyria and send them to me. I have written to the officials and overseers . . . and no one shall withhold a tablet from you; and when you see any tablet or ritual about which I have not written to you, but which you perceive may be profitable for my palace, seek it out, pick it up, and send it to me.[3]

Royal palaces[4] were not the only places in which valuable tablets were kept. All the capital cities and the main provincial towns of Assyria had temple libraries and even perhaps private libraries. There were important libraries at Assur and Nimrud, and Anglo-Turkish excavations at Sultan Tepe, near Harran, have brought to light a rich collection of literary and religious texts belonging to a priest of the moon-god Sin called Qurdi-Nergal and including, besides such well-known pieces as the Gilgamesh Epic, the Legend of Narâm-Sin and the 'Tale of the Righteous Sufferer', masterpieces of literature – like the amusing 'Tale of the Poor Man of Nippur' – which were formerly unknown.[5]

Once the ancient tablets had been brought to Assyria, they were either kept as they were or copied in the small, neat cuneiform script characteristic of the period. Many texts were partly or entirely rewritten and adapted to the fashion of the day, but others were copied to the letter, and it often happened in such cases that the scribe left in blank words or sentences which had been destroyed on the original, added his own commentary or wrote in the margin *ul idi*, 'I do not understand', or *hepu labiru*, 'old break'. Sometimes the scribe did not impress his style into clay but into wax spread over ivory or wooden boards, several boards being bound together by means of metal hinges like a miniature folding screen. In 1953 a number of such writing boards, some of them still bearing traces of an astronomical composition, were discovered at Nimrud in a well where they had been thrown during the sack of the city.[6] While administrative and commercial documents were usually stored in jars or baskets, library tablets seem to have been stored on shelves, but since they were invariably found scattered on the floors of ruined buildings, it is extremely difficult to understand the method of classification followed. We know, however, that tablets belonging to the same series were numbered, or ended with a catch-line announcing the first sentence of the next tablet. For instance, tablet III of *Enuma elish* (the epic of Creation) ends with the sentence:

They founded for him a princely chamber

which opens the narrative in tablet IV. Tablet XI of the Assyrian version of 'Gilgamesh' has the following 'colophon':

Table XI of 'He Who Saw Everything' (of the series of) Gilgamesh.
Written down according to the original and collated.
Palace of Ashurbanipal, King of the Universe, King of Assyria.

The diligence with which these written relics of the past were collected and the care with which they were preserved do honour not only to the scribes but to the kings, their masters. Paradoxically, the Assyrians who caused so much destruction saved for posterity a great deal of the spiritual treasures of Sumer, Akkad and Babylon and of their own country.

Mesopotamian Science

It is unlikely that Ashurbanipal's library was much used by the king himself. He might, for his lordly pleasure, have deciphered 'the stones from before the flood', or read the great epic tales – Gilgamesh, Etana, Adapa – but he hardly had the time or the inclination to read the thousands of tablets assembled on his orders. The palace library must have been accessible to the palace and temple scribes who could find there the reference document they required. It might have been part of an 'academy' (*bît mummi*, 'House of Knowledge'), such as flourished in various cities at various periods, perhaps founded to attract and fix in Nineveh the learned men of Mesopotamia. At their disposal were not only literary, historical and religious compositions in large numbers but also philological works, lists of

plants, animals and minerals, geographical lists, medical prescriptions, mathematical tables, astronomical observations, in a
word a corpus of scientific documents, an encyclopedia, as it
were, of Assyro-Babylonian knowledge. These documents are as
invaluable to us as they were to the ancient scholars, though for
different reasons, but while they call for a general survey of
Mesopotamian science, alone they are insufficient for this purpose. We have therefore in this chapter made use of sources
more recent or more ancient than the seventh-century Kuyunjik
tablets, in particular scientific texts from Nippur, Tell Harmal,
Assur and Uruk ranging from the end of the third millennium
to approximately the third century B.C.[7]

The Greeks who knew – and admired – the 'Chaldaeans'
mostly as magicians and fortune-tellers have done considerable
harm to their memory. It is true that magic in the broader
sense of the term (i.e. words or actions purporting to influence
supernatural forces) had always been closely associated with
Sumero-Akkadian religion and that the diviner's art had been
perfected and codified in Mesopotamia at a very early date, but
the vulgarization of magical practices did not come into full
play until the end of the pre-Christian era. Far from being the
last word in Babylonian wisdom, witchcraft and popular astrology developed as a sign of decay in a dying civilization, and we
now know for certain that Sumerians and Assyro-Babylonians
alike were blessed with almost all the qualities required for a
truly scientific attitude of mind. They had, first of all, an
insatiable curiosity, the curiosity that prompted them to collect
ancient tablets, establish museums of antiquities and bring
home from distant countries rare species of plants and unknown
animals. They had a patience, a devotion to detail apparent in
all their activities, from the compilation of accounts to their
works of art. They possessed an acute sense of observation,
studied nature with enthusiasm, recorded and correlated a vast
amount of data, not so much for practical purposes as for the
sake of pure knowledge, and at least in some fields, went a long
way on the road to discovery. Finally, their mathematics prove

that they were capable of abstract thinking to a degree rarely found in pre-classical antiquity. The only talent they lacked seems to be a sense of synthesis.

As soon as he went to school[8] the would-be Mesopotamian scribe had occasions to apply these inborn qualities. Teaching was essentially verbal – no textbook on any subject has ever been found – and therefore developed his auditive memory. Then, the intricacies of cuneiform writing, where each sign could be read either as a word or as a syllable with several phonetic values, and the fact that two widely different languages – Sumerian and Akkadian – had to be mastered obliged him to embark at once upon fairly complex philological studies. Instead of an alphabet, he had to memorize long lists of signs with their names, their pronunciation and their meaning in both languages. Several of these 'syllabaries' have survived, which is most fortunate, since without them we could never have understood the Sumerian language. In a second stage the student made use of conjugation tables, of vocabularies – lists of objects, technical terms or expressions belonging to the same category – and of bi- or tri-lingual dictionaries including Sumerian dialects, Kassite, Hittite and, later, Greek. Of special interest are tablets engraved with archaic pictographic signs side by side with their Neo-Assyrian counter-parts. Since pictograms had fallen into disuse about 2,600 years before these tablets were written and could hardly be of any practical value to the Assyrians, this is further proof of their love for pure research work. Science in general lay in the realm of the god Enki-Ea and was under the protection of the god Nabû, son of Marduk, while the goddess Nisaba, 'who in her hand holds the stylus', presided over the difficult and much honoured art of writing.

This system of education naturally inclined the Assyro-Babylonian scholar to record his observations and offer them to his colleagues and pupils in the form of lists.[9] Mesopotamian zoology, botany and mineralogy, for instance, have come to us in vocabularies, sometimes disconcertingly arranged, nevertheless representing a serious effort towards the classification of a vast material.[10] Geographical texts consist mostly of lists of countries, mountains, rivers or cities, and of itineraries which are extremely useful to the modern historian, especially when they indicate in *bêru*, or 'double-hours' (approximately ten kilometres), the distance between two towns. As far as we know, there were no true maps, but plans of fields and cities have been recovered, the most interesting being a plan of Nippur which remarkably matches the survey of the ruins made by modern archaeologists. We also possess a rudimentary 'map of the world' on clay, dating from the sixth century B.C.: the earth is a flat surface bound by a circular 'Bitter River'; in the middle flows the Euphrates; unfamiliar countries at the four points of the compass are described in a few words, the northernmost being called 'land where the sun is never seen' – which might refer either to a (mythical) dark region, as found in some literary texts, or to the fact that seen from Mesopotamia the sun never passes through the northern portion of the sky.[11] If we leave aside royal annals and building inscriptions, which were really not historical but propaganda and votive texts, we find that history was also presented in tabular form: king-lists, lists of eponyms and dynasties, synchronous lists, etc. Even Babylonian chronicles, which are nearer to continuous historical narratives, are in fact no more than developed lists of events. In addition, we have mathematical and astronomical tables and medical lists of symptoms and prognoses – to say nothing of the lists of gods, temples, feasts, omens and so forth. Indeed, Mesopotamian science has been called, somewhat derisively, 'a science of lists', but it must be emphasized that tuition being solely verbal, the documents that have survived are 'manuals' or 'vade-mecums' rather than textbooks. There is no doubt that the Assyro-Babylonians knew much more than it would appear from their literature: the transport and erection of huge blocks of stone, for instance, or the construction of long aqueducts, postulate an advanced knowledge of several laws of physics; similarly, certain principles of chemistry, carefully hidden under secret recipes, were successfully applied in the preparation of drugs and pig-

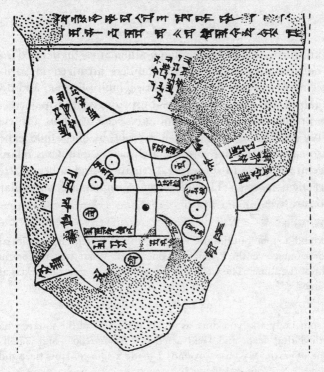

Babylonian 'Map of the World', 6th century B.C. (see text).
From B. Meissner, Babylonien und Assyrien, *1925.*

ments and the manufacture of coloured glass[12] and enamelled bricks. Moreover, in at least two domains – mathematics and astronomy – we are able to understand the mental mechanism that presided over scientific development, and it is precisely in those fields that the Mesopotamians made their greatest strides.

In a country where almost the entire population was illiterate, the scribes, frequently issued of families of scribes, well-paid and universally respected, played a crucial role; indeed the most important role in all periods, since without them Mesopotamian society would have been non-existent, or would have collapsed.[13]

Mathematics and Astronomy

Our knowledge of Mesopotamian mathematics[14] is derived from two categories of texts: lists of numbers arranged in various ways (increasing and decreasing series, multiplication and division tables, etc.) and problems. Surprisingly, the majority of these problems are exercises for advanced students (or even possibly intellectual recreations) and not, as one would expect in a so-called 'primitive' or 'archaic' society, problems relating to architecture, land-surveying, irrigation and other matters of practical interest. The following examples are particularly demonstrative:

Problem No. 1

'I found a stone but did not weigh it; then I added one seventh and I added one-eleventh. I weighed: one *mana*. What was the original weight of the stone? The weight of the stone was: 1 *mana*, 8 shekels and $22\frac{1}{2}$ "lines".'[15]

Problem No. 2

'If somebody asks you thus: as much as the side of the square which I made I dug deep, and I extracted one *musaru* (60^3) and a half of volume of earth. My base (ground) I made a square. How deep did I go?

'You, in your procedure operate with 12. Take the reciprocal of 12 and multiply by 1,30,0,0 which is your volume. 7,30,0 you will see. What is the cube root of 7,30,0? 30 is the cube root. Multiply 30 by 1, and 30 you see. Multiply 30 by another 1, and 30 you see. Multiply 30 by 12, and 6,0 (360) you see. 30 is the side of your square, and 6,0 (360) is your depth.'[16]

The sentence introducing the first problem shows that it is purely hypothetical. The solution is given, but the way to reach it must have been verbally indicated by the teacher. In the second problem, on the contrary, the procedure is fully developed. It will be seen that Babylonian mathematicians were fully conversant with cube roots, and this as early as the seventeenth or eighteenth century B.C., which is the date of this tablet. They also knew, of course, of square roots and were able to calculate the square root of 2 with only a very minute error (1.414213 instead of 1.414214). The calculations involved also point to the two main characteristics of Mesopotamian mathematics: they were based on the sexagesimal system, and while all systems of numeration used in antiquity (including the Roman system) were 'juxtapositional', they alone used a place-value notation or 'positional' system, that is to say a system where the value of a given numeral varies according to its position in the written number. (This is what we do when we write, for instance, 3,333, the same numeral being worth 3,000, 300, 30 and 3 respectively.) Both the sexagesimal and the positional systems offered definite advantages for calculations, but unfortunately, the decimal system was also used within units of the sexagesimal one, and the figure 'zero' was unknown until the Seleucid period. The interpretation of Mesopotamian problems is therefore often fraught with difficulty, even for experts, and we must assume that in many cases the students were verbally supplied with the necessary indications.

Another point to be emphasized is that without using symbols Babylonian mathematicians operated by algebraical rather than by arithmetical methods. The terms of many of their problems show that they could only be solved by a process equivalent to the use of quadratic equations. For instance, a problem like[17]

'I have added 7 times the side of my square and 11 times its surface: the result is 6,15 (in sexagesimal numeration). Write down 7 and 11'

postulates the equation $11x^2 + 7x = 6,15$.

It would also appear from some tablets that the Babylonians were familiar with functions and that their calculations occasionally involved serial, exponential and logarithmic relations. They thought in abstractions; they liked numbers for their own sake, almost forgetting their practical uses. For this reason, their geometry was much less advanced than their algebra.[18] They were aware of some fundamental properties of the triangle, the rectangle and the circle, but failed in their attempts to demonstrate them and measured polygonal surfaces by rough approximation. When tablets are inscribed with geometrical figures these are usually meant to illustrate arithmetical problems. Contrary to the Greeks, the Babylonians were less interested in the properties of lines, surfaces and volumes than in the intricate calculations suggested by their mutual relations.

Mathematics found in astronomy a wide field of application and gave this science a degree of precision unrivalled in antiquity.[19] The need for studying the movements of celestial bodies arose in Mesopotamia from a double preoccupation: metaphysical and chronological. The belief that what happened in heaven was reflected on earth, and the thought that if planets and constellations were identified with gods, kings and countries, and if their mutual relations could be foreseen, it would be possible to predict the future alleviated, to some extent, the dramatic uncertainty which was at the root of Mesopotamian philosophy. Astrology therefore was the foundation of astronomy, although the system adopted was never rigid and left room for divine and human initiative, predetermination in the form of horoscopes appearing only during the Achaemenian period. On the other hand, the Mesopotamians had to solve the problem of the lunar calendar. As far as we can go back in the past, the cycle of the moon had been taken as a convenient means of measuring time. The year began on the first New Moon following the spring equinox and was divided into twelve months of twenty-nine or thirty days. Each day began at sunset and was divided into twelve 'double hours' (*bêru*), themselves divided into sixty 'double-minutes' – a system which we still follow and owe to the Babylonians. Unfortunately, the lunar year is shorter than the solar year by approximately eleven days, so that after nine years the difference amounts to one full season. Moreover, the lunar month began in the evening when the New Moon was visible for the first time, but those who have lived in Iraq know that the Oriental sky is not always as clear as Europeans imagine and clouds, dust or sandstorms may render this observation impossible. How, then, were the official astronomers to decide that the month had begun, and how could they calculate in advance the exact date and time at which any month would begin? What were, in other words, the laws of the lunar cycle and – since the motions of the moon are linked with those of the sun – what were, the laws of the solar cycle?

The amazing results obtained by Mesopotamian astronomers in this field are obviously not due to the perfection of their instruments – they had only the gnomon (a rudimentary sun-dial), the clepsydra (a clock worked by flow of water) and the polos (an instrument registering the shadow projected by a minute ball suspended over a half-sphere). They are due to constant, accurate observation and to the use of mathematics for the extrapolation of the data obtained. At an early date the 'roads' of the sun and planets were determined and divided into twelve 'stations', themselves divided into thirty degrees (the origin of our Zodiac). We possess observations of Venus (Ishtar) written down under the First Dynasty of Babylon[20] and detailed catalogues of stars from the eighth and seventh centuries B.C. Soon, eclipses of the moon and, later, eclipses of the sun could be predicted with a fair degree of accuracy. For centuries the difficulty created by the difference between the solar year and the lunar year was solved arbitrarily, the king deciding that one or two intercalary months should be added to the year, but in the eighth century B.C. astronomers remarked that 235 lunar months made up exactly nineteen solar years, and on their advice King Nabû-naṣir, in 747 B.C., decreed the intercalation of seven extra months in nineteen lunar years. The 'Nabonassar calendar' became standardized between 388 and 367 B.C.[21] Meanwhile, a considerable amount of work had been done on the preparation of lunar, solar and stellar ephemerides. The tables of new and full moons and of eclipses drawn by Nabû-rimâni (the 'Naburianus' of Strabo) at the beginning of the fourth century are incredibly accurate,[22] and the greatest of all Babylonian astronomers, Kidinnu (Cidenas), who practised in about 375 B.C., gave the exact duration of the solar year with an error of only 4 minutes and 32.65 seconds. His error in the value of the motion of the sun from the node was actually smaller than that made by the modern astronomer Oppolzer in 1887.[23]

Admirable as it was, Mesopotamian astronomy lacked what we would call synthesis. Contrary to the Greek astronomers, who lived at the same time as the latest and best of them, the Babylonian astronomers never tried to assemble the numerous data they collected into coherent cosmic theories, such as the heliocentric system of Aristarchus of Samos or the geocentric system of Hipparchus. The reason for this probably was their total submission to the gods, which made them accept the world as it was and not as it could be imagined. Besides, their mind worked differently. To quote a specialist: 'The Greeks were philosophers as well as geometers, the Chaldaeans were empiricists and sophisticated calculators.'[24] As we shall see, the same defect – if it is one – can also be found in Mesopotamian medicine.

Medicine

No such precision can, of course, be expected from what is still regarded as an art more than a science: medicine. Yet Mesopotamian medicine is worthy of a special study for three main reasons: it is copiously documented, highly interesting and often misunderstood.[25]

The Mesopotamians believed that disease was a punishment inflicted by the gods upon men for their sins. The word 'sin' should be taken here in a broad sense including not only crimes and moral offences but also small errors and omissions in the performance of religious duties, or the unintentional breaking of some taboo. The offended gods could strike directly. Thus in the Code of Hammurabi, the Babylonian boundary stones and the political treaties of the ancient Near East they are called upon individually to send all kinds of 'grievous maladies' upon whoever would destroy or alter the document, and physicians as well as priests recognized the 'hand' of various gods in the symptoms exhibited by the patients. The gods could also allow demons to take possession of the sick person, each demon attacking by preference one part of the body; or they could let a man or a woman fall the victim of a spell cast by a sorcerer or witch. Illness was therefore essentially an ethical defect, a black mark, a condemnation which rendered man morally unclean as well as physically unhealthy; and a moral ailment calling for a moral cure, treatment was in many cases magical and religious. The *bâru*-priest, or diviner, was asked to find out by all the methods at his disposal the hidden sin responsible for the divine wrath, the demons were exorcised by the *âshipu*-priest using magical rites and incantations, and the gods were appeased through prayers and sacrifices.

If Mesopotamian medicine had consisted of nothing but moral catharsis it would hardly deserve its name. But an extensive study of the texts in our possession has shown it under another, entirely different aspect. There were in ancient Iraq true physicians who believed in the supernatural origin of most diseases, but who also recognized the causative action of natural agents such as dust, dirt, food or drink and even contagion; who sometimes referred their patients to the *bâru* or the *âshipu*, but who always observed the symptoms with extreme attention, grouped them into syndromes or diseases and applied chemical or instrumental treatments. Side by side with the sacerdotal and magico-religious medicine (*âshiputu*), there had always been in Mesopotamia a rational and pragmatic medicine (*asûtu*).[26]

The physician (*asû*) was neither priest nor witch-doctor, but a professional man belonging to the upper middle-class of the Assyro-Babylonian society. He had spent years at school learning the basic sciences of his time and further years with a senior colleague, mastering his art. The Code of Hammurabi, where nine laws concerning medicine (or rather, surgery) fix the price of certain operations and pronounce mutilation and even death for professional faults (see above, p. 205), gives the impression that the medical profession was controlled by the state and throws discredit on the ability of its members. But these laws are examples of judgements in exceptional cases, and there is no known instance of their having ever been applied. In fact, physicians were held in high esteem at all times and probably established their own fees. Consultants of renown were in great demand, and we know that royal courts exchanged doctors. Thus Tushratta, King of Mitanni in the fourteenth century, sent physicians to the pharaoh Amenophis III, and medical experts from Babylon were dispatched to the Hittite monarch Hattusilis III (1275–1250 B.C.).

We possess a considerable number of lists of symptoms and medical prescriptions written by physicians and several letters addressed to or sent by doctors. From numerous tablets or fragments of tablets written between the eighth and the fifth centuries B.C. but belonging to the same series Professor Labat has been able to reconstruct a complete 'treatise' of medical diagnosis and prognosis.[27] It comprised forty tablets and was divided into five 'chapters'. The first chapter, intended in fact for exorcists, gave an interpretation of the ominous signs which could be observed when proceeding to the patient's house. Thus:

When the exorcist proceeds to the patient's house . . . if he sees a black pig, this patient will die; (or) he will be cured after extreme suffering . . . If he sees a white pig, this patient will be cured; (or) he will be in distress . . . If he sees a red pig, this patient will [die?] on the 3rd month (or) on the 3rd day . . .[28]

Then came the description of a variety of symptoms grouped together by organs, by syndromes or diseases, and by order of occurrence. A last group of six tablets was devoted to gynaecological and infantile diseases. Throughout the treatise emphasis was placed on prognosis rather than on diagnosis proper, and treatments were rarely indicated. Similar texts, or collections of texts, dealt only with the diseases of certain organs, others were more particularly concerned with therapeutics. Here are a few examples chosen among the diseases which can readily be identified:

Epilepsy

If the (patient's) neck is constantly twisted to the left; if his hands and feet are outstretched; if his eyes facing the sky are wide open; if saliva drips from his mouth; if he snores; if he loses consciousness; if, at the end . . . it is an attack of *grand mal*: 'hand' of Sin.[29]

Urinary stone

If . . . for three days he has a stone of the bladder (*aban mushtinni*), this man will drink beer: (thus) the stone will dissolve; if this man, instead of drinking beer drinks much water, he will go to his destiny (i.e. die).[30]

Severe jaundice (Icterus gravis)

If the body of a man is yellow, his face yellow and black, and the surface of his tongue black, it is *ahhazu* . . . For such a disease the physician should do nothing: this man will die; he cannot be cured.[31]

Several texts were devoted to psychiatric diseases, including 'depression' which is not as modern as one may think.[32] While the diagnosis and prognosis of Mesopotamian physicians were a mixture of superstition and accurate observation, their therapeutics owed nothing to magic.[33] The oldest 'pharmacopaeia' known to date is a collection of recipes dating from the Third Dynasty of Ur, which describes the preparation of ointments, lotions and mixtures made from minerals and plants and might have been written two or three hundred years ago. Drugs were administered in every possible way short of injections: mixtures, potions, inhalations, fumigations, instillations, ointments, liniments, poultices, enemas, suppositories. It is often impossible for us to identify some of the simples and salts which entered into their composition, but in many cases ingredients that have only recently fallen into disuse or that are still used in pharmacy can be recognized. In the following recipe, for instance, opium by mouth and emollients in local application are prescribed for urinary retention:

Crush poppy seeds in beer and make the patient drink it. Grind some myrrh, mix it with oil and blow it into his urethra with a tube of bronze. Give the patient anemone crushed in *alappanu*-beer.[34]

And here is the complex, though rational formula of a poultice to be applied in case of 'stricture of the lungs':

Take ... parts of the kidney of a sheep; $\frac{1}{2}$ *qa* of dates, 15 *kisal* of firtree turpentine, 15 *kisal* of pinetree turpentine, 15 *kisal* of laurel, 13 *kisal* of opopanax, 10 *kisal* of resin of galbanum, 7 *kisal* of mustard, 2 *kisal* of cantharis ... Grind these drugs in a mortar together with fat and dates. Pour the mixture on a gazelle's skin. Fold the skin. Put it on the painful area and leave it in place for three days. During that time the patient shall drink sweet beer. He shall take his food very hot and stay in a warm place. On the fourth day, remove the poultice, etc ...[35]

In some cases the physician acted instrumentally. In a letter to Ashurbanipal the king's personal physician, Arad-Nanna, expresses his views on the treatment of epistaxis:

As regards the nose-bleeding ... the dressings are not properly applied. They have been placed on the side of the nose, so that they interfere with respiration and the blood flow into the mouth. The nose should be plugged up to its end that the air entry be blocked, and the bleeding will cease.[36]

Modern physicians would not change a word of this procedure.

Finally, we must quote an amazing text which proves that, contrary to general belief, the Mesopotamians had some notions of hygiene and preventive medicine. Zimri-Lim, King of Mari, who lived *c.* 1780 B.C. once wrote to his wife Shibtu:

I have heard that the lady Nanname has been taken ill. She has many contacts with the people of the palace. She meets many ladies in her house. Now then, give severe orders that no one should drink in the cup where she drinks, no one should sit on the seat where she sits, no one should sleep in the bed where she sleeps. She should no longer meet many ladies in her house. This disease is contagious (*mushtahhiz*, from the verb *ahâzu*, to catch).[37]

Thus Mesopotamian medicine, although still shrouded in superstition, had already some features of a positive science. Transmitted in part to the Greeks, together with Egyptian medicine, it paved the way for the great Hippocratic reform of the fifth century B.C. Yet in its two thousand years of existence it made very little progress. The physicians of Mesopotamia, like her astronomers, founded their art upon metaphysical doctrines and thereby closed the door to a fruitful quest for rational explanations. They knew the answers to many of the 'whens' and 'whats', but they lacked the curiosity to ask themselves 'how?' and 'why?'. They never attempted to build up theories, but modestly – and perhaps wisely – devoted their efforts to the collection of data. It is only fair to say that they often surpassed in their achievements the other learned men of the ancient East.

CHAPTER 23

THE CHALDAEAN KINGS

In 612 B.C., less than thirty years after Ashurbanipal celebrated his triumph, the palaces of Nineveh collapsed in flames and with them collapsed the Assyrian state. The Chaldaean kings of Babylonia, responsible with their allies the Medes for this sudden, violent and radical destruction, remained sole masters in Mesopotamia. Their rule witnessed a colossal amount of building work in southern Iraq, and Babylon – now the largest, most beautiful city in the Near East – became the centre of a movement of architectural, literary and scientific renaissance. It looked as though another Nineveh was born, and indeed the campaigns of Nebuchadrezzar II in the west suggest that a Babylonian empire was on the verge of replacing the Assyrian empire. But the brilliant 'Neo-Babylonian period'[1] was short-lived. The last great Mesopotamian monarch was succeeded by weak, irresponsible princes incapable of resisting the new, formidable enemy that had arisen in the East. In 539 B.C. Babylon fell without resistance into the hands of the Persian conqueror Cyrus.

Such are, in their tragic simplicity, the events which fill the last chapter in the history of Mesopotamia as an independent country, and which must now be told in greater detail.

The Fall of Nineveh

After 639 B.C. the annals of Ashurbanipal come to an abrupt end, leaving in complete darkness the last twelve years of his reign. The reason for this silence is unknown, but it seems to be due to a combination of civil strife and military setbacks. Herodotus, practically our only source of information for this period, tells us that Phraortes, King of the Medes, attacked the

Assyrians but lost his life on the battlefield and was succeeded by his son Cyaxares (*Uvarkhshatra*). Soon, however, the Medes were overpowered by the Scythians, to whom they were forced to pay tribute for twenty-eight years. The wild horsemen also poured over the Zagros, raided Assyria, Syria and Palestine and would have entered Egypt if Psammetichus had not bribed them off. Eventually Cyaxares recovered his freedom by massacring their drunken chieftains at a banquet. The same author, referring to another war, states that a Median onslaught on Nineveh was relieved by a Scythian army – which is quite credible, since we know that Ashurbanipal had made an alliance with the Scythian chief Madyes (see p. 332).[2] These events appear to have taken place between 653 (date of Phraortes's death) and 630 B.C. How they affected Assyria we are not told, but if Herodotus's account of the Scythian invasion is trustworthy the fact that their hordes could ride across the entire empire and safely return home is eloquent proof of the extraordinary state of debility into which the Assyrian Army had fallen. Without any doubt, the key to the final disaster of 614–609 B.C. lies in these obscure years.

It is now generally agreed that Ashurbanipal died in 627 B.C., and there is evidence that Kandalanu, the puppet king he had installed in Babylon, died in the same year. According to the latest and perhaps most plausible reconstruction of the events which occurred in that poorly documented period,[3] the ageing King of Assyria had abdicated in 630 B.C., leaving the sceptre to one of his sons called Ashur-etil-ilâni.* During three years all went well, but immediately after Kandalanu's death trouble began in Babylonia. Sin-shum-lishir, an Assyrian general posted in that region, revolted but was promptly ousted by the royal troops. Sin-shar-ishkun,† another of Ashurbanipal's sons, took possession of Babylon and proclaimed himself King of Babylonia. Early in 626 B.C. there were street battles in his

---

* 'Ashur, hero of the gods.'
† 'The god Sin has appointed the King.'

capital city, probably stirred up by Nabû-apla-usur * (Nabopolas-sar), often held as a member of the *Kaldu* (Chaldaean) tribe, who had made himself King of the Sea-Land. Sin-shar-ishkun fled to Nineveh, leaving Babylon to the Chaldaean. The year 626 B.C. was considered by Nabopolassar and his successors the official beginning of the Eleventh and last dynasty or, as we call it, the Chaldaean (perhaps wrongly) ⁴ or Neo-Babylonian dynasty. Then, war broke out between Ashur-etil-ilâni and his brother, and it lasted for three years, with several towns of southern Mesopotamia passing from one hand to another. In 623 B.C. Ashur-etil-ilâni was killed in battle near Nippur, and Sin-shar-ishkun became King of Assyria. As he could not accept much longer the secession of Babylonia, he declared war on Nabopolassar, and for another seven years this unfortunate country was the theatre of cruel battles around the fortified cities still held by the Assyrians. But the Chaldaean resisted, occupied the key city of Nippur and, in 616 B.C., remained in full control of the whole of Sumer and Akkad. By a happy coinci-dence, 616 also marks the starting-point of a series of Babylonian chronicles which enable us to follow step by step and almost day by day the history of Mesopotamia, including an invaluable account of the fall of Nineveh and other Assyrian cities.⁵

Meanwhile, the political situation outside Mesopotamia was deteriorating rapidly. There was little to be feared from the north: Urartu had been neutralized by its powerful neighbours, and the Cimmerians, now under Scythian domination, showed no signs of aggressiveness. But in Iran Cyaxares was reorganiz-ing his army, turning it into a powerful instrument of war. From Ecbatana (Hamadan), his capital city, he ruled over 'the three Medias', from Lake Urmiah to the region of Teheran, and indirectly over the Persians established farther south. In the east, the Elamites had recovered some degree of independ-ence, and the border town of Dêr had revolted. In the west the Phoenician cities seem to have severed their ties with Nineveh,

* 'O Nabû, protect (my) son!'

and so ineffective was the Assyrian control over Palestine that Josiah, King of Judah, was able to promote his religious reform in the province of Samaria, former kingdom of Israel.[6] In April–May 616 B.C., Nabopolassar left Babylon and marched along the Euphrates up to the district of Harran and along the Tigris as far as Arrapha (Kirkuk) and Assur, which he besieged without success. In order to win the friendship of the Elamites he returned the statues of their gods held captive in Babylonia; but he failed to obtain their armed support and dared not launch alone a full-scale offensive against his rival. Sin-shar-ishkun, on the other hand, driven onto the defensive and seeing his authority challenged within his own country, sought and obtained the alliance of the Egyptians, who had not forgotten their narrow escape from the Scythian invasion and observed with alarm the progress being made by the Medes in Iran and Asia Minor. The fact that Egypt was now called to the rescue by her former conquerors is significant of the desperate straits in which Assyria found herself. The Egyptians, however, did not actively support their allies until 612/611 B.C., already much too late.

The Assyrians might have resigned themselves to accepting the autonomy of Babylonia, and a compromise could perhaps have been reached if the Medes, acting independently, had not thrown their weight into the balance. At the end of 615 B.C. they suddenly invaded Assyria and took Arrapha. During the following winter they marched against Nineveh, but instead of attacking it, moved southwards and fell upon Assur, which they captured (614 B.C.):

He (the Mede), says our Chronicle, made an attack upon the town . . . and the city-wall (?) he destroyed. He inflicted a terrible massacre upon the greater part of the people, plundering it (the city) and carrying off prisoners from it.[7]

The Babylonians arrived too late to take part in the action. Nabopolassar met Cyaxares (called by the Babylonians *Umakish-tar*) under the walls of Assur and 'they established mutual friendship and peace'. The alliance was later sealed by the marriage of Nabopolassar's son, Nebuchadrezzar, with Cyaxares' daughter, Amytis.[8] From then on Babylonians and Medes were to fight hand in hand, and Assyria was doomed.

The following year was spent by Nabopolassar in unsuccessful campaigns along the Euphrates, and it was not until the summer of 612 B.C. that the final assault was launched against Assyria's main city, Nineveh. The town was strongly defended, and Babylonians and Medes at first made very slow progress. After three months of siege, however,

A strong attack they made against the city and in the month of *Ab* (July–August), the . . . th day, the city was captured, a great defeat of the chief (people) was made. On that day Sin-shar-ishkun, the Assyrian king, [was killed?]. The great spoil of the city and temple they carried off and turned the city into a ruin-mound (*tilu*) and heaps of debris.[9]

By the end of 612 B.C. the three capital cities of Assyria – Assur, the religious metropolis, Nineveh, the administrative centre, and probably Nimrud, the military headquarters – as well as all the main Assyrian towns[10] had been destroyed. Yet the ghost of an Assyrian kingdom survived for three years. Sin-shar-ishkun having been killed, one of his officers sat on the throne under the name of Ashur-uballiṭ, the same name, ironically, as that of the great monarch who in the thirteenth century had freed his country from the Hurri-Mitannians (see above p. 260). Rallying what was left of the Assyrian Army, he shut himself up in Harran with a few Egyptian troops at last sent to the rescue. In 610 B.C. the Babylonians and the *Umman-manda* (Medes?)[11] marched against Harran. The Assyro-Egyptians abandoned it to take refuge beyond the Euphrates, and the city fell into the hands of the Medes. The following year, after an unsuccessful attempt to recover his stronghold, Assur-uballiṭ disappeared.

Thus ended miserably within the short space of three years the giant who for three centuries had caused the world to tremble with fear. In a few words Nabopolassar wrote his epitaph:

'I slaughtered the land of Subarum (Assyria), I turned the hostile land into heaps and ruins.

'The Assyrian, who since distant days had ruled over all the peoples, and with his heavy yoke had brought injury to the people of the Land, his feet from Akkad I turned back, his yoke I threw off.'[12]

No one, as far as we know, sat on the ruins of Nineveh to write a lamentation.[13]

Nebuchadrezzar

The Medes do not appear to have laid claim to the kingdom which they had contributed to overthrow, but they kept troops for some time in Harran, possibly as a potential starting-point for further conquests in Asia Minor. The Babylonians remained in full possession of an Assyria which had virtually been wiped off the map, and except for a few provincial towns such as Arrapha (Kirkuk) apparently spared by the war, they did not occupy it; nor did they repair the damage they had caused. All their efforts were devoted to the religious and cultural revival of southern Mesopotamia, and in the field of foreign policy, to the protection of the Taurus frontier and the subjection of Syria-Palestine. The latter country had been rid of its Assyrian masters only to fall into Egyptian hands. In a belated and fruitless effort to save his allies, pharaoh Necho II had invaded it in 609 B.C., defeating and killing Josiah, King of Judah, who foolishly tried to bar his way,[14] and now Egyptian troops held Karkemish and the crossing of the Euphrates. The possession of Karkemish and the control of the Phoenician coast and hinterland were even more important to the Babylonians than they had been to the Assyrians, since practically all their trade was now with the West. The Chaldaean kings could forsake all hope of reconstructing the Assyrian empire; they could abandon to the Medes the lands beyond the mountains; but they could not accept being deprived of rich provinces, nor seeing their gateway to the Mediterranean blocked by the Egyptians, the Aramaeans of Syria or the Phoenicians themselves. Their reigns are filled with repeated campaigns in 'the land of Hatti', and their so-called conquests were in fact nothing but an endless struggle to secure the vital sources of Babylonian prosperity.

After his final victory over the Assyrians, Nabopolassar, who was now ageing, relied more and more upon his son Nabû-kudurri-uṣur ('Nebuchadrezzar') for the conduct of military operations. In 607 B.C. the young and energetic crown prince was entrusted with the task of dislodging the Egyptians from Syria. After two years of unsuccessful attempts at establishing bridgeheads at other points of the Euphrates valley, Nebucha-drezzar mustered his army and attacked Karkemish (May–June 605 B.C.). The Egyptian garrison, reinforced by Greek mercenaries, put up strong resistance, but was finally overwhelmed and massacred or captured:

As for the rest of the Egyptian army which had escaped from the defeat (so quickly that) no weapon had reached them, in the district of Hama the Babylonian troops overtook and defeated them so that not a single man escaped to his own country.[15]

The whole of Syria-Palestine now lay open to the Babylonians. They had already advanced as far as Pelusium, on the Egyptian border, when Nebuchadrezzar heard of his father's death. Wasting no time – the death of an Oriental monarch was always a critical moment – he returned to Babylon 'in twenty-three days' and was crowned upon his arrival in the capital-city (23 September 605 B.C.).[16]

The Babylonians should have known that if invading Syria had been relatively easy, holding it would be extremely difficult. The northern Syrians would be generally submissive, but neither the Phoenicians, nor the Philistines, nor the Jews could whole-heartedly accept paying Babylon a tribute which they had just ceased paying – so reluctantly – to Nineveh. Moreover, Egypt, which had just seen its age-old dream of a Syrian 'colony' take shape and vanish, would now more than ever throw oil on the fire. Soon Nebuchadrezzar found himself compelled to display his strength almost every year in the Mediterranean areas and to quell rebellion after rebellion, as Sargon and his successors had done. Twelve months after the battle of Karkemish he was in Syria again, collecting tribute from Damascus, Tyre, Sidon and Jerusalem, but also destroying Ascalon, whose ruler had revolted. In 601 B.C. the Chronicle mentions a great, though inconclusive, battle between the King of Babylon and the King of Egypt – 'they fought with each other in close battle and inflicted grave havoc on each other'. In 599 B.C. from one of his Syrian camps Nebuchadrezzar 'sent out his companies scouring the desert' against the Arabs of Qedar.[17] During the winter of 598/97 B.C. Jehoiakim, King of Judah, deaf to the warnings of Jeremiah the prophet, refused to pay tribute then died. Babylonian retaliation came swiftly. On 16 March 597 B.C. Jerusalem was captured, its young king Jehoiakin was deported, together with 3,000 Jews, and replaced by one Mattaniah nicknamed Zedekiah.[18] An unfortunate gap in the series of Babylonian Chronicles deprives us of a continuous narrative covering the following years, but we know from other sources that Necho's successor, Psammetichus II, led an expedition to Syria (c. 600 B.C.) and that pharaoh Apries (588–562 B.C.) captured Gaza and attacked Tyre and Sidon.[19] The proximity of an Egyptian army and the belief that he could rely upon its assistance probably encouraged Zedekiah to revolt. From his headquarters at Riblah, near Homs, Nebuchadrezzar directed the operations. After a siege of eighteen months Jerusalem was captured by storm on 29 July 587. Zedekiah, who had fled towards Jericho, was taken prisoner:

So they took the king and brought him up to the King of Babylon to Riblah; and they gave judgment upon him. And they slew the sons of Zedekiah before his eyes, and put out the eyes of Zedekiah, and bound him with fetters of brass, and carried him off to Babylon.[20]

Thousands of Jews were deported with their king, while others took refuge in Egypt. A native governor was appointed over Judah. Jerusalem was looted, its walls were 'broken down round about' and the House of the Lord, the temple that Solomon had built, was burnt down. Thus 135 years after Israel, 'Judah was carried away out of the land'.[21]

The last action of Nebuchadrezzar in Syria, of which we have a record, is a siege of Tyre which lasted, we are told, no less than thirteen years and ended with the capture of the city and the replacement of its king by another. A fragmentary tablet in the British Museum alludes to a campaign against pharaoh Amasis in 568 B.C. and mentions an Egyptian town, but this cannot be regarded as suffucent proof that the Babylonians ever set foot in the Nile valley.[22] Ten years at least before the end of the reign the western districts were firmly in Nebuchadrezzar's hands, and Mount Lebanon, that inexhaustible source of timber, was open to regular exploitation:

'I made that country happy by eradicating its enemy everywhere. All its scattered inhabitants I led back to their settlements. What no former king had done I achieved: I cut through steep mountains, I split rocks, opened passages and I constructed a straight road for the (transport of the) cedars. I made the inhabitants of Lebanon live in safety together and let nobody disturb them.'[23]

Meanwhile, the Medes were progressing in a north-westerly direction, invading successively Armenia (c. 590) – and Cappadocia. In 585 B.C., when Cyaxares the Mede and Alyattes of Lydia found each other face to face at the 'Battle of the Eclipse' and unable to solve their conflict by arms, Nebuchadrezzar acted as referee, negotiated a truce between the two countries and fixed their common frontier on the Halys River (Kizil Irmak).[24] But, either in agreement with his ally or as a precaution against a possible Median invasion from the north, he occupied Cilicia and fortified several towns 'along the border of Urartu'.

The last years of Nebuchadrezzar's reign are obscure. All we know is that this great king died of an illness in the first days of October 562 B.C. His son Amêl-Marduk ('Evil-Merodach' of the Old Testament) ruled for only two years. According to Berossus,[25] 'because he managed affairs in a lawless and outrageous fashion he was plotted against and killed by his sister's husband Neriglisaros ('Neriglissar', Nergal-shar-usur), a businessman whom Nebuchadrezzar had entrusted with official functions. Apart from the restoration of temples and other public works mentioned in his inscriptions, the only major achievement we know of in his four years of reign (559–556 B.C.) was a victorious military campaign against Appuashu, King of Pirindu (West Cilicia) who had plundered the coastal plain of East Cilicia, then in Babylonian hands, and captured some of its inhabitants.[26] After his death, Neriglissar was succeeded by his son Labâshi-Marduk who was still a child but, we are told, exhibited such signs of wickedness that his friends plotted and, nine months later, tortured him to death. The conspirators then met and decided to raise to the throne one of them, Nabû-na'id* (Nabonidus), (June 556 B.C.). But in the previous four years events had taken place in Iran which were of such importance that they were to change, once again, the fate of the Ancient World.

The Fall of Babylon

Nabû-na'id or, as we call him after the Greeks, Nabonidus (556–539 B.C.) is one of the most enigmatic and fascinating figures in the long series of Mesopotamian monarchs.[27] He was the son of a certain Nabû-balatsu-iqbi, who belonged to the Babylonian nobility but was not of royal blood, and of a votaress of the god Sin in the city of Harran. A man in his sixties when he ascended the throne, he had held important administrative functions under Nebuchadrezzar and Neriglissar. Extremely fond of his mother – she died in 547 B.C., at the age of one hundred and four, and was buried with royal honours[28] – he had inherited from her a keen interest in religious affairs and a special, almost exclusive devotion to the god she had served all her life. After the death of Nabû-na'id, the pro-Persian

---

* 'The god Nabû has exalted' (the king).

Babylonians, anxious to please their new sovereign, did everything in their power to sully his memory. In a libel known as
'the Verse Account of Nabonidus' they accused him of being a
madman, a liar boasting of victories he had never won and,
above all, a heretic who blasphemed Marduk and worshipped
under the name of Sin 'a deity which nobody had ever seen in
the country'.[29] These vicious accusations met with a success that
their authors themselves could hardly have expected. Though a
confusion of names they gave birth to the story of Nebuchadrezzar's madness, as told in the Book of Daniel, and found an echo
in a fragment of the famous Dead Sea Scrolls.[30] Even the most
cautious of modern historians are obliged to admit that they
contain a spark of truth. Some at least of Nabonidus's inscriptions suggest that Sin ranked higher in his esteem than the
national god Marduk, and the sanctuaries of the moon-god
throughout the country were the objects of his special attention:
not only did he splendidly restore the ziqqurat and several
temples of Ur but the rebuilding of E.hul.hul, the temple of Sin
in Harran, which had been 'destroyed by the Medes during the
war against Assyria, appears to have been the *idée fixe* of his
reign. To say, however, that Nabû-na'id for political and senti-
mental reasons wanted to replace Marduk by Sin at the head
of the Babylonian pantheon is perhaps going too far. Other
temples in Mesopotamia – including the great temple of Marduk
in Babylon – also benefited from his zeal, and the eagerness
with which, before building anew, he sought the *temenu*, or
foundation-deposit, which authenticated the sacred ground testifies to his attachment to the religious traditions of Sumer and
Akkad. On account of his lengthy excavations in search of these
written documents, Nabonidus has been nicknamed 'the royal
archaeologist', though neither his aims nor his methods had
anything to do with archaeology. Nevertheless, the king certainly shared with his subjects that passion for the study of the
past which characterizes his epoch. During the Neo-Babylonian
period – and indeed during the following Achaemenian period
– a number of ancient chronicles were copied, king lists compiled

and antiquities collected with fervour. To quote an amusing example: when Sir Leonard Woolley was excavating at Ur the palace of En-nigaldi-Nanna (formerly read Bêl-shalti-Nannar) – Nabonidus's daughter and high-priestess of Sin – he was puzzled to find in the same building and in the same occupation-level objects of widely different periods, such as a Kassite *kudurru*, a fragment of a statue of King Shulgi and a clay cone of one of the kings of Larsa. Only later did he realize that he had been exploring the private museum of the priestess.[31]

In complete contrast with this devout and apparently weak monarch stands the formidable figure of Cyrus II, 'Great King, the Achaemenian, King of Parsumash and Anshan', who ascended the Persian throne in 559 B.C., three years before Nabonidus was crowned.

The Persians – an Indo-European speaking people – had entered Iran from the north at the end of the second millennium, at the same time as the Medes with whom they were closely related. Moving slowly across the Iranian plateau, they had eventually reached and occupied the mountainous range still known as Fars, along the Arabo-Persian Gulf. At the close of the seventh century B.C., when their history becomes better known, they were divided into two kingdoms ruled by the descendants of Teispes, son of Achaemenes (*Hahamanish*). In Persia proper (*Parsa* or *Parsumash*), i.e. the region between Isfahan and Shiraz, reigned the family of Ariaramnes, elder son of Teispes, while farther west, along the border of Elam, the country of Anshan (or Anzan) was ruled by the family of Ariaramnes's brother, Cyrus I. Both kingdoms were vassals of the Medes. For one or two generations the House of Ariaramnes held sway over the House of Cyrus, but Cyrus's son, Cambyses I (*c.* 600–559 B.C.), reversed the situation and added to his prestige by marrying the daughter of Astyages, his Median overlord. From this marriage was born Cyrus II. At the beginning of Nabonidus's reign Cyrus (*Kurash*) from his palace at Pasargadae ruled over a large but isolated district of Iran, paying tribute to his grandfather. But the Persian prince lacked neither ambition nor intelligence. He had already started reducing to obedience the Iranian tribes of the neighbourhood and was slowly enlarging his kingdom, when the King of Babylon himself gave him an opportunity to acquire an empire.

We have seen that Nabonidus's most cherished dream was to rebuild the temple of Sin in Harran. Not only was this sanctuary dear to his heart but the possession of the market-place and strategic city commanding the roads from northern Mesopotamia to Syria and Asia Minor was of extreme importance to the economy and security of the Babylonian kingdom. Unfortunately, Harran had been in the hands of the Medes since 610 B.C., and against the Medes Nabonidus alone was powerless. Seeing in the Persians the true successors of the Elamites upon whose assistance the Babylonians had often relied in the past, he called upon Cyrus for help. Cyrus accepted. Astyages got wind of the plot, summoned his grandson to Ecbatana, but met with a refusal to obey. A bitter war ensued, ending with the victory of the Persians. Betrayed by his own general, Astyages was captured by Cyrus, who in one day found himself the master of both the Persian and the Median kingdoms (550 B.C.). This important event, long known to us from the works of classical authors,[32] is also mentioned in contemporary cuneiform texts. In one of his inscriptions[33] Nabonidus tells us that Marduk appeared to him in a dream and ordered him to rebuild E.hul.hul in Harran. As the king objected that Harran was in the hands of the 'Umman-manda' (Medes), Marduk replied:

'The Umman-manda of whom you speak, they and their land and the kings who side with them no longer exist. In the coming third year I shall make Cyrus, King of Anzan, their young slave, expel them. With his few troops, he will disperse the widespread Umman-manda.

'He (Cyrus) captured Astyages (*Ishtumegu*), King of Umman-manda and took him prisoner to his country.'

Another, more precise account of the conflict is given in the so-called 'Nabonidus Chronicle':

King Ishtumegu called up his troops and marched against Cyrus, King of Anshan, in order to meet him in battle. The army of Ishtumegu revolted against him and in fetters they delivered him to Cyrus.[34]

Following his victory over the Medes, Cyrus embarked upon a series of brilliant military campaigns which after ten years gave him an empire considerably larger than anything the world had ever witnessed. His first objective was Lydia, where reigned the fabulously rich Croesus. Rather than cross the Armenian highlands, Cyrus led his troops along the road that ran parallel to the Taurus range, through the steppe of Jazirah. Crossing the Tigris below Nineveh and marching westward via Harran, he occupied Cilicia, then a vassal-state of Babylon, thereby breaking the alliance he had just formed with Nabonidus and throwing the Babylonians on the side of Lydia and her traditional allies, the Egyptians. But neither the Egyptians nor the Babylonians could send troops to the aid of Croesus, who met the Persians alone and was defeated at Pteryum (547 B.C.). Lydia absorbed, the Greek cities of Ionia fell one by one, and the whole of Asia Minor submitted to Persian rule. No sooner was the conquest achieved than Cyrus turned his weapon in the opposite direction. Successively, Parthia and Aria, kingdoms of eastern Iran, Sogdia and Bactria in Turkestan and Afghanistan, and part of India fell into his hands. The Persian empire now stretched from the Aegean to the Pamirs, a distance of almost five thousand kilometres. Confronted with such a giant, Babylon had no hope of surviving.

During that time Nabonidus was in Arabia. We read in the Chronicle that in his third year he went to Syria, raised troops in 'the land of Hatti' (as Syria was then called), entered the Arabian desert and besieged Edom (al-Jauf, 450 kilometres due east of Akaba), an important settlement once occupied by the Assyrians. Whether he returned home after this campaign is uncertain owing to an unfortunate break in the tablet, but the entries for the seventh to the eleventh years state that 'the king was in Temâ', with the result that the New Year Festival could not be celebrated in Babylon.[35] Temâ (Arabic Teima) is a large oasis in western Arabia, and from Temâ Nabonidus could easily wander from oasis to oasis as far away as Iatribu (Yathrib, Medina), as we learn from an inscription discovered at Harran.[36] What the King of Babylon was doing in Arabia is one of the most vexing problems in the history of ancient Iraq. Various suggestions have been put forward,[37] the most plausible, perhaps, being that Temâ lay at the intersection of several trade routes in the Arabian peninsula, as well as being an important centre of the cult of Sin, and Nabonidus endeavoured to weave close ties with the Arabs in order to secure their alliance against the Persians. The official reason, given in the document known as the Harran inscriptions, is that he voluntarily abandoned Babylonia in the throes of civil war and famine. Yet none of these explanations can account for those *ten* years of uninterrupted absence from the capital-city, unless we suppose that Nabû-na'id was prevented by his enemies from returning to Babylon. He had left the government in the hands of his son Bêl-shar-uṣur ('Belshazzar' of the Old Testament), a capable soldier but a poor politician, whose authority was challenged by an increasingly influential pro-Persian party, for in almost every country which his victories had placed under Persian rule it had been Cyrus's policy to win the goodwill of his new subjects rather than frighten them into obedience, to pose as liberator and treat his prisoners with mercy, to respect and even encourage local cults, traditions and customs. He was therefore extremely popular throughout the Near East, and among the Babylonians many thought that they would lose little by becoming the subjects of such a good prince. The writing was on the wall: Babylon would be an easy prey.

Cyrus attacked Babylonia in the autumn of 539 B.C. Nabonidus, who had at last returned from Arabia, ordered Belshazzar to deploy his troops along the Tigris in order to cover the capital-city. But the Persians had overwhelming numerical superiority. Moreover, Gubaru (Gobryas), governor of Gutium (i.e. Assyria), who ought to have protected the left flank of Belshazzar's army, went over to the enemy. The subsequent events are described in detail in the Nabonidus Chronicle.[38]

In the month of *Tashritu* (September–October), when Cyrus attacked the army of Akkad in Opis on the Tigris, the inhabitants of Akkad revolted, but he (Nabonidus) massacred the confused inhabitants.

The fifteenth day, Sippar was seized without a battle. Nabonidus fled.

The sixteenth day, Gubaru, the governor of Gutium, and the army of Cyrus entered Babylon without a battle. Afterwards, Nabonidus was arrested in Babylon when he returned (there).

Till the end of the month, the shield-carrying Gutians were staying within Esagila (the temple of Marduk), but nobody carried arms in Esagila and its buildings. The correct time (for a ceremony) was not missed.

In the month of *Arahsamnu* (October–November), the third day, Cyrus entered Babylon. Great twigs were spread in front of him. The state of 'peace' was imposed on all the city. Cyrus sent greetings to all Babylon . . .

Belshazzar was killed in the battle at Opis, and Nabonidus probably lost his life in Babylon, although, according to other sources, Cyrus appointed him governor of Carmania (Central Iran).[39] Far from being destroyed, as its rival Nineveh had been, Babylon was treated with the utmost respect. From the first day of Persian occupation (12 October 539 B.C.), care was taken not to offend the Babylonians in any way, and every effort was made to resettle them in their homes, to enforce law and order throughout the country. The gods of Sumer and Akkad, whom Nabonidus had brought into Babylon during the war, were reinstalled in their chapels, 'the places which make them happy', and even the gods of Assyria, once taken captive by the Medes, were returned and their temples rebuilt. Cyrus made it known to all that he considered himself as the successor of the national rulers, that he worshipped Marduk and 'praised his great godhead joyously.' Indeed, we can believe the Persian conqueror when, in an inscription written in Akkadian on a clay cylinder,[40] he declares that the Babylonians accepted his rule with enthusiasm:

All the inhabitants of Babylon, as well as of the entire country of Sumer and Akkad, princes and governors, bowed to him (Cyrus) and kissed his feet, jubilant that he had received the kingship, and with shining faces happily greeted him as a master through whose help they had come to life from death and had all been spared damage and disaster, and they worshipped his name.

CHAPTER 24

THE SPLENDOUR OF BABYLON

Short as it was (626–539 B.C.) the rule of the Chaldaean kings has left deep traces in the records of history. Monuments, royal inscriptions, letters, legal and commercial documents in great number concur to help us form of the Neo-Babylonian kingdom a fairly complete and accurate picture, and from this collection of data two main features emerge which give the whole period a character of its own: a religious revival combined with extensive architectural activity, and a resurgence of the temples as major social and economic units.

Geography, circumstances and the will of her rulers had turned Assyria into an expanding military nation. The same factors, acting through a thousand years of political abeyance, had made Babylonia the heir and guardian of Sumero-Akkadian traditions, the 'sacred area' of Mesopotamia, acknowledged as such and generally respected by the Assyrians themselves. A Babylonian renaissance in the sixth century B.C. was therefore bound to take the form of a religious revival. To the rebuilding of sanctuaries, the restoration of age-old rites, the celebration of religious festivals with increased ceremonial display, the Chaldaean kings devoted much time, energy and money. In their official inscriptions the stress was constantly laid on their architectural rather than their warlike performances. They could have claimed, like their predecessors, kingship over 'the Universe' of 'the Four Quarters of the World'; they preferred to call themselves 'Provider (*zaninu*) of Esagila and Ezida'* – a title which appears on thousands of bricks scattered throughout southern Iraq. Their colossal work of reconstruction involved

* Respectively the temples of Marduk in Babylon and his son Nabû in Barsippa.

all the main cities of Sumer and Akkad, from Sippar to Uruk and Ur, but the capital-city was given, as expected, preferential treatment: rebuilt anew, enlarged, fortified and embellished, Babylon became one of the world's marvels. Jeremiah the prophet, while predicting its fall, could not help calling it 'a golden cup in the Lord's hand, that made all the earth drunken', and Herodotus, who is believed to have visited it *c.* 460 B.C., admiringly proclaimed: 'It surpasses in splendour any city of the known world.'[1]

Was this reputation deserved or was it, as in other instances, the product of Oriental exaggeration and Greek credulity? The answer to this question should not be sought in the barren mounds and heaps of crumbling brickwork which today form most of this famous site, but in the publications of R. Koldewey and his co-workers, who, between 1899 and 1917, excavated Babylon on behalf of the Deutsche Orient Gesellschaft.[2] It took the Germans eighteen years of hard and patient work solely to recover the plan of the city in broad outline and unearth some of its main monuments, but we now possess enough archaeological evidence to complete, confirm or amend Herodotus's classical description and often share his enthusiasm.

Babylon, the Great City

Unquestionably, Babylon was a very large town by ancient standards. It covered an area of some 850 hectares, contained, we are told, 1,179 temples of various sizes, and while its normal population is estimated at about 100,000, it could have sheltered a quarter of a million people, if not more. The city proper, roughly square in plan, was bisected by the Euphrates, which now flows to the west of the ruins, and was surrounded by an 'inner wall'. But 'in order that the enemy should not press on the flank of Babylon', Nebuchadrezzar had erected an 'outer wall', about eight kilometres long, adding 'four thousand cubits of land to each side of the city'. The vast area comprised between these two walls was suburban in character, with mud-houses and reed-huts scattered amidst gardens and palm-groves, and contained, as far as we can judge, only two official buildings: Nebuchadrezzar's 'summer palace', whose ruins form in the north-eastern corner of the town the mound at present called Bâbil, and perhaps the *bît akîtu*, or Temple of the New Year Festival, not yet exactly located.

Reinforced by towers and protected by moats, the walls of Babylon[3] were remarkable structures, much admired in antiquity. The inner fortified line surrounding the city proper consisted of two walls of sun-dried bricks, separated by a seven-metre wide space serving as a military road; its moat, about fifty metres wide, contained water derived from the Euphrates. The outer fortification, some eight kilometres long, was made of three parallel walls, two of them built of baked bricks. The spaces between these walls were filled with rubble and packed earth. According to Herodotus, the twenty-five metre wide top of this outer town wall could accommodate one or even two chariots of four horses abreast, enabling a rapid movement of troops from one end of the town to the other. When tested, however, this formidable defensive system proved useless: probably helped by accomplices in the city, the Persians entered Babylon through the bed of the Euphrates at low water and took it by surprise, proving that every armour has its faults and that the value of fortifications lies in the men behind them.

Eight gates, each of them named after a god, pierced the inner wall. The north-western gate, or Ishtar Gate, which played an important part in the religious life of the city, is fortunately the best preserved, its walls still rising some twelve metres above the present ground-level.[4] Like most city gates in the ancient Near East, it consisted of a long passage divided by projecting towers into several gateways, with chambers for the guard behind each gateway. But the main interest of Ishtar Gate resides in its splendid decoration. The front wall as well as the entire surface of the passage were covered with blue enamelled bricks on which stood out in relief red-and-white dragons (symbolic of Marduk) and bulls (symbolic of Adad), arranged

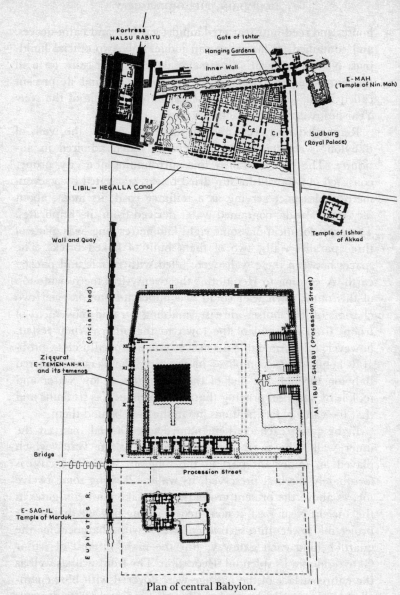

Plan of central Babylon.
Montage of the author after the plans of R. Koldewey, Das wieder erstehende
Babylon, *1925*.

in alternating rows. Even the foundations were similarly decorated, although not with enamelled bricks. The total number of animal figures has been estimated at 575. The passage was roofed over, and the sight of these strange creatures shining in the dim light of torches and oil-lamps must have produced the most startling, awe-inspiring effect.

The Ishtar Gate was approached from the north through a broad, truly magnificent avenue called by the Babylonians *Ai-ibur-shabu*, 'may the enemy not cross it', but better known today as 'Procession Street'. The avenue, more than twenty metres wide, was paved with slabs of white limestone and red breccia and was bordered by two thick walls which were no less impressive than those of the Gate, for on each side sixty mighty lions (symbolic of Ishtar) with red or yellow manes were cast in relief on blue ceramic. Behind these walls were three large buildings called by the Germans 'Northern Citadel' (Nordburg), 'Main Citadel' (Hauptburg) and 'Advanced Work' (Vorwerk). All three formed part of the defensive system of the city, though the Hauptburg seems to have also been used as a royal or princely residence or as a kind of museum.[5] It ruins have yielded a number of inscriptions and sculptures ranging from the second millennium to the fifth century B.C., among which the basalt statue of a lion trampling on a man, known as 'the lion of Babylon'. The origin of this colossal, roughly made piece of work is unknown, but foreign as it is to all that we know of Mesopotamian sculpture, it conveys such an impression of strength and majesty that it has become a symbol of the glorious past of Iraq. Beyond Ishtar Gate, Procession Street continued, somewhat narrower, through the city proper. It passed in front of the Royal Palace, crossed over a canal called *Libil hegalla* ('may it bring abundance'), skirted the vast precinct of the ziqqurat and, turning westwards, reached the Euphrates at the point where the river was spanned by a bridge of six piers shaped like boats. It divided the city into two parts: to the east lay the tangle of private houses (mound of Merkes),[6] to the west and south were grandiose palaces and temples.

Immediately behind the city-wall and close to the Ishtar Gate lay the 'Southern Citadel' (Südburg), 'the House the marvel of mankind, the centre of the Land, the shining Residence, the dwelling of Majesty' – in simpler words, the palace built by Nebuchadrezzar over the smaller palace of Nabopolassar, his father.[7] This very large building was entered from Procession Street through one single monumental gate and comprised five courtyards in succession, each of them surrounded by offices, reception rooms and royal apartments. The throne-room was enormous (c. 52 by 17 metres) and seems to have been vaulted. In contrast with the Assyrian palaces, no colossi of stone guarded the doors, no sculptured slabs or inscribed orthostats lined the walls. The only decoration – obviously intended to please the eye rather than inspire fear – consisted of animals, pseudo-columns and floral designs in yellow, white, red and blue on panels of glazed bricks. Of special interest was a peculiar construction included in the north-eastern corner of the palace. It lay below ground-level and was made of a narrow corridor and fourteen small vaulted cellars. In one of the cellars was found an unusual well of three shafts side by side, as used in connection with a chain-pump. It was extremely tempting to see in this construction the understructure of roof gardens, the famous 'hanging gardens of Babylon' described by classical authors and erected – so one legend tells us – by Nebuchadrezzar for the pleasure of his wife, the Median princess Amytis.[8] Recent excavations there have yielded less romantic results: these rooms merely served as stores for administrative tablets.[9]

To the south of the royal palace, in the middle of a vast open space surrounded by a buttressed wall, rose the 'Tower of Babel', the huge ziqqurat called *E-temen-an-ki*, 'the Temple Foundation of Heaven and Earth'. As old as Babylon itself, damaged by Sennacherib, rebuilt by Nabopolassar and Nebuchadrezzar, it was, as will be seen, completely destroyed, so that only its foundations could be studied by the archaeologists. Any reconstruction of Etemenanki therefore rests essentially upon the meagre data yielded by these studies, upon the eye-witness description of Herodotus, and upon the measurements given in rather obscure terms in a document called 'the Esagila tablet'.[10] It was certainly a colossal monument, 90 metres wide at its base and perhaps of equal height, with no less than seven tiers. On its southern side a triple flight of steps led to the second tier, the rest of the tower being ascended by means of ramps. At the top was a shrine (*sahuru*) 'enhanced with bricks of resplendent blue enamel', which, according to Herodotus,[11] contained a golden table and a large bed and was occupied by a 'native woman chosen from all women' and occasionally by Marduk, this statement being sometimes taken as referring to a 'Sacred Marriage' rite in Babylon, for which there is no other evidence.

E-sag-ila, 'the Temple that Raises its Head', was the name given to the temple of Marduk, the tutelary god of Babylon and the supreme deity of the Babylonian pantheon since the reign of Hammurabi. It was a complex of large and lofty buildings and vast courtyards lying to the south of Etemenanki, on the other side of Procession Street and not at the foot of the ziqqurat, as did most Mesopotamian temples. All the kings of Babylon had bestowed their favours upon the greatest of all sanctuaries, and Nebuchadrezzar, in particular, had lavishly rebuilt and adorned 'the Palace of Heaven and Earth, the Seat of Kingship':

Silver, gold, costly precious stones, bronze, wood from Magan, every-thing that is expensive, glittering abundance, the products of the mountains, the treasures of the seas, large quantities (of goods), sumptuous gifts, I brought to my city of Babylon before him (Marduk).

In Esagila, the palace of his lordship, I carried out restoration work. *Ekua*, the chapel of Marduk, Enlil of the gods, I made its walls gleam like the sun. With shining gold as if it were gypsum ... with lapis-lazuli and alabaster I clothed the inside of the temple ...

Du-azag, the place of the Naming of Destiny ... the shrine of kingship, the shrine of the god of lordship, of the wise one among the gods, of the prince Marduk, whose construction a king before me had

adorned with silver, I clothed with shining gold, a magnificent orna-
ment . . .

My heart prompts me to rebuild Esagila; I think of it constantly.
The best of my cedars, which I brought from Lebanon, the noble
forest, I sought out for the roofing of *Ekua* . . . Inside (the temple),
these strong cedar beams . . . I covered with shining gold. The lower
beams of cedar I adorned with silver and precious stones. For the
building of Esagila, I prayed every day.[12]

The wealth of Esagila is also emphasized by Herodotus who,
having described the ziqqurat, speaks of a 'lower temple':

Where is a great golden image of Zeus (Marduk), sitting at a great
golden table, and the footstool and chair are also of gold; the gold of
the whole was said by the Chaldaeans to be of 800 talents' weight (3
tons). Outside the temple is a golden altar. There is also another great
altar, whereon are sacrificed the full-grown of the flocks. Only sucklings
may be sacrificed on the golden altar, but on the greater altar the
Chaldaeans even offer a thousand talents' weight of frankincense
yearly . . .[13]

Twenty-three centuries after Herodotus visited Babylon however, the great temple of Marduk lay buried under more than
twenty metres of earth and sand, making extensive excavations
almost impossible. At the cost of a considerable effort, the
Germans were able to unearth the main sanctuary ('Hauptbau')
where, among the many rooms symmetrically arranged around
a central courtyard, they identified *Ekua*, the shrine of Marduk,
the smaller chapel of Marduk's consort, the goddess Sarpanitum
and chapels devoted to other deities, such as Ea and Nabû. Of
an adjacent building ('Anbau'), only the outer walls and gates
could be traced. Thoroughly plundered in antiquity, Esagila
yielded practically no object of value. On top of the artificial
hill that concealed it the tomb of 'Amran ibn 'Ali, a companion
of the Prophet, perpetuates for the Moslems the sacred character
attached to that part of Babylon.

The New Year Festival

Once a year, in the spring, the religiosity diffused throughout Sumer and Akkad crystallized in Babylon. For several days the thoughts of the entire population were focused on the ceremonies which took place in the capital-city, because they offered an answer to the fears and hopes of every Mesopotamian. It was felt that mankind shared in the great renewal undergone by nature, that the past was abolished, that the cosmos momentarily reverted to chaos, that the fate of the country depended upon the judgement pronounced by the gods. Nothing short of a complex ritual loaded with magical virtues could solve the unavoidable crisis and put an end to the terrible uncertainty that overwhelmed the human race.

The New Year Festival, or *akîtu*, as celebrated in Babylon during the first millennium B.C.,[14] resulted from the confluence of two powerful currents of religious thought: an extremely old Fertility Cult, consisting of seasonal feasts and a 'Sacred Marriage' ceremony, which is only attested in certain cities and up to the first half of the second millennium B.C., and a comparatively more recent cosmogony developed by the theologians of Nippur, wherein the creation of the world was attributed to Enlil following his victory over Tiamat and the forces of Chaos. After the world was created, a general assembly of the gods presided by the 'Lord Wind' decreed the Destinies of the Land, the fate of humanity. Creation and the naming of Destiny were not unique and final, but annual and conditional. The great cosmic struggle was believed to take place every year and its outcome was unpredictable. In the Babylonian *akîtu*-festival, the passage of nature from want to fruitfulness was made to coincide with the restoration of divine order, and the main role was played by Marduk, who combined the personality of Enlil, champion and king of the gods, with his own personality of fertilizing city-god.

The New Year Festival began on the day called *zagmuk*, in the month of Nisan (March–April), and lasted eleven or twelve

397

days. The tablets which describe it are unfortunately damaged, but enough is legible for us to follow, albeit with some gaps, the ceremonies of the first six days. From what remains concerning the first day we can only gather that a priest unlocked the 'Lofty Gate' of Esagila and opened its great courtyard. On the second day the great-priest (*sheshgallu*) rose before dawn and washed himself with Euphrates water; he then entered the temple, recited a secret prayer asking Marduk to bestow his favours on Babylon and its people, and let in the *erib bîti* priests, the incantators (*kalû*) and the singers, who performed their rites. What follows is too fragmentary to be understood, but it seems that it referred to difficult times, speaking of 'forgotten rites', 'enemies' and 'malediction of Marduk'. The third day began very much like the second day, but three artisans were summoned and provided with material to make two statuettes of wood adorned with precious stones and clad in red garments; one statuette was brandishing a serpent, the other a scorpion. On the fourth day prayers to Marduk and his spouse Sarpanitum were chanted in the early morning, and after the second meal, in the late afternoon, the *sheshgallu*-priest recited the long poem *Enuma elish* (the Epic of Creation) in its entirety, whilst Anu's tiara and Enlil's seat remained covered by deference to these gods who, in the Epic, had been replaced by Marduk.

The first part of the fifth day was devoted to the purification of the temple. A specialized priest, the *mashmashu* went around Esagila with a censer and a torch, sprinkled its walls with Tigris water and smeared them with cedar resin. A slaughterer was then called in to cut off the head of a sheep, take its body around inside the temple and, with the help of the priest, throw head and body into the river, the 'scapegoat' being supposed to take away all the sins of the previous year; whereupon both the *mashmashu* and the slaughterer left Babylon to remain in the open country until the end of the Festival. The *sheshgallu* – who had kept away from these ceremonies to avoid becoming impure – ordered craftsmen to cover the shrine of Marduk's son, Nâbu,

– who was then travelling by boat from Barsippa (Birs Nimrud)[15] to Babylon – with a veil of blue material embroidered with gold.

In the evening, the king proceeded to Esagila. Before the statue of Marduk, he surrendered the insignia of kingship – the sceptre, the circle and the mace – to the *sheshgallu*-priest, who deposited them on a chair in front of Marduk, and then struck the king on the cheek:

He (the priest), says the ritual to which we owe these details, shall accompany him (the king) into the presence of the god Bêl . . . he shall drag him by the ears and make him bow down to the ground . . . The king shall speak the following (only) once:

'I did not sin, lord of the countries. I was not neglectful of your godship. I did not destroy Babylon; I did not command its overthrow . . . The temple Esagila, I did not forget its rites. I did not rain blows on the cheek of a subordinate . . . I did not humiliate them. I watched out for Babylon; I did not smash its walls . . .'

The priest reassured the king:

'Have no fear . . . The god Bêl will listen to your prayer . . . He will magnify your lordship . . . He will exalt your kingship . . . The god Bêl will bless you for ever. He will destroy your enemy, fell your adversary.'

The king was given back his insignia and struck once more:

He (the priest) shall strike the king's cheek. If, when he strikes the king's cheek, the tears flow, (it means that) the god Bêl is friendly; if no tears appear, the god Bêl is angry: the enemy will rise up and bring about his downfall.[16]

The symbolism of this humiliating ritual is clear: the king, scapegoat of the community, atoned for his sins and was reminded that he owed his powers to none but the gods. Later in the night, he took part in other ceremonies involving the burning of a bull in a fire of reeds.

All we know about the sixth day is that Nabû arrived from Barsippa and that, at the same time, the two 'statuettes of evil', which had been made three days before, were decapitated and their heads cast into fire. Our main narrative breaks off here, but other texts indicate that other gods reached Babylon, notably from Sippar, Kutha and Kish. On the ninth day, the king entered Marduk's shrine, 'took his hand' – a gesture which came to summarize the royal participation in the Festival[17] – and installed him in the *ubshukkinna* chapel, together with the other deities. In this first divine assembly was proclaimed the sovereignty of Marduk, as stated in the Epic of Creation and the Destinies were named for the first time. A great, solemn cortège was then formed, including the statues of all the gods and goddesses. Headed by Marduk on his chariot glittering with gold and precious stones and led by the king, it went down Procession Street across Babylon in an aura of incense, songs and music, while people were kneeling down in adoration as it passed by. Through Ishtar Gate the cortège left the city, and after a short journey on the Euphrates, reached the *bît akîtu*, a temple filled with plants and flowers in the middle of a large park.[18] We lack details concerning the ceremonies which took place there but the triumph of Marduk over the forces of evil was certainly celebrated.[19] The gods stayed in the *bît akîtu* for three days. On the eleventh of Nisan they returned to Esagila, where they assembled again to decree, once more, 'the Destinies of the Land'. What is meant by this vague expression, we do not know exactly. Perhaps oracles concerning definite events, such as wars, famines, inundations, etc., were pronounced; perhaps the gods simply reaffirmed their protection over the Babylonians and their monarch in general terms. The session ended in a huge banquet accompanied by music and prayers. On the twelfth of Nisan all the gods who had come to Babylon returned to their respective cities, the priests to their temples, the king to his palace. The great New Year Festival was over.

Economic Life

From the lofty summits of religious thought to the mundane realities of economic life the distance in Chaldaean Babylonia was not very great, since in many places the clergy cared for both the spiritual and material needs of the population. For instance, the archives of E-Anna, the great sanctuary of Uruk, show that the temple owned large estates which were partly let out to tenants, carried out extensive trade within and outside Mesopotamia and formed a social and economic unit almost independent of the central government.[20] These various activities were directed by an 'administrator' (*shatammu*), assisted by an 'overseer' (*qipu*) and by the head scribe (*tupshar bîti*). The temple employed a considerable number of people: notables (*mâr bâni*) and artisans (*ummanê*) engaged in various professions. Hired men and slaves ploughed and harvested its fields, dug and maintained its canals, grazed its cattle and flocks, and assured the transportation and storage of goods. Among the temple servants special mention should be made of the *shirkê* (sing. *shirku*), literally 'consecrated', men and women of different social classes who had been 'offered' in perpetuity to the temple, performed various tasks, received no pay, but were fed and kept by the clergy.[21] The produce of the land, the profits of trade, the rent of fields and houses, taxes levied on the community and part of the offerings and sacrifices – in theory optional, but in practice compulsory – constituted the revenues of the temple. A similar organization probably existed in other cities, though most of the documents from Babylon, Sippar, Nippur, Barsippa and Ur published up to now deal mainly with transactions between individuals.[22]

The importance assumed at least by some temples under the Chaldaean dynasty probably originated in the tenth and eleventh centuries B.C. Prior to that date, the general trend in history had been towards a gradual reduction of the temples' privileges through the creation of large royal estates and the development of private property. But during the 'dark age' of

401

Aramaean invasion events took a different course. Despite the lack of written evidence, we may reasonably assume that while the invaders ransacked and occupied the open country, the Mesopotamian farmers and craftsmen took refuge in or immediately around the cities, and put themselves at the service of the only remaining authority, the local clergy. The temples then became the social, economic and cultural centres of southern Mesopotamia – a state of affairs reminiscent of the role played by the monasteries in our Middle Ages – with unlimited facilities for enlarging their domains. Under the Assyrian domination, when texts again become available, it appears that the wealth of Babylonia was concentrated in her 'holy cities'. The kings of Assyria, who relied a great deal upon the temples to maintain the political stability of Babylonia, bestowed their favours upon them and generally exempted them from taxes and duties; but they also kept them under tight administrative control and, on occasion, 'borrowed' from their treasures.[23] The collapse of Assyria to a great extent freed the temples from governmental interference, and if Nabopolassar and Nebuchadrezzar, out of personal devotion and faithfulness to a well-established tradition, materially rebuilt and adorned the sanctuaries, they abstained from interfering with their organization and contented themselves with a twenty per cent return on their revenue. Nabonidus, however, attempted to bring the temples' business under closer royal scrutiny. We know that in 553 he appointed two high officials – the 'Royal Officer Lord of the Appointment' and the 'Royal Officer over the King's Coffer' – over the E-Anna of Uruk, with instructions to supervise its transactions and ensure the regular collection of royal tithe and taxes. In all probability it was this, more than the king's 'heresy', which alienated the priests from him and threw them on Cyrus's side.

This new, unpopular policy was no doubt dictated by serious financial difficulties. Nebuchadrezzar had spent fabulous sums in the rebuilding of Babylon and other cities, and the 'archaeological' activities of Nabonidus himself were hardly less costly. In addition, the government had to support a large and permanent army. With the exception of Elam, all the northern and eastern countries were now practically closed to Mesopotamian trade, and if Syria–Palestine was still in Babylonian hands, frequent revolts made these distant provinces a burden more than an asset. Moreover, the Phoenician cities had lost much of their former wealth. The sixth century B.C. was precisely the great period of Greek maritime and colonial expansion, and the main commercial centres of the eastern Mediterranean were no longer on the Lebanese coast, but in Greece, Ionia, Lydia, Cilicia and Egypt. Increased expenditures and reduced income drained heavily on the royal treasury and deeply affected the general economy of Babylonia. A study of the hire and sale contracts reveals a marked increase in prices between the beginning and the end of the Neo-Babylonian period. Thus a male slave costing 40 shekels of silver about 600 B.C., cost 50 shekels some fifty years later. Under Nebuchadrezzar 1 shekel could buy from 2 to 4 *qa* of cultivated land, but only 1 to 2 *qa* under Nabonidus.[24] A similar increase affected foodstuffs, clothes and other daily necessities. For various reasons it is difficult to draw an exact scale of wages, but they seem to have remained fairly low throughout the period. The average monthly salary of an unskilled labourer, for instance, was about 1 shekel; with this, he could purchase 2 bushels of grain and 3 bushels of dates, just enough for him to feed his family. In consequence, people took to borrowing money on a long-term basis, and credit inflation rendered the Babylonian economy even more unhealthy.

The term 'money' here should not be taken in its ordinary sense, for minted coins – said to have been invented by the Lydians in the seventh century B.C. – did not circulate widely in the Near East before the reign of Darius I (521–486 B.C.). What the Babylonians used as currency were bits of silver of various shapes and standardized weights: the *shiqlu* (shekel), weighing about three-tenths of an ounce; the *mana* (mine or pound) of 60 shekels, weighing about 18 ounces; and the *biltu* (talent) of 60 mines, weighing about 67 pounds. In current use were also the half-shekel and, occasionally, the *she*, literally a 'grain' of silver. The system was very old, since ingots of bronze stamped with some inscription or image which guaranteed their fineness appear in Mesopotamia as early as the second millennium B.C., and the Assyrians used cast objects of silver, lead and, later, copper in their commercial dealings. What was novel in the Neo-Babylonian period was the adoption of the silver standard, the ratio of silver to gold varying between 14 and 10 to 1. Standardized currency taken as a system of reference made accounting considerably easier and facilitated transactions, but the silver standard also encouraged the development of credit, for the simple reason that silver 'coins' were easy to store and manipulate. 'Usury, mortgages and enslaved debtors followed the new medium of exchange wherever it was introduced.'[25] Private business on a scale hitherto unknown flourished in Babylonia during the sixth century B.C., and while most of the population endured considerable hardship, a few 'dynasties' of capitalists and businessmen – such as the Egibi family in Babylon – made a fortune in real estate, slave trade, money-lending societies, commercial and agricultural companies and banking operations, such as loans and the handling of deposits on behalf of their clients.[26]

The emergence of a monetary system and the development of capitalism are phenomena the importance of which cannot be overstressed; but the resurgence of the temples as major social and economic units is equally important. Both help to explain what happened after Babylonia had lost her political autonomy. Economic depression contributed to the decline of the Mesopotamian civilization, but the temples kept it alive for almost six hundred years. By a remarkable coincidence, this civilization was to die as it was born: under the wings of the gods.

CHAPTER 25

DEATH OF A CIVILIZATION

Not very long ago, the great city which we have just described lay buried beneath a thick blanket of earth, as did all the towns and villages of ancient Iraq. Here and there on these 'tells' could be seen a brick inscribed with a writing no scholar could read. Of the monuments of art, of the masterpieces of literature, of the works of science produced in Mesopotamia during three thousand years of history, practically nothing was known. The Mesopotamian civilization was dead and forgotten, and even today no one, when confronted with the most desolate of ruins, can help wondering when, how and why it died.

If the Persians had dealt with Babylon as the Medes and Babylonians had dealt with Nineveh there would be no problem. The Near East offers, besides Assyria, other examples of nations and cultures which disappeared almost overnight, the victim of devastating wars – the Hittite kingdom of Boghazköy, Urarṭu and Phrygia, for instance. But the Persians did not destroy Babylon, nor did they destroy the other cities of Babylonia, and a number of monuments and inscriptions dating from the Achaemenian, Hellenistic and Parthian periods testify to a partial survival of the Mesopotamian civilization down to the first century A.D. How then did it slowly decline and ultimately vanish?

There are, it seems, two main reasons why this extremely important question has not yet received all the attention it deserves. On the one hand it encompasses three separate fields of scholarly research. Historians of the Semitic Near East, Hebraists or Assyriologists by training, are naturally reluctant to encroach on the domain of Greek and Iranian studies with which they are not fully conversant, while Hellenists and Iranologists, struggling with wider problems, tend to treat

Mesopotamia as a marginal subject beyond the normal scope of their work. On the other hand, the decline and fall of a civilization anywhere in the world is always a complicated process, dependent upon multiple political, ethnic, linguistic, religious, economic and even geographical factors which, in this particular case, are too often beyond the grasp of our knowledge. Nevertheless, we feel that, having described at length how the Mesopotamian civilization was born, we should at least endeavour to examine how it died. Carrying this work a few centuries beyond that fateful date of 539 B.C., when Babylonia lost its independence for ever, we shall give here a condensed account of Mesopotamian history during the three relevant periods of foreign domination:

> the Achaemenian period (539–331 B.C.)
> the Hellenistic period (331–126 B.C.)
> the Parthian period (126 B.C.–A.D. 227)

The Achaemenian Period

To many Babylonians the conquest of their country by the Persians may have appeared as a mere change of dynasty. Soon after Babylon was captured, life between the Tigris and the Euphrates resumed its normal course, and business was carried on as usual, the only difference being that contracts were now dated in the years of '*Kurash*, King of Babylon, King of the Lands', instead of in the years of Nabû-na'id.[1] The government of Babylonia was first entrusted to Nabonidus's former general, Gobryas, but in Nisan 538 B.C. Cyrus's own son, Cambyses (*Kambuziya*) 'took the hand of Bêl' in the New Year Festival and from then on acted as viceroy, with headquarters in Sippar and a staff of native officials. In 528 B.C. after Cyrus had been killed on a distant battlefield, Cambyses, already associated with the throne, became King of Persia. We have very little information concerning this period, except that Babylonian soldiers were enrolled in the Persian Army and took part in the conquest of Egypt, but whatever truth there may be in the story of the king's mad behaviour in the Nile valley, it seems certain that Babylonia enjoyed complete peace throughout his reign.

The death of Cambyses, early in 522 B.C., marks the end of this honeymoon. Bardiya, his brother, who had usurped the throne, was defeated and slain eight months later by Darius;[2] but although Darius was of royal blood – he was a descendant of Ariaramnes and therefore belonged to the Achaemenian family – his authority was immediately challenged. Several of the satraps appointed by Cyrus refused to obey the new king, while a second Phraortes in Media and a pseudo-Bardiya in Persia rallied many supporters. The Babylonians, hitherto submissive, were not slow in joining the rebels, for among them were men in whose hearts the flame of freedom was still burning high. In the long cuneiform inscription in three languages – Old Persian, Babylonian, Elamite – carved in the rock at Behistun (near Kermanshah) to commemorate Darius's victories over his foes,[3] the Persian monarch himself tells us how a Babylonian called Nidintu-Bêl recruited an army by declaring that he was 'Nebuchadrezzar, son of Nabonidus' and seized kingship in Babylon. Darius in person marched against him, routed the Babylonians on the Tigris and on the Euphrates and pursued the rebel to his capital-city, where he was captured and executed. According to dated receipts, 'Nebuchadrezzar III' reigned from October to December 522 B.C. In August 521 B.C., while Darius was fighting for his throne in Media and Persia, the Babylonians 'broke the truce for the second time'. The pretender – who also claimed to be 'Nebuchadrezzar, son of Nabonidus' – was an 'Armenian' (Urartian) called Arakha, son of Haldita. Against him Darius dispatched one of his generals, Vindafârna:

'I said to him: "Go forth! Fight this Babylonian army which does not declare itself for me!" Vindafârna marched against Babylon with the (Persian) army. Ahuramazda lent me his assistance. By the will of

Ahuramazda, Vindafârna fought the Babylonians and took them captive. Twenty-two days of the month Margazana had elapsed when he captured Arakha and the nobles, his main followers. Whereupon, I gave an order: "This Arakha and the nobles, his main followers, shall be impaled in Babylon!" '[4]

'Nebuchadrezzar IV' was put to death on 27 November 521 B.C. He had 'reigned' only four months.[5] At the beginning of 520 B.C. Darius, finally rid of all his enemies, was recognized as king throughout most of the Near East and immediately set out to promote a number of major reforms aimed at consolidating his power and cementing together the various regions of his vast empire. The administrative system was re-shaped, largely on the Assyrian model. The number of satraps was increased and their authority further limited by the creation of military governors, tax collectors and royal inspectors. Royal couriers rode swiftly from the Aegean to the Gulf on an admirable network of roads. A common law, reminiscent in style of the Code of Hammurabi, was imposed upon all subject peoples. The monetary systems were unified and based on a gold standard, the coinage used in trade and banking now being the gold *daric* worth twenty shekels of silver. Reorganized, cleared of corruption, heavily taxed and subjected to tight royal control, Babylonia remained quiet during the rest of Darius's long reign (522–486 B.C.).

In the fourth year of Xerxes, however, the Babylonians made a last attempt at recovering their freedom (482 B.C.). Contracts from Dilbat, Barsippa and Babylon show that Bêl-shimanni and Shamash-eriba were successively accepted as kings, the former in August, the latter in September, while we learn from other sources that the satrap Zophyrus was killed and that Xerxes, greatly angered, sent his brother-in-law Megabysus to crush the revolt.[6] The repression was brutal, the rebels were tortured and slain, but the exact amount of damage inflicted upon Babylon itself is difficult to assess. If Herodotus really visited, some twenty years later, the city which he describes, we may conclude that it had suffered very little harm – indeed, the 'Father of

History' merely states that Xerxes took from Esagila the colossal golden statue of Marduk. Yet Arrian, Ctesias and Strabo suggest that the city-walls were dismantled and the temples razed to the ground. Since Esagila and other sanctuaries are mentioned in later texts, it is probable that they were only partly damaged and that they fell into ruin through lack of maintenance in the course of the following centuries rather than through violent destruction.

The failure of the Babylonians to restore a national monarchy had consequences that went far beyond a simple loss of prestige. From time immemorial the Mesopotamian kings had been responsible to the gods for the welfare of their subjects. The cities owed to them their temples, their palaces, their fortifications and often their parks and gardens. They had never failed to ensure that canals were dug, kept open and extended, that dykes and dams were built, that land rights were safeguarded. In a country like ancient Iraq these functions were of vital importance. No matter what the temples could achieve in their own spheres, only a king residing permanently in the country and constantly aware of its needs could raise the funds and mobilize the labour required for such undertakings on a nation-wide scale. Without her own rulers Mesopotamia was to a great extent paralysed. Sooner or later, it could be predicted, buildings left unattended would crumble down, canals would become silted-up and part of the land would revert to desert.

The first Persian kings, conscious of their duties towards one of their richest and most civilized provinces, carried out some of the royal tasks traditional in Mesopotamia. We know, for instance, that Cyrus restored the precinct of the temple of Sin at Ur and that he and Darius repaired the E-Anna of Uruk. In Babylon, his winter residence, Darius built an arsenal, a palace for the crown prince and an *apadana* (i.e. a hall supported by columns, in the Persian style) for his own palace.[7] But Xerxes and his successors, engaged in an endless and costly war against Greece, do not seem to have cared much for their Babylonian satrapy. The entire period between the accession of Xerxes (485

B.C.) and the conquest of Alexander (331 B.C.) is exceedingly poor in architectural remains and building inscriptions. In southern Iraq business documents found *in situ* prove that Babylon, Barsippa, Kish, Nippur, Uruk and Ur – to mention only the main cities – were alive, some of them even fairly prosperous,[8] but none of their monuments appears to have been rebuilt or repaired. As for the North, it was still suffering from the great destructions of the years 614–609 B.C. We learn from a letter[9] that in about 410 B.C. five 'towns' in that region were administrative centres and that a Persian nobleman possessed a domain there, but with the exception of Arba'il (Erbil), these were only big villages away from the Tigris valley. Xenophon, who marched through Assyria in 401 B.C. with ten thousand Greek mercenaries, describes Nimrud (which he calls 'Larissa') as 'deserted', and did not even recognize the walls of Nineveh in the 'large undefended fortifications' which he saw near Mescila (Mosul).[10]

Adverse economic conditions perhaps contributed to the decline of the Mesopotamian civilization. The main artery of the Persian empire, the 'Royal Road' from Sardis to Susa, ran at the foot of the mountains and by-passed Babylon. Trade with India and the East in general was monopolized by the Persians, nearer to these countries. Syria had been detached from Mesopotamia by Darius or Xerxes. Babylonia and Assyria, forming together the ninth satrapy, were grossly overtaxed: they paid to the Crown an annual tribute of one thousand talents of silver and supplied the Persian court with food during four months of the year. In addition, they had to bear the full burden of a greedy local administration.[11] If we are to believe Herodotus, the satrap of Babylonia received daily the content of an *artaba* (about 57 litres) of silver and kept 800 stallions and 16,000 mares, while his Indian dogs were fed by four villages![12] For all these reasons, the upward trend of prices, already noticed during the Neo-Babylonian period, continued under the Achaemenians: within the century following the death of Darius the cost of living doubled without corresponding increase in wages, and the rent of an average house passed from fifteen shekels per month under Cyrus to forty shekels under Artaxerxes I (464–424 B.C.).[13] Naturally, the great bankers and usurers benefited from these conditions. The Murashû family of Nippur, for instance – a powerful firm which operated in southern Mesopotamia between 455 and 403 B.C. – specialized in farming out the lands which Persian officials and collectives (hatru) of soldiers and civil-servants owned but refused to cultivate; they supplied oxen, agricultural tools and water for irrigation and took a share in the revenues. They also lent clothes, food and equipment to people called up for war duties and money (at 40–50 per cent interest) to those who could not pay their debts or taxes.[14]

No less important were the ethnic and linguistic changes brought about by the Achaemenian domination. The population of Babylonia, already mixed with Medes, Arabs, Jews, Egyptians, Urartians and other foreigners in Assyrian and Babylonian times, received a strong influx of Persian blood under Darius and Xerxes: many Persians were granted estates by the king; others were appointed judges or given major or minor administrative posts.[15] With these men the gods of Iran entered the Tigris–Euphrates valley. There is, it is true, no evidence that they were at that time the object of an organized cult, and the decree of Xerxes forbidding the worship of deities other than Ahuramazda was never obeyed; but the mere fact that a number of Babylonians changed their Semitic name for a name composed with Aryan gods betrays a certain dwindling of private devotion. For all these people of various origins and tongues there could be only one common language: Aramaic. Already widely spoken in Western Asia, easy to learn, eminently suitable for writing on papyrus or parchment, officially adopted by Darius as the lingua franca throughout the empire, Aramaic replaced Babylonian in the homes, streets and shops. Only learned men and temple scribes could still read and write the Akkadian and Sumerian languages in their cuneiform script. The numerous literary, religious and historical texts copied during the Achaemenian period, as well as the remarkable works of astronomers such as Nabû-rimani and Kidinnu (see above, p. 365) are proof that the traditional culture of Mesopotamia was still very much alive in these restricted circles; yet for the great majority of the population inscriptions on clay were meaningless, and history tells us that a nation which forgets its language forgets its past and soon loses its identity.

Oppressed, impoverished and partly 'denationalized', such was Mesopotamia, it would appear, in the last decades of the fourth century B.C., when Alexander came to give her a new, though entirely different life.

The Hellenistic Period

The battle of Gaugamela,[16] on 1 October 331 B.C., opened for Alexander the road to Babylonia and Persia, as the battle of Issus, two years before, had opened for him the road to Syria and Egypt. The Persian troops stationed in Babylon surrendered without fighting, and the Macedonian conqueror made a triumphal entry into the old Semitic metropolis. Realizing, like Cyrus, that he could never rule over 'a hundred different nations' unless he won their hearts, he made sacrifice to Marduk and ordered the rebuilding of the temples thought to have been destroyed by Xerxes – a gigantic task which was never to be completed.[17] The Babylonians hailed him as their liberator and immediately acknowledged his kingship. After a month's stay in Babylon he proceeded to Susa and thereafter embarked upon the great armed expedition to the East which took him as far as the River Ganges. When he returned, nine years later, his mind was full of grandiose projects: Babylon and Alexandria in Egypt were to become the twin capital-cities of his empire; they would be linked by sea around the Arabian peninsula, shortly to be conquered; the coasts of the Indian Ocean would be explored; the Euphrates would be rendered navigable up to the Gulf; a great port would be built at Babylon and another at the mouth of the river. But most of these plans remained a dead letter: on 13 June 323 B.C. Alexander died in Babylon, probably of malaria, at the age of thirty-two.

At that date Alexander's only son, the future Alexander IV, was not yet born, and it was his brother, Philip Arrhideus, who was proclaimed king in Macedonia. But the authority of this young and mentally retarded prince remained purely nominal. The real power lay in the hands of Alexander's generals – the *diadochi* – who, having divided the empire between themselves, struggled for forty-two years to prevent each other from reconstructing it. During this period – one of the most complex in the history of antiquity – Babylon changed hands several times. At first the seat of a military junta presided over by the regent Perdiccas, it was allotted to Seleucus, chief of the Macedonian cavalry, by his colleagues in 321 B.C., after they had murdered Perdiccas. In 316 B.C. Antigonus, the ambitious satrap of Phrygia, dislodged Seleucus from Babylon, forcing him to take refuge with Ptolemy in Egypt. But Seleucus came back in 312 B.C., recovered his satrapy, and for four years successfully protected it from repeated attacks launched by Antigonus and his son Demetrius. It was a fierce and bitter war which brought terrible suffering upon Babylon and its territory – 'there was weeping and mourning in the land' repeats as a *leitmotif* a Babylonian chronicle describing these events.[18] Finally, Antigonus was defeated and killed at Ipsus in Phrygia (301 B.C.), and Seleucus added to Babylonia the satrapy of Syria and the eastern half of Asia Minor. The war, however, continued, this time in the west, between Seleucus, Ptolemy, Demetrius and the Macedonian ruler of Thrace, Lysimachus. In September 281 B.C.,[19] a few months after he had defeated Lysimachus at Korupedion (near Sardis), Seleucus was stabbed to death by a son of Ptolemy. He had taken the title of king in 305 B.C., but for the Babylonians the 'years of *Silukku*', the Seleucid era, began on the first New Year's Day following his return from Egypt: 3 April 311 B.C. It was the first time that a continuous dating system was used in Mesopotamia.

After Ipsus Seleucus ruled directly or indirectly over a huge territory extending from the borders of India to those of Egypt and from the Black Sea to the Persian Gulf. But this empire lacked cohesion and started disintegrating almost as soon as it was formed. By 200 B.C. the descendants of Seleucus had lost practically all their provinces and protectorates beyond the Taurus and the Zagros, and after Babylonia had been conquered by the Parthians (126 B.C.), all that remained was a small state in northern Syria, torn apart by dynastic crises, which fell an easy prey to the Romans in 63 B.C. In actual fact, ever since Seleucus founded Antioch on the Orontes, in May 300 B.C., and made it his favourite residence, the Seleucid kingdom had always been essentially a Syrian kingdom. If we except an unsuccessful attempt made by Antiochus III (222–187 B.C.) to recover the Eastern districts, the diplomatic and military activities of its rulers were almost entirely absorbed in an endless conflict with the Ptolemies of Egypt for the possession of the Phoenician ports and hinterland. This meant peace for the Babylonians who must have been relieved to see the ravages of war removed from their own country to '(the country) across the river' (*ebir nâri*), as they now called Syria, but it also meant that Babylon lost the privileged position it would have held had it remained the capital-city of the Macedonian dominion, as geography and history destined it to be. For many years to come, the world's political, cultural and economic centre had shifted from the banks of the Euphrates to the shores of the Mediterranean.

Undoubtedly the most durable achievement of Alexander and his successors was the foundation in Egypt and Western Asia of numerous cities organized on the model of the Greek *poleis* and populated by Greco-Macedonian settlers as well as by Oriental subjects. Whether by so doing they merely wished to create a network of political and military strongholds, or aimed at promoting the Greek culture and way of life in the Orient is a much debated problem.[20] But the results obtained are obvious: the Near East became 'hellenized' to various degrees, and the pattern of urban life in these regions was profoundly altered.

We know of at least a dozen such cities in Mesopotamia[21] alone, from Edessa-Antioch in the extreme north to Alexandria–Charax on or near the Gulf. They were, as a rule, built beside or on top of ancient towns and villages, though their layout and architectural characteristics were entirely new. Seleucia-on-the-Tigris (Tell 'Umar, opposite Ctesiphon), founded by Antiochus I in 274 B.C., probably on the site of Semitic Upâ (Opis), was the largest city not only of Mesopotamia but of the whole Seleucid kingdom, with a population of about 600,000. Aerial photographs clearly show its 'grid-plan', the blocks of habitations being separated by straight avenues and streets crossing each other at right angles. Excavations conducted there before the war and since 1964 have uncovered a number of buildings and numerous objects (clay figurines, statues, coins, jewels, pottery) in the Seleucian city, the ruins of which were buried under an equally large and rich city of the Parthian period.[22] A similar situation confronted archaeologists at Dura-Europus (Salahiyeh, on the Euphrates, fifty kilometres upstream of ancient Mari), and here again remains of Greek monuments – a fortress, a palace and at least one temple – could be traced underneath the Parthian buildings.[23]

These Hellenistic cities were all situated on the great trade-routes which linked Central Asia with the Mediterranean, and thrived on transit operations. Seleucia, in particular, was the meeting-point of two land-routes coming from India (one through Bactria and the north of Iran, the other through Persepolis and Susa), of the important sea-route from India through the Gulf, and of several tracks crossing the Arabian peninsula. From Seleucia gold, ivory, spices, incense and precious stones, as well as the products of Mesopotamia itself – wheat, barley, dates, woollens and bitumen – were transported to Syria, either along the Euphrates via Dura-Europus, or along the Tigris and across Jazirah via Nisibin (Antioch in Mygdonia) and Edessa. Commercial intercourse between Europe, Asia and part of Africa was extremely active in Hellenistic times, and there is little doubt as to the prosperity of the

Seleucid kingdom in general – at least during the third century B.C. Our information on Babylonia is regrettably scanty, but the few commercial texts published (mainly from Uruk) show that a fair amount of business was carried out even within the older towns, and that prices had fallen much below the levels they had reached in Achaemenian times.[24]

The new economic and demographic conditions prevalent in Seleucid Mesopotamia exerted a deep, though diverse influence upon the older cities. Thus Nimrud owed to its situation on the Tigris route its revival as a small but prosperous village. Similarly, Nineveh, Mari and Arslan-Tash were reoccupied after long years of abandonment.[25] Ur died slowly, probably killed by competition from Alexandria–Charax as much as by hydrographic changes in the region. Babylon was severely affected. It is true that sporadic efforts were made by the Macedonian rulers to revive and modernize the half-ruined city. In the last royal inscription in Akkadian that we possess Antiochus I (281–260 B.C.) calls himself 'provider of Esagila and Ezida', like the Chaldaean kings, and declares that he 'formed with his august hands' and brought from 'Hatti' (Syria) the first bricks of these temples.[26] A tablet dated in the reign of Seleucus III (225–223 B.C.) shows that regular offerings were still made to a number of Babylonian gods in their own shrines. Remains of Hellenistic architecture were discovered on the mound of Bâbil and on the site of Nebuchadrezzar's palace. Under Antiochus IV (175–164 B.C.) – the king who did most to propagate the Greek culture – Babylon received a gymnasium and a remarkable Greek theatre, later enlarged by the Parthians.[27] Yet not only was Babylon no longer the seat of the royal government, but it was already partly deserted, a great number of its inhabitants having been transferred to Seleucia when the city was founded.[28] We do not know what happened in Sippar, Kish and Nippur, but Uruk seems to have enjoyed considerable prosperity, judging from the impressive monuments erected during the Seleucid period. A huge terrace constructed around the E-Anna ziqqurat completely transformed the sacred area, while in other parts of the city were built two large temples: *Irigal* (or, better, *Esh-gal*), dedicated to Ishtar, and the so-called *Bît rêsh*, dedicated to Anu.[29] Both had the conventional features of Babylonian temples, though a long inscription on glazed bricks which ran on the walls of the cult-room of Irigal was, significantly, in Aramaic script and language. Equally typical of the period are the Greek names conferred by the kings to the two city-magistrates who built these temples Anu-uballiṭ Nicarachus and Anu-uballiṭ Kephalon. A study of contracts on clay tablets and of *bullae* * bearing Greek or Aramaic inscriptions shows that Uruk (called by the Greek *Orchoi*) gave shelter to an important Greek community, but retained its ancient laws and customs and was exempted from certain royal taxes. Most of the business transactions were carried out by the temple organization in the activities of which ordinary citizens could be financially interested by means of a system not very different from our modern shareholding.[30] The existence of semi-independent temple-states is well attested in Asia Minor in Hellenistic times, and it is probable that Uruk owed a similar status to the liberal policy of the Seleucids.

It was in temples like those of Uruk, Sippar, Babylon and Barsippa that the Sumero-Akkadian culture was preserved. Throughout the Seleucid period temple astronomers and astrologers continued to record on tablets the motions of celestial bodies, while temple scribes wrote down contemporary events in the form of chronicles and copied a number of very ancient myths, rituals, hymns and omens. It would seem *a priori* that the much-advanced Greek culture, which flourished in cities such as Seleucia, exerted a strong attraction on the less conservative members of the Babylonian *intelligentsia*; but if a long list of Greek authors native from Mesopotamia can be compiled,[31] it is often difficult to distinguish between those who were of pure Greco-Macedonian descent and those who, born Babylonian,

* Small balls of clay attached by a string to official documents on papyrus or parchment.

417

had adopted a Greek name. In fact, the evidence available seems to indicate a movement in the opposite direction: the Greeks became interested not so much in Mesopotamian history and literature as in the scientific and pseudo-scientific works of the 'Chaldaeans'. In the second and third centuries B.C. the Babylonian Sudinês translated into Greek the writings of Kidinnu and other astronomers, and Berossus, priest of Marduk, wrote in Greek a strange mixture of astrology and historical narratives called *Babyloniaca*,[32] which he dedicated to Antiochus I. Limited as they were, these cultural contacts saved for posterity some of the most remarkable achievements of Mesopotamian scientists, while the most objectionable end-product of the Mesopotamian belief in predestination, astrology, permeated and corrupted the religions of the West.

The Parthian Period

The Parthians – a branch of the Scythians – appear for the first time in history *c.* 250 B.C., when Arsaces led his nomadic tribesmen out of the steppes of Turkestan to settle in the north-eastern corner of Iran.[33] By 200 B.C., the 'Arsacids' were firmly established between the Caspian Gate (Hecatompylos) and the region of Meshed (Nisaia). Between 160 and 140 B.C. Mithridates I conquered the Iranian plateau in its entirety and, reaching the Tigris, pitched his camp at Ctesiphon, opposite Seleucia. The Seleucid Demetrius II succeeded in recovering Babylonia and Media for a few years, but in 126 B.C. Artabanus II reasserted his authority over these regions, and from then on the Tigris-Euphrates valley remained in Parthian hands – save for two brief periods of Roman occupation under Trajan and Septimus Severus – until it fell under Sassanian domination with the rest of the Parthian kingdom in A.D. 227.

To govern their empire the Arsacids could only rely upon a small, if valorous, Parthian aristocracy, but they had the intelligence to utilize the social organizations created by the Seleucids, or those which had grown upon the ruins of the

Seleucid kingdom. They encouraged the development of Hellenistic cities and tolerated the formation of independent vassal kingdoms, such as Osrhoene (around Edessa-Urfa), Adiabene (corresponding to ancient Assyria) and Characene (near the Arabo-Persian Gulf).[31] Towards the beginning of the Christian era Ḥaṭra, an old caravan city on the Wadi Thartar, 58 kilometres west of Assur, acquired its autonomy and became the centre of a small but prosperous state known as Araba.[34] The Arsacids and their vassals were rich, since they controlled practically all the trade-routes between Asia and the Greco-Roman world, with the result that the second and first centuries B.C. were marked in Mesopotamia by intensive building activities resulting from governmental or regional initiative. Not only were Seleucia, Dura-Europus and, presumably, other prosperous market-places provided with a large number of new monuments, but towns and villages which had been lying in ruins for hundreds of years were reoccupied. In southern Iraq traces of Parthian occupation were found on almost every site excavated, in particular Babylon, Kish, Nippur, Uruk and even forgotten Girsu. In the north Assyria was literally resurrected: Nuzi, Kakzu, Shibanniba were inhabited again, and Assur, rebuilt anew, became at least as large a city as it had been in the heyday of the Assyrian empire.[35] But it must be emphasized that the revived settlements had very little in common with their Assyrian or Babylonian precursors. Several of them, if not all, had straight streets, often lined with columns, a citadel, usually built on top of the old ziqqurat, and an agora wherever possible. Walls of stone or ashlar-masonry replaced the traditional walls of mud bricks, while the buildings themselves, with their lofty vaulted chambers wide open on one side (*iwan*), their elegant peristyle and their decoration of moulded stucco, differed from the buildings erected by Mesopotamian architects as markedly as the Greco-Iranian statues of the rulers of Ḥaṭra differed from those of Gudea or Ashurnaṣirpal.

These archaeological data, combined with textual evidence, point to a massive influx of foreign population. The Greek and

Macedonian settlers, probably not very numerous at the beginning, had lived side by side with the Babylonians with relatively few social contacts; they had preserved their nationality, their institutions, their art, their language, their 'Greekhood' in a word, and were still keeping it under the protection of enlightened monarchs who called themselves 'philhellen'. But the newcomers – mostly Aramaeans, Arabs and Iranians – settled in Mesopotamia in very large numbers, and mixed with the native population more easily since they were of Oriental, often Semitic stock and spoke the same language. Each city, old or new, gave shelter to several foreign gods. At Dura-Europus, for instance, were brought to light two Greek temples, an Aramaean sanctuary, a Christian chapel, a synagogue and a Mithreum, let alone the shrines of local deities and of the gods of Palmyra. Similarly, the Sumero-Akkadian god Nergal, the Greek god Hermes, the Aramaean goddess Atar'at and the Arabian deities Allat and Shamiya had their temples in Haṭra, around the majestic sanctuary of Shamash, the sun-god common to all Semites. Even at Uruk, the ancestral home of Anu and Ishtar, can still be seen a charming little temple, more Roman than Greek in style, dedicated to the Iranian god Gareus, and the remains of an extraordinary apsidal building believed to be a temple of Mithra.[36] Jews were numerous in Mesopotamia, and from about A.D. 30 to 60 or even more, a local family converted to Judaism ruled over Adiabene from its capital city Arbela (Erbil).[37] According to the Oriental tradition, during the same period Christianity began to penetrate into northern Mesopotamia, coming from Antioch and Edessa.

This flood of people and ideas submerged what was left of the Sumero-Akkadian civilization. A handful of contracts, about two hundred astronomical or astrological texts and two or three very fragmentary chronicles and Babylonian–Greek vocabularies constitute all the cuneiform literature in our possession for that period.[38] The last cuneiform text known so far – an astronomical 'almanac' – was written in A.D. 74–5.[39] It is quite possible that the Babylonian priests and astronomers continued for several

generations to write in Aramaic on papyrus or parchment, but
no work of this kind is likely to be found. We know that some of
the ancient temples were restored, that Ashur was worshipped
in his home town and that a cult was rendered to Nabû in
Barsippa until, perhaps, the fourth century A.D. But there is no
evidence that Esagila, the temple of the former national god
Marduk, was kept in repair. Indeed, Babylon probably suffered
more damage in the repression which followed the revolt of a
certain Hymeros in 127 B.C., or in the civil war between
Mithridates II and Orodes in 52 B.C., than in the hands of
Xerxes. When Trajan, in A.D. 115, entered the once opulent
city, it was not to 'take the hand of Bêl', but to sacrifice to the
manes of Alexander. Eighty-four years later, Septimus Severus
found it completely deserted.[40]

Very little is known of the administrative, social and economic
status of Mesopotamia under the Sassanians (A.D. 224–651).
We learn from Greek and Latin authors that the northern
part of the country was ravaged by four centuries of almost
uninterrupted war between Romans (or Byzantines) and Persians[41] and that Assur was destroyed by Shapur I in A.D. 256 as
radically as it had been destroyed by the Medes. At Ctesiphon
can be admired the remains of a magnificent palace attributed
to Chosroes I while the more modest residence of another
Sassanian king has been excavated at Kish.[42] At Uruk, not far
from the city-wall originally built by Gilgamesh, a local ruler
(?) was buried with his crown of golden leaves.[43] Sherds of
Sassanian pottery testify to the occupation or reoccupation of
other ancient sites. But at the beginning of the seventh century
A.D. shortly before the Islamic conquest, the usual combination
of military setbacks, internal strife and economic difficulties
brought about the decline of the Sassanian kingdom and the
ruin of Mesopotamia. Many canals left unattended dried up;
the rivers, unchecked, could meander freely; scattering to out-
lying villages, people abandoned the towns deprived of water,
and the ancient cities of Iraq were gradually buried beneath
the sand of the desert and the silt of the valley. Those which

survived were much damaged by the formation, in A.D. 629, of the 'Great Swamp' that throughout the Middle Ages covered the whole area of ancient Sumer,[44] or by the terrible destructions systematically performed by the Mongols in the thirteenth century, or again, sadly, by the re-utilization of building materials by poor and or illiterate people to whom the history of ancient Iraq meant virtually nothing.

EPILOGUE

Thus perished one of the oldest and most remarkable civilizations of the ancient world. Brutally destroyed in Assyria at the end of the seventh century B.C., it survived in Babylonia for about six centuries to disappear with the last cuneiform inscription at the beginning of the Christian era. Born during the Uruk and Jemdat Nasr periods (*c.* 3500–3000 B.C.), it had lasted for more than three thousand years.

In its slow decline (500 B.C.–A.D. 100), economic conditions played a smaller part than is sometimes believed, and the geographical changes – the wandering of the Twin Rivers, the silting-up of canals, the salinization of the soil – responsible for the abandonment of many ancient towns and villages and the depopulation of vast areas did not assume large-scale proportions until the end of the Sassanian period (fifth–sixth centuries A.D.). All considered, the decay and death of the Mesopotamian civilization can be ascribed to three main causes: the absence of a national government, the foundation by Alexander and his successors of new cities competing with and eventually superseding the older settlements and, above all, the profound ethnic, linguistic, religious and cultural changes introduced by successive waves of invaders – Persians, Greeks, Aramaeans, pre-Islamic Arabs – who could be neither kept at bay nor assimilated. In the course of her long history Mesopotamia had been invaded many times. Guti, Amorites, Hurrians, Kassites and Aramaeans had found in the Tigris-Euphrates valley a young and vigorous culture immensely superior to their own and had invariably adopted it. But to the highly civilized Greeks of the third century B.C., to the disciples of Plato and Aristotle, the Babylonians had little to offer besides the abstruse works of their astronomers; and nothing was less suited to the requirements of the cosmopolitan society then taking roots in Iraq than the intricate cuneiform script which the Babylonians themselves were giving up. What the Greco-Macedonian and Oriental settlers found in that country was a culture in many ways antiquated and 'fossilized', perpetuated by a few priests in a few temples. Spontaneity and creativeness were absent from literature since the time of Hammurabi; sculpture had died with the Assyrians; architecture under the Chaldaean and Seleucid dynasties still produced some impressive monuments, but adhered to traditional blueprints; as for the various sciences, they had apparently reached their limits, with the notable exception of mathematics and astronomy. Attachment to tradition, which was perhaps the dominant character of the Sumero-Akkadian civilization, had ensured its cohesion and continuity for three millennia, but it had now become a handicap rather than an asset. The crucial period for Mesopotamia, the Hellenistic period, can be compared with the sixteenth-century Renaissance, or indeed, with our own age. The new world heralded by Alexander was a fast changing world bent on extensive commercial intercourse, bursting with curiosity, eager to reappraise most of its religious, moral, scientific and artistic values.[1] There was no room in such a world for a literature which none but a few scholars could read, for an art which drew its inspiration from outdated ideals and models, for a science which evaded rational explanations, for a religion which did not admit scepticism. The Mesopotamian civilization, like its Egyptian counterpart, was condemned. If it were permissible to enclose a highly complex phenomenon into one single and necessarily inaccurate formula one could say that it died of old age.

Civilizations, however, rarely die without leaving any trace and even we, men of the twentieth century, must acknowledge our debt towards the ancient inhabitants of Mesopotamia. While we are harnessing the atom and exploring the planets, it is appropriate to remember that we owe the Babylonians the basic principles of our mathematics and astronomy, including our 'positional' numeration and the sexagesimal system by which we still divide our circle and our clocks. We also owe them – though this is of more doubtful value – the bulk of an astrology which, judging from the number of modern publications devoted to this pseudo-science, has lost nothing of its appeal to the masses. To this heritage must be added the rudiments of an efficient administration (undoubtedly a creation of the Assyrians), some institutions, such as the coronation of our kings, a number of symbols mainly used in religious art (the crescent, the Maltese cross, the 'tree of life', for instance), a few words that have come to us through the channels of Greek or Arabic – e.g. cane (Akkadian *qânu*), alcohol (*guhlu*), dragoman (*targumanu*), gypsum (*gaṣṣu*, myrrh (*murru*), saffron (*azupiranu*), naptha (*naptu*) in English, or corne (*qarnu*) and mesquin (*mushkênu*) in French[2] and, last but not least, the Mesopotamian elements detectable in the Bible. All this may appear exceedingly light compared with the enormous weight of our Greco-Roman heritage, but lists of this kind, even when they are exhaustive, fall short of doing full justice to the importance assumed by the Sumero-Akkadian civilization in the history of mankind. To reckon only with those Mesopotamian relics that have survived up to now is like counting the pieces of furniture inherited from remote ancestors, forgetting that these ancestors have shaped the lives of our forefathers and, indirectly, our own life.

Seventy centuries before the birth of Christ, the inhabitants of Jarmo and other Neolithic sites in Northern Iraq took an active part in the invention of agriculture, a crucial revolution in the development of mankind, and their immediate descendants were among the first to make and decorate pottery, mould and bake clay bricks, fashion metallic objects. It is on the banks of the Tigris River and its tributaries, at Tell al-Sawwan and Choga Mami, that were carried out, about 5,000 years B.C., the first experiments in irrigation agriculture, a novelty soon adopted and perfected in the great Euphrataean plain, where some 2,000 years later the wheel, the sail and the sowing-plough were also invented, the first large cities with their temples and 'prestige houses' were built, and almost perfect pieces of art appeared. In approximately 3300 B.C., about two centuries before the Egyptians, the Sumerians invented writing, another fundamental revolution which enabled man to communicate with distant other men; to refine and develop his thoughts; to transmit them from one generation to the other, making them immortal since they were engraved on stones and, more often, on clay, both imperishable materials. Together with the Mesopotamian Semites (Akkadians, Babylonians and Assyrians), the Sumerians used this wonderful tool not only for their accounts, but also to retain memories of the past; to assemble in a coherent system a number of hitherto disparate religious concepts; to honour and serve their gods and obtain from them a glimpse of their own future; to glorify their kings; to codify their laws; to classify the fascinating world around them and lay the foundations for scientific research; to use myths, legends, epic tales and 'counsels of wisdom' in order to express their properly philosophical ideas, ranging from the creation of the cosmos and man to the insoluble problem of Good and Evil; and for thousands of other things which cannot be listed here, for no other peoples in pre-classical antiquity has left us so many texts of all kinds. This is the true 'Mesopotamian heritage', rather than a few institutions, a few symbols and a few words. It is to this impressive series of technical discoveries and intellectual achievements that Mesopotamia owes its '*organic* position in the line of our own past'.[3] It is important to note that the civilization which flourished between the Twin Rivers did not remain within the confines of South-West Asia; It has reached Europe and eventually all of us in two stages: first from place to place during prehistory, regarding its technical aspects, then through the twin channels of our Judeo-Christian tradition and of the Greek culture, regarding its spiritual and artistic contents.

Classical scholars, long dazzled by the so-called 'Greek miracle', have now come to realize the full impact of Oriental influences upon the formative phase of Greek thought, art and ethics[4] – and the Orient, throughout most of pre-classical

antiquity, was to a great extent culturally dependent upon
Mesopotamia. Long before Alexander brought Greece into Asia,
the Aegean countries were in direct contact with Hittite lands and
in commercial relations by sea with Canaan and Egypt. Merchants, craftsmen, ambassadors, princes, royal couriers, physi-
cans and even priests travelled widely within and outside the
Near East. We know that early in the second millennium B.C.
there were Assyrian colonies in the heart of Asia Minor; between
1500 and 1200 B.C. Mycenaean traders lived in Ugarit on the
Syrian coast and cylinder seals of lapis lazuli dating to the Kassite
period (they were probably gifts from an Assyrian king) have
been found in the palace of the Greek Thebes,[5] while Mesopotamian epics and myths were copied on the banks of the Nile in
their original cuneiform script. We should not therefore be
surprised to find that the Greek civilization was 'built upon
East Mediterranean foundations'[6] largely made up of Mesopotamian material. It has already been suggested that Assyro-
Babylonian medicine paved the way for the great Hippocratic
reform of the fourth and fifth centuries B.C.,[7] and it is highly
probable that early Greek mathematicians, such as Pythagoras
(sixth century B.C.), drew largely upon the work of their
Babylonian predecessors. The analysis of Oriental influences
upon Greek art and literature is fraught with difficulties, since
it is not always easy to distinguish between stimulus, parallel
though independent creation and sheer borrowing. Yet, to
quote only undisputable examples, it is now generally recognized that the Aesopian fable had Sumero-Akkadian anteced-
ents and that Gilgamesh was the prototype of both Heracles
and Ulysses,[8] while a glance at the archaic statues and figurines
of continental and insular Greece reveals at once strong affinities
with earlier or contemporary Mesopotamian works.[9]

If Mesopotamia can be shown to have influenced Greece it is
not unreasonable to believe that she exerted an even greater
influence upon other Near Eastern countries. The case has been
repeatedly proven with regard to the Hittites, the Hebrews,
Canaan, Urarṭu, Media and Achaemenian Persia. But what of

the Mesopotamian heritage in later Oriental civilizations? What of Parthian and Sassanian Iran, of Hellenistic, Roman and Byzantine Anatolia? What of Arabia? What of the Islamic religion and institutions? What of Iraq itself, from Parthian times down to the present day? Going even farther afield, Professor Rostovtzeff – one of the few scholars equally at ease in the Hellenistic and Oriental worlds – could write, fifty years ago: 'We are gradually learning how great was the influence of Babylonian and Persian Art on the artistic development of India and China.'[10] The material available is already substantial, if scattered; yet no one, it seems, has undertaken to study it from this particular point of view. But this can wait. So many *tells* in Syria and Iraq are awaiting the spade, so many tablets and other inscriptions need to be published, revised or republished, so many points in the long history of ancient Mesopotamia require elucidation that generations of Assyriologists, archaeologists and historians will be kept fully busy for centuries to come.

LIST OF ABBREVIATIONS
USED IN THE BIBLIOGRAPHY

AAO   H. FRANKFORT, *The Art and Architecture of the Ancient Orient*, Harmondsworth, 1954

AAS   *Annales Archéologiques de Syrie*, Damascus

AASOR   *Annual of the American Schools of Oriental Research*, New Haven

ABC   A. K. GRAYSON, *Assyrian and Babylonian Chronicles*, Locust Valley, N.Y., 1975

AfO   *Archiv für Orientforschung*, Berlin/Graz

AJA   *American Journal of Archaeology*, Concord, New Haven

Akkadica   *Akkadica*, Brussels (*Musées Royaux d'Art et d'Histoire*)

AM   A. PARROT, *Archéologie Mésopotamienne*, Paris, 1946–53

ANET   *Ancient Near Eastern Texts Relating to the Old Testament* (edited by J. B. PRITCHARD), Princeton, N.J., 1950, 2nd edition, 1955

AOAT   *Alter Orient und Altes Testament* (series), Neukirchen-Vluyn

ARAB   D. D. LUCKENBILL, *Ancient Records of Assyria and Babylonia*, Chicago, 1926–7

ARI   A. K. GRAYSON, *Assyrian Royal Inscriptions*, 2 vol., Wiesbaden, 1972–6.

ARM   *Archives Royales de Mari Traductions*, Paris, 1950 ff

BASOR   *Bulletin of the American Schools of Oriental Research*, New Haven

BBS   L. W. KING, *Babylonian Boundary Stones*, London, 1912

BHT   S. SMITH, *Babylonian Historical Texts*, London, 1924

Bi. Or.   *Bibliotheca Orientalis*, Leiden

BaM   *Baghdader Mitteilungen*, Berlin

Bo. Stu.   *Boghazköy Studien*, Leipzig

CAH   *Cambridge Ancient History* (Revised edition), Cambridge

EA   J. A. KNUDZTON, *Die El-Amarna Tafeln*, Leipzig, 1915

HBS   S. N. KRAMER, *History Begins at Sumer*, New York, 1959. 1st edition, 1956

Iraq   *Iraq*, London (British School of Archaeology in Iraq)

IRSA	E. SOLLBERGER and J.-R. KUPPER, *Inscriptions Royales Sumériennes et Akkadiennes*, Paris, 1971
ISA	F. THUREAU-DANGIN, *Les Inscriptions de Sumer et d'Akkad*, Paris, 1905
JAOS	*Journal of the American Oriental Society*, New Haven
JCS	*Journal of Cuneiform Studies*, New Haven
JESHO	*Journal of the Economic and Social History of the Orient*, Leiden
JNES	*Journal of Near Eastern Studies*, Chicago
JSOR	*Journal of the Society of Oriental Research*, Chicago
JSS	*Journal of Semitic Studies*, Manchester
KB	*Keilinschriftliche Bibliothek*, Berlin, 1889 ff.
KING	L. W. KING, *Chronicles Concerning Early Babylonian Kings*, London, 1907
MARI	*Mari, Annales de Recherches Interdisciplinaires*, Paris
MAOG	*Mitteilungen der Altorientalischen Gesellschaft*, Leipzig
MDOG	*Mitteilungen der deutschen Orient-Gesellschaft*, Berlin
MDP	*Mémoires de la Délégation en Perse*, Paris
MVAG	*Mitteilungen der vorderasiatisch-aegyptischen Gesellschaft*, Berlin
NBK	S. LANGDON, *Die neubabylonischen Königsinschriften*, Leipzig, 1912
OIC	Oriental Institute Communications, Chicago
OIP	Oriental Institute Publications, Chicago
Orientalia	*Orientalia*, Rome (Pontifical Biblical Institute)
PKB	J. A. BRINKMAN, *A Political History of Post-Kassite Babylonia*, Rome, 1968
RA	*Revue d'Assyriologie*, Paris
RCAE	LEROY WATERMAN, *Royal Correspondence of the Assyrian Empire*, Ann Arbor, 1930–36
RGTC	*Répertoire Géographique des Textes Cunéiformes* (series), Wiesbaden
RHA	*Revue hittite et asianique*, Paris
RIMA	A. K. GRAYSON (ed.) *The Royal Inscriptions of Mesopotamia, Assyrian Rulers* (series), Toronto
RISA	G. A. BARTON, *The Royal Inscriptions of Sumer and Akkad*, New Haven, 1929
RLA	*Reallexikon der Assyriologie*, Berlin
SAA	*State Archives of Assyria* (series) Helsinki

SKL	T. JACOBSEN, *The Sumerian King List*, Chicago, 1939
Sumer	*Sumer*, Baghdad
Syria	*Syria*, Paris
UE	*Ur Excavations*, London, 1927 ff.
UET	*Ur Excavations Texts*, London, 1928 ff.
UVB	*Uruk vorläufiger Berichte* (= Vorläufiger Berichte über die . . . Ausgrabungen in Uruk-Warka), Berlin
VDI	*Vestnik Drevney Istorii* (= Journal of Ancient History), Moscow
WISEMAN	D. J. WISEMAN, *Chronicles of Chaldaean Kings* (626–556 B.C.), London, 1956
WVDOG	*Wissenschaftliche Veröffenlichungen der deutschen Orient-Gessellschaft*, Leipzig
ZA	*Zeitschrift für Assyriologie*, Leipzig/Berlin
ZZB	D. O. EDZARD, *Die Zweite Zwischenzeit Babyloniens*, Wiesbaden, 1957

BIBLIOGRAPHY AND NOTES

Chapter 1

1. For physical geography: P. BEAUMONT, G. H. BLAKE and J. M. W. WAGSTAFF, *The Middle East, a Geographical Study*, London, 1976. For historical geography (and often much more): J. B. PRITCHARD (Ed.), *The Times Atlas of the Bible*, London, 1989; the *Tübinger Atlas des Vorderen Orients*, Wiesbaden, 1977 ff., and the subsidiary series: *Répertoire Géographique des Textes Cunéiformes* (*RGTC*), 1974 ff.; M. ROAF, *Cultural Atlas of Mesopotamia and the Ancient Near East*, Oxford, 1990.

2. On fauna: E. DOUGLAS van BUREN; *The Fauna of Ancient Mesopotamia as Represented in Art*, Roma, 1939; F. S. BODENHEIMER, *Animal and Man in Bible Land*, Leiden, 1960; B. LANDSBERGER, *The Fauna of Ancient Mesopotamia*, Roma, 1960 (philological study); B. BRENTJES, *Wildtier und Haustier im alten Orient*, Berlin, 1962. On flora: M. ZOHARI, *Geobotanical Foundations of the Middle East*, Stuttgart, 1973; E. GUEST et al., *Flora of Iraq*, Baghdad, 1966 ff.; M. B. ROWTON, 'The woodlands of ancient western Asia', *JNES* XXVI (1967), pp. 261–77.

3. K. W. BUTZER, *Quaternary Stratigraphy and Climate of the Near East*, Bonn, 1958, and *CAH*, I, 1, pp. 35–62; J. S. SAWYER (ed.), *World Climate from 8000 to 0 B.C.*, London, 1966; W. NUTZEL, 'The climate changes of Mesopotamia and bordering areas, 14000 to 2000 B.C.', *Sumer*, XXXII (1976), pp. 11–24.

4. HERODOTUS, II, 5.

5. Put forward by PLINY, *Hist. Nat.*, VI, xxxi, 13, as early as the first century A.D., this theory was codified by DE MORGAN in *MDP*, I (1900), 4–48.

6. G. M. LEES and N. L. FALCON, 'The geographical history of the Mesopotamian plains', *Geogr. Journal*, CXVIII (1952), 1, pp. 24–39.

7. C. E. LARSEN, 'The Mesopotamian delta region: a reconsideration of Lees and Falcon', *JAOS*, XCV (1975), pp. 43–57. P. KASSLER, 'The structural and geomorphic evolution of the Persian Gulf' in

B. H. PURSUER, *The Persian Gulf*, Berlin, Heidelberg, New York, 1973, pp. 11–32. W. NUTZEL, 'The formation of the Arabian Gulf from 14000 B.C.', *Sumer* XXXI (1975), pp. 101–11.

8. G. ROUX, 'Recently discovered ancient sites in the Hammar-Lake district', *Sumer*, XVI (1960), pp. 20–31.

9. M. S. DRAWER, 'Perennial irrigation in Mesopotamia', in *A History of Technology*, London, 1955, I, p. 545 ff.; P. BURINGH, 'Living conditions in the lower Mesopotamian plain in ancient times, *Sumer*, XIII (1957), pp. 30–46; R. MCC. ADAMS, 'Historic patterns of Mesopotamian irrigation agriculture', in T. E. DOWNING and MCG. GIBSON (eds.), *Irrigation Impact on Society*, Tucson, 1971, pp. 1–6.

10. For some scholars, an extensive salinization in southern Iraq between 2400 and 1700 B.C. was the reason for the decline of the political power of the Sumerians. See: T. JACOBSEN and R. MCC. ADAMS, 'Salt and silt in ancient Mesopotamian agriculture' in *Science*, CXXVIII (1958), pp. 1251–8; T. JACOBSEN, *Salinity and Irrigation Agriculture*, Malibu, 1982. For a different opinion, see: M. L. A. POWELL, 'Salt, seed and yields in Sumerian agriculture', *ZA*, LXV (1985), pp. 7–38.

11. M. IONIDES, *The Régime of the Rivers Euphrates and Tigris*, London, 1937.

12. S. N. KRAMER, *HBS*, pp. 65–9; *The Sumerians*, Chicago, 1963, pp. 105–9 and 340–42. Also see: B. LANDSBERGER, 'Jahreszeiten in Sumerisch-Akkadischen', *JNES*, VII (1949), pp. 248–97.

13. HERODOTUS, I, 193; STRABO, XVI, 14.

14. T. JACOBSEN, in *Sumer*, XIV (1958), p. 81, quoted 2537 litres of barley per hectare (2.47 acres) in the vicinity of Girsu (Tello) *c.* 2400 B.C., as against 1,165 to 1,288 litres in the same region during the fifties. The reliability of ancient texts on this subject is discussed by K. BUTZ in E. LIPINSKI (ed.), *State and Temple Economy in the Ancient Near East*, Leuven, 1979, pp. 257–409. Detailed studies on ancient Mesopotamian agriculture are published in *Bulletin on Sumerian Agriculture*, Cambridge, 1984 ff.

15. A. H. PREUSSNER, 'Date culture in ancient Babylonia', *AJSL*, XXXVI (1920), pp. 212–32; W. H. DOWSON, *Dates and Date Cultivation in Iraq*, Cambridge, 1923; B. LANDSBERGER, 'The date-palm and its by-products according to the cuneiform sources', *AfO*, XVII (1967).

16. According to R. ELLISON, 'Diet in Mesopotamia', *Iraq*, XLIII (1981), pp. 35–43, the diet in Mesopotamia at different periods provided 3,495 calories per day on average.

17. On this desert in general, see: C. P. GRANT, *The Syrian Desert*, London, 1937 (with extensive bibliography).

18. On this region, see: A. M. HAMILTON, *Road through Kurdistan*, London, 1958; R. J. BRAIDWOOD and B. HOWE, *Prehistoric Investigations in Iraqi Kurdistan*, Chicago, 1960, pp. 12–17.

19. W. THESIGER, 'The marshmen of southern Iraq', *Geogr. Journal*, CXX (1954), pp. 272–81; *The Marsh Arabs*, London, 1964.

20. R. J. FORBES, *Bitumen and Petroleum in Antiquity*, Leiden, 1936; *Studies in Ancient Technology*, I, Leiden, 1955, pp. 1–118.

21. Numerous books and articles have been published on Mesopotamian trade. See notably: A. L. OPPENHEIM, 'The seafaring merchants of Ur', *JAOS*, LXXIV (1954), pp. 6–17; W. F. LEEMANN, *Foreign Trade in the Old Babylonian Period*, Leiden, 1960; *Trade in the Ancient Near East*, London, 1977 (articles from *Iraq*, XXXIX (1977); N. YOFFEE, *Explaining Trade in ancient Western Asia*, Malibu, 1982; T. STETCH and V. C. PIGOTT, 'The metals trade in southwestern Asia in the third millennium B.C.', *Iraq*, XLVIII (1986), pp. 39–64. On particular metals: J. D. MUHLY, *Copper and Tin*, Hamden, Conn., 1973; K. R. MAXWELL-HYSLOP, 'Sources of Sumerian gold', *Iraq*, XXXIX (1977), pp. 84–6.

22. J. LEWY, 'Studies in the historic geography of the ancient Near East', *Orientalia*, XXI (1952), pp. 1–12; 265–92; 393–425; A. GOETZE, 'An Old Babylonian itinerary', *JCS*, VII (1953), pp. 51–72. D. O. EDZARD and G. FRANTZ-SZABO. 'Itinerare' *RLA*, V (1977) 216–20.

23. W. W. HALLO, 'The road to Emar', *JCS*, XVIII (1964), pp. 57–88, and remarks by A. GOETZE, *ibid.*, pp. 114–19.

24. SIR ARNOLD T. WILSON, *The Persian Gulf*, London, 1954.

25. For Bahrain, see: G. BIBBY, *Looking for Dilmun*, Penguin Books, London, 1972; D. T. POTTS (ed.), *Dilmun, New Studies in the Archaeology and Early History of Bahrain*, Berlin, 1983; SHAIKHA HAYA ALI AL-KHALIFA and M. RICE (ed.), *Bahrain Through the Ages: the Archaeology*, London, 1986. For Saudi Arabia and the United Arab Emirates, consult the *Proceedings of the Seminar for Arabian Studies*, London, from 1971. Reports of excavations and other papers are published in a variety of scientific journals. For

a general view, see: D. T. POTTS, *The Arabian Gulf in Antiquity*, vol. I, Oxford, 1990.

Chapter 2

1. On Mesopotamian archaeology in general, cf.: A. PARROT, *Archéologie Mésopotamienne*, 2 vols, Paris, 1946–53; H. FRANKFORT, *The Art and Architecture of the Ancient Orient*, Harmondsworth, 1954; SETON LLOYD, *The Archaeology of Mesopotamia*, London, 1978.
2. Up to the end of the third millennium B.C., temples and palaces were, with rare exceptions, made of sun-dried bricks. Baked bricks were almost exclusively used for the pavement of open courtyards, bathroom floors and drains. In many buildings of later periods only the lower part of the walls was built of kiln-baked bricks.
3. The Akkadian (Assyro-Babylonian) word is *tilu*. Sentences such as: 'I turned this town into a mound (*tilu*) and a heap of ruins (*karmu*)' are frequently found in Assyrian royal inscriptions.
4. More details on excavation methods can be found in SETON LLOYD, *Mounds of the Near East*, Edinburgh, 1962. Cf. also A. PARROT, *AM*, II, pp. 15–78. On certain sites where buildings are not too deeply buried, time and money can be saved by 'scraping' the superficial layers of debris. This provides a kind of 'map' of the town and enables the archaeologists to detect areas worthy of true excavations. Tell Taya, in northern Iraq, is an example of this method (*Cf.* J. CURTIS (ed.), *Fifty Years of Mesopotamian Discovery*, London, 1982, figs. 57 and 58).
5. M. B. ROWTON, *CAH*, I, 1, p. 197.
6. *ANET*, pp. 269–70.
7. *ANET*, p. 271.
8. *ARAB*, II, p. 433.
9. TH. JACOBSEN, *The Sumerian King List*, Chicago, 1939.
10. A. UNGNAD, *RLA*, II, 1938, p. 412 ff.
11. For a general survey of this complicated problem, cf.: A. PARROT, *AM*, II, pp. 332–438. The dates 1792–1750 B.C. were proposed by SIDNEY SMITH in *Alalakh and Chronology*, London, 1940, and accepted by an increasing number of scholars (*cf.* M. B. ROWTON, 'The date of Hammurabi', *JNES*, XVII (1958), pp. 97–111).

12. W. F. LIBBY, *Radio-carbon Dating*, Chicago, 1955. For details on the technique, limits and problems of the Carbon 14 method, see: C. RENFREW, *Before Civilization*, Harmondsworth, 1976, pp. 53–92 and 280–94.

13. For details, cf.: S. A. PALLIS, *Early Explorations in Mesopotamia*, Copenhagen, 1954, and SETON LLOYD, *Foundations in the Dust*, London, 1980.

14. XENOPHON, Anabasis, iii, 4.

15. STRABO, XVI, 5.

16. For details, see: C. H. FOSSEY, *Manuel d'Assyriologie*, vol. I, Paris, 1904; S. A. PALLIS, *The Antiquity of Iraq*, Copenhagen, 1956; C. BERMANT and M. WEITZMAN, *Ebla*, London, 1979, pp. 70–123.

17. S. N. KRAMER, *The Sumerians*, Chicago, 1963, p. 15.

18. D. J. WISEMAN, *The Expansion of Assyrian Studies*, London, 1962.

19. Summaries and preliminary reports of these 'salvage excavations' in Iraq have been published in a variety of specialized journals, notably *Sumer*. XXXV (1979) ff. and *Iraq*, XLIII (1979) ff. Some final reports are available in book form. For a general view of the 'Assad dam project' in Syria, see J. C. MARGUERON (ed.), *Le Moyen Euphrate*, Leiden, 1980.

Chapter 3

1. H. FIELD, *Ancient and Modern Man in Southwestern Asia*, Coral Gables, Calif., 1956.

2. R. J. BRAIDWOOD and B. HOWE, *Prehistoric Investigations in Iraqi Kurdistan*, Chicago, 1960; T. C. YOUNG, P. E. L. SMITH and P. MORTENSEN (ed.), *The Hilly Flanks and Beyond*, Chicago, 1984.

3. R. SOLECKI, *Shanidar, the Humanity of Neanderthal Man*, London, 1971.

4. K. W. BUTZER, *CAH*, I, 1 (1970), pp. 49–62.

5. H. E. WRIGHT JNR, 'The Geological Setting of Four Prehistoric Sites in North Eastern Iraq', *BASOR*, 128 (1952), pp. 11–24; 'Geologic Aspects of the Archaeology of Iraq', *Sumer*, XI (1955), pp. 83–90.

6. D. A. E. GARROD and J. G. D. CLARK, *CAH*, I, 1, pp. 74–89 and 118–21.

7. M. L. INIZAN, 'Des indices acheuléens sur les bords du Tigre, dans le nord de l'Iraq', *Paléorient*, XI, 1 (1985), pp. 101–102

8. NAJI-AL-'ASIL, 'Barda Balka', *Sumer*, V (1949), pp. 205–6; H. E. WRIGHT, JNR and B. HOWE, 'Preliminary Report on Soundings at Barda Balka', *Sumer*, VII (1951), pp. 107–10.

9. D. A. E. GARROD, 'The Palaeolithic of Southern Kurdistan: Excavations in the Caves of Zarzi and Hazar Merd', *Bulletin No 6, Amer. School of Prehist. Research*, New Haven (1930).

10. Preliminary reports in Sumer, VIII (1952) to XVII (1961). Also see: R. SOLECKI, 'Prehistory in Shanidar valley, northern Iraq', *Science*, CXXXIX (1963), pp. 179–93, and the book quoted above, note 3.

11. E. TRINKHAUS, 'An inventory of the Neanderthal remains from Shanidar Cave, northern Iraq', *Sumer*, XXXIII (1977), pp. 9–47.

12. A. LEROI-GOURHAN, 'The flowers found with Shanidar V, a Neanderthal burial in Iraq', *Science*, CXC (1975), pp. 562–4.

13. R. J. BRAIDWOOD, 'From Cave to Village in Prehistoric Iraq', *BASOR*, 124 (1951), pp. 12–18. R. J. BRAIDWOOD and B. HOWE, *Prehistoric Investigations in Iraqi Kurdistan*, Chicago, 1960, pp. 28–9, 57–9, 155–6.

14. For more detail on the Mesolithic and Neolithic periods in the Near East, consult: P. SINGH, *Neolithic Cultures of Western Asia*, London and New York, 1974; J. MELLAART, *The Neolithic of the Near East*, London, 1975 and D. and J. OATES, *The Rise of Civilization*, Oxford, 1976.

15. R. SOLECKI, *An Early Village Site at Zawi Chemi Shanidar*, Malibu, Calif., 1980.

16. R. J. BRAIDWOOD and B. HOWE, *Prehistoric Investigations*, op. cit., pp. 52 and 170.

17. R. J. BRAIDWOOD and B. HOWE, *ibid.*, p. 50.

18. M. VAN LOON, 'The Oriental Institute excavations at Mureybet, Syria', *JNES* XXVII (1968), pp. 264–90. J. CAUVIN, *Les Premiers Villages de Syrie-Palestine du IXe au VIIe Millénaire avant J.-C.*, Lyon/Paris, 1978.

19. F. HOLE, K. V. FLANNERY, J. A. NEELY, H. HELBAEK, *Prehistory and Human Ecology in the Deh Luran Plain: an Early Village Sequence from Khuzistan, Iran*, Ann Arbor, Conn. 1969.

20. For more detail on this subject, see: H. J. NISSEN, *The Early History of the Ancient Near East, 9000–2000 B.C.*, Chicago, 1988, pp. 15–27.

21. J. R. HARLAN and D. ZOHARY, 'Distribution of wild wheat and barley', *Science*, CLIII (1966), pp. 1075–80; J. R. HARLAN, 'A wild harvest in Turkey', *Archaeology*, XX (1967), pp. 197–201.

22. L. R. BINFORD, 'Post-Pleistocene adaptations' in S. R. and L. R. BINFORD (ed.), *New Perspectives in Archaeology*, Chicago, 1968, pp. 313–42; K. V. FLANNERY, 'Origins and ecological effects of early domestication in Iran and the Near East' in J. A. SABLOFF and C. C. LAMBERG-KARLOWSKY (ed.), *The Rise and Fall of Civilizations*; Menlo Park, Calif., 1974, pp. 245–68.

23. R. J. and L. BRAIDWOOD, 'Jarmo: a village of early farmers in Iraq', *Antiquity*, XXIV (1950), pp. 189–95; J. MELLAART, *The Neolithic of the Near East*, pp. 80–82.; P. SINGH, *Neolithic Cultures*, pp. 116–21.

24. P. MORTENSEN; *Tell Shimshara: the Hassuna Period*, Copenhagen, 1970.

25. To our knowledge, only summaries have yet been published in *Iraq*, XLI (1979), pp. 152–3 and XLIII (1981), p. 191.

26. D. SCHMANDT-BESSERAT, 'The use of clay before pottery in the Zagros', *Expedition*, XVI (1974), pp. 11–17.

27. On the origins and significance of pottery, see H. J. NISSEN, op. cit., pp. 27–32.

Chapter 4

1. On Mesopotamian proto-history in general, in addition to the books listed in note 14 of Chapter 3, see: J. MELLAART, *Earliest Civilizations of the Near East*, London, 1965; M. E. L. MALLOWAN, *Early Mesopotamia and Iran*, London, 1965; SETON LLOYD, *The Archaeology of Mesopotamia*, London, 1978; C. L. REDMAN, *The Rise of Civilization*, San Francisco, 1978.

2. SETON LLOYD and FUAD SAFAR, 'Tell Hassuna', *JNES*, IV (1945), pp. 255–89.

3. C. S. COON, 'Three Skulls from Hassuna', *Sumer*, IV (1950), pp. 93–6.

4. T. DABBAGH, 'Hassuna pottery', *Sumer*, XXI (1965), pp. 93–111.

5. R. J. BRAIDWOOD, L. BRAIDWOOD, J. G. SMITH and C. LESLIE, 'Matarrah, a southern variant of the Hassunan assemblage, excavated in 1948', *JNES*, XI (1952), pp. 1–75.

6. Danish excavations in 1957–8. Cf. P. MORTENSEN, *Tell Shimshara. The Hassuna Period*, Copenhagen, 1970.

7. Excavated by a Soviet team since 1969. For a summary of the results, see N. Y. MERPERT and R. M. MUNCHAEV, 'Early agricultural settlements in the Sinjar plain, northern Iraq', *Iraq*, XXXV (1973), pp. 93–113; 'The earliest levels at Yarim Tepe I and Yarim Tepe II in northern Iraq', *Iraq*, XLVI (1987), pp. 1–36.

8. Preliminary reports by D. KIRKBRIDE in *Iraq* from vol. XXXIV (1972) to vol. XXXVII (1975). Also see, by the same author, 'Umm Dabaghiyah' in J. CURTIS (ed.), *Fifty Years of Mesopotamian Discovery*, London, 1982, pp. 11–21.

9. Excavated by the Yarim Tepe team. Summaries in 'Excavations in Iraq' in *Iraq*, XXXV (1973), XXXVII (1975), XVIII (1976) and XXXVIII (1977).

10. Japanese excavations from 1956 to 1965, resumed in 1976. Final reports by N. EGAMI *et al.*: *Telul eth-Thalathat*, 3 vols., Tokyo, 1959–74.

11. E. E. HERTZFELD, *Die Ausgrabungen von Samarra*, V, Berlin, 1930.

12. Preliminary reports by B. ABU ES-SOOF, K. A. AL-ʿADAMI, G. WAHIDA and W. YASIN in *Sumer*, XXI (1965) to XXVI (1970). For a global view of the results: J. MELLAART, *The Neolithic of the Near East*, London, 1975, pp. 149–55.

13. H. HELBAEK, 'Early Hassunan vegetables from Tell es-Sawwan, near Samarra', *Sumer*, XX (1964), pp. 45–8.

14. J. OATES, 'The baked clay figurines from Tell es-Sawwan', *Iraq*, XXVIII (1966), pp. 146–53.

15. In the Hamrin basin, Samarran houses, pottery and implements have been found by Japanese archaeologists at Tell Songor and by Iraqi archaeologists at Tell Abada. K. MATSUMOTO, 'The Samarra period at Tell Songor A' in J. L. HUOT (ed.), *Préhistoire de la Mésopotamie*, Paris, 1987, pp. 189–98; SABAH ABBOUD JASIM, 'Excavations at Tell Abada', *Iraq*, XLV (1983), pp. 165–86.

16. Preliminary reports by J. OATES in *Sumer*, XXII (1966), pp. 51–8 and XXV (1969), pp. 133–7; *Iraq*, XXXI (1969), pp. 115–52 and XXXIV (1972), pp. 49–53. By the same author, 'Choga Mami' in J. CURTIS (ed.), *Fifty Years* ... pp. 22–9; 'The Choga Mami traditional' in J. L. HUOT (ed.), *Préhistoire de la Mésopotamie*, pp. 163–80.

17. M. FREIHERR VON OPPENHEIM, *Der Tell Halaf*, Leipzig, 1931. Detailed publication: *Tell Halaf*, I, *Die prähistorischen Funde*, Berlin, 1943.

18. R. CAMPBELL THOMPSON and M. E. L. MALLOWAN, 'The British excavations at Nineveh', *AAA*, XX (1933), p. 71 ff.

19. M. E. L. MALLOWAN and C. ROSE, 'Prehistoric Assyria. The excavations at Tell Arpachiyah', 1933, *Iraq*, II (1935), pp. 1–78.

20. M. E. L. MALLOWAN, 'The excavations at Tell Chagar Bazar', *Iraq*, III (1936), pp. 1–86; IV (1937), pp. 91–117.

21. ISMAIL HIJARA *et al.*, 'Arpachiyah, 1976', *Iraq*, XLII (1980), pp. 31–54; J. CURTIS; 'Arpachiyah', in *Fifty Years . . .*, pp. 30–36.

22. P. J. WATSON, 'The Halafian culture: a review and synthesis', in T. C. YOUNG, P. E. L. SMITH, P. MORTENSEN (ed.), *The Hilly Flanks and Beyond*, Chicago, 1983, pp. 231–50.

23. D. FRANKEL, *Archaeologists at Work: Studies on Halaf Pottery*, London, 1979.

24. This is a physico-chemical technique giving very precise measurements of about 30 elements commonly found in clay, A clay of a specific origin has a specific chemical composition which is both characteristic and unique, like a chemical fingerprint. Since pottery is usually made of the local clay, this method is used to determine the origin of a given piece of pottery (I. PERLMAN, F. ASARO, H. V. MICHEL in *Annual Review of Nuclear Science*, XXII (1972), pp. 383–426). On its application to the Halaf period, see: T. E. DAVIDSON and H. MCKERRELL, 'The neutron activation analysis of Halaf and 'Ubaid pottery from Tell Arpachiyah and Tepe Gawra', *Iraq*, XLII (1980), pp. 155–67.

25. J. MELLAART, *The Neolithic of the Near East*, London, 1975, pp. 169–70.

26. H. R. HALL and C. L. WOOLLEY, *Al-'Ubaid*, London, 1927 (*UE*, I).

27. FUAD SAFAR, MOHAMMED ALI MUSTAFA and SETON LLOYD, *Eridu*, Baghdad, 1982.

28. Some French archaeologists have questioned the religious nature of these buildings and prefer to call them 'prestige buildings'. They claim that they might have housed eminent members of the communities or served as community halls similar to the *mudhifs* of the Marsh Arabs. However, the majority of archaeologists believe that most of them were temples.

29. C. ZIEGLER, *Die Keramik von derQalʿa des Ḥaǧǧi Mohammed*, Berlin, 1953.

30. D. STRONACH, 'Excavations at Ras al 'Amiya', *Iraq*, XXIII (1961), pp. 95–137.

31. Y. CALVET, in *Larsa et Oueili, Travaux de 1978–1981*, Paris, 1983, pp. 15–70; and in *Préhistoire de la Mésopotamie*, Paris, 1987, pp. 129–52.

32. J. L. HUOT, 'Un village de basse Mésopotamie: Tell el 'Oueili à l'Obeid 4', in *Préhistoire de la Mésopotamie*, pp. 129–52.

33. M. D. ROAF, 'The Hamrin sites: Tell Madhhur' in *Fifty Years . . .* pp. 40–46.

34. J. OATES, 'Ubaid Mesopotamia reconsidered' in T. C. YOUNG *et al.* (Ed.), *The Hilly Flanks and Beyond*, Chicago, 1983, pp. 251–72. These 45 apparently intermittent settlements are spread from the southern border of Kuwait to Bahrain and Qatar; another has been found in Bushir peninsula (Iran). They seem to have been camps of fishermen using 'Ubaid 2, 3 or 4 pottery made in Mesopotamia and local flint tools.

Chapter 5

1. See, in particular: C. H. KRAELING and R. MCC. ADAMS (eds.), *City Invincible*, Chicago, 1960; M. B. ROWTON, *The Role of Watercourses in the Growth of Mesopotamian Civilization*, Neukirchen-Vluyn, 1969; P. J. UCKO, R. TRINGHAM and G. W. DIMBLEBY (eds.), *Man, Settlement and Urbanism*, London, 1972; T. E. DAWNING and MCGUIRE GIBSON (eds.), *Irrigation's Impact on Society*, Tucson, 1974.

2. R. MCC. ADAMS and H. J. NISSEN, *The Uruk Countryside*, Chicago, 1972; MCGUIRE GIBSON, *The City and Area of Kish*, Miami, 1972. R. MCC. ADAMS, *Heartland of Cities*, Chicago, 1981.

3. The results of the German excavations at Uruk-Warka (1928–39 and 1952 onwards) are published in a series of preliminary reports known as *Uruk Vorläufiger Berichte* (abbreviated *UVB*). In addition, volumes of monographs (*Ausgrabungen der Deutschen Forschungsgemeinschaft in Uruk-Warka*) deal with particular aspects of the excavations.

4. H. LENZEN, *Die Tempel der Schicht Archaisch V in Uruk*, *ZA*, 49 (1949), pp. 1–20.

5. SETON LLOYD and FUAD SAFAR, 'Tell Uqair', *JNES*, 11 (1943), pp. 131–58.

6. Excavated by the Iraqis in the late sixties. Preliminary reports by B. ABOU-ES-SOOF and I. H. HIJARA in *Sumer*, XXII (1966), XXIII (1967), XXV (1969) and XXIX (1973).

7. German excavations. Preliminary reports by H. HEINRICH *et al.*, in *MDOG*, CI (1969) to CVIII (1976). General book on the subject: E. STROMMENGER, *Habuba Kabira, eine Stadt von 5000 Jahren*, Mainz, 1980.

8. An excellent introduction to glyptics can be found in D. COLLON, *First Impressions: Cylinder Seals in the Ancient Near East*, London, 1987.

9. Published by A. FALKENSTEIN, *Archaische Texte aus Uruk*, Leipzig, 1942.

10. D. DIRINGER, *Writing*, London, 1962; I. J. GELB, *A Study of Writing*, Chicago, 1974; D. HAWKINS, 'The origin and dissemination of writing in Western Asia' in P. R. S. MOOREY (ed.), *The Origins of Civilization*, Oxford, 1979; C. B. F. WALKER, *Reading the Past: Cuneiforms*. London, 1987.

11. D. SCHMANDT-BESSERAT, *An Archaic Recording System and the Origin of Writing*, Malibu, Calif., 1977.

12. Khafaje: *OIC*, XX (1936), p. 25; Habuba Kabira: *AfO*, XXIV (1973), fig. 17; Tell Brak: *Fifty Years of Mesopotamian Discovery*, London 1982, p. 65, fig. 51.

13. E. MACKAY, *Report on Excavations at Jemdet Nasr, Iraq*, Chicago, 1931; H. FIELD and R. A. MARTIN, 'Painted pottery from Jemdet Nasr', *AJA*, 39 (1935), pp. 310–18. For more recent excavations, see: R. J. MATTHEWS *Iraq*, LI (1989), pp. 225–48 and LII (1990), pp. 25–40. For discussions on this period, consult U. FINKBEINER and W. RÖLLIG (ed.), *Gamdat Nasr: Period or Regional Style?* Wiesbaden, 1986.

14. H. HEINRICH, *Kleinfunde aus den archaischen Tempelschichten in Uruk*, Leipzig, 1936, pp. 15–16, pl. 2–3, 38. Hunt stele in *UVB*, V (1934), pp. 11–13, pl. 12–13. Woman's head in *UVB*, XI (1940), frontispiece.

15. W. A. WARD, 'Relations between Egypt and Mesopotamia from prehistoric times to the end of the Middle Kingdom', *JESHO*, VII (1974), pp. 121–35; I. E. S. EDWARDS, in *CAH*, I, 2, pp. 41–5.

16. SETON LLOYD, 'Iraq Government soundings at Sinjar', *Iraq*, VII (1940), pp. 13–21.

17. P. DELOUGAZ and SETON LLOYD, *Pre-Sargonid Temples in the Diyala Region*, Chicago, 1942.

18. The main articles have been conveniently gathered in T. JONES (ed.), *The Sumerian Problem*, New York, 1969. See also: A. PARROT *AM*, II, pp. 308–31.

19. There is still considerable uncertainty as regards the meaning of KI.EN.GI. Some scholars think that *Shumer* and *Kengi/Kengi(r)* are different pronunciations of the same word in the two Sumerian dialects, *emeku* and *emesal*. Others believe that KI.EN.GI is a 'compound ideogram', but they disagree on the way it should be read. On this subject, see F. R. KRAUS, *Sumerer und Akkader*, Amsterdam, 1970, pp. 48–51.

20. On the question of early contacts between Sumerians and Semites, see: F. R. KRAUS, op cit., and the articles by D. O. EDZARD, W. VON SODEN, I. J. GELB, S. N. KRAMER and P. AMIET in *Geneva*, VIII (1960), pp. 241–314.

21. Skulls from Kish (S. LANGDON, *Excavations at Kish*, Paris, 1924, pp. 115–25), from Ubaid (*UE*, I, 1927, pp. 214–40), from Ur (*UE*, II, 1934, pp. 400–407) and from Eridu (*Sumer*, V, 1949, p. 103).

22. H. FRANKFORT, *The Birth of Civilization in the Near East*, London, 1954, p. 50, n.1.

Chapter 6

1. For general studies on Mesopotamian religion, see: S. N. KRAMER, *Sumerian Mythology*, New York, 1961; W. H. P. RÖMER, 'The religion of ancient Mesopotamia' in J. BLEEKER and G. WINDENGREN (ed.), *Historia Religionum*, I, Leiden, 1969; H. RINGGREN, *Religions of the Ancient Near East*, London, 1973, pp. 1–123; T. JACOBSEN, *The Treasure of Darkness: a History of Mesopotamian Religion*, London, 1976. The most recent and complete book on mythology is that of J. BOTTERO and S. N. KRAMER, *Lorsque les Dieux faisaient l'Homme*, Paris, 1989.

2. Excellent translations of Sumerian and Akkadian religious texts can be found in R. LABAT, A. CAQUOT, M. SZNYCER and

M. VIEYRA, *Les Religions du Proche-Orient*, Paris, 1970; J. B. PRITCH-
ARD (ed.), *Ancient Near Eastern Texts Relating to the Old Testament*,
3rd edition, Princeton, 1969; A. FALKENSTEIN and W. von
SODEN, *Sumerische und Akkadische Hymnen und Gebete*, Stuttgart,
1953.

3. W. G. LAMBERT, 'The historical development of the Mesopotamian pantheon' in H. GOEDICKE and J. J. M. ROBERTS (ed.),
   Unity and Diversity, Baltimore/London, 1975.

4. E. CASSIN, *La Splendeur Divine*, Paris, 1968.

5. H. VORLANDER, *Mein Gott*, Neukirchen-Vluyn, 1975. This personal
   god is often represented on cylinder-seals of the Ur III period.

6. T. JACOBSEN, *The Treasures of Darkness*, p. 20.

7. Possibly in the first centuries of the Early Dynastic period, after
   Enmebaragesi, King of Kish, had built the temple of Enlil in
   Nippur. [S. N. KRAMER, *Geneva*, VIII (1960), p. 277, note 25.]

8. Hymn to Enlil: *ANET*, 3rd Edition, p. 575.

9. List of *me* in S. N. KRAMER, *The Sumerians*, Chicago, 1963, p. 116.

10. Myth 'Enki and the World Order': S. N. KRAMER, *Sumerian
    Mythology*, pp. 59–62; *The Sumerians*, pp. 172–83; J. BOTTERO
    and S. N. KRAMER, *Lorsque les Dieux . . .*, pp. 165–88.

11. W. W. HALLO and J. VAN DIJK, *The Exaltation of Inanna*, New
    Haven/London 1968 (cf. *ANET*, pp. 579–82). Also see the
    hymns and prayers to Inanna in R. LABAT *et al.*, *Les Religions du
    Proche-Orient*, pp. 227–57.

12. S. N. KRAMER, *The Sacred Marriage Rite*, Bloomington, 1969; *Le
    Mariage Sacré*, Paris, 1983.

13. D. REISMAN, 'Iddin-Dagan's Sacred Marriage hymn', *JCS*, XXV
    (1973), pp. 185–202.

14. Sumerian version in *ANET*, pp. 52–7; Assyrian version, *ibid.*, pp.
    106–9. J. BOTTERO and S. N. KRAMER, *Lorsque les Dieux . . .*, pp.
    275–300 and 318–30.

15. R. GRAVES, *The Greek Myths*, London, 1955.

16. On these legends, cf.: S. G. F. BRANDON, *Creation Legends of the
    Ancient Near East*, London, 1963, and A. HEIDEL, *The Babylonian
    Genesis*, Chicago, 1951.

17. W. THESIGER, *Geogr. Journal*, CXX (1954), p. 276.

18. A. HEIDEL, *The Babylonian Genesis*, Chicago, 1954; E. A. SPEISER
    in *ANET*, pp. 60–72 and 501–3. J. BOTTERO and S. N.
    KRAMER, *Lorsque les Dieux . . .*, pp. 602–79.

19. As suggested by TH. JACOBSEN in *The Intellectual Adventure of Ancient Man*, Chicago, 1946, p. 170. Others see in *mummu* an epithet of Tiamat: 'mother Tiamat', 'creator Tiamat' or the like [cf. A. HEIDEL, 'The meaning of *mummu* in Akkadian literature', *JNES*, VII (1948), pp. 98–105].

20. M. J. SEUX, *Hymnes et Prières aux Dieux de Babylonie et d'Assyrie*, Paris, 1976. Also see A. FALKENSTEIN and W. VON SODEN, op. cit., note 1 above.

21. W. G. LAMBERT, *Babylonian Wisdom Literature*, Oxford, 1960, p. 101.

22. The Gilgamesh Epic, Old Babylonian version, III, iv, 6–8. (Transl. E. A. SPEISER, *ANET*, p. 79).

23. 'Inanna's Descent to the Netherworld', Obv. 8–11 (Transl. A. HEIDEL, op. cit., p. 121).

24. '*Ludlul bêl nemeqi*', II, 36–42, 48 (W. G. LAMBERT, op. cit., p. 41).

Chapter 7

1. S. N. KRAMER, *Enmerkar and the Lord of Aratta: a Sumerian Epic Tale of Iraq and Iran*, Philadelphia, 1952.

2. S. N. KRAMER, 'Enki and Ninhursag: a Paradise myth' in *ANET*, pp. 37–41.

3. E. A. SPEISER, 'Adapa' in *ANET*, pp. 101–3; S. A. PICCHIONI, *Il Poemetto di Adapa*, Budapest, 1981.

4. G. ROUX, 'Adapa, le vent et l'eau', *RA*, LV (1961), pp. 13–33.

5. TH. JACOBSEN, 'Primitive democracy in ancient Mesopotamia', *JNES*, II (1943), pp. 159–72; 'Early political development in Mesopotamia', *ZA*, LII (1957), pp. 91–140.

6. TH. JACOBSEN, *The Sumerian King List*, Chicago, 1939.

7. *Bad-tibira* has been identified with Tell Medain, near Telloh [V. E. CRAWFORD, *Iraq*, XXII (1960), pp. 197–9]. *Larak* might be Tell el Wilaya, near Kut-el-Imara [*Sumer*, XV (1959), p. 51]. *Sippar* is modern Abu Habba, about 32 kilometres south-west of Baghdad, partly excavated by H. RASSAM in 1881–2, by V. SCHEIL in 1894 and by W. ANDRAE and J. JORDAN in 1927 (cf. *AM*, I, pp. 101, 159, 326). *Shuruppak* is Tell Fara, about 64 kilometres south-east of Diwaniyah, excavated by the Germans in 1902–3 (H. HEINRICH and W. ANDRAE, *Fara*, Berlin, 1931)

and by the Americans in 1931 [E. SCHMIDT, *Museum Journal*, (Philadelphia) XXII (1931), pp. 193–245].

8. 'Gilgamesh', tablet XI, 9–196 (quotations from A. HEIDEL's translation). See also: E. SOLLBERGER, *The Flood*, London, 1962.

9. Usually identified with mount Pir Omar Gudrun, 2,612 metres, in the Zagros range, south of the Lower Zab [E. A. SPEISER, *AASOR*, VIII (1928), pp. 18, 31].

10. For these early versions, cf.: *ANET*, pp. 42–4, 99–100, 104–6, 512–14, and W. G. LAMBERT and A. R. MILLARD, *Atra-hasis. The Babylonian Story of the Flood*, Oxford, 1969.

11. SIR LEONARD WOOLLEY, *AJ*, IX (1929), pp. 323–30; X (1930), pp. 330–41; *Ur of the Chaldees*, London, 1950, p. 29; *Excavations at Ur*, London, 1954, pp. 34–6; *UE*, IV, pp. 15 ff.

12. Among recent publications on this subject, cf.: M. E. L. MALLOWAN, 'Noah's Flood reconsidered', *Iraq*, XXVI (1964), pp. 62–82; H. J. LENZEN, 'Zur Flutschicht in Ur', *BM*, III (1964), pp. 52–64; R. L. RAIKES, 'The physical evidence for Noah's Flood', *Iraq*, XXVIII (1966), pp. 52–63.

13. A. D. KILMER, 'The Mesopotamian concept of overpopulation and its solution reflected in mythology', *Orientalia*, XLI (1972), pp. 160–77.

14. H. DE GENOUILLAC, *Premières Recherches Archéologiques à Kich*, 2 vol., Paris, 1924–5; S. LANGDON, L. C. WATELIN, *Excavations at Kish*, 3 vol., Paris, 1924–34. Updating by P. R. S. MOOREY, *Kish Excavations*, 1922–3, Oxford, 1978. Present name of the site: al-Uhaimir.

15. English translation by E. A. SPEISER in *ANET*, pp. 114–18. The latest, most complete study is that of J. V. KINNIER WILSON, *The Legend of Etana, a New Edition*, Warminster, 1985.

16. S. N. KRAMER, 'Gilgamesh and Agga', *ANET*, pp. 44–7; W. H. P. RÖMER, *Das Sumerische Kurzepos Bilgamesh und Akka*, Neukirchen-Vluyin, 1980.

17. For Enmerkar, see note 1 above, plus: A. BERLIN, *Enmerkar and Ensuhkeshdanna: a Sumerian Narrative Poem*, Philadelphia, 1979. For Lugalbanda, C. WILCKE, *Das Lugalbanda Epos*, Wiesbaden, 1969.

18. Located near lake Urmiah by E. I. GORDON, *Bi.Or.*, XVII (1960), p. 132, n. 63; near Kerman, in central Iran, by Y. MADJIZADEH, *JNES*, XXXV (1976), p. 107; around Shahr-i

Sokhta, in eastern Iran, by J. F. HANSMAN, *JNES*, XXXVII (1978), pp. 331–6.

19. On the Sumerian cycle of Gilgamesh, see *HBS*, pp. 174–81 and 190–99; *ANET*, pp. 45–52; *Gilgamesh et sa Légende*, Paris, 1960.

20. In 1960 the Gilgamesh epic had been translated into twelve languages (*Gilgamesh et sa Légende*, pp. 24–7), and this figure is probably much higher now. Among the main English translations are those of A. HEIDEL, *The Gilgamesh Epic and Old Testament Parallels*, Chicago, 1949; E. A. SPEISER and A. K. GRAYSON in *ANET*, pp. 72–9 and 503–7 (from which we quote), and J. GARDNER, J. MAIER and R. HENSHAW, *Gilgamesh*, New York, 1984.

21. Beside various Iraqi sites (notably Nineveh), fragments of tablets of the Gilgamesh epic have been found in Palestine (Megiddo) and Turkey (Sultan Tepe, Boghazköy). The Hittite and Hurrian translations were found at the latter site.

Chapter 8

1. Inscriptions found in 1973 at al-Hiba have shown that this site is ancient Lagash, whilst Telloh is Girsu. The two towns are 30 kilometres apart, but together with Shurgal (Nina) they were part of the same city-state named 'Lagash'. V. E. CRAWFORD, 'Lagash', *Iraq*, XXVI (1974), pp. 29–35.

2. Fifteen campaigns of excavations were carried out in Girsu (then called Lagash) between 1877 and 1910, and four campaigns between 1929 and 1933. For a review of the overall results, see A. PARROT, *Tello*, Paris, 1948.

3. D. O. EDZARD, 'Enmebaragesi von Kish', *ZA*, 53 (1959), pp. 9–26.

4. Abu Salabikh is 20 kilometres from Nippur. It has been excavated by the Americans from 1963 to 1965 and by the British since 1975. Preliminary reports in *Iraq* since 1976. Overall results of excavations by N. POSTGATE in J. CURTIS (ed.), *Fifty Years of Mesopotamian Discovery*, London, 1982, pp. 48–61. The ancient name of this town could be Kesh (not to be confused with Kish).

5. The Italian excavations at Ebla began in 1964 and are still in progress. General books on archaeology and texts: P. MATTHIAE;

Ebla, an Empire Rediscovered, New York, 1980; G. PETTINATO, *The Archives of Ebla. An Empire Inscribed in Clay*; Garden City, N.Y., 1981. The texts are published in two parallel series: *Materiali Epigrafici di Ebla*, Napoli, since 1979, and *Archivi Reali di Ebla*, Roma, since 1985. Numerous studies in the periodical *Studi Eblaiti*, Roma, since 1979 and many other publications.

6. Preliminary reports of the first twenty-one campaigns of excavations at Mari (1933–9 and 1951–74) in *Syria* and *AAAS*. Four volumes of final reports have been published. The temples, sculptures and inscriptions of the Early Dynastic period can be found in *Mission Archéologique de Mari*, vol. I, *Le Temple d'Ishtar*, Paris, 1956; vol. III, *Les Temples d'Ishtarat et de Ninni-zaza*, Paris, 1967, vol. IV, *Le Trésor d'Ur*, Paris, 1968. For an overview, see: A. PARROT, *Mari, Capitale Fabuleuse*, Paris, 1974. The French excavations at Mari have been resumed and are going on.

7. W. ANDRAE, *Das wiedererstandene Assur*, Leipzig, 1938, 2nd revised edition, Munich, 1977. For more detail, by the same author: *Die archaischen Ischtar-Temple in Assur*, Leipzig, 1922.

8. British excavations from 1967 to 1973. Preliminary reports in *Iraq*, XXX (1968) to XXXV (1973). Overall results by J. E. READE in J. CURTIS (ed.), *Fifty Years . . .*, pp. 72–8.

9. German excavations under A. MOORTGAT, since 1958. Preliminary reports 1969–73 by A. MOORTGAT *et al.*, *Tell Chuera in Nordöst Syrien*, Köln and Opladen, 1960–75.

10. Eight volume of reports on the Chicago Oriental Institute excavations in the Diyala basin have been published between 1940 and 1967 in the series 'Oriental Institute Publications' (*OIP*). Six of them concern the third millennium B.C. For a short description see SETON LLOYD, *The Archaeology of Mesopotamia*, London, 1978, pp. 93–134.

11. O. TUNCA, *L'Architecture Religieuse Protodynastique en Mésopotamie*, 2 vol., Leuven, 1984. Also see. H. E. W. CRAWFORD, *The Architecture of Iraq in the Third Millennium* B.C., Copenhagen, 1977, pp. 22–6 and 80–82.

12. Cf. A. PARROT, *Sumer*, 2nd edition, 1981, fig. 13–15, 127–30, 133, 134 (Tell Asmar); 131, 132 (Khafaje); 137–8 (Tell Khueira); 30, 148, 153, 154 (Mari); 139–41 (Nippur), 135 (Eridu), 136 (Telloh); 144 (al-Ubaid).

13. A. PARROT, *Sumer*, 1981, p. 148.

14. SETON LLOYD, *The Archaeology of Mesopotamia*, London, 1978, pp. 132–4; G. M. SCHWARTZ, 'The Ninevite V period and current research', *Paléorient*, 11, 1985, pp. 52–70; M. ROAF, R. KILICK, 'A mysterious affair of style: the Ninevite V pottery of Northern Mesopotamia', *Iraq*, XLIX (1987), pp. 199–230.

15. SETON LLOYD, op. cit., pp. 124–7; D. COLLON, *First Impressions. Cylinder Seals in the Ancient Near East*, London, 1987, pp. 20–31.

16. Numerous studies have been devoted to this subject. Among these, see: A. FALKENSTEIN, 'La cité-temple sumérienne' in *Cahiers d'Histoire Mondiale* I, Paris, 1954, pp. 784–814; S. N. KRAMER, *The Sumerians*, Chicago, 1963, pp. 73–112; I. J. GELB, 'The ancient Mesopotamian ration system', *JNES*, XXIV (1965), pp. 230–43; C. C. LAMBERG-KARLOVISKY; 'The economic world of Sumer' in D. SCHMANDT-BESSERAT (ed.), *The Legacy of Sumer*, Malibu, Calif., 1976, pp. 59–68.

17. I. M. DIAKONOFF, *Sale of Land in Presargonic Sumer*, Moscow, 1954.

18. W. W. HALLO, *Early Mesopotamian Royal Titles*, New Haven, 1967; M. J. SEUX, *Epithètes Royales Akkadiennes et Sumériennes*, Paris, 1967.

19. Kish: E. MACKAY, *A Sumerian Palace and the 'A' Cemetery at Kish*, Chicago, 1929; P. R. S. MOOREY, *Kish Excavations*, Oxford, 1978, pp. 55–60; Mari: A. PARROT, *Syria*, XLII (1965) to XLIX (1972); *Mari, Capitale Fabuleuse*, Paris, 1974, pp. 73–88; Eridu: F. SAFAR, *Sumer*, VII (1950), pp. 31–3.

20. C. L. WOOLLEY, *Ur, the Royal Cemetery* (*UE* II), London, 1934; *Ur of the Chaldees* (updated by P. R. S. MOOREY), London, 1982, pp. 51–103.

21. C. J. GADD, 'The spirit of living sacrifice in tombs', *Iraq*, XXII (1960), pp. 51–8.

22. *ANET*, p. 51 [cf. S. N. KRAMER, *Iraq*, XXII (1960), pp. 59–68].

23. P. R. S. MOOREY, 'What do we know about the people buried in the Royal Cemetery?', *Expedition*, XX (1977–8), pp. 24–40; G. ROUX, 'La grande énigme des tombes d'Ur', *L'Histoire*, (Paris), LXXV (1985), pp. 56–66.

24. M. LAMBERT, 'Les réformes d'Urukagina', *RA*, LI (1957), pp. 139–44, and *Orientalia*, XLIV (1975), pp. 22–51; S. N. KRAMER, *The Sumerians*, pp. 79–83; B. HRUSKA, 'Die Reformtexte Urukaginas', in *Le Palais et la Royauté*, pp. 151–61.

25. The very important site of Ur (el-Mughayir, 15 kilometres

south-west of Nasriyah) was excavated by a British-American team from 1922 to 1934. Final reports in *Ur Excavations (UE)*, London, 10 volumes published. Texts in *Ur Excavations Texts (UET)*, London/Philadelphia, 9 volumes published. For an overview see C. L. WOOLLEY *Ur of the Chaldees*, London, 1982.

26. A. PARROT and G. DOSSIN, *Le Trésor d'Ur*, Paris, 1968. On the problems raised by this discovery, cf. M. E. L. MALLOWAN, *Bi.Or.*, XXVI (1969), pp. 87–9; E. SOLLBERGER, *RA*, LXIII (1969), pp. 169–70, and G. DOSSIN, *RA*, LXIV (1970), pp. 163–8.

27. As told by Entemena: *ISA*, pp. 63 ff.; *RISA*, pp. 57 ff., *IRSA*, pp. 71 ss. Latest study: J. S. COOPER, *Reconstructing History from Ancient Inscriptions: the Lagash-Umma Border Conflict*, Malibu, Calif., 1983.

28. Akshak is probably to be located to the east of the Tigris, between the Diyala and the Lesser Zab.

29. This text was initially published by G. PETTINATO, notably in *Oriens Antiquus*, XIX (1980), pp. 231–45, as a campaign of Eblaites against Mari. This was challenged on grammatical grounds by D. O. EDZARD in *Studi Eblaiti*, XIX (1980) and interpreted by him, followed by other scholars, as described here.

30. A. ARCHI, 'Les rapports politiques et économiques entre Ebla et Mari' in *MARI*, IV, Paris, 1985, pp. 63–83.

31. F. PINNOCK, 'About the trade of early Syrian Ebla', *ibid.*, pp. 85–92.

32. Excavated by the University of Chicago in 1903–4. E. J. BANKS, *Bismaya, or the Lost City of Adab*, New York, 1912.

33. *ISA*, pp. 90 ff.; *RISA*, pp. 89 ff.; S. N. KRAMER, *The Sumerians*, pp. 322–3.

34. *ISA*, pp. 218 ff.; *RISA*, pp. 97 ff.; TH. JACOBSEN, *ZA*, 52 (1957), pp. 135–6; S. N. KRAMER, *The Sumerians*, pp. 323–4.

Chapter 9

1. Condensed information on the Semites in general can be found in: S. MOSCATI, *The Semites in Ancient History*, Cardiff, 1959.

2. For criticism of the 'Arabian theory', cf. J. M. GRINZ, 'On the

original home of the Semites', *JNES*, XXI (1962), pp. 186–203. But we cannot agree with the author's views that northern Mesopotamia and southern Armenia were the cradle of the Semites.

3. On nomads in the ancient East, see: J. R. KUPPER, *Les Nomades en Mésopotamie au Temps des Rois de Mari*, Paris, 1957, and the penetrating studies of M. B. ROWTON in *Orientalia*, XLII (1973), pp. 247–58; *JNES*, XXXII (1973), pp. 201–15; *JESHO*, XVII (1974), pp. 1–30.

4. S. N. KRAMER, *Genava*, VIII (1960), p. 277.

5. A. GUILLAUME, *Prophecy and Divination among the Hebrews and other Semites*, London, 1939.

6. R. D. BIGGS, 'Semitic names in the Fara period', *Orientalia*, XXXVI (1967), pp. 55–66.

7. On this subject, see the articles by D. O. EDZARD and L. J. GELB in *Aspects du Contact Suméro-Akkadien*, Geneva, 1960, and F. R. KRAUS, *Sumerer und Akkader*, Amsterdam/London, 1970.

8. *ANET*, p. 119; B. LEWIS, *The Sargon Legend*, Cambridge, Mass., 1980; J. S. COOPER and W. HEIMPEL, 'The Sumerian Sargon Legend', *JAOS* CIII (1983), pp. 67–92.

9. We are referring to Sargon's inscriptions, many of which are second-millennium copies. See: *IRSA*, pp. 97–9; *ANET*, pp. 260–68 and H. E. HIRSCH, 'Die Inschriften der Könige von Agade', *AfO*, XX (1963), pp. 1–82.

10. The various sites suggested are listed in *RGTC*, I, p. 9 and II, p. 6. The hypothesis that Agade was the present Mizyiad, 6 kilometres north-west of Kish (H. WEISS, *JAOS*, XVC (1975), pp. 442–51) has been disproved by Iraqi excavations of that mound.

11. 'Hymnal prayer of Enheduanna: the adoration of Inanna in Ur', *ANET*, pp. 579–82 (transl. S. N. KRAMER).

12. Unidentified city (*RGTC*, I, p. 76), probably in northern Syria and perhaps Irim of the Ebla texts.

13. On the bronze head, see M. E. L. MALLOWAN in *Iraq*, III (1936), p. 104 ff. On the texts, see I. J. GELB, *Old Akkadian Writing and Grammar*, Chicago, 1961, pp. 194–5.

14. W. ALBRIGHT, 'The epic of the King of the Battle', *JSOR*, VII (1923), pp. 1 ff.; E. F. WEIDNER, 'Der Zug Sargons von Akkad nach Kleinasien', *Bo.Stu.*, VI (1922).

15. J. NOUGAYROL, 'Un chef d'oeuvre inédit de la littérature babylo-

nienne', *RA*, XLV (1951), pp. 169 ff. On a late text purporting
to describe the geography of Sargon's empire, see: A. K. GRAY-
SON, 'The Empire of Sargon of Akkad', *AfO*, XXV (1974–7),
pp. 56–64.

16. KING, *Chronicles*, I, pp. 27–156; *ABC*, pp. 152–4; *ANET*, p.
266.

17. A. GOETZE, 'Historical allusions in Old Babylonian omen texts',
JCS, I (1947), p. 256, No. 13. For a discussion of the weapons
involved (stone tablets, heavy seals, other cylindrical objects?),
cf. D. J. WISEMAN, 'Murder in Mesopotamia', *Iraq*, XXXVI
(1974), p. 254.

18. *IRSA*, p. 104.

19. P. MATTHIAE, *Ebla, in Impero Ritrovato*, Torino, 1977, pp. 47, 182.
It seems that the Early Dynastic palace of Mari was destroyed
on the way.

20. This huge tell was first excavated in 1937–8, then from 1976
onwards. For an overall view of the results, see: M. E. L. MAL-
LOWAN in *Twenty-five Years of Mesopotamian Discovery*, London,
1956, pp. 24–38, and D. OATES in J. CURTIS (ed.), *Fifty Years of
Mesopotamian Discovery*, London, 1982, pp. 62–71. Recent reports
in *Iraq*. To the vast 'Narâm-Sin Palace' (in fact a fortified
administrative building) must now be added several houses and
a temple.

21. Rock sculpture of Darband-i-Gawr in S. SMITH, *History of Early
Assyria*, London, 1928, p. 97. Stele of Narâm-Sin: J. DE MORGAN,
MDP (1900), pp. 144 ff.; V. SCHEIL, *MDP*, II (1900), pp. 53 ff.;
A. PARROT, *Sumer*, pls. 212–13.

22. So called because it was written on an apocryphal stele allegedly
deposited in Kutha (Tell Ibrahim). Cf. O. GURNEY, *Anatolian
Studies*, V (1955), pp. 93–113. In another inscription, Narâm-Sin
admits defeat; his numerous troops were crushed and he could
only defend Agade; but the text is incomplete. Cf. A. K. GRAYSON
and E. SOLLBERGER, 'L'insurrection générale contre Narâm-
Suen', *RA*, LXX (1976), pp. 103–28.

23. *MDP*, IV, pl. XI; *ISA*, pp. 246 ff.; *RISA*, p. 151.

24. J. S. COOPER, *The Curse of Agade*, Baltimore/London, 1983.

25. S. PIGGOTT, *Prehistoric India*, Harmondsworth, 1950; SIR MOR-
TIMER WHEELER, *The Indus Civilization*, Cambridge, 1962; *Civilizations of the Indus Valley and beyond*, London, 1966; G. L. POSSEHL

(ed.) *Harappan Civilization*, Warminster, 1982. Commercial relations with the Indus valley were already established during the Early Dynastic period (*UE*, II, pp. 397 ff.).

26. A five-foot-high pyramidal block of diorite covered with an Akkadian inscription in sixty-nine columns and known as the 'obelisk of Manishtusu' refers to the purchase by the king of a large estate in central Mesopotamia. Translation by V. SCHEIL, *MDP*, II (1900), pp. 1–52. See also: H. HIRSCH, *AfO*, XX (1963), p. 14.

Chapter 10

1. On the Guti, see: C. J. GADD, *CAH*, I, 2, pp. 457–63 and W. W. HALLO, article 'Gutium' in *RLA*, 3 (1971), pp. 708–20.

2. R. KUTSCHER, *The Brockmon Tablets at the University of Haifa. Royal Inscriptions*, Haifa, 1989, pp. 49–70.

3. *IRSA*, p. 132; W. H. P. RÖMER, 'Zur Siegensinschrift des Königs Utu-hegal von Unug (*c.* 216–2110 v.Chr.), *Orientalia*, LIV (1985), pp. 274–88.

4. S. N. KRAMER, 'The Ur-Nammu law-code: who was its author?', *Orientalia*, LII (1983), pp. 453–56.

5. The main studies concerning ziqqurats are: H. J. LENZEN, *Die Entwicklung der Zikkurat*, Leipzig, 1941; TH. BUSINK, *De Babylonische Tempeltoren*, Leiden, 1949; A. PARROT, *Ziggurats et Tour de Babel*, Paris, 1949; W. ROLLIG, 'Der Turm zu Babel' in A. ROSENBERG (ed.), *Der babylonische Turm. Aufbruch ins Masslose*, München, 1975.

6. S. N. KRAMER and A. FALKENSTEIN, 'Ur-Nammu law code', *Orientalia*, 23 (1954), pp. 40–51. E. SZLECHTER, 'Le code d'Ur-Nammu', *RA*, XLIX (1955), pp. 169–77. J. J. FINKELSTEIN, 'The laws of Ur-Nammu', *JCS*, XXII (1968–9), pp. 66–82.

7. C. L. WOOLLEY, *The Ziggurat and its Surroundings* (*UE*, V), London, 1939; SIR LEONARD WOOLLEY and R. P. S. MOOREY, *Ur of the Chaldees* London, 1982, pp. 138–47.

8. A. FALKENSTEIN, *Die Inschriften Gudeas von Lagash*, 1, Rome, 1966. Bibliography in W. RÖMER, 'Zurn heutigen' Stande der Gudeaforschung', *Bi.Or.*, XXVI (1969 pp. 159–71. The quotations given here are from: Cylinder A, translation M. LAMBERT and R. TOURNAY, *RB*, 55 (1948), pp. 403–23 (cf. A. L. OPPEN-

HEIM in *ANET*, p. 268); Statue E, translation M. LAMBERT, *RA*, XLVI (1952), p. 81.

9. A. PARROT, *Tello*, Paris, 1948, pp. 147–207; *Sumer*, pp. 220–32. Some doubt has been expressed as to the authenticity of some of these statues: F. JOHANSEN; *Statues of Gudea Ancient and Modern*, Copenhagen, 1978.

10. S. N. KRAMER, 'The death of Ur-Nammu and his descent to the Netherworld', *JCS*, XXI (1967), pp. 104–22.

11. W. W. HALLO, 'Simurrum and the Hurrian frontier', *RHA*, XXXVI (1978), pp. 71–82. *Shashrum* is Shimshara; *Urbilum* is modern Erbil; *Harshi* might be at or near modern Turz Kurmatli; *Simurrum* has not been identified but could be between Arbil and Kirkuk.

12. A. FALKENSTEIN and W. VON SODEN, *Sumerische und Akkadische Hymnen und Gebete*, Stuttgart, 1953, pp. 114–19; J. KLEIN, *The Royal Hymns of Shulgi, King of Ur*, Philadelphia, 1981.

13. SIR LEONARD WOOLLEY and R. P. S. MOOREY, *Ur of the Chaldees*, pp. 163–74.

14. Ur-Nammu had married one of his sons with the daughter of Apil-kin, king of Mari (M. CIVIL, *RA*, LVI (1962), p. 213.

15. T. B. JONES and J. W. SNYDER, *Sumerian Economic Texts from the Third Ur Dynasty*, Minneapolis, 1961, pp. 280–310; J. P. GREGOIRE, *Archives Administratives Sumériennes*, Paris, 1970, pp. 61–2 and 201–2.

16. On this institution, cf. W. HALLO, 'A Sumerian amphictyony', *JCS*, XIV (1960), pp. 88–114.

17. P. MICHALOWSKI, 'Foreign tribute to Sumer during the Ur III period', *ZA*, LXVIII (1978), pp. 34–49.

18. These texts have been and are still being published in a wide variety of periodicals. So far, there is no global study on the subject, but much information can be drawn from the books cited in note 15 above.

19. E. SOLLBERGER; 'L'opposition au pays de Sumer et d'Akkad' in A. FINET (ed.), *La Voix de l'Opposition en Mésopotamie*, Bruxelles, 1973, pp. 29–30.

20. H. LIMET, *Le Travail du Métal au Pays de Sumer au Temps de la Troisième Dynastie d'Ur*, Paris, 1960.

21. H. WAETZOLDT, *Untersuchungen zur neusumerischen Textilindustrie*, Roma, 1972.

22. On this controversial subject, see: M. A. POWELL, 'Sumerian merchants and the problem of profits', *Iraq*, XXXIX (1977), pp. 23–9; D. C. SNELL, 'The activities of some merchants of Umma, *ibid.*, pp. 45–50; H. LIMET, 'Les schémas du commerce néosumérien', *ibid.*, pp. 51–8.

23. I. J. GELB, 'Prisoners of war in early Mesopotamia', *JNES*, XXII (1973), pp. 70–98.

24. I. J. GELB, 'The ancient Mesopotamian ration system', *JNES*, XXIV (1965), pp. 230–41.

25. M. CIVIL, 'Shu-Sin's historical inscriptions: collection B', *JCS*, XXI (1967), pp. 24–38; W. W. HALLO, in *RAH*, XXXVI (1978), p. 79.

26. A. UNGNAD, article 'Datenlisten' in *RLA*, II, p. 144; *IRSA*, p. 52. This in fact was a wall, 275 kilometres long, which linked the Euphrates to the Tigris somewhere north of modern Baghdad.

27. On the Amorites generally, see: K. M. KENYON; *Amorites and Canaanites*, London, 1963; G. BUCCELLATI, *The Amorites of the Ur III period*, Napoli, 1963; A. HALDAR, *Who were the Amorites?*, Leiden, 1971; M. LIVERANI, 'The Amorites' in D. J. WISEMAN (ed.), *Peoples of Old Testament Times*, Oxford, 1972, pp. 101–33.

28. E. CHIERA, *Sumerian Epics and Myths*, Chicago 1934, Nos 58 and 112.

29. E. CHIERA, *Sumerian Texts of Varied Contents*, Chicago, 1934, No. 3.

30. On the reign of Ibbi-Sin and the fall of Ur, see: T. JACOBSEN, 'The reign of Ibbi-Suen', *JCS*, VII (1953), pp. 36–44; E. SOLLBERGER, article 'Ibbi-Sin' in *RLA*, V, pp. 1–8; J. VAN DIJKE, 'Ishbi-Erra, Kindattu, l'homme d'Elam et la chute de la ville d'Ur', *JCS*, XXX (1978), pp. 189–207.

31. S. N. KRAMER, 'Lamentation over the destruction of Ur' *ANET*, pp. 455–63. There is also a lamentation over the destruction of Sumer and Ur (*ibid.*, pp. 611–19) and fragmentary lamentations over the destruction of Nippur, Uruk and Eridu; cf. S. N. KRAMER, 'The weeping goddess: Sumerian prototype of the Mater Dolorosa', *Biblical Archaeologist*, 1983, pp. 69–80.

Chapter 11

1. On the socio-economic conditions of Mesopotamia in that period, see: A. L. OPPENHEIM, *Ancient Mesopotamia*, Chicago, 1964, pp. 74–125, and C. J. GADD in *CAH*, II, 1, pp. 190–208. Numerous articles have been published on the subject.

2. W. F. LEEMANS, *The Old Babylonian Merchant*, Leiden, 1950; *Foreign Trade in the Old Babylonian Period*, Leiden, 1960.

3. F. R. KRAUS, 'The role of temples from the third dynasty of Ur to the first Babylonian dynasty', *Cahiers d'Histoire Mondiale*, I, 1954, p. 535.

4. Isin is Ishan Bahriyat, 25 kilometres south of Nippur. German excavations started in 1973 are still in progress. First final reports: B. HROUDA, *Isin-Ishan Bahriyat*, I and II, München, 1977, 1981. Larsa is Senkereh, 48 kilometres north of Nasriyah and not far from Uruk. French excavations in progress since 1968. Interim reports by J. C. MARGUERON, then J. L. HUOT in *Sumer*, XXVII (1971) ff. and *Syria*, XLVII (1970) ff. Also see: J. L. HUOT (ed.), *Larsa et 'Oueili, Travaux de 1978–1981*, Paris, 1983.

5. W. P. H. ROMER, *Sumerische 'Königshymnen' der Isin-Zeit*, Leiden, 1965. A list of these hymns has been published by W. W. HALLO in *Bi. Or.*, XXIII (1966), pp. 239–47.

6. A. L. OPPENHEIM, 'The seafaring merchants of Ur', *JAOS*, LXXIV (1954), pp. 6–17.

7. S. N. KRAMER, 'The Lipit-Ishtar Lawcode' in *ANET*, pp. 159–61. E. SZLECHTER, 'Le code de Lipit-Ishtar', *RA*, LI (1957), pp. 57–82; 177–96, and *RA*, LII (1958), pp. 74–89.

8. On the substitute King, cf.: H. FRANKFORT, *Kingship and the Gods*, Chicago, 1955, pp. 262–5. J. BOTTERO, 'Le substitut royal et son sort en Mésopotamie ancienne', *Akkadica*, IX (1978), pp. 2–24.

9. A. K. GRAYSON, *ABC*, p. 155.

10. Marad is Wanna es-Sa'dun, 24 kilometres north of Diwaniya. On these small Amorite kingdoms, see: D. O. EDZARD, *Die Zweite Zwischenzeit Babyloniens*, Wiesbaden, 1957.

11. H. FRANKFORT, SETON LLOYD, TH. JACOBSEN, *The Gimilsin Temple and the Palace of the Rulers at Tell Asmar*, Chicago, 1940, pp. 116–200. Also see D. O. EDZARD, op. cit., pp. 71–4; 118–21; 162–7.

12. E. SZLECHTER, *Les Lois d'Eshnunna*, Paris, 1954; A. GOETZE, *The Laws of Eshnunna*, New Haven, 1956; *ANET*, pp. 161–3.

13. TAHA BAQIR, *Tell Harmal*, Baghdad, 1959. The texts from Tell Harmal have been published in *Sumer*, VI (1950) to XIV (1958) and in *JCS*, XIII (1959) to XXVII (1975).

14. *Assur* (Qal'at Sherqat) was excavated by a German expedition under W. ANDRAE between 1903 and 1914. Final reports were published in the *WVDOG* collection until the middle fifties. For a condensed account of the results, cf. W. ANDRAE, *Das widererstandene Assur* (2nd edition revised by B. HROUDA), München, 1977.

15. A. POEBEL, 'The Assyrian King List from Khorsabad', *JNES*, I (1942), pp. 247–306; 460–95. A similar list has been published by I. J. GELB in *JNES*, XIII (1954), pp. 209–30. On these lists, see: F. R. KRAUS, *Könige, die in Zelten wohnten*, Amsterdam, 1965, and H. LEWY in *CAH*, I, 2, pp. 743–52.

16. On the beginnings of the Assyrian kingdom, see D. OATES, *Studies in the Ancient History of Northern Iraq*, London, 1968, pp. 19–41.

17. The inscriptions of the early kings of Assyria have been published in *ARI*, I, pp. 4–18 and in *RIMA*, I, pp. 14–46.

18. On the palace, see: J. MARGUERON, 'L'architecture de la fin du IIIe millénaire à Mari' in *Miscellanea Babylonica*, Paris, 1985, pp. 211–22. On the history: J. M. DURAND, 'La situation historique des *shakkanakku*: nouvelle approche', *MARI*, 4, 1985, pp. 147–72.

19. D. CHARPIN, J. M. DURAND, '"Fils de Sim'al": les origines tribales des rois de Mari', *RA*, LXXX (1986), pp. 141–83.

20. G. DOSSIN, 'L'inscription de fondation de Iahdun-Lim, roi de Mari, *Syria*, XXXII (1955), pp. 1–28.

21. D. CHARPIN, in *Miscellanea Babylonica*, pp. 60–61.

22. Tell Leilan, excavated by a team of Yale University since 1979, has yielded a super temple with spiral columns and a large building containing tablets and cylinder-seals. Latest interim report in *AJA*, XCXIV (1990), pp. 529–81. Also see. H. WEISS, 'Tell Leilan and Shubat-Enlil', *MARI*, 4, pp. 269–92.

23. M. T. LARSEN, in *RA*, XLVIII (1974), p. 16. This opinion is shared by D. CHARPIN and J. M. DURAND.

24. The 20,000 odd tablets (most, but not all letters) which form the royal archives of Mari are published in transliteration and translation as *Archives Royales de Mari* (*ARMT*), Paris, 1950 ff.

In 1991, this series, not yet completed, had twenty-six volumes. Many other texts or studies are published separately in *MARI* (= *Mari, Annales de Recherches Interdisciplinaires*); Paris, created in 1982 (seven volumes published), and in other periodicals such as *RA, Iraq, Syria*, etc.

25. *ARMT*, I, 124. The three quotations that follow are taken from *ARMT* (volume and number), IV, 70; I, 61 and I, 69 respectively.

26. J. R. KUPPER, *Les Nomades en Mésopotamie au temps des Rois de Mari*, Paris, 1957.

27. *Qatna*, modern Mishrifeh, 18 kilometres north-east of Homs, was excavated by the French between 1924 and 1929: R. DU MESNIL DU BUISSON, *Le Site Archéologique de Mishrifé-Qatna*, Paris, 1935.

28. *ARMT*, V, 6.

29. *ARMT*, IV, 88.

30. Inscription of Samsi-Addu in *ARI*, I, p. 26.

31. BAHIJA KHALIL ISMAIL, 'Eine Siegesstele des Königs Dadusa von Esnunna', in W. MEID and H. TRENKWALDER, *Im Bannkreis des Alten Orients*, Innsbruck, 1986, pp. 105–8.

32. *ARMT*, I, 93; IV, 5, 14.

33. *ARMT*, V, 56.

Chapter 12

1. For example the head of Hammurabi (?) at the Louvre Museum and the top of the stele with Hammurabi's 'Code of Laws' (A. PARROT, *Sumer*, 1981, figs. 282 and 280 respectively).

2. Illustrations corresponding to these examples can be found in A. PARROT, op. cit., pp. 257–98.

3. W. G. LAMBERT, *Babylonian Wisdom Literature*, Oxford, 1960, p. 10.

4. T. JACOBSEN, *The Treasures of Darkness*, New Haven, 1976, p. 147.

5. W. G. LAMBERT, *op. cit.* above.

6. On the reign in general, see: TH. DE LIAGRE BOHL, 'King Hammurabi of Babylon in the setting of his time', in *Opera Minora*, Leiden, 1953, pp. 339–63; H. SCHMÖKEL, *Hammurabi von Babylon*, Oldenbourg, 1958; H. KLENGEL, *Hammurapi von Babylon und seine Zeit*, Berlin, 1976; C. J. GADD in *CAH*, II, 1, pp. 176–220.

7. The date-formulae of Hammurabi are given in German translation by UNGNAD in *RLA*, II, pp. 178–82. English translation by A. L. OPPENHEIM in *ANET*, pp. 269–71. It has been suggested that in these first campaigns Hammurabi acted as ally, or even as vassal of Shamshi-Adad of Assyria (C. J. GADD, *CAH*, II, 1, p. 177).

8. D. CHARPIN, J. M. DURAND, 'La prise du pouvoir par Zimri-Lim' in *MARI*, 4, 1985, pp. 318–19.

9. On a recently published seal of Zimri-Lim, this king calls himself 'son of Hadni-Addu' (*MARI*, 4, pp. 336–8), This does not necessarily mean that his true father was not Iahdun-Lim, as Zimri-Lim might have been adopted by Hadni-Addu (otherwise unknown) when he was in exile.

10. B. LAFONT, 'Les filles du roi de Mari, in J. M. DURAND (ed.), *La Femme dans le Proche-Orient Antique*, Paris, 1987, pp. 113–25.

11. A. T. CLAY, *The Empire of the Amorites*, New Haven, 1919, p. 97.

12. L. KING, *The Letters and Inscriptions of Hammurabi*, London, 1900–1902; F. THUREAU-DANGIN, 'La correspondance de Hammurabi avec Shamash-haṣir', *RA* XXI (1924), pp. 1–58.

13. D. O. EDZARD, *The Near East*, New York, 1967, pp. 213–14; R. HARRIS, *Ancient Sippar*, Leiden, 1975, pp. 39–142; N. YOFFEE, *The Economic Role of the Crown in the Old Babylonian Period*, Malibu, Calif., 1977, p. 148; R. HARRIS, 'On the process of secularization under Hammurabi', *JCS*, XV (1961), pp. 117–20.

14. Code of Hammurabi, Prologue, I, 1–30. Marduk, in Sumerian AMAR-UTU, 'bullock of the Sun-god' seems to have been a solar deity of minor rank. Although the patron god of Babylon, the capital-city of the first great Babylonian kingdom, he did not figure at the head of the pantheon until the second half of the second millennium B.C. See: H. SCHMÖKEL, 'Hammurabi und Marduk', *RA*, LIII (1959), pp. 183–204.

15. The Code of Hammurabi has been translated into several languages and copiously commented. The most recent English translations are in *ANET*, pp. 163–80 (TH. J. MEEK) and in G. R. DRIVER and G. C. MILES, *Babylonian Laws*, Oxford, 1955–6. Vol. I: Legal Commentary; vol. II: Translation and Philological Commentary.

16. G. R. DRIVER and G. C. MILES, *Babylonian Laws*, pp. 48 ff.; F. R. KRAUS, 'Ein zentrales Problem des altmesopotamischen Rechtes:

was ist der Codex Hammu-rabi?', *Genava*, VIII (1960), pp. 283–96; J. J. FINKELSTEIN, 'Ammiṣaduqa's edict and the Babylonian "Law Codes"', *JCS*, XV (1961), pp. 91–104; D. J. WISEMAN, 'The Laws of Hammurabi again', *JSS*, VII (1962), pp. 161–72.

17. Part of the stele was erased in antiquity, resulting in the loss of five to seven columns of text and approximately thirty-five laws. Fragments of the Code on clay tablets help fill the gap.

18. E. A. SPEISER, 'Mushkênum', *Orientalia*, XXVII (1958), pp. 19–28. The *mushkênum* is already mentioned in the Laws of Eshnunna, §§ 12, 13, 24, 34, 50.

19. The Babylonian marriage was essentially a contract (*CH*, § 128). Before the ceremony, the future husband presented his father-in-law with a 'bridal gift' (*terhatum*), and the bride's father gave her a dowry (*sheriqtum*) of which she had perpetual possession.

20. Neither the Laws of Eshnunna nor the Sumerian Laws (Ur-Nammu, Lipit-Ishtar) mention the *ilkum* which might have been introduced by Hammurabi as a political measure. Note, however, that the absence of this institution in these Law Codes could be due to the fact that they are not so well preserved as the Code of Hammurabi.

21. Code of Hammurabi, Epilogue, xxiv, 30–59 (transl. TH. J. MEEK).

Chapter 13

1. H. W. F. SAGGS, *Everyday Life in Babylonia and Assyria*, London, 1965; S. DALLEY, *Mari and Karana, Two Old Babylonian Cities*, London, 1984, pp. 50–111.

2. On Shimshara: J. LASSØE, *The Shemshara Tablets, a Preliminary Report*, Copenhagen, 1959; *People of Ancient Assyria*, London, 1963. Tell al-Rimah lies 60 kilometres west of Mosul. British excavations from 1964 to 1971. Preliminary reports in *Iraq*, XVII (1965) to XXIV (1972). Summary by D. OATES in J. CURTIS (ed.), *Fifty Years of Mesopotamian Discovery*, London, 1983, pp. 86–98. The identification of this mound as ancient *Karana* is debated. Archives published by S. DALLEY, C. B. F. WALKER and J. D. HAWKINS: *The Old Babylonian Tablets from Tell al-Rimah*, London, 1976.

3. Street chapels of PA.SAG, Ninshubur and unidentified minor gods at Ur: SIR LEONARD WOOLLEY, *AJ*, X (1930), pp. 368–72; *Excavations at Ur*, pp. 190–92; D. J. WISEMAN, 'The goddess Lama at Ur', *Iraq*, XXII (1960), pp. 166–71; SIR LEONARD WOOLLEY, SIR MAX MALLOWAN and T. C. MITCHELL (ed.), *Ur Excavations: The Old Babylonian Period* (*UE* VII), London, 1976.

4. Examples: temple of Hani and Nisaba at Tell Harmal, *Sumer*, II (1946), pp. 23–4; temple of Ishtar-Kititum at Ischâli, *IOC*, XX (1936), pp. 74–98.

5. The principal temples in that period are those of Ischâli, Assur, Tell Leilan, Tell al-Rimah and Larsa, and the temple of the goddess Ningal at Ur. General view in E. HEINRICH, *Die Tempel und Heiligtümer im alten Mesopotamien*, Berlin, 1982.

6. For details on temples and cults, apart from general books on Mesopotamian religion, see: *Le Temple et le Culte, compte-rendu de la XXe Rencontre Assyriologique Internationale*, Leiden, 1972.

7. R. S. ELLIS, *Foundation Deposits in Ancient Mesopotamia*, New Haven and London, 1967.

8. On the difficult subject of Mesopotamian music, as reconstructed from Hurrian tablets of 'score', see: D. WULSTAND, *Music and Letters*, LII (1971), pp. 365–82; A. KILMER, *RA*, LXVIII (1974), pp. 69–82; M. DUCHESNE-GUILLEMIN, 'Déchiffrement de la musique babylonienne', *Academia dei Lincei*, Roma, 1977, pp. 1–25.

9. The studies on Neo-Sumerian feasts published by H. SAUREN and H. LIMET in *Actes de la 17ème Rencontre Assyriologique Internationale*, Ham-sur-Heure, Belgium, 1970, pp. 11–29 and 59–74, would probably apply to the Old Babylonian period with minor changes.

10. F. THUREAU-DANGIN, *Rituels Accadiens*, Paris, 1907, p. 10 ff. (Cf. *ANET*, pp. 334–8.) This ritual dates, in fact, to the Hellenistic period, but it certainly reproduces a much older original.

11. The fundamental study on priests in the Old Babylonian period is that of J. RENGER, 'Untersuchungen zum Priestertum der altbabylonischen Zeit', *ZA*, XXIV (1967), pp. 110–98; XXV (1969), pp. 104–230.

12. See: R. HARRIS, article 'Hierodulen' in *RLA*, IV, pp. 151–5; J. BOTTERO, article Homosexualität' in *RLA*, IV, pp. 459–68.

13. R. HARRIS, 'The *naditu* woman'. in *Studies presented to A. L. Oppenheim*, Chicago, 1964, pp. 106–35, and *Ancient Sippar*, Leiden, 1975, pp. 305–12.

14. The priests received part of the offerings and of the animals sacrificed in proportions fixed by royal decree. See, for instance, the stone-tablet of Nabû-apal-iddina, King of Babylon, in *BBS*, pp. 120–27.

15. A. PARROT, *Mission Archéologique à Mari*, III, Le Palais, 3 vol., Paris, 1958–9. J. MARGUERON, *Recherches sur les Palais Mésopotamiens de l'Age du Bronze*, Paris, 1982, pp. 209–380. Three other palaces are known for that period: Sin-kashid's palace at Uruk, the palace of the kings of Eshnunna at Tell Asmar and the palace at Tell al-Rimah. All three figures in Margueron, op. cit.

16. H. VINCENT, *Revue Biblique* (1939), p. 156.

17. G. DOSSIN, *Syria*, XVIII (1937), pp. 74–5.

18. A. PARROT, *Le Palais, II*; *Sumer*, fig. 254–9; B. PIERRE, 'Décor peint à Mari et au Proche-Orient', *MARI*, 3, Paris, 1984.

19. A. PARROT, *Mari, une Ville Perdue*, Paris, 1938, p. 161.

20. J. BOTTERO, article 'Küche' in *RLA*, VI, pp. 277–98. 'La plus vieille cuisine du monde', *L'Histoire* (Paris), XLIX (1982), pp. 72–82.

21. *ARMT*, I, 64; IV, 79.

22. Modern Tell Ashara, on the Euphrates, 72 kilometres north of Mari. American excavations are in progress. Preliminary reports in *Syro-Mesopotamian Studies*, Malibu, Calif., since 1977.

23. *ARMT*, III, 62.

24. G. DOSSIN, 'Une révélation du dieu Dagan à Terqa', *RA*, XLII (1948), pp. 125–34.

25. A town on the lower Khabur, probably Tell Fedain.

26. Examples taken from *ARMT*, II, 106; VI, 43; I, 89; II, 112 respectively.

27. This was the usual opening sentence for letters. The sender spoke to the scribe who was to read the letter to the addressee.

28. SIR LEONARD WOOLLEY, *UE*, VII, pp. 12–39; 95–165; *Ur of the Chaldees*, London, 1982, pp. 191–213.

29. C. J. GADD, 'Two sketches from the life at Ur', *Iraq*, XXV (1963), pp. 177–88.

30. For details, see: H. W. F. SAGGS, *Everyday Life in Babylonia and Assyria*; On house furniture and equipment: A. SALONEN, *Die Möbel der alten Mesopotamien*, Helsinki, 1963; *Die Hausgeräte der alten Mesopotamien*, Helsinki, 1965–6.

31. On Mesopotamian schools, pupils and teachers, see: C. J. GADD,

Teachers and Students in the oldest Schools, London, 1956; A. W. SJOBERG, 'Der Vater und sein missratener Sohn', *JCS*, XXV (1973), pp. 105–19; 'The Old Babylonian Eduba' in *Sumerological Studies in Honor of Thorkild Jacobsen*, Chicago, 1976, pp. 158–79.

31. *AJ*, XI (1931), pp. 364–6. *Excavations at Ur*, pp. 186–7.

32. A. L. OPPENHEIM, *JAOS*, 74 (1954), pp. 15, 17; W. F. LEEMANS, *The Old Babylonian Merchant*, Leiden, 1950, pp. 78–95; *Foreign Trade in the Old Babylonian Period*, Leiden, 1960, pp. 121–3 and 136–9.

Chapter 14

1. As can be expected, there is a vast literature on the Indo-Europeans. For a general view of the subject, see R. A. CROSSLAND, 'Immigrants from the North', *CAH*, I, 2, pp. 824–76; G. CARDONA, H. M. HOENIGSWALD and A. SENN (ed.), *Indo-European and Indo-Europeans*, Philadelphia, 1970, J. P. MALLORY, *In Search of the Indo-Europeans*, London, 1989.

2. V. G. CHILDE, *The Dawn of European Civilization*, London, 1957; P. BOSCH-GIMPERA, *Les Indo-Européens: Problèmes Archéologiques*, Paris, 1961; M. GIMBUTAS, *Bronze Age Cultures in Central and Eastern Europe*, The Hague, 1965.

3. According to C. RENFREW, *Before Civilization*, Harmondsworth, 1976, the development of metallurgy in the Balkans was independent of Asiatic influences.

4. J. L. CASKEY, *CAH*, I, 2, pp. 786–8, and II, 1, pp. 135–40; cf. M. I. FINLEY, *Early Greece: the Bronze and Archaic Ages*, London, 1970.

5. See J. CHADWICK, *The Decipherment of Linear B*, Cambridge, 1959. See also: S. DOW and J. CHADWICK, *CAH*, I, 1, pp. 582–626.

6. On the Minoan civilization, cf. F. MATZ in *CAH*, I, 1, pp. 141–64 and 557–81. See also: S. HOOD, *The Minoans: Crete in the Bronze Age*, London, 1971, and N. PLATON, *Crete*, London, 1971.

7. SIR MORTIMER WHEELER, 'The Indus civilization', *CAH* (Supplementary Volume), 2nd ed., Cambridge, 1960; *Civilization of the Indus Valley and Beyond*, London, 1966.

8. G. F. DALES, 'Civilizations and floods in the Indus Valley',

Expedition, VII (1965), pp. 10–19; J. P. AGRAWAL and S. KUSUM-GAR, *Prehistoric Chronology and Radiocarbon Dating in India*, London, 1974.

9. J. MELLAART, *Çatal Hüyük: a Neolithic Town in Anatolia*, London, 1967; *The Neolithic of the Near East*, London, 1975, pp. 98–111.

10. R. J. and L. S. BRAIDWOOD, *Excavations in the Plain of Antioch*, I, Chicago, 1960; M. J. MELLINK, 'The prehistory of Syro-Cilicia', *Bi.Or.*, XIX (1962), pp. 219–26.

11. J. MELLAART, 'Anatolia *c.* 4000–2300 B.C.', *CAH*, I, 2, pp. 363–416.

12. P. GARELLI, *Les Assyriens en Cappadoce*, Paris, 1963; L. L. ORLIN, *Assyrian Colonies in Cappadocia*, The Hague/Paris, 1970; M. T. LARSEN, *Old Assyrian Caravan Procedures*, Istanbul, 1967; *The Old Assyrian City-State and its Colonies*, Copenhagen, 1976; K. R. VEEN-HOF, *Aspects of Old Assyrian Trade and its Terminology*, Leiden, 1977.

13. On the Hittites generally, see: O. R. GURNEY, *The Hittites*, London, 1980; J. G. MACQUEEN, *The Hittites and their Contemporaries in Asia Minor*, London, 1986.

14. On the Hurrians generally, see: I. J. GELB, *Hurrians and Subarians*, Chicago, 1944; F. IMPARATI, *I Hurriti*, Firenze, 1964; G. WILHELM, *The Hurrians*, Warminster, 1989. Also see the articles published in *RHA*, XXXVI (1978) and in *Problèmes Concernant les Hurrites*, 2 vol., Paris, 1977–84.

15. *Alalah* is modern Tell Atchana, between Aleppo and Antioch. British excavations in 1936–9: SIR LEONARD WOOLLEY, *Alalah*, London, 1955; *A Forgotten Kingdom*, 2nd ed., Harmondsworth, 1959. Texts published by D. J. WISEMAN, *The Alalah Tablets*, London, 1953.

16. The ancient town of Gasur, re-baptized Nuzi by the Hurrians, is Yorgan Tepe, 13 kilometres south-west of Kirkuk. American excavations from 1925 to 1931: R. F. S. STARR, *Nuzi: Report on the Excavations at Yorgan Tepe, near Kirkuk*, Cambridge, Mass., 1937–9. Bibliography on texts from Nuzi in M. DIETRICH, O. LORETZ and W. MAYER; *Nuzi Bibliography*, Neukirchen-Vluyn, 1972. Recent studies in M. A. MORRISON and D. I. OWEN (eds), *Studies on the Civilization and Culture of Nuzi and the Hurrians*, Winona Lake, Ind., 1981.

17. A. J. TOBLER, *Excavations at Tepe Gawra, II*, Philadelphia, 1950; Tell Billa (Assyrian *Shibbaniba*), near Bashiqa (16 kilometres north-east of Mosul), was also excavated by the Americans from

1930 to 1933. Reports in *BASOR*, Nos. 40 to 60. The Hurrian
level has yielded houses and pottery, but no texts.

18. On horses in the Near East, see. A. SALONEN, *Hippologica Accadica*,
Helsinki, 1956; A. KAMMENHUBER, *Hippologica Hethitica*, Wies-
baden, 1961; J. A. H. POTRATZ, *Die Pferdestrensen des alten Orients*,
Roma, 1966.

19. K. KENYON, *Archaeology in the Holy Land*, London, 1960; J. MELLART,
Earliest Civilizations in the Near East, pp. 22–46 and 57–62; *The
Neolithic of the Near East*, pp. 22–69; 227–43. See also the chapters
by J. MELLAART, M. E. L. MALLOWAN and R. DE VAUX in *CAH*, I, 1,
pp. 264–70, 282–4, 413–21, 499–538; and *CAH*, I, 2, pp. 208–37.

20. Syria: H. KLENGEL, *Geschichte Syriens im 2. Jahrtausend v.u.Z*,
3 vol., Berlin, 1965–70; *Geschichte und Kultur Altsyriens*, Wien-
München, 1980. Palestine: R. DE VAUX, *Histoire Ancienne d'Israël
des Origines à l'Installation en Canaan*, Paris, 1971. Egypt: A. H.
GARDINER, *Egypt of The Pharaohs*, Oxford, 1961.

21. Ugarit (modern Ras Shamra) lies about 10 kilometres north of
the Syrian port of Lattaqieh. French excavations since 1928.
Preliminary reports in *Syria*, 1929 ff. and *AAAS*, 1951 ff. Short
synthesis in *Ras Shamra 1929–1979*, Lyons, 1979. Also see: G.
SAADE, *Ougarit, Métropole Cananéenne*, Beirut 1979.

22. W. A. WARD, 'Egypt and the East Mediterranean in the early
second millennium B.C.', *Orientalia*, XXX (1961), pp. 22–45,
129–55.

23. W. F. ALBRIGHT, *The Archaeology of Palestine*, Harmondsworth,
1954, p. 80.

24. R. DE VAUX, op. cit., pp. 245–53, with discussion on the date
of Abraham's entry into Palestine.

25. J. BOTTERO, *Le Problèmes des Habiru à la 4ème Rencontre Assyriologique Internationale*, Paris, 1954; M. GREENBERG, *The Hab/piru*,
New Haven, 1955. See also: J. BOTTERO, 'Habiru', *RLA*, IV
(1972), pp. 14–27.

Chapter 15

1. N. YOFEE, *The Economic Role of the Crown in the Old Babylonian
Period*, Malibu, Calif., 1977, pp. 143–51; J. RENGER in E.
LIPINSKI (ed.), *State and Temple Economy in the Ancient Near East*,
I, Leuven, 1979, p. 252.

2. J. BOTTERO, 'Désordre économique et annulation de dettes en Mésopotamie à l'époque paléo-babylonienne', *JESHO*, IV (1961), pp. 113–64.

3. MCG. GIBSON, 'Violation of fallow and engineered disaster in Mesopotamian civilization' in T. E. DOWNING and MCG. GIBSON (ed.), *Irrigation Impact on Society*, Tucson, Ariz., 1974, pp. 7–19.

4. The main sources for the period are the royal inscriptions (*IRSA*, pp. 220–9), the year-names published by A. UNGNAD in *RLA*, II, pp.182–92 and by B. E. MORGAN in *Manchester Cuneiform Studies*, II (1952), pp. 31 ff., 44 ff., and III (1953), pp. 56 ff., 72 ff. and 76 ff., and the Babylonian chronicle published by KING, *Chronicles*, II, pp. 15–24. On the period in general, cf. C. J. GADD in *CAH*, II, 1, pp. 220–4, and M. STOL, *Studies in Old Babylonian History*, Istanbul, 1976.

5. SIR LEONARD WOOLLEY and P. R. S. MOOREY, *Ur of the Chaldees*, London, 1982, p. 191; W. HINZ in *CAH*, II, 1, p. 266.

6. Little is known about this dynasty which, according to the Babylonian Royal Lists A and B (*RLA*, VI, pp. 91–100), had eleven kings and lasted 368 years (*sic*). Its capital-city, Urukug, has not yet been identified. The name of its first king can also be read Iliman.

7. Inscription of Esarhaddon, *ARAB*, II, § 576. Cf. *ARI*, I. p. 31.

8. A *Kashtiliash* whose name appears among the Semitic rulers of Hana is probably the same person as the second successor of *Gandash* who founded the Kassite dynasty outside Babylon during the reign of Samsu-iluna.

9. F. R. KRAUS, *Ein Edikt des Königs Ammi-ṣaduqa von Babylon*, Leiden, 1958. Cf. J. J. FINKELSTEIN, 'The edict of Ammiṣaduqa, a new text', *RA*, LXIII (1969), pp. 45–64 and 189–90.

10. F. CORNELIUS, 'Die Annalen Hattushilish I', *Orientalia*, XXVIII (1959) pp. 292–6; F. IMPARATI and C. SAPORETTI, 'L'autobiografia di Hattushili I', *Studi Classici e Orientali*, XIV (1965), pp. 40–85.

11. Inscription of Telepinus (*c.* 1500 B.C.). Cf. F. HROZNY, 'Eine Inschrift des Königs Telepinus', *Bo.Stu*, III (1919), pp. 202–4.

12. So far, the only synthetic studies on the Kassites are those of T. H. CARTER, *Studies in Kassite History and Archaeology*, Bryn Mawr, 1962 (dissertation) and of E. CASSIN in *Fischer Weltgeschichte*, III, Frankfurt, 1966, pp. 12–70. To be completed by J. A. BRINKMAN,

'The monarchy in the time of the Kassite dynasty' in P. GARELLI (ed.), *Le Palais et la Royauté*, Paris, 1974, pp. 395–408, and by the article 'Kassiten' in *RLA*, V, pp. 464–73.

13. K. BALKAN, *Kassitenstudien*, I, *Die Sprache der Kassiten*, New Haven, 1954.

14. Published by F. E. PEISER and H. WINCKLER in *KB*, I (1889), pp. 194–203. See now: A. GRAYSON, *ABC*, pp. 157–70.

15. The inscription was published by F. DELITZCH, *Die Sprache der Kossäer*, Leipzig, 1904. Agum states that he brought the statues 'from the country of Hani'. Is this a scribal error for Hatti, or did the Hittites leave the statues in the country of Haña (the region of Terqa) on their way home? On this problem see: K. JARITZ; 'Quellen zur Geschichte der Kashshu dynasty', *Mitteilungen des Instituts für Orientforschung*, VI (1958), pp. 205–7.

16. *Synchr. History*, I, 1–17.

17. J. JORDAN, *UVB*, I (1930), p. 30; *AAO*, pp. 63–4, pl. 70a.

18. TAHA BAQIR, 'Excavations at 'Aqar Quf', *Iraq*, Supplement 1944–5, and *Iraq*, VIII (1946), pp. 73–92.

19. See Chapter 15, note 18.

20. Most Kassite *Kudurrus* have been published by L. KING in *Babylonian Boundary Stones*, London, 1912.

21. U. SEIDL, 'Die babylonischen *Kudurru*-Reliefs', *BM*, IV (1968), pp. 7–220.

22. On these seals, see T. BERAN, 'Die Babylonische Glyptik der Kassitenzeit', *AfO*, XVIII (1958), pp. 255–87, and A. LIMET, 'Les Légendes des Sceaux Kassites', Bruxelles, 1971. Also see D. COLLON, *First Impressions*, London, 1987, pp. 58–61.

Chapter 16

1. Details and bibliography on the events briefly described in this chapter can be found in *CAH*, II, particularly chapters 8, 10, 15, 17–20, 21 (a), 24, 25, 29, 31 and 32. Shorter accounts are available in all general histories of the ancient Near East, e.g. W. HALLO and K. SIMPSON, *The Ancient Near East, a History*, New York, 1971.

2. *ARAB*, I, § 47–59; *ARI*, I, pp. 32–41; Synchronistic History I, 5'–7' (*ABC*, pp. 158–9).

3. American (1940) and German (1955–6) excavations at Tell Fekheriyeh, near Ras-el-'Ain, on the Khabur, have failed to confirm the traditional identification of this site with Washukkanni. For an interesting attempt at finding that city, using neutron-activation analysis of clay from royal Mitannian letters, cf. A. DOBEL, W. J. VAN LIERE and A. A. MAHMUD, *AfO*, XXV (1974–7), pp. 259–64.

4. S. SMITH, *The Statue of Idrimi*, London, 1949. Cf. *ANET*, pp. 557–8; *CAH*, II, 1, pp. 433–6. In this inscription, Idrimi recounts how he lost and recovered his throne.

5. R. S. F. STARR, *Nuzi* II, Cambridge (Mass.), 1937, pl. 118; H. KLENGEL, 'Mitanni: Probleme seiner Expansion und politische Struktur', *RHA*, XXXVI (1978), pp. 94–5.

6. Treaty between Mattiwaza and Suppiluliumas, Rev. 8–10 (E. WEIDNER, Politische Dokumente aus Kleinasien, *Bo.Stu*, VIII (1923), p. 39.

7. *EA*, 29.

8. *EA*, 17, 29.

9. *CAH*, II, 1, p. 679; O. R. GURNEY, *The Hittites*, London, 1980, p. 27.

10. These tablets (abbreviated *EA*) were found at el-Amarna (ancient Akhetaton in Egypt), the ephemeral capital-city under Amenophis IV, but they are now dispersed in various museums. They were first gathered and published by J. A. KNUDTZON, *Die El-Amarna Tafeln*, Leipzig, 1915: English translation: S. A. MERCER, *The Tell el-Amarna Tablets*, Toronto, 1939. Latest French translation: W. L. MORAN, *Les Lettres d'Amarna*, Paris, 1987. Apart from one letter in Hurrian and two in Hittite, they are all written in Akkadian with a few glosses in Cananaean.

11. For a general survey of the period, cf. E. CAVAIGNAC, *Subbiluliuma et son Temps*, Paris, 1932; K. A. KITCHEN, *Suppiluliuma and the Amarna Pharaohs*, Liverpool, 1962 and A. GOETZE, *CAH*, II, 2, pp. 1–20, 117–29 and 252–73.

12. *EA*, 7, lines 69–72.

13. *EA*, 7, lines 53–4.

14. *EA*, 14.

15. Treaty between Suppiluliumas and Mattiwaza, Rev. 50 [*Bo.Stu*, VIII (1923), p. 17].

16. *EA*, 15–16.

17. *Synchr. Hist.*, I, 8–17. Also the so-called 'Chronicle P', I, 9–14. (*ABC*, pp 159 and 172).

18. 'Chronicle P', III, 10–19. (*ABC* pp. 174–5).

19. Cf. M. C. ASTOUR, 'The partition of the confederacy of Mukish-Nuhashshe-Nii by Shuppiluliuma', *Orientalia*, XXXVIII (1969), pp. 381–414.

20. Identified with Tell Kazel, north of Tripoli [M. DUNAND and N. SALIBY, *AAS*, VII (1957), pp. 3–16].

21. Qadesh is Tell Nebi Mend, in the Orontes river valley, 25 kilometres south of Homs. So far, this site has been the object of only limited excavations: M. PEZARD, *Mission Archéologique à Tell Nebi Mend*, Paris, 1931. On the battle of Qadesh, see: *CAH*, II, 2, pp. 226–8 and 253–4, with bibliography p. 952.

22. *ANET*, pp. 199–203.

23. J. FRIEDRICH, *Der Alte Orient*, XXIV, 3 (1925), p. 26. Cf. J. M. MUNN-RANKIN, *CAH*, II, 2, pp. 274–9.

24. *ARAB*, I, § 73; *ARI*, I, p. 58.

25. *Synchr. Hist.*, I, 24–31 (War between Adad-nirâri and Nazi-Maruttash). Cf. *ABC*, pp. 160–61.

26. *ARAB*, I, § 116; *ARI*, I, p. 82.

27. This magnificent site has been excavated by a French mission in Iran in the 1950–60 period. Cf. R. GHIRSHMAN *et al.*, *Tchoga-Zanbil (Dur Untash)*, Paris, 1966–70.

28. W. G. LAMBERT, 'Three unpublished fragments of the Tukulti-Ninurta epic', *AfO*, XVIII (1957–8), pp. 38–51 (gives a complete translation). Cf. E. WEIDNER, 'Assyrischen Epen über die Kassiten-Kämpfe', *AfO*, XX (1963–4), pp. 113–16. Inscriptions of Tukulti-Ninurta in *ARI*, I, pp. 101–134.

29. *ARAB*, I, § 145; *ARI*, I, pp. 119, 126.

30. *Chronicle P*, IV, 8–9 (cf. *ARAB*, I, § 141). Cf. *ABC*, p. 176.

31. *Ibid.*, IV, 9–13. *Kâr-Tukulti-Ninurta* (modern Tukul Akir), two kilometres north of Assur, on the left bank of the Tigris, was excavated by the Germans in 1913–14: W. BACHMANN, *MDOG*, 53, pp. 41–57; W. ANDRAE, *Das widererstandene Assur*, pp. 121–5.

32. On the fall of the Kassite dynasty, see: D. J. WISEMAN, *CAH*, II, 2, p. 446 and R. LABAT, *ibid.*, pp. 486–7. Contrary to K. JARITZ, op. cit., pp. 224–5, the Elamite king Shilhak-Inshushinak did not take part in these events, though he later campaigned in northern Iraq.

Chapter 17

1. R. D. BARNETT, 'The Sea-Peoples', *CAH*, II, 2, pp. 359–78; N. K. SANDARS, *The Sea-Peoples, Warriors of the Ancient Mediterranean, 1250–1150 B.C.*, London, 1978; R. A. MACALISTER, *The Philistines, their History and Civilization*, Chicago, 1965.

2. Later, the *Parsua* moved to the south-western part of Iran, occupied a district in the Bakhtiari mountains close to Elam and gave it their name: *Parsu(m)ash*, Persia, Fars. (See. R. GHIRSHMAN, *Iran*, Harmondsworth, 1954, pp. 91 and 119.)

3. W. F. ALBRIGHT, *From the Stone Age to Christianity*, 2nd ed., New York, 1957, pp. 13 and 255. See also: O. EISSFELD, *CAH*, II, 2, pp. 307–30. This author favours a date of *c.* 1400 B.C. for the entry into Egypt.

4. *I Kings* i-ix; *II Chronicles* i–ix. O. EISSFELD, 'The Hebrew Kingdom', *CAH*, II, 2, pp. 537–605.

5. Cf. A. SCHAEFER, *Ugaritica* I, Paris, 1939, pp. 43–6; J. NOUGAYROL, 'Guerre et paix à Ugarit', *Iraq*, XXV (1963), pp. 120–21. M. C. ASTOUR, 'New evidence for the last days of Ugarit', *AJA*, LXIX (1965), pp. 253–8.

6. *I Kings* v. 1–12; vii. 13 ff.; ix. 11–14; *II Chronicles* ii. 3–16; iv. 11–18.

7. On the civilization of the Phoenicians, see: D. HARDEN, *The Phoenicians*, London, 1962; S. MOSCATI, *The World of the Phoenicians*, London, 1973; A. PARROT, M. H. CHEHAB, S. MOSCATI, *Les Phéniciens*, Paris, 1975.

8. On the alphabet, cf. G. R. DRIVER, *Semitic Writing*, Oxford, 1948; D. DIRINGER *The Alphabet*, London, 1948; J. G. FEVRIER, *Histoire de l'Ecriture*, Paris, 1948; I. J. GELB, *A Study of Writing*, London, 1952.

9. C. H. GORDON, *Ugaritic Literature*, Roma, 1949; G. R. DRIVER, *Canaanite Myths and Legends*, Edinburgh, 1956; *ANET*, pp. 130–55.

10. On the Neo-Hittites generally see: O. GURNEY, *The Hittites*, London, 1980, pp. 41–7; J. D. HAWKINS, article 'Hatti, the first millennium B.C.' in *RLA*, IV, pp. 152–9. On writing and grammar, E. LAROCHE, *Les Hiéroglyphes Hittites*, Paris, 1960. For a list of hieroglyphic inscriptions, see E. LAROCHE, 'Liste des documents hiéroglyphiques', *RHA*, XXVII (1969), pp. 110–31.

11. SETON LLOYD, *Early Anatolia*, Harmondsworth, 1956, pp. 177–82. Good summary in the articles by I. J. GELB and M. J. MELLINK in *Bi.Or.*, VII (1950), pp. 129–50.

12. J. D. HAWKINS, 'Assyrians and Hittites', *Iraq*, XXXVI (1974), pp. 67–83.

13. On the Aramaeans in general, cf. S. SCHIFFER, *Die Aramäer*, Leipzig, 1911; E. G. KRAELING, *Aram and Israel*, New York, 1918; R. T. O'CALLAGHAN, *Aram Naharaim*, Rome, 1948, pp. 93–130; A. DUPONT-SOMMER, *Les Araméens*, Paris, 1949; A. MALAMAT, 'The Aramaeans', in D. J. WISEMAN (ed.), *Peoples of Old Testament Times*, London, 1973, pp. 134–55.

14. *Deuteronomy* xxvi. 5.

15. *ARAB*, I, § 166.

16. S. MOSCATI, 'The Aramaean Ahlamû', *JSS*, IV (1959), pp. 303–7.

17. M. FREIHERR VON OPPENHEIM, *Der Tell Halaf*, Leipzig, 1931, pp. 71–198, and *Tell Halaf II, Die Bauwerke*, Berlin, 1950; A. MOORTGAT *Tell Halaf, III, Die Bildwerke*, Berlin, 1955; B. HROUDA, *Tell Halaf IV, Die Kleinfunde aus historischer Zeit*, Berlin, 1962.

18. P. GARELLI, 'Importance et rôle des Araméens dans l'administration de l'empire assyrien' in H. J. NISSEN and J. RENGER (ed.), *Mesopotamien und seine Nachbarn*, Berlin, 1982, II, pp. 437–47; H. TADMOR, 'The aramaization of Assyria: aspects of western impact', *ibid.*, pp. 449–70.

19. On this and following periods, see: J. A. BRINKMAN, *A Political History of Post-Kassite Babylonia (1158–722)*, Rome, 1968.

20. On this curious text of 'lamentation', see H. TADMOR, 'Historical implications of the correct rendering of Akkadian *dâku*', *JNES*, XVII (1958), pp. 138–9. Cf. *CAH*, II, 2, p. 501.

21. L. KING, *BBS*, No. VI, pp. 29–36.

22. W. G. LAMBERT, 'The reign of Nebuchadnezzar I: a turning point in the history of ancient Mesopotamian religion' in W. S. MCCULLOUGH (ed.), *The Seed of Wisdom*, Toronto, 1964, pp. 3–13.

23. *ARAB*, I, § 257 (Inscription of Tiglathpileser I).

24. *ARAB*, I, § 300–303; *ANET*, pp. 274–5.

25. *ARAB*, I, § 309. Cf. E. WEIDNER, 'Die Feldzüge and Bauten Tiglatpilesers I, *AfO*, XVIII (1958), pp. 342–60.

26. Stone tablet of Nabû-apal-iddina (885–852 B.C.), Col. I, 4–5. (L. KING, *BBS*, p. 121.)

27. L. W. KING, *Chronicles*, II, pp. 143–79. Cf. in particular, the 'Religious chronicle' (*ABC*, pp. 133–8); some parts of the 'Dynastic chronicle' (*ABC*, pp. 139–44) and a fragment of Assyrian chronicle (*ABC*, p. 189).

28. P. GÖSSMANN, *Das Erra-Epos*, Würzburg, 1955; L. CAGNI, *L'epopea di Erra*, Rome, 1969. Cf. R. BORGER and W. G. LAMBERT, *Orientalia*, XXVII (1958) pp. 137–49.

29. 'Religious chronicle', III, 4–15 (*ABC*, pp. 137–8).

30. M. DIETRICH, *Die Aramäer Südbabyloniens in der Sargonidenzeit (700–648)*, Neukirchen-Vluyn, 1970. Cf. F. MALBRAN in *Journal Asiatique*, Paris, 1972, pp. 15–38.

Chapter 18

1. Exactly since Ninurta apal-ekur (1192–1180 B.C.).

2. The main sources for the political history of the so-called Neo-Assyrian period are (1) the Assyrian royal inscriptions translated by D. LUCKENBILL, *Ancient Records of Assyria and Babylonia* (*ARAB*), 2 vol., Chicago, 1926–7, and, partly, by A. K. GRAYSON, *Assyrian Royal Inscriptions* (*ARI*), 2 vol., Wiesbaden, 1972–6; (2) the Babylonian royal inscription to be found in J. A. BRINKMAN, *A Political History of Post-Kassite Babylonia* (*PKB*), Roma, 1967: (3) the Assyrian and Babylonian Chronicles translated by A. K. GRAYSON, *Assyrian and Babylonian Chronicles* (*ABC*), Locust Valley (New York), 1975; (4) the royal correspondence from Nineveh published by R. F. HARPER, *Assyrian and Babylonian Letters belonging to the Kuyunjik Collection of the British Museum* (*ABL*), 14 vol., London/Chicago, 1892–1914, and translated by LEROY WATERMAN, *Royal Correspondence of the Assyrian Empire* (*RCAE*), 4 vol., Ann Arbor, Mich., 1930–36; (5) the royal correspondence from Nimrud published and translated by D. J. WISEMAN, H. W. SAGGS, J. V. KINNIER WILSON and B. PARKER in *Iraq*, XII (1950) to XXVIII (1966); the remarkable series *State Archives of Assyria* (*SAA*), K. DELLER et al. (ed.), 5 volumes published, Helsinki, 1987 ff.; the *Old Testament*, notably *II Kings, II Chronicles, Prophets*. For a general view of the Assyrians and

Assyria, see: H. W. F. SAGGS, *The Might that was Assyria*, London, 1984.

3. Inscriptions of Adad-nirâri II in *ARAB*, I, §§ 355–99 and *ARI*, II, § 394–460.

4. *ARAB*, I, § 360; *ARI*, II, §§ 420, 422; *Synchr. History*, III, 1–6 (*ABC*, p. 166). Cf. *PKB*, pp. 177–80.

5. *Synchr. History*, III, 9–21 (*ABC* p. 166). Cf. *PKB*, pp. 180–82.

6. *ARAB*, I, § 402–34; *ARI*, II, § 464–88. Also see: W. SCHRAMM, 'Die Annalen des assyrischen Königs Tukulti-Ninurta II', *Bi.Or.*, XXVII (1970), pp. 147–60.

7. On this subject see W. G. LAMBERT, 'The reigns of Assurnaṣirpal II and Shalmaneser III, an interpretation', *Iraq*, XXXVI (1974), pp. 103–6; H. TADMOR, 'Assyria and the West: the ninth century and its aftermath' in H. GOEDICKE and J. J. ROBERTS (ed.), *Unity and Diversity*, Baltimore, 1975, pp. 36–48; A. K. GRAYSON, 'Studies in Neo-Assyrian history: the ninth century B.C.', *Bi.Or.*, XXXIII (1976), pp. 134–45; M. LIVERANI, 'The ideology of the Assyrian empire' in M. T. LARSEN (ed.), *Power and Propaganda*, Copenhagen, 1979, pp. 297–317; J. READE, Ideology and propaganda in Assyrian Arts', *ibid.*, pp. 329–43.

8. D. G. HOGARTH, *The Ancient Near East*, London, 1950, p. 25.

9. It was only in the Middle-Assyrian period (XIII–XIth centuries) that Ashur became a dominant war god. In an Assyrian version of the Epic of Creation (*enuma elish*), he replaces Marduk at the second rank of the Mesopotamian pantheon.

10. F. M. FALES; 'The enemy in the Neo-Assyrian inscriptions: the "moral judgement"', in H. J. NISSEN and J. RENGER (ed.), *Mesopotamien und seine Nachbarn*, Berlin, 1982, II, pp. 425–35.

11. *ARAB*, I, § 466, 501–2; *ARI*, II, §§ 574, 641. The talent (*biltu*) was about 33 kilos and the *gur*, about 70 litres.

12. See A. T. OLMSTEAD, *History of Assyria*, New York, 1923, pp. 530–32.

13. J. N. POSTGATE, *Taxation and Conscription in the Assyrian Empire*, Rome, 1974, pp. 201–2.

14. *AAO*, pl. 82; A. PARROT, *Assur*, Paris, 1961, pls. 22–3.

15. Inscriptions of Ashurnaṣirpal in *ARAB*, I, §§ 436–552 *ARI*, II §§ 529–869. Also: E. MICHEL, 'Die Texte Assur-naṣir-aplis II', *Die Welt der Orient* II (1954), pp. 313–21, 404–7.

16. *ARAB*, I, § 443. *ARI*, II, § 587.

17. *ANET*, p. 276; *ARAB*, I, §§ 479, 518; *ARI*, II, § 586.

18. *Tushhan* is Kurkh, twenty miles south of Diarbakr. *Kar-Ashurnaṣir-pal* and *Nibarti-Ashur*, facing each other on either side of the Euphrates, are probably Zalabiyah and Halabiyah, between Raqqa and Deir-ez-Zor.

19. *ARAB*, I, §§ 443, 445, 472; *ARI*, II, §§ 547, 549, 579.

20. For a reappraisal of Assyrian 'cruelty', see H. W. F. SAGGS, 'Assyrian prisoners of war and the right to live', *AfO, Beiheft* 19 (1982), pp. 85–93. Also see the remarks of A. T. OLMSTEAD, 'The calculated frightfulness of Ashur-naṣir-apal', *JAOS*, XXXVIII (1918), pp. 209–63.

21. *ARAB*, I, § 489; *ARI*, II, § 653.

22. A. H. LAYARD, *Nineveh and its Remains*, London, 1849; *Nineveh and Babylon*, London, 1882.

23. British excavations from 1949 to 1963. Preliminary reports in *Iraq*, XII (1950) to XXV (1963). Final report: M. E. L. MALLOWAN, *Nimrud and its Remains*, 2 vol., London, 1966. Summaries in M. E. L. MALLOWAN, *Twenty-five Years of Mesopotamian Discovery*, London, 1956, pp. 45–78, and in J. CURTIS (ed.), *Fifty Years of Mesopotamian Discovery*, London, 1982, pp. 99–112. Polish excavations from 1972 to 1982. Summarized by R. SOBOLEWSKI in *ZA*, LXXI (1982), pp. 248–73. Iraqi restorations and excavations since 1970.

24. D. J. WISEMAN, 'A new stele of Assur-naṣir-pal', *Iraq*, XIV (1952), pp. 23–39.

25. *AAO*, pl. 93.

26. D. OATES, 'Fort Shalmaneser. An interim report', *Iraq*, XXI (1959), pp. 98–129; 'The excavations at Nimrud', 1960, *Iraq*, XXIII (1961), pp. 1–14, J. LAESSØE, 'A statue of Shalmaneser III, from Nimrud', *Iraq*, XXI (1959), pp. 147–57.

27. H. RASSAM, *Asshur and the Land of Nimrod*, New York, 1897; D. OATES, 'Balawat (Imgur-Enlil)', *Iraq*, XXXVI (1974), pp. 173–8; J. CURTIS, 'Balawat', in *Fifty Years of Mesopotamian Discovery*, pp. 113–19. On the gates: L. W. KING, *Bronze Reliefs from the Gates of Shalmaneser*, London, 1915. Cf. *AAO*, pl. 91, 92; A. PARROT, *Assur*, pl. 121–9.

28. To the inscriptions published in *ARAB*, I, §§ 553–612, add now; G. G. CAMERON, 'The annals of Shalmaneser III, a new text', *Sumer*, VI (1950), pp. 6–26; FUAD SAFAR, 'A further text of

Shalmaneser III', *Sumer*, VII (1951), pp. 3–21; J. LAESSØE, 'Building inscriptions from Fort Shalmaneser', *Iraq*, XXI (1959), pp. 38–41. Poetic version of the campaign in Urarṭu: W. G. LAMBERT, 'The Sultantepe tablets, VIII, Shalmaneser in Ararat', *Anatolian Studies*, XI (1961), pp. 143–58. J. V. KINNIER WILSON, 'The Kurba'il statue of Shalmaneser III', *Iraq*, XXIV (1962), pp. 90–115.

29. French excavations 1929–31: F. THUREAU-DANGIN and M. DUNAND, *Til-Barsib*, Paris, 1936.

30. *ARAB*, I, § 611; *ANET*, p. 279. Note that this is the first historical mention of the Arabs.

31. *ARAB*, I, § 681. Cf. *II Kings* viii. 7–15.

32. *BBS*, pp. 120–27.

33. *ARAB*, I, § 624. *Synchr. Hist.* III, 22–35 (*ABC*, p. 167).

34. A throne-base found at Nimrud shows Shalmaneser shaking hands with Marduk-zakir-shumi. Cf. D. OATES, *Iraq*, XXV (1963), pp. 20–21, and P. HULIN, *ibid.*, pp. 48–69.

Chapter 19

1. Inscriptions of Shamshi-Adad V in *ARAB*, I, §§ 713–29 and in *JNES*, XXXII (1973), pp. 40–46. On the chronology of the reign, see A. K. GRAYSON in *Bi.Or*, XXXIII (1976), pp. 141–3.

2. *ARAB* I, § 731. The presence of this stele among those of the Assyrian kings, and the dedication, by the governor of Kalhu, of a statue for the life of Adad-nirâri and that of Sammuramat (*ARAB*, I, § 745) suggest that Sammuramat had a considerable power, even though it has not been proven that she exerted the regency (S. PAGE, *Orientalia*, XXXVIII (1969), pp. 457–8).

3. Among recent studies on Semiramis, see: H. LEWY, 'Nitokris Naqui'a', *JNES*, XI (1952), pp. 264–86; W. EILERS, *Semiramis: Entstehung und Nachhall einer altorientalische Sage*, Wien, 1971; G. ROUX, 'Semiramis, la reine mystérieuse de l'Orient', *L'Histoire*, LXVIII (1984), pp. 20–32; G. PETTINATO, *Semiramide*, Milano, 1985.

4. DIODORUS SICULUS, *Bibl. Hist.*, II, 4–20.

5. HERODOTUS, *Hist.*, I, 184; BEROSSUS, *Babyloniaca*, in *Sources for the Ancient Near East*. Malibu, Calif., 1978, p. 164.

6. Inscriptions of Adad-nirâri III in *ARAB*, I, §§ 732–43. For other inscriptions, see H. TADMOR, 'The historical inscriptions of Adad-nirâri III', *Iraq*, XXXV (1973), pp. 141–50.

7. A. R. MILLARD and H. TADMOR, 'Adad-nirâri III in Syria', *Iraq*, XXXV (1973), pp. 57–64.

8. F. THUREAU-DANGIN, 'Linscription des lions de Til-Barsib', *RA*, XXVII (1930), pp. 1–21.

9. The reigns of these three kings are mostly known from the lists of eponyms (*ARAB*, II, § 1198).

10. 'Eclectic chronicle', lines 7–15 (*ABC*, pp. 182–3); *PKB*, pp. 223, 225–6.

11. Intermittent British excavations since 1960. Preliminary reports by SETON WILLIAMS *et al.*, in *Iraq*, XXIII (1961), XXIX (1967) and XL (1978).

12. According to D. STRONACH (*Iraq*, XXXVI, 1974, pp. 239–48), the Persians migrated across the Iranian plateau and reached the north-eastern fringe of Elam soon after 700 B.C.

13. If we judge from the valuable objects found during the American excavations at Hasanlu, south of Lake Urmiah, from 1959 to 1977. For bibliography see: 'Bibliography of the Hasanlu Project' in L. D. LEVINE and D. W. YOUNG (ed.), *Mountains and Lowlands*, Malibu, Calif., 1977.

14. Among the recent books devoted to Urarṭu, see: C. BURNEY and D. H. LANG, *The Peoples of the Hills: Ancient Ararat and Caucasus*, London, 1971; B. PIOTROVSKII, *Ourartou*, Geneva, 1970. Origins and development: M. SALVINI, *Nairi e Ur(u)atri*, Roma, 1967. Inscriptions: F. KONIG, *Handbuch der Chaldischen Inschriften*, *AfO*, Beiheft 8, 1955. On art: B. PIOTROVSKII, *Urartu, the Kingdom of Van and its Art*, London, 1967.

15. On these titles and the organization of the peripheral Assyrian provinces, see: R. A. HENSHAW, 'The office of *shaknu* in Neo-Assyrian times', *JAOS*, LXXXVII (1967), pp. 717–25; LXXXVIII (1968), pp. 461–83. J. N. POSTGATE, 'The place of the *shaknu* in Assyrian government', *Anatolian Studies*, XXX (1980), pp. 69–76. J. PEČIRKOVA, 'The administrative organization of the Neo-Assyrian empire', *Archiv Orientalni*, XLV (1977), pp. 211–28.

16. F. MALBRAN-LABAT, *L'Armée et l'Organisation Militaire de l'Assyrie*, Geneva/Paris, 1982, pp. 59–61.

17. *ARAB*, I, §§ 770, 772, 795, 806.

18. On this question, see the thorough study of B. ODED, *Mass Deportation and Deportees in the Neo-Assyrian Empire*, Wiesbaden, 1979.

19. Inscriptions of Tiglathpileser III in *ARAB*, I, §§ 761–822. To these must be added the fragments discovered at Nimrud and published by D. J. WISEMAN in *Iraq*, XIII (1951); XVIII (1956) and XXVI (1964). Also see: L. D. LEVINE, *Two Assyrian Stelae from Iran*, Toronto, 1972, and N. POSTGATE, 'The inscription of Tiglath-Pileser III at Mila Mergi', *Sumer*, XXIX (1973), pp. 47–59.

20. *ARAB*, I, § 772; *II Kings* xv. 19–20.

21. French excavations in 1928: F. THUREAU-DANGIN *et al.*, *Arslan Tash*, Paris, 1931. Cf. G. TURNER, *Iraq*, XXX (1968), pp. 62–8. Tiglathpileser III had his own palace at Nimrud.

22. R. GHIRSHMAN, *Iran*, Harmondsworth, 1954, p. 94.

23. Nimrud letter published by H. W. SAGGS in *Iraq*, XVII (1955), p. 128. Cf. M. COGAN, 'Tyre and Tiglat-Phalazar III', *JCS*, XXV (1973), pp. 96–9.

24. *II Chronicles* xxviii, 5–8; *II Kings* xv, 29–30; xvi, 5–9; Cf. *ANET*, pp. 283–4.

25. The royal inscription in *ARAB*, I, §§ 829–30 is, in reality, an inscription of Esarhaddon. On the meagre sources for this reign, see *PKB*, p. 244.

26. Inscriptions of Sargon in *ARAB*, II, §§ 1–230. The reference edition is that of A. G. LIE, *The Inscriptions of Sargon II of Assyria*, I, *The Annals*, Paris, 1929. Add: C. J. GADD, 'Inscribed prisms of Sargon from Nimrud', *Iraq*, XVI (1954), pp. 172–202. The correspondence of Sargon has now been published by S. PARPOLA and G. B. LANFRANCHI in *SAA*, I (1987) and V (1990). On the chronology of the reign, see: H. TADMOR, 'The campaigns of Sargon II of Assur', *JCS*, XII (1958), pp. 22–40, 77–100.

27. *Babyl. Chronicle* I, 33–7. C. J. GADD, 'Inscribed barrel cylinder of Marduk-apal-iddina II', *Iraq*, XV (1983), pp. 123–34

28. *ARAB*, II, § 5; *ANET*, p. 285; R. BORGER, 'Das Ende des aegyptischen Feldern Sib'e = Sô', *JNES*, XIX (1960), pp. 49–53.

29. *ARAB*, II, §§ 30, 62; *ANET*, p. 286. Cf. H. TADMOR *ibid.*, pp. 83–4.

30. *RCAE*, esp. Nos. 101, 123, 145, 148, 251, 380, 381, 424, 444, 515. Nimrud letters: H. W. SAGGS, *Iraq*, XX (1958), pp. 182–212.

31. F. THUREAU-DANGIN, *Une Relation de la Huitième Campagne de Sargon*, Paris, 1912. *ARAB*, II, §§ 139–89. On the so-called 'Letters to the Gods', see A. L. OPPENHEIM, 'The city of Assur in 714 B.C.', *JCS*, XIX (1960), pp. 133–47.

32. F. THUREAU-DANGIN, op. cit., p. 7.

33. French excavations in 1843–4 and 1852–4: P. E. BOTTA and E. FLANDIN, *Les Monuments de Ninive*, Paris, 1849–50; V. PLACE, *Ninive et l'Assyrie*, Paris, 1867–70. American excavations in 1930–5; G. LOUD, *Khorsabad*, Chicago, 1936–8.

34. *ARAB*, II, § 89.

35. J. A. BRINKMAN; *Prelude to Empire*, Philadelphia, 1984, p. 54, n. 254.

Chapter 20

1. D. D. LUCKENBILL, *The Annals of Sennacherib* (*OIP*, II), Chicago, 1924; *ARAB*, II, §§ 231–496; A. HEIDEL, 'The octagonal prism of Sennacherib in the Iraq Museum' *Sumer*, IX (1953), pp. 117–88; A. K. GRAYSON, 'The Walters Art Gallery Sennacherib inscription', *AfO*, XX (1963), pp. 83–96; J. READE, 'Sources for Sennacherib: the prisms', *JCS*, XXVII (1975), pp. 189–96.

2. U. CUZZOLI, *I Cimmeri*, Roma. 1968; A. KAMMENHUBER, article 'Kimmerier' in *RLA*, V, pp. 594–98.

3. *RCAE*, Nos 146, 197. The kingdom of Urarṭu survived until 590, when it was conquered by the Medes. Inscriptions of Argishti II and Rusas II, a contemporary of Ashurbanipal, have been found.

4. BEROSSUS, *Babyloniaca* III, 2. Cf. J. ELAYI and A. CAVAIGNAC, *Oriens Antiquus*, XVIII (1979), p. 70.

5. Text of this campaign in *ARAB*, II, §§ 233 ff. and in *ANET*, pp. 287–8. The capitulation of Lakish is represented on a relief from Nineveh: *AAO*, pl. 101.

6. *II Kings* xviii. 13–xix. 34; *II Chronicles* xxxii. 1–22; *Isaiah* xxxvi. 1–xxxvii. 38. W. VON SODEN, 'Sanherib vor Jerusalem, 701 B.C.', in *Festschrift Erich Stier*, Munster, 1972, pp. 43–51.

7. *II Kings* xix. 35; HERODOTUS, II, 141; BEROSSUS in JOSEPHUS, *Jewish Antiquities*, X, i, 4–5.

8. See the studies by J. A. BRINKMAN, 'Sennacherib's Babylonian problem: an interpretation', *JCS*, XXV (1973), pp. 89–99; L. D. LEVINE, 'Sennacherib's southern front: 704–869 B.C.', *JCS*, XXXIV (1982), pp. 28–58.

9. *ARAB*, II, § 242.

10. *ARAB*, II, §§ 246–7, 318–22, 350, 353.

11. Tell 'Umar, on the Tigris, south of Baghdad.

12. S. PARPOLA, 'A letter from Shamash-shum-ukin to Esarhaddon', *Iraq*, XXXIV (1972), pp. 21–34.

13. Assyrian version of the battle in *ARAB*, II, §§ 253–4. The 'Babylonian Chronicle' (*ABC*, p. 80) talks of an 'Assyrian retreat'. Hallulê is probably to be located near the lower Diyala river.

14. *ARAB*, II, §§ 339–41. The 'Babylonian Chronicle' (*ABC*, pp. 80–81) simply says: 'On the first day of the month of *kislimu* the city was taken. Mushezib-Marduk was captured and taken to Assyria'.

15. *II Kings* xxx. 36–7; 'Babylonian Chronicle' (*ABC*, p. 81); *ARAB*, II, § 795. See: E. G. KRAELING, 'The death of Sennacherib', *JAOS*, LIII (1933), pp. 335–46; S. PARPOLA, 'The murder of Sennacherib' in B. ALSTER (ed.), *Death in Mesopotamia*, Copenhagen, 1980, pp. 171–82.

16. Nebi Yunus is built up and has hardly been touched by archaeologists. Kuyunjik has been the object of several campaigns of excavations since the pioneer work of LAYARD in 1847. For a general description of the site, cf. R. CAMPBELL THOMPSON, *A Century of Exploration at Nineveh*, London, 1929; T. MADHLOOM and A. M. MEHDI, *Nineveh*, Baghdad, 1976.

17. *ARAB*, II, § 366.

18. T. JACOBSEN and SETON LLOYD, *Sennacherib's Aqueduct at Jerwan*, Chicago, 1935; J. READE, 'Studies in Assyrian geography I, Sennacherib and the waters of Nineveh', *RA*, LXXII (1978), pp. 47–72 and 157–180.

19. W. BACHMANN, *Felsreliefs in Assyrian*, Leipzig, 1927; L. W. KING, 'Some unpublished rock inscriptions of Sennacherib on the Judi-Dâgh', *PSBA*, XXXV (1913), pp. 66–94.

20. Most of Esarhaddon's inscriptions are to be found in R. BORGER,

Die Inscriften Asarhaddons, König von Assyrien, Graz, 1956. Other inscriptions have since been published, including *Sumer*, XII (1956), pp. 9–38; *AfO*, XVIII (1957–8), pp. 314–18; *Iraq*, XXIII (1961), pp. 176–8; XXIV (1962), pp. 116–17; XXVI (1964), pp. 122–3; *JCS*, XVII (1963), pp. 119–31.

21. *ARAB*, II, §§ 501–5; *ANET*, pp. 288–90.

22. *ARAB*, II, § 639–87. Cf. J. NOUGAYROL, *AfO*, XVIII (1957–8). On the role played by the queen Naqi'a/Nakûtu in this reconstruction, see: H. LEWY, 'Nitokris-Naqîa', *JNES*, XI (1952), pp. 264–86.

23. 'Babylonian Chronicle', II, 39–50; IV, 1–2, 9–10 (*ABC*, pp. 82–3); 'Esarhaddon's Chronicle', 10–11–35–37 (*ABC*, pp. 126–7).

24. On this treaty, see now: S. PARPOLA, K. WATANABE, *Neo-Assyrian Treaties and Loyalty Oaths* (*SAA*, II), Helsinki, 1988, pp. 24–7.

25. On the Scythians generally, see: T. TALBOT RICE, *The Scythians*, London, 1957; B. D. GRAPOW, *Die Skythen*, Berlin, 1978; A. M. KHAZANOV, 'The dawn of Scythian history', *Iranica Antiqua*, XVII (1982), pp. 49–63.

26. A. SPALINGER, 'Esarhaddon in Egypt', *Orientalia*, XLIII (1974), pp. 295–306. On Egypt in that period, see: K. A. KITCHEN, *The Third Intermediate Period in Egypt*, Warminster, 1973.

27. A. K. IRVIN, 'The Arabs and Ethiopians' in D. J. WISEMAN (ed.), *People of Old Testament Times*, Oxford, 1973, p. 291. Texts in *ARAB*, II, §§ 518–36, 551; *ANET*, pp. 191–2.

28. *ANET*, p. 293. In reality, bloody battles were fought at Memphis, and the kings of the Delta remained on their throne. Statues of Taharqa and of the Egyptian goddess Anuqet have been discovered at Nineveh (Nebi Yunus). Cf. V. VIKENTIEV, *Sumer*, XI (1955), pp. 111–14; XII (1956), pp. 76–9.

29. D. J. WISEMAN, 'The vassal-treaties of Esarhaddon', *Iraq*, XXX, (1958), pp. 1–99. Cf. *ANET*, pp. 534–41. Also see *SAA II*, pp. 28–58.

30. The so-called 'Zakûtu treaty', *SAA*, II, pp. 62–4.

31. *ARAB*, II, 762–1129; M. STRECK, *Assurbanipal*, 3 vols., Leipzig, 1916. T. BAUER, *Das Inschriftwerk Assurbanipals*, Leipzig, 1933; A. C. PIEPKORN, *Historical Prism Inscriptions of Ashurbanipal*, Chicago, 1933. Other texts or fragments: W. G. LAMBERT, *AfO*, XVIII (1957–8), pp. 382–98; D. J. WISEMAN, *Iraq*, XXVI (1964), pp.

118–24; E. KNUDSEN, *Iraq*, XXIX (1967), pp. 49–69; A. MIL-
LARD, *Iraq*, XXX (1968), pp. 98–114; R. BORGER, *AfO*, XXIII
(1970), p. 90.

32. J. H. BREASTED, *Ancient Records of Egypt*, Chicago, 1906–7, IV,
pp. 919 ff. Also see: A. SPALINGER, 'Assurbanipal and Egypt: a
source study', *JAOS*, XCIV (1974), pp. 316–28.

33. *ANET*, pp. 294–5 (cf. *ARAB*, II, § 772).

34. Ashurbanipal (*ARAB*, II, §§ 784–5, 849, 909–10) says that
Gyges sent him a messenger with a letter stating that he had seen the
god Ashur in a dream, who had told him to 'seize the feet of the King
of Assyria and evoke his name to fight the enemy'.

35. *ARAB*, II, § 855.

36. HERODOTUS, II, 152.

37. *AAO*, pl. 114; D. FRANKEL, *Ashurbanipal and the Head of Teumman*,
London, 1977.

38. *RCAE*, No. 301.

39. See the text published by KNUDSEN in *Iraq*, XXIX (1967),
pp. 55–6, where mention is made of cannibalism.

40. This is the famous 'suicide' of Sardanapallus', as told by DIO-
DORUS SICULUS II, 27, who confused Ashurbanipal (Sarda-
napallus) with his brother. The text published by M. COGAN and
H. TADMOR in *Orientalia*, L (1981), pp. 229–40 confirms that
Shamash-shum-ukîn died in a fire, but does not speak of suicide.

41. The belief that Kandalanu was the name taken by Ashurbanipal
as King of Babylon is rejected by most scholars. Cf. J. A.
BRINKMAN, *Prelude to Empire*, Philadelphia, 1984, pp. 105–6;
H. W. F. SAGGS, *The Might that was Assyria*, pp. 114, 117.

42. Texts in *ARAB*, II, §§ 817–30, 868–70, 878–80, 940–43, 946–50,
and in *ANET*, pp. 297–301. Detailed study by WEIPPERT,
'Die Kampfe des assyrischen Königs Assurbanipal gegen die
Araber', *Die Welt des Orients*, VII (1973–4), pp. 38–85.

43. *ANET*, p. 299.

44. Good summary in W. HINZ, *The Lost World of Elam*, New York,
1971.

45. *ARAB*, II, §§ 810–11.

46. According to *II Chronicles* xxxiii. 11, the Assyrians took Manasseh,
King of Judah, and 'carried him to Babylon'. This event is not
mentioned in the (incomplete) Assyrian records.

47. *Nahum*, 7, 15, 19.

Chapter 21

1. J. N. POSTGATE, 'The economic structure of the Assyrian empire', in T. LARSEN (Ed.), *Power and Propaganda*, Copenhagen, 1979, pp. 193–221 (esp. pp. 194–217).

2. LORD BYRON, 'The Assyrian came down like the wolf on the fold', *The Destruction of Sennacherib*, canto I, line 1.

3. On this subject in general, cf. R. LABAT, *Le Caractère Religieux de la Royauté Assyro-Babylonienne*, Paris, 1939, and H. FRANKFORT, *Kingship and the Gods*, Chicago, 1948.

4. This site has been briefly excavated by Layard in 1850 and Rawlinson in 1852. Cf J. E. CURTISS and A. K. GRAYSON, *Iraq*, XLIV (1982), pp. 87–94.

5. *ARAB*, II, § 986.

6. A. HALLER, *Die Gräber und Grüfte von Assur*, Berlin, 1954, pp. 170–80. J. McGINNIS, 'A Neo-Assyrian text describing a royal funeral', *SAA Bulletin*, I, 1, 1987, pp. 1–11.

7. These tombs have not yet been studied and published scientifically. To our knowledge, at the time of writing the only information available comes from newspapers and magazines.

8. H. FRANKFORT, op. cit., p. 259; Also see R. LABAT, p. cit., pp. 82–7; J. RENGER, article 'Inthronization' in *RLA*, V, pp. 128–36.

9. R. FRANKENA, *Tâkultu*, Leiden, 1954 (in Dutch with summary in English). J. LAESSØE, *Studies on the Assyrian Ritual and Series bît rimki*, Copenhagen, 1955; R. BORGER, 'Das dritte "Haus" der Serie *bît rimki*', *JCS*, XXI (1967), pp. 1–17.

10. H. FRANKFORT, op. cit., p. 259.

11. *RCAE*, No. 437 (R. LABAT, op. cit., p. 359; H. FRANKFORT, op. cit., p. 264).

12. R. CAMPBELL THOMPSON, *The Reports of the Magicians and Astrologers of Nineveh and Babylon*, London, 1900, remains fundamental. Among studies on Mesopotamian divination and magical practices, the most penetrating is that of J. BOTTERO, 'Symptômes, signes, écriture', in J. P. VERNANT et al. (eds.), *Divination et Rationalité*, Paris, 1974.

13. *RCAE*, No. 1237.

14. *RCAE*, No. 137.

15. J. V. KINNIER WILSON, *The Nimrud Wine List*, London, 1972. See also: E. KLAUBER, *Assyrisches Beamtentum*, Leipzig, 1910, and P. GARELLI, 'Remarques sur l'administration de l'empire assyrien', *RA*, LXVII (1974), pp. 1129–40. Also see Chapter 19, note 15.

16. C. PREUSSER, *Die Wohnaüser in Assur*, Berlin, 1955, pp. 15–60. G. LOUD and CH. B. ALTMAN, *Khorsabad*, II, Chicago, 1938.

17. J. N. POSTGATE, *Neo-Assyrian Grants and Decrees*, Rome, 1969.

18. C. J. JOHNS, *An Assyrian Doomsday Book*, Leipzig, 1901; J. N. POSTGATE, *op. cit.* G. VAN DRIEL, 'Land and people in Assyria', *Bi.Or.*, XXVII (1970), pp. 168–75; F. M. FALES, *Censimenti e Castati di Epoca Neo-Assyria*, Roma, 1973.

19. Sargon forced Egypt to open trade relations with Assyria (C. J. GADD, *Iraq*, XVI, 1954, p. 179) and Esarhaddon encouraged the Babylonians to engage in commerce with 'all countries' (R. BORGER, *Die Inschriften Asarhaddons*, pp. 25 ff.).

20. A. L. OPPENHEIM, *Ancient Mesopotamia*, pp. 93–4, and 'Essay on overland trade in the first millennium B.C.', *JCS*, XXI (1967), pp. 236–54.

21. G. VAN DRIEL, 'Land and people in Assyria: some remarks', *Bi.Or.*, XXVII (1970), pp. 168–75; P. GARELLI, 'Problèmes de stratification sociale dans l'empire assyrien', in *Gesellschaftsklassen im alten Zweistromland*, München, 1972, pp. 73–9.

22. To the fundamental and still valid study of W. MANITIUS, 'Das stehende Herr der Assyrerkönige und seine Organization', *ZA* (ancient series), XXIV (1910), pp. 97–148 and 185–224, must now be added that of F. MALBRAN-LABAT, *L'Armée et l'Organisation Militaire de l'Assyrie*, Geneva/Paris, 1982. Also see: Y. YADIN, *The Art of Warfare in Biblical Lands*, London, 1963.

23. J. N. POSTGATE, *Taxation and Conscription in the Assyrian Empire*, Rome, 1974, pp. 218–26.

24. H. W. SAGGS, 'Assyrian warfare in the Sargonid period', *Iraq*, XXV (1963), pp. 145–54 (esp. pp. 146–7).

25. A. L. OPPENHEIM, 'The eyes of the Lord', *JAOS*, LXXXVIII (1968); F. MALBRAN-LABAT, op. cit., pp. 13–29; 41–57.

26. J. E. READE, 'The Neo-Assyrian court and army: evidence from the sculptures', *Iraq*, XXXIV (1972), pp. 87–112.

27. Pieces of equipment and weapons were found in 'Fort Shalmaneser' at Nimrud: D. STRONACH, 'Metal objects from the 1957 excavations at Nimrud', *Iraq*, XX (1958), pp. 169–81.

28. Among the numerous publications devoted to Assyrian reliefs, see: C. J. GADD, *The Stones of Assyria*, London, 1936, and *Assyrian Sculptures in the British Museum, from Shalmanezer III to Sennacherib*, London, 1938; E. WEIDNER, *Die Reliefs der assyrischen Könige*, Berlin, 1939; R. D. BARNETT and M. FALKNER, *The Sculptures of Assur-nasir-apli, Tiglathpileser III, Esarhaddon from the Central and South-West Palaces at Nimrud*, London, 1962; R. D. BARNETT and N. FORMAN, *Assyrian Palace Reliefs in the British Museum*, London, 1970; R. D. BARNETT, *Sculptures from the North Palace of Ashurbanipal at Nineveh*, London, 1976. See also: *AAO*, pls. 77, 83–114. Excellent photographs in A. PARROT, *Nineveh and Babylon*, London, 1961, and E. STROMMENGER, *The Art of Mesopotamia*, London, 1964.

29. A. WALTER, *Kultrelief aus dem Brunnen des Assur Tempels zu Assur*, Leipzig, 1931; *AAO*, pl. 72.

30. A. WALTER, *Farbige Keramik aus Assur*, Berlin, 1923; G. LOUD and CH. B. ALTMAN, *Khorsabad, II*, Chicago, 1938, pl. 89.

31. A. PARROT, *Assur*, fig. 109–111; 343–5.

32. See, in particular, the splendid embroidered coat of Ashurnaṣirpal in *AAO*, p. 104; fig. 41.

33. M. E. L. MALLOWAN, *The Nimrud Ivories*, London. 1978. Cf. R. D. BARNETT, *A Catalogue of the Nimrud Ivories in the British Museum*; London, 1975; M. E. L. MALLOWAN *et al.*, *Ivories from Nimrud*, 4 vol., London, 1966–74 ff. On the difficult problem of the origin of ivory and of the styles of ivory objects, see: R. D. BARNETT, *Iraq*, XXV (1963), pp. 81–5; I. J. WINTER, *Iraq*, LXI (1981), pp. 1–22; D. COLLON, *Iraq*, XXXIX (1977), pp. 219–22.

Chapter 22

1. SETON LLOYD, *Foundations in the Dust*, London, 1980, p. 126.

2. C. BEZOLD, *Catalogue of the Cuneiform Tablets ... in the British Museum*, London, 1889–99, with supplements by L. W. KING in 1914 and by W. G. LAMBERT and W. G. MILLARD in 1968.

3. *RCAE*, IV, p. 213, No. 6 (transl. E. CHIERA, *They Wrote on Clay*, Chicago, 1938, p. 174). Cf. also *RCAE*, Nos. 18, 255, 688.

4. Among other royal libraries is that of Tiglathpileser I. Cf. E. WEIDNER, 'Die Bibliothek Tiglathpilesers I', *AfO*, XVI (1952), p. 197 ff.

5. These texts have been published by O. R. GURNEY, W. G. LAMBERT and J. J. FINKELSTEIN in *Anatolian Studies*, II (1952) to XXII (1972). On the last named piece, see: J. S. COOPER, 'Structure, humour and satire in the Poor Man of Nippur, *JCS*, XXVII (1975), pp. 163–74. Also: J. BOTTERO in *Les Pouvoirs Locaux en Mésopotamie*, Bruxelles, 1980, pp. 24–8.

6. S. PARPOLA, 'Assyrian library records', *JNES*, XLII (1983, pp. 1–29); D. J. WISEMAN, 'Assyrian writing-boards', *Iraq*, XXVII (1955), pp. 3–13.

7. On Mesopotamian sciences in general: O. NEUGEBAUER, *The Exact Sciences in Antiquity*, Providence, Rhode Island, 1957; R. LABAT, 'La Mésopotamie' in *La Science Antique et Médiévale, Histoire Générale des Sciences*, I, Paris, 1957, pp. 73–138. In spite of its date, B. MEISSNER, *Babylonien und Assyrien*, II, Heidelberg, 1925, is still extremely useful.

8. On schools, see Chapter 13, note 31.

9. On these lists, see A. L. OPPENHEIM, *Ancient Mesopotamia*, Chicago, 1964, pp. 180, 248, 371.

10. B. LANDSBERGER, *Die Fauna des alten Mesopotamien*, Leipzig, 1934; R. C. THOMPSON, *A Dictionary of Assyrian Chemistry and Geology*, Oxford, 1936; *A Dictionary of Assyrian Botany*, London, 1949; M. LEVEY, *Chemistry and Chemical Technology in Ancient Mesopotamia*, Amsterdam, 1959.

11. W. HOROWITZ, 'The Babylonian map of the world', *Iraq*, L (1988), pp. 147–65.

12. A. L. OPPENHEIM et al., *Glass and Glassmaking in Ancient Mesopotamia*, Corning, N.Y., 1970.

13. This point has recently been emphasized by J. C. MARGUERON, *Les Mésopotamiens*, Paris, 1991, Vol. II, pp. 179–81.

14. Good summary on mathematics by R. CARATINI in R. LABAT, op. cit., pp. 103–37 (with bibliography). See also: O. NEUGEBAUER, 'Ancient mathematics and astronomy', in C. SINGER et al. (eds.), *A History of Technology*, I, Oxford, 1954, pp. 785–804; E. M. BRUINS, 'Interpretation of cuneiform mathematics', *Physis*, IV (1962), pp. 277–340. More recently: G. IFRAH, *Histoire Universelle des Chiffres*, Paris, 1981; J. FRIBERG, 'Methods and tradi-

tions of Babylonian mathematics', *Historia Mathematica*, VIII
(1981), pp. 277–318; *Id.*, 'Index of publications on Sumero-Akkadian mathematics and related topics', *AfO Beiheft*, XIX (1982),
pp. 225–32; R. BRADLEY, 'Mathematics in ancient Mesopotamia', *Ur* (Baghdad), 1981/3, pp. 28–31.

15. R. LABAT, op. cit., p. 112.

16. TAHA BAQIR, *Sumer*, VII (1951), p. 30.

17. R. LABAT, op. cit., p. 113.

18. H. GOETSCH, 'Die Algebra der Babylonier', *Archive for History of
Exact Sciences*, Berlin and New York, 1968, pp. 79–153.

19. O. NEUGEBAUER, *Astronomical Cuneiform Texts*, 3 vol., London,
1955; 'Ancient mathematics and astronomy', in C. SINGER *et al.*,
A History of Technology, Oxford, 54; *A History of Ancient Mathematics
and Astronomy*, New York, 1975. Good summaries in R. LABAT,
op. cit., note 7, pp. 123–37 and in H. W. F. SAGGS, *The Greatness
that was Babylon*, London, 1962, pp. 453–9.

20. S. LANGDON and J. K. FOTHERINGHAM, *The Venus Tablets of
Ammizaduga*, London, 1928, and J. D. WEIR, *The Venus Tablets of
Ammizaduga*, Istanbul, 1972; E. REINER, *Same title*, Malibu, Calif.,
1975.

21. R. A. PARKER and W. H. DUBBERSTEIN, *Babylonian Chronology*,
Providence, Rhode Island, 1956, pp. 1–3.

22. A. T. OLMSTEAD, *History of the Persian Empire*, Chicago, 1948, p. 206.

23. A. T. OLMSTEAD, op. cit., p. 457.

24. G. SARTON, 'Chaldaean astronomy in the last three centuries
B.C.', *JAOS*, LXXV (1955), pp. 166–73 (citation p. 170).

25. Most medical texts have been published by F. KÖCHER, *Die
babylonisch-assyrische Medizin in Texten und Untersuchungen*, 6 vol.,
Berlin, 1963–80. General studies in G. CONTENAU, *La Médecine
en Assyrie et en Babylonie*, Paris, 1938; H. E. SIGERIST, *A History of
Medicine*, I, Oxford, 1951, pp. 377–497; A. L. OPPENHEIM, 'Mesopotamian medicine', *Bulletin of the History of Medicine*, XXXVI
(1962), pp. 97–108.

26. E. K. RITTER, 'Magical expert ($=ašipu$) and physician ($=asû$):
notes on two complementary professions in Babylonian medicine', *Assyriological Studies*, Chicago, XVI (1965), pp. 299–
321.

27. R. LABAT, *Traité Akkadien de Diagnostics et Pronostics Médicaux*,
Leiden, 1951.

28. R. LABAT, *Traité*, op. cit., p. 3.
29. R. LABAT, *Traité*, p. 81.
30. R. LABAT, *Traité*, p. 173.
31. F. KUCHLER, *Beiträge zur Kentniss der Assyrisch-Babylonischen Medizin*, Leipzig, 1904, p. 60.
32. J. V. KINNIER WILSON. 'An introduction to Babylonian psychiatry', *Festschrif Benno Landsberger*, Chicago, 1965, pp. 289–98; *Id.*, 'Mental diseases in ancient Mesopotamia', in *Diseases in Antiquity*, Springfield, III, 1967, pp. 723–33.
33. L. LEGRAIN, 'Nippur old drug store', *University Museum Bulletin*, VIII (1940), pp. 25–7; M. CIVIL, 'Prescriptions médicales sumériennes', *RA*, LIV (1960), pp. 57–72; S. N. KRAMER, *The Sumerians*, Chicago, 1963, pp. 93–8; P. HERRERO, *La Thérapeutique Mésopotamienne*, Paris, 1984.
34. R. C. THOMPSON, 'Assyrian prescriptions for disease of the urine', *Babyloniaca*, XIV (1934), p. 124.
35. R. C. THOMPSON, 'Assyrian prescriptions for diseases of the chest and lungs', *RA*, XXXI (1934), p. 23.
36. *RCAE*, No. 108.
37. A. FINET, 'Les Médecins au royaume de Mari', *Annuaire de l'Institut de Philologie et d'Histoire Orientales et Slaves*, Bruxelles, XV (1954–7), pp. 123–44

Chapter 23

1. The principal sources for the political history of this period are: 1. The six Babylonian chronicles assembled by A. K. GRAYSON in *ABC*, pp. 87–111; 2. A few letters published by E. EBELING, *Neubabylonische Briefe*, München, 1949; 3. The Old Testament, notably *II Kings*, *II Chronicles* and the Prophets; 4. Some classical authors (Herodotus, Diodorus Siculus, Josephus, Berossus); 5. The royal inscriptions published by S. LANGDON, *Die Neubabylonischen Königsinschriften (NBK)*, Leipzig, 1912; their bibliography has been updated by P. R. BERGER under the same title in *AOAT*, IV, Neukirchen-Vluyn, 1973.
2. HERODOTUS, I, 102 ff. Cf. DIODORUS SICULUS, II, 26, 1–4.
3. R. BORGER, 'Der Aufstieg des neubabylonischen Reiches', *JCS*, XIX (1965), pp. 59–78; J. OATES, 'Assyrian chronology, 631–612 B.C.', *Iraq*, XXVII (1965), pp. 135–59; W. VON SODEN,

'Aššuretillilani, Sinsariškun, Sinšum(u)liser, und die Ereignisse im Assyrerreich nach 635 v.Chr.', *ZA*, LVIII (1967), pp. 241–55; J. READE, 'The accession of Sinsharishkun', *JCS*, XXVIII (1970), pp. 1–9.

4. See the reservations expressed by J. A. BRINKMAN, *Prelude to Empire*, Philadelphia, 1964, p. 110, note 551, on the ethnic origin of Nabopolassar.

5. This very important chronicle was first published by C. J. GADD, *The Fall of Nineveh*, London, 1923, then, with additions, by D. J. WISEMAN, *Chronicles of Chaldaean Kings*, London, 1956 and lately by A. K. GRAYSON in *ABC*, pp. 90–96. Cf. *ANET*, pp. 303–5.

6. *II Kings* xxiii. 4, 15–19; *II Chronicles* xxxiv. 6.

7. D. J. WISEMAN, *Chronicles*, p. 57; *ABC*, p. 93.

8. Discussion by C. J. GADD, *The Fall of Nineveh*, pp. 10–11.

9. D. J. WISEMAN, *Chronicles*, pp. 59–61; *ABC*, p. 94.

10. Kalhu (Nimrud) is not mentioned in the chronicle. It seems that it was taken in 614 and destroyed in 610 B.C. (D. OATES, *Iraq*, XXIII (1961), pp. 9–10).

11. The term *Umman-manda*, first used in the second millennium B.C. to designate Indo-European warriors on chariots (F. CORNELIUS, 'ERIN-manda', *Iraq*, XXV, 1963, pp. 167–70), then loosely used for the Cimmerians and/or the Scythians, here seems to apply to the Medes (D. J. WISEMAN, *Chronicles*, p. 16).

12. *NBK*, p. 61; A. T. OLMSTEAD, *History of Assyria*, p. 640.

13. Joyful reactions in Judah: *Zephaniah* ii. 13 ff.; *Nahum* ii. ff., *Ezekiel* xxxi. 3 ff.; xxxii. 22 ff.

14. *II Kings* xxiii. 29; *II Chronicles* xxxv. 20; *Jeremiah* xiv. 2; HERODO-TUS, II, 159.

15. D. J. WISEMAN, *Chronicles*, pp. 59–61; *ABC*, p. 99.

16. The most recent general studies on this king and his reign are: A. BOYD and T. S. R. BOASE, *Nebuchadnezzar*, London, 1972; D. J. WISEMAN, *Nebuchadrezzar and Babylon*, Oxford, 1985.

17. 'Chronicle of the early years of Nebuchadnezzar II', lines 6–7 and 9–10, *ABC*, p. 101.

18. *II Kings* xxiv.17; *Jeremiah* xxxvii. 1; JOSEPHUS, *Antiq. Jud.*, X, 6; D. J. WISEMAN, *Chronicles*, pp. 32–5, 73.

19. Cf. A. GARDINER, *Egypt of the Pharaohs*, pp. 260–61.

20. *II Kings*, xxv. 6–7 (cf. *II Chronicles* xxxvi. 13–20; *Jeremiah* xxxiv. 1–18).

21. Five years later, however, Jerusalem revolted and other Jews were deported (*Jeremiah* lii. 30). It has been estimated that 15,000 men with their families were deported in 587 B.C. and that the three deportations involved in all some 50,000 people.

22. D. J. WISEMAN, *Chronicles*, pp. 30, 94–5.

23. From an inscription of Nebuchadrezzar in Wadi-Brissa, Lebanon: *NBK*, p. 175; *ANET*, p. 307.

24. HERODOTUS, I, 74.

25. BEROSSUS, III, 108–10. Also see the Nabonidus stele in *ANET*, pp. 308–11. On Neriglissar, see: R. H. SACK, 'Nergal-šarra-uṣur, King of Babylon, as seen in the cuneiform, Greek, Latin and Hebrew sources', *ZA*, LXVIII (1978), pp. 129–49.

26. D. J. WISEMAN, *Chronicles*, pp. 37–42, 75–7.

27. General studies on Nabonidus's reign: R. H. SACK, 'Nebuchadnezzar and Nabonidus in folklore and history', *Mesopotamia*, XVII (1982), pp. 67–131; P. A. BEAULIEU, *The Reign of Nabonidus king of Babylon 556–539 B.C.*, New Haven/London, 1989.

28. Nabonidus had written a biography of his mother after her death, in two stelae. Texts in *ANET*, pp. 311–12 and 560–62.

29. S. SMITH, 'The verse account of Nabonidus', *Babylonian Historical Texts*, London, 1924, pp. 83–97. Cf. *ANET*, pp. 312–15.

30. *Daniel*, IV, 28–33. Cf. R. MEYER, *Das Gebete des Nabonid*, Berlin, 1962; W. DOMMERHAUSEN, *Nabonidus im Buche Daniel*, Mainz, 1964.

31. SIR LEONARD WOOLLEY and P. R. S. MOOREY, *Ur of the Chaldees*, London, 1982, pp. 251–3; J. OATES, *Babylon*, 1979, pp. 160–62.

32. HERODOTUS, I, 127–30; STRABO, XV, 3, 8; DIODORUS SICULUS, II, 34, 6.

33. *NBK*, p. 221. Cf. A. L. OPPENHEIM, *The Interpretation of Dreams in the Ancient Near East*, Philadelphia, 1956, p. 250, no. 12.

34. Nabonidus Chronicle, II, 1–4 (*ABC*, p. 106; *ANET*, pp. 305–7).

35. Nabonidus Chronicle II, 5–25.

36. C. J. GADD, 'The Harran inscription of Nabonidus', *Anatolian Studies*, VII (1958), pp. 35–92.

37. See notably: W. RÖLLIG, 'Nabonid und Tema', *Compte rendu de la XIe Rencontre Assyriologique Internationale*, Leiden, 1964, pp. 21–32; W. G. LAMBERT, 'Nabonidus in Arabia', *Proceedings of the Vth Seminar for Arabian Studies*, London, 1972, pp. 53–64; P. A. BEAULIEU, op. cit., note 27, pp. 178–85.

38. Nabonidus Chronicle, III, 12–19 (*ABC*, pp. 109–10; *ANET*, p. 306).

39. JOSEPHUS, *Contra Apionnem*, I, 21; EUSEBIUS, *Praep. Evang.* IX, 41.

40. F. H. WEISSBACH, *Die Keilinschriften der Achaemeniden*, Leipzig, 1911, pp. 2 ff.; *ANET*, pp. 315–16.

Chapter 24

1. *Jeremiah*, li., 7; HERODOTUS, I, 178. The Hebraic and Greek or Latin sources on Babylon have been assembled by W. H. LANE, *Babylonian Problems*, London, 1923, and the cuneiform sources by E. UNGER, *Babylon, die heilige Stadt nach der Beschreibung der Babylonier,* Berlin, 1970.

2. Each important part of the site has been published separately in the series: *Wissenschaftliche Veröffentlichungen der Deutschen Orient-Gesellschaft* (*WVDOG*), Berlin. Overall review of the results by R. KOLDEWY, *Das viedererstehende Babylon*, Leipzig, 1925 reprinted in Zurich in 1981. Also see: J. WELLARD, *Babylon*, New York, 1974, and J. OATES, *Babylon*, London, 1979, pp. 144–59.

3. F. WETZEL, *Die Stadtmauern von Babylon* (*WVDOG*, 48), Leipzig, 1930.

4. R. KOLDEWEY, *Das Ischtar-Tor in Babylon* (WVDOG, 32), Leipzig, 1918; J. OATES, *Babylon*, pp. 153–6, fig. 105–9; A. PARROT, *Nineveh and Babylon*, London, 1961; fig. 220–22.

5. R. KOLDEWEY and F. WETZEL, *Die Königsburgen von Babylon*, II (*WVDOG*, 55), Leipzig, 1932.

6. O. REUTHER, *Merkes, die Innenstadt von Babylon* (*WVDOG*, 47), Leipzig, 1926.

7. R. KOLDEWEY and F. WETZEL, *Die Königsburgen von Babylon*, I (*WVDOG*, 54), Leipzig, 1931.

8. DIODORUS SICULUS, II, 10; STRABO, XVI, i, 5; QUINTUS CURTIUS, *Hist Alex.*, V, i, 31–5; BEROSSUS in JOSEPHUS, *Antiq. Jud.*, X, 226–7; *Contra Apionnem*, I, 19.

9. J. OATES, *Babylon*, p. 151. Lists of rations for the Jews exiled in Babylon have been found among these tablets (Cf. *ANET*, p. 308). On the 'Hanging Gardens', see: W. NAGEL,' 'Wo lagen die "Hängenden Gärten" in Babylon', *MDOG*, CX, (1978), pp. 19–28.

10. F. WETZEL, E. WEISSBACH, *Das Hauptheiligtum des Marduk in Babylon : Esagila und Etemenanki* (*WVDOG*, 59), Leipzig, 1938. On ziqqurats see the publications referred to in chapter 10, note 5.

11. HERODOTUS, I, 182–3.

12. *NBK*, pp. 125–7.

13. HERODOTUS, I, 183.

14. The New Year Festival can be reconstructed from various texts, the most important being the *akîtu*-ritual dating to the Seleucid period published by F. THUREAU-DANGIN, *Rituels Accadiens*, Paris, 1921, pp. 127–54 (*ANET*, pp. 331–4). Descriptions and studies in: A. PALLIS, *The Babylonian Akîtu Festival*, Copenhagen, 1926; R. LABAT, *Le Caractère Religieux*, pp. 166–76; H. FRANKFORT, *Kingship and the Gods*, pp. 313–33. Important article by A. FALKENSTEIN, *akiti*-Fest und *akiti*-Festhaus, in *Festschrift Johannes Friedrich*, Heidelberg, 1959, pp. 147–82. Outside Babylon, New Year Festivals were celebrated in Assur, Nineveh, Erbil, Harran, Dilbat and Uruk, but at different dates.

15. Partially excavated by the Germans in 1902 [R. KOLDEWEY, *Die Tempel von Babylon und Borsippa* (*WVDOG*, 15), Leipzig, 1911, pp. 50–59]. Important remains of the ziqqurat and of the temple.

16. *ANET*, p. 334.

17. For the significance of th' gesture and its relationship with the legitimacy of the king, see A. K. GRAYSON, 'Chronicles and the *akîtu* festival', in A. FINET (ed.), *Actes de la XVIIe Rencontre Assyriologique Internationale*, Ham-sur-Heure (Belgium), 1970, pp. 160–70.

18. The *bît akîtu* of Assur, described by Sennacherib (*ARAB*, II, §§ 434–51c) has been excavated (*RLA*, I, p. 188; *AM*, I, pp. 228–30). Excavations at Uruk (*UVB*, 1956, pp. 35–42) have yielded the plan of its *bît akîtu*. According to A. FALKENSTEIN op. cit., there were three *akîtu*-temples in Babylon during the Neo-Babylonian period.

19. W. G. LAMBERT, 'The great battle of the Mesopotamian religious year: the conflict in the akîtu house', *Iraq*, XXV (1963), pp. 189–90.

20. The main study on this subject is that of D. COQUERILLAT, *Palmeraies et Cultures de l'Eanna d'Uruk* (*559–520*), Berlin, 1968. See also: H. F. LUTZ, *Neo-Babylonian Administrative Documents from*

Erech, Berkeley, 1927; R. P. DOUGHERTY, *Archives from Erech*, New Haven, 1927–33. On the temple administration, H. W. F. SAGGS, 'Two administrative officials at Erech in the sixth century B.C.', *Sumer*, XV (1959), pp. 29–38, and *The Greatness That Was Babylon*, op. cit., pp. 261–8; P. GARELLI in *Le Proche-Orient Asiatique*, II, pp. 159–64 and 287–90.

21. R. P. DOUGHERTY, *The shirkûtu of Babylonian Deities*, New Haven, 1923.

22. O. KRUCKMANN, *Neubabylonische Rechts- und Verwaltungstexte*, Leipzig, 1933; H. H. FIGULLA, *Business Document of the New Babylonian period* (*UET*, IV), London, 1949; M. SAN NICOLO and H. PETSCHOW, *Babylonische Rechtsurkunden aus dem 6. Jahrhundert vor Chr.*, München, 1960.

23. A. T. OLMSTEAD, *History of Assyria*, pp. 256–7.

24. B. MEISSNER, *Warenpreise in Babylonia*, Berlin, 1936; W. H. DUBBERSTEIN, 'Comparative prices in later Babylonia', *AJSL*, LVI (1930), pp. 20–43. 1 *qa* was worth 10 *gar*, or 675 square feet. For a radically different opinion, cf. P. GARELLI, op.cit., pp. 285–7.

25. G. CHILDE, *What Happened in History*, Harmondsworth, 1942, p. 193.

26. A. UNGNAD, 'Das Haus Egibi', *AfO*, XIV (1941–4), pp. 57–64; R. BOGAERT, *Les Origines Antiques de la Banque de Dépôt*, Leiden, 1966, pp. 105–18.

Chapter 25

1. On these dates and their historical implications, see R. A. PARKER and W. H. DUBBERSTEIN, *Babylonian Chronology 626 B.C.–A.D. 75*, Providence, Rhode Island., 1956.

2. For a discussion of the events leading to the 'usurpation' of Darius, see A. T. OLMSTEAD, *History of the Persian Empire*, Chicago, 1948, pp. 107–13.

3. F. H. WEISSBACH, *Die Keilinschriften der Achaemeniden*, Leiden, 1911; F. W. KONIG, *Relief und inschrift des Koenigs Daraios I. am Felsen von Bagistan*, Leiden, 1938. Cf. G. G. CAMERON, 'The Old Persian text of the Bisitun inscription', *JCS*, V (1951), pp. 47–54.

4. Behistun, § 50.

5. On these two revolts: TH. DE LIAGRE BÖHL, 'Die babylonischen Prätendenten zur Anfangzeit des Darius (Dareios), I', *Bi.Or.*, XXVI (1968), pp. 150–53.

6. R. A. PARKER and W. H. DUBBERSTEIN, op. cit., p. 17; HERODOTUS, I, 183; STRABO, XVI, i, 5; ARRIAN, *Anabasis*, VII, xvii, 2; DIODORUS, II, ix, 4 ff.; CTESIAS, *Persica*, Epit. 52–3; F. M. TH. DE LIAGRE BOHL, 'Die Babylonischen Prätendenten zur Zeit Xerxes', *Bi. Or.*, XIX (1962), pp. 110–14.

7. SIR LEONARD WOOLLEY and P. R. S. MOOREY, *Ur of the Chaldees*, London, 1982, p. 259; *UVB*, XII–XIII (1956), p. 17; pp. 28–31; F. WETZEL, E. SCHMIDT and A. MALLWIST; *Das Babylon der Spätzeit, (WVDOG*, 62), Berlin, 1957, pp. 25–7.

8. A. T. CLAY, *Legal and Commercial Transactions dated in the Assyrian, Neo-Babylonian and Persian Periods*, Philadelphia, 1908; A. TREMAYNE, *Records from Erech, Time of Cyrus and Cambyses*, New Haven, 1925.

9. This was a letter of introduction, written in Aramaic, given to a tradesman who returned from Babylonia to Egypt via Assyria: D. OATES, *Studies in the Ancient History of Northern Iraq*, London, 1968, pp. 59–60.

10. XENOPHON, *Anabasis*, II, 4 to III, 5; D. OATES, op. cit., pp. 60–61; G. GOOSENS, 'L'Assyrie après l'empire', *Compte rendu de la IIIe Rencontre Assyriologique Internationale*, Leiden, 1854, p. 93.

11. A. T. OLMSTEAD, op. cit., p. 293; M. W. STOLPER, *Management and Politics in Later Achaemenid Babylonia*, 2 vol., Ann Arbor, 1974.

12. HERODOTUS, I, 192; A. T. OLMSTEAD, op. cit., p. 293.

13. A. T. OLMSTEAD, op. cit., pp. 299–301.

14. G. CARDASCIA, *Les Archives des Murashû*, Paris, 1951.

15. R. ZADOK, 'Iranians and individuals bearing Iranian names in Achaemenian Babylonia', *Israel Oriental Studies*, VII (1977), pp. 89–138.

16. Often called, wrongly, the battle of Arbela (Erbil). The battle took place in the plain of Keramlais, 23 kilometres east of Nineveh. Cf. SIR AUREL STEIN, *Geographical Journal*, C (1942), p. 155.

17. ARRIAN, *Anabasis*, III, xvi, 4; VII, xvii, 2; STRABO, XVI, i, 5.

18. 'Chronicle concerning the Diadochi', *ABC*, pp. 115–19.

19. A. J. SACHS and D. J. WISEMAN, 'A Babylonian King List of the hellenistic period', *Iraq*, XVI (1954), pp. 202–11.

20. Discussion in M. ROSTOVTZEFF, *The Social and Economic History of the Hellenistic World*, Oxford, 1941, I, pp. 499–504.

21. The term 'Mesopotamia' is taken here in its broader sense. During the Seleucid period, the country was divided into three satrapies: Mesopotamia in the north, Babylonia in the south and Parapotamia along the Euphrates.

22. American excavations in 1927–32 and 1936–7. Italian, then Italian–Iraqi excavations from 1964 to 1974, resumed in 1985. Preliminary results in *Mesopotamia*, I (1966) to VIII (1973–4), then XXI (1986). Summary of results by A. INVERNIZZI, 'Ten years research in the al-Mada' in area: Seleucia and Ctesiphon', *Sumer*, XXXII (1976), pp. 167–75.

23. French excavations 1922–3; American excavations, 1928–39. Several Preliminary and Final Reports published. For a general account of the excavations, M. ROSTOVTZEFF, *Dura-Europus and its Art*, Oxford, 1938.

24. A. T. CLAY, *Legal Documents from Erech dated in the Seleucid Era*, New Haven, 1913; O. KRÜCKMAN, *Babylonische Rechts- und Verwaltungsurkunden aus der Zeit Alexanders und die Diadochen*, Weimar, 1931. Also see: G. K. SARKISIAN in *VDI*, I (1955), pp. 136–70 and *Forschungen und Berichte*, XVI (1975), pp. 15–76.

25. Nimrud: D. and J. OATES, 'Nimrud, 1957: the Hellenistic Settlement', *Iraq*, XX (1958), pp. 114–57. Seleucid graves at Mari: A. PARROT, *Syria*, XVI (1935), pp. 10–11; XXIX (1952), pp. 186–7; XXXII (1955), pp. 189–90. Remains of a Greco-Oriental temple at Arslan-Tash, F. THUREAU-DANGIN, *Arslan-Tash*, Paris, 1931.

26. *ANET*, p. 317.

27. F. WETZEL *et al.*, op. cit., pp. 3–21. The theatre has recently been re-excavated and restored by the Iraqi Directorate of Antiquities. Cf. *Iraq*, XXXIV (1972), pp. 139–40.

28. PLINY, *Naturalis historia*, VI, 122; PAUSANIAS, *Descriptio Graeciae*, I, xvi, 3.

29. R. NORTH, 'Status of the Warka Excavation', *Orientalia*, XXVI (1957), pp. 206–7, 228–33, 327–41 (with bibliography).

30. M. RUTTEN, *Contrats de l'Epoque séleucide conservés au Musée du Louvre*, Paris, 1935. On temple organization and functions, see: G. J. P. McEWAN, *Priest and Temple in Hellenistic Babylonia*, Wiesbaden, 1981.

31. W. RÖLLIG, 'Griechische Eigennamen in den Texten der Babylonische Spätzeit', *Orientalia*, XXIX (1960), pp. 376–91; A. KUHRT, 'Assyrian and Babylonian traditions in classical authors: a critical synthesis', in H. J. NISSEN and J. RENGER (ed.), *Mesopotamien und seine Nachbarn*, Berlin, 1982, II, pp. 538–41.

32. Latest English translation: S. M. BURSTEIN, *The Babyloniaca of Berossus*, in *Sources for the Ancient Near East*, I, 5, Malibu, Calif., 1978.

33. N. C. DEBEVOISE, *A Political History of Parthia*, Chicago, 1938.

34. German excavations, 1903–14 (W. ANDRAE, *Hatra*): Iraqi excavations since 1951. Preliminary reports in *Sumer*, VIII (1952) ff. For a general description of the site, see: D. HOLMES-FREDERICQ *Hatra et ses Sculptures Parthes*, Leiden, 1963, and W. I. AL-SALIHI, *Hatra* (Historical Monuments of Iraq, 2), Baghdad, 1973.

35. H. LENZEN, *Die Partherstadt Assur* (*WVDOG*, 57), Leipzig, 1933.

36. R. NORTH, *Orientalia*, XXXVI (1957), pp. 241–3; *UVB*, XIV (1958), pp. 18–20; XVI (1960), pp. 13–21; *BaM*, VI (1960), pp. 104–14.

37. JOSEPHUS, *Antiq. Jud.*, XVIII, 310–79.

38. J. N. STRASSMAIER, 'Arsakideninschriften', *ZA*, III (1888), pp. 129–42. TH. J. PINCHES and H. SAYCE, *PSBA* (1902), pp. 108 ff.; TH. J. PINCHES, *The Old Testament in the Light of the Historical Records of Assyria and Babylonia*, London, 1902, pp. 481–6; J. KOHLER and A. UNGNAD, 100 *ausgewählte Rechtsurkunden der Spätzeit des babylonischen Schrifttums*, Leipzig, 1909; A. J. SACHS and J. SCHAUM-BERGER, *Late Babylonian Astronomical and Related Texts*, Providence, Rhode Island, 1955.

39. A. J. SACHS and J. SCHAUMBERGER, op. cit., No. 1201 (mentioned but not published).

40. DION CASSIUS, LXXI, 2; AMMIANUS MARCELLINUS, XXIII, vi, 34; ZONARAS, XI, 22, XII, 2. L. DILLEMANN, 'Ammien Marcellin et les pays de l'Euphrate et du Tigre', *Syria*, XXXVIII (1961), pp. 86–158.

41. V. CHAPOT, *La Frontière de l'Euphrate*, Paris, 1907; A. POIDEBARD, *La Trace de Rome dans le Désert de Syrie*, Paris, 1934; D. OATES, *Studies in the Ancient History of Northern Iraq*, Oxford, 1968, pp. 67–117; *Id.*, 'Ain Sinu', in J. CURTIS (ed.), *Fifty Years of Mesopotamian Discovery*, London, 1982, pp. 120–22.

42. Ctesiphon was studied by German, then German and American archaeologists in 1931–2 and, more recently, by the Italians working in Seleucia (see note 22 above). On the Kish palace: s. LANGDON, 'Excavations at Kish and Barghutiat', *Iraq*, I (1934), pp. 113–22; P. R. S. MOOREY, *Kish Excavations 1923–1933*, Oxford, 1978, p. 180 ff.

43. H. LENZEN, 'Ein Goldkranz aus Warka', *Sumer*, XIII (1957), pp. 205–6. On this tomb, the date of which has not been determined with certainty, cf. *UVB*, XV (1959), pp. 27–34; XVI (1960), pp. 23–9.

44. G. LE STRANGE, *The Lands of the Eastern Caliphate*, 3rd ed., London, 1966, pp. 26–9.

Epilogue

1. W. W. TARN, *La Civilisation Hellénistique*, Paris, 1936, pp. 219–37.

2. A list of these words will be found in H. W. F. SAGGS, *The Greatness that was Babylon*, London, 1962, pp. 493–5. This book also contains other examples of our Mesopotamian heritage.

3. J. BOTTERO, 'L'Assyriologie et notre histoire', *Dialogues d'Histoire Ancienne*, VII, Paris, 1981, p. 95.

4. Numerous studies have been devoted to the relations between the Greek and Oriental civilizations. They include: R. M. HAYWOOD, *Ancient Greece and the Near East*, London, 1965; M. L. WEST, *Early Greek Philosophy and the Orient*, London, 1971; H. A. HOFFNER (ed.), *Orient and Occident*, (*AOAT*, 22), Neukirchen-Vluyn, 1973; D. KAGAN, *Problems in Ancient History*, I, *The Ancient Near East and Greece*, New York, 1975.

5. E. PORADA, 'The cylinder seals found at Thebes in Beotia', *AfO*, XXVIII (1981–2), pp. 1–70; J. A. BRINKMAN, 'The Western Asiatic seals found at Thebes in Greece', *ibid.*, pp. 73–7.

6. C. H. GORDON, *Before the Bible*, London, 1962, pp. 9, 132.

7. J. FILLIOZAT, 'Pronostic médicaux akkadiens, grecs et indiens', *Journal Asiatique*, CCXL (1952), pp. 299–321; M. SANDRAIL, *Les Sources akkadiennes de la Pensée et de la Méthode hippocratiques*, Toulouse, 1953.

8. C. H. GORDON, op. cit., pp. 49–97, 218–77. R. GRAVES, *The Greek Myths*, Harmondsworth, 1957, II, p. 89.

9. See, for instance, R. D. BARNETT, 'Ancient Oriental influences on archaic Greece', in *The Aegean and the Near East, Studies presented to H. Goldman*, New York, 1956, pp. 212–38; R. A. JAIRAZBHOY, *Oriental Influences in Western Art*, London, 1965.

10. M. ROSTOVTZEFF, *The Social and Economic History of the Hellenistic World*, Oxford, 1941, I, p. 84.

CHRONOLOGICAL TABLES

I. PREHISTORY

DATES B.C.	PERIOD	MESOPOTAMIA NORTH	SOUTH	TECHNICAL AND CULTURAL DEVELOPMENT IN MESOPOTAMIA
c.70000	MIDDLE PALEOLITHIC	Barda Balka **Shanidar D** (c. 60–35000) Hazar Merd		*Neanderthal hunter-gatherers living in caves and rock shelters.*
35000				
25000	UPPER PALEOLITHIC	**Shanidar C** (c. 34–25000)		*Homo sapiens sapiens. Improvement and diversification of stone implements. Wider food spectrum.*
12000		(Hiatus) Shanidar B2 **Zarzi.** Palegawra		
9000	MESOLITHIC	Shanidar B1 Zawi Chemi Shanidar Karim Shehir Mlefaat **Mureybet**		*Microlithic tools and weapons. Obsidian imported. Bone work. First clay figurines. First groups of dwellings. Beginnings of animal domestication.*
8000			Bus Mordeh	
7000	NEOLITHIC	**Jarmo**	Ali Kosh	*Progressive domestication of animals and edible plants. Villages. Invention of pottery. First baked bricks.*

Date (BC)	Period	Cultures / Sites	Developments
6000	CHALCOLITHIC	Umm Dabaghiuah	*Use of copper. First mural paintings. Irrigation agriculture. First seals. First temples. Decorated luxury ware. Clay and alabaster figurines. Wide use of brick.*
		HASSUNA Yarim Tepe 1, Matarrah	
5500		**SAMARRA** T. Sawwan	
		HALAF Yarim Tepe 2, Arpachiya → Choga Mami	
5000		**OUEILI** (Ubaid 0)	
		ERIDU (Ubaid 1)	
		HAJJI MUHAMMAD (Ubaid 2)	
4500		**NORTH UBAID** Tepe Gawra and numerous other sites →	*Temples and houses of increasing size and complexity. Terracotta sickles and pestles.*
		SOUTH UBAID el-'Ubaid, Ur and numerous other sites	
4000		**URUK PERIOD**	*Urbanization. Potter's wheel. Swing-plough. Sail. Metal work (bronze, gold, silver). First cylinder-seals. Invention of writing (c. 3300). Development of sculpture. Expanding trade.*
3750		Tepe Gawra, Qalinj Agha, Grai Resh, Habuba Kabira and numerous other sites	
		Uruk, Tell 'Uqair and numerous other sites	
		Tell Brak	
3000	ANCIENT BRONZE	**NINEVEH V**	
		JEMDAT NASR	
2700	HISTORIC	**Early Dynastic I**	**SUMERIAN CIVILIZATION** *City-states. Fortified towns. Development of writing. Administrative archives from Fara and Abu Salabikh.*
		Early Dynastic II	
2500		**Early Dynastic III**	

II. EARLY DYNASTIC PERIOD (c. 2900–2384 B.C.)

DATES B.C.	SUB-PERIODS	KISH	URUK	UR	LAGASH	MARI	EBLA	OTHER DYNASTIES
2750	E.D. I	**KISH I**	**URUK I**					
	E.D. II	21 kings (Etana included) from the Flood to:	4 'mythical' kings Meskiangasher Enmerkar Lugalbanda Dumuzi in about one century down to:					
2700		Enmebaragesi (c. 2700)	Gilgamesh					
		Agga						
2650			6 successors of Gilgamesh between c. 2660 and c. 2560					
2600	E.D. IIIA			Royal cemetery Meskalamdug Akalamdug (c. 2600)				
		Uhub (c. 2570)		**UR I**	En-hegal (c. 2570)	**DYNASTY OF MARI** According to the Sumerian King List. 6 kings : 136 years ?	**AWAN**	**ADAB** Nin-kisalsi
2550		**Mesilim** (c. 2550)		**Mesannepadda** (c. 2560–2525)				3 kings
				A-annepadda (c. 2525–2485)		Ilshu (c. 2500)		**Peli** 13 kings down to c. 2250
2500	E.D. IIIB	**KISH II** 6 kings (+ Zuzu of Akshak ?) from c. 2520 to:			**Lugal-shag-engur** (c. 2500)	Lugal-shag-engur (c. 2500)		Me-durba Lugal-dalu

Chronological chart of Early Dynastic rulers (c. 2450–2300 BC).

Date	KISH / AKKAD	URUK	UR	LAGASH (Ur-Nanshe)	MARI (Lamgi-Mari)	EBLA	HAMAZI / AKSHAK / AKKAD
			Meskiagnunna (c. 2485–2450)	Ur-Nanshe (c. 2490)	Lamgi-Mari	Igrish-Halam	HAMAZI c. 2450 — AKSHAK
			Elili (c. 2445)	Akurgal (c. 2465)	Ikun-Shamash	Irkab-Damu	Hataanish
2450							Zizi = ? — Zuzu
	Enbi-Ishtar (c. 2430)	URUK II — En-shakush-anna (c. 2430–2400)	Bailli — UR II	Eannatum (c. 2455–2425)	Ikun-Shamagan	Ar-Ennum	Unzi
	KISH III			Enannatum I (c. 2425)	Iblul-il		Puzur-Nirah
					Mari exerts control over Ebla		Ishu-Il
2400	Ku-Baba (*Female inn-keeper*)	Lugal-kinishe-dudu (c. 2400)	4 kings (*names unknown*)	Entemena (c. 2400)			Shu Sin
	KISH IV — Puzur-Sin	Lugalkisalsi		Enannatum II / En-entarzi / Lubalanda / Uru-inimgina (c. 2350)		Ebrium	
2350	Ur-Zababa (c. 2340)	URUK III — Lugalzagesi (c. 2340–2316)					DYNASTY OF AKKAD — Sharru-kin (Sargon) (c. 2334–2279)
	AKKAD					Ibbi-Sipish	
2300							

The chronology of this period is uncertain. All dates are approximate. The order of the kings of Mari attested by their inscriptions (and apparently different from those of the Sumerian King List) is not established.

III. DYNASTIES OF AKKAD, GUTIUM AND UR III (c. 2334–2004 B.C.)

DATES B.C.	AKKAD/UR	URUK/ISIN	GUTI/LARSA	LAGASH	MARI
	DYNASTY OF AKKAD				
	Sharru-kin (Sargon) (2334–2279)	Lugalzagesi			*Sargon takes Mari and Ebla*
2300	Rimush (2278–2270) Manishtusu (2269–2255)				
2250	**Narâm-Sin** (2254–2218)				*Narâm-Sin conquers Mari and destroys Ebla* **SHAKKANAKKU** Ididish
2200	Shar-kalli-sharri (2217–2193)		**DYNASTY OF GUTIUM** *21 Guti Kings down to 2120*	Lugal-ushumgal (2230–2200)	Shu-Dagan Isma-Dagan (2199–2154)
	Anarchy				

	Ur / Uruk	Guti / Larsa	Isin	Ensi of Lagash / Governors	
2150	Shu-Turul (2168–2154)			**ENSI OF LAGASH** (2155–2142) Ur-Baba (2155–2142)	Nur-Mēr Ishtup-Ilum Ishkun-Addu
	URUK IV Ur-nigina (2153–2147) Ur-gigira (2146–2141) + 3 kings	*The Guti invade Akkad and Sumer*		**Gudea** (2141–2122) Ur-Ningirsu (2121–2118) Pirig-me (2117–2115) Ur-gar (2114) Nam-mahazi (2113–2111)	Apil-Kin (2126–2091)
	URUK V Utu-hegal (2123–2113)	Tiriqan (x–2120)			
	UR III Ur-Nammu (2112–2095)			**GOVERNORS OF LAGASH VASSALS OF UR** Ur-Ninsuna	
2100	**Shulgi** (2094–2047)			Ur-Ninkimara	Iddin-Ilum Ilum-Ishtar Turam-Dagan (2071–2051)
				Lu-kirilaza	
		DYNASTY OF LARSA Naplânum (2025–2005)	**DYNASTY OF ISIN** Ishbi-Erra (2017–1985)		
2050	Amar-Sin (2046–2038) Shu-Sin (2037–2029) **Ibbi-Sin** (2028–2004)			Ir-Nanna	Puzur-Ishtar (2050–2025) Hilal-Erra Hanun-Dagan (2016–2008)
2000	*Fall of Ur* (2004)	Emisum (2004–1977)		*Lagash becomes independent* (2023)	

IV. ISIN-LARSA, OLD BABYLONIAN AND OLD ASSYRIAN PERIOD (c. 2000–1600 B.C.)

DATES B.C.	ISIN	LARSA	BABYLON	MARI	ASSYRIA	ESHNUNNA	ANATOLIA
2025	**DYNASTY OF ISIN** **Isbbi-Erra** (2017–1985)	**DYNASTY OF LARSA** **Naplānum** (2025–2005)				*Eshnuna becomes independent* *Ilushu-ilia (c. 2028)*	
		Emisum (2004–1977)			Ushpia		*Cappadocian culture*
2000	Shu-ilishu (1984–1975)				Kikkia	Nūr-ahum	
		Samium (1976–1942)			Akkia **DYNASTY OF PUZUR-ASHUR**	Kirikiri	
	Iddin-Dagan (1974–1954)				Puzur-Ashur I	**Bilalama**	
	Ishme-Dagan (1953–1935)				Shallim-ahhé	Ishar-ramashshu	
1950		Zabaia (1941–1933)				Usur-awassu Azuzum	
	Lipit-Ishtar (1934–1924)	**Gungunum** (1932–1906)			**Ilushuma**	Ur-Ninmar Ur-Ningizzida Ibiq-Adad I	*Colonies of Assyrian merchants in Cappadocia (Kārum Kanesh I)*
	Ur-Ninurta (1923–1896)	Abi-saré (1905–1895)	**BABYLON I** **Sumu-abum** (1894–1881)		Erishum I (c. 1906–1867)	Sharria Belakum	
1900	Bur-Sin (1895–1874)	Sumu-El (1894–1866)	Sumu-la-El (1880–1845)			Warasa Ibal-pi-El I	*abandoned kārum Kanesh*
	Lipit-Enlil (1873–1869) Erra-imitti (1868–1861) Enlil-bāni (1860–1837)	Nūr-Adad (1865–1850) Sin-iddinam (1849–1843) Sin-eribam, Sin-iqisham Silli-Adad (1842–1835)	Sabium (1844–1831)	**AMORITE DYNASTY** Iaggid-Lim (c. 1830–1820)	Ikūnum Sharru-kin (Sargon I) Puzur-Ashur II	Ibiq-Adad II	Pitkhana
1850	Zambia, Iterpisha, Urdukuga (1836–1828) Sin-magir (1827–1817)	Warad-Sin (1834–1823)	Apil-Sin (1830–1813)	Iahdun-Lim (c. 1820–1796)	Narām-Sin Erishum II	Narām-Sin	*kārum Kanesh II*

Date	Sealand / Isin	Larsa	Babylon (First Dynasty)	Mari / Kassites	Assyria	Eshnunna	Hittites
	(1816-1794)		Sin-muballit (1812-1793)	*Iasmah-Adad* (1796-1776)	(1809-1776)	(c. 1805-1780)	Anitta
1800	*Hammurabi conquers Isin* (1787)		**Hammurabi** (1792-1750)	**Zimri-Lim** (1776-1761) *Hammurabi destroys Mari*	Ishme-Dagan (1780-1741) *Hammurabi conquers Assur (?)*	**Ibal-pi El II** ... *Hammurabi conquers Eshnunna*	
		Hammurabi conquers Larsa (1763)					
1750	**DYNASTY OF THE SEALAND**	Rim-Sin II (1741-1736)	**Samsu-iluna** (1749-1712)	**KASSITES** Gandash (c. 1730)	Mut-Ashkur	Iqish-Tiskpak Anni *Samsu-iluna destroys Eshnunna*	
	Iluma-ilum (Iliman) (c. 1732)			Agum I	Rimush		
	Itti-ili-nibi			Kashtiliash I *King of Hana*	Asinum		
1700			Abi-eshuh (1711-1684)		*Anarchy: 8 usurpers from Puzur-Sin to Adari*		
	Damiq-ilishu		Ammi-ditana (1683-1647)	Ushshi	Bēlu-bāni (1700-1691)		**OLD HITTITE EMPIRE** Labarnas I (c. 1680-1650?)
				Abirattash	Libaia (1690-1674)		
1650	Ishkibal		Ammi-saduqa (1646-1626)	Kashtiliash II	Sharma-Adad I (1673-1662)		**Hattusilis I** (1650-1620)
	Shushshi		Samsu-ditana (1625-1595)	Urzigurumash Harbashihu	IPtar-Sin (1661-1650)		**Mursilis I** (1620-1590)
			c. 1595: Babylon conquered by the Hittites	Tiptakzi	Bazaia (1649-1622)		
1600	Gulkishar		Agum II	**Agum II**	Lullaia (1621-1618)		**Hantilis I** (1590-1500)
					Kidin-Ninua (1615-1602)		
					Sharma-Adad II (1601)		
					Erishum III (1598-1586)		
	5 other kings to Ea-gamil (c. 1460)				Shamshi-Adad II (1585-1580)		

V. KASSITE PERIOD (c. 1600–1200 B.C.)

DATES B.C.	BABYLONIA	ASSYRIA	HURRI-MITANNI	ANATOLIA	SYRIA-PALESTINE	EGYPT	ELAM
							DYNASTY OF EPARTI *(since c. 1850)*
1600	*c. 1595: Babylon conquered by the Hittites*	Erishum III		**OLD HITTITE EMPIRE** *(since c. 1680)*		*Hyksos period*	Tata (1600–1580)
	KASSITE DYNASTY	Shamshi-Adad II					Atta-merra-halki (1580–1570)
	Agum II kakrime	Ishme-Dagan II		Hantilis I		**NEW EGYPTIAN EMPIRE**	Pala-ishshan (1570–1545)
	(c. 1570)	Shamshi-Adad III	Kirta	(1590–1560)	*The Hyksos expelled from Egypt*	*XVIIIth DYNASTY*	
1550		Ashur-nirari I	**Shuttarna I** (c. 1560)			**Amosis** (1576–1546)	Kur-Kirwesh (1545–1520)
	Burnaburiash I	(1547–1522)	*Formation of the Kingdom of Milanni*	Zidantas I	Idrimi, King of Alalah	Amenophis I (1546–1526)	
		Puzur-Ashur III	Parattarna (c. 1530)	Ammunas			Kuk-nahhunte (1520–1505)
		(1521–1498)		Huzziyas I		**Thutmosis I** (1526–1512)	
1500	**Kashtiliash III**	Enlil-nasir	**Saustatar** (c. 1500)	Telepinus (1525–1500)	*Egyptian campaigns in Syria*	Thutmosis II (1512–1504)	Kutir-nahhunte II (1505–?)
		Nur-ili	*Assyria under Milannian rule*	Alluwanash		**Thutmosis III** (1504–1450)	
	Ulamburiash	Ashur-rabi I	*Archives of Nuzi*	Hantilis II	*Syria conquered by the Egyptians*		
				Zidantas II			
1450	Agum III	Ashur-nadin-ahhe I		Huzziyas II		**Amenophis II** (1450–1425)	
	Kadashman-harbe I	Enlil-nasir II	Artatama I (c. 1430)	**NEW HITTITE EMPIRE**	*Amenophis' campaigns in Syria-Palestine*		
	Karaindash	Ashur-nirari II		**Tudhaliyas I** (1450–1420)		Thutmosis IV (1425–1417)	
	Kurigalzu I	Ashur-bel-nisheshu		Arnuwandas I (1420–1400)			
		Ashur-rem-nisheshu	Shuttarna II (c. 1400)				
1400	Kadashman-Enlil I	Ashur-nadin-ahhe II		Tudhaliyas II	*el-Amarna period (c. 1400–1350)*	**Amenophis III** (1417–1379)	
		Eriba-Adad I	Artatama II **Tushratta**	Hattusilis II		Amenophis IV	
	Burnaburiash II (1375–1347)	(1392–1366)		Tudhaliyas III (1395–1380)	*Northern Syria conquered b)*	(Akhenaten) (1379–1362)	
		Ashur-uballit I (1365–1330)					

Babylonia (Kassite)	Assyria	Mitanni	Hatti	Events	Egypt	Elam
			(c. 1380–1336)		(1361–1352)	Ige-halki (1350–1330)
Kurigalzu II (1345–1324)	Enlil-nirari	Shutarna III			Ay (1352–1348)	Hurpatila
Nazimaruttash (1323–1298)	Arik-den-ili (1319–1308)	Shuattarra = ? Shuttaara I	Mattiwaza	Archives of Ugarit Alphabetic cuneiform writing	Horemheb (1348–1320)	Pahir-ishshan I (1330–1310)
	Adad-nirari I (1307–1275)		Arnuwandas II Mursilis II (1335–1310)		*XIXth DYNASTY*	Attar-kitah (1310–1300)
Kadashman-Turgu (1297–1280)		Wasasatta		*Battle of Qadesh* (1300)	Rameses I (1319–1317) Sethi I (1317–1304)	Humban-numena (1300–1275)
Kadashman-Enlil II (1279–1265)	**Salmanasar I** (1274–1245)	Shattuara II	**Muwatallis** (1309–1287)		**Rameses II** (1304–1237)	**Untash-napirisha** (1275–1240)
Kudur-Enlil Shagaraku-Shuriash (1255–1243)	**Tukulti-Ninurta I** (1244–1208)		**Hattusilis III** (1286–1265)	*Egyptian–Hittite treaty* (1286)		
Kashtiliash IV			Tudhaliyas IV (1265–1235)	*Moses and Exodus*		Unpatar-napirisha Kiten-Hutran (1235–1210?)
Assyrian governors (1235–1227)	Ashur-nadin-apli Ashur-nirari III Enlil-kudurri-usur		Arnuwandas III (1235–1215)		Merneptah (1237–1209)	*SHUTRUKIDS*
Enlil-nadin-shumi Adad-shuma-iddina Adad-shuma-usur (1218–1189)	Ninurta-apal-Ekur (1192–1180)		Suppiluliumas II (1215–?)			Hallutush-Inshushinak (1205–1185)
Melishipak (1188–1174)			*The Phrygians and Gasgas destroy the Hittite Empire.* (c. 1200)	*Invasion of the Peoples of the Sea*	*XXth DYNASTY* **Rameses III** (1198–1166)	**Shutruk-nahhunte** (1185–1155)
Marduk-apal-iddina (1173–1161)	**Ashur-dân I** (1179–1134)			*Philistines. The Israelites begin to conquer Canaan*		
Zababa-shuma-iddina Enlil-nadin-ahhê (1159–1157) *End of the Kassite dynasty* (1157)					Rameses IV to Rameses XI (1166–1085)	Kutir-nahhunte **Shilhak-Inshushinak** (1150–1120)

The number, order and chronology of the kings of the Kassite dynasty who reigned before Burnaburiash II are extremely uncertain. The same applies to the last kings of the Old Hittite Empire.

DATES B.C.	BABYLONIA		ASSYRIA	PHENICIA-SYRIA	
1150	**BABYLON IV (ISIN II)**	Marduk-kabit-ahhêshu (1156–1139)	Ashur-dân I (1179–1134)		
		Itti-Marduk-balaţu Ninurta-nadin-shumi	Ashur-rêsh-ishi I (1133–1116)		
		Nebuchadrezzar I (1124–1103)	**Tiglathpileser I** (1115–1077)		
1100		Enlil-nadin-apli Marduk-nadin-ahhê		*Neo-Hittite kingdoms in Northern Syria*	
		Marduk-shapik-zêri	Asharid-apal-Ekur Ashur-bêl-kala (1074–1057)		
1050		Adad-apla-iddina (1067–1046)	Shamshi-Adad IV Ashurnaşirpal I (1050–1032)	*Aramaeans settle in Syria and expand towards Mesopotamia*	
		Marduk-zêr-x			
		Nabû-shum-libur (1032–1025)	Shalmaneser II (1031–1020)		
	BABYLON V	Simbar-shipak (1024–1007) 2 kings (1007–1004)	Ashur-nirâri IV Ashur-râbi II (1016–973)	**BYBLOS** Ahiram (c. 1000)	**DAMASCUS** Hadadezar
1000	**BABYLON VI**	Eulma shakin-shumi (1003–987) 2 kings (986–984)			
	BABYLON VII	Mâr-bîti-apla-uşur		Itobaal (c. 980)	**TYRE** Hiram (c. 969–931)
	BABYLON VIII	Nabû-mukin-apli (977–942)	Ashur-rêsh-ishi II Tiglathipileser II (967–935)	Abibaal (c. 940)	
950		Ninurta-kudurri-uşur Mar-bîti-ahhê-iddina (941–?)	Ashur-dân II (934–912)	Yehimilk (c. 920)	
		Shamash-mudammiq (?–c. 900)	**Adad-nirâri II** (911–891) Tukulti-Ninurta II	Elibaal	
900		Nabû-shuma-ukîn (899–888?) Nabû-apla-iddina (887–855?)	**Ashurnasirpal II** (883–859)	Shipitbaal	**DAMASCUS** Ben-Hadad I (880–841)
850		Marduk-zakir-shumi I (854–819)	**Shalmaneser III** (858–824)	*Battle of Qarqar* (853)	Hazael (841–806)
800		Marduk-balassu-iqbi Baba-aha-iddina 5 unknown kings	Shamshi-Adad V (823–811) **Adad-nirâri III** (810–783)		Ben-Hadad II (806–?)
		Ninurta-apla-x			
		Marduk-bêl-zêri			
		Marduk-apla-uşur	Shalmaneser IV		
		Eriba-Marduk (769–761)	Ashur-dân III (772–755)		
		Nabû-shuma-ishkun (760–748)	Ashur-nirâri V (754–745)		

SSYRIAN PERIODS (*c.* 1150–750 B.C.)

ALESTINE		ANATOLIA	EGYPT
			XXth DYNASTY
ERIOD OF THE JUDGES		*Lydian Kingdom founded (Heraclides)* (c. *1205–700*)	*Last Ramessides*
hniel			
ud			
rak, Deborah		*Assyrian campaigns against the Mushki*	**THIRD INTERMEDIATE PERIOD**
deon			*XXIst DYNASTY*
phthah			Smendes (c. 1085)
mson			
muel		*First colonies of Ionians, Eolians and Dorians on the Aegean coast* (c. *1100–950*)	Psusennes I (c. 1050)
ONARCHY			
ıl (1030–1010)			
vid (1010–970)			
			Amunemope (c. 1000)
			Siamon (c. 975)
lomon (970–931)			*XXIInd DYNASTY*
			Sheshonq I (945–924)
DAH	**ISRAEL**		Osorkon I (924–889)
hoboham	Jeroboam I		
31–913)	(931–910)		
bijam			
a	Nadab		
ı1–870)	Baasa (909–886)		
	Ela (886–885)		Takelot (889–874)
	Zimri. Omri (885–874)		Osorkon II (874–850)
oshaphat	Ahab	**KINGDOM OF URARTU**	Takelot II (850–825)
70–848)	(874–853)	Arame (c. 850)	
ram (848–841)	Ahaziah Joram		
haziah	Jehu (841–814)	Sardur I (832–825)	Sheshonq III (825–773)
thalia		Ishpuini (824–806)	*XXIIIrd DYNASTY*
ash (835–796)			(Libyan)
	Jehahaz (814–798)	Menua (805–788)	(c. 817–730)
			5 kings
maziah	Jehoash (793–783)	Argishti I (787–766)	
96–781)	Jeroboam II		Pami
zariah	(783–743)	Sardur II (765–733)	Sheshonq V
81–740)			(767–730)

DATES B.C.	BABYLONIA	ASSYRIA	PHENICIA-SYRIA	PALESTINE	
				JUDAH	**ISRAEL**
	BABYLON IX (since 977)				
750					
	Nabû-našir (Nabonassar) (747–734)	**Tiglathpileser III** (744–727)	**DAMASCUS** Razin (740–732)	Jotham (740–736)	Menahem (743–738)
	2 kings (734–732) Nabû-mukin-zêri	**Shalmaneser V** (726–722)	732: conquest of Damascus	Achaz (736–716)	Peka Hoshea (732–724)
	Merodach-Baladan II (721–710)	**Sargon II** (721–705)	Neo-Hittite and Aramaean kingdoms incorporated in the Assyrian Empire (747 to 704)	Ezechiah (716–687)	722: Conquest of Samaria
	3 kings (703–700)	**Sennacherib**			
700	Ashur-nadin-shumi (699–694)	(704–681)	**SIDON** Lullè		
	2 kings (693–689)			Manasseh (687–642)	
		Esarhaddon (680–669)	**SIDON** Abdi-milkuti		
	Shamash-shuma-ukîn (668–648)	**Ashurbanipal** (668–627)			
650	Kandalanu (647–627)		Assyrian campaigns in Phoenicia	Amon Josiah (640–609)	
	BABYLON X CHALDAEAN DYNASTY Nabû-apla-uṣur (Nabopolassar, 625–605)	Ashur-etil-ilâni Sîn-shumu-lishir Sîn-shar-ishkun Ashur-uballiṭ II			
600	**Nebuchadrezzar II** (604–562)	612–609: conquest of Assyria by the Medes and the Babylonians	Battle of Karkemish	Jeoahaz Jeoiakim Jeoiakin Zedekiah (598–587)	
			573: Tyre conquered by Nebuchadrezzar	587: Jerusalem conquered by Nebuchadrezzar	
	Evil-Merodach Neriglissar				
550	Nabû-na'id (Nabonidus)				
	539: Cyrus conquers Babylon				

* Classically, the Neo-Assyrian period begins with the reign of Ashurnaṣirpal II (883–859) noted on table VI.

ANATOLIA		IRAN		ELAM	EGYPT
URARTU	PHRYGIA	MEDES	PERSIANS	LAST DYNASTIES	
Sardur II (765–733)				Humoash-tahrah (?760–742)	XXIVth DYNASTY (Kushite) / Piankhi (751–716)
	Midas (c. 740–700)			Humban-nikash I (742–717)	XXVth DYNASTY / Tefnakht
Rusa I (730–714)		Deioces (c. 728–675)			Bocchoris
Argishti II (714–?)				Shutruk-nahhunte II (717–699)	Shabaka (716–701)
			Achemenes		Shabataka (701–689)
	LYDIA MERMNADES			Hallutush-Inshushinak (699–693) / Humban-nimena (692–687) / Humban-haltash I (687–680)	Taharqa (689–664)
	Gyges (685–644)	Phraortes (675–653)	Teispes (675–640)	Urtaki (674–663)	Assyrian campaigns in Egypt / SAITE RENAISSANCE / XXVIth DYNASTY
Rusa II				Tempt-Humban-Inshushinak (Teuman, 668?–653)	Psammetichus I (664–609)
		Cyaxares (653–585)		Tammaritu I (653)	653: Assyrians expelled from Egypt
	Ardys (644–615)		Cyrus I (640–600)	Humban-haltash III (648–644?)	
Sardur III				Ashurbanipal conquers Susa and plunders Elam	
	Sadyattes (615–610) / Alyattes (610–561)				
Rusa III			Cambyses (600–559)	610: Elam divided between Babylonians and Medes	Necho II (609–594)
					Psammetichus II (594–588)
Urartu conquered by the Medes		Astyages (585–550)			Apries (588–568)
	Cresus (561–547)		Cyrus II (559–530)		Amasis (568–526)
Cyrus conquers Lydia, then Anatolia		Cyrus King of the Medes			

VIII. ACHAEMENIAN AND HELLENISTIC PERIODS (539–126 B.C.)

DATES B.C.	GREECE	IRAN	MESOPOTAMIA
	Solon, archon (since *c.* 620)	*ACHAEMENIDS* (since *c.* 700)	
550			*539: Cyrus conquers Babylon*
	Pisistratus (tyrant) (539–528)	Cambyses II (530–522)	**ACHAEMENIAN PERIOD** *Revolts of Nebuchadrezzar III and Nebuchadrezzar IV (522–521)*
		Darius I (522–486)	
500	*Median wars (490–478)*	**Xerxes I** (485–465)	*Revolts of Bêl-shimanni and Shamash-eriba (482). Xerxes sacks Babylon*
		Artaxerxes I (464–424)	*c. 460: Herodotus in Babylon? The Murashû family, bankers at Nippur (455–403)*
450	Pericles (strategus) (443–430)		
	Peloponnesian war (431–404)	Darius II (423–405)	*Nabû-rimânni and Kidinnu astronomers*
400		Artaxerxes II (404–359)	*401: Xenophon in Babylonia*
	Philip of Macedonia (359–337)	Artaxerxes III (358–338)	
350	**Alexander the Great** (336–323)	Darius III (335–331)	*Gaugameles (331), Alexander enters Babylon and dies there in 323*
	DIADOCHI Seleucos I (305–281) **SELEUCIDS**		**HELLENISTIC PERIOD** *311: beginning of the era of Seleucos*
300	**Antiochos I** (281–260)		*c. 300, Seleucia-on-the-Tigris founded*
	Antiochos II (260–246)	**ARSACID PARTHIANS**	*Last royal inscriptions in Akkadian (Antiochos I) Berossus writes the 'Babyloniaca'.*
250	Seleucos II (245–226)	Arsaces (250–248) Tiridates I (248–211)	
	Antiochos III (222–187)		*Temples built in Uruk*
200		Artabanus I (211–191)	
	Antiochos IV (175–164)	**Mithridates I** (171–138)	*Greek theatre at Babylon*
	Demetrios I (162–150)		
150	Demetrios II (145–126)	Artabanus II (128–124)	*144: Mithridates founds Ctesiphon Demetrios reconquers Babylonia*
	Antiochos VIII (126–96)	Mithridates II (123–88)	*126: Artabanus II snatches Babylonia from the Seleucids*
100			**PARTHIAN PERIOD** *Major building works Assyria repopulated* Kingdoms of ADIABENE (Assyria), OSRHOENE (Edessa = Urfa) and CHARACENE (ancient sea-land).
		Orodes I (80–76)	
	Antiochos XIII (69–65)	Phraates III (70–57)	
	64: Pompey conquers Antioch	Orodes II (57–37)	*Crassus defeated at Carrhae (Harran) (53 B.C.)*
50			

IX. PARTHIAN AND SASSANIAN PERIODS (126 B.C.–637 A.D.)

DATES B.C.	ROME	IRAN	MESOPOTAMIA
50	Caesar and Antony	Phraates IV (37–2)	*38: Labienus' war against the Parthians*
	ROMAN EMPIRE		
	Octavius Augustus (– 27 to 14)		
A.D.		Artabanus III (11–38)	
	Tiberius (14–37)		
	Caligula (37–41)		
	Claudius (41–54)	Vologazes I (51–78)	
50	Nero (54–68)		*Foundation of Hatra*
	Vespasian (70–79)	Pacorus II	*(c. 70?)*
	Domitian (81–96)	(78–115)	*74/75: Last known cuneiform text*
	Trajan (98–117)		
100		Osroes (109–128)	*Temple of Gareus at Uruk (c. 110)*
	Hadrian (117–138)		*114–117: Trajan's campaigns in Mesopotamia takes Ctesiphon and reaches the Arabo-Persian Gulf*
	Antoninus (138–161)	Mithridates IV (128–147)	
150		Vologazes III (148–192)	*Kingdom of HATRA (c. 160–240)*
	Marcus Aurelius (161–180)		
	Commodus (180–192)		*164: Cassius, legate of Syria, conquers Nisibin and Ctesiphon*
	Septimus Severus (193–211)	Vologazes IV (192–207)	*197: Septimus Severus conquers Ctesiphon Caracalla murdered at Carrhae (Harran)*
200		Artabanus V (208–226)	
	Caracalla (211–217)	**SASSANIDS**	**SASSANIAN PERIOD**
		Ardeshir I	*226: Ardeshir conquers Mesopotamia*
	Alexander Severus (222–235)	(224–241)	*232: Unsuccessful campaign of Alexander Severus.*
		Shapur I	*240: Ardeshir destroys Hatra*
250	Valerian (253–260)	(241–272)	*256: Shapur destroys Assur*
			260: Valerian prisoner of Shapur I
	Aurelian (270–275)	Bahram II	*262: Odenath (Palmyra), allied to the Romans, marches on Ctesiphon*
		(276–293)	
	Diocletian (285–305)		
300		Narses (293–302)	*296: War against Narses, then peace. Rome gains provinces in Mesopotamia*
	Constantine (312–337)	Shapur II (309–379)	
	Constantius II (337–361)		*338–350: Wars, then peace between Constantius and Shapur II. The Romans invade Mesopotamia, then withdraw because of starvation.*
350	Julian the Apostate (361–363)		
	Jovian (363–364)		*Jovian evacuates Roman strongholds in Northern Mesopotamia.*
	Theodosus (379–395)	Bahram IV (388–399)	*Florut of Christian literature in Syriac at Edessa, Nisibin and Arbela (Erbil) Intermittent wars between Byzantines and Sassanids. Economic decline of Mesopotamia.*
400	**BYZANTINE EMPIRE** (395–1453)	Yezdegerd I (399–420)	
	↓	↓ 651	*637: Beginning of the conquest of Mesopotamia by Moslem Arabs.*

MAPS

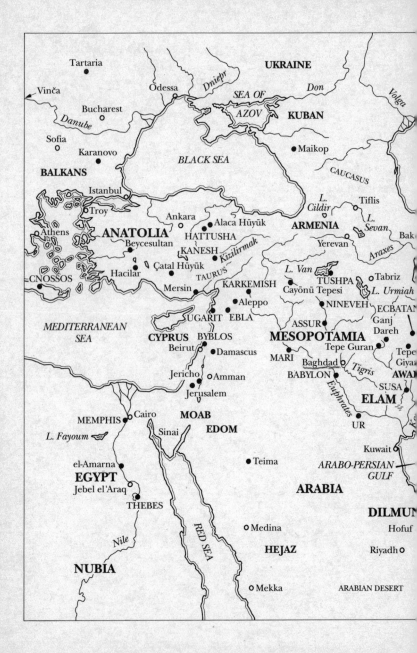

Near and Middle East
in Early Antiquity

Modern towns ○ Baghdad

Ancient towns or
Archaeological sites ● NINEVEH

0   500 km

*ARAL
SEA*

*Iaxartes
(Syr Darya)*

TURKMENISTAN

○Bukhara   ○Samarkand   *Oxus
(Amu Darya)*

KARAKORUM
DESERT

●Dashliji Tepe

*ASPIAN
SEA*

●Anau   ●Namazga Tepe   ●Balkh   PAMIR

●Tureng Tepe
Gurgan   ○Meshed   HINDU-KUSH

ELBURZ

○Tehran   ●Tepe Hissar   Peshawar○

IRANIAN PLATEAU   Herat○   Kabul○

●Tepe Sialk   **IRAN**   **AFGHANISTAN**   **PAKISTAN**

○Ispahan   DASHT-I KEVIR
DESERT   Harappa●

ANSHAN   ○Yazd

ANSHAN
epe Malyan)   ○Kerman   Kandahar○   **MELUHHA**

●PERSEPOLIS   Zahédan○   Qetta○

Shiraz   Tepe Yahya●   **BALUCHISTAN**   *Indus*

○Bushir   FARS MOUNTAIN   Mohenjo-Daro●

SHERIHUM   Nal●

Bahrain   Amri●   Chanhu-Daro●

QATAR   Kulli●   Karachi

AKHDHAR

MAGAN   Muscat○   *INDIAN OCEAN*   Lothal●

JABAL.

OMAN

Southern Mesopotamia

Modern towns   ○ Baghdad
Ancient towns and present name   ● UR (T. Mughayir)
Ancient towns of uncertain location ◑ LARAK
Prehistoric sites   ▲ T. Uqair
Approximate course of the
Euphrates c. 2000 B.C.   — — —
Modern borders   .—..—..—..—.
T = tell
Marshes   ⠶

0   100 km

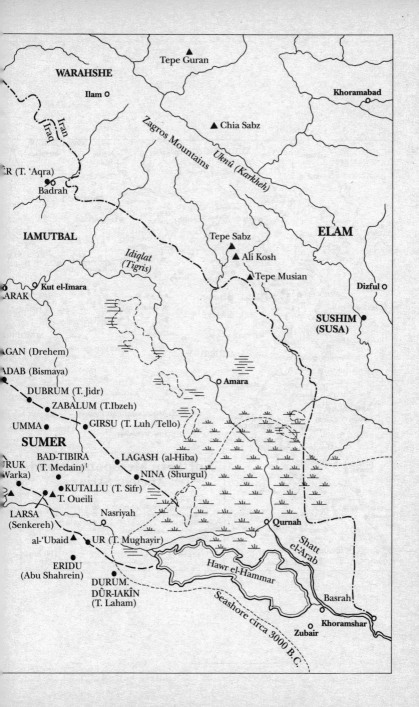

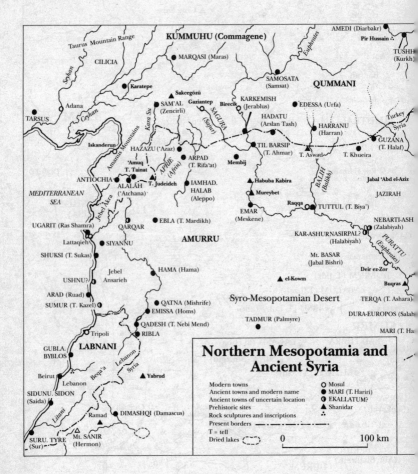

Northern Mesopotamia and Ancient Syria

Modern towns	○ Mosul
Ancient towns and modern name	● MARI (T. Hariri)
Ancient towns of uncertain location	◑ EKALLATUM?
Prehistoric sites	▲ Shanidar
Rock sculptures and inscriptions	⋰
Present borders	— ·· — ·· —
T = tell	
Dried lakes	

0   100 km

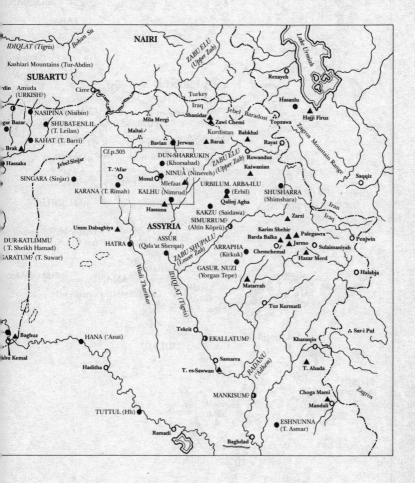

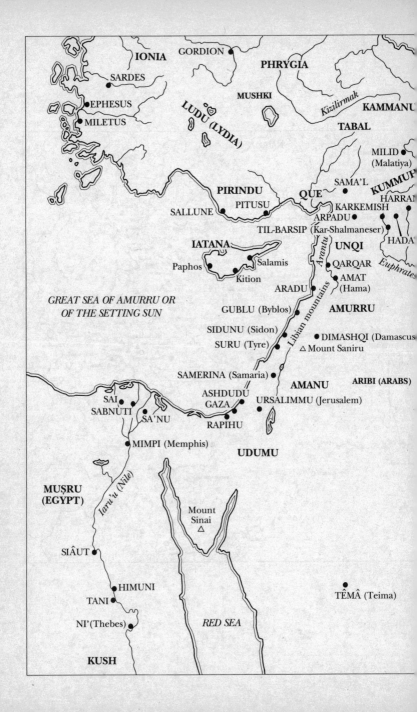

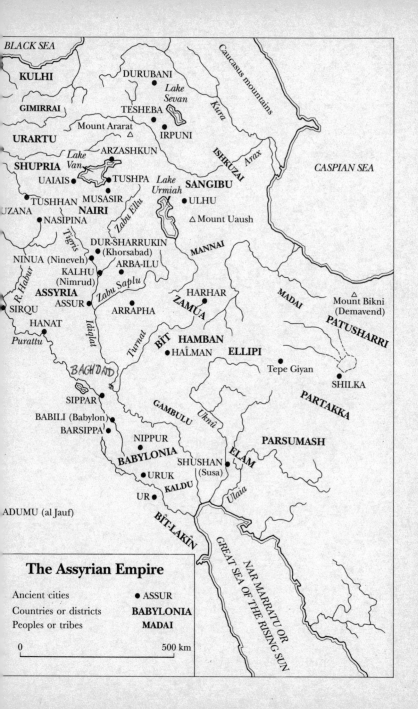

The Assyrian Empire

Ancient cities   ● ASSUR
Countries or districts   **BABYLONIA**
Peoples or tribes   **MADAI**

0   500 km

INDEX

Modern geographical names are in italic.
The names of deities are followed by an asterisk.

Discover more about our forthcoming books through Penguin's FREE newspaper...

Penguin
Quarterly

It's packed with:

- exciting features
- author interviews
- previews & reviews
- books from your favourite films & TV series
- exclusive competitions & much, much more...

READ MORE IN PENGUIN

In every corner of the world, on every subject under the sun, Penguin represents quality and variety – the very best in publishing today.

For complete information about books available from Penguin – including Puffins, Penguin Classics and Arkana – and how to order them, write to us at the appropriate address below. Please note that for copyright reasons the selection of books varies from country to country.

In the United Kingdom: Please write to *Dept. EP, Penguin Books Ltd, Bath Road, Harmondsworth, West Drayton, Middlesex UB7 ODA*

In the United States: Please write to *Consumer Sales, Penguin USA, P.O. Box 999, Dept. 17109, Bergenfield, New Jersey 07621-0120.* VISA and MasterCard holders call 1-800-253-6476 to order Penguin titles

In Canada: Please write to *Penguin Books Canada Ltd, 10 Alcorn Avenue, Suite 300, Toronto, Ontario M4V 3B2*

In Australia: Please write to *Penguin Books Australia Ltd, P.O. Box 257, Ringwood, Victoria 3134*

In New Zealand: Please write to *Penguin Books (NZ) Ltd, Private Bag 102902, North Shore Mail Centre, Auckland 10*

In India: Please write to *Penguin Books India Pvt Ltd, 706 Eros Apartments, 56 Nehru Place, New Delhi 110 019*

In the Netherlands: Please write to *Penguin Books Netherlands bv, Postbus 3507, NL-1001 AH Amsterdam*

In Germany: Please write to *Penguin Books Deutschland GmbH, Metzlerstrasse 26, 60594 Frankfurt am Main*

In Spain: Please write to *Penguin Books S. A., Bravo Murillo 19, 1° B, 28015 Madrid*

In Italy: Please write to *Penguin Italia s.r.l., Via Felice Casati 20, I–20124 Milano*

In France: Please write to *Penguin France S. A., 17 rue Lejeune, F–31000 Toulouse*

In Japan: Please write to *Penguin Books Japan, Ishikiribashi Building, 2–5–4, Suido, Bunkyo-ku, Tokyo 112*

In Greece: Please write to *Penguin Hellas Ltd, Dimocritou 3, GR–106 71 Athens*

In South Africa: Please write to *Longman Penguin Southern Africa (Pty) Ltd, Private Bag X08, Bertsham 2013*

READ MORE IN PENGUIN

HISTORY

The Making of Europe   Robert Bartlett

'Bartlett does more than anyone before him to bring out the way in which medieval Europe was shaped by [a] great wave of internal conquest, colonization and evangelization. He also stresses its consequences for the future history of the world' – *Guardian*

The Somme Battlefields   Martin and Mary Middlebrook

This evocative, original book provides a definitive guide to the cemeteries, memorials and battlefields from the age of Crécy and Agincourt to the great Allied sweep which drove the Germans back in 1944, concentrating above all on the scenes of ferocious fighting in 1916 and 1918.

Ancient Slavery and Modern Ideology   M. I. Finley

Few topics in the study of classical civilization could be more central – and more controversial – than slavery. In this magnificent book, M. I. Finley cuts through the thickets of modern ideology to get at the essential facts. 'A major creative achievement in historical interpretation' – *The Times Higher Education Supplement*

The Penguin History of Greece   A. R. Burn

Readable, erudite, enthusiastic and balanced, this one-volume history of Hellas sweeps the reader along from the days of Mycenae and the splendours of Athens to the conquests of Alexander and the final dark decades.

The Laurel and the Ivy   Robert Kee

'Parnell continues to haunt the Irish historical imagination a century after his death ... Robert Kee's patient and delicate probing enables him to reconstruct the workings of that elusive mind as persuasively, or at least as plausibly, as seems possible ... This splendid biography, which is as readable as it is rigorous, greatly enhances our understanding of both Parnell, and of the Ireland of his time' – *The Times Literary Supplement*

READ MORE IN PENGUIN

HISTORY

A History of Wales   John Davies

'Outstanding ... Dr Davies casts a coolly appraising eye upon myths, false premises and silver linings ... He is impartial. He grasps the story of his country with immense confidence and tells it in vigorous and lucid prose ... Its scope is unique. It is the history Wales needed' – *Daily Telegraph*

Daily Life in Ancient Rome   Jerome Carcopino

This classic study, which includes a bibliography and notes by Professor Rowell, describes the streets, houses and multi-storeyed apartments of the city of over a million inhabitants, the social classes from senators to slaves, and the Roman family and the position of women, causing *The Times Literary Supplement* to hail it as a 'thorough, lively and readable book'.

The Anglo-Saxons   Edited by James Campbell

'For anyone who wishes to understand the broad sweep of English history, Anglo-Saxon society is an important and fascinating subject. And Campbell's is an important and fascinating book. It is also a finely produced and, at times, a very beautiful book' – *London Review of Books*

Customs in Common   E. P. Thompson

Eighteenth-century Britain saw a profound distancing between the culture of the patricians and the plebs. E. P. Thompson explains why in this series of brilliant essays on the customs of the working people, which, he argues, emerged as a culture of resistance towards an innovative market economy. 'One of the most eloquent, powerful and independent voices of our time' – *Observer*

The Habsburg Monarchy 1809–1918   A J P Taylor

Dissolved in 1918, the Habsburg Empire 'had a unique character, out of time and out of place'. Scholarly and vividly accessible, this 'very good book indeed' (*Spectator*) elucidates the problems always inherent in the attempt to give peace, stability and a common loyalty to a heterogeneous population.

READ MORE IN PENGUIN

ARCHAEOLOGY

Breaking the Maya Code Michael D. Coe

Over twenty years ago, no one could read the hieroglyphic texts carved on the magnificent Maya temples and palaces; today we can understand almost all of them. The inscriptions reveal a culture obsessed with warfare, dynastic rivalries and ritual blood-letting. 'An entertaining, enlightening and even humorous history of the great searchers after the meaning that lies in the Maya inscriptions' – *Observer*

The Ancient Economy M. I. Finley

One of M. I. Finley's most influential contributions to ancient history, this study examines the structure, character and operation of the ancient economy, illustrating, for example, that the Roman Empire was for centuries a single political unit operating within a 'common cultural-psychological framework'.

The Pyramids of Egypt I. E. S. Edwards

Dr Edwards offers us the definitive work on these gigantic tombs, drawing both on his own original research and on the work of the many archaeologists who have dug in Egypt. This revised edition includes recent discoveries and research.

Lucy's Child Donald Johanson and James Shreeve

'Superb adventure . . . *Lucy's Child* burns with the infectious excitement of hominid fever . . . the tedium and the doubting, and the ultimate triumph of an expedition that unearths something wonderful about the origins of humanity' – *Chicago Tribune*

Archaeology and Language Colin Renfrew
The Puzzle of Indo-European Origins

'The time-scale, the geographical spaces, the questions and methods of inquiry . . . are vast . . . But throughout this teeming study, Renfrew is pursuing a single, utterly fascinating puzzle: who are we Europeans, where do the languages we speak really stem from?' – *Sunday Times*